THE NEW ILLUSTRATED
ENCYCLOPEDIA OF
AIRCRAFT

THE NEW ILLUSTRATED
ENCYCLOPEDIA OF
AIRCRAFT

EDITED BY DAVID MONDEY

Revised and updated by Michael Taylor

GREENWICH EDITIONS

First published in England by
Greenwich Editions
10 Blenheim Court
Brewery Road
London N7 9NT

A member of the Chrysalis Group plc

AN OCEANA BOOK

ISBN 0-86288-268-0

QUMEOAF

This book is produced by
Quantum Publishing Ltd
6 Blundell Street
London N7 9BH

Project Manager : Joyce Bentley
Designer : Rod Teasdale
Editor : Phillip Jarrett
Author : Michael Taylor

Printed in Singapore by Star Standard Pte Ltd
Manufactured in Singapore by United Graphics Pte Ltd

CONTENTS

THE
HISTORYOF
FLIGHT

MAN BECOMES AIRBORNE

I t is unlikely that we shall ever know the name of the person who first commented that, if God had intended men to fly, he would have given them wings. It could quite easily have been a Chinese spectator of an unsuccessful launch of a man-lifting kite, perhaps a century or more before the birth of Christ. That is a possible date for the first men to become airborne, although it was not until the famed Marco Polo travelled to Cathay (China) in the 14th century that proper records were made of genuine flights by tethered man-carrying kites. Indeed, the desire to fly like the birds could well stretch back to prehistoric man, conscious of the ease with which winged creatures could elude land-bound predators.

Myth and fantasy fill the years between the wishes of those prehistoric ancestors and the first thinking men to consider seriously, but unsuccessfully, the mechanics of flight. Leonardo da Vinci (1452-1519), Italian artist-inventor, produced many designs for ornithopter (flapping-wing) aircraft but prudently made no practical experiments. A hundred and fifty years after his death, in 1670, a Jesuit priest, Francesco de Lana-Terzi, had heard of the invention of the vacuum pump. This seemed to him to be a useful tool in achieving flight, based upon the assumption that a thin metallic globe from which the air had been evacuated could be lighter than air and thus would float in the air. He failed to see the simple fact, about which most present-day school children could have advised him, that if his metallic spheres had been light enough to lift they would have been crushed by atmospheric pressure at the moment of evacuation.

THE FIRST LIGHTER-THAN-AIR CRAFT

Since schooldays most of us have believed that the brothers Etienne and Joseph Montgolfier were the first to launch a hot-air balloon. More recent research has shown that another priest, the Brazilian Bartolomeu de Gusmào, demonstrated a practical model of a hot-air balloon at the court of King John V of Portugal in 1709. On 8 August that year, before a distinguished gathering of reliable witnesses, de Gusmào showed the amazed audience that his small paper balloon, with burning material suspended below the open neck of the envelope, could rise in free flight within the confines of the Ambassador's drawing-room. Its brief journey was brought to an end when two servants, fearing it might set

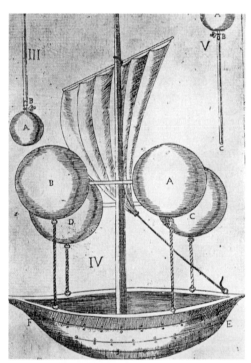

Bladud, (above), fabled ninth king of Britain, was an early 'jumper', who fixed artificial wings to his arms. De Lana Terzi's flying-machine (centre), was also a non-starter. The work of men like Leonardo da Vinci (right) gave a starting point to later thinkers. The first free flight in a Montgolfière balloon(left) was undertaken by de Rozier and the Marquis d'Arlandes. The engraving (far right) records de Rozier's fatal cross-Channel attempt in a composite hot-air/hydrogen balloon. Both de Rozier and his companion, Jules Romain, were killed.

the curtains alight, dashed it to the ground. A lighter-than-air craft had thus been demonstrated 74 years before the first flight of a Montgolfier hot-air balloon took place.

This in no way detracts from the achievements of the Montgolfiers. Their first hot-air balloon was launched, probably at Annonay, France, on 25 April 1783. Some 12 m (39 ft) in diameter, it climbed to a height of about 305 m (1,000 ft) before the hot air in the envelope cooled and it began its descent. The Montgolfier brothers are said to have been unaware that hot air alone was the lifting agent for their balloons, believing that a specially light gas was generated by the mixture of wool and straw which they burned below the open neck of the envelope.

A second demonstration, at Annonay, was given on 5 June 1783, but just before a third, command performance at the Court of Versailles on 19 September of that same year, when a sheep, a duck and a cock became the first living creatures to be artificially airborne, Professor J. A. C. Charles had successfully demonstrated a small hydrogen-filled balloon at Paris, on 27 August 1783.

Events then moved quickly. On 15 October 1783 Francois Pilâtre de Rozier became the first man in the world to be carried aloft in a balloon, sole passenger of a Montgolfière balloon tethered to the ground by a 26 m (84 ft) rope. Just over a month later, on 21 November 1783, de Rozier, accompanied by the Marquis d'Arlandes, made the first free flight in a balloon, remaining airborne for 25 minutes, during which time they travelled about 8.5 km (5.5 miles) from their launch point. Free flight in a lighter-than-air craft had at last been realised. And although this was a beginning, it was also virtually the end of the Montgolfière-type balloon until the 'reinvention' of modern hot-air ballooning almost two centuries later. It was generally (though not totally) superseded at that early time by the infinitely superior and practical hydrogen-filled balloon developed by J. A. C. Charles, in which he and one of the Robert brothers who had assisted in its construction made a free flight from the gardens of the Tuileries, Paris, on 1 December 1783. Their flight was one of 43 km (27 miles), their ascent being witnessed by a crowd estimated at some 400,000. Their balloon was so well designed that it was essentially similar to the gas-filled balloon used to this day. The hydrogen balloon made long journeys possible, and by 1785 the English Channel had been crossed by air, with longer and more hazardous over-sea attempts then being planned.

MAKING THE BALLOON NAVIGABLE

The expansion of ballooning as a sport was very rapid. At last man was properly free of the Earth which had been his habitat for so many centuries, and there was no telling what achievements might now be possible. Within days of de Rozier's first flight in a Montgolfière had come an appreciation of the potential which such a vehicle held for military pursuits, especially for reconnaissance; by 1794 the man-carrying balloon had actually been used in war by the French Republican Army at Maubeuge, Belgium, during the Battle of Fleurus.

While the balloon made ascending and sustained flight possible, the direction of flight when untethered from the ground was dictated by the direction of the wind. There had to be some method of steering, for the balloon at the mercy of the slightest wind. Grandiose ideas involving oars, sails and propellers were of no avail; it had to be understood that if an airborne vehicle was to be steerable it must be capable of independent movement, instead of being carried by the wind, so that movable aerofoil surfaces and/or overriding motive power could impose the chosen direction of travel. From this realisation stemmed the initial airship designs, the envelope becoming elongated instead of spherical, with the provision of a powerplant to provide forward motion independently of the breeze. This latter word is chosen advisedly: there was then no question of trying to fly in anything that might be classed as a wind.

The first published design for an airship appeared in France as early as 1784, with a cigar-shaped envelope and two large propellers to be turned by a crew of eighty. It was not built, but later that year a cylindrical airship was constructed by the Robert brothers, and flew on 15 July. This also had the important innovation of a ballonet, a small gas-tight compartment inside the main envelope which could be inflated with air to maintain envelope volume and shape or deflated to adjust flying altitude; ballonets would subsequently be used to maintain envelope shape during variations in gas volume, and to adjust trim, the former requirement being amply demonstrated on this first flight, when the envelope had to be pierced to relieve gas pressure.

The major problem, and the one which was also to frustrate the pioneers of heavier-than-air craft, was the non-availability of a suitable lightweight and compact powerplant. Thus Frenchman Henri Giffard, who recorded the first flight of a manned, powered dirigible (Latin for 'able to be directed') on 24 September 1852, used a 2.2 kW (3 hp) steam-engine driving a 3.35 m (11 ft) diameter propeller. The use of the word 'dirigible' in that record is rather open to question, for anything more than the merest suggestion of a breeze would have made it unsteerable. To Charles Renard and Arthur Krebs, officers of the French Corps of Engineers, goes the distinction of flying La France, the world's first fully controllable and powered dirigible. In this craft, on 9 August 1884, Renard and Krebs flew a circular course of about 8km (5 miles), taking off from and returning to Chalais-Meudon, near Paris. Powered by a 6.7kW (9hp) Gramme electric motor driving a 7.01 m (23 ft) diameter propeller, La France achieved a maximum speed of 23.5 km/h (14.5 mph) during its 23-minute flight. Increased power had provided the speed necessary to make the vehicle controllable, but this seemingly small improvement had taken 101 years from the first flight of the Montgolfier balloon.

THE FIRST HEAVIER-THAN-AIR CRAFT

The beginning of heavier-than-air flight is the story of many men mostly working independently towards a common goal, some of whom stand out because of their advanced thoughts or brilliant innovations.

First must come the man now regarded as the 'Father of Aerial Navigation', the English Baronet Sir George Cayley (1773-1857). In 1804 he built what is generally regarded as the first successful model glider. This consisted of little more than a rod to which was mounted a kite-shape monoplane wing; at the aft end of the 'fuselage' were vertical and horizontal tail surfaces to provide control. With this device he was able to confirm that the principles of heavier-than-air flight were entirely feasible, and it was able to demonstrate stable flight over quite long distances.

From this first model he evolved gliders capable of carrying a small schoolboy in flight (1849), and later his reluctant coachman (1853). Both were passengers only, with no means of controlling their aircraft in flight. In addition to his practical work, Cayley suggested the use of an internal combustion engine for powered flight, demonstrated how a curved aerofoil surface provides lift, and pointed out that biplane or triplane wings would provide maximum lift from a lightweight, robust structure. Cayley's 'Father' title was well-earned.

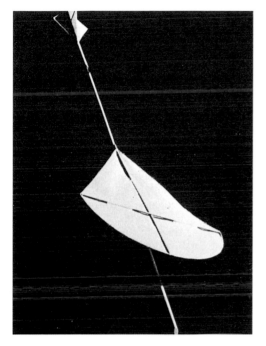

Cayley's model glider (top, left), with its adjustable aerofoil surfaces, enabled him to experiment with the problems of gliding flight, leading to the 'boy lifter' of 1849 (left). Clément Ader's Éole steam-powered monoplane (top) was the first aircraft to lift itself from the ground, but failed to fly. Fèlix du Temple's monoplane (model above) made a short hop after launch down a ramp, powered by a hot-air or steam engine.

Cayley died in 1857, and in that same year a French naval officer, Félix du Temple, constructed and flew the world's first powered model aeroplane to fly successfully, although some aviation historians support John Stringfellow's claim to have flown his steam-powered model at Chard in England in 1848. Félix du Temple's 'first' was achieved with a clockwork motor, and subsequently his little monoplane was powered with a steam engine. Seventeen years later this same inventor was flight testing a full-size man-carrying aeroplane, which was powered by either a hot-air engine or a steam engine. Piloted by an unknown sailor, at Brest, this aircraft was the first in the world to achieve a short hop into the air, after launch down an inclined ramp.

Although men were beginning to learn how to construct a fixed-wing aircraft that could travel through the air, their problem was now the same as that of the balloonist who wanted to steer his vessel. Both needed a suitable powerplant. A practical working layout for a suitable powerplant was to be demonstrated by the German engineer Nicholas Otto, in 1876. The four stroke cycle of operations for an internal combustion engine, which Otto evolved at that time, is still the basic principle upon which most piston-engines work, especially those for motor cars and aircraft. But Otto's invention was in the future. The more practical among the pioneer aviators accepted the reality of the situation, and spent the period most profitably in improving airframe design, learning the best means of lightweight construction, and trying to discover practical means of controlling the aircraft when it became airborne.

SUSTAINED HEAVIER-THAN-AIR FLIGHT

The most important of this group of pioneers was the German Otto Lilienthal (1848-1896), whose beautifully built lightweight gliders enabled him to make many thousands of flights. These were not just pleasure flights; Lilienthal was a practical researcher, building, modifying, improving, and at all times recording meticulously the results of his experiments for the benefit of other researchers.

Lilienthal's gliders were of the configuration which we would now call hang gliders, designed so that the mass of his body was disposed about the aircraft's centre of gravity when the craft was in a stable flying position. By body movements he could influence a degree of control on the craft's flight but, unfortunately, this did not allow rapid response to changing flight conditions. Despite his experience, Lilien-

thal was gravely injured in a flying accident on 9 August 1896, brought about by a control problem to which he could not respond quickly enough, and he died on the following day. This was unfortunate in more ways than the obvious, as he had been studying control surfaces and had considered adding power to one of his gliders.

Lilienthal was a source of inspiration to many, but especially influenced the work of the British pioneer builder/pilot Percy Pilcher (1866-1899), who flew his first glider in 1895. Pilcher travelled to Germany to meet and talk with Otto Lilienthal, from whom he obtained a great deal of practical advice, and he also flew his gliders. But Pilcher, too, was to die two days after his Hawk glider crashed to the ground near Market Harborough on 30 September 1899.

There was a third important glider pioneer (a builder, not a flyer) who collected information from every possible source, publishing this pot-pourri under the title *Progress in Flying Machines*. American railway

Hiram Maxim's giant steam-powered craft (top), spanning 31.7 m (104 ft) developed so much lift that it broke away from its safety rails. At the same time, Otto Lilienthal (right) was flying well-built hang-gliders. Despite an advanced engine, Langley's Aerodrome (above) failed to fly, both attempts ending in the river.

The historic picture (above) is of the first flight of the Wright Flyer on 17 December 1903. Orville Wright, who was at the controls, later wrote: "The course of the flight up and down was exceedingly erratic. The contol of the front rudder (elevator) was difficult. As a result, the machine would rise suddenly to about ten feet, and then suddenly dart for the ground.
A sudden dart when a little over 120 feet from the point at which it rose into the air ended the flight." Three others followed, the last and the best that day covering 260 m (852 ft), but ended with the elevator being damaged when the Flyer landed. When it was overturned by a gust of wind more damage followed. The ironical feature of these flights was that the world failed to learn that a man had been airborne and in control of a powered heavier-than-air craft. It was not until three years later, in November 1906, that the little Brazilian Alberto Santos-Dumont electrified aviation progress in Europe by recording a first flight in his No. 14bis of nearly 61 m (200 ft). Both aircraft were really dead-end designs, but their achievement and influence inspired new ideas and efforts. In the short term more powerful engines were the key to success.

engineer Octave Chanute (1832-1910), the compiler of that book, was to develop the Lilienthal-type craft into a classic glider. More importantly for powered flight, his book, his advice and his friendship were to inspire the brothers Orville and Wilbur Wright.

There are many links in the chain of progress towards the realisation of powered flight, some big and many small. All contribute to the end result, and it is unfortunate that space will not allow us to relate them all. One of the final links was undoubtedly Germany's Gottlieb Daimler, who in 1885 developed the world's first single-cylinder internal-combustion engine. This employed the four-stroke principle of operation devised by his fellow countryman, Nicholas Otto, and used petrol (gasoline) as its fuel. As it was developed to provide a power-to-weight ratio far superior to any other form of engine then available, the would-be aviators realised that the necessary powerplant had arrived.

Unfortunately this was to be of no avail to American Samuel Pierpont Langley. Langley, a scientist and Secretary of the Smithsonian Institu-

tion, built a series of large steam-powered model aeroplanes that were the first in history to make truly sustained flights (from 1896), of up to 1,280 m (4,200 ft). Using a $50,000 State subsidy to continue his research, Langley built a quarter-scale model of his intended manned version, which in June 1903 flew well using a petrol engine, the first aeroplane ever to make a sustained flight using such a powerplant. His collaboration with Charles Manly to build and fly his full-size and manned (by Manly) Aerodrome aircraft resulted in the creation by Manly and his associate Stephen Balzer of a remarkably advanced 39 kW (52 hp) five-cylinder radial petrol engine. Despite this advantage, Langley's full-size manned aircraft failed to become airborne on two occasions when launched from a roof-top structure on a houseboat. Both times, on 7 October and 8 December 1903, the aircraft crashed into the Potomac River. Most observers believed the Aerodrome fouled its launching device on both dates, but it has been suggested that the aircraft's structure collapsed. Either way, the stage was clear for the Wright brothers, who had been fully aware of Langley's trials.

MANNED AND POWERED FLIGHT BECOMES REALITY

The achievement of the Wright brothers on that cold Thursday, 17 December 1903, has been told many times but is still exciting, especially, perhaps, for those who have learned to fly; who understand that moment of magic when the aircraft loses contact with the ground and becomes a living creature, free in three-dimensional space: so very nearly a bird in flight.

The brothers Orville and Wilbur deserved their success because of their determination to overcome the very real difficulties that beset them by embarking on a remarkable research programme. If they lacked something they made it; if it did not work, they found out why and changed their design. And when the Flyer was dismantled on that historic day it was an end to the first phase of powered flight. The world's first powered, sustained and controlled flight had been accomplished. It was also a beginning; the expansion of aviation to facilitate world travel and inaugurate a hoped-for era of peace.

PIONEERS OF POWERED FLIGHT

It is ironical that the 'beginning' with which we closed the last chapter was then, so far as the world is concerned, no beginning at all. In fact it was not until almost three years later, on 23 October 1906, when the Brazilian Alberto Santos-Dumont achieved a flight of less than 60 m (200 ft), in Paris, that the world fully realised that the first flight of a powered heavier-than-air craft had been accomplished. This was because the Paris flight was observed by thousands, photographed and recorded in the world's newspapers. Almost three weeks later, on 12 November, Santos-Dumont covered 220 m (722 ft) in the same aircraft, his so-called 14bis, and this was recognised as the first European sustained flight by a manned and powered aeroplane. It also set the first-ever distance record officially ratified by the Fédération Aéronautique Internationale, though by then the Wrights had built new versions of their Flyer able to cover distances of many miles.

Santos-Dumont's aircraft was a strange-looking machine, with box-kite-like wings. It seemed even more odd when it was realised that it flew with the tail way out in front and the wings at the back. This configuration earned the name 'canard', because such craft resemble a duck in flight. The box-kite wings stemmed from the original research of Lawrence Hargrave in Australia. Hargrave had perfected the design of the box-kite in 1893, and the lightweight and robust construction of this device, together with its good lifting characteristics, encouraged a number of European designers to adopt this form of structure for their early attempts to build the ideal aircraft.

By 1907 the Wright design was beginning to have an influence upon European constructors, leading to a combination of Wright features with the Hargrave box-kite. It is worth explaining at this point that the powerplant of this type of aircraft was mounted so that the propeller was not only behind the engine, but also aft of the main wing structure in what was known as a pusher configuration. A considerable number of the new designs emerging in Europe were quite different, comprising monoplane and biplane aircraft with the engine mounted at the forward end of the fuselage, with the propeller at the front of the engine. This was known as the tractor configuration, the propeller pulling the entire machine through the air. A little thought will bring the realisation that the propeller in a pusher configuration is doing exactly the same thing, but it has proved convenient, even to this day, to call

Noting the marginal capability of such aircraft as Santos-Dumnt's 14bis, other pioneers examined new ideas to achieve the aim of 'flight like the birds'. Paul Cornu's twin-rotor helicopter (top left) recorded the first rotary-wing flight on 13 November 1907: the Ecquevilly multiplane (left) was one of the proposals to gain more lift from a short span; Karl Jatho's aircraft (top right) was nearly the first to fly in Germany; Trajan Vuia's machine (above) could only hop.

By 1908, when Wilbur Wright demonstrated the Flyer A (below) in France, the two brothers had refined its design almost to the ultimate. In Europe the pioneers were still trying to evolve a really practical aeroplane. Aircraft such as the Koechlin Boxkite (right) and Blériot/Voisin with cellular wings (below right) owed much to the work of the Australian Lawrence Hargrave.

the forward-mounted propeller a tractor, and the aft-mounted version a pusher.

By the beginning of 1908 there was better progress in Europe, but control of the aircraft in flight had not graduated beyond the elementary stage. Men were airborne in powered aircraft, but their flight was far from emulating that of a bird; they were certainly in the air, but very limited in their flight control. To illustrate the point, the first flight in Europe to exceed one minute's duration was recorded by Henry Farman, flying his Voisin-Farman I biplane, on 10 November 1907. On 13 January 1908 the same combination of aircraft and pilot recorded completion of the first 1km (0.62 mile) circle flown in Europe, in a time of 1min 28sec. At the then current stage of aviation development in Europe, this was no mean achievement, and won for Henry Farman the 50,000 francs Deutsch/Archdeacon Grand Prix d'Aviation. But changes were imminent.

THE MOMENT OF TRUTH

In the summer of 1908 Wilbur Wright visited France, bringing with him a Wright Flyer A with which to give a series of demonstration flights. He based himself initially at Hunaudiéres, near Le Mans, and very soon had uncrated and assembled his aircraft.

On 8 August, in the cool, windless, near-twilight of that summer evening, he prepared to take off before a highly critical audience of European (mostly French) pilots. Collectively they considered themselves the hub of aviation development and achievement. After all, there was really no certainty that the Wrights had flown before the great achievement of Santos-Dumont. And, with a nudge of the elbow: "You know how these Yankees exaggerate".

There was a sudden roar from the engine, focusing attention, but by then Wilbur and the Flyer were airborne. And look, here indeed was the legendary birdman, climbing, turning, banking with unbelievable perfection and grace. Man and machine were one, weaving dream patterns in a sunset sky. The audience was silent, breathless, eyes almost blinded by emotion. Too soon it ended as, with engine throttled back, Wilbur set the Flyer calmly and gracefully on the ground. The spectators were still silent, still breathless. Then suddenly cheers rang out; cheers of amazement, of appreciation and of congratulation. Wilbur had demonstrated, convincingly, the considerable lead which the Wrights then held in aviation, and their complete mastery of control. From that moment forward European aviation was spurred to progress in leaps and bounds.

NEW ACHIEVEMENTS: NEW POWER

The European pilots were soon to discover that Wilbur was indeed one of the brotherhood, prepared to talk about design and improvements, and his demonstrations and influence had a profound effect on the rapid development of European aviation. By the end of 1908, flying from Auvours, France, Wilbur had made more than 100 flights totalling in excess of 25 flying hours. His last flight of the year, on 31 December, lasted 2 hrs 20 min 23 sec, during which he covered a distance of 124 km (77 miles) to set a new world record and win the Michelin prize.

While Wilbur was busy in Europe, Orville Wright had been demonstrating at Fort Myer, Virginia, the Wright Model A which had been ordered by the United States Army but still had to pass acceptance trials. These demonstrations began on 3 September 1908, and people came in their thousands to see an aeroplane in flight for the first time. They were as thrilled and excited as the European spectators, but trag-

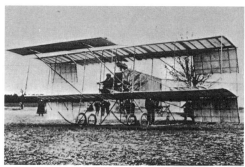

Three aircraft showing the evolutionary changes in basic design. The Voisin (top) was typical of the structure evolved from the box-kite. Farman's biplane (above) showed a blend of Wright and Voisin ideas. A. V. Roe's triplane (left) was typical of new tractor-propeller layouts.

ically, within a matter of two weeks, the flights came to an end when the aircraft crashed. Orville was seriously injured, and his passenger, Lt Thomas E. Selfridge, was killed; powered aeroplane flying had claimed its first victim. Subsequent investigation showed that a propeller blade had split, causing unequal thrust, and had then severed a guy line supporting the rudder, which had twisted out of position and forced the machine into the ground.

Lessons were being learned in the very active European area, too, with the first use of ailerons for lateral control, the first powered aeroplane flight in Britain being recorded by American S. F. Cody, the first aeroplane passengers being carried in Europe (including the first woman anywhere in the world), and the first-ever full-sized triplane to fly (the French Goupy I in September 1908). Another lesson learned by hard experience was that overloaded engines overheat, lose power and quickly lose the ability to keep their aircraft in the air. One prime requirement of a good aviator was to keep a constant lookout for suitable emergency fields so that, when the engine overheated and failed, a quick and safe landing could be made in the chosen area.

It was all part of the sport of aviation, and did not matter a great deal at a time when there was even enjoyment to be had in stripping, repairing and rebuilding a troublesome engine. It was likely to prove disconcerting, however, if aircraft were to be developed for the regular carriage of passengers, and unless engines of increased power became available there would be little scope for enlarging or reinforcing the 'stick-and-string' airframe of the day.

INTRODUCTION OF THE ROTARY ENGINE

Louis and Laurent Seguin, in France, began to investigate the problems associated with existing engines so that they could develop a new powerplant which would satisfy the requirement of the day and meet the needs of the future. Engines in use at that period were of two main types: in-line, which stemmed directly from the motor-car industry; and radial (with the cylinders disposed radially around a circular crankcase), which had been developed as an aircraft powerplant. The former were penalised at the outset by their origin, tending to be exces-

The historic moment of Blériot's arrival at Dover (above) gave some idea of the potential of the aeroplane. In early 1910, Henri Fabre (right) recorded the first flight from water of a powered aircraft.

sively heavy and having the added disadvantage of needing a water-cooling system, including a drag-inducing radiator. The radial engine relied upon air cooling, then far from effective because of bad cylinder design, and had a large frontal area which reduced the forward speed of the entire aircraft; a vicious circle of inefficiency.

The Seguins adopted a new air-cooled engine configuration in which the cylinders and crankcase, to which the propeller was rigidly attached, rotated around a fixed crankshaft. The resulting powerplant, with its cylinders rotating through the air, was adequately cooled yet light, permitting the development of far more powerful engines. In addition, the flywheel torque of the revolving engine produced smooth power, even at small throttle openings. Despite the rather awesome appearance which a rotary engine presented on the first encounter, it proved to be a most important interim power source, presenting airframe designers, for the first time, with as much power as they needed at the time.

One disadvantage was that, because the cylinders were rotating, a conventional carburettor set-up could not be used to supply the com-bustible mixture. Instead, a fuel/air mixture was admitted to the crankcase, entering the cylinders via ports in the cylinder walls. This raised lubrication complications, making essential the use of an oil not miscible with petrol. The resulting need for castor oil meant that engines had a characteristic smell which is associated nostalgically with rotary engines to this day. And because centrifugal force ensured that large quantities of oil passed straight through the engine, out of the exhaust ports and into the slipstream, both airframe and pilot were coated liberally. The oil consumption of a rotary engine could be from 25 to 50 per cent of the total fuel consumption, which meant that, in the long term, engines of this type would have proved totally unsuitable for long-range flight. Apart from that, when larger and more powerful engines were needed, the gyroscopic effect of the rotary engine would have made handling the aircraft very difficult.

In those early years these factors were unimportant, and Gnome engines, as the Seguins named their creations, were to power many significant aircraft during the seven or eight years following their entry into service in 1909.

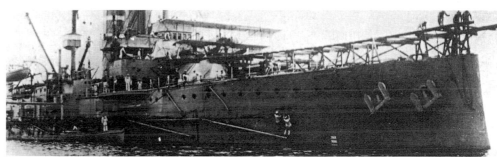

Later in 1910 Eugene Ely flew a Curtiss biplane off the cruiser USS Birmingham *(above); in May 1912 Commander Samson took off from the deck of the battleship HMS* Hibernia *(right), while it was under way, the first aviator to perform this feat.*

ELIMINATION OF NATURAL BARRIERS

1909 was to see another important event in early aviation, the attainment of a milestone of great future significance. On 25 July, at approximately 05.12 hours, a frail-looking monoplane landed on the Northfall Meadow, close alongside Dover Castle, Kent. Piloted by Frenchman Louis Blériot, this machine had just completed the first crossing of the English Channel by a heavier-than-air aircraft. Blériot's Type XI monoplane, which had made the crossing in 37 minutes, was powered by a three-cylinder air-cooled Anzani engine of only 18.6kW (25hp). Subsequently, similar Blériot monoplanes, though usually with rotary engines of significantly greater power, were to make many important pioneering flights, but few could have caused such military concern as this first Channel crossing. For the first time it was clear that an island's geographic insularity was no longer adequate protection, and that reliance could not be placed solely upon its 'moat' of surrounding sea, policed by a strong navy. Blériot monoplanes made the first flight over the Alps (23 September 1910), the first London-Paris nonstop flight (12 April 1911), and were the first officially to carry airmail in Britain (9 September 1911) and the United States (23 September 1911). One of the type also became the first aeroplane used in war (by Italy, 22 October 1911).

MOVES TOWARD MILITARY AIRCRAFT

Regardless of the growing capability of the aeroplane, few military leaders could appreciate its potential other than for reconnaissance purposes. And this, despite the fact that, as early as 30 June 1910, Glenn Curtiss in America had demonstrated it was possible to drop weapons from an aircraft in flight. Subsequently, the first rifle was fired from an aeroplane (on 20 August 1910), the first live bomb was dropped (on 7 January 1911), and later that same year a torpedo was launched from an aircraft for the first time.

Meanwhile, the potential of the aeroplane for naval operations had not gone unnoticed. On 14 November 1910 Eugene Ely had flown a Curtiss biplane off the American cruiser USS *Birmingham*; on 18 January 1911, he landed a similar aircraft on the cruiser USS *Pennsylvania*. In Britain, Lt C. R. Samson flew from the battleship HMS *Africa* on 10 January 1912, having possibly made an earlier 'secret' flight in December 1911. Four months later, during the Naval Review off Portland in May 1912, the then-promoted Commander Samson was the first to fly an aeroplane off a ship under way, taking off from the forecastle of HMS *Hibernia*.

Lack of military acceptance was of little concern to the pioneers. Their aim from the outset, on the whole (but not exclusively), had been to give to man the wings of a bird, perhaps even those of a dove of peace. Orville Wright was to comment: '... we [Orville and Wilbur] thought that we were introducing into the world an invention which would make future wars practically impossible'. A British pioneer, Claude Grahame-White, in a book written in association with British aviation journalist Harry Harper, was to state '... the globe will be linked by flight, and nations so knit together that they will grow to be next-door neighbours'.

The aim, from the outset; the belief, throughout these early years of development; and the hope, so frequently expressed by the pioneers of aviation, was that the aeroplane would prove an instrument of peace in the world.

While people of all nations gazed at the aeroplane in wonder, as daring young men accomplished those first flights which are the delight of today's historians, one nation began quietly assembling the biggest military air force in the world. When the First World War began, on 4 August 1914, Germany had 258 aircraft available for use by its army and navy. Britain and France combined had only slightly more aircraft in military service, and Belgium had only 24. Significantly, the military potential of the aircraft in German use was, at that time, superior to that of the machines available to the Allies. In any event, few aircraft in 1914 were very lethal, except to their occupants, but this was only the beginning. The aeroplane was very quickly to show that, properly used, it could be a military weapon of the greatest importance.

THE FIRST WAR IN THE AIR

When Britain entered the First World War the Royal Flying Corps (RFC) comprised 105 officers and just 63 aircraft. The Royal Naval Air Service (RNAS) had 130 officers, 700 petty officers and men, 39 landplanes, 52 seaplanes and 7 airships, of which about half of the aeroplanes and six of the airships were immediately available for use. The RFC, therefore, could hardly be considered a potent military force. What was worse, only a very small number of officers of the British Army believed that the aeroplane had the capability of being used in wartime operations that were still dominated by land forces. And there was, at the outset, little point in considering the air forces for major offensive purposes, as they were generally unarmed. To be fair, though, pilots could carry a revolver, if they could gain access to it beneath the voluminous clothing worn to keep them reasonably warm in the open cockpits.

Orders for British pilots on the initial Channel crossing to join the British Expeditionary Force were to ram any Zeppelin airship which might be encountered en route, since this was the only hope they had of destroying such craft. This was not a happy prospect, as it would have meant certain death. In one respect, though, a pilot's safety equipment was first class. The inflated rubber inner-tube around his waist promised security if engine failure dictated a forced landing in the Channel. He had no problems with carrying a parachute; he did not have one. High authority believed that the provision of such a device might encourage the pilot to abandon a damaged aircraft prematurely, instead of using his skill to get it back to base.

It was believed, however, that provided the weather was fairly calm it should be possible to use aircraft as reconnaissance platforms for trained observers. Reduced to the simplest terms, few had faith in the military aeroplane, and the aeroplanes available to the military were hardly suitable for day-to-day, all-weather use.

There was a contradictory problem with stability. Because the only role envisaged for the aircraft was one of observation, it was assumed that the observation platform should be as stable as possible. Aircraft designers worked hard to provide their aeroplanes with this characteristic. Among the most successful was the young British designer Geoffrey de Havilland of the Royal Aircraft Factory at Farnborough, Hampshire, whose B.E.2 biplane was a superb example of the inher-

ently-stable aircraft. Flying a B.E.2b, Lt Gilbert Mapplebeck, in company with Capt (later Air Chief Marshal Sir) Philip Joubert de la Ferté in a Blériot XI monoplane, flew the first RFC reconnaissance flight on 19 August 1914. The B.E.2 in its developed version, the B.E.2c, was perhaps the most perfect observation aircraft of the First World War. Unfortunately, this very characteristic of stability was to prove a serious problem at a later stage, as it made the aircraft an easy target for subsequent highly-manoeuvrable fighting aircraft.

RECONNAISSANCE AIRCRAFT PROVE THEIR VALUE

At the war's beginning the German advance was breathtakingly fast. By the time it had been slowed to a halt on the banks of the River Marne, the new and previously untried appendages of the British and French forces had already demonstrated that aerial reconnaissance was of vital importance. Without its use in this initial stage of the First World War, the conflict might have ended in the first few weeks, with the German armies in Paris. This early use of air power not only showed that an observation aircraft could report on enemy positions, the movement of reinforcements and supplies, and the sites chosen for munition dumps, but also proved, very quickly, that by spotting for batteries of field guns and directing their fire, this hit-and-miss weapon had gained new importance and a much higher degree of lethality. Air-to-ground communications initially relied upon message-dropping and visual signalling, but these methods were soon superseded by wireless telegraphy. And to make sure that an observer missed no small detail which might be of significance, aircraft were soon provided with cameras so that photographs could be studied and examined minutely for any information they might reveal.

It should not be imagined that such developments were confined to the Allied air forces, however. The German High Command also realised the potential of these new eyes in the sky, and it became clear to all combatant nations that serious efforts should be made to prevent enemy reconnaissance aircraft from overflying home territory. This was especially true in areas where important troop movements were in progress, or where poker tactics were being used to hold a weak point in the line with minimal strength.

Following trials with the Royal Aircraft Factory B.E.2a, the B.E. 2c evolved as a prime example of an inherently stable aircraft, which meant it could even be flown hands-off. When 'gusted' off an even keel it could usually right itself.

The airship represented the first true achievement of the pioneers towards the realisation of practical flight. The balloon was a great sporting vehicle, but if flight was to become commercial, the vehicle must have a means of being steered from point to point and be able to carry a worthwhile payload. Airships such as that demonstrated by Roy Knabenshue in America (right) represented the first minimal advancement towards this aim in the early 1900s. The military potential of the developing airship was soon appreciated. and vessels such as the Italian semi-rigid P-type (top) were used for reconnaissance and bombing attacks in 1912. It was Count Ferdinand von Zeppelin in Germany, however, who succeeded in designing and building very large airships (below) which, initially, were successfully used for passenger flights and later became formidable weapons in WW1.

The Bristol Fighter (foreground), known to WW1 pilots as the "Biff", first flew on operations in April 1917. Its debut was disastrous, but the machine developed to excellence, remaining in RAF service until 1932. The Sopwith Pup (behind), which went into service in 1916, was considered a superior aircraft by German air ace von Richthofen.

MILITARY AIRCRAFT FOR DIFFERENT ROLES

From this need stemmed the entire family of military aeroplanes: firstly, arms for the reconnaissance aircraft; then escort fighters to accompany them over enemy territory; fighters to take on enemy fighters; bombers to attack the bases from which an enemy's reconnaissance or fighter aircraft were deployed; and bombers to attack factories building such aircraft, their engines and weapons. On the ground, steadily improving anti-aircraft guns were developed to ensure that their high-velocity shells would keep observation aircraft at an altitude where they would be less able to carry out their task effectively.

The reconnaissance task was not limited to heavier-than-air craft. Large numbers of gas-filled tethered observation balloons were used initially by most combatant nations, until such time as they became sitting targets for fast aircraft armed with incendiary bullets. Germany, in particular, had also developed a fleet of large long-range Zeppelin airships, the majority of which were intended originally for use as naval reconnaissance vessels. Only as the war developed were they used instead as long-endurance strategic bombers.

These latter vessels were awe-inspiring weapons which seemed able to roam at will over British targets. Their size alone was frightening, with a length of more than 195 m (640 ft). But as defending fighter aircraft gained the ability to climb above the airships' operational height, and to attack them with newly devised incendiary bullets, they became far too vulnerable. When, on 5 August 1918, the pride of the German Naval Airship Division, the 211m (692 ft 3 in) long L.70, was shot down over the North Sea, the use of airships as offensive weapons finally came to an end.

DEVELOPMENT OF FIGHTER AIRCRAFT

The need to prevent an enemy's reconnaissance aircraft from having the freedom of the sky above one's own territory or lines meant that some way had to be devised to destroy the intruders. Anti-aircraft guns were one of the weapons chosen for the task, but the likelihood of hitting a moving target some thousands of feet in the air was then a question of luck rather than judgement. They served to keep enemy aircraft flying high and, if the barrage was heavy enough, to keep them away from a particular area.

In the air, initial combat involved opposing pilots taking pot-shots at each other with pistols; their observers soon joined in, often using rather more accurate rifles. There was an element of medieval combat about these early encounters, with rather more than a hint of knightly conduct on both sides. It was not to last, because the need to prevent an enemy from getting back to base with important photographs or information was vital, and so was the task of eliminating an aircraft that was directing the fall of heavy shells against one's own defensive positions.

As a result, machine-guns were taken into the air, fired initially by the observer from a movable mounting. This was practical for two-seaters, but was of little use to the pilot of a single-seat aircraft, who needed a machine-gun that was fixed rigidly to the aircraft and fired forwards. Moreover, it was difficult to aim such a weapon if it was not in the pilot's direct line of sight, and if it jammed it was useless, unless it was within the pilot's reach. One solution was to mount the gun centrally, so that the pilot aimed his aircraft at the enemy, but there was still the problem of access to the gun for clearing stoppages and, in

Britain's Sopwith Snipe (above) was one of the best fighter-scouts of WW1. When the United States became involved in the war they had no significant combat aircraft, and had to rely on supplies from their Allies. They built, however, and excellent trainer in the Curtiss JN series, and a JN-4 is shown (left). Typical of fighter-scouts used by France was the French Nieuport 28C-1 (opposite top right), The Fokker Dr.1 triplane (below) was one of the best remembered German aircraft, flown by Manfred von Richthofen, but the Fokker D.VII (above right) is regarded as one of the great warplanes of all time; armistice terms demanded that all D.VIIs were surrendered to the Allies.

the case of a Lewis gun, of reloading with new drums of ammunition. The ideal position was on the upper fuselage, directly forward of the pilot's windscreen, but this meant that the stream of bullets would have to pass through the disc of the rotating propeller.

French pilot Roland Garros and French aircraft designer Raymond Saulnier mounted a machine-gun in the ideal position on a Morane-Saulnier single-seat fighter, attaching steel deflector plates to the backs of the propeller blades to deflect any bullets which would otherwise splinter the wooden blades. Garros quickly demonstrated the effec-

tiveness of such a weapon, destroying at least three enemy aircraft before force-landing in enemy territory.

The significance of the machine-gun and deflector plates was appreciated quickly by the Germans who inspected the captured aircraft. Initially they wanted to copy this crude system, but designers Leimberger and Luebbe of the Fokker Company devised an interrupter gear which timed the discharge of bullets from a forward-mounted machine-gun so that they would pass between the rotating propeller blades. The resulting combination of aircraft and gun system produced

The Zeppelin Staaken R.VI (above) was one of Germany's so-called giant bombers, spanning 44.21 m (138 ft 5 ¹/₂ in), which had sufficient range to carry its load of eighteen 100kg bombs to attack not only targets on the Eastern and Western fronts, but to the heart of England's capital city. Maximum take-off weight of the R.VI was 11,460 kg (25,265 lb). The superb Avro 504k (below) training aircraft has a unique place in aviation history, because the foundation of modern flying training was evolved with this aircraft in the hands of the instructors of the RFC's School of Special Flying, men who used the techniques of flying training developed by Major R. R. Smith-Barry. But even this diminutive trainer had started life as a reconnaissance aircraft, and had won its spurs bombing Zeppelin sheds in Germany. When, on 21 November 1914, Royal Navy Air Service Avro 504s recorded the first ever strategic bombing attack by a formation aircraft, each carried the diminutive load of four 20 lb bombs.

the highly manoeuvrable Fokker Eindecker monoplanes with forward-firing machine-guns that proved a serious problem to the Allies.

The RFC, in particular, found itself at a grave disadvantage. The inherently stable B.E.2c was virtually defenceless when attacked and unable to outmanoeuvre the enemy and, because the observer was armed with a machine-gun that was restricted in its field of fire by the wings, struts and bracing wires, he was unable to fight back effectively. Within no time at all the observation aircraft of the Allies were being driven from the sky by a relatively small number of German Eindeckers. This was the beginning of the period of dominance by the German air force known as the 'Fokker Scourge', lasting from October 1915 until May the following year.

It soon became essential for Allied reconnaissance aircraft to be escorted by a mass of fighters, although, without an immediately available suitable interrupter system to enable Allied tractor single-seaters to be converted into machines with line-of-sight guns firing through the turning propeller, machine-guns had to be hastily fitted outside the propeller arc on the upper wing of a tractor biplane or installed into the nose of purpose-designed 'pusher' biplanes such as the RFC's Airco D.H.2 that slowly came into service.

Although these early fighters helped tame the Eindecker, it was essential for the the Allies to evolve a new family of very manoeuvrable and hard-hitting fighter aircraft that could deal with the even better German fighters that were taking over from the Eindecker from 1916, such as the sleek and much faster Albatros. Above all, they required an interrupter gear. The intended source to meet the RFC's requirements was the government's Royal Aircraft Factory, which produced the S.E.5 fighter for use from 1917. But private companies pulled their weight too, including Sopwith, which gave the RFC the Pup and Camel, and the British & Colonial Aeroplane Co (later Bristol), which produced its F.2 Fighter.

The British Admiralty relied only upon the private manufacturers, with Sopwith as a major source, providing its Triplane to the RNAS, among other types. The French aircraft industry followed similar lines of development, as involvement in the same theatres of war brought identical experience. This nation's industry was to benefit from the fact that it had been well established before the war, enabling it not only to produce excellent aircraft for the needs of its own armed forces, but to build aircraft in quantity for its Allies. This was to be of considerable importance in April 1917, when the United States entered the war, for although that nation's armed forces possessed some 250 aircraft, none were more effective than the simplest training aircraft of the belligerent nations. At the end of the First World War about 75 per cent of United States military aircraft operating at the Western Front had been supplied from French or British manufacturing sources.

THE DEVELOPMENT OF BOMBER AIRCRAFT

Germany's early reliance upon Zeppelin airships to fulfil the long-range strategic bombing requirement had meant reduced priority for the development of heavier-than-air craft to carry out both tactical and strategic bombing attacks. The Allies, on the other hand, had never

Germany's A.E.G. G.IV (right) was another of the significant bomber aircraft that evolved during WW1. Its range proved inadequate and the majority were used for short-range tactical missions. The Vickers Vimy (below) was intended as a strategic bomber to attack industrial targets in Germany. It was too late to see operational service in WW1, but made many important post-war flights, including the first heavier-than-air North Atlantic crossing.

envisaged the deployment of airships in such a role, both Britain and France confining the activities of such aircraft to maritime patrol in the North Sea and Mediterranean respectively. Both nations found them to be valuable anti-submarine weapons, not by taking direct action themselves but by calling upon naval sea forces to deal with these vessels.

As a result, the Allies were rather quicker to become involved in the development of suitable aeroplanes to satisfy the tactical or strategic attack role. The earliest attacks against Zeppelin sheds had been made by undefended RNAS Avro 504 scouts in late 1914, each carrying a small number of light bombs, but gradually, as the importance of attacks against military targets and supply bases and factories became apparent, manufacturers in Britain and France began to embark on the development of proper bombing aircraft.

One of the most important early aircraft to enter service with the RFC in the bomber capacity was the Airco D.H.4 day bomber, which hit the enemy hard under the operational guidance of the RAF's legendary father-figure, Hugh Trenchard. By 1917 both the RFC and the German air force were making use of specially-developed heavy bombers, Britain deploying the multi-engined Handley Page O/100 alongside the smaller Royal Aircraft Factory F.E.2b pusher biplane that had helped end the 'Fokker Scourge' in its fighter capacity and was now being pressed into service as a night bomber.

Germany had evolved the Gotha heavy bomber and Zeppelin-Staaken series of giant bombers, among other types. When the former made daylight attacks on London in June and July 1917, appearing

to range freely over the capital without any sign of opposition, the resulting public outcry ensured that the subject of this alarming gap in Britain's defences was debated in Parliament and, following enquiry and investigation, resulted in the creation of the independent Royal Air Force (RAF) on 1 April 1918.

The first Chief of the Air Staff was Major-General Sir Hugh (later Lord) Trenchard, and when he found difficulty in working with the Secretary of State for Air he resigned as Chief of the Air Staff and returned to France to create the Independent Force in June 1918. A firm believer in the capability of air power, Trenchard was the ideal man to establish the Independent Force, which initially comprised day bombers transferred from the RAF, plus Handley Page O/400s borrowed from the former RNAS and then integrated into the RAF. In the closing stages of the war an even bigger bomber was being developed by British manufacturer Handley Page, the V/1500. Both this and the smaller Vickers Vimy entered production too late to be used on wartime operations.

When the war ended, on 11 November 1918, all of the nations involved had gained an appreciation of the capability of air power. In particular, Hugh Trenchard in Britain, William ('Billy') Mitchell of the US Army Air Service and Giulio Douhet of the Italian Air Force had become dedicated protagonists of air power, convinced that a nation which possessed a potent air force could dominate the army and navy of an aggressor. We shall see how, in the inter-war years, these beliefs helped to shape the air forces which were to become involved in the Second World War.

THE CONQUEST OF THE GLOBE

There still exists a widespread belief that wartime use of aircraft in a combat or offensive role had brought about complete emancipation of the aeroplane. In fact, no such thing had happened. In the main, an airframe still relied upon a mass of struts and bracing wires to maintain its rigidity. The real change had come in the development of far more powerful engines: the 37.3-74.6 kW (50-100 hp) engines with which the various nations had gone to war had been replaced by engines that were no less reliable but had outputs ranging from 149-224 kW (200-300 hp).

Thus, the constant cry of the aircraft designer for more power had been met. But instead of developing 'clean' aircraft, free from drag-inducing struts and bracing wires, designers had tended to follow their noses, building bigger, better equipped machines that relied upon the increased power of their engines to drag them through the air. The external appearance of a biplane of 1918 tended to differ little, except in size, from that produced by the same company in the early days of the war.

The growing capability of aircraft during the war was clearly recognised by those interested in the post-war development of civil air services. As early as 5 October 1916 George Holt Thomas in Britain had registered a company named Aircraft Transport and Travel Ltd; shortly afterwards, in France, Pierre Latécoére planned how he might link his native country with Morocco. His ultimate dream was an air service for passengers, cargo and mail, spanning the South Atlantic to South America.

They, and others like them, had failed to appreciate that considerable development of specialised aircraft was necessary before such air services became routine. They had also overlooked the fact that the potential air traveller was not yet ready to accept the aeroplane as the best means of getting from one place to another. The majority of people who, in those early post-war years, would have the need to travel for business or pleasure, were still under the impression that flying was for heroes, certainly not for the mere person in the street.

THE FIRST POST-WAR CIVIL AIRLINE SERVICES

On 25 August 1919 Aircraft Transport and Travel inaugurated the first post-war scheduled civil air service between London and Paris. This was followed first by Handley Page Transport and then by S. Instone and Co, both operating services over the same route. France had also started civil operations, recording the first scheduled international passenger service between Paris and Brussels, on 22 March 1919. Compagnie des Messageries Aériennes and Compagnie des Grands Express Aériens also began services between London and Paris, with the result that too many aircraft were chasing a non-existent queue of passengers. Within a few years the competing private companies operating these and other European services found themselves in grave financial difficulties, leading to the formation of national airlines such as Air Union (later to become Air France), Deutsche Luft Hansa, Imperial Airways and Sabena.

The Swallow (above) was typical of the open-cockpit biplanes with which men such as Charles Lindbergh first pioneered the airmail routes of North America.

With the aircraft that were available to the early airlines in the immediate post-war years, flying was uncomfortable rather than unsafe. The only machines immediately obtainable were ex-military, with limited accommodation adapted for the carriage of passengers. What had been the gunner's position in a D.H.4 day-bomber, for example, could be provided with seats for two passengers, crammed face-to-face in the narrow fuselage, beneath a celluloid-windowed fuselage lid. Ventilation just happened; heating could be provided by heavy clothing, rugs and a hot-water bottle. A pair of household wooden steps was provided to make it easier to board the aircraft. The single fare could cost you about £16 from London to Paris. For the current equivalent sterling value one could fly from London to New York and return today.

Travel by air was expensive and unpopular. Only the wealthy or the brave took up the challenge. For them it was probably a good investment, for the passengers of an aircraft which had made one or more forced landings would have acquired a fund of exciting anecdotes which would ensure their selection as dinner guests for months ahead. Believe it or not, one of Aircraft Transport and Travel's 'airliners' made a record 22 forced landings on a single 'flight' between London and Paris.

THE BEGINNING OF THE GREAT FLIGHTS

Some catalyst was needed, powerful enough and widely reported, which would convince the 'person in the street' that anyone could fly as a passenger. In Britain, the *Daily Mail* newspaper had, from the date of the first powered flight in Europe, done much to sponsor aviation progress by the promise of substantial prizes for specific achievements. There had been, for example, £1,000 for the first cross-Channel flight, £10,000 for the first London-Manchester flight, and £10,000 for the winner of the first 'Round Britain' air race. All of these prizes had been won before the war and, so far as the public was concerned, long forgotten.

The Vickers Vimy (above) was the type used by Alcock and Brown to record the first historic non-stop west-east crossing of the North Atlantic; the Ryan Monoplane Spirit of St. Louis (left) carried Charles Lindbergh on the first great New York-Paris flight, an epic solo achievement. The airship R.100 (right), designed by Barnes N. Wallis (later Sir), also flew the North Atlantic, to and from Canada in the Summer of 1930. The Vimy's flight was made without the aid of any sophisticated navigational devices. Lindbergh's achievement was one of indomitable courage and skilful navigation; his primary problem was to keep awake for almost 34 hours of flight. The R.100, with 44 people on board, made its double Atlantic crossing with such ease that it seemed that the future of long-range transportation could be satisfied by such aircraft. It was wishful thinking: a number of fatal accidents soon showed that airships were not the answer.

The *Daily Mail* had offered another £10,000 prize for the first non-stop crossing of the North Atlantic, and this was won by Capt John Alcock and Lt Arthur Whitten Brown, who flew from St John's, Newfoundland, to Clifden, County Galway, Ireland (Eire) during 14-15 June 1919. Their aircraft was a specially-prepared Vickers Vimy, which, it will be recalled, had been developed as a long-range strategic bomber late in the war. This was the first of the great achievements that, over a period of time, would convince the non-flying public that a new and safe method of fast travel was developing rapidly.

Less than six months after Alcock and Brown's North Atlantic crossing, the Australian brothers Capt Ross and Lt Keith Smith (and two mechanics) set off to make the first flight between England and Australia. They, too, used a specially prepared Vimy, completing the 18,175km (11,294-mile) flight between 12 November and 10 December 1919, to win a £10,000 prize offered by the government of Australia.

From that moment on, the pace of progress got faster and faster. The first flight across Australia was accomplished between 16 November and 12 December 1919; the first flight between Britain and South Africa from 4 February to 20 March 1920; the first non-stop crossing of the United States during 2-3 May 1923; and the first round-the-world flight between 6 April and 28 September 1924.

All of these flights gained world headlines and brought some measure of confidence in the aeroplane. But something was still needed to capture the hearts and imagination of ordinary people all over the world. Then, at 07.52 hrs on 20 May 1927, a small (14 m; 46 ft span) and very overweight single-engined monoplane literally staggered off a rain-soaked field at Long Island, New York. Heavily laden with fuel, it only just cleared obstructions at the end of the field and climbed slowly, almost reluctantly, into lowering skies. The pilot, little-known except to his colleagues involved in carrying the US Air Mail, headed his aircraft out over the Atlantic, aiming for the diminutive target of Le Bourget airport, Paris. Thirty-three hours and 39min later, in the glare of car headlights and before an almost unbelieving crowd of cheering people, the little Ryan monoplane *Spirit of St Louis* came in to land at Le Bourget. Never again could its pilot claim anonymity, for this was the now-legendary Charles Lindbergh. His flight, the first solo non-stop crossing of the North Atlantic, was that which more than any other enchanted the peoples of the world. If, they argued, one man in a small aeroplane with only one engine could fly safely from New York to Paris, a distance of 5,810km (3,610 miles), then air travel must be safe for anyone wanting to travel over domestic and short-range intercontinental services. This single achievement gave a tremendous fillip to air services everywhere, and especially to domestic services in the United States.

On the subject of achievements, during the two years which followed Charles Lindbergh's Atlantic crossing, Costes and Le Brix made the first non-stop flight across the South Atlantic; 'Bert' Hinkler flew solo from England to Australia; Charles Kingsford Smith and Ulm with

a two-man crew achieved the first true trans-Pacific flight; and Sqn Ldr Jones Williams and Flt Lt Jenkins of the RAF flew non-stop from England to India. In August 1929 the German *Graf Zeppelin* airship made a round-the-world flight in just three weeks.

DEVELOPMENTS IN LIGHTER-THAN-AIR CRAFT

The post-war development of airships had seemed to offer an important means of travel on very long-distance routes. When, between 2 and 6 July and 9 and 13 July 1919 the British airship R.34 flew to Canada and back to accomplish the first airship crossing and the first two-way crossing of the North Atlantic, the protagonists of lighter-than-air craft were convinced that there was immense potential for cruise-liner type services over long ranges.

Germany, at first forbidden to build any new aircraft by the terms of the Treaty of Versailles (though this was soon relaxed in part), attempted to resuscitate the airship service between Berlin and Friedrichshafen which had operated so successfully pre-war, but this was soon stopped by the Allied Control Commission. Count von Zeppelin had died before the war's end, and his associate from the early days, Dr Hugo Eckener, had taken over control of the company. They were difficult times, but Dr Eckener ensured the continuance of the company by building the LZ.126 by way of German reparations to the United States of America. This airship, named the USS *Los Angeles*, was an immense success in US Navy service, accumulating well over 5,000 flight hours before being scrapped in 1939.

The Zeppelin company went on to build the highly successful *Graf Zeppelin*, first flown on 18 September 1928, and subsequently the world's largest airship, the LZ.129 *Hindenburg*, which was 245m (803.81 ft) long and had a maximum diameter of 41 m (134.5 ft).

Britain also built two large airships for civil air services, the R.100, designed for the Airship Guarantee Company by a team under the leadership of Barnes Wallis (later Sir), and the R.101, designed and built at the Air Ministry's Royal Airship Works at Cardington, Bedfordshire. Between 29 July and 16 August 1930 the R.100 flew to Canada and back on a proving flight which was highly successful. The R.101, on the contrary, crashed at Beauvais, France, on its proving flight to India, killing 48 of its 54 occupants. This event brought to an end the development of British rigid airships, and the R.100 was scrapped.

In America both the army and navy operated a number of airships, the latter having a large quantity of non-rigid vessels in service at various times. In addition to operating the LZ.126, the US Navy subsequently acquired two more large rigid airships that were unique for carrying and air-launching/retrieving fighters, the USS *Akron* and USS *Macon*. When both of these were lost at sea, in 1933 and 1935 respectively, the navy's rigid airship programme was brought to an end.

In Germany, the *Graf Zeppelin* was going from success to success. It seemed that a vessel had been designed and built which could provide the long-range civil services which it was believed were within the capability of such aircraft. By the time this airship was scrapped, in 1940, it had accumulated 17,178 flying hours, made 140 Atlantic crossings (among nearly 600 flights), and had carried 13,100 passengers. The Zeppelin company had every reason to believe that, as a result of their experience with the *Graf Zeppelin*, the subsequent Hindenburg would recoup the company's fortunes, and that airline operators would want to acquire similar craft to inaugurate prestigious long-range services. It was not to be. Because supplies of non-inflammable helium could not be obtained from overseas by then-Nazi Germany to inflate the *Hindenburg*, its gas cells were filled instead with hydrogen. When the giant airship approached the mooring mast at Lakehurst, New Jersey, USA, on 6 May 1937, static electricity ignited the airship and, within seconds, the *Hindenburg* collapsed in a blazing mass. By a miracle, 62 of the 97 people on board escaped with their lives, but this disaster was the last straw. Large commercial airship development had come to an end; at least, that is, until the latest revival in the late 1990s

The Ford Trimotor, or 'Tin Goose' as it was known popularly (left), had been produced originally in the 1920s. It utilised the corrugated metal skin which had been pioneered by Hugo Junkers in Germany, hence its nickname. Junkers later produced a tri-motor monoplane, but of low-wing configuration.

The Handley Page W9 Hampstead (below) was developed from the earlier W8b 12-passenger airliner. It differed by having three engines instead of two, providing a higher cruising speed, and could seat 14 passengers in wicker chairs.

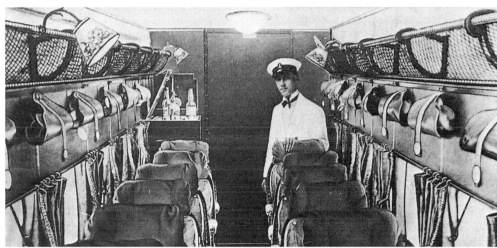

The first post-war civil aircraft were somewhat casual conversions of machines which had been used by the air forces during WW1. The austere accommodation available in the immediate post-war years did little to enthuse travellers to take to the air, and it was not until purpose-built airliners began to enter service that the passenger was able to find a degree of comfort. The Argosy airliners of Imperial Airways in 1927 had a steward to serve a buffet lunch to the 18 passengers of its Silver Wing service (right). Very different is the interior of a wide-body jet airliner such as the McDonnell Douglas DC-10 (above) which provided accommodation for a maximum of 380 passengers in air-conditioned luxury. The original 'wide-body airliner, Boeing's Model 747 'Jumbo-Jet', can carry well over 500 passengers.

START OF THE FLYING CLUBS

Just a couple of years before Lindbergh's North Atlantic flight an important aircraft had been designed and built by Geoffrey de Havilland in Britain. This was the de Havilland D.H.60 Moth, the prototype of which flew for the first time on 22 February 1925. A lightweight biplane powered by a four-cylinder in-line engine, it was the aircraft chosen to start the government-sponsored British Flying Club Movement. It was built subsequently in America, Australia, Canada, Finland, France and Norway, and is regarded generally as being responsible for the start of the worldwide flying club movement.

The de Havilland Moth was one link in the chain which made people aware of the potential of air travel. Subsequent achievements by ordinary people flying Moths added new links to the chain, including the first solo flight from England to Australia by a woman, accomplished by Amy Johnson between 5 and 24 May 1930. (Such is the affection for the Moth that, in early 1978, Flt Lt David Cyster flew one from Darwin to London to commemorate the 50th anniversary of Hinkler's solo flight to Australia in 1928.)

NEW AIRLINERS ENTER SERVICE

Next came another link, in 1931, when Britain's Imperial Airways introduced a fleet of Handley Page H.P.42/45 four engined biplane airliners. Despite having a cruising speed of only 160 km/h (100 mph), so that Anthony Fokker described them as having 'built-in headwinds', these majestic aeroplanes gained such a reputation for safety and comfort that, in the 1930s, they carried more passengers between

London and the Continent of Europe than all other airlines combined. The E and W versions of the H.P.42 carried 24 and 38 passengers respectively, the latter serving on the short-haul European routes. They accommodated the flight crew within the fuselage on a flight deck for the first time; it was finally understood that the pilot and his crew would be able to work far more efficiently under such conditions than if they were frozen to the marrow and exposed in an open cockpit to the worst the weather could offer.

Even greater changes were coming in America, where domestic air routes had expanded rapidly following the stimulus of Lindbergh's Atlantic flight. They had a good basis on which to develop, for the US Air Mail Service had linked major towns across the nation with navigational beacons, airfields and other facilities. All that was needed was a new generation of specially-designed transport aircraft.

On 8 February 1933 a very significant prototype aircraft made its first flight as the Boeing Model 247, which set entirely new standards. A low-wing monoplane of all-metal construction, powered by two 410 kW (550 hp) Pratt & Whitney air-cooled radial engines, it introduced several important innovations that would add considerably to the performance of aircraft the world over. These included retractable landing gear, variable-pitch propellers, control surface trim tabs, deicing equipment and an automatic pilot. It was the first twin-engined monoplane capable of climbing with a full load on the power of one engine, a fact which added considerably to safety in the critical areas of take-off and landing.

When the Model 247 was introduced into service by United Air Lines (UAL), a passenger could travel coast-to-coast across America in less than 20 hours, and this high-speed service sparked off a spate of

In the early 1930s this scene at Croydon Airport gave immense pride to those who worked hard to put civil aviation on a sound footing in the UK. This Handley Page H.P.42W Horatius of Imperial Airways was one of four Croydon-based 42Ws which linked London with Europe. But the Boeing Model 247 (above), a smaller contemporary, made these reliable biplanes look as if they had originated in another age.

development as a result of which the US manufacturers gained a lead in the production of civil transport aircraft which they held on to through most of the remaining years of the 20th century, indeed until recently equalled by the European Airbus Industrie.

Other US airlines, losing revenue to UAL, decided to approach the Douglas Company to produce a competing aircraft. The resulting DC-2 proved to be even more comfortable than the 247, carried four more passengers, was faster, and introduced wing trailing-edge flaps which improved take-off and landing performance. From the DC-2 Douglas evolved a wider-fuselage DST (Douglas Sleeper Transport), followed by one of the most famous aircraft in the history of civil aviation, the 21-seat DC-3. In the period 1939-1940, when some 80 per cent of civil transports used by America's domestic airlines were DC-3s, a 100 per cent safety record was maintained. Even at the end of the 20th century numbers of these remarkable aircraft remained flying around the world.

DEVELOPMENT OF INTERCONTINENTAL ROUTES

With the establishment of domestic routes in Europe and North America, airlines began to investigate the possibility of inaugurating intercontinental services over long ranges. Not surprisingly, most countries decided to use aircraft which could operate from water for such services. After all, 70 per cent of the Earth's surface is covered with water, and the development of flying-boats appeared to make good sense. Thus, when Britain decided to introduce the Empire Air Mail Scheme in late 1934, which meant that Imperial Airways would carry all mail for Commonwealth countries, the airline ordered a fleet of four-engined C-class flying-boats from Short Brothers. Designated S.23, the first of

The Douglas C-47 (left) was a military variant of the DC-3. Both earned a unique place in aviation history, primarily because of their reliability. The contemporary German Junkers Ju 52/3m (bottom left) gained equal respect; the name Tante Ju bestowed by Luftwafe pilots showed their trust in this multipurpose transport aircraft.

Once upon a time flying-boats dominated the long-range air travel scene. There was a romantic and almost magical aura about these great vessels. Open waterways used for take-off meant there was no serious restriction to the length of run, so flying 1-1 boats were usually much bigger than landplanes of the same era. The Boeing 314 (top right) provided the first regular transatlantic services. The Sikorsky S-42 (centre right) surveyed both Atlantic and Pacific routes . The Grumman Goose (bottom right) operates both from land and water, making it a true amphibian.

these, named *Canopus*, made its first revenue flight on 30 October 1936, and by mid-1938 S.23s were operating a through service from Southampton to Sydney, Australia.

America looked out across the vast reaches of the Pacific Ocean, planning a route via island stepping stones. Bases were therefore prepared on Midway Island, Wake Island and Guam (all US territory) to permit a route from San Francisco via Honolulu, Midway, Wake and Guam to Manila, the first stage, to Honolulu, being the longest (3,853km; 2,394 miles). The Martin Company built three four-engined flying-boats for this service, to the specification of Pan American Airways, and the first of these M-130 boats, the *China Clipper*, inaugurated the first trans-Pacific mail service on 22 November 1935. It was not until 21 October 1936 that fare-paying passengers were first carried.

France and Germany were both interested in developing a route across the South Atlantic. France began by establishing a service between Toulouse and Dakar, but it was 1928 before it was possible to open a route between Toulouse and Buenos Aires. This was not, however, a full air route, the ocean sector being operated by ships. It was not until 12 May 1930 that legendary French pilot Jean Mermoz took off from Senegal in the Latécoère seaplane *Comte de La Vaulx* to make the first direct crossing to Natal. More suitable aircraft were needed before a regular service could be established, and the three-engined Couzinet 71 landplane and four-engined Latécoère 300 flying-boat *Croix du Sud* began a South Atlantic mail service from 28 May 1934. But passengers were not carried over this route until after the Second World War.

Germany initially opted to use the *Graf Zeppelin* across the South Atlantic, the first trial flight from Friedrichshafen to Rio de Janeiro beginning on 18 May 1930. This proved successful, and airship services between Germany and Recife, Brazil, were inaugurated on 20 March 1932 and continued at an average of one return trip per month into 1936. The alternative German plan was to use Dornier flying-boats to link Africa and South America, with landplanes providing the service over the remainder of the route. To ensure that the flying-boats could take off with maximum fuel and full payload, a method of catapulting them from depot ships was adopted, enabling regular air mail services to begin on 7 February 1934. Subsequently, improved Dornier Do 26s were able to make direct unassisted crossings, and well over 300 crossings had been completed by various Dornier flying-boats when the Second World War brought the service to an end.

CONQUEST OF THE NORTH ATLANTIC

What about the North Atlantic? It seems strange that this, the first ocean to be conquered by both airship and aeroplane, should not have been the first to have regular air services linking the Old and New World.

It was not for want of enthusiasm that the North Atlantic was the last of the oceans to be conquered by air, for the commercial potential was apparent to all. Distance, unreliable weather and strong prevailing westerly winds conspired to make such a service impossible until reliable aircraft with long-range capabilities were available for the task.

Not until the late 1930s was the time considered right, and the interested nations began experimental flights. France used a six-engined flying-boat, the Latécoère 521, which made its first crossing to New York, via Lisbon and the Azores, in August 1938. Germany experimented with the depot ship technique which had been used on the South Atlantic route, several crossings being made by this method in

1936 and 1937 by Dornier Do 18 flying-boats and Blohm und Voss Ha 139 seaplanes. And in 1938 a specially-prepared Focke-Wulf Fw 200 Condor landplane made successful Berlin-New York and return flights, pointing the way to the future.

Interim British solutions included the Short-Mayo composite, the S.21 *Maia* flying-boat taking off with the S.20 *Mercury* seaplane carried pick-a-back. The *Mercury* could thus be air-launched with a maximum fuel load and payload, at a weight that would otherwise have prevented it from taking off without assistance. On 21-22 July 1938 *Mercury* made the first commercial crossing of the North Atlantic by a heavier-than-air craft, flying non-stop from Foynes to Montreal. It was, however, an impractical solution, and proved to be of no commercial use. Britain also experimented with inflight refuelling of Short C-class flying-boats, refuelled to maximum capacity by Handley Page Harrow tankers after take-off, and successfully completed a series of survey flights from 5 July 1937. Refuelled flights became weekly from August 1939, but were terminated on 30 September 1939 after eight crossings, because Britain had become involved in the Second World War.

It remained for America's Pan American Airways, which had been making experimental flights simultaneously with those of Imperial Airways, to inaugurate the first regular transatlantic mail service, on 20 May 1939. Finally, on 8 July 1939, Pan Am's Boeing 314 Yankee Clipper flying-boat carried 17 passengers and the mail on the inaugural northern route transatlantic service.

It had taken so long to achieve success on this, the most difficult ocean route in the world, that it seems unjust that the achievement was overshadowed and overlooked as a result of the gathering war clouds in Europe. By the end of the Second World War, a complete new generation of civil airliners was in prospect.

THE NEW AIRBORNE ARMIES

With the signing of the Versailles Treaty the 1914-18 'war to end wars' was over. The cost in human lives was almost unbelievable; the cost in monetary terms was to bring enormous problems to all the nations which had been involved. Germany was at first forbidden to build engine-driven aircraft; the other nations, believing that the four years of madness would have taught an unforgettable lesson, reduced their armed forces to a minimum.

Apart from the reductions in manpower and the disposal of surplus equipment, it meant that for some years ahead air forces would have to make do with the types of aircraft that had equipped their squadrons at the war's end. For aircraft manufacturers it was a bleak prospect as contracts for thousands of machines were cancelled. To stay in business many had to move into different fields of manufacture, often turning to the production of furniture, other domestic goods, motorcycles, buses and other items of which their national home markets had been starved during the war. As we have seen, the world was not then ready for a large civil aviation industry and, in consequence, there was little demand for the development of new civil aircraft, although a few early and purely commercial aircraft for passenger carrying did appear in 1919, such as the de Havilland D.H.16. In general, virtually the only aviation work available was the conversion of wartime aircraft for civil use, and even this requirement was very limited.

NATIONAL DEVELOPMENTS

With the end of the war, Hugh Trenchard was reappointed Chief of the Air Staff in Britain (in 1919). He took with him to the Air Ministry his profound belief in strategic air power and a determination to ensure that before he relinquished the reins he would build the foundation of an air force that could deal with any eventuality.

The United States Army Air Service (USAAS) had ended the war with a rapidly growing force. In immediate tactical command of its front-line squadrons at the Western Front was Colonel William ('Billy') Mitchell, a disciple of Trenchard. After a period with the Army of Occupation he returned to America to find that the USAAS had been reduced to a mere shadow of its wartime strength. Appointed Assistant Chief of the USAAS, Mitchell, too, was determined to bring about changes, convinced of the doctrine of strategic air power, as well as of the need to make the Air Service an independent force, free of Army control.

There was yet another prophet of air power, the Italian General Giulio Douhet, who in 1921 published a treatise The *Command of the Air,* expressing his convictions that stategic air power should be the dominant feature of military planning, since both armies and navies would eventually become subservient to air power.

France, which with Belgium had been the main board on which the battles of the First World War had been played, was thinking primarily in terms of defence. The immense and costly fortifications called the Maginot Line were constructed, in the firm belief that it would prove more than adequate to prevent another invasion from Germany.

Japan had no significant aircraft industry until the early 1920s, and before that only small numbers of aeroplanes of European design had been built under licence. Realising that its small army and navy air forces needed practical instruction in military aviation, a service mission was invited from France in 1919 to provide essential education for the army air force in aerial combat, gunnery, reconnaissance and bombing techniques. This was so successful that, in 1921, the Japanese Navy invited a similar mission from Britain. This also proved of great importance, providing technical instruction which covered subjects from the basics of flight control to aerial photography, the use of torpedo-launching aircraft, and operations from aircraft carriers (*Hosho,*

These between-wars military aircraft have a disparity in size, but both played a significant role in RAF training. The de Havilland Tiger Moth primary trainer (left) remained in service for 15 years. The Vickers Virginia (above) was an important night bomber, teaching skills invaluable in WW2, when RAF Bomber Command was primarily a night force.

the first purpose-built Japanese aircraft carrier, being commissioned in December 1922). The lessons were well learned, and in just 20 years the Japanese had created formidable air forces.

In Russia, after the holocaust of the Communist Revolution, a new and powerful air force was created gradually. Much assistance in the later development of the Red Air Force came from German sources, in return for facilities at Lipezk, in Russia, where for eight years the new Luftwaffe was trained in secret.

TRENCHARD PLANS THE FUTURE RAF

A most important event in British military aviation came in 1919, with the publication in December of an official document which has found its way into history as Trenchard's White Paper. In this, the Chief of Air Staff advocated the retention of an independent air force, with small units to be trained especially for co-operation with the navy and army. This led to the creation at a later date of the Fleet Air Arm and Army Air Corps. But the most important section of this document was that which detailed Trenchard's proposals for the training of an RAF which,

though small, could be expanded as needed in a time of national crisis. Furthermore, this high quality and careful training, allied to the practical experience which the air force gained while helping to maintain law and order abroad, or as a result of involvement in the small-scale wars and insurrections which persisted almost continuously between the First and Second World Wars, was to provide an élite corps of airmen, both in the air and on the ground. When the real challenge came, in 1939, they were ready for it.

THE IMPORTANCE OF THE SCHNEIDER TROPHY

The surplus of aircraft which the RAF inherited at the end of the First World War meant that, in the main, they had to soldier on for many years, sometimes into the early 1930s, before any significant new machines became available to replace them. When replacements did materialise, some bore the imprint of the influence on aircraft and engine design which had resulted from the Schneider Trophy Contests initiated by Jacques Schneider, in France, in late 1912. Schneider's original aim had been to speed the development of aircraft which could operate from water, believing that the future of air transport would be linked closely with waterborne aircraft, or hydro-aeroplanes as they were then known. But these international contests evolved into air races between high-speed seaplanes and became matters of national pride, most purpose-developed aircraft having just about sufficient room within their streamlined fuselage to accommodate a pilot.

In the development of these aircraft, designers learned a great deal about building sleek monoplane and biplane structures, the impor-

New generations of fighter aircraft were developed between the wars. The Boeing P-26 of the US (left) and the high-wing monoplane built by Emile Dewoitine in Switzerland (bottom left) had similar bluff lines, being built around radial engines. R.J. Mitchell's Supermarine S 6B racer (below) had the streamlined form that later graced the Spitfire fighter.

tance of streamlining and the significance of an aircraft's shape in keeping drag to a minimum. At the same time, specialist designers evolved far more powerful engines. These were, of course, short-life racing engines, but the experience they gained in building, testing and operating such machines led to new powerplants of greater reliability and much improved power/weight ratio. The Curtiss D-12 engine and Curtiss/Reed propeller developed in America was one of these remarkable powerplants of the early 1920s, a small-diameter propeller allowing the construction of an engine which needed no reduction gear drive to ensure that the propeller tips did not exceed a certain critical speed. This simplification not only reduced the overall weight of the engine, but meant that power normally needed to drive the reduction gearing was available instead for propulsion. In the UK the Rolls-Royce R (racing) engine of 1,752 kW (2,350 hp), which speeded the Supermarine S.6B seaplane to victory in 1931, finally winning the Schneider Trophy outright for Britain, was developed initially into a new 746 kW (1,000 hp) military engine called the Merlin. The Supermarine S.4, S.5 and S.6 series of racing seaplanes designed by R. J. Mitchell led him to the creation of the famous Spitfire monoplane eight-gun fighter, which was powered by the Merlin. In aviation, as in the automobile industry, the spur of competition improved not only the capability of the vehicle, but also its mechanical efficiency and reliability.

DEVELOPMENT OF AIR FORCES

In America, Billy Mitchell campaigned ceaselessly for an independent air force, demonstrated (though under unrealistic conditions) that aircraft had the capability of sinking capital ships, and, following persistent campaigning and criticism of senior command, was court

martialled. He was sentenced to five years suspension from duty, but instead he resigned from the Service so that he could continue to use every means at his disposal to influence the creation of the kind of air force which he was certain the United States needed.

Despite Mitchell's efforts, America retained army and navy air forces, the former service operating primarily for army co-operation until the provision of long-range bombers and defensive fighters in the 1930s brought a change of policy. In the inter-war period the US Navy built six aircraft carriers and procured a series of shipboard aircraft, mostly with dive-bombing capability. When, in 1926, a navy squadron of dive-bombers dramatically demonstrated the potential of such aircraft, not only did the US Navy adopt such tactics as standard for anti-shipping operations, but both Germany and Japan made due note of this information.

Germany's Ernst Udet, previously a First World War fighter ace, was so impressed by the potential of dive-bombing that he influenced the development of aircraft with such capability to serve with the Luftwaffe, the creation of which service was announced officially on 9 March 1935, though it was internationally illegal. The idea of dive-bombing was taken up enthusiastically, to the extent that a special dive-bomber was created as the Junkers Ju 87 Stuka, and the Luftwaffe directed that new bombers being developed by the German industry must also have a dive-bombing capability. There was little support for a long-range strategic bomber, except from the Luftwaffe's first Chief of Staff, Lt-Gen Wever. After his death, in 1936, he was superseded by Gen Kesselring, an advocate of tactical support for the army, with the result that Germany had no long-range strategic bombers for operations throughout the war. Instead, design and production was concentrated on short-range lightly-armed bombers intended for daylight use. The first standard single-seat fighter to be operated by the Luftwaffe was

Classic trainer of the USAAC and USN, the Stearman Kaydet earned fame for its rugged reliability; more than 8,000 were built.

the rugged-looking Heinkel He 51 biplane, but this was soon followed by Willy Messerschmitt's superb Bf 109 single-seat fighter which, in progressively developed versions, was to serve the German air force throughout the Second World War.

Aircraft produced in Italy during this period were mostly of biplane configuration, their performance limited somewhat by the quality of the engines provided to power them. In retrospect, this seems ironic during a period when the Italian aircraft industry was producing some excellent aircraft and powerful engines to compete in the Schneider Trophy contests. Even after the Macchi-Castoldi M.C.72 had achieved a new world speed record, in 1934, the aircraft industry was instructed to continue the production of radial aircooled engines for military use. Not until Italy was able to obtain higher-powered Daimler-Benz inline engines from Germany during the war did production of high-performance combat aircraft become a reality. Two exceptions to this were the Fiat C.R.32 biplane fighter and Savoia-Marchetti S.M.79 bomber, both remarkable aircraft. The latter was numbered among the best land-based bombers of the Second World War.

Japan had been busy building up the strength of its air forces from the time that the French and British missions had visited that country. The navy's air arm expanded most dramatically, with new and effective aircraft equipping the six aircraft carriers that were built between the wars.

Germany's announcement of the creation of the Luftwaffe caused great concern in both Britain and France, especially as German propaganda was designed to exaggerate the size and capability of this new force. Immediately, both nations initiated massive rearmament programmes. In the case of Britain it led to the design and development of aircraft such as the Spitfire and Hurricane fighters, and Blenheim and Wellington bombers with which the war was begun, as well as the important four-engine strategic bombers that entered service as it progressed. France was not so successful; her aircraft industry was newly-nationalised and in a state of disorder, with the result that the only significant new aircraft entered service too late to be of any use in the nation's defence.

Most of the nations which were to become involved in the Second World War had, during the inter-war years, had some opportunity of using their air forces operationally, thus gaining valuable experience. Britain had used her air force for policing and air control in the Middle East and on the North West Frontier of India. Germany, Italy and Russia had been actively involved in the Spanish Civil War. Italy had been at war with Abyssinia and Albania, Japan with China and Russia. America's policy of neutrality had sufficed to keep the nation from war, but this meant that when war broke out in Europe, on 1 September 1939, the capability of her Army Air Corps was far behind that of the European nations.

WORLD WAR IN THE AIR

The invasion of Poland by German forces on 1 September 1939 was not such a shock as was the speed and efficiency with which this brave nation, possessing only a small and outdated air force, was ruthlessly eliminated as a fighting unit by Germany. The German Blitzkrieg technique, with Stuka dive-bombers providing close support for massive Panzer divisions of tanks and armoured vehicles, swept all before it. Within seventeen days it was all over, and Germany and Russia were busy dividing the first spoils of their uneasy alliance.

When the first air raid sirens sounded in Britain, on 3 September 1939, soon after Prime Minister Neville Chamberlain had told the nation by radio that Britain and France were again at war with Germany, most civilians believed that bombs would soon come raining from the sky.

This was not surprising, for they had been conditioned to expect it by a concentrated year of Air Raid Precautions, from newsreel pictures of air raids during the Spanish Civil War, and by early BBC reports of the invasion then in progress in Poland.

GERMANY OVERRUNS WESTERN EUROPE

At that time, Hitler then had no intention of fighting simultaneously on two fronts, and it was not until 3 April 1940, when there had been time to prepare for the new campaign in the West, that his war machine was unleashed again in massive strength, first against Denmark, then against Norway, Belgium, Holland and France. By June 1940 the German army and air force could stand and look across the English

The Spitfire (right) and the Hurricane (below) were both eight-gun fighters and both were powered by Rolls-Royce engines.

This Spanish-built version of the Messerschmitt Me Bf 109 (left) gives an authentic impression of the Luftwafte's fighter which took part in the Battle of Britain. Opposing bombers are pictured (opposite): the Vickers Wellington (right) and Dornier Do 217 (bottom right) were both eventually used in a variety of roles.

Channel and see their next target; Britain. But the British Isles were not to prove quite so easy to overcome.

The year which Britain had gained when Neville Chamberlain signed the 1938 Munich peace (or, arguably 'appeasement') agreement with Adolf Hitler was put to good use by the RAF and the nation's aviation industry. Worthwhile numbers of eight-gun Hurricane and Spitfire fighters were deployed, and Britain's development of radar, allied to the reporting network of the Observer Corps and RAF Control Centres, meant that the fighters could be used to maximum effect. It was not necessary to fly endless patrols in case the enemy attacked. Instead, the fighters could wait and be directed to attack the enemy aircraft as and when necessary. This multiplied the effectiveness of the outnumbered British aircraft and saved aircraft, pilots, maintenance, fuel and stress.

Contrary to popular belief, Germany had also developed a radar system, but had not provided the back-up which existed in Britain to direct defending fighters to meet hostile aircraft. In any event, such a comprehensive system proved unnecessary in the first stages of the war, because German defences proved more than adequate to deal with daylight attacks; so effective, indeed, that British bombers could only be sent over German targets by night if high losses were not to be sustained.

BATTLE OF BRITAIN

Thus, when Germany launched its air force to knock out Britain's air defences in preparation for invasion, the RAF had some 700 front-line fighters and about 300 more aircraft in reserve, ready for the fight which has since become known as the Battle of Britain. By the time the Battle was over, in early September 1940, the Germans had been driven from the daylight sky over Britain. Henceforth, German bombers had to operate by night. As well as providing a psychological and practical victory for the RAF and the nation it protected, the German Luftwaffe had lost many of its most experienced pilots and invasion was impossible.

Space does not permit a detailed coverage of the aircraft involved in the Second World War: instead we must look at the trends which developed as the war itself progressed.

DEVELOPMENTS IN BRITAIN

Most of the nations which were involved in the war still had biplanes in service at the time of their entry. Britain's air arms all had fairly large quantities of such aircraft, but only the Gloster Gladiator remained in first-line service as a fighter, and it was soon to disappear. One biplane that remained in front-line service until after VE-Day was the Fleet Air Arm's famous 'Stringbag', the Fairey Swordfish torpedo-bomber. The Hawker Hurricane was gradually superseded by the Hawker Typhoon and Tempest but, in many differing variants, the Supermarine Spitfire

remained in service until after peace was restored. The Bristol Company, well known for the Blenheim I fighter and Blenheim IV medium bomber, produced the Beaufighter, which enjoyed considerable success as a nightfighter and was developed subsequently for use in a wide variety of duties.

De Havilland, renowned for its family of inter-war light aircraft, built the 'Wooden Wonder', better known as the Mosquito, which served as fighter, bomber and reconnaissance aircraft, flying high and fast enough so that for most of the war nothing could catch it. In 1936 Britain had begun the development of modern long-range strategic bombers, resulting in the four-engined Handley Page Halifax, Short Stirling and Avro Lancaster bombers which ranged over Germany by night as the war developed. But in the initial stages the Blenheim, Armstrong Whitworth Whitley, Vickers Wellington and Handley Page Hampden were the mainstay of Bomber Command.

REGIA AERONAUTICA AND THE LUFTWAFFE

Italy, under the dictatorship of Mussolini, had developed its Regia Aeronautica into a large air force, and experience gained during its operations in Abyssinia (Ethiopia) and in the Spanish Civil War should have ensured that it would prove a potent and valuable ally for the Luftwaffe. This did not prove to be the case, for despite the development of some excellent fighter and bomber aircraft, it lacked the esprit de corps which distinguished the achievements of the Luftwaffe, RAF, Commonwealth air forces, and the United States Army Air Force (USAAF).

As mentioned previously, the Messerschmitt Bf 109 was the Luftwaffe's primary fighter at the beginning of the war. It was to be joined by another superb fighter, designed by Kurt Tank, the Focke-Wulf Fw 190. This aircraft rather dumbfounded the 'experts', who had believed for so long that a fighter had to have an inline engine if it was to be sleek and fast. Kurt Tank and BMW showed that a properly cowled bluff-fronted radial engine, with air ducted to a cooling fan, could provide sparkling performance, and was free from the weight and vulnerability of a liquid-cooling system. For bombing capability, Germany relied initially upon three medium bombers, the Dornier Do 17, Heinkel He 111 and Junkers Ju 88. The Ju 87 had its initial glory in the first blitzkrieg attacks, but also proved an important aircraft for deployment against Germany's one-time ally, Russia, which was invaded with considerable early success on 22 June 1941. The famous Stuka, however, was slow and vulnerable to enemy fighters, and therefore useless unless Germany was in complete control of the sky.

RUSSIAN AIRCRAFT PRODUCTION

Like Napoleon before him, Hitler had not appreciated sufficiently the vast areas of land into which the Russians could retreat strategically to blunt the enemy's attack and plan new campaigns. Neither had he been prepared for the ferocious severity of the Russian winter; and it

At dawn on the morning of 7 December 1941, a Japanese naval task force was steaming close to Hawaii. At 07.40 hours 183 carrier aircraft were over Oahu Island and streaking to attack Pearl Harbor. As this first group finished its mission, a second wave of 167 aircraft came in to add to the devastation on the ground. Taken completely by surprise, and while Japanese diplomats were still negotiating peace terms in America, the US Pacific fleet had been virtually eliminated as a fighting unit for some time to come. Happily for the US Navy, but unknown to the Japanese, US aircraft carriers were at sea, escaping the fate of Battleship Row, where four battleships, two destroyers, a target ship and a minelayer had been sunk and numerous aircraft and facilities destroyed. Four battleships, two cruisers and a destroyer also lay seriously damaged. When, three days later, the British battleships *Prince of Wales* and *Repulse* and an escorting destroyer were sunk at sea by Japanese naval aircraft, the beliefs expressed by Billy Mitchell were shown to be valid. No longer could surface vessels afford to ignore the danger in the sky.

Japan had learnt well from the teachings of the Western military missions, especially the navy, which had realised from an early date the potential of the aircraft carrier. And despite the reports which had come to the Western nations from China, none had appreciated that Japan had developed such a wide range of high-performance aircraft. They were to discover, in due course, that in many cases this performance resulted from lightweight structures void of armour protection for the crew and without adequate precautions to make fuel and hydraulic systems safe from attack. American pilots soon learned that, even if an enemy had superior performance, he needed only to be hit hard once to be destroyed.

Japanese innovation provided some excellent aircraft as the war progressed, but no missions were more devastating than the Kamikaze ('Divine Wind') suicide flights which, in the final ten months of the war, accounted for no less than 48.1 per cent of all US warships damaged and 21.3 per cent of all ships sunk during the whole of the Pacific War.

is doubtful whether anyone could have believed that despite the disruption and chaos of a full-scale invasion, the Russians would be able to move their aircraft industry far behind the fighting areas and resume production surprisingly quickly. From such conditions came a series of Yakovlev fighter aircraft able at last to confront the Luftwaffe on equal terms. Further supplies of large numbers of fighter aircraft from Britain and the United States enabled Russia also to divert resources into other types of aircraft and, in particular, the Ilyushin Il-2 Sturmovik ground-attack aircraft proved hugely valuable. Heavily armoured to protect it from ground fire, the Il-2 was armed with guns, rockets and bombs to provide a most effective tank-destroying capability, taking heavy toll of German armour.

JAPAN GOES TO WAR

In 1941 Japan had decided that national interest, as a result of sanctions imposed by the United States, made it essential for Japan to gain access to supplies of aviation fuel and/or crude petroleum. Indonesia was the nearest source of supply, but this would be available to the Japanese only as conquerors. As Japan was cut off from external fuel supplies, its reserves were dwindling rapidly because of the continuing war against China. It was now or never, and it had the large forces to wage war in the Pacific over huge distances, allied to much combat experience.

AMERICA'S EUROPEAN/PACIFIC INVOLVEMENT

American involvement in the war after the Japanese attack on Pearl Harbor meant that, in the long run, success for the Western Allies was inevitable. Britain no longer stood alone at arms. Even before Amer-

American bombers included the Douglas DB-7 (Havoc and Boston) light bomber (right), the most extensively-built and widely-used aircraft in this category. The Boeing B-17 Flying Fortress (centre) is known especially well in Britain for its vital contribution to round-the-clock bombing of European targets during WW2. The Boeing B-29 Superfortress (bottom), designed to meet the USAAF's requirement for a long-range strategic bomber, proved of vital importance in the closing stages of WW2, destroying Japanese cities with incendiary weapons, and is remembered also for its two atom bomb attacks.

The Gloster-Whittle E.28/39 (left) was Britain's first aircraft to take to the air under the power of a gas turbine engine, the work of Sir Frank Whittle. The first turbojet-powered aircraft to fly, on 27 August 1939, was the German Heinkel He 178, powered by a gas turbine engine developed by Dr. Pabst von Ohain.

ica was precipitated into battle, the Japanese Navy had expressed the opinion that in a long-drawn-out war America must win, because of the enormous productive capacity at that nation's disposal.

Britain and the USA came to an agreement on production of aircraft: in the main Britain would concentrate on short/medium-range aircraft for combat in the European theatre of operations, while America would build long-range bombers and transports, plus suitable fighter aircraft, with which to fight the long-range island-hopping war in the Pacific Ocean and contribute to the European theatre.

Thus, in Europe, British bombers were deployed against enemy targets by night and US bombers by day, to provide round-the-clock attacks. Escorting the bombers over enemy territory by day were such classic American aircraft as the Lockheed P-38 Lightning, North American P-51 Mustang (especially after it was fitted with the Merlin engine) and Republic P-47 Thunderbolt. The escorted aircraft were mainly Boeing B-17 Flying Fortresses and Consolidated B-24 Liberators.

RAF Bomber Command concentrated on large-scale attacks by night, with targets pinpointed by Pathfinders which illuminated the bombing area for the masses of Halifax, Lancaster and Stirling bombers following behind. The primary result of such concentrated strategic bombing was to reduce Germany's supplies of fuel to a point where it was impossible to prevent the relentless attacks from the air.

As the war neared its end, in 1944, both Britain and Germany were to deploy aircraft using a completely new powerplant, the gas turbine, which had been developed independently by Frank Whittle in Britain and Pabst von Ohain in Germany. The USA and Japan also developed jet fighters, but these were not to become operational in this war. Germany was also to use operationally the world's first rocket-powered interceptor, the Messerschmitt Me 163B. However, none of these aircraft was built in sufficient quantity or appeared early enough to have significant influence on operations.

In its final attempts to avoid defeat, Germany launched pilotless V-1 flying bombs and V-2 ballistic rockets against Britain and selected targets in continental Europe, Britain being the principal target as the base from which British and US aircraft took off to attack Germany, and from which the D-day invasion was launched. But such missile attacks came too late to have any effect on the war's final outcome. The German forces were overrun and defeated, and with Adolf Hitler dead and Germany itself besieged by Britain, America and their Allies in the West, and the Russians fighting in a devastated Berlin, war in Europe ended on 8 May 1945.

In the Pacific theatre, heroic and bitter fighting by the American Army and Marines had driven the Japanese back towards their home islands. The availability of the Boeing B-29 Superfortress meant that massive incendiary attacks could be launched against Japanese targets. One such raid on Tokyo, on 9 March 1945, destroyed a quarter of the capital, and nearly 84,000 people lost their lives. Five months later, on 6 August and 9 August, the world's first operational atomic bombs were dropped over the cities of Hiroshima and Nagasaki respectively. The prospect of continuing annihilation of Japanese citizens and property on such a scale was inconceivable, though for a short time the war continued. Then, on 19 August, two Mitsubishi transports flew the Japanese surrender delegation to Ie Shima and later, on 2 September 1945, the surrender documents were signed on board the battleship USS *Missouri*. Six years and one day after Germany's invasion of Poland, the Second World War was over. From first to last it was a conflict which had shown the impact of aviation as a primary military weapon.

KEEPING THE BALANCE OF POWER

At the beginning of the Second World War the two fastest opposing fighters, the Messerschmitt Bf 109 and the Supermarine Spitfire, were capable of approximately the same maximum speed at optimum altitude, that is about 571 km/h (355 mph). By the end of the war both had gained 30-40 per cent in weight, had engines with anything up to double the power, and speeds as much as 25 per cent faster, despite the increased weight. In the main, the increased weight came from extra equipment, more armament, and additional fuel capacity to increase range and to cope with the demand of higher-powered engines.

THE PROBLEM OF COMPRESSIBILITY

This was the trend for most aircraft which were in military use over a period of years and, with certain specific exceptions, the increased speed, as well as overall improvement in performance, came from engines of greater power and more efficient propellers. But as the war progressed and new aircraft entered service, generally improved technology made it possible for level flight speeds in excess of 708 km/h (440 mph) to become fairly commonplace. In the latter stages of the war it was not uncommon for aircraft such as the British Hawker Typhoon and the American Lockheed P-38 Lightning to exceed these speeds in a dive, their pilots reporting violent shuddering of flying surfaces. In some cases control surfaces, wings and tail units were torn away, and many pilots lost their lives as a result; for the first time they were encountering the effects of compressibility, a phenomenon then known primarily in advanced aerodynamic theory.

When an aerofoil surface approaches the speed of sound, the air ahead of the aerofoil is unable to move aside fast enough, and a shockwave forms at the leading and trailing edges of the aerofoil. If the wing has not been specially designed, not only will it (or any other aerofoil surface) be buffeted by this shockwave, but additional drag will also be induced.

Considerable research on this problem was carried out in Germany during the war, especially in relation to the Messerschmitt Me 163 Komet, the world's first rocket-powered combat aircraft which, in the Me 163B-1a version, was capable of a speed of 959km/h (596mph) at 3,000 m (9,840 ft). It was discovered that a swept wing, that is one in which the angle between the wing leading edge and the centreline of the fuselage forms an angle of less than 90 degrees, was able to be flown at above-normal speeds without the onset of buffeting. This sort of research information became available to the world's aircraft manufacturers in the early post-war years.

At that time Britain held a considerable lead in the development of turbine engines, and the RAF's Gloster Meteor F.3s, which were powered by 8.90kN (2,000 lb st) Rolls-Royce Derwent I turbojets, formed the equipment of the RAF's first jet-fighter wing in 1945. The maximum speed of this version was 668 km/h (415 mph), but the piston-engined de Havilland Hornet F.1, which entered RAF service in 1945, had a maximum speed of 760 km/h (472 mph). At that time the newly-developed turbine engine had not attained the propulsive efficiency of which the engine/propeller combination was capable at the peak of its development.

SUPERSONIC FLIGHT

The power output of gas turbines began to grow rapidly, and it was soon clear that the time was fast approaching when it would be possible for aircraft to travel at more than the speed of sound. This represents a velocity of about 1,193 km/h (741 mph) in dry air at 0C (32F), such speed being expressed as Mach 1.0, after the 19th century Austrian Ernst Mach, who studied the propagation of sound waves. Thus, Mach 0.75 represents three-quarters of the speed of sound. Before new generations of aircraft could travel in excess of Mach 1 as a matter of routine, it was necessary to build a research aircraft which would have a very strong structure to survive aerodynamic buffeting and use most or all then-known aerodynamic improvements, together with a powerful engine to provide the necessary thrust.

Under contract to the National Advisory Committee for Aeronautics (NACA), the Bell Aircraft Company in America designed and built such an aircraft, designated X-1, powered by a rocket engine but minus the kind of swept-wing technology Germany had already researched, using instead thin-section straight wings. Air-launched at 9,145m (30,000ft) altitude from a B-29 Superfortress mother plane, this aircraft was flown progressively nearer to the speed of sound by a young USAF pilot, Charles 'Chuck' Yeager. At times the aircraft was buffeted so badly that it seemed an impossible task. Then, on 14 October 1947, Yeager slipped through what the media had dubbed 'the sound barrier' to the smoothness of supersonic flight. Subsequently he flew the Bell X-1A at a speed of 2,655km/h (1,650mph), and the knowledge gained from this research was to make possible a whole new range of combat aircraft which was developed all over the world.

THE BERLIN AIRLIFT

It is unlikely that any serious-thinking person imagined that the Second World War would prove the latest 'war to end wars'. It left behind far too many new and potentially hazardous situations. One of these situations was the partition of Berlin, partly occupied by the Soviet Union, while West Berlin was controlled by British, French and US powers. Vitally, the Soviet Union controlled the surface routes for transport into and out of West Berlin that went through East Germany. The Soviets therefore believed that by closing the surface routes 'for technical reasons' and effectively isolating West Berlin from West Germany, the Western Allies would leave Berlin for good. This was a miscalculation. Instead, West Berlin was sustained from the air in an important oper-

The first operational turbojet-powered aircraft to enter service in the UK was the Gloster Meteor, and the picture (opposite page) shows Meteors of the RAF's No. 77 Squadron operating in Korea. But at that time there was still a lot to be learnt about gas turbines and the design of aircraft to reap the full potential of the immense power that such engines promised. In the meantime piston-engined aircraft such as the US Navy's Douglas AD-1 Skyraider (above) proved still valuable in post-WW2 conflicts. So did the North American F-82 Twin Mustang (right), developed as a long-range escort fighter.

ation known as the Berlin Airlift, and for more than a year, from 26 June 1948, military and civil pilots ferried essential materials and food into Tempelhof, Gatow and, in the latter months, Tegel. Indeed, the flights became so regular that special arrangements had to be made to unload aircraft while others approached. The Allies had effectively demonstrated that they were prepared to face any cost to ensure continuing peace and prevent the expansion of communism. Furthermore, this warning of potential danger to peace in Europe speeded up the formation of the North Atlantic Treaty Organisation (NATO), which took place in April 1949.

THE KOREAN WAR

The next major trial of strength was to come in Korea when, at 04.00 hours on 25 June 1950, the communist North Korean infantry, spearheaded by Soviet-built tanks, streamed in their thousands across the 38th Parallel to attack the Republic of Korea. The United Nations Security Council called immediately upon all member nations to assist in repelling the attackers, and troops from many countries were to be involved in bitter combat on Korean soil. In the air the battle was fought

primarily by the USAF, USN and RAAF, and in this three-year struggle there came three developments important for military aviation; a rebirth of aerial reconnaissance, the introduction of tactical air co-ordinators (known later as Forward Air Controllers), and the rapid evolution of the helicopter as a military weapon. There came also, in this conflict, the first air battles between jet fighters.

Large-scale reconnaissance was needed in this new type of war, resulting in the introduction of new techniques and new equipment, as well as the realisation that reconnaissance capability of the highest order would be permanently essential for the prevention of more general war. At the beginning of the evolution of these new techniques was the tactical air co-ordinator. A pilot and observer, flying in a lightweight aircraft, maintained visual reconnaissance over a battle area until relieved, relaying constantly by radio to an operations centre the state of the battle below. They could call in strike aircraft and direct them to a target, making a very valuable contribution to the battle on the ground. Also in this conflict helicopters, which had seen just a taste of experimental/operational use before the Second World War ended, were to prove invaluable. Because of their go-anywhere capability, they were able to carry troops and supplies into forward areas inac-

cessible to any other form of transport. On their return journey to base they could operate as air ambulances, carrying men injured in battle for immediate treatment at field hospitals. By this action, the death rate from wounds in Korea was reduced to the lowest figure then recorded in military history. Helicopters were able to demonstrate also that if armed, even with comparatively simple weapons, they could be developed into an important close-support aircraft for tactical operations.

CUBAN CRISIS

The Cuban crisis of 1962 was another shock to all nations, creating potentially the greatest threat of a Third World War and again highlighting the importance of reconnaissance in a world which, thanks to the development of a whole armoury of nuclear (or thermonuclear) armed intercontinental ballistic missiles, had achieved the ability to destroy itself. Routine reconnaissance of Cuba had been initiated by the USA, after Fidel Castro had shown that close links existed between

New types of aircraft evolved soon after WW2. Helicopters such as the Bell H-13 Sioux (opposite top) proved themselves vitally important in the Korean War. Flight refuelling techniques (below) made it possible to deploy aircraft over vast ranges. Spy-planes like the Lockheed U-2 (left) could provide important intelligence information.

his regime and the Soviet Union. When surface-to-air missile (SAM) sites of Russian origin were discovered on the island, US reconnaissance was stepped up which eventually led to the discovery that Russian-built medium-range ballistic missiles were being installed and trained against the highly-industrial areas of the USA.

American President John F. Kennedy advised his NATO allies of the situation, put the massive US deterrent forces into an action alert state and called upon the missiles to be withdrawn or face the consequences. Soviet Premier Nikita Khrushchev, having challenged the US right to be concerned over Cuban matters but equally anxious to prevent a US invasion of Cuba and the possibility of US-Soviet conflict, agreed to order a stop to the construction of the sites and ship the missiles back to the Soviet Union.

IMPORTANCE OF RECONNAISSANCE

When this crisis was resolved, on 29 October 1962, there was no doubting the importance of a first-class reconnaissance capability, and this desirable aim was pursued energetically by governments all over the world. Not only was the aeroplane involved heavily in such work, but gradually a whole family of pilotless drone aircraft was developed to carry out such tasks; development of tactical and theatre reconnaissance UAVs (unmanned air vehicles, to use the latest terminology) continues to this day, ranging from the tiniest camera-carrying vehicles that fit into the palm of a hand to huge aircraft with full stealth capability such as the USAF's planned Global Hawk for service in the 21st century that has a wing span of 35.4 m (116 ft 2 in) and can loiter on station some 5,550 km (3,450 miles) from base for up to 24 hours, while allowing its controller to flick between radar, infrared and visual surveillance modes as required. And as man learned to make his first journeys into space, and evolved the technique of placing satellites into Earth orbit, these too enhanced reconnaissance capability, as part of a delicately-balanced deterrent policy which has prevented highly-destructive conventional or nuclear war between the major powers.

It has not proved adequate, however (and neither has the gradual development of even more advanced and potent combat, close-support and strategic aircraft), to prevent smaller regional conflicts fought for political, nationalistic or economic reasons, which have plagued mankind since the end of WW2.

Space does not permit a detailed list of military aircraft which have evolved in the post-Second World War years. Instead, it is possible only to mention briefly the trends of development, which have been similar among the major powers. And because, with one or two notable exceptions, lesser powers are unable to face the astronomical research and development costs of a new significant military aircraft, they too have equipped their air forces with many of the weapons developed by the major powers of the East or West.

SUPERBOMBERS

The Boeing B-29 Superfortress bomber, which had been instrumental in bringing about final victory for the Allies over Japan in 1945, was, in a very true sense, the first 'superbomber'. It was designed to a requirement for a 'hemisphere defence weapon', and its many important innovations included pressurized crew compartments connected by a crawl tunnel, and a series of small remotely-controlled gun turrets to offer a high degree of defence. The B-29 was the USAAF's principal strategic bomber in 1946 when Strategic Air Command (SAC) was formed as one of three new commands for USAAF combat units, the others becoming Tactical Air Command and Air Defense Command, and it remained in service long enough to see action in the Korean War. Its more powerful and slightly modified B-50 derivative was the first new bomber taken into service by SAC, by which time the USAAF had transformed into a fully independent service under the new title of United States Air Force (USAF), a consequence of the 1947 National Security Act.

Now, with the Cold War hotting up, the post-war run-down of the USAF was reversed and new B-50s became medium bombers, serving alongside a veritable giant bomber with a 70 m (230 ft) wingspan and six large piston engines driving 'pusher' propellers, the Convair B-36. This intercontinental bomber was the last USAF strategic bomber to have piston engines, in its final developed form having the ability to deliver a 39,000 kg (86,000 lb) bombload, assisted by the addition of four podded turbojet engines to boost its power. Its long legs were

amply demonstrated in December 1948, when one completed an unrefuelled non-stop flight from Texas to Hawaii and back, a distance of 15,128 km (9,400 miles).

The B-36 finally left the USAF in early 1959, its strategic role having passed to the huge eight-turbojet Boeing B-52 Stratofortress, while the six-turbojet Boeing B-47 Stratojet had become the principal strategic medium bomber. The Stratojet was phased out in the 1960s, but in 1999 the remaining B-52H Stratofortresses were still a major component of the USAF's Air Combat Command, founded in 1992 to amalgamate USAF bomber and continental US combat aircraft units. The B-52 gave the USAF truly global bomber coverage, demonstrated in January 1962 when a B-52H was flown unrefuelled from Okinawa, in the Ryukyu Islands, to Madrid, Spain, a distance of 20,169 km (12,532 miles).

In the Soviet Union, its own copy of the B-29, the Tupolev Tu-4, was superseded in the intermediate-range strategic role during the early 1950s by the Tupolev Tu-16, codenamed 'Badger' by NATO and with twin turbojets neatly faired into the wingroots of its sweptback wings. For the heavy long-range turbine bomber requirement the Soviets chose two quiet different designs, the four-turbojet Myasishchev M-4 (NATO 'Bison') and the incredible Tupolev Tu-95 (NATO 'Bear'). Both were first flown over the winter of 1952-53, the Tu-95 having a unique powerplant of four massively powerful turboprop engines, each driving two four-blade coaxial contrarotating propellers, and it is this aircraft type that has matched the B-52 for longevity of service into the 21st century.

As a point of interest it should be remembered that a twin-jet tactical Soviet bomber that first flew in 1947, the widely operated Ilyushin II-28 (NATO 'Beagle'), preceded all three of the larger Soviet types. Similarly, the USAF fielded three light tactical jets; the North American B-45 Tornado, a Martin-built version of the Canberra known as the B-57 (the first non-US aircraft to join the post-war USAF, which, in its long-span RB-57 high-altitude reconnaissance version, was also used for sorties over Soviet territory), and the Douglas B-66 Destroyer. The last was developed from the US Navy's Skywarrior carrier-based attack bomber.

Above: A B-52G, one of the 744 Stratofortresses built by Boeing between 1953 and 1962 for the USAF.

Left: The Convair B-36 intercontinental bomber in developed form with six piston engines and four turbojets.

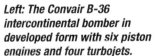

Right: Martin-built B-57B, used for night intrusion and tactical bombing by the USAF.

SUPERSONIC AND SWING-WINGS

Meanwhile, at the end of the 1940s, the USAF had formulated a requirement for a supersonic medium bomber able to deliver either a nuclear or conventional warload. At that time Convair led US work on delta wings for high-speed aircraft, having flown in 1948 its XF-92A delta-winged research aircraft, designed with the assistance of Dr Alexander Lippisch, who had conducted similar research in Germany during the Second World War. To meet the bomber requirement Convair conceived the B-58 Hustler, which first flew in November 1956, over two years after Convair had first flown another of its new deltas, the smaller F-102 Delta Dagger supersonic interceptor, the design of which had begun in 1950. F-102 became the first US operational fighter armed only with missiles and rockets. To allow a speed of 2,230 km/h (1,385 mph), the Hustler had an area-ruled fuselage, four high-powered turbojets pod-mounted under the large delta wings, used lightweight composite/metal honeycomb sandwich construction for skin panels in many areas of the airframe, and featured individual escape capsules for the three crew members, to permit supersonic ejection. This last feature was first tested at high speed in March 1962, with a bear as the occupant, by which time the Hustler had been in USAF active service for two years. Most importantly, the Hustler carried its warload and fuel for the outward part of a mission in a detachable underfuselage pod, which could be jettisoned for the return flight.

The Hustler was retired in 1970, in which year the USAF became operational with the replacement General Dynamics FB-111A two-seat supersonic strategic bomber, developed from the F-111 tactical fighter-bomber that had itself been the first US operational warplane with variable-geometry or 'swing-wings'. Interestingly, when the FB-111A was retired from its strategic role in the 1990s, many were converted to F-111Gs for conventional attack.

However, a shock lay around the corner. Unknown to the West, in 1969 the Soviets had flown the prototype of a vastly superior intermediate-range bomber and missile carrier, which later became known in service as the Tupolev Tu-22M (NATO 'Backfire'). Designed to replace the Tu-16 and the Tupolev Tu-22 (NATO 'Blinder') medium bombers (the latter of which had first been seen in public in 1961 as a twin-jet and swept-wing type, and was the first Soviet supersonic bomber, with a speed of Mach 1.4), the new swing-wing Tu-22M had been required to reach targets in Western Europe and China while carrying nuclear bombs or missiles (or conventional weapons), to have a dash speed of 2,000km/h, and to have a low-level penetration speed of Mach 0.9. Deliveries to operational units began in 1975, but by then Tupolev had already begun work on an even more formidable strategic bomber, the larger swing-wing Tu-160 (NATO 'Blackjack'), designed as a long-range platform for launching cruise missiles. The original requirement had been for a bomber able to cruise at up to 3,500km/h and cover a range of up to 18,000km, but in 1970 this was scaled down to a dash speed of 2,000km/h and 14,000-16,000km range, allowing the prototype to make its first flight in 1981 and production aircraft to enter service from 1987.

Before the appearance of the Tupolev bombers, in 1967, the West had been surprised and greatly worried by the first sighting of the Soviet Mikoyan MiG-25 (NATO 'Foxbat') interceptor and reconnaissance aircraft. This very-high-powered aircraft had a maximum speed of over Mach 3, and had originally been conceived to intercept the US North American B-70 Valkyrie strategic bomber then under development. Intended as a B-52 replacement, the Valkyrie had been designed to fly its entire long-range mission at Mach 3, thus making it the most formidable bomber of all time. However, even before the first of two prototypes flew in 1964, the same year as the MiG-25, it had already

The General Dynamics F-111 Aardvark first flew in 1964, and was introduced into combat in Vietnam in 1968, initially with disastrous consequences. It became, however, a much-prized warplane with the USAF until it was retired in 1997, leaving only Royal Australian Air Force F-111s in service.

Above: The Russian-built Tupolev Tu-160 'Blackjack' supersonic bomber can fire cruise missiles or short-range attack missiles from rotary launchers in its two bomb bays.

Right: The Avro Vulcan was the RAF's longest-serving 'V' bomber in its intended role, finally being used in the first British attack of the 1982 Falklands conflict. When first introduced into service it was the world's largest delta-winged aircraft.

Below: The Panavia Tornado in strike form, here operated by the Royal Saudi Air Force.

Reworked to reduce detectability by an enemy during long-range penetration missions, the more stealthy but slower Lancer, as it was later named, first flew in 1984 and became operational from 1986.

Supersonic bombers for nations outside the USSR and USA took very different forms. Britain, having put its first jet bomber into service in 1951 as the light and subsonic English Electric Canberra, followed by three types of subsonic long-range medium 'V' bombers for strategic use, the Vickers Valiant, Avro Vulcan and Handley Page Victor, all for service from the mid-1950s, developed the BAC TSR 2 as a Mach 2-plus attack bomber. This first flew in 1964 but was cancelled in favour of US aircraft which were in turn subsequently cancelled. The TSR 2 became the RAF's last and lost chance to deploy this type of dedicated weapon, and since the 1980s this air arm has instead relied on the capability of the internationally developed, smaller, two-seat, swing-wing Panavia Tornado to perform its heaviest interdiction and strike missions, though its nuclear role was withdrawn in 1998. A second version of Tornado was developed as a long-range interceptor, known as the Air Defence Variant, which entered RAF service at the same time. Germany and Italy, as partner nations in the Tornado programme, also received production aircraft, and Germany's special electronic combat and reconnaissance version of Tornado was used in September 1995 to execute the Luftwaffe's first combat missions since the end of WW2, flying sorties over former Yugoslavia from a base in Italy, in support of the United Nations.

been cancelled as a bomber and was thereafter flown only for aerodynamic research. This did not stop Soviet production of the MiG-25, however, as its performance was so high.

The next attempt to replace the ageing B-52 came with the Rockwell International B-1, the USA's own concept for a large swing-wing heavy strategic bomber, capable of twice the speed of sound. First flown in 1974, it too was cancelled in 1977 in favour of cruise missile development for strategic attack. But a manned bomber offered much greater flexibility of use, and in 1981 the programme was reactivated as the modified B-1B, with a much smaller number of bombers anticipated for service, to supplement B-52s rather than replace them.

For French service in the supersonic strategic nuclear bomber role, Dassault developed the Mirage IV, first flown in 1959, which looked like a scaled-up Mirage III delta-winged fighter. This remained in ser-

vice as a bomber until 1996, so completing 33 years in the role, although five strategic reconnaissance conversions will continue operations until 2005. A version of the Mirage 2000 combat aircraft now performs France's low-altitude nuclear or conventional penetration role, while the latest Dassault Rafale will also include nuclear strike among its many combat roles.

PROGRESS TOWARDS STEALTH

The importance of strategic reconnaissance after the start of the Cold War between East and West, as mentioned earlier, led to the development of some remarkable and unique aircraft. In the 1950s work began at Lockheed's top-secret 'Skunk Works' on a dedicated and jet-powered strategic reconnaissance aircraft, which first flew in 1955. To hide its real mission it was given a 'U' designation, which normally denoted 'utility', although in the case of the resulting U-2 it was a spyplane. Subsonic, it relied on its very high operating altitude to escape detection, while its huge wingspan allowed it to glide power-off for periods while gathering intelligence. Incredibly, the U-2 Dragon Lady in its latest 'S' version remains operational today. The Soviet equivalent took until the 1980s to appear, as the Myasishchev M-17/M-55 (NATO 'Mystic'), although work on the aircraft had originally begun in 1970 for an entirely different role, that of high-altitude interception to destroy US unmanned reconnaissance balloons.

In 1966 a far more incredible strategic reconnaissance aircraft entered USAF service, the SR-71. Another product of the secret Lockheed Skunk Works, this was designed for speeds well in excess of Mach 3, and the adoption of some low-observable or 'stealth' technologies in airframe design and construction gave it low 'visibility' to enemy radar. Indeed, such was its performance that an interceptor compatriot was also flown but not funded for service. Consequently,

when the US authorities requested the secret development of a new attack-fighter of low radar signature in 1974, it came as no surprise when Lockheed's Skunk Works eventually won the bid.

This new attack-fighter was to be like nothing before it. For the first time an attempt was to be made to exploit virtually every known stealth technology, and thereby produce an aircraft that could evade even complex enemy defences during night attacks on carefully selected high-value or important targets. For its stealth mission the subsonic aircraft was to avoid detection by giving off the very lowest possible radar and infrared signatures, while being visually difficult to see and acoustically hard to detect. Control of 'give-away' contrails and engine smoke was essential, and electromagnetic emissions were to be suppressed. The engines would have no afterburning, and no radar would be carried. As a first step Lockheed built two sub-scale XST Have Blue technology demonstrators for flight testing of the strange airframe shape at Groom Lake, the first flying in 1977. These were followed by 5 development aircraft and 60 full-production single-seat F-117A Nighthawks, although the USAF accepted only 59 F-117As for service, as one crashed before delivery. Initial operational capability was declared in 1983, but it took another five years for the USA to announce the F-117's existence to the public, so secret was its conception.

It is impossible to gauge the work conducted in the Soviet Union/Russia on stealth aircraft, but there is little doubt that this important technology must have been recognised as a vital avenue of research.

Meanwhile, back in the USA, a programme was initiated only a year after the first XST flew, to develop in secret a fully stealthy, very large subsonic strategic bomber. This time Northrop became the chosen developer, having worked on flying-wing designs since the 1940s, including huge piston- and jet-powered flying-wing bombers that very nearly reached USAF service. The B-2A Spirit, as the stealth bomber

Left: The latest French combat aircraft is the Dassault Rafale, which is going into service with both the air force and navy. Its wide range of missions can include attack with Apache missiles that each deploy many submunitions. (F. Robineau - Dassault/Aviaplans)

Right: The first warplane to make genuine use of stealth technology was Lockheed's SR-71A Blackbird Mach 3+ strategic reconnaissance aircraft.

Below: The many flat-plate airframe surfaces of the amazing Lockheed Martin F-117A stealth fighter-bomber help it to defeat enemy radars.

The USAF's Northrop Grumman B-2A Spirit became the world's first operational stealth strategic bomber. There are no vertical flying or control surfaces to spoil the blended airframe.

became known, first flew as a prototype in 1989, and 21 joined the USAF from 1993 to supplement the B-52H and B-1B, although original plans had been for 132.

SUPERFIGHTERS FOR THE 21ST CENTURY

Although termed a 'fighter', the F-117A is an attack aircraft, and it is interesting that even the most modern genuine fighters for service well into the 21st century call upon only limited aspects of stealth technology. In Russia, where some of the world's most advanced combat aircraft are being developed, greater emphasis has recently been placed on developing thrust-vectoring nozzles for conventional fighters, to improve manoeuvrability, rather than on the incorporation of major stealth technologies. However, some Russian designers are reportedly sceptical of the benefit of thrust vectoring for Mach 2 aircraft, as the manoeuvring advantages offered are usually obtained at low speed, below Mach 0.5.

In the USA, the new Lockheed Martin F-22 Raptor fighter for USAF operational service from 2005 uses more stealth technology than its contemporaries. This includes the ability to achieve supersonic cruis-ing speed without use of its engine afterburners (known as 'super-cruise'), a low radar cross-section, internally-carried weapons, avionics intended not to betray its position, and more; but it is still not as fully 'stealthy' as might have been possible, and again has thrust vectoring.

As for Europe, the excellent Swedish Saab Gripen and the multinational Eurofighter only pay lip service to stealth, despite the fact that they are intended also for attack and reconnaissance roles in very hostle environments.

SPEED IS NOT ALL

The fighters of the 1950s had introduced Mach 1 and then Mach 2 performance. And, while most fighters became larger and heavier as the years passed, France, the Soviet Union and Sweden continued to achieve considerable success with much lighter aircraft: the Mirage III/5, MiG-21 and Saab Draken and Viggen types respectively. Of course, considerably heavier Soviet warplanes followed in very rapid succession, but none was produced in such huge numbers for world-wide use as the MiG-21 (well over 10,000 built in the Soviet Union alone).

Left: Sukhoi's latest range of combat aircraft is among the most advanced in the world. It includes this Su-37 with thrust-vectoring nozzles for very high manoeuvrability, a side-stick controller to ease the pilot's workload, and 'glass cockpit' multifunction display screens.

Below: The lastest Swedish combat aircraft is the Saab JAS 39 Gripen, designed to be capable of undertaking fighter, maritime, ground-attack or reconnaissance roles at the flick of a computer switch, and yet to be turned-around under combat conditions by five conscripts and one technician in just 10 minutes. (Johnny Lindahl/Saab)

Bottom: The Soviet-designed Mikoyan MiG-21 is still built and developed in China as the Chengdu J-7, seen here in J-7B form.

The USA had entered the Vietnam War in the mid-1960s, expecting to assist the South in quickly breaking the North's incursions through the deployment of vastly better-equipped and better-trained forces. Helicopters, so useful in Korea in the 1950s, had grown in status and size, while multi-million-dollar jet combat aeroplanes were expected to fly freely against a lesser-equipped enemy. It was not to be so simple. Raids over the North met complex defences comprising surface-to-air-missile sites and radar-guided guns, while the large and heavy US jets often found that the small but growing number of lighter, more manoeuvrable and less sophisticated opposing MiG-17 and then MiG-21 fighters were equal to the task, not least because they could often intercept and then dart back across borders where US warplanes were forbidden to follow. Moreover, some combat aircraft being introduced into the theatre by the USA, such as the McDonnell F-4C Phantom, were missile fighters and had no cannon, a mistake that proved costly in dogfights and had to be rectified. Indeed, Vietnam proved in many ways to be a 'retro' war, as particular operations, such as counterin-surgency, were best suited to much slower and more easily maintain-able warplanes. The USAF, US Navy, US Marine Corps and South Vietnamese Air Force found themselves scratching around for old

In the early post-war years came the first of the supersonic fighters. Aircraft such as the US Navy's LTV F-8 Crusader (above) and USAF's Lockheed F-104 Starfighter (left) evolved from research programmes that investigated problems of supersonic flight and how to build airframes to fly at such speeds.

Right: Boeing's AH-64D Apache Longbow, a highly effective counter-weapon to armoured vehicles, performs a nap-of-the-Earth low-flying exercise.

piston-engined Skyraiders and Trojans, and investigations were even conducted into whether or not to put the wartime Mustang back into production and service.

By 1968 the US forces had lost well over 600 aircraft, the vast majority to non air-to-air combat causes, and this led to the deployment of specialised electronic countermeasure aircraft to jam enemy radars. Such aircraft remain vital to present-day operations, and are typified by the US Northrop Grumman EA-6 Prowler, which can escort attacking warplanes to degrade or suppress enemy defences.

Other aircraft developments resulting from experience in Vietnam included specially-designed but slow light-attack and forward-air-control types such as the 451 km/h (281 mph) and turboprop-powered North American Rockwell OV-10 Bronco, while the Bell Helicopter Company developed the world's first specially designed helicopter gunship for service in Vietnam, the AH-1 HueyCobra, which proved devastating as an anti-armour and escort machine. Whereas the Bronco ethos later spawned such subsonic tankbusters as today's Fairchild Republic A-10 Thunderbolt II, with its 7,257kg (16,000lb) weapon load and hard-hitting seven-barrel nose cannon to fire 1,174 rounds of 30mm armour-piercing ammunition, the HueyCobra was the precursor of all modern attack helicopters, up to today's Boeing AH-64 Apache, Boeing Sikorsky RAH-66 Comanche, and foreign types such as the Russian Mil Mi-28 'Havoc', South African Rooivalk, Italian Agusta A.129 Mangusta and European Eurocopter Tiger.

EXTENDED RANGE

Before the Second World War, Britain had led the world in trials to demonstrate in-flight refuelling to extend the range of both military and civil aircraft, and continued to be a leader post-war. With the coming of fast military jets and the requirement to deploy forces rapidly across the world, the need for suitable in-flight refuelling tankers became obvious. Many early tankers were produced by converting ex-airline or military piston-engined transports, but such were the operating altitudes and speeds of some military jets that a completely new breed was required. One answer came with the conversion of surplus jet bombers into tankers, and this was done, but when Boeing chose to develop a purpose-designed tanker for the USAF it was to change aviation for ever. As a private venture, Boeing designed and developed a four-turbojet transport, which first flew as the Model 367-80 prototype on 15 July 1954. After demonstrations with a flight refuelling boom the potential was obvious, and later that same year the aircraft was ordered in massive numbers for the USAF as the KC-135 Stratotanker.

Knowing that it had a winning design, in July 1955 Boeing gained permission to build a commercial airliner derivative alongside the KC-

Above: First flight of the Lockheed Martin F-22 Raptor advanced tactical fighter for the USAF in Engineering and Manufacturing Development (EMD) form (September 1997).

135, leading to the first-ever US turbojet airliner, the famous Model 707. In-flight refuelling has made it possible for air forces to deploy an attacking or `policing' force anywhere in the world at short notice, and some long-range transports and helicopters are also able to take fuel from tankers to enable them to carry men and equipment to far-away destinations in hours instead of days. The idea of using in-flight refuelling for commercial applications, though, never took off.

VERTICAL-TAKE-OFF AEROPLANES

The vulnerability of airfields, and other tactical reasons, suggested to post-Second World War planners that vertical take-off fixed-wing aeroplanes could make very useful additions to military arsenals. In the event, all manner of strange aircraft were tested from the 1950s, but

it was Britain once again that led the world when, in 1960, Hawker Siddeley first hovered its incredible P.1127 Kestrel, a prototype tactical fighter and close-support aircraft that eventually led to full development and deployment of the renowned Harrier 'jump jet' by the RAF, the US Marine Corps and others. A naval version for aircraft-carrier operation was the Sea Harrier, one of the mainstays of the 1982 Falklands conflict.

The Soviet Union also developed a similar type of aircraft for naval use, the Yakovlev Yak-38 'Forger', which first flew in 1971. But this, like its intended but later abandoned Yak-41 'Freestyle' replacement, used both a main engine with rear thrust vectoring to direct thrust at the required angle for vertical or horizontal flight, and small almost vertically mounted 'lift-jets' in the mid-fuselage for use in vertical operations only; a far more complicated and ultimately unsuccessful system than the Harrier's use of a single jet engine with front and rear thrust-vectoring nozzles. As the world's first operational vertical/short take-off and landing (V/STOL) fixed-wing aeroplane, the Harrier has been continuously developed, and current versions are in widescale service and remain unique among world warplanes.

BRIDGING THE GAP BETWEEN HELICOPTERS AND AEROPLANES

Rotating-wing aircraft, better known as helicopters and autogyros, have been an everyday part of the military and civil scene for many decades, but historically were more difficult to develop. The many operating benefits offered by the helicopter have to be weighed, however, against its fairly low speed and short range, and sometimes low internal carrying capacity. While these limitations are unimportant for many uses, they have concerned military planners wishing to combine vertical lift with greater speed, operating economy and capacity. The answer to this difficult problem has now appeared in the form of

Above: First flown in 1954, the Lockheed XFV-1 was one of the most interesting early concepts to produce a vertical take-off fighter, in this case intended as a carrier-based naval escort.

Below: The British Aerospace (BAe) Harrier was the world's first VTOL combat aircraft, developed from the earlier P.1127 Kestrel. The BAe Nimrod (bottom), developed from the de Havilland Comet jet airliner, became an important maritime patrol and ASW aircraft.

the Bell Boeing V-22 Osprey, a tilt-rotor transport and multipurpose aircraft which has its turboshaft engines and huge 11.58 m (38 ft) diameter proprotors (propeller/rotors) mounted at the tips of its wings. This enables the proprotors to be positioned horizontally for vertical flight and then tilted down for fast cruising, permitting a maximum speed of approximately 699km/h (434 mph) to be attained, combined with a self-deployment range of over 3,800 km (2,400 miles) and an internal payload capacity of 9,072 kg (20,000 lb). First flown in 1989, the Osprey is now joining the US forces. Bell has also developed a quite separate 10/12-passenger civil tilt-rotor aircraft, the BA 609, which is being co-produced with Agusta of Italy.

Of course, conventional helicopters will continue to be built and developed for traditional markets, and for an ever-expanding number of roles that now include such diverse activities as firefighting and air-to-air combat.

FINAL THOUGHTS

All in all, military aircraft have been developed to a point where they are capable of an almost frightening kill capability. On the face of it, this would have been abhorrent to the aviation pioneers, who hoped and believed that the aeroplane would be an instrument of peace. Nevertheless, the potential of the modern aeroplane has done much to ensure the avoidance of WW3 between the world's major powers, with its potentially catastrophic consequences, and has often provided the transport capacity to haul vast quantities of life-saving food and medicines to disaster or famine areas all over our world.

Above: The Bell Boeing V-22 Osprey, seen here in vertical flight, bridges the gap between helicopters and aeroplanes.

Below: A Lockheed Martin Hercules turboprop transport on a dirt landing strip, bringing vital food to the starving people of Somalia under the United Nations World Food Programme.

Universal transport

The reader will recall that the First World War had brought little improvement in airframe structures. Powerplants, however, had been developed from reasonably reliable low-power units to engines of four or five times the power, with good reliability. The Second World War brought about more wide-ranging changes, including extensive improvements in the aircraft structures and systems. Radar, which had been almost in an embryo state at the war's beginning, developed as a navigational aid, providing an aircrew with a map of the terrain below which was unaffected by clouds or darkness. Radio was not only capable of providing reliable round-the-world communications, but had been harnessed to create new and accurate navigational systems and bad-weather landing aids, all precursors of today's incredibly accurate satellite-based global navigation systems. America's involvement in the war with Japan, in the far reaches of the Pacific Ocean, had necessitated the development of transport and cargo aircraft with long-range capabilities as a priority requirement.

Once again, the persistent cry from airframe designers for more power had resulted in the evolution and production of piston engines of up to 2,610 kW (3,500 hp). Not only were they more powerful, but most were supremely reliable. In addition, the 'jet' or gas turbine engine had begun its development. Germany had flown the world's first aircraft to be powered by a turbojet, the Heinkel He 178, on 27 August 1939. Britain's Gloster/Whittle E.28/39 had not flown until 15 May 1941, but just over three years later, on 27 July 1944, the twin-engined Gloster Meteor fighter, powered by two 7.6 kN (1,700 lb) thrust Rolls-Royce Welland I turbojet engines, was used in action for the first time. At this early date the gas turbine was already proving a practical engine, and would very quickly be developed to produce almost unbelievable power.

There was one other contributory factor which had great significance in the enormous post-war expansion of civil aviation. During the war years many thousands of people had travelled by air as routine. They had learned that flying was no longer fit only for heroes; if transport

The eight-engined Bristol Brabazon airliner, designed to carry 100 passengers, was too advanced to gain sales interest.

aircraft were able to carry people from one side of the world to the other for military purposes, then most certainly they would be capable of carrying them around the world on peaceful business. If air fares were low enough, they would also prove a wonderful means of speeding holiday travel.

THE END OF THE FLYING-BOAT ERA

America had established the first transatlantic passenger services with Boeing flying-boats, and these were maintained throughout the war. Other nations, too, attempted to keep their commercial routes open, and even embattled Britain ensured that some long-range links with Commonwealth countries were operated throughout the war. These were really the last great years of the flying-boat, for, with the return to peace, long-range landplane transport aircraft which had spanned the world in military service were hastily converted for civil use. Suitable airfields, with all essential services, had been built all over the world for the operation of such aircraft, and it made good sense to continue to use these aeroplanes, with which air and ground crews were familiar, for the carriage of fare-paying passengers.

The USA, which had concentrated on producing long-range bombing and transport aircraft during the war, was in a strong position to supply the needs of civil airlines, which would soon be clamouring for passenger and cargo transport aircraft. This factor, plus the pre-war lead gained in this field due to the excellence of civil airliners pro-

duced by the Boeing, Douglas and Lockheed companies, was to make the USA dominant in this field of aviation until the 1970s and the arrival in a big way of the rival European consortium Airbus Industrie, which has gone on to produce a complete family of jet airliners to challenge Boeing and others. Indeed, international collaboration in funding and developing new programmes, and/or in the construction of sub-assemblies on behalf of the prime manufacturer, has become very widespread in modern times, bringing many less-prominent countries into the airliner construction business.

Britain had been aware during the war years that a return to peace would mean a struggle for the British builders and operators of civil aircraft, and had endeavoured to establish guidelines by means of the Brabazon Committee of 1942/43, which had the task of drawing up plans for the development and construction programmes that would be initiated upon the return of peace. The speed of development and innovative progress was such that it was not possible for that Committee to forecast with complete accuracy the post-war needs of civil aviation. As a single example, the Saunders-Roe SR.45 Princess giant flying-boat, developed as a Brabazon recommendation, was born into a world which no longer needed such aircraft. Perhaps the most important work of this Committee was to encourage designers and manufacturers to take a brief look into the future. Had it done no more than recommend that designer/manufacturers should examine the possibilities of the gas turbine engine, the Brabazon Committee would have been well worth while.

In the immediate post-war years the first generation of new airliners were developed from wartime aircraft: the Boeing Stratocruiser (left) owed its origin to the B-29. Not so for de Havilland in Britain when it built a new airliner to utilise the newly-emerging and powerful gas turbine engine, the Comet 1. When this failed in service, the new Comet 4 (above) emerged.

FIRST POST-WAR AIRLINERS

So, in the first post-war stage, quick conversions or derivatives of wartime bombers, and demilitarised military transports, served the airlines until a new generation of aircraft appeared. Thus, in Britain, the Wellington led to the 21/27-seat Vickers Viking, and aircraft such as the Lancastrian and York were evolved from the Lancaster family. In America, an interim airliner which evolved from the Boeing B-29 Superfortress was to prove of great importance when put to work on the North Atlantic route in 1949. This was the Boeing Model 377 Stratocruiser, powered by four 2,610 kW (3,500 hp) Pratt & Whitney radial engines which gave it a maximum speed of about 560 km/h (350 mph) and a range of up to 6,400 km (4,000 miles). It was followed by aircraft such as the Douglas DC-6 and DC-7, and Lockheed L.1049 Super Constellation and L.1649 Starliner. The DC-7C Seven Seas and L.1649A Starliner represented the piston-engined airliner at the peak of its evolution.

In Britain, new-generation airliners were being developed around the gas turbine engine, this nation holding a considerable lead in the construction of such engines. First to appear was the Vickers Viscount, the Type 630 prototype of which flew for the first time on 16 July 1948. On 29 July 1950 this very aircraft was used by British European Airways on the world's first scheduled passenger service by a turbine-powered airliner. It had a pressurised cabin to accommodate 32 passengers, and each of its four 1,029 kW (1,380 hp) Rolls-Royce Dart gas turbine engines had a reduction-gear drive to a four-blade

constant-speed propeller. This type of engine, known as a turboprop, is beautifully smooth in operation, the power unit being devoid of reciprocating components. The expanding gases produced for combustion drive the turbine, which in turn powers the compressor section of the engine and drives the reduction gear. For speeds up to about 560 km/h (350 mph), such a powerplant is more fuel efficient than a pure jet (turbojet) engine. The production Viscount 700 which evolved from the 630 prototype was an immediate success, with accommodation for 47-60 passengers, and a total of 445 was built.

FIRST TURBOJET AIRLINERS

Also in Britain, at about this same time, the de Havilland company was completing the construction of a turbojet powered aircraft. This was the Comet 1, the prototype of which flew for the first time on 27 July 1949. The Comet inaugurated the world's first turbojet airliner service, operated by the British Overseas Airways Corporation (BOAC) on 2 May 1952, on its London-Johannesburg route. Soon these aircraft were also speeding between London and Singapore, and London and Tokyo, cutting previous scheduled flight-times in half. There was every reason to believe that British manufacturers were in a position to gain a substantial share of the world market for airliners. Then came disaster; three Comets disintegrated in flight. Subsequent investigation showed that metal fatigue was responsible for the structural failure, information which enabled aircraft manufacturers across the globe to initiate new fail-safe methods of construction. By the time de Havilland had incorporated such features into a new Comet 4 version, Britain had lost its lead in these new-generation airliner types, and never regained it.

In America, the Boeing company had been busy during this period with the design and construction of a turbojet transport, and the prototype Model 367-80, known as the Dash Eighty to Boeing workers, flew successfully for the first time on 15 July 1954. Its development as the KC-135 military tanker/transport for the USAF has already been recounted. Its commercial version was the superb Boeing 707, of which (together with the similar Model 720) 1,010 were built up to 1992, mainly for airlines all over the world up to 1982, but for the final decade as base airframes for special military aircraft. After this basic design, Boeing developed the short/medium-range 727 with three engines and short-range 737 with two. The 737 remains in production in 1999 in very advanced forms, incorporating modern 'glass cockpit' display screens that replace electromechanical instruments for the crew, and it is the world's best-selling airliner, with well over 4,000 ordered. From McDonnell Douglas came the DC-8, and Britain attempted, unsuccessfully, to join this big league with the introduction of the Vickers VC10 in April 1964, and the larger (163-seat) Super VC10 which went

Boeing's Next Generation 737-700 airliner during its debut in 1997.

into service a year later. Of course, Boeing and McDonnell Douglas, as well as Lockheed plus other companies in Europe, followed up their early turbine airliners with newer types, and since the 1997 merger of Boeing and McDonnell Douglas to form the world's largest aerospace company, the Boeing range of available commercial and military transports has grown considerably.

The Soviet Union followed a similar pattern of post-war development for commercial transports, with the piston-engined Ilyushin Il-12 and Il-14 carring the bulk of air traffic until 1956, when the nation's first tur-

bojet airliner, the Tupolev Tu-104, entered service. It revolutionised air travel in the Soviet Union, offering immense reductions in route times. As in the West, Russian designers also showed early interest in the development of turboprop-powered airliners, attracted by their economical operation, and large numbers of Ilyushin Il-18s were built for service from 1959. This type was roughly equivalent to the US Lockheed's L.188 Electra and, like the Electra, was also developed

The failure of the Comet 1 was due to metal fatigue. From the investigation of this problem manufacturers learned to build new fail-safe structures. Boeing produced the superb Model 707 (top left) which served airlines all over the world, and evolved a related series of airliners such as the Model 727 (centre left). The Model 747 (bottom left) was the world's first wide-body jet, later followed by such aircraft as the Lockheed TriStar, McDonnell Douglas DC-10 (right), and the slightly smaller A300B Airbus (above) developed by a consortium of European aerospace manufacturers.

into a shore-based military anti-submarine aircraft (the Electra becoming the Orion and the Il-18 becoming the Il-38 'May', just as the British Comet was developed into the Nimrod). And in the same way that manufacturers like Boeing evolved a family of long-, medium- and short-range aircraft, the Tupolev design bureau followed a similar pattern with the Tu-114, -124, -134 and -154, followed by new types. Similarly, the Russian/Ukrainian Antonov bureau produced a family of military and commercial transport aircraft, but this time most notably as freighters, recently including the world's two largest aeroplanes, the four-turbofan An-124 'Condor' of 73.3 m (240 ft 6 in) wingspan and weighing 392,000 kg (864,210 lb) at take-off, and the even larger six-engined An-225 Mriya 'Cossak' with a take-off weight of 600,000 kg (1,322,770 lb).

SUPERSONIC TRANSPORT AIRCRAFT

The development of the supersonic civil transport began with agreements between the British and French governments, and between the British Aircraft Corporation and Sud-Aviation, in November 1962, to collaborate on such an aeroplane. Construction of the first two prototypes began in 1965, the year in which a model of a Soviet supersonic transport, the Tupolev Tu-144, was shown at the Paris Salon. Subsequently, on 1 May 1967, the US Federal Aviation Administration signed a contract with The Boeing Company for the construction of two Boeing 2707 SST prototypes. However, the shortlived American project was cancelled by the US Senate in 1971, by which time the Tu-144 and first Concorde prototype had flown, on 31 December 1968 and 2 March 1969 respectively. On 21 January 1976 Concordes of Air France and British Airways inaugurated the world's first supersonic passenger services, though the Tupolev Tu-144 had been the first to fly commercially, on 26 December 1975, carrying airmail and freight. However, the Tu-144 was not successful and, although it began scheduled passenger services on 1 November 1977, only 102 flights were made before the services were terminated for good. Interestingly, the fifteenth Tu-144 (one of only two remaining airworthy) was brought up to Tu-144LL standard and reflown in 1996 to help the US and Russian

Left: The Lockheed Martin Orion in modern P-3C form, a military aircraft produced from the commercial L.188 Electra turboprop airliner.

The ultimate in civil air transportation has been an airliner that can carry passengers at supersonic speed. The Anglo/French Concorde (right) and Soviet Tupolev Tu-144 (bottom left) both reached commercial service, but only Concorde proved successful and lasting.

industries in the development of next-generation supersonic transports, as the only type of supersonic airliner available for modification and testing. The Concordes were unavailable because of their continuing and superb commercial operations, which will continue well into the 21st century.

THE WIDE-BODY TRANSPORT

Wide-body civil transport aircraft originated in the USA. An announcement in April 1966 gave the news that Boeing had received a contract for 25 Model 747s from Pan American World Airways. Few then appre-

ciated just what the 747 was all about, but as it became known that its wings spanned 59.64 m (195ft 8 in), that its 57 m (187 ft) long cabin was 6.13 m (20ft 1 in) wide and 2.54m (8ft 4in) high, and that it could accommodate up to 500 passengers, the media immediately dubbed it the 'Jumbo Jet', a name which has stuck. The 747 first entered service on Pan Am's New York-London route on 22 January 1970, and well over 1,300 of these hugely-successful aircraft have since been ordered and development of new versions continues. As a wide-body, the 747 was followed into service by the McDonnell Douglas DC-10

Ilyushin's Il-86 was the first Russian wide-body airliner.

Above: An impression of the Airbus A3XX, showing its huge size compared with double-deck buses.

Below: Raytheon employees surround the 3,000th Beech Bonanza A36 to be built.

(August 1971), Lockheed TriStar (April 1972), Airbus Industrie Airbus A300 (May 1974), and Ilyushin Il-86 (December 1980).

The design of a very-high-capacity airliner is the latest milestone for commercial aviation. The Airbus A3XX, featuring a full double-deck passenger layout for up to 854 passengers, is expected to become the first in the world, for delivery from the year 2004.

GENERAL AVIATION

Civil aviation is made up of so much more than merely commercial transports, and the term 'general aviation' can be regarded as covering all other aspects of civil flying, from lightplanes and business jets to agricultural aircraft. This field has expanded enormously since the war. The `Big Three' in America, Beechcraft (now part of Raytheon), Cessna and Piper (now New Piper), have collectively built hundreds of thousands of aircraft, the greater percentage of these since 1946, with a predominance of lightplanes. Elsewhere, but particularly in France, construction of general-aviation aircraft remains buoyant, with important designs also coming from such faraway places as Australia, South America, the Czech Republic, India, Israel and Malaysia, to name but a few.

Large airliners and stylish jet fighters capture our attention, but vast numbers of less exciting general aviation aircraft became important to our everyday lives. The DHC Twin Otter (above) was designed to provide regular air services in remote areas; the Taylorcraft Topper (right) did the equally important job of crop dusting, or spreading fertilisers to boost crop production.

In America, the Experimental Aircraft Association has fostered the development of homebuilt/kitplane aircraft, helping its members to achieve for themselves the dream of flight. Tens of thousands of these aircraft have been constructed all over the world, plus many others originating in virtually every air-minded nation of the world. Some of these have been very basic indeed, some of advanced design, and some have even become production aircraft, but most show in their standards of construction a loving care that would have gladdened the hearts of the pioneers.

BACK INTO HISTORY

Harking backwards into aviation history is the rediscovered sport of hang gliding, following development of the Rogallo flexible wing and the even more efficient Jalbert Parafoil. All over the world people have been building and flying hang gliders as an exhilarating tisport, perhaps unaware that they are emulating the pioneers who provided the final stimulus for the achievement of powered flight. An even more astonishing event, and one which would have been regarded as a miracle by the pioneers, was the achievement of Dr Paul MacCready in the USA during 1977. Taking off at Shafter, California, on 23 August, his Gossamer Condor aircraft, powered and controlled by racing cyclist

Above: One of the seemingly 'impossible' dreams of flight became a reality in 1977, when Dr. Paul McCready's Gossamer Condor *man-powered aircraft (left) recorded a first flight. .*

Right: An American Blimp Corporation A60+ Lightship, currently used for advertising purposes.

Bryan Allen, was flown in a figure-of-eight around two pylons 0.8km (0.5 mile) apart. This was the world's first significant human-powered flight, and won for Paul McCready the £50,000 Kremer Prize, which had been so long finding a claimant. Another MacCready aircraft, the Gossamer Albatross, won the £100,000 Kremer Prize on 12 June 1979 by becoming the first human-powered aircraft to fly the English Channel.

Another seeming throwback in time was achieved on 7 January 1973, when Cameron Balloons in Britain flew the world's first hot-air airship. Airships of gas and hot-air types are now, once again, a fairly commonplace sight, used for advertising, surveillance, passenger carrying, research and other roles. Examples have been built in Britain, Canada, China, the Czech Republic, France, Germany, Hungary, Japan, Russia and the USA, their number including new Zeppelin airships from Germany. In the Netherlands, design began in 1995 of a 174 m (570 ft) rigid airship known as the Navigator, with an expected 22-day duration and accommodation for up to 230 passengers. The first example was originally intended to take part in Dutch millennium celebrations. And, with hot-air balloons prevalent at many sporting events, plus the recent successful circumnavigation of the world in a balloon, it seems that aviation has rediscovered its roots. These aircraft, together with sophisticated and modern-technology kites flown daily by enthusiasts the world over, provide a poignant reminder that it has taken 2,000 years of development to make possible the brilliant achievements of modern aviation.

THE
A-Z
OF THE WORLD'S
AIRCRAFT

Left: Stearman Aircraft Company became a subsidiary of Boeing in 1934, and soon after produced a classic biplane trainer, the Stearman Model 75, of which about 10,000 were built.

A

AAA • International

Advanced Amphibious Aircraft was established as international programme to develop a twin-turboprop amphibian for various civil and military roles, including fire-fighting, surveillance, pollution control, search and rescue and transportation. Original concept by Alenia of Italy and Dornier of Germany, with Alenia undertaking initial research from 1990 to 1992; Germany withdrew 1992 but programme joined by Hellenic Aerospace Industry, Yugoslav Directorate of Supply and Procurement, and Per Udsen of Denmark, with SOKO of Yugoslavia and OGMA of Portugal as associate members of the programme. Programme put on hold in 1994.

AAC • USA

American Aviation Corporation; formed in 1964 to develop and manufacture the AA-1 Yankee side-by-side two-seat monoplane (formerly called Bede BD-1) using aluminium honeycomb fuselage construction and metal-to-metal bonding throughout. Also produced a trainer version (American Trainer) and a four seater (American Traveler). Became part of Grumman American Aviation Corporation (q.v.) in January 1973.

AACHENER SEGELFLUGZEUGBAU GMBH • Germany

In 1920 Aachen Flugzeugbau was successful with gliders built to the designs of Prof Klemperer. In 1921 the name was changed and in 1923 the K. F. glider-related light aeroplane (also a Klemperer design) was in production. In 1924 a two-seat low-wing monoplane was also flown.

AAMSA • Mexico

Aeronáutica Agrícola Mexicana SA was formed in 1971, after agreement between Rockwell International (USA) and Industrias Unidas SA of Mexico to take over manufacture of Quail Commander and Sparrow Commander agricultural monoplanes. The Sparrow programme finished, and the Quail Commander (a more powerful development with larger hopper) was built as AAMSA Quail.

ABBOTT-BAYNES AIRCRAFT LTD. • UK

See Carden-Baynes Aircraft Ltd.

ABRAMS AIRCRAFT CORPORATION • USA

Formed in 1937 to build the Explorer twin-boom pusher monoplane to the design of Talbert Abrams, president of the Abrams Aerial Survey Corp.

ACA INDUSTRIES INC. • USA

Designed series of joined-wing aircraft as single-seat research types under JW designations.

AAMSA Quail (formerly Quail Commander) agricultural aircraft

Adam R.A. 14 two-seat lightweight sporting aircraft

ACAZ • Belgium

Ateliers de Constructions Aéronautiques Zeebrugge was formed after the First World War. Built in 1924-1925 the T.2 light two-seat cabin monoplane, largely of duralumin, with cantilever wing and low-drag undercarriage. Began construction of a two-seat fighter in 1926.

ACE AIRCRAFT CO • USA

Markets plans and kits for the Baby Ace D single-seat parasol-wing monoplane, as a 1956 update of the original 1930s aircraft designed by 'Ace' Corben, and plans and kits for the Junior Ace E two-seat version of Baby Ace D.

ACES HIGH LIGHT AIRCRAFT LTD. • Canada

Markets Cuby 1 in kit form as a single-seat cabin microlight, plus the side-by-side two-seat Cuby II.

ACME AIRCRAFT CORPORATION • USA

Established in 1928 to build light rigidly-braced sporting biplanes.

ACME • USA

Air Craft Marine Engineering Company, formed in Los Angeles, California, in September 1954 to build a prototype of the Anser four-seat twin-jet amphibian.

ACRO SPORT INC. • USA

Markets plans and some components for the Acro-Sport I single-seat aerobatic/competition biplane and Super Acro-Sport for unlimited aerobatics, two-seat Acro-Sport II aerobatic biplane, Pober Junior Ace two-seat parasol-wing monoplane, Pober Pixie and Poper Super Ace single-seat parasol-wing monoplanes, and Nesmith Cougar I two-seat high-wing cabin monoplane.

ADA • India

See Aeronautical Development Agency

ADAM • France

Etablissements Aéronautiques R. Adam, specialists in light aircraft, which were built in small numbers during the early 1950s. R.A.14 and 15 were side-by-side two-seaters; R.A. 17 an agricultural derivative. R.A. 14 intended for amateur construction, but also delivered complete.

ADAMS INDUSTRIES INC. • USA

Produced T211 two-seat lightplane, designed by John Thorpe from the original T-11 Sky Scooter of 1946.

ADC AIRCRAFT LTD. • UK

Formed March 1920 to take over from His Majesty's Disposals Board surplus aircraft not required for use by the

AEA Research Explorer 350R

diminishing RAF. Value of stock about £100 million, stored in six depots, main one at Waddon Aerodrome, Croydon, Surrey. Specimen aircraft demonstrated in many parts of the world, and drawing office formed under J. Kenworthy, formerly with Austin and Westland. Many modifications (e.g. Lamblin radiators) made on standard military types, notably Martinsyde F.4, which was developed later as the ADC 1 with Armstrong Siddeley Jaguar radial engine. Eight of this type sold to Latvia in 1926, in which year Nimbus Martinsyde (with ADC Nimbus engine) appeared. Ceased trading 1930.

ADLERWERKE GMBH • Germany

Formed in 1934 at Frankfurt as Adlerwerke vorm. Heinrich Kleyer AG, to take over Frankfurter Flugzeugbau Max Gerner GmbH (q.v.). First product was the Adler G.IIR light two-seat biplane (formerly Gerner G.IIR).

ADVANCE AIRCRAFT COMPANY • USA

See Waco Aircraft Company

ADVANCED AERODYNAMICS & STRUCTURES INC. • USA

Followed Aerodynamics and Structures Inc. in the development of the Jetcruzer business and multipurpose aircraft, featuring composites-built fuselage, rear mounted metal wings with winglets, metal canards, and rear mounted turboprop engine with pusher propeller. Original unpressurised Jetcruzer-450 prototype first flew January 1989, followed by first to production standard September 1992, with certification June 1994. Jetcruzer-450 not put into production but followed by lengthened Jetcruzer-500 for six persons, first flown August 1997 and to be pressurised in production form (deliveries starting 1999). Stratocruzer-1250 is 13-seat intercontinental business jet, with basically similar layout except for swept canards, addition of fin and high-mounted tailplane, and use of twin turbofan engines, prototype not flown by 1998.

ADVANCED AIRCRAFT CORPORATION • USA

See Riley

ADVANCED TECHNOLOGY AIRCRAFT CO INC. • USA

Developed Model 480 Predator composites-built and turboprop-powered agricultural aircraft, with prototype built by Scaled Composites and first flown 1984.

ADVENTURE AIR • USA

Has produced kits for 2 + 2 Amphibian (2 + 2 seating) and Adventure Twin two-seat amphibian, Super Adventurer and Adventurer 4-Place.

AEA RESEARCH PTY. LTD. • Australia

Founded 1992 and is developing the eight-seat piston-engined Explorer 350 and ten-seat turboprop-powered Explorer 500 light aircraft, for delivery from the year 2001 (first flown January 1998)

AEG • Germany

Allgemeine Elektrizität Gesellschaft; the Flugtechnische Abteilung of this great electrical company built its first aircraft in 1910, and soon established a flying school. Early designs included a Wright-type biplane, a monoplane, flying-boat and floatplane, but the Z 6 (B 1) biplane of 1914 was the first type built in quantity, and introduced the company's characteristic steel-tube construction. Also in 1914 came the Z 9 (B II) which saw limited war service, though less than the later C II-C IV types. By far the most notable products were the twin-engined G I-G IV, relatively small three-seat multi-purpose aircraft, for tactical rather than strategic use. Best known was the G IV (in service late 1916); G V was a larger three-bay design, entering service 1918. Production of G series totalled 542, 50 G IVs being used for night bombing behind Allied lines in August 1918. Other wartime types (experimental) included single-seaters and 'Giants'. The J II civil cabin biplane built 1918 had a two-seat cabin in place of the gunner's position, as well as a door and steps. The company made other contributions to the development of German airlines, and the G V was converted for service with Deutsche Luft-Reederei.

AERAUTO SA • Italy

Formed shortly before the Second World War to build a two-seat roadable monoplane.

AERIAL DISTRIBUTORS INC. • USA

In the early 1970s was developing Distributor Wing monoplane, prototype of which had flown in 1965. Agricultural equipment was an integral part of the aircraft; power for spraying and dusting was by a separate engine.

Aerial Distributors DW-1 Distributor Wing agricultural aircraft

Aeritalia G222 twin-turboprop transport in Italian Air Force service

AERIAL SERVICE CORPORATION • USA

Formed 1920. Built Mercury night-mail biplane with Liberty engine, an unusual inverted sesquiplane configuration.

AERITALIA SPA. • Italy

Formed 12 November 1969 by equal shareholding of Fiat and IRI-Finmeccanica to combine Fiat aerospace activities (except engines) and those of Aerfer and Salmoiraghi. Fully operational January 1972. In September 1976 IRI-Finmeccanica bought Aeritalia stock owned by Fiat. Had cooperation agreement with Boeing. Then comprised Combat Aircraft, Transport Aircraft, and Diversified Activities Groups. Main products were Aeritalia G91Y twin-jet development of very successful single-jet Fiat G91; Aeritalia G222 twin-turboprop high-wing transport (first flown 1970); Aeritalia (Lockheed) F-104S serving with Italian and Turkish Air Forces (delivered from 1969). Took control of Partenavia in 1981-1992 under its General Aviation Group. As Panavia partner, designed and developed variable-geometry wing and other important features of Tornado multirole aircraft. Became partner in AMX programme (see AMX International), and joined Aerospatiale of France in establishing ATR (q.v.). Merged with Selenia in December 1990 to form Alenia Aerospazio (q.v.).

AERMACCHI • Italy

Name for Macchi after 1961, as a subsidiary of Aeronautica Macchi (see Macchi entry for MB.326 programme). Production began 1960 of Aermacchi-Lockheed AL.60

SIAI-Marchetti S211A jet trainer, which is now marketed by Aermacchi

light cabin monoplane, built under rights obtained from Lockheed of USA. 1981 reorganisation of Aeronautica Macchi into a holding company, with Aermacchi SpA as a subsidiary undertaking aircraft activities. First flight in August 1976 of current MB-339 jet trainer and light attack aircraft, while in 1996 Aermacchi took over L-90TP RediGO from Valmet of Finland (since redesignated M-290TP RediGO). In January 1997 Aermacchi acquired SIAI Marchetti, inheriting the S211 jet trainer and SF260 piston/turboprop light aircraft. Partner programmes include the AMX combat aircraft with EMBRAER of Brazil and Alenia of Italy (see AMX International), and Yak/Aem-130 jet trainer with Yakovlev of Russia. Other work includes production of major components and assemblies for foreign military and commercial aircraft.

Aero Boero 180 three-seat lightweight cabin monoplane

AERO BOERO SA. • Argentina

Founded 1959 and based at Córdoba. Three-seat Aero Boero 95 (first flown March 1959) was development of the Piper Cub. AB 115 derived from AB 95 and first flown February 1973; still in production in basic training and recreational form and as AB 115/150 higher-powered version that can undertake agricultural work. AB 180 four-seater first flew in 1960s and remains available in AB 180 AG agricultural, PSA military pre-selection and RVR glider-towing forms. From AB 180 was developed lower-powered AB 150 series. AB 260 AG first flew December 1972 as a basically single-seat agricultural aircraft.

AEROCAD INC. • USA

Produced composites-built AeroCanard four-seat monoplane with pusher engine and canards, intended for construction from kits.

Aermacchi MB-339A advanced jet trainers

AEROCAR ASSOCIATES • USA

Has marketed plans to construct Mini-Imp single-seat metal/composites monoplane with tail-mounted pusher propeller, and Coot-A two-seat amphibian (see former Aerocar Inc.).

AEROCAR INC. • USA

From February 1948 had under development a flying automobile designed by M. B. Taylor. Prototype completed October 1949. Aerocar Model I, with Lycoming O-320 engine, used for tests which led to FAA Airworthiness Certification of the Aerocar on 13 December 1956. Extensive development undertaken to enhance flight and road performance. Accumulated road travel on six Aerocars exceeded 321,865 km (200,000 miles) and more than 5,000 flying hours. Other light aircraft made, including Coot and Sooper-Coot amphibians.

AERO COMMANDER INC. • USA

History dates from 1944 in Culver City, California, as Aero and later Aero Design and Engineering Company (q.v). Associated particularly with fast twin-engined monoplanes, mainly for executive use. Entered general aviation 1952 with Aero Commander 520. Rockwell-Standard re-formed company as Aero Commander division 1960, and after North American Rockwell Standard merger in 1967 the single-engined and twin-engined types continued in development. In 1965 Rockwell-Standard acquired Snow Aeronautical, continuing to produce agricultural aircraft at Olney as Snow Commanders (as division of Aero Commander), and acquired Intermountain Manufacturing Company (IMCO) 1966. Single-engined Model 112 delivered to customers from 1972. Low-wing twin-engined Rockwell Commander 700 produced jointly with Fuji in Japan. Thrush Commander was very notable specially-designed agricultural aircraft. The entire Thrush Commander range sold to Ayres Corp and then became known by the Ayres name. Shrike Commander 500S terminated 1980 but Commander Jetprops continued by Gulfstream American Corporation. See Israel Aircraft Industries.

Aerocar Model I, Moulton Taylor's practical roadable aircraft

Aero Commander Model 500, typical high-wing executive transport

Aero Commander 200, developed from Meyers 200B light aircraft

AERO-CRAFT MANUFACTURING COMPANY • USA

The firm was established at Detroit, Michigan, in 1928, and exhibited its first product, the 3-seat Aero Coupe, at the 1928 Detroit Acro Show.

AERO DESIGN & ENGINEERING • USA

Formed as Aero in 1944 to build Aero Commander twin-engined high-wing light transport monoplane, becoming Aero Design and Engineering 1950. Aero Commander 520 certificated 30 January 1952. Succeeded by Model 560 in 1954. Aero Commander 680 Super in production in late 1955. Various models supplied to US Army as L-26, and by 1957 more than 550 Aero Commanders of several models in worldwide service. Became known as Aero Commander Inc. (q.v.) 1960.

AERO DESIGNS INC. • USA

Produced Pulsar series (first flown 1988) as composites-built two-seat versions of Mark Brown's Star-Lite, offered in kit form for home construction.

AERO-DIFUSIÓN SL • Spain

Registered as a company at Santander to manufacture, overhaul and repair aircraft. As an experiment in 1954 built a Jodel lightplane; under name Popuplane made licence-built versions of Jodel D.112 and D.119, and under new management made a refined version of the Aero-Difusión Jodel D.1190S, which was called the Compostela.

AERODIS AMERICA INC. • USA

Established 1982 to develop AA200 Orion four-seat composites lightplane with tail mounted propeller, AA300 Rigel tandem two-seat jet trainer and AA330 Theta single-seat light tactical jet. Assets of Aerodis acquired by P.T. Cipta Restu Sarana Svaha of Indonesia 1991.

Aero-Difusión D.119 Popuplane, a licence-built Jodel design

AERODYNAMICS AND STRUCTURES INC. • USA

See Advanced Aerodynamics & Structures Inc.

AERODYNE SYSTEMS ENGINEERING LTD. • USA

Bought assets of Texas Helicopter Corporation (q.v.) in 1985 and continued development of Wasp as single-seat agricultural and utility helicopter based on Bell Model 47 and known as ML74 Wasp, plus M79 Hornet (certification 1985) as tandem two-seat and turbine-engined armed helicopter based on former Texas Helicopter Jet Wasp II.

AEROFAN AIRCRAFT MANUFACTURING COMPANY • USA

Work on the prototype SingleTwin pusher-engined eight-passenger business aircraft took place during 1980s.

AERO-FLIGHT AIRCRAFT • USA

In late 1940s built Streak two-seat monoplane and derivatives. Metal construction and slotted flaps were features. Three models built were all fast, though low-powered.

AERO HOLDING JOINT STOCK COMPANY • Czech Republic

Founded in 1990. Has important interests in Aero Vodochody, Let Kunovice, Letov Praha, Walter Praha, Technometra Praha - Radotin, AXL Semlly, and the VZLÚ research and test institute.

AERO INTERNATIONAL (REGIONAL) • France/Italy/UK

Founded January 1996 to merge the businesses of ATR (q.v.) and British Aerospace Regional Aircraft (which comprised Avro International Aerospace and Jetstream Aircraft) in terms of marketing, sales, support and aircraft development of their transport aircraft and to oversee future programmes. Organisation disbanded July 1998, with ATR and British Aerospace Regional Aircraft (BARAL) regaining full independence.

AERO-JEAN SA • Spain

Produces kits to build the AJ.1/RF-5 Serrania, a variant of the French Fournier RF-5.

AERO KUHLMANN • France

First flew in May 1996, the Scub two-seat braced high-wing cabin lightplane which is offered in production form.

AEROLITES INC. • USA

Produced low-wing AeroMaster AG and high-wing Ag Bearcat as single-seat agricultural monoplanes, and Bearcat as single-seat recreational parasol-wing monoplane, made available in kit form.

AERO-M JSC • Russia

Is developing the twin piston-engined A-209 nine-seat passenger and utility transport.

AEROMARINE KLEMM CORPORATION • USA

Formed 1928 as a component of Aeromarine Plane & Motor Co Inc. to make German-designed Klemm low-wing monoplanes, under licence granted to the new company in New York City. US-built Le Blond engines fitted. Model AKL-26 had 37-95mph (60-153kmh) speed range. Sales inhibited by economic depression 1930-1931.

AEROMARINE PLANE & MOTOR CO INC. • USA

Established before First World War at Keyport, NJ. In 1917 received from US Navy largest single order for aircraft then placed by that Service: 50 Model 39-A and 150 Model 39-B biplane trainers (wheel or float undercarriage). Model 700 served for early torpedo-dropping tests. Two 39-B used for deck-landing experiments. Type also made first landing (1922) on US Navy's first carrier (USS *Langley*). AS-1 and 2 were fighters, but more important were company's flying boats (200 Model 40F ordered 1918). After the war, converted D.H.4s, built 25 Martin bombers (completed winter 1923/24) and undertook flying-boat conversions for civil use, thus making significant contributions to commercial flying (e.g., New York-Atlantic City service

Aeromarine flying-boat, typical of such aircraft in the 1920s

1919). Two F-5Ls (Aeromarine Model 75) with accommodation for 12 passengers used on Key West-Havana run until 1923, when air mail subsidies withdrawn. In 1923 built metal-hulled flying-boat and biplane mail-carrier. PG-1 low-level fighter completed by Boeing.

AERO MERCANTIL SA • Colombia

Distributor of Piper aircraft. Began development of Gavilán transport. See El Gavilán.

AEROMERE SPA • USA

Based at Trento in 1950s. Acquired from Aviamilano licence for Falco series (F.8 Falco, designed by Stelio Frati, was first flown in June 1955). Falco was noted internationally for high performance on low power, owed to smooth wooden construction and aerodynamic refinement. Company became Laverda SpA.

AERONASA • Spain

Constructora Aeronaval de Levante SA, established factory in Castellon de la Plana, near Valencia. Licence-builder in 1960s of Piel Emeraude French light aircraft.

AERONÁUTICA AGRICOLA MEXICANA SA • Mexico

See AAMSA

AERONÁUTICA ANSALDO SA • Italy

See Ansaldo

AERONÁUTICA D'ITALIA • Italy

Aeronàutica d'Italia SA was the aeronautical branch of Fiat, occupying the factories of the old Ansaldo company which it had absorbed by the 1920s, although the Ansaldo

name was still used. For this company and the Società Italiano Aviazione the name Fiat (or Fiat-Aviazione, or Fiat-Divisione Aviazione) was used after 1924. For an outline of development of Fiat types see under Fiat.

AERONAUTICA INDUSTRIAL SA. • Spain

See AISA

AERONÁUTICA MACCHI GROUP • Italy

Holding organization for Aermacchi and other companies, following 1981 reorganization. See Aermacchi and Macchi.

AERONÁUTICA MILITAR ESPAÑOLA • Spain

Established at Cuatro Vientos, near Madrid, headquarters of the Spanish Military Air Service. Had its own workshops and laboratory and before 1931 was said to have produced several types of aircraft.

AERONAUTICAL CORPORATION OF AMERICA • USA

Incorporated November 1928 at Cincinnati, Ohio. Famous for Aeronca series of high-wing wire-braced monoplanes. These had two-cylinder engines of Aeronca design, or those of other manufacturers and, despite low power, these aircraft were sometimes fitted with Edo floats. Original landplane model had empty weight of only 180 kg (398 lb). C-2 and C-3 series well known in 1930s, and C-2 held many class records. Refinement of C-3 continued through early 1930s. Also built low-wing cantilever type Model L, or C-70 from 1935. Flight of 16,093 km (10,000 miles) in early-model Aeronca (Peterborough, England to Johannesburg, South Africa in 130 hr flying time) proved dependability of very light aircraft and supported company claim to have built and marketed first aeroplane of this class in USA. Name Aeronca also used for strutbraced Scout and Chief series of high-wing monoplanes built in late 1930s.

AERONAUTICAL CORPORATION OF GREAT BRITAIN LTD. • UK

Registered in London to build Aeronca light monoplanes developed by Aeronautical Corporation of America (q.v.). Based at Peterborough in the mid-1930s, its output was small. Used Aeronca engines built in England as Aeronca JAP (J. A. Prestwich, also builder of motorcycle engines). Chairman was H. V. Roe, who with his brother A. V. Roe had founded A. V. Roe & Co Ltd. in 1913. Pending production of British model called Aeronca 100, 16 American-built C-3 airframes assembled at Hanworth, London.

AERONAUTICAL DEVELOPMENT AGENCY • India

Founded in 1990 and based at Bangalore, the ADA is a government organisation managing the Light Combat Aircraft (LCA) programme, to provide the Indian Air Force with the first modern fighter to be designed and produced in India. First flown in 1998, the LCA has brought together many years of scientific and technological research, including test facilities, computer simulation, composite materials and digital flight control system. Operational trainer and naval carrier-borne versions are also under development. Construction is undertaken by HAL (q.v.). Has also proposed a twin-turbine 120-passenger airliner, as MTA 120.

AERONAUTICAL INDUSTRIAL ENGINEERING AND PROJECT MANAGEMENT COMPANY LTD. • Nigeria

AIEP established 1979 to assemble kits of the US Van's RV-6A, known locally as Air Beetle and used by the Nigerian Air Force as the T18 trainer.

AERONAUTICAL PRODUCTS INC. • USA

Formed in Detroit, Michigan, in 1935. In 1942 began development of cheap helicopter. First flown April 1944.

Aeronautical Development Agency Light Combat Aircraft

new types. Also had licence for Erco 'two control' system. Champion two-seat strutbraced high-wing monoplane was particularly successful, and between 1946 and 1951 company built over 10,000 Champions and over 600 Army liaison derivatives. Champion production ended 1950. Many variations, including Chief (1947), Super Chief (1948). Arrow marked low-wing departure. Since 1950 company has been a sub-contractor, but towards the end of the 1960s undertook, in conjunction with American Jet Industries Inc. (q.v.), development of a light strike version of the Super Pinto, built originally as a jet primary trainer. In January 1978 entered an agreement to build the Foxjet twin-turbofan light transport aircraft designed by Tony Team Industries Inc. but later terminated (see Foxjet International).

Improved type (A-3) tested 1945. Both had nose-mounted engines.

AERONAUTICAL RESEARCH & DEVELOPMENT CORPORATION • USA

See ARDC

AERONAUTICAL SYNDICATE LTD. • UK

Formed June 1909 by pioneer Horatio Barber (1875-1964). After building an unsuccessful tractor monoplane the Syndicate became identified with the Valkyrie series of canard (pusher) monoplanes. From Sallsbury Plain, Wilts., moved its scene of operations, in September 1910, to Hendon Aerodrome, London, leasing three of the eight hangars belonging to the Blériot Company. On 4 July 1911 the Valkyrie B was used to transport the first air cargo in Britain (a box of Osram lamps). Several Valkyrie canard pushers built. Not easy to fly, but used successfully for training. Early in 1912 twin-propeller Viking biplane built. This was the last of Barber's designs, for in April 1912 he retired as an active designer, after making a very substantial contribution to the early development and promotion of Hendon as an aeronautical centre.

Model L3, one of many lightplanes built by Aeronca during the 1920-1930s

AERONAUTICS INDIA LTD. • India

See Hindustan Aeronautics Ltd.

AERONAUTIC SUPPLY COMPANY • USA

See Benoist Aircraft Company

AERONCA AIRCRAFT CORPORATION • USA

Incorporated originally as Aeronautical Corporation of America (q.v.), but name changed in 1941. Quantity production of Fairchild trainers and liaison aircraft ceased 1944, and for post-war production company developed

Aeronca 65, a typical example of the company's high-wing designs

AERONICS (PTY.) LTD • South Africa

Following agreement of 1978 with Sequoia Aircraft Corporation of USA, gained production rights for Sequoia
Model 300 and Model 301 in South Africa.

AERONOVA COSTRUZIONI AERONAUTICHE • Italy

Established in the 1940s to manufacture a roadable monoplane designed by Ing. Pellarini. Designated Aeronova
A.E.R.1, it was powered by a Lycoming flat-four engine,
and the prototype made its first flight on 9 May 1948.

Aeroplastika LAK-X lightplane

AEROPLASTIKA • Lithuania

Based in Kaunas, this company developed the LAK-X lightplane, which is built by Avia Baltika (q.v.).

AEROPRACT • Russia

Offers various light aircraft, including the A-21 very small
single-seat lightplane for recreational, agricultural and civil
patrol uses, A-23M tandem two-seat lightplane that can
be purchased assembled or as a kit (first flown January
1993), A-25 Breeze four-seat amphibian (November
1994), and A-27 twin-float lightplane (first flown June
1998).

Aeropract A-25 Breeze amphibian

AEROPRAKT LTD. • Ukraine

Aeroprakt aircraft are marketed by Global Aero Design
Centre headquartered in Singapore. Currently produces
the A-20 tandem two-seat ultralight (first flown 1991) and
A-22 side-by-side two-seat very light cabin monoplane
for recreational and other uses (first flown 1996), and is
developing the A-24 two-seat amphibian.

AEROPROGRESS INC. • Russia

Aeroprogress was founded in 1990. The Aviation Department of the Khrunichev State Space Research Centre is
affiliated to Aeroprogress and has been responsible for
designing several light aircraft (q.v.). Also associated is
Washington Aeroprogress in the USA (q.v.). Aeroprogress
offers the T-101 Gratch 10-seat civil/military STOL transport (first flown 1994), Aeroprogress/Khrunichev T-411
Aist and T-421 five-seat STOL multipurpose lightplane
(first flown 1993), T-417 Pegas hot-and-high braced high-
wing lightplane for Peru, T-420 Strizh twin-engined light
aircraft with twin tail booms and an upward-lifting rear
cabin door for cargo carrying, T-430 Sprinter business
twin, T-440 Mercury twin-turboprop business aircraft, and
other types.

Right: Aeroprogress/Khrunichev T-411 Aist

Aero Resources Super J-2 autogyro

AERO RESOURCES INC. • USA

This company assumed responsibility in 1974 for continued production of the J-2 gyroplane, designed by D. K. Jovanovich, and manufactured previously by McCulloch Aircraft Corporation (q.v.). It developed also an improved version, with 200 hp engine, designated Aero Resources Super J 2.

AERORIC SCIENCE AND PRODUCTION ENTERPRISE • Russia

Has developed the Dingo passenger (up to 9 seats) or cargo amphibious lightplane of unusual design, featuring an air cushion landing system which enables it to land on any surface; has twin-boom tail unit and single turboprop engine with pusher propeller. Mock-up displayed 1992, and prototype displayed in 1995 in incomplete form but not flown by 1998.

AEROSPACE GENERAL COMPANY • USA

Produced series of strap-on and sit-on single-seat helicopters under the Mini-Copter name (first flown 1973).

AEROSPACE INDUSTRIAL DEVELOPMENT CORPORATION • Taiwan

See AIDC

AERO SPACELINES INC. • USA

Formed at Van Nuys, California, in 1961 for Boeing Stratocruiser and C-97 conversions. Built Pregnant Guppy, Super Guppy and Mini Guppy, with extremely deep high-capacity fuselage, intended initially for transportation of large rockets and spaceflight equipment

AEROSPACE TECHNOLOGIES OF AUSTRALIA LTD. • Australia

ASTA founded 1987 to replace former Government Aircraft Factories (GAF; q.v.) and Aircraft Technologies of Australia. Undertook aircraft maintenance, repair and modification, including Airbus and Boeing airliners. Sold 1994 as part of Government privatisation programme, with Rockwell Australia Ltd. buying Commonwealth's shareholding of ASTA Components, Defence and Engineering divisions; currently ASTA Components division of Boeing Australia Ltd. with new programmes including work on an AEW&C aircraft under Project Wedgetail.

Aero Spacelines Super Guppy transport

Pregnant Guppy, like Super Guppy (above), intended for transport of outsize equipment

AEROSPATIALE • France

Société Nationale Industrielle Aérospatiale was formed 1 January 1970 by French government decision, as a result of merger of Sud-Aviation, Nord-Aviation and SEREB. Thus became biggest aerospace company in Common Market on European Continent. Concorde supersonic transport developed in co-operation with British Aircraft Corporation Ltd.; Airbus A300 in co-operation with international partners (see European Airbus and Airbus Industrie); and Transall turboprop-powered transport with MBB and VFW-Fokker. Aérospatiale products included N262 and Frégate high-wing light transports; and Corvette turbofan-powered light transport. Light piston-engined aircraft produced through subsidiary Socata. Helicopter activities covered design and production of several types, with more modern types including 5/6-seat Ecureuil, 10-seat Dauphin and Super Frelon (up to 37 seats). Agreements with Westland in UK covered joint development and production of Puma and Gazelle helicopters and Westland-designed Lynx. Main Aérospatiale organisation then divided between Aircraft, Helicopter, Tactical Missiles and Space and Ballistic Systems Divisions. Eurocopter (q.v.) formed 1992, with Aérospatiale and Daimler-Benz Aerospace of Germany (q.v.) having 60 per cent and 40 per cent respectively of Eurocopter Holding SA, which in turn owned 75 per cent of Eurocopter SA. Owns 37.9 per cent of Airbus Industrie (q.v.), and partner with Alenia of Italy in ATR (q.v.). Company reorganised under Aérospatiale Group in 1998, with Aircraft and Space & Defence subsidiaries. Aircraft subsidiary includes Socata, Aerostructures, Aérospatiale Airbus and Aérospatiale ATR.

Aérospatiale SA 360 Dauphin helicopter

Aérospatiale SA 330 Puma

Aérospatiale Corvette multi-purpose twin-turbofan transport

Aérospatiale Alouette III helicopters in Royal Netherlands Air Force markings

AeroSPORT Supa Pup 4 being loaded into trailer, with wings folded

AEROSPORT PTY. LTD. • Australia

Offers its Supa Pup 4 single-seat cabin lightplane in assembled or kit forms (first flown 1994).

AEROSTAR AIRCRAFT CORPORATION • USA

Formed 1 July 1970, following an agreement the previous November between Butler Aviation International Inc. and American Electronic Laboratories Inc. to acquire Mooney Aircraft Corp, a subsidiary of the latter organisation. The Aerostar Ranger was, in prototype form, the former Mooney Mark 21; Aerostar Chaparral was an updated version of the Super 21.

AEROSTAR SA • Romania

Formed out of IAv Bacau (q.v.) in 1991. Continues to produce the Yak-52 and aero engines. With Elbit of Israel offers MiG-21 fighter upgrade as the Lancer, as performed in Romanian Air Force MiG-21s (first flew in August 1995).

AEROSYSTEMS • USA

Plans made available to construct two-seat Cadet STF as representation of 1941 Culver Cadet monoplane.

AERO TALLERES BOERO SRL • Argentina

see Aero Boero

Aerotechnik EV-97 Eurostar with wings folded

AEROTEC • Brazil

Sociedade Aerotec Ltda., Engenharia Aeronáutica formed 1968. Designed and built Uirapuru which, as T-23, was ordered by Brazilian, Bolivian and Paraguayan air forces and civil flying clubs. In the Brazilian Air Force the T-23 succeeded the locally-built Dutch Fokker types. Developed A-132 Tangará as potential replacement for T-23 (first flown 1981) but further developed into A-135 Tangará II. Aerotec also produced wings for EMBRAER Ipanema agricultural aircraft, starter pods and components

AEROTECHNIK CZ SRO • Czech Republic

Produced the L 13 Vivat motorgliders, recently out of production. Developed with Evektor Ltd. of same address in Kunovice the EV-97 Eurostar two-seat light or ultralight monoplane. Also offers the P 220 UL sports two-seater in kit form in light and ultralight versions, and is marketing the braced high-wing two-seat Fox (a variant of the German Ikarusflug Eurofox, with Evektor of the Czech Republic having undertaken important design work, and Aeropro of Slovakia building airframes for Fox and Eurofox).

AEROTECHNIK ENTWICKLUNG UND APPARATEBAU GMBH • Germany

In early 1960s began development of cheap, easy-to-fly helicopter, a prototype of which was completed in 1968. Other single-seat models followed, but development of WGM22 two-seater ended mid-1970s.

Aerotec T-23 Uirapuru two-seat primary trainer

Aerotechnik WGM21 helicopter prototype

Aerotécnica AC-14 light helicopter

AEROTÉCNICA SA • Spain

Formed to develop and build helicopters of French (Jean Cantinieau) design. Also licensed for Matra-Cantinieau production. Two prototypes of AC-12 built in Madrid by mid-1950s (first one flown July 1956) and a few delivered to Spanish Air Force. Type was unorthodox in layout and featured transmission and reduction gear on automobile principles. AC-14 development flew July 1957, but Aerotécnica organisation dissolved in 1962.

AEROTEK • South Africa

Produces the Hummingbird two-seat light plane (first flown May 1993), designed for observation role and capable of stable low-speed flying.

AERO TOVARNA LETADEL Dr KABES • Czechoslovakia

Founded in Prague 1919. Owned originally by a lawyer, this company made accessories as well as building aircraft. Built copies of Austrian Phönix (Brandenburg) biplanes, but later developed own designs. A-11 and A-30, both international record-breakers, were two-seat reconnaissance biplanes of 1920s and 1930s; A-34 was a light two-seater; A-35 a four-passenger monoplane; A-38 a nine-seat cabin biplane. By early 1930s company was making A100 two-seat multipurpose aircraft and A102 fighter. Aero M.B.200 was French Marcel Bloch bomber, licence-built, and partly subcontracted to Avia; Aero 204 was 8-passenger civil monoplane; a military development of this aircraft was designated Aero 304. A fast medium bomber was tested in 1938, but war prevented its production.

AEROTRADE SRO • Czech Republic

Currently produces the Racak 2 composited-built ultralight.

Aero Vodochody L-59 carrying light bombs

AERO UNION CORPORATION • USA

Founded 1959 for aerial firefighting, and produced firefighting conversions of many aircraft of all sizes.

AEROVANT AIRCRAFT CORPORATION • USA

Markets plans to construct the Acroduster 1 single-seat aerobatic biplane that was formerly the Stolp SA-700 Acroduster.

AERO VODOCHODY LTD. • Czech Republic

Current name for Aero Vodochody Narodni Podnik. In May 1997 the Board selected a consortium made up of Boeing, the former McDonnell Douglas and CSA Czech Airlines to take a major stake in the company as strategic investors. Product range comprises the L-39 Albatros, L-59, L-139 Albatros 2000 (using US engine and avionics) and L 159 ALCA jet trainers and light combat aircraft, and the Ae 270 Ibis transport as a partner with AIDC in Ibis Aerospace.

Aero Vodochody L-139 Albatros 2000 jet trainer and light attack aircraft

Aero L-29 Delfin jet trainer

AERO VODOCHODY NARODNI PODNIK • Czechoslovakia

Established 1 July 1953, perpetuating the old Czech name Aero. Received Red Banner award of the Ministry of Engineering and UVOS seven times. Achieved technical distinction and international success 1963-1974, when major product (for several countries) was Delfin jet trainer (first flown April 1959; more than 3,000 built). Type succeeded in production in late 1972 by L-39 Albatros jet trainer and light attack aircraft (first flown November 1968), following its selection as standard jet trainer of all Warsaw Pact countries except Poland; L-39 as part of training system, comprising also special simulator, ejection training simulator and mobile automatic test equipment. See Acro Vodochody Ltd.

AERO WOOD SPECIALITIES INC. • USA

Markets kits to construct the Avocet 1-A four-seat amphibian aircraft.

AESL • New Zealand

Aero Engine Services Ltd. was established in 1954 and until 1966 did engine repair and overhaul. Early 1967 acquired rights for Victa Airtourer, thenceforth produced as AESL Airtourer. Also made AESL Airtrainer two/three-seater. Amalgamated 1 April 1973 with Air Parts (NZ) Ltd. (q.v.) to form New Zealand Aerospace Industries Ltd.

AFIC (PIY) LTD. • South Africa

Formed 1967 to build developed version of Italian Partenavia P.64B, designated RSA 200. Production was suspended pending new arrangements for manufacturing facilities.

AG-CAT CORPORATION • USA

Formed 1995 from former Malden Ag-Craft Inc. to manufacture Ag-Cat agricultural biplane (first flown May 1957 as Grumman AgCat; see Grumman and Gulfstream).

AGO-FLUGZEUGWERKE GMBH • Germany

Initials of Ago were those of Aerowerke Gustav Otto (founded 1912), but the name was first applied in 1911 to products of Aeroplanbau G. Otto and Alberti. Modified biplane of Gustav Otto (German aviation pioneer, 1883-1926) and developments of Farman design were early products, but in 1912/13 came a seaplane of original design, followed by other types. During 1915/16 developed three pusher reconnaissance types: C I, C II and C III with twin tail-booms, but showing high efficiency despite layout. C I caused a stir on introduction at the Western Front by reason of twin-boom design, for which Swiss engineer A. Haefeli (earlier with Farman) was responsible. C IV was tractor biplane with sharply tapered wings; about 70 in service 1917/18. Experimental types included seaplanes. Ago name disappeared until late 1930s, but during the Second World War was again current for Ago 192 Kurier light twin-engined monoplane (built 1938).

AGOSTINI • Italy

Società Aeroplani Livio Agostini was founded by Livio Agostini and Adriano Mantelli. Products were marketed as Alaparma (q.v.).

Ag-Cat Corporation Ag-Cat agricultural biplane

AESL CT/4A two/three-seat Airtrainer

AFIC RSA 200 four-seat light monoplane

Above: Agusta AZ-8 Zappata-designed four-engined civil transport

AGROCOPTEROS LTDA. • Colombia

Produced the Scamp B development of the Aerosport Scamp, and the MXP-640 and MXP-740 versions of the Zenair CH-601 and CH-701 respectively in assembled and kit forms.

AGROLOT FOUNDATION • Poland

Has been developing the PZL-126P Mrówka very small single-seat agricultural aircraft (first flown 1990), with the unusual feature of detachable wingtip spray tanks with atomisers for low-volume spraying.

Right: Agusta-Bell 204AS anti-submarine helicopter

AGUSTA • Italy

Costruzioni Aeronàutiche Giovanni Agusta SpA. Foundations of the company were laid in 1907, when Giovanni Agusta built his first aeroplane. Several more built before First World War. Firm revived 1923, specialising in light aircraft; Ag.2 of 1927 was a small parasol monoplane, AZ-10 twin-engined civil transport of 1954 was designed by Filippo Zappata (noted for his work with CANT and Breda). After Second World War built fixed-wing four-seater. In 1952 Agusta was granted a licence to build Bell Model 47 helicopters. First Agusta-built example flew May 1954, and over 1,200 were built before production ended in mid-1970s. The company also produced Bell Iroquois models as Agusta-Bell 204B and 205, twin-engined Model 212 (still offered as AB-212 Naval/Skyshark) and Model 206 JetRanger (still offered as AB-206B JetRanger III) helicopters. In 1967, under Sikorsky licence, production of

Right: Agusta-designed A 109 eight-seat helicopter

SH-3D helicopters began, and in 1974 production of HH-3F (S-61R); production of final HH-3F Combat SAR version lasted into mid-1990s. Together with Elicotteri Meridionali (q.v.), SIAI-Marchetti (q.v.) and other Italian companies, Agusta became involved in production of the Boeing Vertol CH-47C Chinook. Other licence-built helicopters include AB-412EP/Griffon/Maritime Patrol versions of the Bell 412EP and Griffon, AMD-500E version of the McDonnell Douglas (now Boeing) MD 500E, and Agusta-Boeing 520N NOTAR helicopter.

Agusta-designed helicopters include the twin-turboshaft A 109 civil/military multi-purpose type (flown August 1971), A 119 Koala single-turboshaft widebody helicopter (first flown February 1995), and A 129 Mangusta tandem two-seat attack helicopter (first flown September 1983) and its more-powerful International variant with five-blade main rotor as standard (first flown January 1995). Partnered with GKN Westland (q.v.) on the EH 101 helicopter programme (see E.H. Industries Ltd.) and with Eurocopter Deutschland, Eurocopter and Fokker on NHIndustries NH90 helicopter.

Left: Agusta A 109 Power, latest version of A 109 type

AHRENS AIRCRAFT CORPORATION • USA

Developed AR 404 twin-turboprop passenger or cargo transport, intended to be simple to maintain and having a constant square-section fuselage to provide maximum volume. Prototype first flown December 1976, followed by first production-standard aircraft built at Puerto Rico production factory October 1979, but programme halted through lack of funding.

AICHI TOKEI DENKI KABUSHIKI KAISHA • Japan

Established 1899, but first built aeroplanes in 1920 and aero engines in 1927. From 1920s essentially a supplier to the Japanese Navy, but built civil types also, including a mail plane for the Japan Air Transport Company. Had technical agreement with Heinkel in Germany and imported specimen aircraft, which it developed for Japanese Navy requirements. Resulting aircraft (D1A type of 1934) sank US gunboat *Panay* in 1937. Later D3A monoplane was perhaps the most famous of the company's types, duplicating German interest in dive-bombers. Code-named 'Val' by the Allies, this type attacked Pearl Harbor 7 December 1941, and was also successful against British warships in the Indian Ocean. H9A1 twin-engined flying-boat was built in numbers; also notably E10A reconnaissance float plane; B7A attack bomber; and the M6A catapult-launched submarine-borne bomber, intended to attack such targets as the lock gates of the Panama Canal.

Above: Agusta A 129 in more-powerful International form

Right: Aichi D1A1, Type 94, carrier-based dive-bomber

Right: Aichi M6A1-K Nanzan (Southern Mountain) conversion trainer

AIDC XT-CH-1A turboprop trainer

AIDC • Taiwan

Aerospace Industrial Development Corporation (current Chinese name Han Hsiang Aerospace Industry Co Ltd.), established 1 March 1969 under auspices of Ministry of National Defence (reorganised 1996 under Ministry of Economic Affairs; to be privatised 1999?), in succession to Bureau of Aircraft Industry (set up in Nanking in 1946, moved to Taiwan 1948). In 1968 a branch of the Bureau built the first Chinese-constructed PL-1B, a version of the US Pazmany PL-1. In 1969 AIDC began production of Bell helicopters for Chinese Nationalist Army. Later undertook production of US Northrop F-5 Tiger II tactical fighter. Developed T-CH-1 turboprop trainer (flown November 1973; 50 production aircraft built) and AT-3 Tzu-Chiang advanced jet trainer and light attack aircraft (first flown September 1980; 62 built 1977-1989, with upgrades thereafter). Has developed and is producing the Ching-Kuo indigenous defence fighter, which first flew in May 1989 and achieved initial operational capability in 1995 (to replace Starfighters and Tiger IIs). Produces components for the F-16 fighter, and since 1995 has also been involved in non-military programmes, including becoming a partner with Aero Vodochody of the Czech Republic in the Ibis Aerospace company (q.v.), and produces components for the Boeing 717, Falcon 900 and 200 bizjets, Sikorsky S-92 helicopter, plus engines.

AI(R) • France/Italy/UK

See Aero International (Regional)

AIRBUS INDUSTRIE • International

The company was established in 1970 as a 'Groupement d'Intérât Economique' to manage the development, manufacture and marketing of the A300 widebodied short/medium range twin-engined transport (A300B first flown 28 October 1972). Airbus consortium owned by Aérospatiale of France (37.9 per cent), DaimlerChrysler of Germany (37.9 per cent), British Aerospace (20 per cent) and CASA of Spain (4.2 per cent), which are also the main industrial participants in design, development and manufacture. Associate members of the consortium are Belairbus of Belgium and Fokker Aviation of the Netherlands (q.v. all). Airbus Industrie is being restructured into a limited-liability company in 1999. Divisions include Airbus Industrie Asia, formed with Alenia of Italy (q.v.) to develop a new airliner in partnership with AVIC of China and ST Aero of Singapore; Airbus Military Company to develop the FLA military freighter (taking over from former Euroflag, q.v.); and Large Aircraft, founded in 1996 to progress work on the ultra-large A3XX airliner.

Initial Airbus A300B2/B4 airliners delivered 1974 to 1986; current version of A300 is A300-600 for 231-361 passengers (first flown July 1983), delivered from 1984.

AIDC Ching-Kuo indigenous defence fighters in two-seat form

Above: Airbus Industrie A300-600R in EgyptAir livery

Right: Airbus Industrie A310 flown by Aerolineas Argentinas

Airbus Industrie A320 operated by Dragonair

A310 first flew April 1982 as 191-280 short/medium-range widebody airliner; A319 first flew August 1995 as shortened variant of A320, for 124-145 passengers; A320 short/medium-range airliner first flew February 1987, for 137-180 passengers; A321 lengthened version of A320 for 185-220 passengers, first flown March 1993; A330 medium/extended-range widebody airliner for 295-440 passengers, first flown November 1992; and A340 four-engined companion of A330 for long-range and medium-density services, first flown October 1991 and accommodating 250-440 passengers. A3XX expected to enter service in year 2004 as the world's first very-high-capacity and full double-deck airliner, with initial accommodation for 555 passengers in three-class arrangement, but with variants for up to 854; not yet flown. FLA (Future Large Aircraft) military freighter expected to enter service in year 2004, but not yet flown.

Above: Airbus Industrie A330 twin-engined companion of A340

Right: Airbus Industrie A340-200 in Austrian Airlines colours

Below: Impression of the ultra-large Airbus Industrie A3XX airliner

AIRCO • UK

The Aircraft Manufacturing Company Ltd. was established by George Holt Thomas (1869-1929), a great promoter of flying in Britain, engaging (for instance) Louis Paulhan for exhibition flights. In 1911 Holt Thomas acquired British rights for Farman aeroplanes, and early in 1912 formed the above-named company. Wishing to establish the firm's own design department he secured, in 1914, the services of Geoffrey (later Sir Geoffrey) de Havilland, who had already achieved success at the Royal Aircraft Factory, Farnborough, Hants. Centred at Hendon, London, the new company made several types of notable military aircraft, more generally known by the prefix D.H. than the strictly correct Airco. These were the D.H.1 and 1A two-seat pushers; D.H.3 and 3A twin-engined pushers; D.H.4 two-seat tractor (representing, as a fast day-bomber, one of the greatest aeronautical advances of the First World War); D.H.5 single-seat tractor with backward stagger; D.H.6 tractor trainer; D.H.9, an extensively developed D.H.4; D.H.9A, an even greater advance; D.H.10 and 10A, built in pusher and tractor forms (notably tractor); D.H.11 twin-engined bomber; and D.H.14 and 15 single-engined bombers.

Early civil transport types were D.H.16 and D.H.18. Other companies controlled by Airco built flying-boats, aero engines and airships. After the war Holt Thomas founded Air Transport and Travel Ltd. and The Aircraft Manufacturing Co was shut down, making way for de Havilland Aircraft Co Ltd. (q.v.). Airco name was temporarily revived January 1958 for production of D.H.121 jet transport.

Airco D.H.9A, used extensively post-WW1 by RAF for air policing

AIR COMMAND INTERNATIONAL INC. • USA

Offers eight versions of its single/two-seat Commander autogyro, as bolt-together kits.

AIRCONCEPT FLUGZEUG UND GERÄTEBAU GMBH UND CO KG. • Germany

Founded 1976 and marketed VoWi 10 Airbuggy two-seat ultralight.

AIRCORP PTY. LTD. • Australia

Developed two/four-seat Bushmaster braced high-wing lightplane, first flown 1989.

AIRCRAFT DESIGNS (BEMBRIDGE) LTD. • UK

Formed 1978 to develop Sheriff two/four-seat light plane.

AIRCRAFT DESIGNS INC. • USA

Offers the Bumble Bee single-seat ultralight autogyro in plan and kit forms, the two-seat Experimental-category Sportster as plans, and the Stallion four-seat lightplane in kit form (first flown 1994).

AIRCRAFT DISPOSAL COMPANY LTD. • UK

See ADC Aircraft Ltd.

AIRCRAFT INVESTMENT CORPORATION LTD. • UK

Formed 1929 to deal in or build lighter- or heavier-than-air craft. Technical advisor Sir Henry Segrave, pilot and sportsman. This group had interests also in Saunders-Roe Ltd. and Blackburn Consolidated Ltd. (founded 1929). Segrave designed twin-engined Segrave Meteor 1, built by Saunders-Roe, known also as Saro Segrave Meteor 1, and flown in King's Cup Race 1930 by Major A. P. Holt. Segrave killed in Saro-built motorboat during speed record attempt in 1930, but development of Meteor 1 continued by Blackburn.

AIRCRAFT MANUFACTURING COMPANY LTD. • UK

See AIRCO.

AIRCRAFT MANUFACTURING DEPOT • Indian Air Force

Took over hangars at Kanpur (Indian Air Force Station) when a decision was taken to build the Hawker Siddeley 748 as a Dakota replacement. First set of jigs set up at Depot by mid-1960, and first Indian built 748 (delivered unassembled from England) flew 1 November 1961. Production of type continued, in addition to other work, including sailplanes. In June 1964 the Depot was incorporated in Aeronautics (India) Ltd. and later became Kanpur Division of Hindustan Aeronautics Ltd. (q.v.).

AIR CRAFT MARINE ENGINEERING COMPANY • USA

See ACME

AIRCRAFT SPRUCE & SPECIALITY INC. • USA

Markets kits and plans to construct the One Design DR.107 single-seat aerobatic monoplane (first flown 1994), kits for the Rihn DR.109 tandem two-seat aerobatic monoplane, plans for the Wittman W.10 Tailwind side-by-side two-seat cabin monoplane (designed by Steve Wittman in 1953), plans and some components for the Breezy tandem two-seat open-frame monoplane, plans and kits for the Baby Lakes single-seat biplane plus Super Baby Lakes and two-seat Buddy Baby Lakes, plus plans and some components for the the Acrolite single-seat entry-level acrobatic biplane.

AIRCRAFT TECHNOLOGIES INC. • USA

Has plans and kits available to build the Acro I single-seat aerobatic monoplane, designed for the International Aerobatic Club 'One Design' competition. The company also produces plans and kits for the Atlantis two-seat aerobatic monoplane.

Airco D.H.2 single-seat scout

Airco D.H.4 two-seat day-bomber

AIRCRAFT TECHNOLOGY INDUSTRIES • International

See Airtech

AIR CREATION • France

Offered a range of single- and two-seat microlights with flex-rogallo wings.

AIRLIFTS INC. • USA

See Cancargo Aircraft Manufacturing Co Ltd.

AIR-LIGHT GMBH-SÜD • Germany

Markets kits to construct Wild Thing two-seat very light monoplane.

AIR MAGIC ULTRALIGHTS • USA

Markets the Spitfire single-seat microlight in assembled or kit forms, plus the quicker Spitfire Super Sport, two-seat Spitfire II and Spitfire II Elite.

AIRMARK LTD. • UK

Formed early 1969. Acquired all rights to T.S.R.3 ultra-light monoplane designed by Tom Storey in 1967. Also undertook development of US Cassutt Special racing monoplane, building three modified examples under the designation Airmark Cassutt 111M and offering construction kits.

AIRMASTER HELICOPTERS LTD. • UK

Founded 1971 to develop very simple and low-cost two-seat helicopter, the resulting H2-B1 first flying 1972.

AIRMASTER INC. • USA

Founded 1980 to develop turboprop amphibians. Proof-of-concept Avalon 680 first flew 1983, but anticipated seven-seat Avalon Twin Star 1000 and military A-1200 Guardian were never flown.

AIR MECHANICS INC. • USA

Revival of Alexander Aircraft Company (q.v.), partly by former employees. Conducted service department of Alexander products, and during the 1930s made D-1 and D-2 two-seater monoplanes of new design.

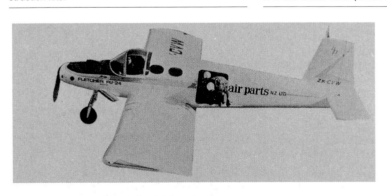

Left: Air Parts Fletcher FU-24 agricultural aircraft

Left: Airmark/Cassutt 111 M US-designed racing monoplane

Above: Air-Metal AM-C 111 STOL transport

AIR-METAL FLUGZEUGBAU UND ENTWICKLUNGS GMBH & CO KG. • Germany

Formed early 1970s for production of STOL transport aircraft. Eight variants planned of this high-wing twin turboprop design, and prototype of AM-C111 version started but programme halted 1978.

AIR-MOD ENGINEERING COMPANY • USA

See Doyn Aircraft Inc.

AIR NAVIGATION & ENGINEERING CO LTD. • UK

See ANEC

AIR NOVA (PTY.) LTD. • South Africa

Formed to make Reed Falcon single-seat aerobatic biplane, developed from Rooivalk of the late 1960s. Also sales and service centres for Beechcraft and Piper aircraft and manufacture of special spraying equipment.

AIR PARTS (NZ) LTD. • New Zealand

In 1957 acquired Australasian sales rights for Fletcher FU-24, and in 1964 acquired manufacturing rights. FU-24 had been designed initially for top-dressing work in New Zealand, to which country initial series of 100 was delivered. Several variants developed, including two turboprop versions. On 1 April 1973 the company was amalgamated with Aero Engine Services Ltd. (see AESL) to form New Zealand Aerospace Industries Ltd.

AIRPLANE DEVELOPMENT CORPORATION • USA

Subsidiary of the Cord Corporation. Founded in the early 1930s, its first product had the designation V-1 allocated by the designer, Gerald Vultee, who was for some years

the chief engineer of the Lockheed Aircraft Company. The V-1 was a clean-looking 8-seat commercial transport of low-wing monoplane configuration. Powered by a 700 hp Wright Cyclone, it had a maximum speed of 225mph (362kmh).

AIRIGHT INC. • USA

Purchased from Ed Swearingen (see Swearingen) rights to the SX300 two-seat monoplane, now continuing to be made available in kit form. SX200 developed to be certificated version with greater wingspan.

AIR & SPACE AMERICA INC. • USA

Produced 68 examples of the Model 18-A autogyro at Muncie in Indiana during 1960s, as slightly modified version of Umbaugh light two-seat autogyro (developed 1957-1962). See Farrington Aircraft Corporation.

AIRSPEED LTD. • UK

Founded February 1931 to build the Ferry 3-engined low-performance biplane, designed specifically for short-range pleasure flying ('joy riding'). Prototype Ferry, to Sir Alan Cobham's specification, went on tour with his National Aviation Day Displays 1932 and 1933; joined by second example 1932. In 1933 two more Ferries (four only built) acquired by John Sword of Midland and Scottish Air Ferries Ltd.

Airspeed Ferry, in which many Britons experienced their first flight

AIRSPEED (1934) LTD. • UK

Established 1934 at The Airport, Portsmouth, Hants. in association with shipbuilding interests of Swan, Hunter and Wigham Richardson. Developed the single-engined Courier monoplane (first British aircraft with retractable undercarriage to go into production), sixteen built. The Envoy was an enlarged twin-engined development (50 built) and was developed into Oxford advanced trainer for RAF. By July 1945 8,751 Oxfords had been built by several makers. During 1946-1948 over 150 Oxfords converted to civil Consul, but most notable civil product (associated also with the Airspeed Division of the de Havilland Aircraft Co, of Christchurch Aerodrome, Hants.) was the Ambassador high-wing, twin-engined airliner, mainly operated by British European Airways. Pre war construction of Queen Wasp radio-controlled target aircraft and Fleet Shadower accentuated company's versatility. In 1950 the de Havilland D.H.115 Vampire Trainer was built by Airspeed.

Airspeed Ambassador, important post-WW2 transport of BEA

AIRTECH • International

Aircraft Technology Industries founded 1980 by IPTN (q.v.) of Indonesia and CASA (q.v.) of Spain. Produces the 44-passenger CN 235 twin-turboprop regional airliner and CN 235 M military freighter variant (plus Persuader and

Airtech CN 235 M operated by South Korea

Airtech Canada DHC/1000 hp Otter conversion

MPA medium-range maritime patrol/surveillance, anti-submarine, anti-surface vessel, over-the-horizon targeting, and search and rescue variants). The C 295 stretched version offers 50 per cent more capacity (for typically 69 troops or freight).

AIRTECH CANADA AVIATION SERVICES LTD. • Canada

Established 1977. In addition to maintenance and repair work for small aircraft, and conversion of aeroplanes and helicopters for medevac roles, currently offers its DHC/1000 hp Otter programme to replace the original engine of de Havilland Canada Otter with a 967 hp WSK PZL-Kalisz ASz-62IR-M18/DHC-3 radial piston engine to improve performance and extend operational life. Also offers a re-engining programme (600 hp) for DHC-2 Beaver.

AIR TRACTOR INC. • USA

Founded 1958. Produces low-wing agricultural monoplanes developed from Snow S-2B, designed in the 1950s. Founder Leland Snow became Air Tractor president. Has built more than 1,650 Air Tractors, with radial piston-engined AT-401B (can be converted to turboprop power), turboprop-powered AT-402A (available since 1997), higher-powered AT-402B with 680 shp engine, heavier and 1,100 shp turboprop-engined AT-502A, 680 shp AT-502B, AT-503A two-seater for agricultural work and train-ing, AT-602 with 1,050 shp engine and the second largest Air Tractor model, AT-802 two-seater and the largest of all Air Tractors suited to agricultural and fire-fighting roles (first flown 1990), and AT-802 single-seat verson, available for purchase.

AIR TRANSPORT MANUFACTURING CO LTD. • USA

In 1938 built a three-engined high-wing six-seat aircraft, unusual in its class for the number of engines.

AISA • Spain

Aeronautica Industrial SA, engaged from 1923 on aircraft manufacture, repair and maintenance. In 1927 built some of earliest Cierva Autogiros, a type originated in Spain. H.M.1 and 5 trainers and H.M.9 glider tug built 1943; H.M.3 seaplane and H.M.7 cabin monoplane 1947; took over Aircraft Department of Iberavia SA (including helicopter designs); flew I-11 1953; built AVD-12 high-wing all-metal monoplane to designs of Emile Dewoitine mid-1950s. Tandem-seat trainer I-115 went into production for Spanish Air Force at same period, also I-11B tourer/trainer. Repair work has embraced several modern types of helicopter, while fixed-wing production continued with Italian-designed Siai-Marchetti four-seater. Rotary-wing work continued with AISA Autogyro GN, having jump take-off capability.

AJEP DEVELOPMENTS • UK

Offered kits to construct modified version of Whittman Tail-wind homebuilt aircraft.

AJI • USA

American Jet Industries Inc. founded 1951; became specialists in modification and repair of executive and transport aircraft, including large cargo types. Successful programme of Cessna turboprop conversions. In June 1968 first flew Super Pinto, a jet primary trainer or light strike aircraft developed from TT-1 Pinto built by Temco (q.v.). Work also done on five-seat executive version. Under 1974 expansion programme, concentrated production facilities at Van Nuys Airport, California, building Hustler, a seven-seat business/utility monoplane with supercritical wing, conventional turboprop and 'standby' turbofan in rear fuselage. First flight 11 January 1978. Purchased Grumman American Aviation Corporation (q.v.) September 1978, being renamed Gulfstream American (q.v.) in 1979. Meantime, AJI renamed Gulfstream American Corporation of California, developing the Peregrine as a jet trainer and business aircraft. All programmes stopped 1985.

AJI Hustler Model 400 prototype

AKASAMITRA HOMEBUILT AIRCRAFT ASSOCIATION • Indonesia

In addition to work with amateur-built aircraft, produced in 1984 the ST-220 two-seat recreational and training lightplane.

AISA's own-design GN autogyro

AISA Avion I-11B two-seat training or sporting monoplane

AJI Super Pinto jet

AKROTECH AVIATION INC. • USA

Offers kits to build Giles G-200 single-seat aerobatic monoplane (first flown 1992) and Giles G-202 tandem two-seat aerobatic monoplane (first flown 1995). See next entry.

AKROTECH EUROPE • France

Subsidiary of Aeronautical Service. Has taken over assets of Avions Mudry et Cie (q.v.), continuing production of the CAP 10B two-seat aerobatic and club trainer (first flown 1968) and CAP 232 single-seat aerobatic competition monoplane (first flown July 1994). Also produces the CAP 222, a version of the US AkroTech Giles G-202 two-seat kit-built aerobatic competition aircraft and trainer.

AKS-INVEST • Russia

Established 1990 to develop the MiG-TA4 general-purpose light plane with air-cushion landing system.

ALAPARMA SPA • Italy

Founded 1945 to develop A.M.6 twin-boom aircraft with engine of pusher configuration, first built 1942. To this formula made ultralight A.M.8, also A.M.10 two-seater. A.M.75 Baldo was one of same series, all designed by Adriano Mantelli.

ALASKA INTERNATIONAL CORPORATION • USA

In 1962 acquired from Silvaire Aircraft Company (q.v.) all rights to the Luscombe Silvaire two-seat all-metal light aircraft.

ALBATROS FLUGZEUGWERKE GMBH • Germany

Established late 1909 at Berlin-Johannisthal by Dr Walter Huth. Original name Pilot-Flugtechnische was only briefly retained. At first built biplanes and (under licence) French Antoinette monoplanes. From 1911 was building highly efficient biplanes and in 1912 turned attention also to marine aircraft. In 1912 and later Hellmuth Hirth and others broke several records on Albatros landplanes. Development benefited from participation of Ernst Heinkel who, in 1913/14, designed large single-engined three-bay biplane, forerunner of numerous reconnaissance and multipurpose types; C III of 1915 remained in service until early 1917 and was built by several other firms.

Historic line of single-seat fighters began with D I and D II, in service 1916. D III (1917) was 'vee-strutter'; W 4 a single-seat fighter seaplane, less known than landplanes though 118 delivered to German Naval Air Service. Decline of Albatros land fighters was marked by company building Fokker D VII in 1918. First civil aircraft was single-engined six-passenger L 58 high-wing cantilever monoplane of 1923; L 73 was twin-engined transport; L 75 was biplane trainer and L 79 a single-seat biplane with symmetrical wing-section specially developed for inverted flight. L 100 was low-wing monoplane; L 101 a parasol monoplane. One Albatros biplane was adapted for advanced research (water tanks for trim, cameras etc.). Aircraft manufacture ceased 1930. Company merged with Focke-Wulf 1930/31.

ALBERT AÉRONAUTIQUE • France

Formed 1926 as Avions Albert to build Albert (licence Tellier-Duhamel) high-wing light monoplanes. Named as above, in early 1930s built A-61 and A-70 two-seat monoplanes and A-140 racer for 1933 Coupe Deutsch de la Meurthe, though this latter machine was not completed in time. Construction was of wood. A-20 of 1929 was a two-seat twin-engined aircraft.

ALBERTA AEROSPACE CORPORATION • Canada

In 1995 the Belgian company Promavia licensed Alberta Aerospace to begin development of an *ab initio* trainer version of its Jet Squalus, under the name Phoenix FanJet. Eventually Promavia sold Alberta Aerospace the flying Jet Squalus prototype for conversion (to include new Williams-Rolls FJ44 turbofan engine in a revised airframe, new 'glass' cockpit, larger flying control surfaces and more), allowing certification in about the year 1999. After Promavia ceased trading, Alberta Aerospace purchased other Promavia assets, allowing eventual production in Canada. Variants of Phoenix Fanjet will include a four-seat personal transport.

ALCO • USA

Allison Airplane Company, established in 1920 to build a small single-seat high-wing monoplane known as the Alco Junior Coupe. Powerplant was a single 40 hp Szekely 3-cylinder radial air-cooled engine.

Right: Albatros CI two-seat general purpose biplane

Right: Albatros D III, one-time mount of Manfred von Richthofen

*Allison Super Convair, turboprop conversion of
Convair 580*

ALENIA AEROSPAZIO • Italy

Founded December 1990 by merger of Aeritalia and Selenia. Has undertaken modernization of Aeritalia-produced
F-104ASAs to improve weapon systems and maintain-
ability. Participates in the Airbus A321, AMX, ATR,
Eurofighter, FLA and Tornado programmes, plus the Dassault Falcon 2000. Provides continuing production and
support for the G222 (most importantly now as the Lockheed Martin Alenia Tactical Transport System C-27J Spartan in association with Lockheed Martin of the USA),
produces aerostructures for the MD-11 and 717 airliners
for Boeing, conducts modification and maintenance programmes for commercial and military aircraft, and takes
part in space programmes among other activities.

ALEXANDER AIRCRAFT COMPANY • USA

Formed August 1925 at Colorado Springs, Colorado, as
division of Alexander Industries Inc. then of Denver. Concentrated on Eaglerock three-seat civil biplane with Curtiss OX-5 engine. When supplies of this cheap engine
exhausted (1928), redesigned aircraft for other engines.
Eleven Eaglerock biplanes still registered in USA in 1960s.
D-2 was two-seat strut-braced high-wing cabin monoplane. Low-wing Bullet series designated by firearm cal-
ibres (.22, .32, .45 etc.). Company succumbed to US
financial depression, but continued manufacture as Air
Mechanics Inc. (q.v.), and in 1934 designed a five-seat
low-wing monoplane.

ALHAMBRA AIRPORT & AIR TRANSPORT
COMPANY • USA

With Allan H. Lockheed as president, built a new version
of his Duo twin-engined monoplane. Type was called Alcor
Duo-6 and was distinctive in having two Menasco engines

placed horizontally. Though Alcor conformed with Lockheed 'star names' system and development was pursued
in 1930s, no production resulted. Alcor was not a Lockheed Aircraft Corporation product.

ALLGEMEINE ELEKTRIZITÄT
GESELLSCHAFT • Germany

See AEG

ALLIANCE AEROPLANE COMPANY LTD. • UK

Founded in London during the First World War by Lord
Waring, and built large assemblies for Handley Page
bombers. Shortly after the war amalgamated with the
British Aerial Transport Co and British Nieuport & General
Aircraft Co; also with other smaller companies including
Ruffy, Arnell & Baumann Aviation Co. With last-named
company the Alliance P.1 biplane trainer originated. For
transatlantic attempt built (1919) a special P.2 Seabird
biplane with 21-hour endurance, powered by Napier Lion
engine; a second example crashed attempting Australia
flight.

ALLIANCE AIRCRAFT CORPORATION • USA

In late 1920s made Argo 3-seat biplane and Hess Warrior 7-cylinder radial engine of 115 hp.

ALLIED AVIATION CORPORATION • USA

Organised January 1941 to make moulded-plywood aircraft structures. In 1943 built large amphibious glider for
US Navy. Was developing in 1945 prototype of Allied Trimmer light twin-engined flying-boat amphibian. Manufacturing rights acquired by Commonwealth Aircraft Inc,
Kansas City, Missouri.

ALLISON AIRPLANE COMPANY • USA

See Alco

ALLISON DIVISION OF
GENERAL MOTORS • USA

Until May 1956 managed at Indianapolis, Indiana, Convair 580 conversion programme then subcontracted to
Pacific Airmotive.

ALON INC. • USA

Formed December 1963 by two former Beech officials.
Acquired all assets of Aircoupe two-seater from former
owners (city of Carlsbad, New Mexico) promoting
improved version as Alon AirCoupe. Alon, of McPherson,
Kansas, merged with Mooney Aircraft Corporation in
October 1967.

Alon X-A4 prototype (foreground) and A-2 Aircoupe

Alpavia Avion-Planeur lightweight aircraft designed by M. Fournier

ALPAVIA SA • France

Founded 1958 by Mm d'Assche and Noin. Made slightly modified Jodel D-117-A (two per month from January 1959). In 1962 partnership with René Fournier resulted in Avion-Planeur RF3 with Volkswagen engine.

ALPHA AVIATION COMPANY • USA

Established early 1970s to manufacture a re-engined and updated version of the Luscombe 11A Sedan under the designation Alpha 11D. Primary changes were the introduction of a fixed tricycle landing gear and provision of a 180 hp engine.

ALPHA JET • International

See Dassault-Breguet/Dornier

NPP ALPHA-M • Russia

Established 1992 as a subsidiary of Myasishchev (q.v.). First flew in 1993 its SL-A light plane, as a derivative of the Interavia SL-90 Leshiy. A-211 is version meeting JAR VLA regulations, while a kit-built version is A-211K.

ALTURAIR • USA

Has flown the Rotorair 2 two-seat air-pressure helicopter (first flown 1986), manufactures components for the BD-5 and Globe Swift, and developed the Alturdyne A650 and AT62 engines.

AMAX • Australia

Developed Eagle and Double Eagle autogyros for construction from plans or kits.

AMBROSINI • Italy

After incorporation of Società Aeronàutica Italiana with Ing A. Ambrosini & Cie (Ambrosini was a pioneer pilot),

specialised in fast tourers and sporting monoplanes, though SAI 1 was biplane. SAI 7 held speed record in its category. S.S.4 was experimental tail-first fighter. SAI207 was light fighter, developed during war. Smooth wooden construction and very clean design gave high performance on low power (as in company's sporting types) and 2,000 were ordered, though only 13 completed, type being replaced for proposed production of SAI 403, work on which finished at war's end. Intended subcontractors were Savoia-Marchetti and Caproni. In 1948 S 1001 Grifo broke more records. S 7 delivered in small numbers and developed into outstanding Super S 7 (1950s). F 7 Rondone was 3/4-seat cabin tourer.

AMECO-HAWK INTERNATIONAL • USA

Joint company of Ameco and Hawk International (q.v.), founded to progress development of GafHawk 125 single-turboprop STOL freighter (first flown 1982 as Hawk Industries Inc. aircraft division, product).

AMERICAN AERONAUTICAL CORPORATION • USA

Formed at Long Island, New York, October 1928 to build two types of Savoia-Marchetti flying-boat. These comprised S-55, as mentioned under Società Idrovolanti Alta Italia, and S-56 three-seat biplane amphibian the latter

having an American Kinner engine. In 1931 the Dayton Airplane Engine Co acquired a controlling interest in the company.

AMERICAN AIRCRAFT COMPANY • USA

Formed 1939 to take over Security Aircraft Corporation, including manufacturing rights for Security S1-B two-seat tourer/trainer, a number of which were in production in the summer of 1939.

AMERICAN AIRMOTIVE CORPORATION • USA

In the late 1950s built in quantity NA-75 agricultural aircraft, a development of Stearman Model 75 (Boeing Kaydet). Alternatively offered new high-lift wings and special modification kits. In eight years more than 200 Stearmans were fitted with new wings, permitting loads of over 2,000 lb (907 kg).

AMERICAN AVIATION CORPORATION • USA

See AAC

AMERICAN AVIATION INDUSTRIES • USA

Founded 1985 and offered Lockheed JetStar business jet re-engining programme as FanStar.

Alpha Jet twin-turbofan close support aircraft

Ambrosini Super 7 lightplane, developed from earlier S 7

Amiot 354 mailplane, used by Vichy for North Africa service in WW2

Privateer amphibian flying-boat developed by Amphibians Inc.

AMERICAN CHAMPION AIRCRAFT CORPORATION • USA

Current manufacturer of former Bellanca/Champion Aircraft two-seat lightplanes, in form of Aurora, Adventure and Explorer based on former Citabria, plus Super Decathlon and Scout.

AMERICAN EAGLE AIRCRAFT CORPORATION • USA

Established 1925 in Kansas City, with E. E. Porterfield as president. In 1926 built three-seat civil biplane with Curtiss OX-5 engine. Specially noted for American Eaglet light parasol monoplane, first two-seat light aeroplane to be granted Approval Type Certificate by US Department of Commerce. Several hundred Eaglets built before company suspended operations in 1930 Depression. Later American Eagle merged with Lincoln Aircraft Company Inc.

AMERICAN EAGLECRAFT COMPANY • USA

In 1942 revived American Eaglet light monoplane by building a new prototype. Tests postponed until after war. By end of February 1960 had built one Eaglet and was supplying plans for amateur builders. Company later sold to John Spach.

AMERICAN EAGLE-LINCOLN AIRCRAFT CORPORATION • USA

Established May 1931 in merger between American Eagle Aircraft Corp and Lincoln Aircraft Co. In early 1930s built American Eaglet two-seat light parasol monoplane, which had particular success. Eagle-Lincoln P.T. biplane was a trainer and Eagle-Lincoln A.P. a three-seat cabin monoplane.

AMERICAN GENERAL AIRCRAFT CORPORATION • USA

Bought rights to Gulfstream Aerospace Corporation's light aircraft 1989, with agreement in 1991 for GA-7 Cougar licence manufacture by Tbilisi Aircraft Manufacturing Association in Georgia.

AMERICAN HELICOPTER COMPANY • USA

Incorporated July 1947 for research and development on XA-5 pulsejet-powered helicopter. Taken over April 1954 by Fairchild Engine & Airplane Corp. Work on the XH-26 pulsejet helicopter was terminated by US Government.

AMERICAN HOMEBUILTS • USA

Markets kits for the John Doe STOL two-seat bush plane (first flown 1994).

AMERICAN JET INDUSTRIES INC. • USA

See AJI

AMERICAN SPORTSCOPTER INC. • USA

Subsidiary of Light's American SportsCopter Inc. (q.v.).

AMERIPLANES INC. • USA

In April 1998 AmeriPlanes took possession of the Mitchell Wing Company, and is remarketing the A-10 and T-10 kit-planes.

AMEUR AVIATION TECHNOLOGIE • France

Produced Balbuzard two-seat composite-built cabin monoplane in kit form, featuring tail-mounted pusher propeller.

AMIOT • France

Avions Amiot products were known formerly by SECM prefix, latterly as SECM-Amiot or generally, Amiot, after founder Felix Amiot. Amalgamated 1929 with Avions Latham. Amiot 101 of late 1920s was monoplane fighter; Amiot 122 was three-seat single-engined bomber, of which about 20 built by 1934. Type served with French Air Force and in Brazil. Firm later concentrated on large all-metal multiengined aircraft, using light-metal stampings, though well before 1940 introduced stressed-skin construction. In the 1930s works at Colombes and Caudebec were reconditioning several types of metal aircraft for French Government. Changes in structural techniques were matched by aerodynamic advances; thus Amiot 143, widely used by French Air Force in 1930s, attained less than 200mph (320kmh), whereas Amiot 350 series of 1940 were about 100 mph (160kmh) faster. As Avions Amiot remained part of France's 'independent' industry.

AMPHIBIANS INC. • USA

Based at Garden City, NY. Built Privateer light civil amphibian flying-boats, with braced monoplane wing and pusher engine, from 1932, with progressive improvements. Tail was carried on streamlined structure attached to hull.

AMX INTERNATIONAL LTD. • International

Founded by Aermacchi and Aeritalia (now Alenia) of Italy and EMBRAER of Brazil to develop the AMX close-air-support, interdiction and reconnaissance jet (known as A-1 in Brazil), first flown May 1984 and delivered from 1989 (192 delivered by 1998 and production continuing).

Right: AMX International AMX combat aircraft in Italian service

Below: American Helicopter XH-26 had pulsejet-driven rotor

Left: Anahuac Tauro 300 Mexican-developed agricultural aircraft

Left: Anatra D two-seat reconnaissance biplane

Left: Anderson Greenwood AG-14 all-metal twin-boom monoplane

Left: Andreasson BA-4B lightweight single-seat biplane

ANAHUAC • Mexico

Fabrica de Aviones Anahuac SA established 1966 to develop agricultural aircraft suited to national requirements. Prototype Tauro 300 first flew 3 December 1968. Improved Tauro 350 with more powerful radial engine (350 hp) followed into production from 1977.

ANATRA • USSR

Zavod A.A. (for Arturo Antonovich) Anatra founded Odessa 1913. Important during First World War, with factories at Odessa and Simferopol, Ukraine. By 1917 company was building own designs, plus Voisins and Nieuports, to a total monthly output of 80. Anatra VI (designed 1915) was essentially a developed Voisin; hence initial letters signifying 'Voisin Ivanov'. From March 1915 one year's output of VI type was intended to total about 150, though this quantity not completed until mid-1918. Anatra D was German Albatros derivative, with distinction of using rotary engine. Later DS had Salmson radial engine. Company activities ceased in early 1920s.

ANDERSON, GREENWOOD & COMPANY • USA

Originally incorporated 1941 for research into private-owner aircraft, but closed down and re-formed after war. Developed AG-14 light pusher monoplane of all-metal construction. First flight October 1947, but company completed only four production models before engaging in subcontract work.

ANDREASSON, BJORN • Sweden

During 1950s designed several types of light aircraft, promoted under the designer's name in San Diego, California. Tiny BA-4B single-seat biplane was designed for amateur construction (still available in plans form). Seventh design (BA-7) was better known as Bölkow Junior, with Swedish and German production.

ANEC • UK

Air Navigation and Engineering Co Ltd. formed at Addlestone, Surrey, as successor to the Blériot and Spad Aircraft Works, which had built Spads and had been awarded a contract for S.E.5a fighters, though name ANEC was associated with new civil aeroplanes. Three monoplanes (ANEC I, IA and II), designed by W. S. Shackleton, were among Britain's earliest ultralight aircraft. ANEC IV Missel Thrush (designer J. Bewsher) was light biplane, but ANEC III was large single-engined transport biplane designed by G. H. Handasyde, who had no production facilities for his own Handasyde Aircraft Co Ltd. First ANEC III flown March 1926. Three of type contributed to development of aviation in Australia, two being converted to Larkin Lascowls, one of which was not retired until June 1932.

Left: ANEC I, one of the first ultra-light aircraft built in UK

Ansaldo A. 400 utility biplane

ANGEL AIRCRAFT CORPORATION • USA

Certificated in 1992 its eight-seat Model 44 Angel STOL missionary, executive and utility aircraft, featuring twin piston engines with pusher propellers. Originally The King's Engineering Fellowship Model 44 Angel, developed by donations for missionary duties and designed by Carl Mortenson. See Evangel Aircraft Corporation.

ANSALDO • Italy

Aeronàutica Ansaldo SA established late in First World War by engineering and shipbuilding firm of Gio. Ansaldo (formed 1896). After the war a separate company was formed, Società Anìnima Aeronàutica, Turin, though title was variously rendered. Ansaldo achieved aeronautical eminence in 1917 by providing a single-seat fighter of original Italian design (Italy having previously used French types). Aircraft was A-1 Balilla. About 150 built; others, licence-built in Poland, served well into 1920s. S.V.A.5 was also a fighter, though more notable for fast recon-

naissance flights and record-breaking, which had Warren-truss wing bracing, later a characteristic of Fiat biplanes. Before Ansaldo merged completely with Fiat, in 1925, company built A.300 two/three-seat multipurpose biplane, extensively produced and used. Hydrofoils fitted to a seaplane development of S.V.A.5 presaged later developments in UK and USA. Initials S.V. signified Savoia Verducci. Ansaldo/Fiat links were implicit in name Rosatelli. Pomilio name also linked by 1918 takeover.

ANT • USSR

Central Aero-Hydrodynamic Institute, Moscow. Founded by Bolshevik government 1 December 1918 under Prof N. E. Zhukovskii; based on Moscow Technical University's pre-Revolution research organisation. Departments for study of propellers, aero engines, aeronautical construction materials, flight testing etc. Separate flight test centre for Soviet Air Force established 1920; alternative centres for aero engines 1930 and materials 1932. Zhukovskii

Ansaldo S.V.A.5 Primo fighter

Angel Aircraft Model 44 Angel STOL transport

Antonov An-12 ('Cub') four-turboprop transport

died 1921; succeeded by S. A. Chaplygin (1921-1941), N. I. Kharlamov, M. N. Shulzhenko and (since early 1960s) V. M. Myasischchev. New facility built 1931 at Stakhanov, Moscow; continued until 1939. Most aircraft designs before Second World War carried ANT designations (for details see under Tupolev); other designers also employed, some eventually heading their own bureaux, e.g. Petlyakov and Sukhoi. Aircraft with TsAGI designations included Komta twin-engined 10-passenger triplane of 1922; 1-EA to 5-EA and A-4 to A-15 series of helicopters and autogyros from various designers between 1928-1940; and TsAGI-44 (MTB-2) four-engined flying-boat bomber, redesignated from ANT-44 after arrest of Tupolev in 1936.

After Second World War TsAGI became purely research centre and moved to new premises at Zhukovskaya, near Ramenskoye. New facilities since provided for new Hydrodynamic Institute at Novosibirsk.

ANTONI • Italy

Società Italiana Brevetti Antoni completed in 1923 an experimental aircraft with variable-camber wing to patents and designs of Ing Guido Antoni. Firm was wound up shortly afterwards. Antoni, an inventor in several fields, was first associated with aviation in 1912.

ANTONOV • USSR/now Ukraine

First aircraft designed by Oleg Konstantinovich Antonov (1924) was OKA-1 glider, followed 1926-1929 by OKA-3 to 7. Continued to build gliders during and after the war. In 1943 was working on Yakolev fighters, but fame rests on An-2 'workhorse' biplane of 1946 (when present Antonov Aviation Scientific-Technical Complex organisation was founded), used for passenger, freight, exploration, ambulance and agricultural work; fitted with wheels, skis or floats and licence-built in Poland and China. Russian production of An-2 series ended in 1965 after almost 3,600 built; An-3 was originally considered as a turboprop development of An-2 but is now offered as a mid-life upgrade of the An-2 to have a turboprop engine and other improvements (first flown 1980). An-12 large four-turboprop high-wing military transport was essentially similar to the widely-used and earlier An-10, but with rear loading and many other refinements (first flown December 1957; some 1,400 built up to 1972; also produced in China as Y8). An-14 was a light twin-piston-engined transport.

An-22 was the world's largest aircraft when first flown in February 1965, powered by four huge Kuznetsov turboprop engines, each driving two contrarotating coaxial propellers; a very heavy freighter for the Soviet Air Force and Aeroflot, it was given a rear loading ramp to provide access to the 86 ft 7 in-long (26.4 m) cargo hold; set many payload-to-height records before production finished in the 1970s. An-24 became an extensively-used twin-turboprop commercial transport (first flown October 1959); An-26 was a development of An-24 for short-haul freight-

Antonov An-2 general-purpose biplane (Piotr Butowski)

ing and troop carrying (first flown May 1969). An-28 twin-turboprop light passenger and cargo transport first flew April 1975 and went into production in Poland (still in production in 1999 by WSK 'PZL-Mielec' as M28). An-30 first flown August 1967 as photogrammetric aircraft. An-32 short/medium-range twin-turboprop transport (first flown July 1976) was development of An-26, suited to operation from hot-and-high airfields. An-38 is small 27-passenger twin-turboprop commuter airliner (first flown June 1994). An-70 medium freighter with four advanced propfan engines was first flown December 1994 and is expected to replace remaining An-12s and also some Il-76s, with projected An-170 heavy transport derivative.

An-71 small tactical airborne early warning and control aircraft with rotating radome above tailfin, known to NATO as *Madcap* (first flown July 1985 but so far without production orders) was based on An-72, the latter a light freighter or passenger transport with two turbofan engines carried ahead of the high-mounted wings (first flown

August 1977); An-72P armed surveillance and maritime patrol aircraft based on An-72; An-74 is civil development of An-72, originally for Arctic operations but since produced in other variants. An-88 is a tactical battlefield surveillance aircraft based on An-72 (also known as An-72R). An-124 very-heavy-lift freighter, first flying December 1982 as then the world's largest aircraft, is powered by four turbofans and has a wing span of 240 ft 6 in (73.3 m) and all-up weight of 864,200 lb (392,000 kg). An-140 short-haul regional airliner is to supersede An-24 (first flown September 1997); An-142 is proposed civil/military derivative of An-140, with rear loading ramp. An-180 is proposed 175-passenger propfan airliner, and An-218 is proposed medium/long-range airliner for 195-400 passengers. An-225 Mriya was produced as an enlarged and six-turbojet development of An-124, first flying in December 1988 but only one completed. An-102 and An-104 are projected agricultural aircraft.

Above: Antonov An-22, once the world's largest aircraft (Piotr Butowski)

Left: Antonov An-140 regional airliner

AOI • Egypt

See Arab Organization for Industrialization

AQUAFLIGHT INC. • USA

Formed in 1946 to build Aqua twin-engined amphibian. Aqua I prototype tested in Philadelphia as a pure flying-boat; Aqua II tested as landplane also. As W-6 the type was developed for small-scale production.

ARAB ORGANIZATION FOR INDUSTRIALIZATION • Egypt

Established in November 1975. Has assembled Gazelle helicopters, and Tucano and Alpha Jet trainers. Also produced aircraft of original design, including the Gomhouria primary trainer and Helwan 2 and 3 lightplanes. Its engine factory assembles the Larzac and PT6A, and overhauls these and other engines. Further work includes manufacture of components for the Mirago 2000 and other aircraft, modification of aircraft for special missions, and weapons production. Work at the electronic factory, one of nine factories in the group, includes avionics and electronic subassemblies for French radars and missiles.

Arado Ar 95 general-purpose torpedo-bomber-reconnaissance seaplane

ARADO FLUGZEUGWERKE GMBH • Germany

In the Second World War a manufacturer of great importance, largely in connection with production of aircraft for other companies, but also in the development and production of its own types. Originated in early 1917 with creation of Werfte Warnemünde der Flugzeugbaus Friedrichshafen as a subsidiary of Flugzeugbau Friedrichshafen GmbH. Aircraft work ceased in 1918, but the factory was acquired 1921 by Hugo Stinnes, and was briefly engaged in shipbuilding. In 1924 Walter Rethel (formerly with Kondor and Fokker) joined as designer, and Stinnes created a Yugoslav subsidiary named Ikarus (q.v.).

Arado Handelsgesellschaft mbH established 1925. S I trainer biplane flown that year, followed by other trainers, SD II and III fighters and civil aircraft, notably VI of 1928 (high-wing transport) and L II light cabin monoplane. Walter Blume (formerly with Albatros) appointed chief engineer 1932; name Arado Flugzeugwerke adopted 4 March 1933. Ar 68 was Luftwaffe's first fighter; Ar 66 trainer also delivered in quantity. Notable designs thereafter were Ar 80 monoplane fighter; Ar 95 multipurpose aircraft and torpedo-carrier; Ar 196 ship's catapult floatplane, extensively used in Second World War; Ar 231 experimental submarine-borne monoplane; Ar 232 military transport, remarkable for unique multiwheel landing gear, Ar 240 heavy fighter/light bomber; and, most significant of all, Ar 234 jet-propelled single-seater, built both with two and four turbojets and tested initially with jettisonable wheeled take-off trolley. Used for reconnaissance and bombing, the Ar 234 was the world's first jet bomber and the second jet-propelled aircraft to enter service.

ARBEITSGRUPPE FÜR LUFT- UND RAUMFAHRT • Switzerland

Attempted to design series of single-seat lightweight combat aircraft of low cost from 1977, under the name Piranha, with single or twin turbojet engines.

ARC ATLANTIQUE AVIATION • France

Produces the RF 47 two-seat lightplane as a version of an original Fournier design.

ARCTIC AIRCRAFT COMPANY • USA

Established at Anchorage, Alaska to build and market as the S.1BE a strut-braced high-wing monoplane known as the Arctic Tern, a developed version of the Interstate S.1A, first flown in the 1950s.

ARDC • USA

Aeronautical Research & Development Corporation acquired all rights to Brantly helicopters from Lear Jet Industries in early 1969, then formed a Brantly Division. Promoted ARDC/Brantly Model B-2E. Five-seat Model 305 with engine of 305 hp first flew in 1964, but is also promoted as ARDC/Brantly type.

AREA DE MATERIAL CORDOBA • Argentina

Established 10 October 1927 as Fábrica Militar de Aviones. In 1928 secured licence for Avro Gosport (British biplane trainer) and eventually made 33 for Argentine Air Force. In 1931 made to original designs the first of a number of light single-engined monoplanes (Ao.C.1). On 20 October 1943 name was changed to Instituto Aerotícnico. On 23 January 1957 became a State enterprise under the title of Dirección Nacional de Fabricaciones e Investigaciones Aeronáuticas (DINFIA). Reverted to its original name 1968.

ARGONAUT AIRCRAFT INC. • USA

First product (1935) was Pirate three-seat monoplane amphibian, with Menasco Pirate engine. Main use of Menasco engines had previously been in racing aircraft.

ARIEL AIRCRAFT INC. • USA

Formed in 1940 to produce a light two-seat cabin monoplane of semi-cantilever low-wing configuration, externally braced below the wing only.

Arado Ar 234B Blitz (Lightning) jet bomber

Arctic Aircraft/Interstate Arctic Tern

ARMSTRONG WHITWORTH, SIR W. G./ AIRCRAFT LTD. • UK

Established 1914 as Aeroplane Department of engineering company Sir W. G. Armstrong, Whitworth & Co Ltd. In September 1914 built unsuccessful F.K.1 single-seater. Later (during the war) F.K.3 and F.K.8 two-seat observation aircraft delivered in quantity, as improvements on Government-designed B.E.2c. Experimental First World War types included quadruplanes and Armadillo and Ara biplane single-seat fighters. Aeroplane Department closed late 1919, but new company, named above, formed 1920. Outstanding products between the wars were Siskin single-seat fighter and Atlas army co-operation aircraft for RAF, both introducing some steel construction. Scimitar fighter (1934) was among the world's fastest with radial engine, partly owing to company's associations with engine-builder Armstrong Siddeley. Notable airliners were the three-engined Argosy biplane (1926), four-engined Atalanta monoplane (1932) and the much larger Ensign (1938). Company's most famous product was Whitley twin-engined bomber of 1936, in which year Hawker Siddeley Group was formed, with Armstrong Whitworth as a member company. In July 1943 the 1,824th Whitley left the assembly line at Baginton, Coventry, the type having achieved several historic 'firsts' in RAF service. Albemarle (600 built) used as glider-tug and transport, and Avro Lancaster bombers built in dispersed factories. After the war, from basic Gloster design, company developed and produced in quantity Meteor two-seat nightfighter. When this type was well advanced undertook development of Hawker Sea Hawk naval fighter. Avro Lincolns, Hawker Hunters and Gloster Javelins also produced. Experiments made with

Armstrong Whitworth Whitley V long-range night bomber

Right: Armstrong Whitworth-built Hawker Sea Hawk carrier-based fighter

Right: Armstrong Whitworth Argosy 20-passenger civil transport

flying-wing aircraft and prone-pilot position. Apollo turbo-prop airliner (1949) had no commercial success, though Argosy twin-boom four-turboprop freighter (1959) gained limited civil and military orders.

ARNET PEREYRA INC. • USA

Sells kits for the Aventura single-seat amphibious ultralight and two-seat Aventura II.

Armstrong Whitworth A.W. 650 Argosy first flew in 1959 as large-capacity freighter

ARPIN, M. B. & COMPANY • UK

At West Drayton, Middlesex, built during 1937-1938 a two-seat pusher cabin monoplane, the A-1, with MacLaren crosswind tricycle undercarriage. Re-engined 1939 for Army evaluation, but not adopted.

ARROW AIRCRAFT & MOTOR CORPORATION • USA

In late 1920s made three models of two-seat sport or training biplane (the Arrow Sport and Arrow Sport Pursuit). Standard type of 1935 was Model F two-seat low-wing monoplane with Ford V-8 converted automobile engine, awarded contract by the Bureau of Air Commerce.

ARROW AIRCRAFT (LEEDS) LTD. • UK

Largely designed by A. C. Thornton (responsible for Blackburn Bluebird of 1924), the Arrow Active 1 of 1931 was a single-seat all-metal aerobatic biplane with military-training potential. Active 2 of 1932 was re-engined and had new centre-section; but though company made aircraft components it built no aeroplanes in quantity.

ARSENAL DE L'AÉRONAUTIQUE • France

Established in 1936 in old Breguet works at Villacoublay. Products generally designated by initials of Vernisse (direc-

Arrow Active 2 single-seat sporting biplane

tor) and Galtier (designer). VG 30 was lightweight fighter; VG 33 a more powerful development (200 ordered and many being assembled by June 1940). Arsenal-Delanne 10 was unorthodox tandem monoplane two-seater, flown 1941. Experimental work on fast and unorthodox aircraft resumed after war, when VB 10 fighter with tandem piston engines and contrarotating propellers was flown. VG 70 had German Junkers Jumo 004 turbojet; VG 90 was naval jet fighter; 5.501 a pilotless aircraft; 0.101 a research monoplane for testing aerofoil sections, spoilers, etc. After 1954 became SFECMAS (Société Française de Construction de Matériaux Spéciaux).

ASAP • Canada

Markets in kit form the Beaver RX-550 tandem two-seat microlight (as a variant of Spectrum Beaver RX-550), the Beaver RX-28 two-seat training model, and the Chinook Plus 2 tandem two-seat microlight.

ASL HAGFORS AERO AB. • Sweden

Marketed a certificated version of the Highlander (q.v.), as the Opus 280.

ASSOCIATE AIR • USA

Markets kits to build Air Liberty 181 four-seat cabin monoplane (first flown 1996).

ASTRA SOCIÉTÉ DE CONSTRUCTIONS AÉRONAUTIQUES • France

Obtained from the Wright Brothers in 1909 a licence to build their aircraft in France. Introduced own modifications, and one Astra-Wright was used for early bombing trials. Triplane also built. During First World War made military aeroplanes and airships, having been famous for lighter-than-air craft before the war. Components also manufactured. In 1921 amalgamated with Nieuport as Nieuport-Astra, thenceforth abandoning airship work entirely.

Arsenal VB 10 tandem-engined experimental fighter

Arsenal VG 90 experimental jet fighter for naval use

ATEC VOS • Czech Republic

Has developed the Zephyr 2 two-seat ultralight.

ATELIERS DE CONSTRUCTIONS AÉRONAUTIQUES BELGES • Belgium

Established in Brussels 1933. In that year LACAB T.7 advanced trainer entered for Belgian Government competition, and in 1934 company began construction to official specifications of the LACAB GR.8 twin-engined multi-seat fighter sesquiplane.

ATELIERS DE CONSTRUCTIONS AÉRONAUTIQUES ZEEBRUGGE • Belgium

See ACAZ

ATELIERS ET CHANTIERS DE LA LOIRE • France

See Gourdou et Leseurre

ATLANTIC AIRCRAFT CORPORATION • USA

Established at beginning of 1923 and started active operations in May, remodelling 100 D.H.4s. Held patent rights and licence to build Fokker aircraft in USA, and largely associated with Anthony Fokker, who went to USA in 1922 and played a part in founding the company at Hasbrouck Heights, NJ. Fokker was also design consultant to other US companies. AO-1 was two-seater of characteristic Fokker biplane form for artillery observation; XLB-2 (officially prefixed Atlantic-Fokker or Atlantic (Fokker)) of 1927/28 was first twin-engined US Air Corps monoplane bomber. Type not adopted despite Fokker's experience with large civil monoplanes. C-2 and C-2A of late 1920s also were typical Fokker-type high-wing cantilever monoplanes.

ATLAS AIRCRAFT COMPANY • USA

Formed in 1949 by J. B. Alexander and Max B. Harlow to build H-10 four-seat cabin monoplane of all-metal stressed-skin construction.

ATLAS AIRCRAFT CORPORATION OF SOUTH AFRICA (PTY.) LTD. • South Africa

Registered as a private company at Kempton Park, Transvaal, in 1964 to establish an aircraft industry in South Africa, jointly with the Industrial Development Corporation. Completed manufacture of Impala (M.B.326M) under Aermacchi licence. Developed C4M Kudu utility STOL light transport, first flown February 1974. First flew in 1986 its Cheetah multirole fighter, fighter-bomber and reconnaissance aircraft conversion of the Mirage III for the SAAF, allowing initial operational capability in 1987. ACE all-composite turboprop trainer first flew April 1991 but later cancelled. Developed Rooivalk attack helicopter, Puma gunship and Oryx. Company also held marketing rights for several

Atlas Impala of SAAF, licence-built Aermacchi M.B.326M

foreign aircraft and undertook extensive maintenance and overhaul work for SAAF. Merged with Simera (q.v.) in April 1996 under new Denel Aviation (q.v.) name, having been a division of Denel (Pty) Ltd. within the latter's Aerospace Group.

Atlas ACE composites trainer

Prototype of South African Atlas C4M STOL light transport

ATR (Avions de Transport Regional) ATR 42-500 48-passenger regional airliner

ATR • International

Founded 1982 by Aérospatiale of France and Alenia of Italy to develop twin-turboprop regional transport aircraft. Initial ATR 42 42/48-seat airliner or freighter first flown August 1984, with production deliveries from 1989. Followed by larger ATR 72 for 66-74 passengers (first flown October 1988 and also delivered from 1989). Both also available in Maritime Patrol form. ATR 52C civil/military multipurpose transport still to fly at time of writing, as shorter derivative of ATR 72 with rear loading ramp for easy access to hold for bulk freight or vehicles. Consideration being given to development of twin-turbofan regional airliners, initially as 70-passenger Airjet 70, with follow-up 58-passenger Airjet 58 and possibly 84-passenger Airjet 84.

Auster's first fully aerobatic aircraft, the Aiglet Trainer

AUBERT, PAUL, AVIONS • France

Aubert-Aviation was formed 1932, but in 1938 name was changed to the above and PA-20 trainer was shown at Paris Salon. Subcontract work on Morane-Saulnier trainers ceased June 1940. After war PA-20 was revived as PA-201 and PA-204 (high-wing cabin monoplanes with cantilever undercarriage; common name Cigale). As Cigale Major PA-204 was certificated in 1951.

AUSTER AIRCRAFT LTD. • UK

Formerly called Taylorcraft Aeroplanes (England), but in March 1946 this was changed to the above and the works were transferred from Thurmaston, Leicester, to Rearsby, Leicester. Auster name was well established in Second World War by light observation (AOP) monoplanes known as Taylorcraft Austers, and many of these made

Right: Auster lightweight ambulance or freight aircraft

Austin Whippet single-seat biplane (33.5 kW; 45 hp Anzani engine)

an important contribution to the development of post-war light aviation. The type mainly concerned was the Auster 5, or Model J, three-seater with Lycoming engine. As war neared its end Taylorcraft designers were already looking to the civil market, and the outcome was the Autocrat, often British-powered and widely used not only for ordinary tasks but also, for instance, to test the Rover TP.90 gas turbine. In the 1950s came the Aiglet and the Autocar, one of the latter being used to test the Saunders-Roe hydro-ski landing gear. Its name notwithstanding, the Aiglet Trainer differed greatly from the Aiglet, and the Agricola was an entirely new low-wing agricultural aircraft, first flown December 1955. To supersede the AOP6 the entirely new military AOP9 was tested in March 1954, by which time the British Army and RAF had received nearly 2,000 Austers.

AUSTFLIGHT ULA PTY. LTD. • Australia

Markets the Drifter tandem two-seat microlight, as a modified variant of former Maxair Drifter.

AUSTIN MOTOR COMPANY (1914) LTD. • UK

Centred at Northfield, Birmingham, Warwickshire, this engineering company became a War Office contractor for aeroplanes during the First World War, building over 2,000 subcontract aircraft. In 1917 the aircraft department, managed by J. D. North (best known for his later Boulton Paul associations) contemplated aircraft of original design. The Osprey (1918) was a triplane single-seater designed by C. H. Brooks; the Greyhound two-seat fighter was flown after the Armistice; and civil types were the Kestrel side-by-side two-seater (awarded 2nd prize in an Air Ministry competition) and the tiny Whippet single-seater, for which high hopes were entertained but only five were built. Aircraft activities ceased 1920, but in 1936 the 'shadow factory' scheme ensured that the Austin name once again had aircraft connections. Production of Fairey Battle began October 1937, first aircraft tested July 1938.

AUSTRALIAN AIRCRAFT CONSORTIUM PTY. LTD. • Australia

Founded 1982 by Commonwealth Aircraft Corporation, Government Aircraft Factories and Hawker de Havilland Australia to develop A10B turboprop trainer. Taken over by Hawker de Havilland (q.v.).

AUSTRALIAN AIRCRAFT & ENGINEERING CO LTD. • Australia

Based at Sydney, New South Wales, in the early 1920s, with works and aerodrome at Mascot. Built six Avro 504Ks for the Royal Australian Air Force, as agent for A.

Austin Osprey single-seat triplane

V. Roe & Co. Also built, to designs of H. E. Broadsmith, a six-seat commercial biplane, and this aircraft was taken over by the Commonwealth Government, but lack of further support caused the firm to go into voluntary liquidation.

THE AUSTRALIAN AUTOGYRO COMPANY • Australia

Developed and marketed Skyhook as a single-seat light autogyro. Company formed 1984.

AUSTRALIAN AVIATION WORKS • Australia

Offers the single-seat Aerolite 1+1 cabin monoplane in plans or kit forms, plans for the single-seat Avromax 1700 Sport, plans for the Karatoo C Model two-seat cabin monoplane, and plans for the Spacewalker single-seat open monoplane.

THE AUTOGIRO COMPANY OF AMERICA • USA

Licensed in 1930 by Cierva Autogiro Co of UK, the US company itself arranged sub-licences to Pitcairn and Kellett. For three years experimented with own AC-35 Autogiro, a roadable cabin type, delivered to Experimental Development Section of Bureau of Air Commerce in 1937. The folding rotor blades had direct control. ('Autogiro' is spelled with an 'i' if it is an aircraft of Cierva origin.)

AUTOGYRO DESIGN BUREAU • Russia

First flew Pelegrin light autogyro prototype in 1991, followed by two-seat Boomerang (lost in accident 1994). Ariel-211 two-seater followed, developed into latest Ariel-212 two-seater (first flown June 1997).

Avia 14 Salon, Czech-built version of the II-14M.

AUTOMEDIA SRO • Czech Republic

Has developed the JK-1 twin-boom single-seat ultralight.

AVGUR AEROSTAT CENTRE • Russia

Has developed a range of manned and unmanned airships for various applications as its main business. Is also developing the Krechet as a light VTOL aeroplane with a thrust/flow vectoring system using ducted propellers under the rear-mounted wings and in the nose, with cascade aerofoils to deflect thrust; vectoring system has been tested on Aerostatika airships.

AVIA • Italy

Azionaria Vercellese Industrie Aeronàutiche; first flew F.L.3 two-seat cabin monoplane in 1939, and 400 built between 1939 and 1942. Production resumed after the war, until the end of 1947, when company was absorbed by Francis Lombardi. Types known as Lombardi (AVIA) included L.M.5 Aviastar, first produced 1945.

AVIA LTD. • Russia

Founded 1991, has developed the Accord-201 seven-seat lightplane with twin piston engines on its high-mounted wing (first flown 1994). A four-seat business jet is under development as the Accord-Jet.

AVIA AKCIOVA SPOLECNOST PRO PRUMYSL LETECKY • Czechoslovakia

Original Avia company founded 1919. Taken over by Milos Bondy a Spol about 1923, but acquired 1926 by Skoda, which also made Hispano-Suiza aero engines under licence. Early Avia designers were Benes and Hajn: hence initials in aircraft designations. BH-1 was light sporting two-seater; BH-3 a low-wing strut-braced single-seat fighter for the Czechoslovak National Defence Ministry; BH-25 a five-seater; BH-26 a two-seat fighter; BH-33 a single-seat biplane fighter developed from the BH-21. Company made Fokker F.VII/3m under licence, and Avia FIV IX was a Fokker-designed bomber. Before the war the company built fast metal-skinned transports of original design: Avia 51, 56 and 57. B 534 biplane was outstanding single-seat biplane fighter (445 built) used by Czechoslovak Air Force and widely considered best of class in Continental Europe. B 71 was Soviet-designed monoplane bomber; S 199 was post-war improvised development of German Bf 109. In 1945 works were reconstituted under Government, but production of Avia 36 light monoplane was resumed and Douglas C-47s were converted for civil use. Soviet Il-14M built as Avia 14.

AVIA AVIATION WORKS • Czechoslovakia

Founded 1936 at Kunovice, renamed Let (q.v.) in 1950.

Czech Avia BH-21 fighter with ski landing gear.

AVIA BALTIKA AVIATION LTD. • Lithuania

Incorporated 1991 and founded from the Kaunas helicopter service and repair factory, currently markets in assembled and kit forms the two-seat composites LAK-X lightplane (first flown 1992 and developed by Aeroplastika). Other work includes overhaul of helicopters and aviation equipment/components, aircraft leasing, transport operations and rescue work using company-owned Mil helicopters.

AVIABELLANCA AIRCRAFT CORPORATION • USA

Company chairman and chief design engineer is August Bellanca, whose father founded the original Bellanca Aircraft Corporation. Has developed the SkyRocket III six-seat composites cabin monoplane (first flown 1995 in SkyRocket II prototype form), which has been marketed in kit form and was intended also to be certificated for full assembled production.

AVIACOR INTERNATIONAL AIRCRAFT CORPORATION JSC • Russia

First flew in 1993 the M-12 Kasatik three-seat recreational and utility lightplane.

AVIAKOMPLEKS JSC • Russia

Established 1989 and has developed the AS-2 two-seat very light recreational monoplane (first flown 1991).

AVIAMILANO COSTRUZIONI AERONAUTICHE • Italy

During 1950s, after production of Falco F8L was transferred, under licence, to Aeromere, the company continued to build P.19 two-seat trainer and F.14 Nibbio four-seat cabin monoplane, a development of Falco. Aviamilano also built prototype of F.250 three-seat cabin monoplane, but sold rights to Siai-Marchetti. Aviamilano Construzioni Aeronàutiche went into liquidation 1968.

AVIAN AIRCRAFT LTD. • Canada

Formed February 1959 to develop a special wingless autogyro type, the Avian 2/180. First flew 1960, but accident delayed development. In 1964 Canadian Government provided financial assistance for further research and development. Certification granted in 1968.

*Above: Aviamilano P.19
Scricciolo lightplane*

*Right: Avian 2/180 Gyroplane
two-seat autogyro*

AVIASPETSTRANS CONSORTIUM • Russia

Created 1990 to develop the Yamal multipurpose amphibian, suited to passenger (15) and cargo transportation, patrol, survey, firefighting, rescue and other roles. MAPO 'Myasishchev' to manufacture. Unusual powerplant; twin turboshafts driving single 6-blade pusher propeller aft of tail unit.

AVIASUD INDUSTRIES • France

Began constructing aircraft in 1980. Produced the AE 206 Mistral two-seat mostly composites-built biplane (first flown 1985), with a twin-engined version principally for advertising and surveillance named Mistral Twin. Also developed AE 209 Albatros (first flown 1991) as two-seat mostly composites ultralight monoplane.

AVIAT INC. • USA

Markets A-1 Husky two-seat cabin light plane (also developed Acro-Husky with clipped wings and inverted fuel/oil systems), Pitts Special aerobatic biplanes in certificated form, and kits for Eagle II aerobatic biplane (former Christen Industries Eagle).

JSC AVIATEHNOLOGIE • Moldova

Has developed the Favorit very light single-seat monoplane (first flown 1996), with a two-seater for training being studied.

AVIATIK • Germany

Automobil and Aviatik AG. was founded in 1910. An Aviatik biplane crashed as early as June that year, but company named as above in 1911. Made French Farman biplanes and Hanriot monoplanes, but developed original types also. On outbreak of war in 1914 transferred works

Aviasud AE 209 Albatros lightplane

Aviatik standard biplane, with unequal span wings

from Mülhausen, Alsace, to Freiburgim-Breisgau. Developed B I reconnaissance aircraft from earlier Pi 5. Although unarmed, B I was used operationally. CI-CIII series (1915 onwards) were armed, and reversed earlier pilot-at-back arrangement. CIII used for bombing also. Company also made a few twin-engined Gotha bombers before working on larger R types. Designed post-war civil aircraft, but activities ceased 1919, and a new company formed to take over the concern, which went into liquidation.

AVIATIKA • Russia

Founded 1991 to bring together several organisations undertaking aviation related work and intending to move into civil aircraft development and production, including Moscow Dementyev Aviation Production Association, Gromov Flight Research Institute and Moscow Aviation Institute. In 1993 received Russian State Certificate as Russia's first commercially operated aircraft manufacturing company. In 1997 Aviatika withdrew from the programme, after which the manufacturer of Aviatika lightplanes became known as KB MAI (q.v.).

AVIATION ENTERPRISES • UK

Markets Chevvron 2-32C two-seat composites microlight-trainer (first flown 1983 in original prototype form).

AVIATION FARM LTD. • Poland

Markets through East European Markets Ltd. the J-5 Marco single-seat very light aircraft/motorglider, originally the Janowski J-5 and then offered by Alpha.

AVIATION FRANCHISING INTERNATIONAL • USA

Company handling progress with the Prescott Pusher II four-seat pusher-engined monoplane.

AVIATION INDUSTRIES OF AUSTRALIA • Australia

Superseded Melbourne Aircraft Corporation as developer of MA-2 Mamba lightplane.

AVIATION INDUSTRIES OF IRAN • Iran

Founded 1993 and affiliated to Iran's Ministry of Industries, Iran Industrial Development and Renovation Organisation (IDRO), thought to be tasked with establishing maintenance and repair facilities for light/medium aircraft, and overseeing production of aircraft and other air vehicles. Developing the IR-H5 five-seat helicopter, a two-seat piston-engined trainer possibly known as IR-02, a 12-seat STOL transport possibly known as IR-12, and the IR-G1

Nasim/AVA 101composites two-seat glider (first flown 1996, and possibly marketed by Iran Hava Commercial Services Company).

AVIATION SCOTLAND LTD. • UK

Took over ARV-1 Super2 from Island Aircraft (q.v.). See Highlander.

AVIATION SPECIALTIES INC. • USA

In January 1971 received certification for a turbine-powered conversion of Sikorsky S-55 helicopter, designated S-55-T. Became Helitec Corporation 1976.

AVIATION TRADERS (ENGINEERING) LTD. • UK

Formed at Bovingdon, Herts 1947 to sell aircraft and spares. In 1949 acquired base at Southend, Essex, to maintain aircraft on Berlin Airlift. During 1952-1955 built Bristol Freighter centre-sections. Sold about 20 civil Percival Prentices. Conversion of the 20-year-old Douglas DC-4 into a cheap car-ferry first considered January 1959; called Carvair, aircraft first flew June 1961; 21 built. Less successful was company's own medium-range airliner, the Accountant, with two Rolls-Royce Dart turboprops, flown July 1957 and backed by managing director F. A. Laker.

AVIATON • Russia

Has developed a four-seat general-purpose lightplane, the Merkury, with twin piston engines mounted on the high wing. First flown 1997.

Aviation Specialties' S-55-T turbine conversion of Sikorsky S-55

Vickers Vanguard formed basis for Merchantman freighter conversion for British European Airways, undertaken by Aviation Traders and first flown 1969. Later operated by Air Bridge

AVIATOR SCIENTIFIC-PRODUCTION ENTERPRISE • Russia

Produces M-9 Marathon as two-seat open-cockpit very light monoplane.

Aviation Traders ATL90 Accountant 1 airliner

Aviation Traders ATL98 Carvair car ferry, converted from the Douglas DC-4

Avibras A-80 Falcão two-seat cabin monoplane

AVIATSIONNYI KOMPLEKS IMENI S.V. ILYUSHINA • Russia

See Ilyushin

AVIBRAS • Brazil

Sociedade Avibras Ltda. in 1963 was testing prototype of A-80 Falcao, a side-by-side two-seat low-wing monoplane of wooden construction with plastic skin. Brazilian government contracts received for several projects, including single-seater with Volkswagen engine, but in 1967 the company withdrew from the aviation industry.

AVID AIRCRAFT INC. • USA

Kits supplied for the Bandit two-seat cabin monoplane, Catalina three-seat amphibian, Magnum two/three-seat cabin monoplane, and Speedwing two-seat cabin monoplane with aerobatic or STOL capabilities.

AVIMETA • France

Société Avimeta was formed in 1926 as a separate aeronautical firm by Établissements Schneider, exploiting use of structural material 'Alférium'. The Avimeta AVM-88 of 1927 was a parasol monoplane two-seat fighter with corrugated skin.

AVIOANE SA CRAIOVA • Romania

See S.C. Avioane SA Craiova

AVIOLANDA MAATSCHAPPIJ VOOR VLIEGTUIGBOUW NV • Netherlands

Founded December 1926. Before Second World War built under licence Dornier Wal twin-engined flying-boats for Royal Netherlands Naval Air Service and Curtiss Hawk biplane fighters for East Indies Army Air Service. After war made assemblies for Gloster Meteor, Hawker Hunter and Lockheed Starfighter. Made N.H.I. Kolibrie helicopter. Developed AT-21 pilotless drone and aircraft components (e.g. passenger ramps). Extensive repair and overhaul work also undertaken.

AVIOLIGHT SRL • Italy

Founded 1988 by Partenavia (q.v.), Tecnam and Avio Interiors to manufacture the Partenavia-developed P.86 Mosquito two-seat lightplane (first flown 1986). Also assigned P.66D Delta two/three-seater.

AVION INC. • USA

Formed 1942 to undertake research, engineering and production of military aircraft. Orders during war included subassemblies for Northrop and Lockheed. In January 1943 received Northrop subcontract for three XP-79 jet fighters, one of which (MX-324) was the first US rocket-propelled aircraft to fly, on 5 July 1944.

AVIONES DE COLOMBIA SA • Colombia

Originally a Cessna dealership (1961), then also assembled selected Cessna aircraft, produced a two-seat training derivative of the Cessna AgTruck, known as AgTrainer, and produced its own single-seat agricultural aircraft, the AC-05 Pijao (1992).

AVIONNERIE LAC ST-JEAN INC. • Canada

Markets partial kits for the Cyclone four-seat cabin monoplane, based on a Cessna 185.

AVIONS AMIOT • France

See Amiot

AVIONS AUTOMOBILES PHILIPPE MONIOT • France

First flew in November 1995 the APM-20-1 Lionceau two-seat light aircraft suited to training and many other roles.

AVIONS CLAUDE PIEL • France

Claude Piel produced a series of light aircraft from the early 1950s, most famous of which was the Emeraude two-seater with, in its original CP.30 form, a 65 hp Continental engine. Hundreds of Emeraudes of varying types were built under licence by companies in a number of countries. This company (instead of original Piel Aviation SA) continues to market Piel aircraft in plans form, including single-seat CP.80 Zef racing monoplane, CP.90 Pinocchio single-seat monoplane (single-seat variant of Emeraude), CP.328 Super Emeraude (also has been commercially built), CP.402 Donald single-seat high-wing cabin monoplane (first flown 1953), CP.605 Diamant three/four-seat cabin monoplane (first flown 1964 in CP.604 prototype form) and is certificated for commercial production, CP.751 Beryl tandem two-seat monoplane, and CP.1320 Saphir three-seat monoplane.

AVIONS CROSES • France

See Croses

AVIONS DE TRANSPORT REGIONAL • International

See ATR

AVIONS H. NICOLLIER • France

First flew in 1902 the HN.400 Menestrel single seat mono plane, available for home construction from plans and some components; redesigned HN.434 also offered. HN.500 Bengali first flew 1988 as side-by-side two-seat monoplane, and HN.700 Menestrel II two-seat version of Menestrel, both available in plans form.

AVIONS JACQUES COUPE • France

Offers plans to construct JC 01 and more powerful (and nosewheel undercarriage) JC-200 two-seat low-wing monoplanes.

AVIONS MARCEL DASSAULT-BREGUET AVIATION • France

Formed in December 1971, following the merger of Dassault and Société des Avions Louis Breguet. Expanded successful Falcon series to include Falcon 50 (1976), Falcon 100 and Falcon 900 (1984). Super Etendard carrier-borne combat aircraft appeared October 1974, Mirage 2000 fighter in 1978 and Mirage 50 in April 1979. Breguet 1150 Atlantic (1961) maritime aircraft continued in production until 1973, with new Atlantique 2 appearing in May 1981. Engaged on the SEPECAT Jaguar with British

Dassault Super Etendard naval strike-fighters (Photo AMD-BA/Aviaplans) – see Avions Marcel Dassault-Breguet

Aerospace. Undertook Alpha Jet twin-jet trainer development and production with Dornier of Germany (later Daimler-Benz Aerospace; see Dassault-Breguet/Dornier). Name changed to current Dassault Aviation in 1990.

AVIONS MUDRY ET CIE • France

See Mudry et Compagnie

AVIONS ROBIN • France

See Robin

AVIONS ROGER DRUINE • France

Roger Druine built his first aircraft in 1938 at the age of 17, and built a single-seat cabin monoplane, the Aigle, in 1948. His 1950 single-seat D.31 Turbulent was produced in small number by Rollason Aircraft & Engines and Stark Flugzeugbau, and remains available in plans form for home construction. Rollason also built the 1954 two-seat D.60 Condor (plans available). Also remaining available in plans form is D.5 Turbi two-seater, first flown 1951, as a development of Turbulent.

AVIOTECHNICA • International

Joint Russian/Bulgarian company (see Interavia).

AVIS FLUGZEUGWERKE UND AUTOWERKE GMBH • Austria

After the First World War built two types of high-wing monoplane trainer and the B.G.VI three-engined transport biplane, the wings of which were cantilevered outboard of struts near fuselage.

AVI SOCIEDAD ANÓNIMA INDUSTRIAL COMERCIAL Y FINANCIERA • Argentina

In October 1958 began development of Avi 205 multipurpose high-wing monoplane. First flight was in September 1960.

AVPK SUKHOI • Russia

Aviatsionnyi Voyenno Promyshlennyi Komplex Sukhoi. Founded December 1996 to oversee activities of Sukhoi and Beriev (q.v.), plus production centres at Irkutsk, Komsomolsk-on-Amur and Novosibirsk. Incorporates Sukhoi Shturmovics Consortium, founded March 1992 and encompassing 47 companies, Sukhoi Advanced Technologies JSC and Sukhoi Design Bureau.

AVRO • UK

See Roe, A.V. & Co Ltd.

AVRO AIRCRAFT LTD. • Canada

Formed as part of Hawker Siddeley Group after acquiring Victory Aircraft Ltd. (Crown-owned) in July 1945. In 1946 Group took over Turbo-Research Ltd. Technical innovations brought company brief world fame. Built C-102 Jetliner, first jet transport on American continent, in 1949, though no sales followed. CF-100 was world's first straight-wing combat aircraft to exceed Mach 1 (in a dive, 18 December 1952). Type first flown January 1950 and developed as two-seat all-weather interceptor through five marks. About 700 built, serving in Canada and Europe and supplied to Belgian Air Force. Was to have been followed in production by CF-105 Arrow, with delta wing. First Arrow completed October 1957 and flew 1958; but project cancelled February 1959 after expenditure of about $400 million. The Arrow was a victim of the widespread belief that the interceptor role could best be performed by a missile. Three years later Canada had to buy McDonnell F-101 Voodoo fighters from the USA. Also experimented with three-engined lift-fan Avrocar.

AVRO INTERNATIONAL AEROSPACE • UK

Established 1993 to manage the regional aircraft of British Aerospace. Became part of Aero International (Regional) for short period. Now British Aerospace Regional Aircraft Ltd. (BARAL) division (see British Aerospace).

AVTEK CORPORATION • USA

Established 1982, flew proof-of-concept prototype for the intended Avtek 400A pressurised, composites-built, six/nine-seat business jetfan in September 1984. Avtek has unusual layout, with rear-mounted main wings, canards, and twin turboprops with pusher propellers. Avtek 400A expected to be certificated in year 2000, with 419 Express 19-seat airliner and Explorer special missions versions proposed.

AYRES CORPORATION • USA

In November 1977 Ayres purchased manufacturing rights to the Rockwell Thrush Commander agricultural aircraft. Production continues in 1999 of various developed models as Turbo Thrush agricultural aircraft with piston and turboprop engines. Has also developed the Loadmaster, a uniquely configured multipurpose transport with two turboprop engines driving a single propeller, intended mainly for carrying bulk and containerised freight but with passenger/troop and reconnaissance variants planned.

AZIONARIA VERCELLESE INDUSTRIE AERONAUTICHE • Italy

See AVIA

Avro CF-105 Arrow, in 1958 one of the most advanced fighter aircraft

Ayres 510 Gallon Turbo Thrush, with 1,931 litre chemical hopper

Ayres Amphibious Loadmaster representation

B

BA • UK

In the mid-1930s Major E. F. Stephen formed at Hanworth, Middlesex, a company originally titled British Klemm Aeroplane Company Ltd. to build under licence the German Klemm L.25 two-seat lightweight sporting aircraft under the name B. K. Swallow. Also built six B.K.1 Eagle 1 three-seat cabin monoplanes, similar to Klemm L.32 but redesigned by G. A. Handasyde. A total of 22 B.A. Eagle 2s was subsequently built.

BAC • UK (1935)

The British Aircraft Company (1935) Ltd. built a series of gliders in the early 1930s. In 1932 one was fitted with landing gear and a Douglas motorcycle engine driving a pusher propeller. A small number were produced before designer and company owner C. H. Lowe Wylde was killed while flying the initial conversion on 13 May 1933. Company taken over by Austrian pilot Robert Kronfeld, becoming Kronfeld Ltd. (q.v.).

BAC • UK (1960)

British Aircraft Corporation formed in February 1960 to unite the aircraft and guided weapon activities of Bristol Aeroplane Company Ltd., English Electric Company Ltd., and Vickers Ltd. It then had four wholly-owned subsidiaries: Bristol Aircraft Ltd., English Electric Aviation Ltd., Vickers Armstrongs (Aircraft) Ltd., and British Aircraft Corporation (Guided Weapons) Ltd., plus a controlling interest in Hunting Aircraft Ltd. On 1 January 1964 British Aircraft Corporation (Operating) Ltd. was formed to be responsible for the business conducted formerly by the subsidiaries. At the same time BAC acquired the remaining shares of Hunting Aircraft Ltd. Merged into British Aerospace (q.v.) in April 1977. Final products using BAC name included One-Eleven short/medium-range airliner (first flown August 1963 in Series 200 prototype form), Strikemaster jet trainer and armed tactical support jet (first flown October 1967), and Concorde supersonic airliner (first flown March 1969) in association with Aérospatiale of France.

BACC • USA

Business Air Craft Corporation, formed on 15 July 1963 to combine Howard Aero Inc (q.v.), Alamo Air Service and Alamo Aviation Inc in a single company. Continued production of the Howard 500 12/16-seat transport, the similar 350 and 250 under the respective designations BACC BA400, Models H-350 and H 250.

Right: The T Mk 5 version of Jet Provost basic jet trainer (seen to rear of Tucano that replaced it in RAF service) did not fly until 1967 and so was produced by BAC at Preston

Above: B.K. Swallow two-seat monoplane – see BA

Right: Howard 250, a conversion of the 10/12-passenger Lodestar L-18 – see BACC

BACH AIRCRAFT COMPANY INC. • USA

Founded in March 1927, the company produced a number of civil aircraft before introducing the Bach Air Yacht in 1928. This was a three-engined commercial transport with a maximum capacity of two crew and ten passengers. Had nose-mounted engine of 220 hp or 400 hp, with one 100 hp or 125 hp engine mounted on the bracing strut beneath each wing.

Right: Concorde was developed jointly by BAC and Aerospatiale

BAC One-Eleven airliner

Above: BAC Strikemaster with 20-mm gun pods

BACHEM-WERKE GMBH • Germany

From 1944 this company, with a design team led by Dipl Ing Erich Bachem (formerly technical director of Fieseler-Werke), began development of the Ba 349 Natter, a vertically-launched rocket-powered piloted missile was intended to attack Allied bomber concentrations. Following launch, the pilot would attack the enemy aircraft with unguided rockets, and complete his sortie with a parachute extraction from the expendable aircraft and descent to the ground. The rear fuselage of the Natter and its Walter rocket motor was also recovered by parachute. So far as is known only one piloted launch was made, in February 1945, when test pilot Lothar Siebert was killed. The Allied advance prevented completion of the project, and none of these aircraft was used operationally.

BACINI E SCALI NAPOLETANI • Italy

This company established an aircraft department in 1923 to carry out repairs to seaplanes and flying-boats on behalf of the Italian Air Ministry. Began in the late 1930s to manufacture components for the Italian aircraft industry and to build aircraft under subcontract for the Regia Aeronàutica.

BACK FORTY DEVELOPMENTS LTD. • Canada

Markets kits for the Tundra tandem two-seat microlight.

BACON • USA

Erle L. Bacon Corporation established at Santa Monica, California, to build an extensively updated version of the North American T-6 tandem two-seat advanced trainer. Known as the Bacon Super T-6, the prototype first flew in April 1957.

BAe • UK

See British Aerospace plc.

BAHNBEDARF AKTIEN-GESELLSCHAFT • Germany

Established in 1922, this company had formerly produced railway equipment. In 1924 it began the production of lightweight sporting aircraft, including the BAG E.1, D.1 and D.11a, the last being a two-seater with folding wings, allowing it to be stored in a garage.

BALDWIN AIRCRAFT CORPORATION • USA

Baldwin Aircraft Corporation acquired the plant and equipment of Ordnance Engineering Corporation to continue production of the Orenco designs.

BALDWIN AIRCRAFT INTERNATIONAL • USA

In 1988 first displayed the prototype composites-built and two-seat ASP-XJ armed surveillance and patrol experimental jet.

BALL-BARTOE AIRCRAFT CORPORATION • USA

Developed JW-1 Jetwing blown-wing research single-seat jet, first flown 1977.

BAOSHAN IRON & STEEL COMPLEX • China

See Venga.

BARCLAY, CURLE & CO LTD. • UK

Barclay, Curle & Company of Whiteinch, Glasgow, built 100 Royal Aircraft Factory B.E.2es under subcontract. Order also received for the construction of 50 Fairey F.22 Campania two-seat patrol seaplanes in 1917.

BARKLEY-GROW AIRCRAFT CORPORATION • USA

Established in 1935 to manufacture an eight-seat twin-engined light transport aircraft designated Barkley-Grow T8P-1. Similar in appearance to the Lockheed Electra, the design incorporated a multispar stressed-skin wing patented by A. S. Barkley, which eliminated the need for ribs or bulkheads in the wing.

BARNETT ROTORCRAFT COMPANY • USA

Offers plans and material kits to construct the J4B single-seat autogyro and J4B2 two-seat autogyro, plus welded steel airframes and completed components.

BARNEY OLDFIELD AIRCRAFT COMPANY • USA

Marketed in plan and kit forms the Baby Lakes, Super Baby Lakes, Buddy Baby Lakes and Great Lakes Sport Trainer single- and two-seat biplanes. See Aircraft Spruce & Speciality.

BARTLETT AIRCRAFT CORPORATION • USA

Immediately after the Second World War the Bartlett Aircraft Corporation of Rosemead, California, began production of a lightweight two-seat cabin monoplane designated the Bartlett LC 13-A Zephyr 150. This aircraft was developed from the Babcock monoplane of the mid-1930s.

BASLER TURBO CONVERSIONS INC • USA

Founded 1957. Developed Turbo-67 as turboprop-powered, re-engineered and lengthened modification of DC-3, plus Turbo-34 lengthened Cessna 337 Skymaster with the original twin piston engines replaced by a single turboprop.

BAT • UK

Founded in 1917 by Samuel (later Lord) Waring in premises previously occupied by Joucques Aviation Company. The British Aerial Transport Company's chief designer was Frederick Koolhoven, formerly with Sir W. G. Armstrong, Whitworth & Company Ltd. His first design for the new company was the BAT F.K.22 Bat, a small single-seat fighter. Failure of the ABC Mosquito engine for which it was designed resulted in a new and smaller aircraft being created, the F.K.23 Bantam, powered by the ABC Wasp. Only nine production aircraft were built, and none saw

Bacon Super T-6 conversion of the North American T-6 trainer

wartime. Other BAT designs included the F.K.24 Baboon, F.K.25 Basilisk and, finally, the F.K.26, a civil transport aircraft with accommodation for four passengers, of which only four were built. The F.K.27 was a single side-by-side, two-seat variant of the Bantam. When the company was disbanded post-war, its assets were distributed between Alliance Aeroplane Company Ltd. and Nieuport & General Aircraft Company, also founded by Samuel Waring.

BATHIAT-SANCHEZ • France

Established at Issy-le-Moulineaux as successors to Roger Sommer, and with a flying school at Bouy, Marne, in 1914 this company was producing a single-seat high-wing monoplane with tractor propeller, and a two-seat biplane with pusher propeller.

BATWING AIRCRAFT CORPORATION • USA

In the mid-1930s this company built a two-seat tailless monoplane aircraft to the design of W. F. McGinty, a member of the instructional staff of the Boeing School of Aeronautics. It had a 75 hp Pobjoy engine with a pusher propeller.

BAUMANN AIRCRAFT CORPORATION • USA

Established in 1945 by J. B. Baumann, a former designer and engineer with the Lockheed Aircraft Corporation. Designed and built the Baumann Model 250 Brigadier prototype; production aircraft were designated Model 290.

Below: BAT F.K.26 four-passenger airliner, first exclusively civil transport built post WW1

BAYERISCHE FLUGZEUGWERKE • Germany

See BFW.

BÄUMER AERO GMBH • Germany

This company was founded by Herr Bäumer, who was killed in July 1927 while flight-testing a high-performance monoplane. In addition to operating a flying school at Hamburg, the company designed and manufactured a number of lightweight aircraft. Best known was the Bäumer Sausewind, a two-seat low-wing monoplane.

BD MICRO-TECHNOLOGIES INC. • USA

Founded by Ed 'Skeeter' Karnes to offer partial kits and plans of the Bede BD-5 to existing builders still undertaking construction.

Above: Baumann Brigadier, with twin engines in a pusher configuration

BEAGLE AIRCRAFT LTD. • UK

Beagle Aircraft Ltd. was, immediately before its dissolution, a state-owned company, acquired in August 1968 to continue the production and development of light aircraft in Britain. The company was founded in 1960, and became in 1962 a subsidiary of British Executive and General Aviation Ltd. before which it had absorbed Beagle-Auster Aircraft Ltd. and Beagle-Miles Aircraft Ltd. The Auster interests were disposed of to Hants & Sussex Aviation Ltd. which continued to provide spares and modification support to all Auster aircraft in service. The company went into voluntary liquidation on 27 February 1970. Beagle produced Auster-designed aircraft, conversions of ex-military Austers, the B.206 twin-engined

Beagle Airedale four-seat touring aircraft

Beagle B.206 twin-engined light transport

light executive transport, of which 20 served with the RAF as the Basset, and the B.121 Pup two/three-seat light aircraft. A military trainer version of the latter aircraft, known as the Bulldog, was also produced; production of this was continued by Scottish Aviation after Beagle went into liquidation.

BEARDMORE, WILLIAM & CO • UK

Large British engineering and shipbuilding company which turned to aircraft construction just before the First World War, obtaining a licence to build German DFW biplanes to be powered by Beardmore-built Austro-Daimler engines. Built large numbers of aircraft under subcontract during war. Under leadership of G. Tilghman Richards produced original aircraft, including W.B.III, a redesigned Sopwith

Pup with folding wings and folding or jettisonable landing gear. Designed and built a small number of civil and military aircraft in the interwar years.

BÉARN • France

Constructions Aéronautiques du Béarn was responsible for production of the Minicab two-seat lightweight cabin monoplane designed by Yves Gardan. Designated Béarn Minicab GY-201, it was powered as standard with a 65 hp Continental flat-four engine.

BEATTY AVIATION COMPANY • UK

American pilot G. W. Beatty visited Britain in 1912 to demonstrate the Gyro aero engine. Returned 1913 and

founded flying-school at Hendon. Built biplane 1916, later powered by engine of own construction. Began construction of aircraft and components in 1918.

BEDE AIRCRAFT CORPORATION • USA

Original Bede Aviation Corporation established 1960 in Kansas to develop advanced STOL aircraft. Early type was BD-1 that first flew 1963 and was later produced by others as Yankee Trainer and Traveler. Subsequent designs included BD-4 two/four-seat sporting monoplane of 1970s, and remarkable and tiny BD-5 Micro single-seat pusher-engined monoplane and its turbojet-powered derivative

Beardmore Inflexible, an experimental design of 1928, powered by three Rolls-Royce engines

Above: Beech T-34Cs of Peruvian Navy

as the BD-5J. Following difficult period, company later re-established as Bede Aircraft Corporation in Missouri, reviving BD-4 and BD-6 for sale in kits and plans forms. BD-12A of 1994 became tandem two-seat variant of BD-5, with larger four-seat BD-14A then put under development.

BEDE JET CORPORATION • USA

Developed the BD-10 two-seat supersonic jet for home construction from kits, first flown July 1992 and kit deliveries from August 1993. See Peregrine Flight International.

BEDEK AIRCRAFT COMPANY • Israel

See Israel Aircraft Industries (IAI).

BEE AVIATION ASSOCIATES INC. • USA

Known originally as Beecraft Associates Inc. this company built the diminutive Wee Bee in 1949, in which the pilot lay in a prone position. It was followed by the larger V-tailed Honey Bee, which first flew on 12 July 1952.

BEECH AIRCRAFT CORPORATION • USA

Founded in 1932 by the late Walter Beech and Mrs Olive A. Beech, to design and manufacture lightplanes. Delivered the 10,000th example of its Beechcraft Bonanza Model 35 in February 1977, and the Bonanza celebrated its 50th anniversary in 1995, with production continuing.

Above: Beech Starship 2000As were delivered before the company was fully merged into Raytheon in 1994

Beechcraft Wee Bee

Beechcraft Honey Bee V-tailed lightweight monoplane

Beech D.17 four-seat lightplane

Beech Bonanza four/five-seat monoplane

Beech Super King Air light transport

Company also supplied military aircraft, and became involved in the construction of aircraft and missile components and missile targets for the US Army. Designed, developed and manufactured the cryogenic gas storage system for NASA's Apollo and Skylab projects. Other work included provision of power reactant storage assembly for NASA's Space Shuttle orbiter. Acquired by Raytheon in 1980, but continued to be operated as an independent company until 1994.

Beech Model 18 light transport. More than 4,000 were built for military service in WW2

BEIJING KEYUAN LIGHT AIRCRAFT INDUSTRIAL CO LTD. • China

Produces the AD-200 Blue Eagle tandem two-seat STOL general-purpose lightplane (first flown September 1988, designed by the Nanjing University of Aeronautics and Astronautics). Features of AD-200 include rear mounted wings with winglet fins, nose canard and pusher piston engine in the rear of the fuselage pod.

B & L HINZ • Germany

Provides plans to construct the BL.1 Kéa two-seat composites monoplane.

BELL AEROMARINE • UK

Markets Flitzer single-seat open-cockpit biplane in plans and kit forms (first flown 1995).

BELL AEROSPACE CORPORATION • USA

See Bell Aircraft Corporation

BELL AEROSYSTEMS • USA

See Bell Aircraft Corporation

Above: Bell Aircraft XV-3 was an experimental tilt-rotor convertiplane that first flew in 1955. Accumulating 250 test flights, it proved the concept was practicable

BELL AIRCRAFT CORPORATION • USA

Original company of 1935, Bell Aircraft Corporation, responsible for P-39 Aircobra and P-63 Kingcobra of Second World War. Built first US turbojet, the P-59 Aircomet fighter/trainer. Built the rocket-powered Bell X-1, in which USAF pilot Charles Yeager was the first to exceed the speed of sound, on 14 October 1947. Subsequent X-1A flown at 1,650mph (2,655kmh) in 1953. Company subsequently known as Bell Aerosystems, then on 5 July 1960 became Bell Aerospace Corporation, a wholly-owned subsidiary of Textron Inc. which had acquired the former Bell Aircraft Corporation. Responsible for the Bell Model D2127 tilting-duct research aircraft; two lunar Landing Research Vehicles (LLRV) for NASA, to train astronauts to land safely on the moon; Automatic Carrier Landing System (ACLS), used on US Navy aircraft carriers; and was involved with an air-cushion landing system that was expected to enable military transports to land and take off from practically any surface. Terminated aircraft production. See Bell Helicopter Textron Inc.

Above: Bell Model D2127 tilting-duct V/STOL research aircraft, tested from 1966 as the X-22A

Bell P-39 Aircobra, which had nose-mounted cannon

Bell X-1 rocket-powered research aircraft

BELL HELICOPTER TEXTRON INC. • USA

Bell Helicopter Company, originally a division of Bell Aircraft, became a branch of Textron Inc. in 1960 and a fully-integrated subsidiary in January 1982. Bell Helicopter Textron Inc is its current name; Bell has produced well over 33,000 helicopters. In 1986 commercial/civil helicopter production moved to Canada (see Bell Helicopter Textron Canada). Came to an agreement with IAR-SA Brasov (q.v.) in 1996 to allow licence manufacture of AH-1W SuperCobra in Romania, tied with the purchase of a majority shareholding in IAR-SA Brasov.

Historically, Bell was responsible for design and construction of the Model 47, the first helicopter to receive Approved Type Certificate from the US Civil Aviation Authority (on 8 March 1946), and which remained in production for more than 25 years. Later helicopters of particular importance included the UH-1 Iroquois (Model 204) military utility helicopter (first flown October 1956), and the world's first purpose-designed tandem two-seat attack helicopter, the Model 209 (military AH-1 HueyCobra), first flown September 1965 and operated by the US Army in Vietnam from 1967. Production of HueyCobra in the USA has ended, but Fuji in Japan is still producing examples in the modern AH-1S version.

Current Bell programmes include remanufacture of 180 AH-1W SuperCobras and 100 UH-1Ns of US Marine Corps into AH-1Zs and UH-1Ys respectively under the H-1 Programme, with upgrades common to both helicopter types including the installaton of General Electric T700 engines, four-blade composite hingless and bearingless rotors, and much more besides; upgrade and life-extension of UH-1Hs of other forces to UH-1H-II or Huey II standard (joint Bell and AlliedSignal programme) by installation of AlliedSignal T53-L-703 turboshaft engine plus airframe improvements; production of the twin-turboshaft AH-1W SuperCobra for

Above: Bell Helicopter Textron AH-1W SuperCobra attack helicopter

Right: Bell Helicopter Textron OH-58D Kiowa Warrior

the US Marine Corps (introduced 1986); and upgrade of 411 US Army OH-58 Kiowa reconnaissance helicopters to OH-58D Kiowa Warrior armed configuration (also for Taiwan). Also development and production of the BA 609, a civil 10/11-seat tiltrotor transport (to fly 1999; production in association with Agusta of Italy, after Boeing's share in the programme was passed to

Bell), and participation in the very important Bell Boeing V-22 Osprey military tiltrotor programme (first flown March 1989) to provide the US forces with a vertical-lift transport and multipurpose aircraft capable also of strike, rescue, amphibious combat assault and anti-submarine work.

Above: Bell VTOL research vehicle

Left: The 47G-5A variant of the Bell Model 47 light helicopter, in production for more than 25 years

Bell Boeing V-22 Osprey military tiltrotor aircraft

Bell Helicopter Textron AH-1F HueyCobras operated by Jordan

Bell/Agusta BA 609 tilt-rotor civil transport mock-up

BELL HELICOPTER
TEXTRON CANADA • Canada

Founded 1984, with a production factory at Mirabel completed 1985 as a division of Textron Canada Ltd. Manufacture of Bell Helicopter Textron Inc commercial/civil helicopters moved from USA to Mirabel 1986, leaving US company free to concentrate on military types. Current production encompasses Model 206B-3 JetRanger III five-seat light helicopter (first flown 1962 in original form and 1977 as JetRanger III) and its TH-67 military trainer variant; seven-seat Model 206L-4 LongRanger IV (first flown 1974 in original form and certificated 1992 as LongRanger IV); Model 206LT TwinRanger as twin-turboshaft variant of LongRanger (certified 1993); 15-seat Model 212, using twinned turboshafts; Model 230 intermediate-twin ten-seat helicopter (first flown August 1991); Model 407 extra-wide variant of LongRanger with a four-blade main rotor (first flown June 1995); Model 412EP 15-seat utility helicopter, also suited to specialised roles such as law enforcement, SAR and medical (first flown 1979); Model 427 eight-seater (first flown December 1997) as a lengthened version of Model 407; and Model 430 derived from the Model 230 but with more engine power and a four-blade bearingless composite main rotor (first flown October 1995).

Bell Helicopter Textron Canada Model 230

Bell Helicopter Textron Canada Model 412EP utility helicopter

Bell Helicopter Textron Canada Model 430 intermediate twin, as used for a round-the-world helicopter speed record attempt in 1996

BELLANCA • USA

See following entries, plus AviaBellanca.

BELLANCA AIRCRAFT CORPORATION • USA

Incorporated December 1927, taking over from original Bellanca Aircraft Corporation of America. Aircraft produced included CH.300 six-seat lightplane, Pacemaker six-seater of 1929 and flown 1931 on an 84 hour 33 minute world non-refuelled endurance record, Skyrocket development of 1930, Airbus 14-passenger commercial transport that was developed into Aircruiser of early 1930s for commercial and military use, Bellanca bomber of 1933 that was basically a twin-engined Aircruiser, 28-90 two-seater and others for air racing, 14-13-3 Cruisair four-seater first

flown November 1945, and 14-19 Cruisemaster development, among many others. Assets acquired by Northern Aircraft (q.v.) 1955 and Bellanca name finally dropped 1959 after merger with non-aviation companies.

BELLANCA AIRCRAFT CORPORATION • USA

Second use of name, though this company originally known as International Aircraft Manufacturing Inc (q.v.), becoming first Bellanca Sales Company (a subsidiary of Miller Flying Service) to manufacture and market versions of the Bellanca Model 14 four-seat light business aircraft designed by G. M. Bollanca. Three versions, known as Bellanca Viking series, became available. Acquired assets of Champion Aircraft Corporation 1970 and changed name

Bellanca of Canada CH-300 Pacemaker

to Bellanca Aircraft Corporation, thereafter building and marketing Citabria, Decathlon and Scout two-seaters produced formerly by Champion Aircraft. Became subsidiary of Anderson, Greenwood and Company, and thereby also became responsible for developing the Aries T-250 five-seat cabin lightplane (had first flown 1973). Also, in 1979, became responsible for producing Eagle Aircraft Company's agricultural aircraft (q.v.). Bellanca went into liquidation 1981 and Viking assets bought by Viking Aviation (q.v.) 1982. See also Champion Aircraft Company Inc.

BELLANCA AIRCRAFT ENGINEERING INC. • USA

Formed by G. M. Bellanca and his son, August T. Bellanca, researching from 1956 use of glassfibre for aircraft construction. Developed from 1963 a six-seat light aircraft as Model 25 Skyrocket, constructed of high strength

Bellanca Model 19-25 Skyrocket II six-seat lightplane

Bellanca Super Viking four-seat light aircraft, powered by a flat-six engine

glassfibre-epoxy laminates, which made its first flight in March 1975 and was evaluated in Aircraft Energy Efficiency programme. Programme ended 1986.

BELLANCA INC. • USA

Formed out of Viking Aviation (q.v.). Produced Viking from 1984 and supported Eagle agricultural aircraft after purchasing certificate and jigs in 1984. Ceased operations 1988.

BELLANCA SALES COMPANY • USA

See Bellanca Aircraft Corporation.

BELLANGER FRERES • France

Once-famous manufacturer of motor cars, built a flying-boat to the design of M. Denhaut, originator of the Donnet-Denhaut aircraft. Subsequently built a number of experimental aircraft designed to improve the lift characteristics of an aircraft's wing.

BENDIX HELICOPTER INC. • USA

Designed and built in 1947 a single-seat experimental helicopter designated Bendix Model K. A four-seat development, the Model J, had completed over 100 hours of flight testing in early 1948 and was to be revised before the start of production.

Rare picture of Benoist biplane flying-boat

BENES & MRAZ TOVARNA NA LETADLA • Czechoslovakia

Founded 1935 by P. Benes, well-known designer of light aircraft, in conjunction with the industrialist J. Mráz. Benes had been a founder of the Avia company, and subsequently chief designer of Ceskoslovenska-Kolben-Danek (CKD Praga, q.v.). Producers of several different types of one- and two-seat lightweight sporting aircraft.

BENNETT AVIATION LTD. • New Zealand

This company built and developed a single-engine agricultural monoplane, designated Bennett P.L.11 Airtruck, designed by Luigi Pellarini. Somewhat similar to the P.L.7 agricultural aircraft, designed by Pellarini for the Kingsford Smith Company in Australia, it flew for the first time on 2 August 1960.

BENOIST AIRCRAFT COMPANY • USA

Known originally as the Aeronautic Supply Company, and established at St Louis, Missouri; built in 1914 a small biplane flying-boat known as the Benoist XIV Air-Boat. Power plant comprised a 70 hp Sturtevant or 75 hp Roberts engine driving a pusher propeller.

BENSEN AIRCRAFT CORPORATION • USA

Founded by Dr Igor B. Bensen, formerly chief research engineer of the Kaman Corporation (q.v.), to develop a series of lightweight autogyros. Examples built and supplied to USAF for research purposes, but marketed primarily in kit form for amateur construction. Also attempted to develop Cargolifter as multi-helicopter lifting platform, with eight-rotor sub-scale prototype flown in early 1980s.

BERGAMASCHI CANTIERI, AERONAUTICI • Italy

Originally operator of a flying school, began in 1927 to build single-seat and two-seat training aircraft, the Bergamaschi C-1 and C-2 respectively, which incorporated improvements to facilitate flying training. These included a well-sprung landing gear and aerodynamic features to

Bensen Super Bug light autogyro

improve stability. Absorbed into Caproni group (q.v.) 1931 as Caproni Aeronàutica Bergamasca.

BERIEV • USSR/now Russia

Starting seaplane design in 1928, G. M. Beriev became the leading designer of Russian waterbased aircraft. Chief designer of the TsKB seaplane group in 1930, he was responsible for the twin-engined MBR-2 flying-boat, Be-2 reconnaissance seaplane and Be-4 flying-boat. Beriev design bureau became centre of Soviet seaplane development in 1945, a major flying-boat project being the twin-jet Be-10. Be-12 twin-turboprop anti-submarine and reconnaissance amphibian manufactured between 1963 and 1973 and served widely with Soviet/Russian Navy until about 1997, when withdrawn; several Be-12s have been modified for civil uses, including transport and firefighting. A-40/Be-40 Albatross *Mermaid* turbofan-powered intermediate-range anti-submarine, search and rescue and patrol amphibian first flown December 1986 and ordered for the Russian Navy in 1992 but not funded. Improved search-and-rescue variant became Be-42, which might eventually join the Russian Navy with propfan engines (sometimes referred to in the West as A-45).

A laser-gun test-bed aircraft based on the Ilyushin Il-76 was produced by Beriev and has been flown since 1980s as A-60, while in 1978 the first flight took place of the Beriev A-50 *Mainstay* airborne early warning and control aircraft, also based on Il-76 and in Russian operational service since

Beriev Be-12P-200 firefighting conversion of the ASW amphibian, with 'tail sting' removed (Piotr Butowski)

1984. Beriev Be-32 16-passenger twin-turboprop transport (first flown 1976), similar to earlier Be-30 (first flown 1968), was still to enter production in 1998. Be-102 multipurpose amphibian designed in 1993 but remained project in 1990. Be-112 Polican larger multipurpose amphibian under consideration for development, while Be-200 twin-turbofan multipurpose amphibian (initially for firefighting) first flew in 1998. Be-103 six-seat light amphibian, also suited to cargo carrying, survey and other roles, first flew July 1997; has twin piston engines carried on mounts either side of the rear fuselage. Very heavy lift cargo and passenger amphibians have been projected as Be-1200 and Be-2500, possibly to fly next century. Company currently named Joint Stock Company 'Taganrog Aviation Scientific-Technical Complex named after G.M. Beriev', and now part of the AVPK Sukhoi organisation.

Beriev MBR-2 flying-boat

Beriev M-12 (Be-12) amphibian flying-boat

BERLINER AIRCRAFT COMPANY INC. • USA

Established in 1926 by H. A. Berliner to build the Berliner Monoplane, intended initially to equip his own Potomac Flying Service. H. A. Berliner was the son of Emile Berliner, designer of an aero engine, a helicopter and the gramophone.

BERLINER-JOYCE AIRCRAFT CORPORATION • USA

See B/J Aircraft Corporation

BERNARD • France

Known originally as A. Bernard, company was founded in the latter years of the First World War. Its title was changed

Berliner-Joyce P-16/PB-1, first to be designated in the USAAC's 'Pursuit, Biplane' category

Blackburn Beverley military transport

in 1924 to Société Industrielle des Métaux et du Bois (SIMB, q.v.). The latter company was wound up in 1926, but the Société des Avions Bernard was established in late 1927 to manufacture the Bernard 190T, a ten-seat transport aircraft designed by SIMB.

BERWICK, F. W., & COMPANY LTD. • UK

This company, established at Park Royal, northwest London, built a number of D.H.4, D.H.9 and D.H.9A aircraft during the First World War under subcontract to The Aircraft Manufacturing Company (AIRCO). Was the recipient of a contract for 1,000 ABC Dragonfly engines which was cancelled when the unreliable behaviour of this new engine became apparent.

BESSON • France

Known originally as Marcel Besson et Cie, Société des Constructions Aéronautiques et Navales Marcel Besson was responsible for construction of some attractive triplane flying-boats, all powered by single engines in a pusher configuration. Built also in 1927 the M.B.35 monoplane seaplane and M.B.36 three-engined flying-boat.

BETA AIR LTD. JOINT VENTURE • Russia

Founded to undertake development of the Be-200 amphibian, combining Beriev, Taganrog and Irkutsk aircraft production associations, and Geneva ILTA Trade Finance SA of Switzerland. Be-200 now recognised as a Beriev programme.

B & F TECHNIK VERTRIEBS GMBH • Germany

First flew in 1985 the FK.6 single-seat high-wing monoplane, currently available for construction from plans. Also offers kits for FK.9 side-by-side two-seat monoplane, FK.9 Mk 3 of 1997 first appearance, and FK.12 Comet tandem two-seat microlight biplane.

BFW • Germany

Began aircraft construction during First World War and produced a number of prototypes, the company originally being called Bayerische Flugzeug-Werke. Post-war, when aircraft construction was forbidden under the Treaty of Versailles, became the still-famous Bayerische Motoren-Werke (BMW), building motorcycles, motor cars and aero engines. Re-formed at Augsberg in 1926, taking over the factory of the former Bayerische Rumpler Werke. Built a number of successful commercial aircraft, including BFW M-20 twelve-seat transport. Willy Messerschmitt joined the company as chief engineer in 1928, evolving the Bf 108 Taifun four-seat cabin monoplane and the Bf 109,

without doubt the most famous German aircraft of all time, before the company became Messerschmitt AG (q.v) in July 1938.

BHARAT HEAVY ELECTRICALS LTD. • India

First flew in November 1990 the prototype of the LT-IIM Swati two-seat metal/wood monoplane, designed by the Technical Centre of Directorate General of Civil Aviation in India, which received certification in 1992 and is marketed.

BINDER AVIATIK KG. • Germany

In conjunction with Schempp-Hirth KG (q.v.) began production in 1966 of the CP 301 S Smaragd. Built under licence, this aircraft was a de luxe version of the Piel Emeraude.

BIRD AIRCRAFT CORPORATION • USA

In 1928 the Brunner-Winkle Aircraft Corporation was founded to manufacture a three-seat open cockpit commercial biplane known as the Bird biplane. In March 1929 the Bird Aircraft Corporation was incorporated, with William E. Winkle as Vice-President, to continue production of the Bird biplane with a variety of engines ranging from 100-165 hp. It was made available subsequently in four- and five-seat forms.

BIRD WING COMMERCIAL AIRCRAFT COMPANY • USA

Founded at St Joseph, Missouri, in 1928 to build a three-seat commercial biplane. Powered by a 90 hp Curtiss engine, the Imperial had a maximum speed of 90mph (145 kmh).

THE BIRMINGHAM CARRIAGE COMPANY • UK

Built D.H.10s during the First World War under subcontract to The Aircraft Manufacturing Company Ltd. IAIRCO, q.v.). Received a contract also for the construction of 70 Handley Page O/400 heavy bombers.

Blackburn Kangaroo bomber, used for anti-submarine patrols in WW1

Blackburn Buccaneer low-level strike aircraft

B/J AIRCRAFT CORPORATION • USA

B/J Aircraft Corporation was the name given to the Berliner-Joyce Aircraft Corporation after it had been acquired by North American Aviation Inc. The company continued production of one type developed by Berliner-Joyce, namely the B/J P-16, a two-seat biplane fighter for the US Army Air Corps. The company ceased to operate in 1934.

BLACKBURN & GENERAL AIRCRAFT LTD. • UK

The Blackburn Aeroplane Company was founded by Robert Blackburn, who had designed and built his first aircraft in 1909. Throughout the company's history the emphasis was on the design and production of naval aircraft; its first for the Royal Navy was the twin-engined GP seaplane of 1916. A similar landplane, the Kangaroo, was supplied to the RAF in 1918. Aircraft to serve with the Navy include the Baffin, Blackburn, Buccaneer, Dart, Firebrand, Ripon, Roc, Shark and Skua. In 1930 acquired Cirrus Hermes Engineering Co. Blackburn Aircraft Company founded 1936. In 1949 merged with General Aircraft Ltd. (q.v.) of Feltham, Middlesex. Latter company founded 1934 and produced such aircraft as Monospar twin-engined light-plane, Cygnet and Owlet. Built pressurised version of Monospar, which was first pressurised aircraft built in UK. Built Hotspur and Hamilcar gliders during Second World War. New 1949 company known as Blackburn & General Aircraft Ltd. Company name reverted to Blackburn Aircraft Ltd. in 1959, when Blackburn & General became the holding company. Became part of the Hawker-Siddeley Group in 1960, losing its individual identity in 1963.

BLANCHARD, CONSTRUCTIONS AÉRONAUTIQUES • France

Founded in January 1923 by M. Blanchard, a designer who had worked for the Farman brothers and Georges Levy. Specialised in the construction of flying-boats. A single-seat racing monoplane was designed to take part in the 1924 Schneider Trophy Contest, which was cancelled because there were not sufficient aircraft ready to compete.

BLÉRIOT, SOCIÉTÉ AÉRONAUTIQUE • France

The French aviation pioneer Louis Blériot achieved a unique place in aviation history by making the first crossing of the English Channel in a powered aircraft (his Type XI monoplane) on 25 July 1909. This success resulted in the formation of the above company to produce the Type XI monoplane, and many significant flights were made with these aircraft. Aircraft of this type, and derivatives such as the Parasol, served with the French forces, the RFC and RNAS at the beginning of the First World War, as well as with other air arms. In post-war years took over the SPAD (q.v.) interests and built many examples of these aircraft.

Blériot 127/2 twin-engined military aircraft; armament of 3 or 4 machine-guns and up to 1,000 kg (2,205 lb) of bombs

Blériot Type XI monoplane, one of the most famous pioneer aircraft

Boeing B-17 Flying Fortress, used extensively in the European theatre of war

BLÉRIOT AND SPAD AIRCRAFT WORKS • UK

Established at Addlestone, Surrey, to provide support for Blériot and SPAD aircraft operated in the UK. Built Avro 504A trainers under subcontract to A. V. Roe Ltd. during the First World War.

BLOCH, MARCEL, SOCIÉTÉ DES AVIONS • France

In 1933 Marcel Bloch established a small factory at Courbevoie, Paris, to build light aircraft. In 1933-34 the company built its first fighter aircraft, the Bloch 130, the first flight of this prototype being made on 29 June 1934. Production Bloch 131s entered service in 1938. Subsequent production included the Bloch 151/152/155 monoplane fighter, Bloch 175 light bomber, and Bloch MB 200 and MB 210 bomber aircraft. Nationalisation of the French

aircraft industry in 1937 combined the Blériot and Bloch companies as Société Nationale de Constructions Aéronautiques de Sud-Ouest (q.v.), with Marcel Bloch as managing director.

BLOHM UND VOSS • Germany

See BV.

BODIANSKY • France

In 1930 Avions Bodiansky produced an advanced two-seat light monoplane, the Bodiansky 20 monoplane, which featured a welded steel-tube fuselage structure, as well as manually and automatically operated leading-edge slots and trailing-edge flaps.

BOEING • USA

Founded 15 July 1916 by William E. Boeing as Pacific Aero Products Corporation. Name changed to Boeing Airplane Company 26 April 1917. Bid successfully for the San-Francisco-Chicago air mail route in 1927 and formed subsidiary Boeing Air Transport to operate the route; as other airlines were acquired, this became Boeing Air Transport System. Merged with Pratt & Whitney, Standard Steel Propeller Co, and two small aircraft manufacturers to form United Aircraft & Transport Corporation in 1929. All continued to operate under original identities; United Air Lines formed as holding company of airlines. In 1934 legislation prevented aircraft and engine manufacturers from operating airlines: those of the former Boeing Air Transport System reorganised into a new United Air Lines. Boeing, together with Stearman (q.v.), a wholly-owned subsidiary, adopted the name Boeing Aircraft Company. The name Boeing Airplane Company was readopted in 1948. In May 1961, following acquisition of Vertol (q.v.) in 1960, became known as The Boeing Company, which remains the name in 1999.

Very important changes in company structure took place in 1996, when on 15 December it was announced that a merger had been agreed with McDonnell Douglas. The two large organisations began operating as a single company from 4 August 1997, under the Boeing name. Also in December 1996 Boeing purchased Rockwell International's aerospace and defence units, these being retitled Boeing North American Inc. and subsequently becoming part of Boeing's Space Systems business unit. Several internal restructures of the Boeing organisation followed, the set-up (at the time of writing) comprising three main groups namely Information, Space and Defense systems Group (ISDS), Boeing Commercial Airplane Group (BCAG), and Boeing Shared Services Group; the latter for information management and computing resources. Within ISDS are various business units comprising Aircraft and Missile Systems (to undertake Boeing's military aeroplane and helicopter programmes, plus oversee tactical missile

Bloch 131 four-seat reconnaissance bomber

Bloch MB 200 night bomber of the between-wars era

Boeing Model 314 Clipper, the type used by Pan American to inaugurate mail/passenger services across the North Atlantic

Boeing Model 247, the first modern airliner

development), Boeing Space Systems (to oversee Boeing's space programmes for DoD and NASA), Information and Communication Systems (programmes include AWACS surveillance systems, communications systems and more), Phantom Works (a previous McDonnell Douglas unit for advanced research and development, with current programmes including research into hypersonic aircraft), and Business Resources. BCAG is headquartered at Renton but has units in various other locations. This group comprises Customer Services, Douglas Products Division (for manufacturing airliners that originated from McDonnell Douglas, such as the MD-80, MD-90, MD-11 and B717), Engineering Division, Fabrication Division (constructing components), Materiel Division (made responsible for materials and sub-contracted components), Propulsion Systems Division (engine preparation for airliners), 737/757 Programs, 747/767 Programs, 777 Program, and Wichita Division (components and subassemblies).

First product B & W Seaplane of 1916, designed by William Boeing in conjunction with Conrad Westervelt. First production order was for Model C seaplane trainer for US Navy (first flown 1916), followed by Model EA land trainer of 1916 for US Army. Improved Model C of 1918 was first mass-produced Boeing aircraft, built alongside Boeing-constructed Curtiss HS-2L flying-boats. First post-First World War design was the B-1 three-seat flying-boat (first flown December 1919), while in 1920 the first flight took place of the first of many Boeing-built DH-4s (based on British Airco D.H.4). Built ten US Army-designed GA-1 armoured ground attack triplanes (first flown May 1921) but just two GA-2s, followed by 200 Thomas-Morse MB-3A pursuit aircraft (first flown 1922).

First real success with own-design military aircraft came in 1923, with the PW-9/FB-1 series, which had a fabric-covered welded-steel-tube fuselage. Other aircraft followed in quick succession, types of particular note including the Boeing Model 40, designed for carriage of airmail plus two (and later four) passengers, used by new Boeing Air Transport. Model 80 12-passenger transports with three Pratt & Whitney Wasp engines introduced by Boeing Air Transport in 1928. World's first airline stewardesses introduced on these aircraft 1930. Model 80A with more powerful Hornet engines and seats for 18 passengers followed. Biggest military order to that date (other than MB-3As) came in 1931, when US Army ordered 135 P-12E single-seat fighters, and US Navy 113 of the similar F4B-3: total of 586 aircraft in this series built by 1933 (prototype Model 83 for P-12 series had flown June 1928). Boeing Model 200 Monomail, mail/cargo aircraft, first flew May 1930; revolutionary aircraft with cantilever all-metal monoplane wing, retractable main landing gear and a specially designed antidrag cowling for its single Hornet engine. A second Monomail, Model 221, had six-seat passenger cabin. Military development of this aircraft resulted in YB-9 bomber (first flown April 1931), forcing evolution

Right: Boeing B-29 Superfortress, the most powerful bomber of WW2

Above: Boeing XB-47, prototype for the six-engine Stratojet medium jet bomber

Boeing B-52G heavy bomber of the USAF

Left: Historic prototypes of the Models 707, 737 and 747

of new fighter types. Boeing produced P-26 single-seat all-metal monoplane fighter (first flown March 1932), of which 136 bought by US Army. Biggest step forward came with the Model 247 (first flown February 1933), most advanced conception of a transport aircraft anywhere in the world at that time. Introduced wing and tail unit leading-edge de-icing, control surface trim tabs and, in production aircraft, controllable-pitch propellers and autopilot. It was the first twin-engined monoplane transport that could climb with a full load on the power of one engine.

Significant military aircraft since the early 1930s have included the B-17 Flying Fortress bomber (first flown July 1935), of which 12,731 examples were built; B-29 Superfortress bomber (first flown September 1942); B-47 Stratojet medium jet bomber (first flown December 1947); B-52 Stratofortress intercontinental strategic bomber (first flown April 1952); E-4 National Airborne Operations Center aircraft (first flown June 1973); E-3 Sentry airborne early warning and control system aircraft (delivered from March 1977); E-6 Mercury survivable airborne communications system aircraft for the US Navy (first flown February 1987); and EC-18 advanced range instrumentation and cruise missile control aircraft. The B-52H Stratofortress continues to form a major component of the USAF, and propos-

als were made in 1998 to re-engine 71 examples of this eight-engined bomber with four very powerful Rolls-Royce RB211-535F-4 turbofans each. Continuing military programmes in 1999 include work in developing the AL-1A Airborne Laser aircraft based on the Model 747 Freighter; development of Boeing's contender for the Joint Strike Fighter programme to produce a multipurpose combat aircraft with CTOL/STOVL flight characteristics to replace a range of present warplanes from about the year 2000; new AWACS aircraft for export based on 737 and 767 airframes (first flight of an E-767 AWACS with structural

Below: Pan American Boeing 727 medium-range tri-jet

Above: Boeing Next-Generation 737-700 poses by the very first 737 of 1967, the latter operated by NASA since 1973 and used for weather research

Above: Boeing 777-200 Increased Gross Weight version on its first flight in 1996, before joining British Airways in 1997

AWACS features for Japan August 1996); and production of the F-15 Eagle, F/A-18 Hornet and Super Hornet, Harrier II and II Plus, and T-45 Goshawk (all ex-McDonnell Douglas, -q.v.).

Aircraft which have made important contributions to global air transport, in addition to those previously mentioned, include the Model 314 flying-boat (first flown June 1938); Model 307 Stratoliner with pressurisation (first flown December 1938); Model 377 Stratocruiser (first flown November 1944 as XC-97 military transport); Model 367-80 turbojet transport (first flown July 1954) which was put into production as a military tanker-transport for the USAF as the KC-135 Stratotanker and as the Model 707 commercial airliner; Model 727 tri-jet short/medium-range airliner (first flown February 1963); Model 737 twin-turbofan short-range airliner (first flown April 1967 and still in production in 1999 in advanced and Next Generation versions, with development continuing and over 4,000 sold); Model 747 four-jet widebody high-capacity airliner

Right: Boeing 747-400 in All Nippon Airlines livery

Boeing F/A-18F Super Hornet, developed from the McDonnell Douglas Hornet but now constructed by Boeing

(first flown February 1969 and given the press nickname 'Jumbo Jet'; still in production in 1999 in latest 747-400 series versions, with new versions under development); Model 757 twin-jet medium-range airliner (first flown February 1982); Model 767 twin-jet wide-body medium/long-range airliner (first flown September 1981); and Model 777 twin-jet widebody long-range airliner.

Since the merger with McDonnell Douglas (q.v.), the Boeing aircraft range now also includes the Model 717 (first flown 1998; formerly the McDonnell Douglas MD-95), C-17A Globemaster III military heavy-lift and long-range transport (first flown September 1991; commercial version proposed as the MD-17); MD-11 medium/long-range tri-jet airliner (see McDonnell Douglas entry; first flown January 1990 but production expected to end in the year 2000); MD-80 twin-jet short/medium-range airliner (first flown October 1979 as follow-on to similar but older DC-9; production to end shortly); MD-90 twin-jet medium-range airliner (first flown February 1993 as longer and advanced development of MD-80; production coming to an end); F-15 Eagle (see McDonnell Douglas entry); F/A-18 Hornet and Super Hornet (see McDonnell Douglas entry); Harrier II and II Plus (see McDonnell Douglas entry); T-45 Goshawk (see McDonnell Douglas entry); and various helicopters (see next paragraph). Since taking over Rockwell International's aerospace and defence units, the B-1B Lancer long-range variable-geometry strategic bomber is technically also a Boeing type, although production of 100 ended in 1988.

Since the merger of Boeing and McDonnell Douglas, Boeing's helicopter range has grown. However, Boeing took the strategic decision to concentrate on military helicopter programmes and sold its 49 per cent share in the Model 609 civil tilt-rotor transport to its development partner, Bell Helicopter Textron (now called BA 609; see Bell Helicopter Textron), while in 1998 it also seemed likely that Bell would purchase the Boeing range of small civil helicopters that came with the merger of McDonnell Douglas (this sale was blocked by US Federal review); the MD 500/520/530/Defender and MD 600N helicopter ranges thereafter (plus MD 900/902 Explorer/Combat Explorer not selected by Bell) remained for sale elsewhere, some using the unique NOTAR anti-torque system (see Hughes Helicopters and McDonnell Douglas). However, Boeing continued its partnership with Bell over development and production of the V-22 Osprey military tilt-rotor transport and multipurpose aircraft for the US forces (first flown March 1989). Not for sale was the inherited AH-64 Apache attack helicopter, currently being produced (also in the UK) in AH-64D Apache Longbow form. Boeing's own H-47 Chinook continues in production (see below), and Boeing remains partnered with Sikorsky in the development of the RAH-66 Comanche multirole battlefield helicopter for the US Army (first flown January 1996).

Boeing 767 AWACS aircraft destined for Japan

Boeing F-15I Ra'am, delivered to Israel in 1998 as F-15E Eagle type

Boeing C-17A Globemaster III military heavy-lift and long-range transport, developed by McDonnell Douglas

BOEING AUSTRALIA LTD. • Australia

Formerly Rockwell Australia (see Rockwell), with diverse activities including manufacture of components for Airbus, Boeing and Aérospatiale.

BOEING VERTOL COMPANY • USA

On 31 March 1960 Vertol (q.v.) became a Division of The Boeing Company with the title Boeing Vertol Company. Continued production of the Vertol-designed Model 107 23/25-seat twin-rotor transport aircraft, built subsequently in civil and military versions. A development of the Model 107, designated KV-107, was built under licence by Kawasaki Kokuki Kogyo Kabushiki Kaisha (q.v.) in Japan. Developed larger transport helicopter as the H-47 Chinook (first flown September 1961) which, in addition to supply to the US Army, serves with many other forces worldwide and continues in production; also built by Agusta in Italy and Kawasaki in Japan. Company later absorbed fully into The Boeing Company (q.v.), initially as the helicopter division of Boeing Defense and Space Group and currently as part of Aircraft and Missile Systems business unit of ISDS.

Right: Boeing Vertol 107 tandem-rotor turbine-engined helicopter

Below: Boeing Vertol UH-46D Sea Knight (Model 107 variant), used mainly by the US Navy for vertical replenishment operations

BOISAVIA • France

Designed and built in the late 1940s a four-seat cabin monoplane known as the Boisavia B-60 Mercurey, the prototype of which first flew on 3 April 1949. Variants included agricultural and glider-tug versions.

BÖLKOW GMBH • Germany

This company was founded on 1 May 1956, becoming established at Ottobrunn bei München in 1958. Until 1 January 1965 was known as Bölkow Entwicklungen KG, adopting above title following acquisition of a one-third

Bölkow BO 208 C Junior two-seat lightweight aerobatic aircraft

interest in the business by Boeing. Bölkow held a 25 per cent interest in Entwicklungsring Süd (EWR, q.v.). Aircraft produced include the BO 207 four-seat light aircraft, BO 208 C Junior (a licence-built version of the Malmö MFI-9) and the BO 105 five-seat light helicopter, which featured a rigid main rotor of glassfibre reinforced plastics. This helicopter continued in production under the designation MBB BO 105, signifying that it was then built by Messerschmitt-Bölkow-Blohm (q.v.), and most recently it has become a Eurocopter (q.v.) product.

BOMBARDIER INC. • Canada

A division of this organisation is the Bombardier Aerospace Group, which combines the activities of Bombardier Inc. Canadair and de Havilland Inc. both based in Canada, plus Learjet Inc. in the USA and Short Brothers PLC in the UK.

BOMBARDIER INC. CANADAIR • Canada

New name for previous Canadair (q.v.), following integration into Bombardier Aerospace Group. Current programmes include 50-passenger and twin-turbofan Regional Jet regional airliner (first flown May 1991) and its Corporate Jetliner business jet and CRJ Series 700 70-passenger airliner derivatives; CL-415 twin-turboprop amphibian (first flown December 1993); Challenger 604 widebody business jet (first flown September 1994); and BD-700 Global Express long-range and high-performance business jet (first flown October 1996).

Bölkow BO 46 helicopter built to test the Derschmidt high-speed rotor system

Bombardier Inc. Canadair Regional Jet in Delta Connection colours

Above: Borel floatplane, one of the first seaplanes used by the Royal Navy

Left: Bombardier Inc. Canadair Challenger 604 wide-body business jet

BONDY, MILOS, & COMPANY • Czechoslovakia

See Avia Akciova Spolecnost pro Prumysl Letecky.

BONOMI • Italy

In 1929 Aeronàutica Vittorio Bonomi built a two-seat cabin monoplane to the design of Ing Abate. This was developed subsequently by Captain Bonomi and produced as the Bonomi 25 Monoplane.

BORDELAISE • France

Derived from the aircraft department of Dyle et Bacalan, Société Aérienne Bordelaise was controlled by the Nieuport-Delage company. Production included the Bordelaise D.B.70, a twin-fuselage tri-motor design with accommodation for 20 passengers. A military version, designated A.B.20, had four engines.

BOREL • France

Formed in 1909 by Gabriel Borel, Établissements Borel was an early constructor of floatplanes. One of the first aircraft to serve with the British Navy was a Borel monoplane, purchased in 1912, and at least eight were in service with the Naval Wing before the beginning of the First World War. A high performance two-seat fighter was built to the design of M. Boccacion, but too late for wartime service. Known subsequently as Société Générale des Constructions Industrielles et Mécaniques (q.v.).

BOULTON PAUL AIRCRAFT LTD. • UK

Established as a building constructor in Norwich, Norfolk, turned to subcontract construction of aircraft in First World War, including RAF F.E.2d, Sopwith 1/2-Strutter and Sopwith Camel. Known originally as Aircraft Department of Boulton & Paul Ltd. As the war neared its end, the company decided to continue in aircraft industry. First original design P.3 single-seat biplane fighter which did not, however, enter production. Designed and built P.6 research aircraft, which provided much data for later P.9. P.7 Bourges twin-engined fighter-bomber built at the end of 1918, followed later by somewhat similar Bugle. Neither entered RAF service. Continued to build small numbers of civil aircraft during inter-war years. Sidestrand 3/4-seat medium bomber entered RAF service with one squadron

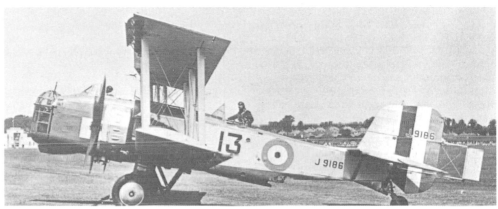

Above: Boulton Paul Overstrand medium-bomber with power-operated gun turret

Boulton Paul P.111 delta wing research aircraft

in April 1928. Replaced by improved Overstrands, with power-operated gun turret, in 1934. When production ended, in 1936, company re-established at Wolverhampton, Staffs. Name of Boulton Paul Aircraft Ltd. adopted 1934. Designed and built P.82 Defiant for RAF, prototype first flew 11 August 1937; two-seat fighter with power-operated gun turret was entirely new concept and enjoyed initial operational success. Production ended 1943 after more than 1,000 built. Designed P.108 Balliol three-seat advanced trainer for RAF, 162 built subsequently as two-seat Balliol T.2, of which 30 built under subcontract by Blackburn Aircraft Ltd. Built P.111 and P.120 for research into behaviour of delta wing at transonic speeds.

BOUNSALL AIRCRAFT • USA

Developed kits and plans to construct Super Prospector single-seat STOL bush plane.

BOWDLER AVIATION INC. • USA

Markets plans and kits to build the Supercat single-seat monoplane, formerly developed by First Strike and first flown 1984.

BOWERS, PETER • USA

First flew in 1960 the Fly Baby 1-A single-seat open-cockpit monoplane, made available to amateur constructors via plans. Biplane version of same aircraft is Fly Baby 1-B.

BRADLEY AEROSPACE • USA

Markets kits to build the Aerobat single-seat aerobatic monoplane.

BRANDENBURGISCHE FLUGZEUGWERKE • Germany

See Hansa und Brandenburgische Flugzeug-Werke GmbH.

BRANTLY HELICOPTER CORPORATION • USA

Founded by N. P. Brantly, who designed the Brantly B-1, with co-axial rotors, in 1943. From this design he developed the improved Model B-2, using the rotor evolved for the B-1, a two-seat helicopter which first flew on 14 August 1956. Subsequently entered production as Model B-2A, superseded by B-2B in 1963. Larger Model 305, a five-

Brantly Model 305 five-seat light helicopter

seat aircraft, first flew in January 1964. Company acquired by Lear Jet Industries Inc (q.v.) in May 1966.

BRANTLY HELICOPTER INDUSTRIES USA CO LTD. • USA

Founded 1989 to continue production of Brantly B-2B and Model 305 helicopters.

BRANTLY-HYNES HELICOPTER INC. • USA

The Brantly helicopter interests, which had been acquired by Lear Jet Industries in 1966, passed to Aeronautical Research and Development Corporation (q.v.) in 1969, and to Brantly Operations Inc in late 1970. On 1 January 1975 Michael K. Hynes founded Brantly-Hynes Helicopter Inc, having gained ownership of the Brantly interests, later becoming just Hynes Helicopter as division of Hynes Aviation Industries Inc. Production of Model B-2B two-seater and Model 305 five-seater continued. Rights to helicopters acquired by businessman James Kimura from Hynes Aviation Industries 1989, forming Brantly Helicopter Industries (q.v.).

BRATUKHIN • USSR

Involved in helicopter development since the late 1930s, I. P. Bratukhin first designed a twin-rotor helicopter, with an engine and related rotor mounted at each end of an outrigger. Designated 2MG Omega, this was completed in 1941. Vibration problems resulted in construction of Omega II in 1943. A series of similar twin-rotor helicopters were built up to 1948.

BREDA • Italy

A large industrial concern based in Milan, Società Italiano Ernesto Breda began the construction of aircraft in 1917. In the immediate post-First World War years, when no production aircraft were being built, concentrated on research and constructed a number of experimental aircraft. Began the construction of all-metal aircraft in 1922. Production

Brantly B-1 co-axial rotor helicopter

Brantly B-2 two-seat light helicopter

Breda Ba 88 Lince (Lynx) twin-engined medium attack bomber

BredaNardi NH-500, a licence-built version of the Hughes 500

BREDANARDI COSTRUZIONI AERONAUTICHE SPA. • Italy

Established on 15 February 1971 by Nardi SA per Costruzioni Aeronàutiche (q.v.), and Breda, a member company of the EFIM state-owned financial group, each with a 50 per cent holding. Initiated manufacture of helicopters under a licence granted by Hughes Helicopters, and is building the Hughes 300C, 500C, 500D, and 500M under the respective designations of Breda Nardi NH-300C, NH-500C, NH-500D and NH-500M-D (TOW). The last is a multirole military helicopter armed with TOW missiles.

BREGUET AVIATION • France

Louis Breguet, founder of Société Anonyme des Ateliers d'Aviation Louis Breguet in 1911, was a French pioneer of rotary-wing flight. The aircraft built by the Breguet brothers lifted a man off the ground on 29 September 1907, but did not constitute a free flight. BU3 biplane bomber prototype of 1915 built under subcontract by Edouard and André Michelin as Breguet-Michelin BUM. Improved SN3 entered production with Michelin 1916 as BUC. Breguet 14 tractor biplane of 1917 was a significant French wartime bomber. Its successor, the Breguet 19 of 1921, remained in service until 1936. One specially-prepared Breguet 19 (*Question Mark*), flown by Costes and Bellonte, made first east-west aircraft crossing of North Atlantic September 1930. Built Short Calcutta flying-boat under licence during 1930s as Breguet Bizerte. Breguet elected not to be included in nationalised industry 1936; his factories were, however, incorporated. Regained some independence in 1939 through purchase of former Latécoère

aircraft have included Breda 15 two-seat lightweight sporting aircraft of 1930, Breda 25 and 28 training biplanes, and the Breda 33 two-seat sports monoplane of 1932, from which time production concentrated mainly on military aircraft. These included Breda Ba 27 single-seat monoplane fighters, which equipped a squadron of the Chinese Air Force in 1937; Ba 65 one/two-seat fighter-bomber/reconnaissance monoplane, which saw service in the Spanish Civil War; Ba 88 Lince twin-engined medium attack bomber, produced also by Meridionali (q.v.) under subcontract. Breda also built a number of Junkers Ju 87Bs under licence as the Breda 201 Picchiatelli before suspension of production soon after the Italian surrender.

Breguet 940 Integral deflected slipstream prototype transport, which led to construction of four 941s

Two-seat Breguet 19 A2, successor to the Breguet 14 night bomber

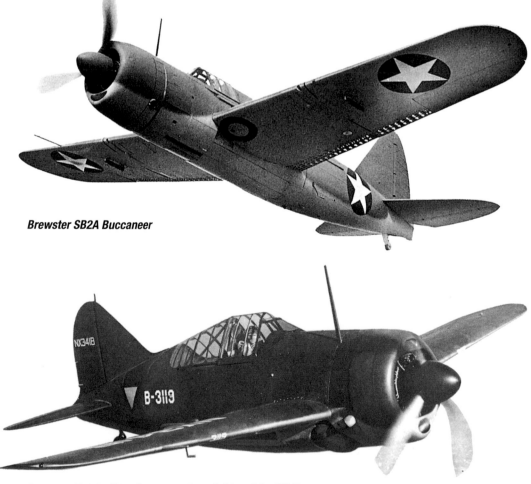

Breguet 765 Sahara 176-troop military transport developed from the Br 763 Deuxponts

Brewster SB2A Buccaneer

Brewster F2A Buffalo, first monoplane fighter of the US Navy

factories. Avions Marcel Dassault became major stockholder 28 June 1967. Anglo-French company Société Européenne de Production de l'Avion École de Combat et d'Appui Tactique (SEPECAT, q.v.) formed between British Aircraft Corporation and Breguet Aviation 1966 to design and develop tactical support/advanced trainer. Built four 941 unpressurised cargo/passenger transports, which used deflected slipstream technique to give STOL capability, for French Air Force trials. Breguet Type 1150 Atlantic maritime patrol aircraft selected by NATO, with prototypes ordered 1959; production aircraft built internationally by Belgium, France, Germany, Netherlands and USA. For later production see Avions Marcel Dassault-Breguet Aviation, reflecting merger of Dassault and Breguet.

BREWSTER AERONAUTICAL CORPORATION • USA

Founded in the mid-1930s, the first product of this company was a two-seat scout/bomber for the US Navy designated SBA. When this aircraft entered production in 1937-1938 the company had inadequate productive capacity and 30 were built by the Naval Aircraft Factory as SBNs. The F2A Buffalo which followed was the first monoplane fighter to serve with the USN, and was also used by the armed forces of Belgium, Britain, Finland and Netherlands East Indies. The later SB2A Buccaneer, though built in quantity, proved totally unsuitable for frontline service.

BRISTOL AEROPLANE COMPANY LTD. • UK

Founded at Bristol, Somerset, in February 1910 as British & Colonial Aeroplane Company Ltd. First began construction of a number of biplanes under licence from Société Zodiac (q.v.), but these were not completed because the sample aircraft received from France could not be induced to take to the air. First aircraft produced were Bristol biplanes, usually known as the Boxkite, which initially were little more than copies of the Henry Farman biplane. Flying schools established at Larkhill, on Salisbury Plain, and at Brooklands, Surrey, 1911. February 1911 Deutsche Bristol-Werke established at Halberstadt, Germany, to operate a flying school and build Bristol aeroplanes; arrangement cancelled 23 June 1914. First military aircraft were monoplanes designed by Henri Coanda; No 105 shared third place with a Deperdussin in the Military Aeroplane Competition of 1912. Bristol Scout, or 'Baby Biplane', evolved by Frank Barnwell 1914. The two-seat Bristol Fighter entered service in 1917 and became regarded as the best general-purpose combat aircraft of the First World War. Between the wars Bristol Bulldog biplanes had equipped nine RAF Squadrons by 1932 and were most widely used fighter until 1936. Bristol Type 138A of 1936 captured world altitude record in September, 1936, then regained it from Italy in June 1937 with an altitude of 53,937 ft (16,440 m). Bristol Type 142, built as executive aircraft for Lord Rothermere, became the military Blenheim,

Bristol Boxkite, more accurately the Bristol biplane of 1910

an important light bomber in the early Second World War period. Beaufighter, first flown July 1939, became RAF's first nightfighter, subsequently an important antishipping aircraft armed with rockets, torpedoes and bombs.

Designed and built prototype of eight-engined 100-passenger Brabazon I, first flew 4 September 1949; scrapped 1953 for financial/political/technical reasons. Type 170 Freighter first flown 2 December 1945 and 213 built subsequently. Turboprop powered Britannia first flew 16 August 1952, made the first non-stop airliner flight London, Vancouver (5,100 miles; 8,208 km) 29 June 1957, and first North Atlantic passenger service to be flown by a turbine-powered airliner on 19 December of the same year. Rotary-wing development resulted from formation of a helicopter department in 1944; initial flight of Bristol Type 171 prototype made 27 July 1947. Subsequently produced as Sycamore, entering service with RAF as its first British-designed helicopter in 1952.

Bristol Fighter (F.2B), nicknamed 'Brisfit', one of the best general-purpose combat aircraft of WW1

Bristol's graceful turboprop Britannia

Bristol Type 170 Freighter cargo aircraft

Bristol Beaufort reconnaissance-torpedo-bomber

Research and development of the tandem-rotor helicopters resulted in Type 192 Belvedere, but by the time this entered service with the RAF, in 1961, Bristol's helicopter department had become the Bristol Helicopter Division of Westland Aircraft Ltd. Company's aircraft activities reorganised as Bristol Aircraft Ltd. in January 1956, wholly owned by Bristol Aeroplane Company Ltd. This company was absorbed into the British Aircraft Corporation (BAC, q.v.) in June 1960. Following the acquisition of the Cosmos Engineering Company in 1920, the Bristol Company was also a major builder of aero engines.

BRISTOL AEROSPACE LTD. • Canada

Has its origins in McDonald Brothers Aircraft (q.v.). Undertakes aircraft modernisation (has included F-5) and other activities within its Aircraft division. Aerocomponents division undertakes important aero engine and aero structure design and construction programmes. Also has a Rockets and Space division.

BRITISH AERIAL TRANSPORT COMPANY • UK

See BAT.

BRITISH AEROSPACE PLC • UK

Nationalised enterprise, founded in April 1977, uniting British Aircraft Corporation, Hawker Siddeley Aviation, Hawker Siddeley Dynamics and Scottish Aviation. Companies retained their identities initially, but subsequently became divisions of British Aerospace. Many aircraft of former constituent companies continued as BAe products, initially under old company names, although former British Aerospace Corporate Jets division sold to Raytheon of the USA in August 1993 (becoming Raytheon Corporate Jets), thereby losing the Hawker bizjets.

BAe recently reorganized into new business units, namely Defence, Commercial Aerospace and British Aerospace Regional Aircraft Ltd. (BARAL), which is the structure in 1999, with additional organisations for international marketing and sales, spares and logistics, Jetstream Aircraft Ltd. (offers engineering management for Jetstream customers), securities, consultancy services, flight training, Farnborough Business Aviation, Sowerby Research Centre, and British Aerospace Holdings Inc. Defence business unit comprises British Aerospace Australia Holdings (as important Australian defence and aerospace company), British Aerospace Defence Systems (Siemens Plessey Defence Systems acquired as core of company), Matra BAe Dynamics (as a European joint venture developing and producing missiles), Military Aircraft and Aerostructures (to develop and manufacture military aircraft and

British Aerospace ATP production ended in 1998

Jetstream 41 production ended in 1998

Avro International Aerospace (British Aerospace Regional Aircraft) RJ85

construct components/subassemblies for civil aircraft), British Aerospace North Sea Range (operating a target range for air combat training), Royal Ordnance (to produce munitions and weapons), BAeSEMA (for naval work), British Aerospace (Systems & Equipment) for instrumentation/avionics systems, and Systems & Services. Commercial Aerospace division encompasses British Aerospace Airbus (working on Airbus airliner programmes), and British Aerospace Asset Management. British Aerospace Regional Aircraft Ltd. (BARAL) encompasses Avro International Aerospace (producing RJ airliners), plus Jetstream Aircraft, and Spares & Logistics Centre.

Current military aircraft activities, some as continuations of programmes begun by pre-BAe companies, include the Hawk basic/advanced jet trainer and light attack aircraft, with air defence capabilities (first flown August 1974 and sales continuing in Hawk 50/60/100 two-seat and Hawk 200 series single-seat versions); development/upgrading/production of STOVL Sea Harrier F/A Mk 2 for Royal Navy; joint development and production with Boeing in the USA (formerly McDonnell Douglas) of land-based STOVL Harrier II (first flown November 1981) and Harrier II Plus (first flown September 1992) plus T-45 Goshawk carrier-capable jet trainer for US Navy (Hawk variant); share of the Eurofighter programme (see EuroFighter Jagdflugzeug GmbH.); share of the Tornado programme (see Panavia Aircraft GmbH.); share of the Jaguar programme (see SEPECAT); development and rework of existing Nimrod maritime patrol aircraft into Nimrod 2000 form for RAF service as MRA Mk 4s from

British Aerospace Hawk Mk 209 in Indonesian service

the year 2003 (first flight 1999; programme involves more than 200 British companies and some foreign suppliers); and work on the Future Offensive Aircraft (first flight of a technology demonstrator possible in 2005) as a stealth Tornado replacement.

Current civil aircraft activities include continued marketing and production of the Avro RJ family of 70- to 128-seat short-range regional airliners and freighters (developed from the previous BAe 146; RJ85 first flew March 1992), and possible future development of the RJ-X twin-turbofan follow-on to the RJs. Manufacture of the

Jetstream 31 (first flown March 1982 in production form) and Super 31 (April 1988), Jetstream 41 (September 1991), ATP (August 1986, as development of former HS/BAe 748) and its derivative Jetstream 61 (1994, but none sold), ended in 1998.

A merger with GEC-Marconi Avionics Ltd. was being finalised in 1999.

Right: British Aerospace Sea Harrier F/A Mk 2

British Aerospace and McDonnell Douglas developed Harrier II, seen here as RAF Harrier GR Mk 7

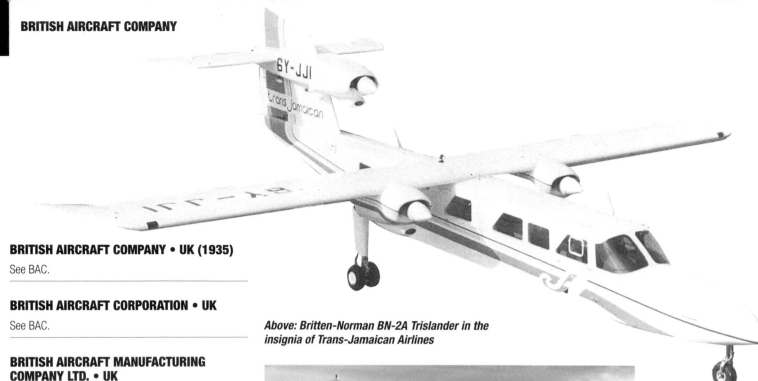

BRITISH AIRCRAFT COMPANY • UK (1935)

See BAC.

BRITISH AIRCRAFT CORPORATION • UK

See BAC.

BRITISH AIRCRAFT MANUFACTURING COMPANY LTD. • UK

See BA.

BRITISH & COLONIAL AEROPLANE COMPANY LTD. • UK

See Bristol Aeroplane Company Ltd.

BRITISH CAUDRON COMPANY LTD. • UK

Established at Cricklewood, London, just before the First World War to provide product support to French Caudron aircraft being operated in Britain. Built nine Caudron G.3s under licence. During the war built D.H.5s under subcontract to Aircraft Manufacturing Co Ltd. B.E.2s under subcontract to the Royal Aircraft Factory and F.1 Camels under subcontract to Sopwith Aviation Company Ltd.

BRITISH KLEMM AEROPLANE COMPANY LTD. • UK

See British Aircraft Manufacturing Company Ltd.

BRITTEN-NORMAN LTD. • UK

Britten-Norman Ltd. was founded in 1955 to specialise in equipment for agricultural aircraft. Flew prototype of BN-2 Islander, a twin-engined feeder-line transport, on 13 June 1965. BN-2A Trislander, with a third engine mounted on vertical tail, first flown 11 September 1970. Military version of BN-2, named Defender, first demonstrated 1971, able to carry 1,150 lb (522kg) of mixed weapons on underwing pylons. Name changed to Britten Norman (Bembridge) Ltd. in November 1971, when company ran into financial difficulties. Assets acquired in August 1972 by Fairey (q.v.). In late 1977 the company was again in financial difficulties, an official receiver being appointed. In 1979 Pilatus of Switzerland took over the company, and it became known as Pilatus Britten-Norman Ltd. However, in July 1998 it was sold to Litchfield Continental Ltd., thereafter reverting to its original name of Britten-Norman Ltd. Manufacture of the Islander, Defender and latest BN2T-4S Defender 4000 continues.

In January 1999 Britten-Norman received approval from the Board of Directors of Romania's State Ownership Fund for its tender offer to acquire Romaero (q.v.).

Above: Britten-Norman BN-2A Trislander in the insignia of Trans-Jamaican Airlines

Left: Britten-Norman BN2T Islander operated by Aviazur in New Caledonia

BRITTEN-NORMAN (BEMBRIDGE) LTD. • UK

See Britten-Norman Ltd. above.

BROCHET • France

In the early 1950s Avions Maurice Brochet designed and built lightweight sporting aircraft. In addition to production versions, some were intended also for amateur construction. These included the M.B.70, M.B.71, M.B.80, M.B.100 and M.B.101.

Below: Brochet M.B.80 lightweight sporting aircraft

BROMON AIRCRAFT CORPORATION • USA

Began developing in 1987 the BR2000 twin-turboprop STOL transport, said to have been influenced by Ahrens 404 and thereby intended to be simple and easy to maintain. Project terminated 1989.

BROOKLANDS AIRCRAFT COMPANY LTD. • UK

New name for Optica Industries (q.v.) from April 1987 and aircraft renamed Optica Scout (also see Edgley). Company ceased trading 1990 (see Lovaux Ltd.).

BRÜGGER, MAX • Switzerland

Plans offered to build Colibri 2 single-seat monoplane.

Above: Bücker Bü 133 Jungmeister single-seat aerobatic trainer

BRUNNER-WINKLE AIRCRAFT CORPORATION • USA

See Bird Aircraft Corporation.

BRUSH ELECTRICAL ENGINEERING COMPANY LTD. • UK

Built Avro 504c, 504J/K and 504K trainers under sub-contract to A. V. Roe & Company Ltd. during the First World War; also seaplanes of the Admiralty Type 830 and Admiralty Type 184 for Short Bros.

BRUTSCHE AIRCRAFT CORPORATION • USA

Offers plans and partial kits to construct Freedom 40 single-seat cabin monoplane, and kits to construct Freedom Sport Utility four-seat STOL utility monoplane.

BTA TOP-AIR SRO • Czech Republic

Company formerly known as Swing spol sro, marketing the two-seat Tango (formerly Swing) light composites-built monoplane.

BUCHANAN AIRCRAFT CORPORATION LTD. • USA

Incorporated 1989 and developed BAC-204 two-seat composites lightplane (first flown 1992).

BÜCKER FLUGZEUGBAU GMBH • Germany

Founded at Johannishal in 1932, its first aircraft was the Bü 131 Jungmann trainer, designed by Swede Anders Andersson. The prototype first flew on 27 April 1934. It was followed by the Bü 133 Jungmeister in 1935 and by the extensively built Bü 181 Bestmann in 1936. Production of the latter continued after Second World War by Zlin in Czechoslovakia and, under Czech licence, by Egypt's Heliopolis Aircraft Works in the 1950s.

BÜCKER PRADO SL • Spain

Offers kits to build the former German Jungmann two-seat aerobatic biplane using original Bücker/CASA Bü 131 jigs, plus Jungmeister single-seat aerobatic biplane.

BUCKEYE POWERED PARACHUTE INC. • USA

Markets kits for single- and two-seat aircraft comprising ram-air parachute and powered trike, in Eagle and Dream Machine series.

BUETHE ENTERPRISES INC. • USA

Markets plans and kits to construct the Barracuda two-seat 200+mph (322kmh) low-wing monoplane (first flown 1975).

BUHL AIRCRAFT COMPANY • USA

Known originally as the Buhl-Verville Aircraft Company, based at Detroit, this company was founded in March 1925, with its head office and works at Marysville, Michigan. Builder of three- and five-seat transport biplanes known as the Airster and Airsedan series.

BUNYARD AIRCRAFT COMPANY • USA

In 1931 K. Bunyard designed and built a small biplane flying-boat, following this with a design for an unusual amphibian which failed to materialise in prototype form. At the end of the Second World War he began production of a three-seat lightweight amphibian flying-boat known as the Bunyard BAX-3 Sportsman. A four-seat version was designated BAX-4.

BUREAU OSOVIKH KONSTRUKTSII • USSR

BOK founded 1930 as an operating unit of Central Aero and Hydrodynamic Institute in Moscow. Developed research aircraft including BOK-1 with pressure cabin, BOK-2 of high-lift design, BOK-5 flying wing and BOK-11 high-altitude reconnaissance aircraft. Moscow offices taken over by Sukhoi in 1939.

BURGESS COMPANY & CURTISS • USA

Established at Marblehead, Massachusetts, originally built Wright types under licence. By arrangement built three single-float seaplane variants of the British Dunne tailless biplane, two of which were sold to the US Navy which carried out its first experiments in aerial gunnery using these aircraft. Produced also in the period 1916-1918 a number of training and experimental seaplanes of original design.

BURGFALKE FLUGZEUGBAU • Germany

Building originally examples of the Schelbe and Vogt sailplanes, Burgfalke developed a two-seat lightweight semi-aerobatic training aircraft designated M-150 Schulmeister. It was based on the WN-16, which had been designed by the Wiener-Neustadt company.

BURKHART GROB LUFT- UND RAUMFAHRT GMBH & CO KG. • Germany

Aviation work began in 1971 and has since built many thousands of motorgliders, lightplanes and other aircraft. Recent aircraft include the G 103 Twin III and G 109 series of gliders/motorgliders (production now ended), piston-engined G 115 two-seat lightplane (some versions suited to training and aerobatics; first flown November 1985), GF 200 pusher piston-engined and pressurised 4/5-seat lightplane (first flown November 1991, with 6-8 seat versions with piston and turboshaft engines anticipated as GF 250, GF 300 and GF 350), turboprop-powered G-520 Egrett and Strato 1 high-altitude and long-duration research platforms capable of carrying different electronic payloads in 12 separate compartments (first flown June 1987 in G-500 Egrett form), and the most recent G-850 Strato 2C high-altitude and long-duration atmospheric/stratospheric/climatic research aircraft with a unique

Buhl LA-1 Bull-Pup ultralight monoplane

Bücker Bü 181 Bestmann cabin monoplane

compound propulsion system using two turbocharged piston engines and two gas generators (first flown March 1995).

BURNELLI AIRCRAFT CORPORATION • USA

Founded 1920, Remington-Burnelli Airliner produced in that year. Vincent Burnelli concentrated on the development of fuselage structures which would contribute some degree of lift, augmenting that of the wing. The Burnelli VB-14B transport of 1936 could accommodate a crew of two and 14 passengers in a fuselage which was virtually an integral part of the wing.

BURNS AIRCRAFT COMPANY • USA

Began development in 1964 of high-performance 6/8-seat business aircraft powered by two Continental flat-six engines. The prototype Burns BA-42 flew for the first time on 28 April 1966.

BUSCAYLET ET CIE • France

Built aircraft under subcontract during the First World War. In 1923 secured services of Louis de Monge as a designer, producing in 1924 a single-seat monoplane fighter with 300 hp Hispano-Suiza engine. It was notable for being of all-metal construction, except for fabric covering of wing and tail surfaces.

Right: Grob G 115C (nearest) and fully aerobatic G 115D

Below: Bushmaster 2000, a modernized version of the Ford Tri-Motor designed by William B. Stout.

BUSHMASTER AIRCRAFT CORPORATION • USA

Formed in August 1970 to produce a modern version of the 1920s Ford Tri-Motor under the designation Bushmaster 2000. This updated design of the aircraft first built by the Stout Metal Airplane Company (q.v.) was evolved by Aircraft Hydro-Forming Inc. This latter company was acquired by the Whittaker Corporation in February 1969, which wished to dispose of the Tri-Motor programme. Improvements, by comparison with the original design, included more powerful lighter-weight engines with constant-speed fully-feathering propellers, and new systems.

BUTTERFLY AERO • USA

Offers plans to construct Banty single-seat parasol-wing microlight.

BV • Germany

Blohm und Voss was a famous shipbuilding concern, based on the Elbe at Hamburg. Its aircraft division, Hamburger Flugzeugbau GmbH. (q.v.), turned to construction of maritime aircraft in the early 1930s. In 1937 Hamburger Flugzeugbau adopted the title of the parent company. Successful designs of Dr Ing Richard Vogt initiated under the Ha designation continued in production becom-

ing designated, for example, Bv 138 instead of Ha 138. True Blohm und Voss developments included the Bv 222 Viking, the largest flying boat to attain operational status in the Second World War, and the even larger Bv 238, evolved too late to enter production before the war's end. The only prototype Bv 238 was destroyed by air attack four days before VE-day.

B W ROTOR COMPANY INC. • USA

Offered plans to construct the Sky Cycle single-seat ultralight pressure jet helicopter.

Above: Blohm und Voss Ha 139 seaplane; type was used for North Atlantic service trials

BX-AVIATION • Switzerland

Markets Brändli BX-2 Cherry two-seat monoplane (first flown 1982).

Below: Blohm und Voss Bv 238 six-engined prototype, largest flying-boat completed in WW2

Blohm und Voss Bv 138 long-range patrol flying-boat

CAARP • France

Cooperative des Atéliers Aéronautiques de la Région Parisienne initially specialised in modification and repairs. Began manufacture of components for sailplanes under licence, and in 1965 contracted from Scintex-Aviation (q.v.) to produce Super Emeraude light aircraft. Prototype only of C.P.100 two-seat version of Emeraude was built. CAARP became associated with Avions Mudry et Cie (q.v.) in manufacture of CAP 10 and 20 aerobatic aircraft in the early 1970s, being responsible for building of CAP 20 and fuselages for CAP 10. Final assembly of the latter was undertaken by Mudry at Berney, the companies being merged in 1978.

CAC • UK

The Civilian Aircraft Company Ltd was formed at Burton-on-Trent by Harold D. Boultbee, formerly assistant chief designer of Handley Page Ltd. Its sole product was the C.A.C. Mk I Coupé, a two-seat, high-wing cabin monoplane tourer built at Hedon, near Hull, and flown July 1929. A novel design for its time, there were initial difficulties and only five were built. Last four designated Mk II Coupé (uprated Armstrong Siddeley Genet Major engine); company closed in 1933.

CAGNY, RAYMOND • France

Put under development an all-composites three-seat training aircraft of unusual design as the Performance 2000, with the piston engine mounted on pylon aft of cockpit (engine was originally to be tail mounted).

CAIN AIRCRAFT CORPORATION • USA

Established 1 January 1931, this company designed and produced a two-seat lightweight sporting aircraft known as the Cain Sport. It was powered by a 95 hp Cirrus engine, licence-built by the US American Cirrus Engine (ACE) Corporation.

CAIRNS AIRCRAFT SYNDICATE • USA

Started in late 1928 as the Cairns Development Company; was taken over by Cairns Aircraft Corporation in August 1929. Began to develop advanced-design all-metal low-wing monoplane. First product was the Model A, first flown April 1930; second design evaluated by the US government but most of the 1930s dedicated to development work. Model A built for a new Cairns-designed engine, and in 1938 Models B and C.

CALIFORNIA HELICOPTER INTERNATIONAL • USA

Produced turbine conversion kits for Sikorsky S-58 helicopter, with rights purchased 1981 after earlier work.

Callair B-1 agricultural aircraft

Campbell Cricket light autogyro

Camair Twin Navion four-seat cabin monoplane

CALLAIR • USA

Call Aircraft Company formed originally as Call-Air in 1940-1941 by Renel, Ivan and Spencer Call to design and develop the Call-Air Model A two-seat light Cabin monoplane with Continental flat-four engine. Updated version with Lycoming flat-four certificated in 1946. Other models were the A-2 (Lycoming) and A-3 (Continental). Named changed to Callair Incorporated around 1950, producing the Model 150 (Callair A4) in 1955. A-5 and A-6 (uprated) were agricultural adaptations. Callair was purchased by Intermountain Manufacturing Company (q.v.) in 1962, and this company continued the development of aircraft for agricultural use.

CAMAIR • USA

Camair Division of Cameron Ironworks Inc took over the Twin Navion programme from Temco (q.v.) in mid-1950s.

Continued under the name Camair 480, for which certification was obtained by the retitled Camair Aircraft Corporation in September 1966. The aircraft was a conversion of twin-engined North American/Ryan Navion four-seat cabin monoplane with two Continental flat-six engines.

CAMPBELL AIRCRAFT LTD. • UK

Based at Hungerford, Berkshire, Campbell acquired UK rights for manufacture and sale of Bensen range of US Gyro-Gliders and Gyro-Copters in 1959. First licence-built example flew August 1960. Bensen range reduced to two models in 1969, when Campbell designed own two-seat light autogyro, the Curlew. Development abandoned in favour of the single-seat Cricket in July 1969; 47 were built by April 1972. Cougar single/two-seat prototype flew March 1973, but was not produced.

CAMS 55 twin-engined flying-boat patrol-bomber

Left: Canadair CL-215 water bomber, scooping water from the Pacific

CAMS • France

Chantiers Aéro-Maritimes de la Seine founded 1921, specialising in production of marine aircraft; technical director and chief designer from 1927 was Maurice Hurel. Best-known products were flying-boats; CAMS 33, built 1923-1926 originally for the Schneider Trophy race; CAMS 37 for shipborne observation/patrol; and the CAMS 51, 53 and 55 family, of which the CAMS 55 was a patrol bomber. Company acquired in 1933 by Société des Avions et Moteurs Henry Potez (q.v.). Factories at Sartrouville and Vitrolles nationalised in 1937.

CANADA AIR R V INC. • Canada

Established November 1988 and currently offering the ARV Griffin two-seat lightplane for home construction.

CANADAIR LTD. • Canada

Formed December 1944 at Cartierville, Montreal, from Aircraft Division of Canadian Vickers Ltd. (q.v.), as a 'Crown Company'. Purchased 1946 by Electric Boat Company of New York; later that year became a subsidiary of General

Above: Canadair Argus maritime patrol aircraft of the RCAF

Left: Canadair CL-84-1 tilt-wing VTOL research aircraft

Canadair CL-215T twin-turboprop amphibian in firefighting role

Dynamics Corporation (q.v.). First contract (1944) to build the DC-4m (Merlin-engined version of the Douglas DC-4) for the RCAF. Eventually built 71, including commercial versions, and converted many wartime C-47s into post-war commercial DC-3s. Since 1949 has licence-built more than 1,900 North American F-86 Sabre jet fighters for the RCAF and the US Military Assistance Programme; more than 700 Lockheed T-33 Silver Star jet trainers; 200 Lockheed F-104 Starfighters for the RCAF; and 240 Northrop F-5s for the Canadian Armed Forces and Royal Netherlands Air Force.

Products of its own design have included the CL-28 Argus Maritime patrol aircraft (32 built); CL-41 jet trainer/ground-attack aircraft (210 for Royal Canadian and Malaysian Air Forces); 39 CL-44 Yukon and Forty Four military/civil transports; three prototypes of the CL-84 tilt-wing VTOL research aircraft; CL-215 twin piston-engined firefighting and utility amphibian (first flown October 1967) and its CL-215T twin-turboprop re-engined derivative (first flown June 1989); and Challenger 600 widebody business jet (first flown November 1978) and 601 follow up. Company was repurchased by the Canadian government in December 1975. Other programmes included the CL-89 battlefield reconnaissance RPV, major subcontract work for the US Navy's P-3C Orion and its Canadian derivative, the CP-140 Aurora, and manufacture of components for other companies. Canadair became part of Bombardier Aerospace Group in 1992, renamed Bombardier Inc. Canadair (q.v.).

Canadair CL-41 two-seat jet trainer, used by the Canadian forces as the CT-114 Tutor

Canadair CF-5D, a Canadian-built version of the Northrop F-5B (Canadian Armed Forces/Vic Johnson)

CANADIAN AEROPLANES LTD. • Canada

Government-sponsored company, formed late 1916 taking over works and staff of Curtiss Canada at Long Branch, Toronto, where over 1,200 Curtiss JN-4C two-seat biplanes were built. In 1918 licence production began of Avro 504K to replace JN-4s at Canadian training establishments. One hundred ordered, but only one or two delivered before the Armistice. Also subcontractor for Felixstowe F.5 maritime patrol flying-boat.

CANADIAN ASSOCIATED AIRCRAFT LTD. • Canada

Founded in 1938; factories at St Hubert, Quebec, and Malton, Ontario. Contracted directly by the British government to speed up British rearmament programme for the RAF. Basically acted as parent company for six Canadian firms: Canadian Car & Foundry Co. Canadian Vickers, Fairchild Aircraft, Fleet Aircraft, National Steel Car Corporation and Ottawa Car & Aircraft. First contract in Autumn 1938 for 80 Handley Page bombers, later increased, but company wound up in 1942.

CANADIAN CAR & FOUNDRY COMPANY LTD. • Canada

Called CCF and later Can-Car; initially the largest company in Canada for the manufacture of railway equipment. In 1937 acquired licence to build Grumman GE-23

Below: Canadian Vickers Vancouver II flying-boat

(FF-1) two-seat biplane fighters, in factory at Fort William, Ontario. Built prototype of little-known FDB-1 fighter biplane in 1938. Orders for large numbers of Avro Ansons, Hawker Hurricanes, Avro Lancasters and Curtiss Helldivers. Seven new factories opened by mid-Second World War.

Early post-war obtained Canadian licence for Burnelli 'lifting fuselage' designs; flew prototype CBY-3 (twin Wasp engines) August 1945. Accommodation was three crew plus 38 passengers or 22 passengers and freight. Development of CBY-3 by subsidiary Cancargo (q.v.). In 1947 acquired assets of Noorduyn Aviation Ltd (q.v.); continued manufacture of Mk V Norseman and variants until early 1950s; resold it to its designer in 1953. In early 1950s designated products 'Can-Car', beginning with North American Harvard Mk 4s built under licence at Fort William for RCAF and NATO air forces. Gained contract to build 100 Beechcraft T-34A Mentor piston-engined trainers in 1952-1953 for USAF and also for RCAF. Retitled Canadian Car Company Ltd in mid/late 1950s.

CANADIAN CURTISS AEROPLANE COMPANY LTD. • Canada

At Long Branch, Toronto, this company built 18 Curtiss JN-3 'Jenny' two-seat biplane trainers in 1915-1916. RNAS order for 100 twin JNs cancelled in 1916; factory acquired in 1916 by Canadian Aeroplanes Ltd. (q.v.).

CANADIAN HOME ROTORS INC. • Canada

Produces the Baby Belle, first flown 1986 as a two-seat light helicopter for home assembly from kits or plans.

CANADIAN VERTOL AIRCRAFT LTD. • Canada

Wholly-owned subsidiary of Vertol Aircraft Corporation (q.v.); formed February 1954 at former RCAF air base Arnprior, west of Ottawa, to repair and overhaul RCAF/RCN Vertol helicopters. Also produced in 1957 small number of Vertol Model 42A, exclusively Canadian civil conversion of RCAF H-21B helicopters used to supply stations of the mid-Canada radar chain.

CANADIAN VICKERS LTD. • Canada

Established 1911 at St Hubert, Montreal, as subsidiary of Vickers Ltd. (q.v.). Aircraft division formed 1922; first Canadian company to build aircraft commercially. First contract was for six UK-designed Viking IV amphibians for Canadian Air Force. These followed from 1924 by 61 Vedette single-engined flying-boats and amphibians, its most successful product, designed in Canada by W. T. Reid. During the 1920s six other designs appeared: the Varuna, Vista, Vanessa, Velos, Vigil and Vancouver. Of these, only the Varuna (eight) and Vancouver (six) flying-boats went into production. In the 1930s the company licence-built Fairchild and Fokker designs and Northrop Deltas. During the Second World War built 40 Supermarine Stranraer flying-boats for the RCAF, 230 Consolidated OA-10 Catalinas for the USAAF and 149 Canso amphibians for the RCAF, plus hulls for 600 more Catalinas and fuselages for 40 Handley Page Hampden bombers. Took over Canadian Associated Aircraft (q.v.) in 1941, and in following year moved to government factory at Cartierville, near Montreal. In December 1944 became a separate autonomous company under new name of Canadair Ltd (q.v.), later to become a subsidiary of General Dynamics.

CANARY, AERO TECHNIK • Germany

In 1967 Jack Canary began licence production of the pre-war Bücker Bü 133D-1 Jungmeister single-seat aerobatic biplane, powered by rebuilt Siemens-Halske Sh 14 A radial or modern alternative. Three built in works of Josef Bitz Flugzeugbau at Augsburg/Haunstetten; production then transferred to Wolf Hirth GmbH at Nabern/Teck. Total of eight ordered (first one flown Summer 1968), but activities suspended after death of Mr Canary in August 1968. Four were completed by Bitz and Hirth; the programme was abandoned as uneconomic in January 1972.

CAN-CAR • Canada

See Canadian Car & Foundry Company Ltd.

CANCARGO AIRCRAFT MANUFACTURING COMPANY LTD • Canada

This wholly-owned subsidiary of the Canadian Car & Foundry Company (q.v.) was formed about 1950 to build the Burnelli Loadmaster transport. Only the CBY-3 prototype was built, by CCF; the rights in this aircraft were acquired in 1952 by Airlifts Inc. of Miami, and reverted eventually to Ballard Aircraft Corporation.

CANSA • Italy

Name of Costruzioni Aeronàutiche Novaresi SA assumed 1 May 1936 by former Aeronautica Gabardini SA (q.v.). Head office and factory at Cameri; began with repair and maintenance work on aircraft and engines. First product was C.5 single-engined one/two-seat training biplane (Fiat or Alfa Romeo engine), built in some numbers in late 1930s for civil market. The C.6 was a less successful development. CANSA then became subsidiary of Fiat (q.v.), producing small numbers of F.C.12 fighter/trainer monoplane (first flown 1940) and also the F.C.20 twin-engined ground-attack aircraft.

CANT • Italy

Company originally called Cantieri Navale Triestino created 1923 as subsidiary of Cantieri Navali di Monfalcone to manufacture civil/military marine aircraft. Most designs produced between 1923-1930 were work of R. Conflenti, including such flying-boats as Cant 6 three-engined biplane bomber; Cant 6 ter, commercial transport version; Cant 7, 7 bis and 7 ter single-engined trainer biplanes; Cant 10 and 10 ter five/six-seat single-engined light transport biplanes; Cant 18 trainer; Cant 22 three-engined eight/ten-seat commercial transport; Cant 25 single-seat fighter. Landplanes included Cant 23 transport and Cant 36 trainer.

Company changed its name in 1931 to Cantiere Riuniti dell'Adriatico. Chief designer Filippo Zappata (formerly of Blériot) completely reorganized the company 1933-1936. From 1934 most aircraft had Z prefixes, marine air-

CRDA Cant Z.506 Airone (Heron) seaplane (see CANT)

craft being numbered in 500 series, beginning with Z.501 Gabbiano biplane reconnaissance/bomber, first flown 1934. Followed by Z.504 two-seat fighter biplane flying-boat and Z.505 twin-float three-engined monoplane, both 1935. Latter developed into Z.506 (1936), built as reconnaissance/bomber/ASR for Regia Aeronàutica (Z.506B Airone) and as commercial transport for Italian airlines (Z.506A and C). Landplane version built by Piaggio (q.v.). Built Z.508 and Z.509, monoplane flying-boat bombers, and world's largest floatplane: Z.511 four-engined trans-Atlantic mail/freight variant, first flown 1943. The Z.515 twin-engined twin-float monoplane (coastal reconnaissance), built 1938-1939.

Landplanes (designated in 1000 series) included Z.1007 and 1007 bis Alcione three-engined bomber; Z.1011 twin-engined medium bomber/transport; Z.1012 three-engined transport; Z.1015 three-engined derivative of Z1017 bis, first flown January 1939 and used in torpedo trials early in the Second World War. Final type was Z.1018 Leone, twin-engined medium bomber intended to replace Alcione, probably Italy's best wartime design but too late to see service. Did not continue aircraft manufacture in the post-war period.

CAP • Brazil

Companhia Aeronàutica Paulista formed at Sao Paulo shortly after the Second World War to produce CAP 1 Planalto low-wing advanced trainer, CAP 4 Paulistinha high-wing cabin monoplane, and similar CAP 5 Carioca. The second was the most successful; improved version

later built by Nieva (q.v.). Company came under control of IPT (q.v.) in late 1940s.

CAPELLA AIRCRAFT CORPORATION • USA

Produces kits to assemble single- and two-seat versions of the Capella high-wing monoplane.

CAPITAL AIRCRAFT CORPORATION • USA

Founded at Detroit, Michigan, in 1928, this company produced a lightweight two-seat sporting and training monoplane known as the Capital Air Trainer.

CAPITAL HELICOPTER CORPORATION • USA

Established January 1954 for continued development of C-1 Hoppi-Copter, built previously by Hoppi-Copters Inc. (q.v.). C-1L, first flown 1954, was a redesigned and simplified version of original 1945 prototype.

CAPRONI • Italy

Italy's oldest and, at one time, largest aircraft manufacturer, the Caproni group comprised more than 20 companies, of which the principal aircraft building members were Aeroplani Caproni Trento, Caproni Aeronàutica Bergamasca, Caproni Vizzola SpA, Compagnia Nazionale Aeronàutica, Aeronàutica Predappio SpA and Officine Meccaniche Reggiane SpA. The Isotta-Fraschini aero-engine company was also part of the group.

Caproni Ca 97 high-wing monoplane

Caproni Ca 33 (Ca 3) three-engined bomber

Caproni Ca 73 of unusual inverted-sesquiplane configuration

Company's founder, Count Gianni Caproni di Taliedo, built and flew his first aircraft in May 1910, thereafter associating with various partners until First World War. Achieved an international reputation with the Ca 1-Ca 5 series of large tri-motor biplane and triplane bombers, built by a company called Società per lo Sviluppo dell'Aviazione in Italia, with factories at Taliedo and Vizzola. Early post-war publicity gained by Ca 60, an enormous eight-engined 'triple-triplane' of 1921, intended to carry 100 passengers. After formation of Regia Aeronàutica in 1923 Caproni achieved success with such military aircraft as the Ca 36, Ca 73 and Ca 74. The following decade produced the Ca 101, Ca 111 and Ca 133 range of 'Colonial' aircraft and a series of multipurpose reconnaissance/light bomber/transport types, production of which was shared with the Bergamasca subsidiary.

Cantieri Aeronàutici Bergamaschi (q.v.) had been absorbed by Caproni in 1931. Initially built Ca 100 and Ca 101, then built the new aircraft to the designs of Ing Cesare Pallavicino. Major production types during 1934-1944 were A.P.1 single-seat fighter, followed by the family of multi-purpose twin-engined aircraft: Ca 309 Ghibli; Ca310/310 bis Libeccio; Ca 311 Libeccio; Ca 312 bis Libeccio; Ca 314 and 316.

More than 2,500 examples of the Ca 100 training/touring biplane were built during the 1930s; the Ca 161 bis, a single-seat single-engined biplane, set an international altitude record of 56,046 ft (17,083 m) that remains unbeaten today in its class. The Caproni-Campini CC-1 of 1940 was Italy's first and the world's second aircraft to fly by jet propulsion, though it was not powered by a turbine. During the Second World War the company was chiefly concerned with the production and development of the Ca 310-Ca 314 multi-purpose twin-engined aircraft and with the Reggiane Re. 2000-Re 2005 series of single-seat fighters. During the lifetime of the group some 180 different types were built, in addition to licenced construction of almost as many by other designers.

The parent company went bankrupt in 1950. Aeroplani Caproni Trento survived the bankruptcy and in May 1952 flew Italy's first postwar jet light aircraft, the F.5, designed by Dott Ing Stelio Frati.

Caproni Vizzola Costruzioni Aeronàutiche SpA was formerly the Scuola Aviazione Caproni, the oldest flying school in Italy, and became the last surviving part of the company until bought by Agusta in 1983, producing the Calif series of sailplanes and finally the C22J Ventura two-seat very light basic trainer with two Microturbo turbojet engines, first flown 1980. Earlier it remodelled the Ca 133 for ambulance and military transport duties and assisted in production of the Breda Ba 65. Its first original design had been the F.4 single-seat fighter designed by Ing F Fabrizi, flown in 1940. Prototype F.6 had more powerful engine.

CARDEN-BAYNES AIRCRAFT LTD. • UK

Sir John Carden was associated with British light aviation after designing the 750 cc ultralight engine for the Gloucestershire Gannet in the early 1920s. Went into partnership with L. E. Baynes in 1930 to produce a one-off single-seat powered glider. In 1936 built a single Bee, a small two-seat high-wing monoplane with two Carden Ford S.P.1 modified car engines, flown in 1937. Development of three-seat B-3 halted by war.

CARDOEN • Chile

See Indústrias Cardoen Ltda.

CARIBE DOMAN HELICOPTERS INC. • Puerto Rico

Acquired assets of Doman Helicopters Inc. (q.v.) in August 1965. Tooling began in January 1966 to produce Doman

Carson conversion of the Bell 47

Carstedt Jet Liner 600, a conversion of the de Havilland Dove

D-10B helicopter; however, rights repurchased by parent company in late 1967, emerging as Berlin Doman Helicopters Inc.

CARLSON AIRCRAFT INC. • USA

Manufactures kits to construct the Sparrow series of micro-light/homebuilt high-wing monoplanes in several single- and two-seat versions, plus the single-seat low-wing Sky-cycle (developed from an original 1945 design).

CARMA MANUFACTURING COMPANY • USA

Established 1948 to manufacture electrical, mechanical, and aircraft control equipment. Aircraft manufacturing division formed in 1954 at Tucson, Arizona, to build a turbo-jet-powered two-seat trainer, the Carma VT-1 Weejot. Prototype first flew 30 March 1956.

CARSON HELICOPTERS INC. • USA

Formed in 1963 at Perkasie, Pennsylvania, to develop conversion schemes to improve payload and performance of standard US light helicopters, i.e., Bell 47 and Hiller UH-12. A four-seat conversion of three-seat Bell 47G called the Carson Super C-4 was also produced. Company later became a helicopter overhaul organisation and charter operator.

CARSTEDT INC. • USA

In December 1966 produced a 'stretched' version of the de Havilland D. H. 104 Dove with AiResearch turboprop engines. It was called the Carstedt Jet Liner 600 and had 18 seats; a small number were built for commuter airline use. Company acquired by Texas Airplane Manufacturing Co Inc. (q.v.) in mid-1970s.

CASA • Spain

Construcciones Aeronáuticas SA formed 3 March 1923, with factory at Getafe, to produce all metal aircraft for Spanish Air Force. Began by licence-building Breguet XIX reconnaissance-bomber biplanes, followed by other air-

CASA-207 Azor military transport

craft of foreign design including Dornier Wal flying boats (at Cadiz), Vickers Vildebeest torpedo-bombers, Gotha Go 145C biplane trainers, Junkers Ju 52/3m transports, Bücker Bü 131 and 133 aerobatic trainers and Heinkel He 111 medium bombers. Opened design department after Second World War; first series product was Dornier Do 27 general-purpose lightplane, followed by CASA-201

Alcotan, CASA-202 Halcon and CASA-207 Alcotan twin-engined transports of own design. Completed 70 Northrop F-5 fighters under licence for Spanish Air Force. In 1972 took over Hispano Aviación, followed by the ENMASA aero-engine concern in June 1973. Currently has three divisions, namely Aircraft, Maintenance and Space: Aircraft division activities include design of aircraft and integrated

CASA C-101BB armed jet trainer operated by Honduras

structures; share in international Airbus, Eurofighter and FLA programmes; manufacture of structural parts and components for Boeing, Eurocopter, Northrop Grumman and Saab aircraft; continuing development and production of C-101 Aviojet advanced and lead-in jet trainer/light attack aircraft (first flown June 1977), C-212 Aviocar (first flown March, and currently offered in Series 400 form as first flown April 1997) in transport and maritime versions, and development of the new ATX family of advanced trainers and light combat aircraft; and production of CN 235 via international Airtech company (q.v.).

Above: CASA C.212 Aviocar twin-turboprop STOL transport

CASA C-212 MP Patrullero maritime patrol aircraft in Argentine service

Caudron G.III biplane trainer of WW1

CASPAR-WERKE AG. • Germany

Established in 1921 in ex-Fokker factory at Travemünde to continue business of Hanseatische Flugzeugwerke Karl Caspar AG. of Hamburg. Started with manufacture of seaplanes, including S.1 twin-float monoplane and Heinkel-designed U.1 and U.2, 1922 prototypes for detachable-wing biplanes to be carried by submarines. A four-seat open-cockpit light transport was followed by the CLE.11 in 1923, a two-seat high-wing cabin monoplane. In 1925 came the CT-1-5 series of light aircraft designed by Karl Theiss, and CLE.12 eight-seat single-engined transport. Lightplane designs C.17, 23, 24 and 26 followed; then in 1926 the C.27 seaplane training biplane; C.30 reconnaissance aircraft; C.32 agricultural biplane (one of the world's first) with payload of 1,984 lb (900 kg); the C.35 Priwall eight-passenger biplane of 1927 (also used by Deutsche Luft Hansa as freighter); and the C.36 reconnaissance aircraft. Lack of orders for these types caused the factory to close in 1928.

EV CASSAGNERES • USA

Offers plans for the Ryan STA, as a representation of the 1930's two-seater.

CATA • France

Construction Aeronautique de Technologie Avancee. First flew in 1994 the LMK.1 Oryx side-by-side two-seat monoplane, offered as a kit.

CAUDRON • France

Gaston and René Caudron established aeroplane factory as Caudron Frères at Romiotte (Seine) in 1910. Initial flight of the first of a series of highly successful biplanes (G.I, II and III) February 1911. G.III considered extremely reliable and used widely as a trainer in the First World War. Single-seat monoplane trainer produced in 1912. G.IIIAs were built for military use in 1914; used extensively by France, UK, Belgium, Russia and Italy as two-seat reconnaissance/artillery observation aircraft. Several hundred built, mostly in France, but also by British Caudron (q.v.) and in Italy. Series continued with G.IV (1915), several military variants; also in that year the prototype R.4 three-seat bomber appeared, very solid and well armed. The R.11 with five Lewis machine-guns was produced a few months before the Armistice was declared.

The company had moved to Issy-les-Moulineaux (Seine) by 1919, and post-war products included C 23 (and/or C 232) two-seat biplane, which inaugurated French commercial air services on 10 February 1919 with flight from Paris to Brussels; C 61 three-engined six/eight passenger biplane; three-engined seven-seat development of C 61; C 183, a further modernisation of two previous aircraft of which one only was built, in 1925.

The company, known as Société Anonyme des Avions Caudron, ran into financial difficulties and was reorganized as Société Caudron-Renault. Next became notable for distinctive streamlined aircraft from its designer Marcel Riffard, who joined in 1932. His C363 took second place in 1933 Coupe Deutsch race; developed versions took first three places in 1934 and 1935, first two places in 1936. Derivatives of these included the Rafale series of single- and two-seat sporting/racing aircraft of the late 1930s. Fifteen C 690Ms built as advanced trainers for the Armée de l'Air; series ended with the C 720. Followed by the single-seat C 580 and C 680; C 600 Aiglon series; C 620/C 630 Simoun four-seat cabin monoplane; C 640 Typhon series; the little-known C 670 ground-attack prototype; and the single-seat C 860, built in 1938 for an attempt (never made) on 1936 Paris-Tokyo flight record established by a Simoun. About 1,700 examples built in about ten years of C 440 (later AA.1) Göeland, twin-engined six-passenger transport. Two series of light fighters developed from Coupe Deutsch racers: following C 710 and C 713 prototypes, four-gun C 714 entered service. Improved variants CR 760 and 770 under development when France collapsed. The factories built aircraft for Germany during the Occupation. Later nationalised as Ateliers Aéronautiques d'Issyles-Moulineaux; incorporated into SNCAN (q.v.) in late 1945

CAVALIER AIRCRAFT CORPORATION • USA

Successor to Trans-Florida Aviation (q.v.), acquired during 1960s type certificate for North American F-51 Mustang, producing tandem two-seat business/sport conversions of F-51D as Cavalier 2000 series, and building new single-seat F-51Ds for the USAF counterinsurgency Military

Caudron Simoun four-seat cabin monoplane

Caudron C23, built originally as a night bomber

Cavalier Aircraft versions of the North American F-51D Mustang

Assistance Programme. Prototype of Mustang II, two-seat COIN patrol/attack version equipped with heavier armament, flew December 1967; prototype Turbo Mustang III (with Rolls-Royce Dart) in 1969. Second prototype flew in April 1971, equipped with Lycoming TSS engine, by which time the programme had been sold to the Piper Aircraft Corporation (q.v.), but then the company was dissolved.

CAVENAUGH AVIATION INC. • USA

Developed Cargoliner conversion for the Mitsubishi MU-2 transport.

CCF • Canada

See Canadian Car & Foundry.

CEA • France

Centre Est Aéronautique formed at Dijon October 1957 by Pierre Robin and Jean Delemontez (ex-Jodel, q.v.); began production with the DR 100 Ambassadeur, a three-seat version of the Jodel D.11, designed by Robin and first flown July 1958; built also by Société Aéronautique Normande. Delivered 500th aircraft in June 1967. Subse-

Centre Est Sicile Record lightweight cabin monoplane

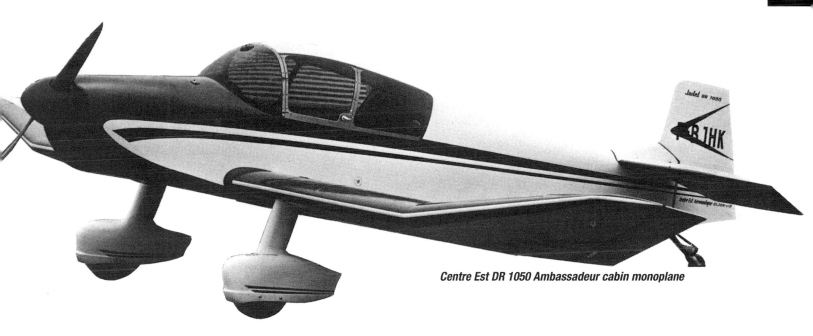

Centre Est DR 1050 Ambassadeur cabin monoplane

quent products also mainly two- to four-seat private-owner models. Name of company subsequently altered to Avions Pierre Robin (Centre Est Aéronautique); the latter part later dropped from marketing name.

CEI • USA

Markets kits to construct the Free Spirit Mk II two-seat low-wing monoplane, originally developed by Cabrinha as the Free Spirit Mk I and first flown 1986.

CELAIR (PTY.) LTD. • South Africa

Developed Eagle 300 six-seat STOL cabin lightplane (first flown 1990); programme later offered for sale. Also developed Celstar CG-1 composites aerobatic glider.

SN CENTRAIR • France

Continues to produce gliders in Alliance, Marianne, 101 Club and Pégase series. In 1980s developed Parafan powered parawing microlight, and was developing Sup'aero as single-seat canard monoplane powered by two Microturbo jet engines and Sup'Air as six-seat composites lightplane with tail-mounted propeller for piston engine.

CENTRAL AERO-HYDRODYNAMIC INSTITUTE • USSR

See ANT.

CENTRALA FLYGVERKSTÅDERNA • Sweden

Royal Swedish Air Force maintenance depots at Malmslätt (CFM, later CVM) and Västerås (CFV, later CVV). Established 1926/27, and from 1928 until mid-1930s built foreign aircraft under licence for RSWAF, including Focke-Wulf Fw 44 Stieglitz, Fokker C.V-D and -E and Hawker Hart.

CENTRALA INDUSTRIALA AERONAUTICA RUMANA • Romania

Authority responsible since 1968 for all Romanian aircraft production. Major factories are IRMA at Bucharest and ICA at Brasov; also produces, in collaboration with Yugoslavia, the Orao twin-jet fighter/ground-attack aircraft (see VTI/CIAR).

CENTRAL AIRCRAFT COMPANY LTD. • UK

Founded in London late 1916, subsidiary of established joinery company, R. Cattle Ltd. Aircraft and components built during 1918 under licence. Produced in 1919, at Northolt, Middlesex, small biplane trainers designed by J. S. Flotcher, the company manager. Original designations were C. F., later changed to Centaur. The Centaur IV (C.F.4) was a three-seat Renault-engined tourer. The next model was the Centaur IIa (C.F.2A) a twin-engined commercial transport biplane with Beardmore engines. Two were built, equipped with seats for six/seven passengers or to carry half a ton of mail or freight.

Below: Century Aerospace Corporation Century Jet entry-level business jet

CENTRO TÉCNICO DE AERONAUTICA • Brazil

See CTA.

CENTRO VOLA A VELA • Italy

See CVV.

CENTRAL STATES AERO COMPANY LTD. • USA

Established at Bettendorf, Iowa, this company produced a small two-seat sporting monoplane known as the Central States Monocoupe. Powered by a 70 hp engine, it was reputedly able to become airborne within five seconds of starting its take-off run.

CENTURY AEROSPACE CORPORATION • USA

Developing Century Jet CJ-1 and CJ-2 as six-seat light entry-level business jets, with single Williams-Rolls FJ44 turbofan engine. First flight anticipated year 2000.

CENTURY AIRCRAFT CORPORATION • USA

Amarillo, Texas, based company which in 1977 certificated a re-engined (TPE 331) version of Handley Page Jetstream Mk 1 twin-turboprop transport; conversion carried out by Volpar Inc (q.v.).

CERVA • France

Consortium Européen de Réalisation de Ventes d'Avions is a joint venture started 1971 by Siren SA and Wassmer Aviation (q.v.) to build and market CE.43 Guépard four-seat light aircraft, an all-metal development of the Wassmer Super 4/21, first flown May 1971. Prototype of generally similar CE.44 Cougar flown October 1974, and CE.45 Léopard late 1975. Partnership ended autumn 1977 owing to bankruptcy of Wassmer.

CESKOMORA VSKA-KOLBEN-DANEK • Czechoslovakia

See CKD-Praga.

CESKOSLOVENSKÉ ZAVODY AUTOMOBILOVÉ A LETECKÉ, NARODNI PODNIK • Czechoslovakia

Blanket title: Czech Automobile and Aircraft Works, National Corporation, covering all national manufacture from 1945 until mid-1950s. The Zavody Letecke (aircraft works) incorporated the former Aero, CKD-Praga and Letov factories, plus Walter (engines), while Avia, Mraz and Zlin plus the Skoda car works came under Závody Automobilové. Built under licence several Soviet types (Ilyushin Il-14 and -28, MiG-15). Czech designations for MiG-15 were CS-102, S-103; Il-14 built as Avia 14. Early indigenous products included the Tom-8 (or L-208) two-seat trainer; L-40 Meta-Sokol four-seat light trainer/tourer; L-60 Brigadyr three/four-seat light STOL monoplane; Zlin 226 Trener and 326 Trener-Master; Aero 145 and Super Aero; L-200 Morava four/five-seat twin-engined air taxi/business aircraft; and HC-2 Heli-Baby and HC-3 light helicopters.

Below: Cessna 208 Caravan in Grand Caravan version, showing the 850th delivery in 1997

CESSNA AIRCRAFT COMPANY INC. • USA

Clyde V. Cessna, originally a motor mechanic, built his first aircraft at Enid, Oklahoma, in the spring of 1911. Built and flew several more before moving to Wichita, Kansas, in 1917. Founded Travel Air Manufacturing Company (q.v.) with Walter Beech and Lloyd Stearman on 5 February 1925. Disagreed with company policy on aircraft design and in 1927 built self-financed monoplane which developed into Airmaster and Model 195 series of four-seat cantilever high-wing cabin monoplanes. Cessna-Roos Aircraft Company established with Victor Roos on 8 September 1927; Roos backed out and on 31 December the present Cessna company was incorporated.

Production of 'A' series (again with cantilever wings) began 1928, as did BW three-seater. Built DC-6 prototype 1929, followed by four-seat DC-6A and 6B. Cessna tried to keep factory functioning during the Depression, producing 300 CG-2 primary gliders, but finally had to close in 1931. Company continued to exist and build several highly successful custom-built racers. Factory reopened 1934, but Clyde sold his interests and company continued to be run by his son, a nephew and T. Salter.

Cessna T-37 Twoot jet trainer

Went on to develop highly successful Airmaster series and in 1939 the first Cessna twin, the T-50 five-seat cabin monoplane. Latter built in large numbers including nearly 1,200 Crane trainer versions for the RCAF. Adopted also by USAAF, US Army and Navy, and over 5,000 produced during Second World War, serving in all theatres.

After the war Cessna began building light aircraft for private and business use. The most successful early models were Models 140 and 170, plus later Models 172, 305, 180 and others which became world-renowned. Model 305 used widely for liaison duties during Korean War and later as L-19/OE-1 Bird Dog (over 3,500 built). In March 1952 acquired Seibel Helicopter Co (q.v.) and the CH-1 four-seat helicopter was developed and built in small numbers. In 1972 Cessna became the world's first company to have produced 100,000 aircraft. Production

has included nearly 2,000 twin-engined jet trainers and A-37 strike aircraft for the USAF and US Military Assistance Programme. Company's Pawnee and Wallace divisions taken into Aircraft division in 1984, but company sold to General Dynamics (q.v.) in 1985 and then to Textron Inc.

In July 1996 Cessna Single Engine Piston Facility opened in Independence, Kansas, to reintroduce production

Cessna Model 525 CitationJet business aircraft

Above: Cessna Citation executive transport

Cessna 150 Aerobat lightplane

of single-engined light aircraft to Cessna range. Currently available Cessna aircraft are Cessna 172R and 172SP Skyhawk four-seat lightplanes as much refined versions of previous Skyhawk, four-seat 182S Skylane as refinement of previous Skylane versions, six-seat 206H Stationair and T206H Turbo Stationair as refinements of previous versions, 208 Caravan (first flown 1982) as single-turboprop commuter, business and cargo aircraft (among other uses) offered in four civil versions plus as U-27A for US foreign military sales, and a range of business jets as six/seven-seat Model 525 CitationJet (first flown April 1991), nine/12-seat Model 550 Citation Bravo (first flown April 1995), nine/ten-seat Model 560 Citation Ultra and latest Ultra Encore (latter first flown July 1998), eight/ten-seat Model 560-XL Citation Excel (first flown February 1996), 15-seat Model 650 Citation VII (first flown February 1991), ten-seat Model 680 Citation Sovereign (for certification in year 2002), 11/14-seat Model 750 Citation X (first flown December 1993), CJ1 (for delivery from year 2000 as successor to CitationJet), and eight-seat CJ2 (to fly 1999).

CFA • France

Compagnie Française d'Aviation established at Billancourt in late 1930s to build a version of pre-war Salmson Cri-Cri. Developed also a post-war variant, the D-7 Cri-Cri Major two-seat high-wing cabin monoplane. Only a few built; superseded by prototypes of D57 Phryganet (first flight 7 November 1950) of similar general layout and D21T-4 Super Phryganet (first flown 30 July 1951). All three designed by Paul J. Deville of Salmson.

CFM AIRCRAFT LTD. • UK

Offers kits to build Streak Shadow and Star Streak two-seat light monoplanes. Company formed from CFM Metal-Fax.

CGS AVIATION INC. • USA

Offers kits to construct single-seat Hawk Classic, two-seat Hawk II Classic, single-seat Hawk Arrow and two-seat Hawk II Arrow, all high-wing microlights.

Cessna Model 402 Businessliner light transport

Cessna A-37B (Model 318E) light strike aircraft

Cessna AGwagon duster/sprayer agricultural aircraft

Champion Olympia high-wing monoplane

Champion Scout light utility aircraft

CH-7 HELICOPTERS HELI-SPORT SRL • Italy

Produces the CH-7 Angel single-seat ultralight kit-built helicopter (well over 130 delivered since 1992 at time of writing) plus the CH-7 Kompress tandem two-seat version (kits delivered since mid-1998).

CHADWICK HELICOPTERS INC. • USA

Founded as subsidiary of Chadwick Inc. (established 1964 to produce helicopter components and equipment) to produce C-122S single-seat ultralight helicopter (completed 1985), with two-seaters then anticipated.

Below: CH-7 Helicopters Heli-Sport CH-7 Angel

CHAMPION AIRCRAFT COMPANY INC. • USA

In 1982 B & B Aviation purchased rights to Champion light-planes from Bellanca, then founding Champion Aircraft Company Inc. to build Citabria, Decathlon and Scout until 1985.

CHAMPION AIRCRAFT CORPORATION • USA

This company was formed by Robert Brown after acquiring rights in the Aeronca Model 7 Champion two-seat training/touring monoplane in June 1954. Aeronca Aircraft Corporation (q.v.) ceased manufacture of the Champion in 1951. Production began at Osceola, Wisconsin, in late 1954; subsequent models included the 7EC Traveler, 7FC Tri-Traveler, Sky-Trac, Challenger and Citabria. By

Above: Champion Citabria aerobatic lightplane

mid-1960s the Citabria had become the main production version. In 1961 Champion Aircraft Corporation produced the single-seat parasol-wing Model 8 Citabria Pro for professional aerobatic pilots. Bellanca Sales Company (q.v.) acquired the company's assets on 30 September 1970, by which time some 1,500 Citabrias had been built.

Chase YC-122 Avitruc light assault transport

CHANCE VOUGHT • USA

Lewis & Vought Corporation (q.v.) renamed Chance Vought Corporation after First World War. From 1922-1926 produced UO-1 observation float biplanes (developed from VE-7/9) and FU-1 catapult fighter seaplanes for US Navy, followed in 1927 by 02U observation landplanes for same customer, first of several Vought designs to bear the name Corsair. Moved to East Hartford, Connecticut, in about 1930, where until 1935 it continued the Corsair series with 03U observation biplanes and similar SU scouts, again for US Navy. Became Chance Vought Division of United Aircraft Corporation (q.v.) in 1934, initially continuing production at East Hartford of 03U/SU Corsairs. These were followed by Vought SBU two-seat scout-bomber, designed in 1932 and produced for US Navy between 1935-1937.

Joined with Sikorsky Division of UAC in April 1939 to form Chance Vought and Sikorsky Aircraft Division of United

Aircraft Corporation (q.v.). Became Chance Vought Aircraft Inc. after becoming separate and independent from UAC on 1 July 1954. Main product during this stage of its history was the unorthodox F7U Cutlass, in production 1952-1955 for the US Navy. Deliveries began also in 1957 of the F-8 (originally F8U) Crusader, development and production of which continued as the LTV F-8 after further company metamorphoses into Chance Vought

Corporation (from 31 December 1960), and a merger on 31 August 1961 with Ling-Temco Electronics Inc. to form Ling-Temco-Vought Inc. (q.v.). Within the latter structure, Vought became, successively, the Aerospace Division of LTV, then Vought Aeronautics Company (Division of LTV Aerospace Corporation). Since 1 January 1976 it has continued its activities as Vought Corporation (q.v.), a subsidiary of the LTV Corporation.

CHANGHE AIRCRAFT INDUSTRIES CORPORATION • China

Founded out of vehicle manufacturing concern. First flew in December 1985 a heavy commercial/military transport and anti-ship helicopter as the Z-8, based on the French Aérospatiale Super Frelon. More recently developed a small multipurpose single-turboshaft helicopter as the Z-11, first flown 1996 and possibly based in part on Eurocopter Ecureuil. Name changed to Jingdezhen Helicopter Corporation in 1998.

CHANTIERS AÉRO-MARITIMES DE LA SEINE • France

See CAMS.

CHANTIERS AÉRONAUTIQUES DE NORMANDIE • France

Name from 1940 of the former Amiot factory at Cherbourg, which contributed to production of the Junkers Ju 52/3m during the occupation of France.

CHASE AIRCRAFT COMPANY INC. • USA

Established New York 1943 by Michael Stroukoff to develop experimental assault/cargo gliders. Produced XCG-14, XCG-14A and CG-18A. Moved to Trenton, New Jersey, late 1946, developing a powered version, 30-troop YC-122 Avitruc, first flown 18 November 1948. Twelve built for USAF trials but no further production. Followed by larger

Chance Vought & Sikorsky VS-44A Excalibur flying-boat

Chance Vought F7U Cutlass carrier-based fighter

C-123 Avitruc, first flown 14 October 1949, derived from XG-20 cargo glider; this project later taken over by Fairchild (q.v.) as C-123B and renamed Provider. An XC-123A prototype (four General Electric turbojets) flew on 21 April 1951: first flight of a US transport powered by jet engines. Chase became wholly-owned subsidiary of Willys Motors Inc. of Toledo, Ohio, in 1953, itself owned by Kaiser-Fraser (q.v.). In June 1953 a USAF contract for 300 C-123Bs was cancelled, a smaller contract going to Fairchild that autumn. See also Stroukoff Aircraft Corporation.

CHEETAH LIGHT AIRCRAFT COMPANY LTD. • Canada

Clairco formed 14 January 1964 at St Jean, Quebec, by David Saunders (an RCAF pilot 1957-1963). Built and flew, in 1962, an all-wood two-seat light aircraft named Cheetah. Founded company to build a four-seat all-metal improved version, the Super Cheetah; prototype built by Aircraft Industries of Canada. This flew September 1964, but no production took place.

CHENGDU AIRCRAFT INDUSTRIAL CORPORATION • China

Founded in 1958 for jet fighter and jet trainer development and production, based on original Soviet designs. J-7 tactical fighter and air-defence interceptor first flew in January 1966, developed from the Soviet MiG-21F-13 following 1960-1961 discussions between the two nations, though technology transfer had not been completed when co-operation came to an abrupt end. J-7 originally assembled by Shenyang but production moved to Chengdu in 1967. Many new versions followed, including F-7 Airguards for export, with production and development

Above: Chengdu FC-1 is under development as J-7 replacement

continuing in 1999. A replacement for J-7/F-7 has been under development as the FC-1. Another early programme led to the JJ-5 which first flew in May 1966 as an advanced lead-in/fighter conversion trainer, based on the Shenyang J-5A single-seat fighter (itself a Chinese-produced variant of the Soviet MiG-17PF), but with a MiG-15UTI style tandem cockpit arrangement. Much more recently, Chengdu has also developed the new J-10 as a very advanced multirole fighter, first flown in March 1998 and possibly using some technology derived from the abandoned Israeli Lavi programme of the 1980s. A further multirole fighter has been under development as J-12, about which little is yet known.

Above: Chengdu J-7s of the PLA Air Force

Chilton D.W.1A single-seat lightplane

CHETVERIKOV • USSR

A 1928 graduate of Leningrad Institute of Transport Engineering, I. V. Chetverikov worked briefly with D. P. Grigorovich (q.v.) before joining the Tsentralnoe Konstruktorskoe Byuro (Central Design Bureau; TsKB). From 1931-1933 was in charge of seaplane development section; responsible for designing MDR-3 reconnaissance flying-boat, OSGA-101 light amphibian, and related SPL submarine-borne small floatplane. His ARK-3 flying-boat was a failure, but the three-seat MDR-6 (or Che-2) of 1937 was produced for Soviet Naval Aviation, 50 being built at Taganrog between 1939 and German invasion of Crimea in 1941. Development, but no further production, of MDR-6 continued during Second World War; after completion in 1947 of three prototypes of the eight-passenger TA-1 flying-boat, this bureau was closed down in 1948 and Chetverikov became a lecturer.

Above: Chetverikov MDR-6 flying-boat

CHICHESTER-MILES CONSULTANTS LTD. • UK

Has developed the Leopard four-seat sports executive jet, powered in latest production form by two Williams International FJX turbofan engines (first flown December 1988 and production deliveries anticipated from the year 2002).

CHILTON AIRCRAFT • UK

Operated from Chilton, near Hungerford, Berkshire, in 1936 to build D.W.1 single-seat light aircraft designed by Hon Andrew W. H. Dalrymple and A. R. Ward, an attractive low-wing open-cockpit wooden monoplane with fixed 'trousered' landing gear and Carden-Ford engine, first flown April 1937. Three D.W.1s built, followed by one faster D.W.1A, first flown July 1939. Design of D.W.2 only half finished when Second World War began and it was never completed.

During the war company did subcontract work for MAP and aircraft industry generally. Dalrymple died in a flying

Below: Chichester-Miles Consultants Leopard sports executive jet

accident in December 1945, and company re-registered on 5 June 1946 as Chilton Aircraft Company Ltd. Prototype Olympia single-seat sailplane built 1947; rights in this sold to Elliotts of Newbury Ltd. (q.v.) in 1952. Company began work in electrical industry.

CHINCUL SACAIFI • Argentina

Wholly-owned subsidiary of La Macarena SA, distributor of Piper Aircraft Corporation (q.v.) products in Argentina. Chincul manufactured Piper aircraft from 1972 including Archer, Arrow, Aztec, Turbo Aztec, Chieftain, Dakota, Pawnee, Cherokee, Cheyenne, Navajo, Seneca, Super Cub and Warrior. Signed agreement with Bell Helicopter Textron 1990 for helicopter co-production.

CHRISLEA AIRCRAFT COMPANY LTD. • UK

Based originally at Heston, Middlesex, in 1936, building joint designs of R. C. Christophorides and B. V. Leak. In 1938 one L.C.1 Airguard was built, a two-seat, low-wing cabin monoplane for Civil Air Guard. Company transferred

Chincul-built Piper PA-28-140 Cherokee cabin monoplane

Chrislea CH.3 (series 2) Super Ace lightplane

to Kentish Town shortly before Second World War, undertaking subcontract work for aircraft industry. Moved again in 1947 to Exeter Airport, where during 1948-1950 a series of four-seat lightplanes were constructed: Series 1 CH.3 Ace, Series 2 CH.3 Super Ace and Series 4 CH.3 Skyjeep. The first of these high-wing cabin monoplanes was flown in August 1946, but high operating costs and unacceptable control system affected sales of the Ace and Super Ace; more conventional system used on 1949 Skyjeep. Total production (all three types) about 26 aircraft. In 1952 assets acquired by C. E. Harper Aircraft Ltd and all surviving models were scrapped.

CHRISTEN INDUSTRIES INC. • USA

First flew in 1977 Eagle II two-seat unlimited-class aerobatic biplane; hundreds of kits sold for amateur construction. In 1983 acquired former Pitts Aerobatics company and this plant at Afton in Wyoming became company headquarters. Thereafter added Pitts Special aero-batic biplane to product line, plus A-1 Husky two-seat cabin monoplane (first flown 1986) as assembled and certificated aircraft. See Aviat and Steen.

CHRYSLER TECHNOLOGIES AIRBORNE SYSTEMS INC. • USA

Founded 1989 and undertook work on special electronic and surveillance aircraft programmes. USAF C-27A Spartan version of Italian Alenia G222 was ordered through company.

CICARÉ AERONAUTICA • Argentina

From late 1960s designed and built Cicaré I and II experimental light helicopters. Followed September 1976 by

Cicaré II three-seat light helicopter

Cierva C.30A Autogiro

C.K.1 (originally CH-III) two/three-seat light helicopter for training and agricultural use, aimed mostly at the South American market.

CIERVA AUTOGIRO COMPANY LTD. • UK

Company founded 24 March 1926 by Air Commodore J. G. Weir, specialising in construction of Autogiros designed by famous Spanish pioneer aviator Juan de la Cierva (1886-1936). Two best-known craft were C.8L, first rotorcraft to fly the English Channel, and C.30A, built by A. V. Roe (q.v.) as Rota for RAF. Production of other Autogiros licenced by Cierva to Airwork (C.30, C. 30P); Avro (C.6, C.8, C.9, C.12, C.17, C.19, C.30A, C.30P); British Aircraft Manufacturing Co (C.40); Comper (C.25); de Havilland (C.24, C.26); George Parnall & Co. (C.10, C.11); and Westland (CL.20). Weir formed a separate company (G. & J. Weir Ltd, q.v.) in 1933, and re-established Cierva Company in 1944. After Second World War evolved (jointly with

above company), the W.9, a two-seat helicopter using jet thrust to counteract torque. The W.11 Air Horse three-rotor design was built for Cierva by Cunliffe-Owen (q.v.); designed specifically for crop-spraying, it was first flown 8 December 1948. The W.14 Skeeter, small two-seat helicopter, first flown 8 October 1948. Both designs taken over in 1951 by Saunders-Roe (q.v.), together with other Cierva projects. Company then concentrated on research; eventually re-emerged as Cierva Rotorcraft Ltd, and bought up Rotorcraft Ltd. (q.v.) in April 1966 and Servotec Ltd. in 1968. The prototype CR.LTH-1 flew 18 October 1969 but was not produced owing to lack of funds.

Cierva three-rotor W.11 Air Horse helicopter

CIRCA REPRODUCTIONS • Canada

Markets plans and kits to build 87 per cent scale replicas of the First World War Nieuport 11 and 12.

Below: Circa Reproductions 87% scale Nieuport 12 replica

CIRRUS DESIGN CORPORATION • USA

Currently offers SR20 four-seat composites light monoplane (first flown March 1995), for delivery to customers from 1999. Previously produced VK30 kitplane (first flown 1988).

CIVILIAN AIRCRAFT COMPANY LTD. • UK

See CAC.

CKD-PRAGA • Czechoslovakia

Ceskomoravska-Kolben-Danek, maker of aero engines from 1915, including several marketed under the name Praga. Began aircraft construction in 1931, subsequent products including the Praga E.40 two-seat training biplane and E.45 single-seat fighter biplane, and a family of two/four-seat light cabin monoplanes designated E.114 Air Baby, E.115, E.210 and E.214. Factory overrun by German invasion, but operated by Germany as Böhmisch-Mührische Maschinenfabriken AG. (Bohemian-Moravian Engineering Works). Re-established post-war under new title of Závody Letecké Praga, producing, *inter alia*, updated models of the E.114 and E.210/211.

CKD-Praga E.114 Air Baby lightplane

CLARK AIRCRAFT CORPORATION • USA

Subsidiary of Fairchild (q.v.) formed 10 February 1938 under presidency of Harold Clark. He developed Duramold process of constructing fuselages in moulded halves of a plastic compound material, joined along top and bottom centrelines. Production of prototype Clark F-46A three/four-seat monoplane followed, using this technique, at Fairchild's Hagerstown, Maryland factory.

CLARK AIRCRAFT INC. • USA

Clark 1000 single-seat agricultural biplane, produced at Marshall, Texas, was first flown March 1956 and put into production the following spring.

CLASSIC AERO ENTERPRISES • USA

Markets plans to build H-2 Honey Bee single-seat biplane, plans and kits for the H-3 Pegasus low-wing microlight, and plans to modify H-3 into HP-40 Warhawk.

CLASSIC AIRCRAFT CORPORATION • USA

Produces the Waco Classic YMF Super biplane as modern version of pre-war Waco Model F open-cockpit three-seater.

CLAUDIUS DORNIER SEASTAR GMBH & CO KG. • Germany

Founded 1982 to develop the Seastar twin-turboprop STOL amphibian (first flown 1984) but became insolvent 1989. Re-formed 1990 as Dornier Composite.

CLAYTON & SHUTTLEWORTH LTD. • UK

Ssubcontractor during First World War for the construction of Handley Page O/100, Sopwith Triplane, Sopwith Camel and Vickers Vimy, all built at Lincoln.

CLEARY AIRCRAFT CORPORATION • USA

Developed CL-1 Zipper single-seat light aircraft with twin booms and pusher propeller, designed and built by Laister Sailplanes and first flown 1983.

CLÉMENT-BAYARD • France

Adolphe Clément-Bayard, former bicycle and car manufacturer, became interested in aeronautics in 1908 and was known primarily as a producer of airships and, in more minor capacity, of aero engines and aircraft. Was pioneer of welded steel tube airframe construction. Built and engined small number of Santos-Dumont Demoiselles 1909-1910. Gnome-engined Clément-Bayard two-seat monoplane set world distance record of 255 miles (410 km) February 1913. Same year other Gnome-engined civil/military monoplanes appeared; also three-seat monoplane. At Olympia Aero Show, London, March 1914, exhibited an all-steel armoured monoplane. In 1928 sold his factory to Citroën.

CLUTTON, ERIC • USA

When living in UK, Eric Clutton designed FRED (Flying Runabout Experimental Design), first flown 1963. Has been offered in Mk I, II and III versions, and plans remain available.

CLYDE ENGINEERING COMPANY LTD. • Australia

Contracted in 1939-1940 to build wing units for Avro Anson twin-engined trainers and assemble Ansons in Australia for Commonwealth Air Training Plan. Merged early 1948 with Fairey Aviation Company Ltd. of UK (q.v.), becoming Fairey Clyde Aviation Company Pty. Ltd. carrying out repair/overhaul of Fairey Firefly and Hawker Sea Fury aircraft for Royal Australian Navy. Renamed Fairey Aviation Company of Australia Pty Ltd (q.v.) in November 1951.

CMASA • Italy

Costruzioni Meccaniche Aeronàutiche SA; previously SA Industrie Aeromarittime Gallinari (q.v.); established 1922 at Marina di Pisa as Società di Costruzioni di Pisa (q.v.) to licence-build Dornier Wal flying-boats. Title CMASA adopted in 1930; became subsidiary of Fiat (q.v.) same year. Production included G.8 two-seat aerobatic training/touring biplane (1934); M.F.4 radial-engined flying-

Top and above: Colemill Enterprises converts Beech, Cessna and Piper aircraft to improve performance

Nacional de Navegaçao Costiera (CNNC, q.v.) around 1941. Produced Muniz M-11 two-seat primary trainer, designated HL-1, with strong resemblance to Piper Cub; batch of 50 HL-6 tandem two-seat low-wing monoplane trainers was begun 1943. Other designs included HL-2 and HL-4. In 1947, improved Series B versions of the HL-1 and HL-6 appeared; the company's activities had ceased by about 1950.

CNNC • Brazil

Companhia Nacional de Navegaçao Costiera, founded at Ilha do Viana, Rio de Janeiro, in late 1930s to manufacture Muniz-designed M-7 and M-9 biplane trainers; basically an Army aircraft workshop. In early 1940s renamed Fábrica Brasileira de Avioes (q.v.); see also Muniz.

CNT • Italy

See Cantiere Navale Triestino.

COBELAVIA • Belgium

Compagnie Belge d'Aviation in the mid-1960s built Nipper single-seat ultralight aircraft at Kortessem. Nipper Aircraft (q.v.) took over sole manufacturing rights of this aircraft in June 1966.

COCKSHUTT MOULDED AIRCRAFT LTD • Canada

Subsidiary of Cockshutt Plow Company, which produced parts for Canadian Ansons in 1940, was formed summer 1942 to manufacture moulded plywood fuselage components for Anson Mks V and VI built in Canada by Federal Aircraft Ltd. (q.v.). Work began late 1942, aircraft delivered between March 1943 and December 1944. Later built fuselages of D. H. Mosquito B Mk 25 for de Havilland Canada (q.v.).

CODOCK • Australia

Cockatoo Dockyard & Engineering Co Ltd. opened an experimental aviation department in the early 1930s, under the guidance of Wg Cdr. L. J. Wackett, formerly in the RAAF. In 1933 designed and built a twin-engined monoplane, the Codock, for Sir Charles Kingsford-Smith, who had made the first Pacific air crossing in 1928. A six-seat monoplane of the cantilever-wing Fokker type, it was powered by two 165 hp Napier Javelin engines.

COLGATE AIRCRAFT • USA

Colgate-Larsen Aircraft Corporation succeeded Spencer-Larsen Aircraft Corporation (q.v.) around 1940, continuing its work at Amityville, Long Island, NY, on novel-design small four-seat amphibian flying-boat, the CL-15 (formerly SL-15). From 1941 engaged on subcontract work for other

boat (1933); M.F.5 (development of Wal); M.F.6 two-seat fighter/reconnaissance floatplane; M.F.10 two-seat fighter/reconnaissance shipborne flying-boat (1935); BGA twin-engined floatplane/bomber (1936); and twin-engined, twin-float R.S.14 reconnaissance seaplane. The latter was the most successful, serving throughout Second World War. Assisted also in production of Fiat fighters in late 1930s/early 1940s. Activities suspended on Italian Armistice (September 1943). The C.S. high-speed monoplane and J.S.54 six-engined civil flying-boat were then under development, but never produced.

CMC • UK

See Chichester-Miles Consultants Ltd.

CNA • Italy

Compagnia Nazionale Aeronàutica, founded in 1920 at Cerveteri Aerodrome, Rome, moving to CNA-owned Littorio civil airport (Rome), eventually becoming a member of Caproni group (q.v.). Mainly a licence builder of others' designs, but in mid/late 1930s own products included C.N.A.15 low-wing and C.N.A.25 high-wing four-seat cabin monoplanes (both CNA-engined). During 1939-1940 said to have produced PM1 two-seat high-wing monoplane with flat-four engine.

CNNA • Brazil

Companhia Nacional de Navegaçao Aérea, took over manufacture of Muniz-designed aircraft from Companhia

Colomban CriCris at Rennes in 1985

military aircraft building programmes, especially after US entry into Second World War.

COLLIER AIRCRAFT CORPORATION • USA

Formed by W. S. Collier in 1939 to build CA-1 Ambassador two-seat light trainer biplane.

COLLINS AERO • USA

Markets plans to build Dipper Amphibian two-seat amphibian of metal and glassfibre construction (first flown 1982).

COLOMBAN, MICHEL • France

Has sold hundreds of sets of plans to build the very unusual CriCri single-seat aerobatic monoplane powered by two 15 hp engines. Also offers plans and some components for the MC-100 Banbi two-seat monoplane (see Dyn'Aero).

COLOMBES, ATELIERS AÉRONAUTIQUES • France

Amiot (SECM) company after nationalisation; AAC came under control of Junkers (q.v.) during the occupation of France in Second World War and began producing Junkers Ju 52/3m transports for the Luftwaffe. After the war continued building these aircraft under French government contract, designated AAC-1 Toucan. More than 400 produced; when order was completed, factory taken over by Aérocentre-SNCA du Centre (q.v.).

COLONIAL AIRCRAFT CORPORATION • USA

David B. Thurston and four other designers founded this company in 1946 to produce the C-1 Skimmer two/three-seat single-engined amphibian. First flown 17 July 1948, certificated 1955, but first major model produced in 1957 (four-seat C-2 Skimmer IV). Manufacturing rights sold October 1959 to Lake Aircraft Corporation (after 1962 the Lake Aircraft Division of Consolidated Aeronautics Inc, q.v.). See also Lake Aircraft.

COLUMBIA AIRCRAFT CORPORATION • USA

During 1928-1929 produced the Triad high-wing wheel/float amphibian at Valley Stream, Long Island, NY, at which time the company was known as Columbia Air liners Inc. Name changed to above and later built 330 Grumman J2F-6 Ducks for the USN. Two Grumman-designed XJL-1 (Duck replacement) prototypes were built. The company was taken over in early 1946 as part of the Commonwealth Aircraft Corporation (q.v.); it went into liquidation in 1948.

Above: Grumman Duck amphibian, built by Columbia as J2F-6 and ordered after Pearl Harbor attack

Below: Colonial Skimmer amphibian flying-boat

COMMANDER AIRCRAFT COMPANY • USA

Formed 1988, after acquiring rights to Rockwell Commander 112 and 114 from Gulfstream Aerospace Corporation (q.v.). First flew in May 1992 new four-seat Commander 114B version, since followed in 1994 by 114TC turbocharged version. Commander 114AT is advanced trainer.

COMMONWEALTH AIRCRAFT CORPORATION PTY. LTD. • Australia

Established Port Melbourne, 1936, as basis of an independent Australian industry. Took over Tugan Aircraft (q.v.) that year and chief designer Wg Cdr L. J. Wackett. First product was North American NA-33, built under licence as CA-1 to CA-16 Wirraway for RAAF, starting in July 1939. Followed by Wackett-designed prototype CA-2 Wackett two-seat trainer, production version designated CA-6. Company also produced the only Australian-designed fighter to serve in Second World War, the CA-12, 13, 14, 19 Boomerang.

Post-war products included the prototype CA-22 and production CA-25 Winjeel trainer for the RAAF, the CA-28 Ceres agricultural aircraft and over 200 North American Mustangs built as CA-17 and 18. First jet aircraft were North American F-86F Sabres, licence-built and modified to use the Rolls-Royce Avon turbojet, thought by many to be the best Sabre variant. Recently CAC has participated with Government Aircraft Factories (q.v.) in licence-production of Dassault Mirage III-0 (CA-29) and III-D, as well as Aermacchi M.B. 326H jet trainers. Became a public company in

1975 and contracted to build 56 Bell 206B JetRanger II helicopters for Australian Army, all delivered by early January 1978. Other contracts included work for Boeing, Sikorsky, Pratt & Whitney and Hawker Siddeley (q.v.). Finally specialised in the manufacture and repair of gas turbine engines. Became part of Hawker de Havilland 1985.

COMMONWEALTH AIRCRAFT INC. • USA

Formed in Kansas City October 1942, after the acquisition of Rearwin Aircraft & Engines Inc. (q.v.) by New York

Right: Commonwealth Wackett two-seat trainer

Below: Australia's nationally-designed Boomerang fighter

interests. In 1943 it received substantial orders for Waco CG-3A and -4A troop-carrying gliders for the USAAF. It obtained manufacturing rights in 1945 for the Trimmer three-seat twin-engined light amphibian (prototype only), formerly built by Allied Aviation (q.v.). In 1946 Commonwealth Aircraft Inc. began producing Model 185, a development of the pre-war Rearwin Model 175. Early that year the company took over the Columbia Aircraft Corporation (q.v.), all manufacturing being transferred to the latter's Valley Stream factory. In March 1946 it acquired a non-aircraft company at Port Washington as a manufacturing

base for the Trimmer, which did not go into series production. The Skyranger model was built in small numbers in 1946-1948.

COMMUTER AIRCRAFT CORPORATION • USA

Founded to develop 60-seat four-turboprop CAC-100 airliner.

COMPAGNIE BELGE D'AVIATION • Belgium

See COBELAVIA.

COMPANHIA NACIONAL DE AVIÕES LTDA • Brazil

See CONAL.

COMPER AIRCRAFT CO LTD. • UK

The company was formed at Hooton Park, Cheshire, on 14 March 1929 by Flt Lt Nicholas Comper and others. Formerly with Airco, Comper had also been responsible for the Cranwell Light Aeroplane Club series of amateur-built lightplanes, the C.L.A. 2, 3 and 4A. The company's first product was the C.L.A. 7 Swift, a single-seat high-wing sporting aircraft, which was first flown in spring 1930 and built between 1930 and 1934 (one was owned by the Prince of Wales, later Edward VIII). The company moved to Heston, Middlesex, in 1933; the one-off three-seat Mouse and single-seat Streak monoplanes were built in that year, followed by a single Kite two-seat tourer developed from the Streak. In 1934 the company closed, to re-register as Heston Aircraft Company (q.v.).

COMPOSITE AIRCRAFT CORPORATION • USA

Founded 1978 to continue production of Windecker Eagle four-seat monoplane, but suffered financial difficulties. Armed counterinsurgency version proposed as Eagle TC.

COMPOSITE AIRCRAFT DESIGN INC. • USA

Markets kits to construct CADI 2001 four-seat monoplane.

COMPOSITE AIRCRAFT INDUSTRIES • South Africa

Established 1986 to develop SE-86 eight-seat executive and multipurpose aircraft, with rear-mounted wings, canards and twin piston or turboprop engines.

COMTE • Switzerland

Flugzeugbau A. Comte built in early/middle 1920s a few German types (e.g. Sablatnig) under licence at Hargen, near Zürich. First own-design was AC-1 fighter prototype of 1927; followed by AC-3 twin-engined bomber. Best known for series of small high-wing cabin monoplanes such as three-seat AC-4 Gentleman, built 1928-1930.

Left: Licence-built Commonwealth Wirraway trainer

CONAIR AVIATION LTD. • Canada

Specialises in converting a wide range of aeroplanes for aerial spraying and discharge, principally for firefighting roles but also for insect and pollution control. Has developed the Helitanker tank for helicopters.

CONAL • Brazil

The name stands for Companhia Nacional de Avioes Ltda. A prototype five-seat high-wing cabin monoplane Conal W 151 Sopocaba was designed and flown in August 1964, but none was produced. The company was licensed for

Prototype of the Conal W-151 cabin monoplane

Comper C.L.A.7 Swift single-seat sports aircraft

Concorde, in 1999 still the world's only commercial supersonic airliner in service

conversions of the Dumod I and Dumod Liner made by the American Dumod Corporation (q.v.), but apparently none was built.

Right: Conroy Airlift, an outsize Canadair CL-44

CONCORDE • International

Anglo-French supersonic transport developed following 29 November 1962 agreements between French and British governments and aircraft/aero-engine companies. Airframe manufacturers BAC and Aérospatiale (both q.v.); engine contractors are Rolls-Royce and SNECMA. Production authorised of two prototype (first flown 2 March 1969), two pre-series and 16 production aircraft (first flown 6 December 1973).

CONROY AIRCRAFT CORPORATION • USA

Formed 1968-1969 by Jack M. Conroy at Santa Barbara airport, California, offering aircraft and services for the petroleum and other 'bulk' cargo industries. First ventures included turboprop conversions of Douglas DC-3 (Conroy Turbo Three) and Fairchild C-119 Flying Boxcar. Conroy developed original Guppy series of giant transports

Right: Conroy Turbo Albatross, a conversion of Grumman's amphibian

Conroy Aircraft Corporation CL-44-O with new upper fuselage of greatly increased volume, as once used by HeavyLift Cargo Airlines

Above: Consolidated PBY Catalina patrol flying-boat

Left: Consolidated PB2Y-3 Coronado flying-boat

CONSOLIDATED VULTEE AIRCRAFT CORPORATION • USA

Amalgamation from 17 March 1943 of Consolidated Aircraft Corporation and Vultee Aircraft Inc., whose wartime production programmes are listed under these separate headings. By the end of Second World War Consolidated Vultee was largest aircraft manufacturing organisation in the USA, with factories at San Diego and Vultee Field, California; Fort Worth, Texas; Nashville, Tennessee; Wayne, Michigan; New Orleans, Louisiana; Miami, Florida; and Allentown, Pennsylvania; plus modification centres at Tucson, Arizona; Elizabeth City, North Carolina; and Louisville, Kentucky.

Late-war/early post-war programmes included B-32 Dominator long-range bomber, L-13 liaison/observation aircraft and multi-engined B-36 intercontinental bomber. The company entered the commercial field with first flight, in summer 1946, of twin-engined Model 110, from which later stemmed well-known 240/340/440 Metropolitan series of medium-sized shorthaul airliners. Various noteworthy military prototypes included the XB-46 jet bomber, XP-81 single-seat mixed-power escort fighter, XF-92 rocket-powered interceptor, XA-41 close-support aircraft and XF2Y Sea Dart hydro-ski fighter. A small number of R3Y Tradewind four-engined transport flying-boats were built for the US Navy. In the early 1950s Consolidated Vultee began calling its products 'Convair' types, and on 30 April 1954 it became the Convair Division of General Dynamics Corporation (q.v.), which was then the major shareholder.

(see Aero Spacelines); also converted Canadair CL-44D-4 swing-tailed, long-range freighter as Conroy CL-44-0, with enlarged-diameter fuselage (flown November 1969); and Stolifter (flown 1969) single-turboprop conversion of Cessna Super Skymaster, with upward-opening aft fuselage. Turboprop conversion of Grumman Albatross amphibian flown February 1970; company ceased trading shortly afterwards.

CONSOLIDATED AERONAUTICS INC. • USA

Parent company after 1962 of Lake Aircraft (q.v.), producer of LA-4-200 Buccaneer four-seat amphibian.

CONSOLIDATED AIRCRAFT CORPORATION • USA

Original factory was quickly outgrown by the company formed 29 May 1923 and moved to Buffalo, NY, in 1924, leasing part of a wartime Curtiss factory. In the 1920s and 1930s produced small numbers of civil types, but main output was military and between 1924-1932 included more than 770 PT-1/311 and NY primary training biplanes for the USAAC and Navy, plus a small batch of similar O-17s for observation duties. Thomas Morse Aircraft (q.v.) acquired 1929. In the 1930s Consolidated specialised in marine aircraft, P2Y twin-engined patrol flying-boats being built 1931-1933; followed by P-30 single-seat fighter monoplanes for the Army in 1933-1935.

In autumn 1935 company moved to San Diego, California, gaining a harbour for testing its maritime designs, which continued with the P3Y/PBY Catalina family. During a ten-year production life 2,400 Catalinas were built by Consolidated and hundreds more by other companies. Production of PB2Y Coronados began in 1939. In 1940 Hall Aluminium Co acquired. Company began a five-year programme of building more than 11,000 B-24/C-87/PB4Y/RY Liberator and Privateer bomber, transport and patrol aircraft for the US Services and the RAF. Liberator production was also undertaken by Ford, Douglas and North American (q.v.). Final wartime product was the TBY Sea Wolf. A 34 per cent controlling interest in Consolidated acquired December 1941 by Vultee Aircraft Inc. (q.v.), and management links from then led to merger of the two companies on 17 March 1943 as Consolidated Vultee Aircraft Corporation (see next entry).

CONSTRUCCIONES AERONAUTICAS SA • Spain

See CASA.

Below: Consolidated B-24 Liberator bomber/reconnaissance aircraft

CONTENDER AIRCRAFT INC. • USA

Founded to develop a series of pressurised business and commuter rear-winged turbojet aircraft, as twin-jet Contender 202 for seven to 19 passengers, triple-engined 11 to 19 passenger Contender 303, and triple-engined Contender 606 for up to 33 passengers in a widebody commuter layout.

CONTINENTAL AIRCRAFT CORPORATION • USA

Based at Amityville, Long Island, NY, in 1919; was then building KB-3T two-seat trainer biplane, designed by Vincent Burnelli and powered by Curtiss OX engine.

CONTINENTAL COPTERS INC. • USA

From 1959 produced assorted versions of the El Tomcat, specialised single-seat agricultural conversions of Bell Model 47 helicopter. Successive variants included Mks IIIA, IIIB, IIIC, V, V A, V-B, VI, VI-A and VI-B, of which many completed; also marketed kits for operator conversion. Developed JC-1 Jet Cat as special agricultural modification of Bell JetRanger. Also assembled Bell 47G series helicopters to order using spare and surplus components.

CONTINENTAL INC. • USA

With Robert E. Fulton Jr as President, company was formed 1945 at Danbury, Connecticut. Prototype Airphibian flew 7 November 1946, a two-seat 'roadable' aircraft, with tricycle landing gear, detachable wings/tail/rear fuselage. Certificated December 1950 as Fulton Model FA-2 Airphibian; production model, designated FA-3, appeared 1954.

Continental Copters E1 Tomcat Mk VI-B

CONVAIR • USA

Convair Division of General Dynamics Corporation; title adopted from 30 April 1954 by Consolidated Vultee (q.v.) following acquisition in 1953 of major shareholdings by General Dynamics. Major products have been the Convair F-102 Delta Dagger and F-106 Delta Dart interceptors, B-58 Hustler supersonic bomber and Convair 880 and 990 four-jet commercial transports. Developed subsequently F-111/FB-111 variable-geometry combat aircraft, now the responsibility of GD's Fort Worth Division (q.v.). Convair was grouped with GD's Fort Worth and Pomona Divisions in September 1970 to form the single Convair

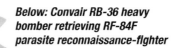

Below: Convair RB-36 heavy bomber retrieving RF-84F parasite reconnaissance-fighter

Below: Convair CV twin-engined short-range airliner

Above: Convair XFY-1 Pogo VTOL tail-sitter experimental fighter

Above: Convair B-58 Hustler supersonic bomber

Above: Convair F-102A Delta Dagger fighter-interceptors

Convair 580 still used in 1990s as parcel freighter

Aerospace Division, but Fort Worth was again made a separate division in June 1974. Convair Division at San Diego became responsible for commercial aircraft and space exploration systems, product support for Convair 240/340/440 and derivatives and the Convair 880/990. It also built major components for McDonnell Douglas DC-10, Space Shuttle Orbiter vehicle and Tomahawk cruise missile.

COOK AIRCRAFT CORPORATION • USA

Founded by John A. Cook in 1968 at Torrance, California, to market JC-1 Challenger four-seat cabin monoplane. Two prototypes built (first flight May 1969). Third prototype flew November 1971, but crashed January 1972, killing Cook. Company continued, hoping for certification with a fourth (modified) aircraft, first flown 1972, but activities ceased in mid-1970s.

CORNELIUS AIRCRAFT CORPORATION • USA

Based at Dayton, Ohio; received order for one XBG-3 glider bomb in 1942, but project was cancelled. In 1944 two prototypes of XFG-1 were built, a fuel-carrying piloted glider to be towed behind long-range bombers and cut adrift when empty. Again, idea not adopted operationally by USAAF.

COSMIC AIRCRAFT CORPORATION • USA

In May 1970 acquired all rights in manufacture of F-23 single-seat agricultural monoplane, produced previously by D. D. Funk Aviation Company Inc. (q.v.). Two models: F-23A (Continental radial) and F-23B (Jabobs radial). Production ceased 1975.

COSMOS • USA

Manufactures in assembled and kit forms a large range of single- and two-seat microlights with Rogallo wings and open trikes.

COSTRUÇOES AERONAUTICAS SA • Brazil

Originated May 1940 as government-backed private company under French designer René Couzinet (q.v.), at Lagoa Santa, Minas Gerais, to build civil and military aircraft. First licence was for North American NA-16 (AT-6 Texan) advanced trainer, but none produced.

COSTRUZIONI AERONAUTICHE TECNAM SRL • Italy

Formed 1986 as a member of the Associazione Italiana Costruttori Aerodine da Diporto e Sportive. Constructs the P92 Echo two-seat braced high-wing ultralight (first flown 1993 and also available in kit form), and the P96 Golf two-seat low-wing ultralight (first flown 1997). In addition,

Technam P92 Echo two-seat ultralight

manufactures components for A 109 and EH 101 helicopters, and ATR and Boeing airliners.

COSY EUROPE • Germany

Markets plans and kits to construct the mostly composites-built Cozy Classic, a two/three-seat pusher-engined canard monoplane; bought rights for Cosy from Nathan Puffer of USA in 1987, original Cosy having flown in 1982 (see Co-Z).

COURIER MONOPLANE COMPANY • USA

Formed 20 December 1928, produced a braced high-wing monoplane powered by a 100 hp Kinner radial engine.

COUZINET • France

Distinguished French engineer, René Couzinet, began manufacturing aeroplanes in 1928 with the stylish tri-motor monoplane Couzinet 10 Arc-en-Ciel prototype, designed for transatlantic flight. It was destroyed by fire, but the Couzinet 70, developed from the Couzinet 30, was also called Arc-en-Ciel and intended for Aéropostale's transatlantic mail service to South America. After route-proving flight by Jean Mermoz in January 1933 it was extensively modified as Couzinet 71 and entered regular service in May 1934. Air Couzinet 10 of 1937 was totally unrelated twin-engined monoplane. Couzinet himself went to Brazil in the late 1930s, assisting with the development of that country's aviation industry.

COVENTRY ORDNANCE WORKS LTD. • UK

Established at Coventry 1911, absorbing former Warwick Wright company (q.v.) and inheriting two excellent designers, Howard T. Wright and W. O. Manning, who designed a biplane of which two were built at Battersea and test-flown at Brooklands as entries for RFC Military trials of August 1912, one with Gnome engine and other with Chenu engine. Neither did very well, though Gnome engined aircraft later flew successfully at Brooklands after modification. No further original designs before First World War. During the conflict C.O.W. acted mainly as subcontractor on Royal Aircraft Factory aircraft, including B.E.2 and B.E.8 series, B.E.12/12a, R.E.7 and R.E.8. Also built Sopwith Snipe single-seat fighters. Aircraft department closed 1919.

Basically acknowledged, however, as armaments firm (e.g. warship gun installations), and developed rapid-firing aircraft gun (1 lb shell) intended for Royal Aircraft Factory F.E.4 fighter/bomber and projected Airco (de Havilland) D.H.8.. A 37 mm development was later mounted in Vickers and Westland F.9/27 fighter prototypes, but its weight prohibited its acceptance for fighters.

COX AIR RESOURCES LTD. • Canada

Offered turboprop conversion of de Havilland Canada DHC-3 Otter 1978.

COX-KLEMEN AIRCRAFT CORPORATION • USA

Based at College Point, Long Island, NY; supplied three TW-2 tandem two-seat biplane trainers for USAAS in 1922.

Followed 1923-25 by six examples for USN of XN-1/XS-2 experimental twin-float scout Seaplanes intended for carriage aboard submarines. Also produced two XA-1 prototype ambulance aircraft for US Army.

CO-Z DEVELOPMENT CORPORATION • USA

Markets plans and components to construct the Cozy Mark III and higher-powered Mk IV four-seat canard monoplanes of composite construction, developed from Nathan Puffer's side-by-side two-seat Cosy Classic, which itself was developed from the Rutan Long-EZ (see Cosy Europe).

CPCA SA • Romania

Centrul de Projiectare Si Consulting Pentru Aviatie SA or Aviation Design and Consulting Center. Established 1991. First flew ADC-XO two-seat ultralight 1997 and DK-10 Dracula two-seat lightplane 1998. ADC-H1 two-seat light piston-engined helicopter expected to fly 1999.

CRAFT AEROTECH • USA

Has offered plans and kits to build the Craft Aerotech 200 two-seat and twin-engined rotorcraft, and the 200 FW two-seat high-wing monoplane.

CRAWFORD ALL-METAL AIRPLANE COMPANY • USA

Established in 1928 at Los Angeles, California, built all-metal aircraft to special order. Production included a six-seat cabin monoplane, designated Crawford 65, which had corrugated alclad sheet covering for the fuselage, wing and tail surfaces, pioneered by Hugo Junkers in Germany.

CROPLEASE PLC • UK

Established 1989 to manage former The Norman Aeroplane Company (q.v.) Fieldmaster programme and take over activities of Croplease Ltd. Firemaster fire-fighting

variant also tested. Rights sold to EPA Aircraft Company Ltd. (q.v.) 1992.

CROPMASTER AIRCRAFT PTY. LTD. • Australia

Amalgamation of Yeoman Aircraft Pty. Ltd. (q.v.) and Yeoman Aviation Pty. Ltd. which, in 1959, began building prototype Yeoman YA1, first flown January 1960. This one/two-seat agricultural low-wing monoplane started production in 1964 as YA1 Cropmaster. A projected tricycle-landing-gear YA5 Fieldmaster was not built, and in 1967 production rights in the YA1 were sold to the Cameron-Gray Aircraft Company of the USA.

CROSBY AVIATION CORPORATION LTD. • UK

At Knutsford, Cheshire, Crosby began producing (around 1974) factory-built versions of the Andreasson (q.v.) BA-4B single-seat homebuilt biplane; also marketed plans and kits.

CROSES • France

Avions Croses produced one of the original and practical modern microlights in 1961 as the EC-3 Pouplume, with pivoting forward wing and fixed rear wing as a Pou-du-Ciel type; still available for home construction via plans. First flew in 1965 the two-seat tandem-wing EC-6 Criquet, available as plans, with concept developed also into three-seat EC-8 Tourisme and six-seat EC-9 Paras Cargo.

CROSLEY AIRCRAFT CO • USA

Established in 1929 at Cincinnati, Ohio, this company was a subsidiary of the Crosley Radio Corporation. It produced two- and three-seat open-cockpit high-wing monoplanes known respectively as the Crosley C-1 and C-2. These two models pioneered the advantages of interchangeability, the complete wing, tail surfaces, landing gear, engines and engine mountings being common to both.

CROWN AIRCRAFT CORPORATION • USA

Originally the Aircraft Division of Crown Motor Carriage Company. Produced to direct order in 1930 the B-3 Custombuilt two-seat sporting/training biplane.

CRUSADER AIRCRAFT CORPORATION • USA

Between 1933-1934 built Crusader AF-4 four-seat cabin monoplane with two Menasco in-line engines and twin-booms carrying twin tail.

CSIR • South Africa

Council for Scientific and Industrial Research developed SARA II (first flown 1972) and SARA III light autogyros.

CTA • Brazil

Centro Técnico de Aeronáutica, established at Sao José dos Campos as aeronautical research centre in late 1950s by Brazilian Air Ministry; CTA originally had two divisions. A group within the IPD (Research and Development Division), Departamento de Aeronaves (q.v.) or PAR, was responsible for the BF-1 Beija-Flir (Humming Bird) two-seat helicopter, first to be designed, built and flown in Brazil.

CTA • Brazil

Centro Técnico Aerospacial developed re-engining programme for Paulistinha lightplane, with IMAER TM 2000 EM1 piston engine, as Paulistinha 65.

CUB AIRCRAFT COMPANY LTD. • Denmark

Created late 1930s at Lundtofte as Scandinavian assembly factory for US Piper Cub light aircraft; doubtful if any were built.

CUB AIRCRAFT CORPORATION LTD • Canada

Established 1937 at Hamilton, Ontario, to build American Piper Cubs. Early 1931 obtained licence to build Harlow PJC-2 all-metal monoplane. New factory at Hamilton was completed 1940. Production resumed in 1945 of Canadian variant known as Cub Prospector; company does not appear to have survived for more than a year or so after this.

CUBITT LTD. • UK

First World War subcontractor for production at Croydon, Surrey, of Airco D.H.9 day bomber.

CULP SPECIALITIES • USA

Sells plans and kits to build the Special two-seat biplane, designed to represent a 1930's type.

Culver Cadet two-seat cabin monoplane

Cunliffe-Owen Concordia medium-range transport

CULVER AIRCRAFT CORPORATION • USA

Formed at Columbus, Ohio, in 1939 by K. K. Culver. Took over manufacturing and sales rights of Dart Model G two-seat low-wing cabin monoplane from Dart Manufacturing Corporation (q.v.) same year. First own product, the Cadet, was a two-seat light cabin monoplane (Continental flat-four engine). In 1940-1941 developed two-seat Models LFA and LCA tourer, based on the Cadet, but with retractable landing-gear. Production ceased when America entered Second World War, company then doing sub-contract work for US aircraft industry. Moved to Wichita, Kansas, 1941, and concentrated entirely on producing radio-controlled pilotless aircraft based on LFA (nearly 2,400 produced) for use as PQ-8/TDC and PQ-14/TD2C gunnery target drones with USAAF and USN. When this ended in 1946, Culver began developing the Model V civil lightplane, first flown September 1945. Four built as drones designated XPQ-15. Company went bankrupt in late 1946; remaining assets acquired mid-1956 by Superior Aircraft Company (q.v.).

CUNARD STEAMSHIP COMPANY • UK

Cunard built factory at Aintree late 1917/early 1918 after receiving contract on 22 November 1917 to build 500 Bristol Fighters. Production began March 1918, although in the previous month factory had been taken over by Ministry of Munitions and renamed National Aircraft Factory No 3 (q.v.). Production ended after only 126 aircraft completed.

CUNLIFFE-OWEN AIRCRAFT LTD. • UK

Company founded 1938 at Southampton Municipal Airport, Eastleigh, Hampshire, to build 'flying wing' (lifting-fuselage) aircraft based on Burnelli (q.v.) concept. First product was improved version of Burnelli UB-14 known as O.A.1 (two crew, 15 passengers). Second version (three crew, 20 passengers) designed as O.A.2, but not produced owing to outbreak of war. France acquired O.A.1 and used it in Africa during the war. Extensive subcontract work for Air Ministry undertaken, mostly 'anglicising' US Consolidated Vultee, Lockheed and Martin Lend-Lease aircraft for RAF. Late 1945 converted a number of Lancaster B.III bombers for air/sea rescue. In 1946 began design of airliner, the Concordia 10-seat passenger transport, first flown May 1947. Prototype and one other built, but work suspended November 1947 owing to insufficient orders. Also built that year the prototype W.10 helicopter for Cierva (q.v.); this project shelved too, and shortly afterwards company abandoned its aviation interests.

CUNNINGHAM-HALL AIRCRAFT CORPORATION • USA

Randolph F. Hall, with other ex-employees of Thomas-Morse Aircraft Corporation (q.v.), formed this company at Rochester, NY, in 1928, in collaboration with the US automobile company James Cunningham, Son & Co. First aircraft was a six-seat passenger transport (twin-engined PT-6), but only two built. Followed by Model X-90(N) tandem two-seat biplane with special high-lift wings, entered for 1929 Guggenheim Safe Airplane Competition. A developed version (also high-lift wings) led to GA-21M all-metal monoplane in 1934, which reappeared after a year or so as GA-36 with Super Scarab engine. In 1937 built PT-6F biplane light freighter, a two-seat development of PT-6 with 1,128 lb (512 kg) payload and Wright Whirlwind engine. Company ceased building complete aircraft and produced subcontract aircraft components for other firms during Second World War. It was dissolved in 1948.

CURTISS AEROPLANE AND MOTOR COMPANY • USA

Created January 1916 from former (though separate) Curtiss Aeroplane Company (Hammondsport, NY) and Curtiss Motor Company, opening new aircraft factory at Buffalo, NY. A third factory (Garden City, Long Island, NY) became boat hull department for flying-boat production. Burgess Company of Marblehead, Massachusetts, became a subsidiary in February 1916. Aircraft built during First World War included A and AH biplanes for USN, Models D and E for US Army, Model F flying-boats for USN, H-4 Small Americas, H-12 Large Americas and H-16 Large Americas (plus 150 by Naval Aircraft Factory, q.v.).

Best-known were JN-4/JN-6 'Jenny' trainers (5,000 built, plus 1,200 by Canadian Curtiss), HS flying-boats, MF flying-boats, N-9 floatplanes, British S.E.5a fighters, Orenco D fighters and 5L flying-boats. Total wartime was 4,014 aircraft and 750 aero engines.

Post-war production, mostly in 1920s, included NC-1/2/3/4 transatlantic flying-boats (four only); Oriole, Eagle and Seagull civil types (little success achieved with the few built). Followed by a series of Army (R-6/R-8 etc.) and Navy (CR/R2C/R3C etc.) racers. Twelve B-2 Condor biplane bombers were followed by PW-8 biplane fighters, P-1/P-6 US Army Hawks, F6C US Navy Hawks and O-1/11/39 and A-3 Falcons for US Army. The few Carrier Pigeons and Larks were followed by one Tanager biplane, which won 1929 Guggenheim Safe Airplane Competition. Subsequently produced N2C Fledgling, F8C/OC Falcon and F8C/O2C Helldivers for USN. Foundation of Curtiss-Robertson division (q.v.) in 1928 was followed by a merger with Wright Aeronautical Corporation (q.v.) on 9 August 1929 to create Curtiss-Wright Corporation (q.v.).

Curtiss JN-4 'Jenny' historic and well-loved US trainer

Above: Curtiss NC-4, the first aircraft to make a North Atlantic crossing (in stages)

Above: Curtiss SB2C Helldivers, carrier-based scout-bombers

CURTISS-REID AIRCRAFT COMPANY • Canada

Founded in Montreal in January 1929 by a merger of the Reid Aircraft Company (founded 1928) and the Curtiss Aeroplane & Motor Co of New York. W. T. Reid, formerly chief designer of Bristol Aeroplane Company (q.v.), had founded Reid Aircraft to build a light biplane of his own design. This was produced by the new company as the Curtiss-Reid Rambler, powered by a licence-built Cirrus engine, and at least six of these aircraft were supplied to the RCAF. Opened flying school in 1930. Built also the Courier, a single-seat lightweight mail-carrying monoplane.

CURTISS-ROBERTSON AIRPLANE MANUFACTURING CORPORATION • USA

Founded at St Louis, Missouri, in 1928 as division of Curtiss-Wright Corporation (q.v.) with William B. Robertson as President. Main products were Robin three-seat high-wing cabin monoplane (noted for its endurance records) and Kingbird seven-passenger development with twin engines. Neither was produced on a large scale.

CURTISS-WRIGHT CORPORATION, AIRPLANE DIVISION • USA

Formed from merger on 9 August 1929 between Curtiss Aeroplane and Motor Co Inc.and Wright Aeronautical Corporation (both q.v.). Subsequent production mainly by Curtiss Airplane Division of Curtiss-Wright (aircraft still being 'Curtiss' types rather than 'Curtiss-Wright', except for those with 'CW' designations. Travel Air (q.v.) became another subsidiary in 1930. In 1936 complete reorganisation dissolved all main subsidiaries except Wright Aeronautical Division. From 1930 onwards main products included F9C Sparrowhawk fighter, carried on board USN airships; F11C/BFC Goshawk for USN and export versions Hawk I/II/III/IV; SBC Helldivers for USN; SOC Seagull for USN; BT-32/CT-32/T-32 Condor bomber and civil/military transport; A-8/10/12 Shrike for USAAC; P-36 for USAAC and export Hawk 75s; one CW-20 prototype (later used by BOAC); C-46 Commando (USAAF) and R5C (USN) transport developments of CW-20; CW-21 Demon fighters; SNC trainers for USN, developed from CW-21; P-40 Warhawk/Tomahawk/Kittyhawk fighters for USAAF and other Allied services, of which 13,738 built during Second World War; C-76 Caravan transports for USAAF; 0-52 Owl observation biplanes for USAAF/USN; S03C Seamew for USN and Fleet Air Arm; SB2C Helldiver; AT-9 Jeep twin-engined trainers for USAAF; SC Seahawk scout seaplanes for USN; Republic P-47 Thunderbolt fighters for USAAF. Total wartime production (1940-1945) was 26,755 aircraft and 223,036 aero engines.

Curtiss P-40 Warhawk, the last of the Curtiss Hawk series

Curtiss-Wright X-19A VTOL research aircraft

After the war many Curtiss factories closed and most aircraft construction discontinued. Some Boeing B-29 modification undertaken until end of 1945, but Curtiss-Wright basically then undertook overhaul and repair of aircraft and manufacture of components, subassemblies and spare parts. By 1952 was concerned exclusively with production of aero engines and propellers. At the end of the 1950s Curtiss-Wright made a brief return to aircraft production with Skydart rocket-propelled target drone and prototype VZ-7AP VTOL 'flying Jeep' for Army trials. Last type produced by the company was the X-19A, a six-seat convertiplane with twin engines driving tandem pairs of tilting propeller/rotors; first flight 26 June 1964, but development discontinued 1966. By 1970s main activities of the corporation included nuclear research, data transmission and research into new advanced engine designs for USAF and NASA, although still made components for Boeing 747 airliners.

CUSTER CHANNEL WING CORPORATION • USA

Set up during early 1950s to develop 'channelwing' concept devised by its President, Willard R. Custer. (Wing contours formed semi-circular channel/duct in which two

pusher engines were suspended). Small-scale experimental aircraft with this configuration flown December 1951; another test aircraft flew shortly afterwards. Followed by Custer CCW-5 (flown July 1953), a modified Baumann Brigadier (built by that company; q.v.) with a channel wing and two Continental engines, and expected to take off in a few feet, rise vertically, hover and land vertically. First production model flew June 1964. Custer

Custer CCW-5 research aircraft

Above: Curtiss-Wright C-46 Commando in Vietnam in 1973, with International Commission for Control and Supervision markings (US Army)

retired early 1968, but remained as consultant throughout prolonged certification programme by DeVore Aviation Service Corporation. Despite its founder's efforts to keep the company solvent, Custer Channel Wing Corporation eventually closed through lack of funds.

CUSTOM FLIGHT COMPONENTS LTD. • Canada

Offers kits to build the Bright Star and North Star tandem two-seat cabin monoplanes, both representing Piper Super Cub layouts.

CVJETKOVIC, ANTON • USA

Offers plans to construct the single-seat CA-61 Mini-Ace and two-seat CA-65 Skyfly monoplanes.

CVV • Italy

Centro Volo a Vela, Politecnico di Milano, fundamentally a research and development centre attached to Milan Polytechnic after Second World War to study soaring flight. Production included gliders and sailplanes, but in the late 1940s/early 1950s the Centro Volo a Vela also produced prototypes of the P.110 three/four-seat cabin monoplane and P.M. 280 Tartuca single-seat low-wing monoplane.

C. W. AIRCRAFT • UK

Established 1936 by C. R. Chronander and J. I. Waddington to design and develop Cygnet two-seat all-metal cabin monoplane, which first flew in 1937. Rights in Cygnet acquired by General Aircraft Ltd. (q.v.) in 1938. C. W. was then re-formed as Chronander Waddington Aircraft Ltd., a company not concerned with the building of aircraft.

DAEWOO HEAVY INDUSTRIES LTD. • South Korea

Aerospace division founded 1984. Current programmes include development and production of the KTX-1 Woong-Bee turboprop trainer, work on F-16 construction and KTX-2 lead in fighter trainer/light combat aircraft programmes under Samsung leadership, component production for commercial transports, and helicopter and UAV programmes.

DAIMLER-BENZ AEROSPACE AG. • Germany

New name from 1995 for Deutsche Aerospace AG. which was founded in 1989 (q.v.). Regional Aircraft division administered by Dornier Luftfahrt (q.v.). In June 1996 Fairchild Aerospace purchased 80 per cent of Dornier Luftfahrt from Daimler-Benz Aerospace, forming Fairchild Dornier Germany Dornier Luftfahrt GmbH (q.v.). Daimler-Benz Aerospace became part of DaimlerChrysler Aerospace AG. in late 1998 (q.v.).

DAR-10F two-seat bomber, only Bulgarian combat aircraft in WW2

Dart Kitten II ultra-light single-seat sportsplane

DAIMLERCHRYSLER AEROSPACE AG. • International

Founded in November 1998 as the aerospace division of the DaimlerChrysler Group, following the merger of Daimler-Benz and Chrysler Corporation. Headquartered in München, civil aircraft business unit includes Daimler-Chrysler Aerospace Airbus, helicopter activities are via Eurocopter SA and Eurocopter Deutschland GmbH, the military aircraft business unit comprises DaimlerChrysler Aerospace AG. and Dornier Flugzeugwerft GmbH, while other business units include Aero Engines via MTU, Space Infrastructure, Satellites, and Defense and Civil Systems. Current programmes include the AT-2000 Mako role-flexible military aircraft.

DAIMLER COMPANY LTD. • UK

A motor car company founded 1897 in Coventry. Built under subcontract during First World War the RAF B.E.2c, B.E.12/12a, R.E.8, and Airco D.H.10. Proposed production of cannon-armed F.E.4 ground-attack aircraft cancelled.

DAIMLER MOTORENGESELLSCHAFT WERKE • Germany

Built Mercedes aero engines from 1910. Constructed Friedrichshafen FF, G III, G IV and other aircraft under licence during First World War. Designed and built G I/R four-engined Giant, 1916; L.8 single-seat fighter, 1918. L.9, L.11, L.14 parasol fighters followed. Ceased production at main works 1919.

DAIMLER-WERKE ATKIENGESELLSCHAFT • Germany

Continued operations when main Daimler works closed. Experimental motorglider developed into L.15 (1923) and L.20 (1924) under chief designer Dr Ing Hans Klemm. Odd parasol-wing twin-engined two-seater for 1925 Rundflug won class prize. In 1927 became Leichtflugzeugbau Klemm.

DARJAVNA AEROPLANNA RABOTILNITZA • Bulgaria

State Aircraft Works, Bojouristhe, Sofia. Aero department of Ministry of Railways, Posts and Telegraphs. Subject to Versailles limitations, but by 1932 had produced DAR-4, three engined transport for state airline. Of several subsequent designs, only the DAR-10F of 1941 reached production.

DARMSTADT AKADEMISCHE FLIEGERGRUPPE • Germany

Established in 1921 by students at the Technical High School, Darmstadt, for building and testing aircraft. Produced a number of sailplanes, and from 1924 a series of advanced light aircraft that held several class records. Work on powered aircraft ended 1939.

DARRACQ MOTOR ENGINEERING COMPANY • UK

Branch of French motor car company of Alexandre Darracq, based at Fulham, London. In First World War built Airco D.H.5, RAF F.E.8 and Sopwith Dolphin under subcontract.

DART AIRCRAFT LTD. • UK

Formed at Dunstable, Bedfordshire, in 1936 to build ultra-light single-seat aircraft to designs of A. R. Weyl. First were Dunstable Dart, later named Dart Pup, and Flittermouse, both with parasol wing and pusher propellers. Three Dart Kittens were built in UK, as well as one in Australia from plans. Ceased operations 1939.

DART MANUFACTURING COMPANY • USA

Formed 1937 at Columbus, Ohio, to manufacture Dart G two-seat light aircraft. This was a version of the aircraft

Dassault Atlantique 2 long-range maritime patrol aircraft (F. Robineau - Dassault/Aviaplans)

known originally as the Monosport, designed and built by the Mono Aircraft Corporation (q.v.). Taken over by Culver Aircraft Company (q.v.) of Columbus in 1939.

DASSAULT AVIATION • France

Name adopted in 1990 for former Avions Marcel Dassault-Breguet Aviation (q.v.). Current programmes include Atlantique 2, Mirage 2000, Rafale air-superiority and strike fighter for the French air force and Navy (first flown July 1986 and entering service circa year 2000), Falcon 50 series, Falcon 900 series and Falcon 2000 (first flown March 1993).

Dassault Super Extended Carrier-based fighter

Dassault Super Mystere single-seat fighter

Dassault Mirage III-R reconnaissance aircraft

Dassault Mystére-Falcon twin-turbofan executive transport

Above: Dassault Mirage 2000 D two-seat all-weather deep penetration combat aircraft (Dassault/Aviaplans)

Left: Dassault Mirage 2000-5 of Armée de l'Air carrying four Mica and two Magic 2 missiles (F. Robineau - Dassault/Aviaplans)

Right: Dassault's latest combat aircraft is the Rafale, seen here in naval M 02 development aircraft form during carrier trials (F. Robineau - Dassault/Aviaplans)

Right: Alpha Jet 2, optimised for ground attack (E. Moreau)

Above: Falcon 50EX replaced Falcon 50 as Dassault's triple-turbofan transcontinental business jet, delivered to customers from 1997 (F. Robineau - Dassault/Aviaplans)

Dassault Falcon 900B triple-turbofan wide-body transatlantic business jet (Dassault Falcon Jet)

DASSAULT BELGIQUE AVIATION SA • Belgium

See SABCA.

DASSAULT-BREGUET • France

See Avions Marcel Dassault-Breguet Aviation.

DASSAULT-BREGUET/DORNIER • International

Following agreement between the French and German governments in 1969 to procure a new subsonic basic and advanced training aircraft, suitable for deployment also in a close-support or battlefield reconnaissance role, Dassault-Breguet and Dornier (both q.v.) developed Alpha Jet, with involvement also by SABCA (q.v.) in Belgium and other French and German companies. Powered by twin turbofan engines, Alpha Jet first flown in October 1973; production eventually totalled 504, the majority going to Armée de l'Air and Luftwaffe, but others to Belgium, Cameroon, Egypt (assembled by AOI), Ivory Coast, Morocco, Nigeria, Qatar and Togo. The final versions available were the Alpha Jet basic trainer, Alpha Jet 2 strike aircraft and Alpha Jet ATS advanced trainer with an advanced 'glass' cockpit, laser designation, ECM and more.

DASSAULT, MARCEL, GÉNÉRAL AÉRONAUTIQUE • France

Marcel Dassault designed under his original name, Marcel Bloch, (q.v.) before Second World War. As Avions Marcel Dassault built the MD 315 Flamant light transport for the Armée de l'Air in 1945. A highly successful line of fighters for France and export began with the Ouragan (1949); followed by swept-wing Mystére (1952). Afterburning Super-Mystère (1959) was first European supersonic production aircraft. Etendard naval fighter appeared 1958. Large family of aircraft included Mirage prototype (1956), Mirage III (1958), Mirage IV supersonic bomber (1959), Mirage V (1967), Mirage III/V VTOL strike fighter prototype (1965), F2 interceptor (1966) and G8 variable-geometry prototypes (1967), Mirage F1 (1966) and Milan (1969). Also produced Mercure airliner (1971) and successful executive Falcon 10 (1970) and 20 (1963) twin jets (originally called Mystère; US production called fan Jet Falcon). Involved in formation of Air-Fouga (Etablissements Fouga), 1956. Dassault acquired majority holding in Breguet Aviation (q.v.), becoming Avions Marcel Dassault-Breguet Aviation (q.v.) in December 1971.

Above: Dassault Mirage V with two 1,300 litre drop tanks

Left: Dassault Mercure 120/162-passenger airliner, taken in small numbers by Air Inter

Right: Dassault Mirage IV-P supersonic bomber, using JATO rockets to boost take-off performance (Avions Marcel Dassault Breguet Aviation)

MDC MAX DÄTWYLER AG. • Switzerland

Max Dätwyler & Co, based at Bleinbach-Leupenthal, produced in 1960 a glider-tug based on the Piper Super Cub, designated MDC-Trailer. Produced subsequently a modernised version of the Bücher Bü 131 Jungmann, known as the Lerche. First flew in 1983 the prototype MD-3 Swiss Trainer. See MDB Flugtechnik AG.

DAVIS AIRCRAFT CORPORATION • USA

Founded at Richmond, Indiana, by Walter C. Davis to take over Vulcan Aircraft Company (q.v.). Production of American Moth continued as Davis V-3, and the D-1 series of fast parasol-wing two-seaters began in 1929.

DAVIS AIRCRAFT CORPORATION • USA

Between 1958 and 1961 Leon D.Davis began development and production of the five-seater DA-1 light aircraft. Designed subsequently a number of light aircraft for construction by amateur enthusiasts.

DAVIS-DOUGLAS CORPORATION • USA

Formed in 1920 at Santa Monica, California, by Donald W. Douglas, with finance from Davis, to produce the first Douglas design, the 1921 Cloudster. Formerly chief engineer of the Glenn L. Martin Company (q.v.), Donald W. Douglas was to found the Douglas Aircraft Company (q.v.) in 1928.

DAYTONA AIRCRAFT CONSTRUCTION INC. • USA

Founded 1990 and bought rights to Jamieson D light aircraft.

DAYTON-WRIGHT AIRPLANE COMPANY • USA

Formed during First World War at Dayton, Ohio, for quantity aircraft production, with Orville Wright as consulting engineer. Built Liberty-engined DH-4 (the 'Liberty plane') and Standard J-1. In 1919 built a limousine version of DH-4, single-seat Messenger, and also a three-seater. In 1920 Milton C. Baumann designed the revolutionary RB Racer,

with solid all-wood wing, totally enclosed cockpit and retractable landing gear linked to rod-operated leading- and trailing-edge camber-changing flaps. Built the USB-1, an Engineering Division redesign of the Bristol Fighter; 1921 twin-engined seaplane; side-by-side two-seat TR-3 (last rotary-engined design for US Army) and single-wheel landing-gear TR-5. In 1922 built Douglas DF-2. In 1923 the parent company, General Motors, abandoned aviation and dissolved Dayton-Wright; aeronautical work of the company taken over by Consolidated Aeronautics Inc (q.v.).

DE CHEVIGNY, HUBERT • France

Hubert de Chevigny commissioned the Explorer amphibian design from Dean Wilson, to provide full living accommodation for five people and carry a vehicle or bulk freight loaded via a swing-open tail. First flown 1991.

Above: Davis-Douglas Cloudster, the first Douglas design, of 1921, with 313 kW (420 hp) Liberty engine

THE DEE HOWARD COMPANY • USA

Specialises in upgrading/modifying civil/commercial jets, recent programmes covering Boeing 727, Douglas DC-8 and Learjets. Has been a subsidiary of Alenia since 1989, after Italian company acquired majority shareholding.

DEEKAY AIRCRAFT CORPORATION LTD. • UK

Built the side-by-side two-seat Knight, designed by S. C. Hart-Still at Broxbourne in 1937. One completed; scrapped during war.

Left: Dayton-Wright K-T Cabin Cruiser three-seat tourer

Left: Dayton-Wright FP-2, designed for Canadian forest patrols

DE HAVILLAND INC. • Canada

See de Havilland of Canada Ltd.

DE HAVILLAND AIRCRAFT COMPANY LTD. • UK

Geoffrey de Havilland built his first (unsuccessful) aircraft in 1909. His second, flown in 1910, was bought by the War Office, and de Havilland was taken on as designer at the Balloon Factory (later Royal Aircraft Factory), where between 1911 and 1914 he designed the F.E.2, S.E.1, S.E.2, B.E.1 and B.E.2. In 1914 he joined the Aircraft Manufacturing Company (q.v.) at Hendon, designing the D.H.2 pusher fighter, D.H.3 and D.H.10 twin-engined bombers, D.H.5 fighter and D.H.4 day bomber. The latter was extensively built in the USA. The D.H.9 and 9a were variations; the 9a equipped post-war RAF bomber squadrons and it, too, was built in the USA. Nearly 3,000 were constructed in Russia as the R-1.

The D.H.53 Humming Bird ultralight was the best entrant in the 1923 Air Ministry Light Aeroplane competition, but de Havilland realised that their passion for lightness was an error, and in 1925 produced the first Moth to more sensible proportions. Perhaps the most famous light aircraft ever built, it was sold all over the world. A number of cabin monoplanes and a military version, the Tiger Moth, followed; over 8,000 Tigers were built for various air forces.

The three-engined D.H.66 Hercules was flown by Imperial Airways from 1926, and in the 1930s many domestic and foreign airlines used the twin-engined D.H.84/09 Dragon/Dragon Rapide and four-engined D.H.86 Express.

In 1934 de Havilland designed the all-wood D.H.88 Comet twin-engined racer for entrants in the 'MacRobertson' England-Australia race. At a fixed unit price of £5,000 this gamble paid off; three were entered, and one of these won the speed prize. By 1939 the firm was producing the D.H.91 Albatross, a fast airliner with four engines; the twin-engined D.H.95 Flamingo feederliner and the diminutive D.H.94 Moth Minor. All production of these ceased at the outbreak of war, which also cut short a promising bomber-trainer, the D.H.93 Don. In 1938 work started on a fast unarmed wooden bomber, the D.H.98 Mosquito. It became one of the most versatile aircraft of its time, and by the end of the war a single-seat fighter version attained a speed of 472mph (760kmh). The Vampire, de Havilland's first turbojet fighter, Venom, Sea Venom and later Sea Vixen, served for a decade after the war.

Back in civil work, the company produced the twin-engined Dove, four-engined Heron and, in 1949, the first jet airliner in the world, the D.H.106 Comet. The Comet 1 ran into constructional problems, but the Mark IV achieved success. The last DH designs were the D.H.121 Trident, a three-engined airliner for BEA, and the D.H.125 executive jet (both first flown 1962). Both were still in production in 1978, long after the company's absorption into the Hawker Siddeley Group (q.v.) in 1960, and the D.H.125's successors were still in production at the turn of the new century.

P.R.34 long-range reconnaissance version of the superb de Havilland Mosquito

de Havilland Tiger Moth two-seat elementary trainer

Airco D.H.10 three-seat bomber

de Havilland Comet 1 jet airliner

DE HAVILLAND AIRCRAFT OF CANADA LTD. • Canada

Formed in 1928 at Downsview, Toronto, as a constructional and service facility. Built 1,553 Tiger Moths (1938-1945), erected about 40 D.H.60M Moths, a Giant Moth, some 25 Puss Moths and 200 Tigers (from UK-built parts). Developed ski and float installations for DH products. Built 1,134 Mosquitoes (1942-1945) and 54 Fox Moths (postwar). Undertook design and construction of the Tiger Moth replacement, the DHC-1 Chipmunk, built in Canada, Britain and Portugal. Further Canadian designs have concentrated on STOL capability: the DHC-2 Beaver transport, DHC-3 Otter transport, DHC-4 Caribou piston-engined freighter (company's first twin), DHC-5 Buffalo twin-turboprop freighter (first flown 1964), DHC-6 Twin Otter twin-

turboprop transport (first flown 1965), DHC-7 Dash 7 quiet STOL four-engined airliner (first flown 1975), and DHC-8 Dash 8Q short-range twin-turboprop regional airliner (first flown June 1983 and remaining in major production, with latest Series 400 for up to 78 passengers first flown January 1998). Special variants of its aircraft have included maritime surveillance, navigation training and airborne over-the-horizon telemetry relay models of the Dash 8. The company became part of the Hawker Siddeley Group in 1960, but retained the name de Havilland. From 1974 owned by Canadian Government, then Boeing (as Boeing Canada) from 1986, and finally sold to Bombardier Inc (q.v.) as part of Bombardier Aerospace Group in 1992 and since known as de Havilland Inc.

Bombardier de Havilland Dash 8Q Series 300

de Havilland Canada DHC-6 Twin Otter

de Havilland Canada DHC-3 Otter

DE HAVILLAND AIRCRAFT OF NEW ZEALAND LTD. • New Zealand

Formed 1939 at Rongotai, Wellington. Produced a small number of Tiger Moths from 1940. After the war reverted to overhaul and servicing, and assembled Devons, Fox Moths and Chipmunks.

DE HAVILLAND AIRCRAFT PTY. LTD. • Australia

Formed 1927 at Melbourne, the first overseas holding by DH, as service agent, assembling imported Moths. Moved to Sydney 1929. Between 1939 and 1942 built 1,085 Tiger Moths and 87 Dragons; 212 Mosquitoes (1942-1947); 120 Vampires (1948-1961). Local designs were the DHA G2 troop-carrying glider and the post-war DHA 3 Drover three-engined transport. Acquired CAC Lidcombe (1959); Bristol Aeroplane Company (Australia) Pty. Ltd. (1962); Fairey Aviation Company of Australia Pty. Ltd. (1963). In 1960 became Australian Hawker Siddeley Company, the name changing in 1963 to Hawker de Havilland Australia Pty. Ltd.

de Havilland Canada E-9A telemetry relay aircraft, used by US Air Force and based on Dash 8 airliner

de Havilland Canada DHC-5 Buffalo

DELANNE • France

Maurice Delanne produced his first design, a light aircraft, the D.II *L'bis Bleu*, at Chateauroux in 1929. Proposed a tandem wing arrangement (the 'Nevadovich biplane') in 1936. Virtues claimed for this arrangement included an exceptional c.g. travel and very low stalling speed. The Delanne 20 research aircraft was built on this principle by the Société Anonyme Française de Recherches Aéronautiques in 1938. A full-scale fighter design, the Arsenal-Delanne A-D 10, was built by Arsenal de l'Aéronautique (q.v.) at Villacoublay in 1939. Completed during the German occupation, it was taken to Germany for further testing.

DELHAMENDE • Belgium

Took over production of the D-158 Tipsy Nipper from Avions Fairey Belge, designed originally by M. Tips to be sold as a kit. Delhamende marketed it under the name Cobelavia from the early 1960s, and sold all Nipper rights to Nipper Aircraft in the UK in 1966.

Del Mar DH-1A Whirlymite

DEL MAR ENGINEERING LABORATORIES • USA

A weapons systems support and training systems designer/manufacturer of Los Angeles, California; produced a series of very original experimental ultralight helicopters from 1940, as well as a helicopter training system. Production ended by 1974.

DELTA DART FLUGZEUGBAU • Germany

Produced Delta Dart II tandem two-seat pusher-engined homebuilt.

DELTA-V SRL • Moldova

Is developing the AK-21 single-seat autogyro.

DE MONGE, LOUIS • France

A propeller designer from the Société Anonyme des Etablissements Lumière who designed and built a single-seat racer in 1921. In 1924 built a 'scale model' of a Burnelli-type flying wing, with two 40 hp engines. Also built the Koolhoven F.K.31 under licence. In 1924 he joined Buscaylet et Cie (q.v.), giving up independent design.

DENEL AVIATION • South Africa

Earlier Denel (Pty.) Ltd. encompassed Atlas Aviation (q.v.) and Simera (q.v.) as divisions of its Aerospace Group. Took present name in April 1996 after merging Atlas and Simera, with new subdivisions created as Tactical Aircraft Support, Transport Aircraft Support, Aircraft Manufacturing and Airmotive. Co-operating with DaimlerChrysler (q.v.) of Germany on AT-2000 Mako programme. Co-operates with Aérospatiale of France on aircraft and missiles. Full range of maintenance, repair and modification facilities, plus component manufacturing. Continuing programmes of former Atlas include Cheetah C and D fighter conversion of Mirage III, development and production of AH-2A Rooivalk anti-armour/attack helicopter (first flown February 1990 and for delivery from 1999), development of the Cirstel (Combined Infra-Red Suppression and Tail rotor Elimination system) tail-rotorless conversion of an Alouette helicopter as a technology demonstrator (first flown 1998), development and production of a variant of the SA 330 Puma helicopter as the Oryx. and development of a modular weapon suite for the Puma helicopter to convert it into a gunship.

Right: Denel Puma Gunship modification includes Helicopter Stabilised Optronic Sighting system for aiming ZT-3 anti-armour missiles

Below: Denel AH-2A Rooivalk anti-armour/attack helicopters

DENNY • UK

William Denny and Brothers, a Dumbarton engineering firm, built 150 RAF B.E.2c/2e aircraft under subcontract in First World War.

DENNY AERO-CRAFT COMPANY • USA

Original Idaho source for the Denny Kitfox two-seat cabin homebuilt with good short-field characteristics, first flown 1984 and hugely successful. Manufactured under licence in Australia, Brazil, Philippines, Portugal and South Africa, and developed into improved variants. See Skystar Aircraft Corporation.

DEPARTEMEN AGKATAN UDARA REPUBLIK INDONESIA, LEMBAGA INDUSTRI PENERBANGAN NURTANIO • Indonesia

Formed at Bandung in 1966 from the Institute for Aero Industry Establishment. LIPNUR built a prototype series of light aircraft and from 1963 began production under licence of the Polish PZL 104 utility aircraft under the name of Gelatik (Rice Bird). Also manufactures the LT-200, a modified Pazmany PL-2 light aircraft, for military and civil training.

DEPARTAMENTO DE AERONAVES (PAR) • Brazil

The aircraft department of the Instituto de Pesquisas e Desenvolvimento (IPD). From 1970 concentrated entirely on research, all design and development being handed over to Embraer. Between 1959 and 1964 it developed

Right: LIPNUR Model 90 Belalang lightweight aircraft

prototypes of the Beija-Flìr two-seat light helicopter, designed especially for Brazilian conditions by Prof Heinrich Focke, formerly of Focke-Achgelis.

DEPARTMENT OF AIRCRAFT PRODUCTION (AUSTRALIAN GOVERNMENT) • Australia

Built the Bristol Beaufort under licence, with a great deal of local redesign of parts and detail. Some 700 were built, 1939-1943, as well as 364 Beaufighters (1943-1945) and some Lancasters. After the war was renamed Division of Aircraft Production, Department of Supply and Development. From 1946 production switched to Lincoln B Mk 30 (73 built). Canberras were produced at the Department's plant at Fisherman's Bend.

DEPERDUSSIN • France

Société Provisoire des Aeroplanes Deperdussin established in 1910, and built during 1912-1913 a series of very advanced monoplane racers with tulip-wood monocoque fuselages. In 1912 a 'Dep' was the first aircraft to exceed 100mph (160kmh), and Prévost flew one to win the 1913 Schneider Trophy race at Monaco. In 1913 Deperdussin was arrested for embezzlement and the company was taken over by Louis Blériot. The same initials were retained, but now stood for Société Pour Aviation et ses Dérivées (SPAD) (q.v.).

DESCAMPS • France

Elysée Alfred Descamps designed a machine-gun-armed fighter in 1913, but this was not put into production. For a time he worked with Aviatik at Mulhouse, then went to Russia in 1914 to become chief engineer to Anatra. After the revolution he returned to France and built several fighter and bomber prototypes. In 1923-1924 he was carrying out experimental work for the French government.

DE SCHELDTE • Netherlands

This Dordrecht company, N.V. Koninklijke Maatschappij De Scheldte, the aircraft division of a shipping organisation, was formed in 1935. It took over the designs of Pander and Zonen (q.v.) when that company went out of business in 1934. Occupied up to 1940 in design and construction of lightweight biplanes. The Scheldemusch was the first production light aircraft with a steerable nosewheel. After 1945 began glider construction and Dakota conversion. In 1951 acquired licence for production of Saab Safir.

DESERT AVIATION • USA

Offers plans or kits to build Staggerlite single-seat biplane with forward-staggered wings (appeared 1997).

DESOUTTER AIRCRAFT COMPANY LTD. • UK

Pioneer pilot Marcel Desoutter re-entered aviation by establishing this company at Croydon in 1929, building 41 examples of a modified version of the Koolhoven F.K.41 three-seater.

DETROIT AIRCRAFT CORPORATION • USA

Formed in 1929 as a parent corporation to take control of several firms hit by the Depression: Lockheed Aircraft Company, Ryan Aircraft Corporation, Eastman Aircraft Corporation, Blackburn Aircraft Corporation, Aircraft Development Corporation, Marine Aircraft Corporation, Parks Airlines Ltd. and the Winton Engine Corporation. The consortium itself failed shortly afterwards.

DEUTSCHE AEROSPACE AG. • Germany

Formed May 1989 to represent the aerospace activities of the Daimler-Benz Group. Owned MTU engine manufacturer and was the major shareholder in Dornier GmbH; took over MBB and Deutsche Airbus. See Deutsche Airbus and Daimler-Benz Aerospace AG.

DEUTSCHE AIRBUS GMBH • Germany

Was Munich-based German partner (37.9 per cent) in Airbus Industrie (q.v.), consisting of Messerschmitt-Bölkow-Blohm (MBB) Transport Aircraft Group, and became responsible for manufacturing the forward fuselage, between the flight deck and wing box, upper centre and rear fuselage and vertical tail surfaces of the A300. See Daimler-Benz Aerospace AG.

DEUTSCHE BRISTOL-WERKE • Germany

Founded at Halberstädt in 1912 to manufacture products of the British & Colonial Aeroplane Company (q.v.), but severed connection with the parent company in 1914. Subsequently it developed and built its own designs under the name of Halberstädter Flugzeugwerke (q.v.).

DEUTSCHE FLUGZEUG-WERKE GMBH • Germany

Formed by Bernard Meyer at Lindenthal, Leipzig, in 1910, it built Maurice Farman biplanes under licence and produced its own Mars biplane and a copy of the Jeannin Taube and Etrich Stahl-taube in 1914. During the war the DFW B series (unarmed) and C (armed) two-seaters were well-known, the C V in particular being licence-built also by Aviatik and Halberstadt. In 1916 DFW produced the R.I. and R.II giant bombers, very clean designs with engines in the fuselage. Planned civil development of these after the war had to be abandoned and they were scrapped, but civil conversions of C types were built. The company built no aircraft after 1920, amalgamating with Allegemeine Transportanlagen Gesellschaft Maschinenbau (ATG).

Above: One of the early successful monoplane aircraft, a French Deperdussin

Left: Desoutter Mk.1, a modified Koolhoven FK 41

*Dewoitine D.500 four-gun
fighter, one of a series of
combat monoplanes*

DEUTSCHE FORSCHUNGSINSTITUT FÜR SEGELFLUG • Germany

Established as the Rhön-Rossiten-Gesellschaft at Wasserkuppe in 1925; became DFS on moving to Darmstadt in 1933 and undertook glider research. Designed and built the successful DFS 230 assault glider in the Second World War, and the DFS 228, an air-launched rocket aircraft used as a research vehicle for the DFS 346, a swept-wing reconnaissance project expected to reach 1,650mph (2,655kmh) at 20,120 m (66,000 ft). Also undertook development of Me 163 and Mistel composite bomber. Experimented with delta designs by Dr Alexander Lippisch and evolved piloted V-1. In 1946 the DFS 346 project and its engineering design staff were taken by the Soviets to Podberczhye, where the project was said to have been completed.

DEWOITINE • France

Founded at Toulouse in 1922 by Emile Dewoitine to build all metal aircraft. His first fighter, the D.1, appeared that year and his ultralight D.7 of 1923 was demonstrated in the USA. Designed and built a number of fighters, of which the D.21 of 1927 was built in Switzerland and France and in 1929 in the Argentine. As no French orders were forthcoming, Dewoitine went to Switzerland in 1927 and formed the Société Aéronautique Dewoitine. Returned to France 1930, establishing a manufacturing agreement with Lioré et Olivier (q.v.), which was entrusted with the redesign of his D.531 to become the D.37 for the Armée de l'Air. He produced two long-range aircraft, both lost on record attempts, and airliners for Air France, but in the main developed a successful family of fighters, the last of which, the D.520 of 1938-1940, was known as the 'French Spitfire'. Merged into SNCAM (q.v.) in 1936. During the war the Group formed the Société Industrielle pour l'Aviation with the organisation that represented General Motors in France, building the Arado Ar 196 and Ar 199 and developing the Ar 296.

DFE ULTRALIGHTS • USA

Sells kits to assemble the Ascender series of single seat trike microlights.

DFL HOLDINGS INC. • USA

Markets kits to build Tango two-seat monoplane.

Dewoitine D.21 prototype, a successful fighter

DFS • Germany

See Deutsche Forschungsinstitut für Segelflug.

DFW • Germany

See Deutsche Flugzeug-Werke GmbH.

DHC • Canada

See de Havilland Aircraft of Canada Ltd.

DIAMOND AIRCRAFT INDUSTRIES CANADA • Canada

Division of Diamond Aircraft Industries GmbH (q.v.), established 1993. See below for production details.

DIAMOND AIRCRAFT INDUSTRIES GMBH • Austria

Name since March 1996, but originated as Hoffmann Flugzeugbau-Friesach GesmbH in 1981, thereafter being known as HOAC-Austria, Flugzeugwerk Wiener Neustadt Gesellschaft mbH after the 1989 management buyout.

Diamond Aircraft Industries Canada is a division (q.v.). Produces the HK 36 Super Dimona motorglider in four versions, but has stopped production of the DV 20 Katana two-seat lightplane in Austria (first flown March 1991 as the HOAC LF 2000, becoming LF2 before DV 20), which is now produced in Canada as the DA 20 Katana. Latest aircraft is the four-seat DA 40 Katana (first flown 1998).

DICK, KERR AND COMPANY • UK

Built 110 Felixstowe F.3 twin-engined flying-boats at its Preston works under subcontract in First World War.

DIETRICH • Germany

Richard Dietrich first built a monoplane at his Hanuske works in 1912, and learned to fly a year later. In 1922 produced the DP1, one of the first light aircraft in Germany. About that time the name was changed to Dietrich-Gobiet, of Kassel. In 1924 built a cantilever biplane resembling a Fokker D.VII, as well as other designs, but by 1925 (when company reverted to original name) was in serious financial trouble, becoming bankrupt in 1927.

DINFIA IA 46 Ranquel lightplane

DINFIA • Argentina

Dirección Nacional de Fabricaciones e Investigaciones Aeronáuticas originally founded in 1927 as the Fábrica Militar de Aviones (FMA) (q.v.) for aeronautical research and production. Became Instituto Aerotécnico in 1943, Industrias Aeronauticas y Mecánicas in 1953. Nationalized 1957, with aircraft works at the Fábrica Militar de Aviones at Córdoba, under DINFIA name. Began with design and construction of IA 46 light aircraft, twin-engined transports IA 35, IA 45, the IA 38 four-engined tailless transport designed by Dr Reimar Horten, and the IA 37, a small delta-wing aircraft. In 1966 began licence construction of Cessna 182 and indigenous light turboprop and piston-engined transports. Reverted to name FMA in 1968, becoming part of Area de Materiel Córdoba division of the Argentine Air Force.

DITS • France

Les Etablissements Henri Dits founded in 1922 to build the designs of pioneer Breguet pilot Réné Moineau, starting with a small metal aircraft for tropical service. During First World War produced an aircraft with twin propellers driven by engine mounted transversely in the fuselage.

DITTMAR • Germany

A designer of high-performance sailplanes, Heine Dittmar produced a motorised version of his Segelmöwein in 1953-1954 as the HD 153 Möwe two-seat light aircraft. Wing and tail detached for road transport. A small number of these aircraft, and of the later HD 156 three-seat aircraft, was built.

DM AEROSPACE LTD. • UK

Offers Thorpe T-211 AeroSport two-seat monoplane, imported from USA in assembled and kit forms.

DOAK AIRCRAFT CO INC. • USA

Incorporated in 1940 in Los Angeles, California, developing the Model 16 VZ-4Da, with ducted propellers rotating at wingtips, under contract to the US Army Transportation Research and Engineering Command, 1958. This was transferred to NASA for further evaluation. Doak sold out to Douglas Aircraft Company (q.v.) in early 1960s.

DINFIA IA 50 Gurani II prototype, twin-engined light transport

DOBLHOFF • Germany

Friedrich Doblhoff began work on a jet helicopter in 1942, with a piston engine delivering ram air via a compressor to tip orifices. Development was taken up by Wiener-Neusätdter Flugzeugwerke (q.v.) and resulted in four models of the WNF 342.

DOCKYARD CONSTRUCTIONAL UNIT • Malta

Between November 1917 and December 1918 the unit built 18 F.3 flying-boats under subcontract to the British government.

DOMAN • USA

Founded in 1945 by Glidden J. Doman at Danbury, New York, to construct rotorcraft with hingeless rotorblades and totally enclosed self-lubricating hub. Produced LZ-1a, LZ-2a Pelican, LZ-4, LZ-5 and a developed version, DB-10B, in 1953. At one time known as Doman-Frasier Helicopters Inc. Doman H-31 of 1952 was licence-built by Hiller Aircraft Company Inc (q.v.). Operations transferred to Puerto Rico, with continued production of DB-10B and name changed in 1967 to Berlin-Doman Helicopters, recognising interests of Chairman Dr Don R. Berlin.

DOMINION AIRCRAFT CORPORATION • USA

Established originally at Vancouver, Canada, but production and development carried out at Renton, Washington. First aircraft produced was the Skytrader 800 STOL twin-engined transport, which flew for the first time on 21 April 1975. Corporation ceased trading 1979. See Skytrader Corporation.

DONG IN INDUSTRIES • USA

Marketed kits to build Wizard two-seat microlight/homebuilt.

DONNET • France

Operated under the name Hydravions J. Donnet at Neuilly-sur-Seine, after Percheron replaced Denhaut as designer in 1918. Did not long survive First World War, but some flying-boats used on the Antibes-Ajaccio service, 1921-1928.

Doak Model 16 VTOL research aircraft

Doman LZ-5 light helicopter

DONNET-DENHAUT AND DONNET-LEVEQUE • France

Based at Ile de la Jatte from 1912, designing and building light, fast, single-engined flying-boats for the French Navy, RNAS and others. Total of 58 2/3-seat flying-boats acquired by US Navy for coastal patrol in European waters in 1918, and two sent to USA.

DORAND • France

In 1916 Colonel Dorand, then head of the Section Technique d'Aviation, designed a two-seat reconnaissance biplane which was produced at the government aircraft factory at Chalais-Meudon and also by Farman.

H F DORNA CO • Iran

Established 1989 and has produced the Blue Bird two-seat composites-constructed touring lightplane (said to have first flown 1997).

DORNIER • Italy

SMCA Dornier founded at Marina di Pisa in 1922 to produce the Dornier Wal flying-boat. A great commercial success, it was built also by Japan, Spain and the Netherlands, and was used on both European and international routes during the 1930s.

DORNIER • Spain

Oficinas Técnicas Dornier was set up after the Second World War by Dr Claude Dornier. First designed the Do 25, from which the very successful Do 27 STOL aircraft was built. Spanish Company Construcciones Aeronáuticas SA (q.v.) produced 50 of these.

DORNIER • Switzerland

By 1926 the German Dornier works at Manzel had become too small, and the main factory was transferred to Altenrhein, in Switzerland. Here, for the next three years, Aktien Gesellschaft fär Dornier Flugzeug was occupied in building three Do X flying-boats, the largest aircraft of their time, powered by 12 engines. Two were sold to Italy. Bomber designs followed, the Do N, P and Y being built 1929-1931. These led to the Do F which, like the Do 11, began in 1933 to re-equip the German Air Force. However, in 1932 production was resumed in Germany. The Swiss factory subsequently became the Eidgenössisches Flugzeugwerk (q.v.).

DORNIER COMPOSITE • Germany

See Claudius Dornier Seastar and Dornier Seastar Malaysia.

DORNIER FLUGZEUGWERFT GMBH • International

Represents part of the Military Aircraft business unit of DaimlerChrysler Aerospace AG. (q.v.).

DORNIER LUFTFAHRT GMBH • Germany

Formerly Dornier Reparaturwerft GmbH, as a subsidiary of Dornier GmbH. Became the Regional Aircraft division of Daimler-Benz Aerospace AG. (q.v.). In June 1996 Fairchild Aerospace purchased 80 per cent of Dornier Luftfahrt from Daimler-Benz Aerospace (q.v.), forming Fairchild Dornier Germany Dornier Luftfahrt GmbH (q.v.).

DORNIER SEASTAR MALAYSIA SDN BHD. • Malaysia

Formerly Flitestar Anokagai, owned by Conrado Dornier and Malaysian interests, had expected to place the German Seastar amphibian (first flown 1984 in Germany) into production.

DORNIER-WERKE GMBH • Germany

Dr Claude Dornier was employed by Count Zeppelin in 1910, and in 1914 was in charge of the design and construction of large all-metal marine aircraft at Zeppelin-Werke Lindau. Here he produced the Rs I in 1915, then the largest aircraft in the world, with a span of 145 ft 9 in (43.5 m). By 1918 three more giant flying-boats had been built, Rs II, III and IV, as well as prototypes of single-seat and two-seat fighters. All employed Dornier's techniques of advanced metal construction. After the war the works were transferred to Manzel, near Friedrichshafen, where some two-seaters for the Swiss Air Force were completed. At Manzel, between 1920 and 1925, appeared the Libelle,

Dornier Do 24 maritime patrol flying-boat

One of the most important flying-boats produced by Dornier, the Wal had influence on later designs

Dornier's Do X was one of the first attempts to provide a large-capacity long-range flying-boat

Dornier Do 13 medium-bomber of the 1930s

Dornier Do 28 D-2 Skyservant STOL transport

Delphin, Komet and Merkur, small civil aircraft, and the Falke, an unsuccessful fighter. In 1922 the company became Dornier Metallbauten GmbH and in 1926, as the Manzel works were too small, it transferred to Altenrhein in Switzerland (see Aktien Gesellschaft für Dornier Fluzeuge). In 1932 production was re-established in Germany, this time as Dornier-Werke GmbH, beginning with the military Wal (later the Do 18) and Do 11 bomber, supplanted later by the Do 23. In 1934 appeared its first modern warplane, the Do 17, evolved from a fast, six-passenger mailplane designed for Deutsche Luft Hansa. The Do 17 and its successor, the Do 217, which served as a nightfighter, were the only Dornier designs to see large-scale production during 1935-1943. Towards the end of

the war the company produced the remarkable Do 335 push-pull twin-engined heavy fighter with a top speed of 474mph (763km/h), probably the fastest piston-engined Second World War fighter.

After the war Dornier became established in Spain (see above). The first post-war aircraft developed completely in Germany was the twin-engined STOL Do 28. An experimental STOL jet transport followed, the Do 31, and the Do 29 research aircraft. From 1966 the company developed the Skyservant and was involved in international programmes. Collaboration with Avions Marcel Dassault-Breguet Aviation (q.v.) on Alpha Jet development and production included research into supercritical wing (see also Dassault-Breguet/Dornier).

Became Dornier GmbH in 1972. A majority shareholding was acquired by Daimler-Benz AG. in 1985. In 1989 Deutsche Aerospace AG. (q.v.) was formed as a corporate unit of Daimler-Benz Group and intended to unite the work of Dornier, MBB, MTU and more, and was renamed Daimler-Benz Aerospace AG. in 1995 (q.v.), with the Regional Aircraft division administered by Dornier Luftfahrt GmbH. In June 1996 Fairchild Aerospace purchased 80 per cent of Dornier Luftfahrt from Daimler-Benz Aerospace, forming Fairchild Dornier Germany Dornier Luftfahrt GmbH (q.v.). For more informaiton see also Daimler Chrysler Aerospace A.G, in which Dornier Flugzeugwerft GmbH represents part of the Military Aircraft business unit.

Dornier Do 28 Skyservant twin-engined utility transport

DOSWIADCZALNE WARSZTATY LOTNICZE •
Poland

Founded in Warsaw in 1933 to take over assets and lia-
bilities of RWD, the aeronautical section of Warsaw Technical High School, which had been building to the designs
of Rogalski, Wigura and Drzwiecki, initially in the school
workshops, later those of the government. Production continued under the RWD name until 1939.

Right: RWD 5 bis ultra light sportplane

DOUGLAS AIRCRAFT COMPANY • USA

The Davis-Douglas Cloudster of 1920, Donald W. Douglas's first design, was followed in 1921 by the DT torpedo-bomber for the US Navy, the largest single-engined aircraft in the USA at the time. Four modified DTs, known as Douglas World Cruisers, made the first round-the-world flight in 1924, with Army crews. The Douglas Aircraft Company was formed in 1928, and in 1932 a former Douglas engineer, Jack Northrop, set up the Northrop Aircraft Company and produced an all-metal low wing dive-bomber, the XBT-1/A-17. Northrop and Douglas merged in 1937 (Douglas with a majority stockholding), and in 1938 it became Douglas-El Segundo. The dive-bomber design progressed, via the Douglas TDB Devastator of 1934, to become the US Navy's first monoplane, and was followed by the Dauntless SBD. Ultimate Douglas development of the single-engined piston-engined attack-bomber was the 1945 Skyraider, which served in many roles until 1968, both in Korea and Vietnam. Last single-engined military designs by Douglas were the small delta-wing F4D Skyray jet fighter (first flown January 1951) and highly-successful A4D Skyhawk jet attack-bomber (first flown June 1954

Left: Douglas SBD Dauntless carrier-based scout/dive-bomber

Below: Douglas DC-2s of Swissair

and 2,960 built up to 1979; current programmes around the world keep substantial numbers of Skyhawks operationally capable with foreign forces).

The first twin-engined Douglas design appeared in 1925; the T2D for the US Navy. The B7 of 1930 was the

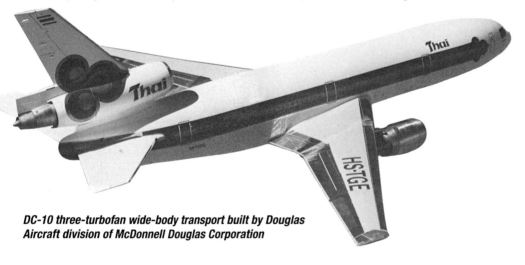

DC-10 three-turbofan wide-body transport built by Douglas Aircraft division of McDonnell Douglas Corporation

first of a series for the US Army, and was followed by the B-18 in 1935. The most famous twin, however, was the DB-7/A-20 Boston (and nightfighter Havoc), which first saw action in June 1940. A total of 7,385 was built, of which 3,125 went to Russia. The A-26/B-26 Invader of 1945, developed from the A-20, served in Korea and Vietnam, and the Boston/Havoc concept was taken into the jet age by the Skywarrior and Skynight. A version of the former became the B-66 Destroyer, Douglas's (and the USAF's) last conventional light attack bomber.

In 1933, under pressure from United Airlines' Boeing 247, Transcontinental & Western Air turned to Douglas to provide a competing aircraft. The first DC-1 (Douglas Commercial) appeared in prototype only, but 131 DC-2s followed in 1932-1936. A wide-bodied sleeper version, the DST, led to the DC-3 in 1936, which was to be the most famous airliner of all time. In 1940 the USAAC ordered it as the C-47 transport. Douglas built 9,255 of the 10,125 produced, and in 1961 1,000 were still in military use, and 600 civil DC-3s remained in operation in the USA in 1974. Douglas, consulting five airlines, developed a four-engined version, the DC-4, in 1941. The Army commandeered all civil DC-4s on US entry into the war, and 1,162 military C-54s were built. After the war many reverted to DC-4 status, to be succeeded by the DC-6 and DC-7. Douglas temporarily lost its lead in transport when Boeing produced the Model 707, but then produced the very effective DC-8 and DC-9 jet.

Douglas C-133A Cargomaster strategic heavy freighter

*Below: The superb, ubiquitous Douglas DC-3, in the insignia
of British European Airways*

Douglas C-124 Globemaster military transport

Military transport design continued with the big C-124 Globemaster in 1950, and C-133 Cargomaster of 1957, a heavy strategic freighter capable of carrying all the then-current IRBMs or ICBMs. In 1947 Douglas went supersonic with the jet D-558-1 Skystreak and D-558-2 rocket Skyrocket, built for NASA. The latter held the world speed record in 1953 at 1,231mph (1,981kmh) and achieved Mach 2.01 at 65,000 ft (19,810 m) in 1953. The later X-3 research aircraft was intended for flight at up to Mach 3. There was a brief involvement with executive jets with the PD-808 Vespa-jet, production being transferred from El Segundo to Rinaldo Piaggio before, in 1967, the company merged with McDonnell Aircraft to become McDonnell Douglas (both q.v.).

Left: Douglas DC-6A converted for freighting

Right: Douglas A-4M Skyhawk II, the last Skyhawk built

Below: Douglas X-3 short span (double wedge) and turbojet-powered research aircraft of 1952

Above: Dragon Fly mod 333 light helicopters

DOWNER AIRCRAFT INDUSTRIES INC. • USA

Formed at Alexandria, Minnesota, in 1959, from the former Northern Aircraft Inc (q.v.) to continue production of the Bellanca Model 14 (see Bellanca Aircraft Corporation). Built the Model 14-19-2 Cruisemaster and the Downer Bellanca 260 Model 14-19-3. Further development was undertaken by Inter-Air Inc (q.v.). Following merger with American Aviation Corp of Freeland, Michigan, supplied parts and conversion kits for Seabee.

DOYLE AERO CORPORATION • USA

Harvey Doyle of Baltimore, Maryland, produced his first light aircraft, the Oriole, in 1929. Before this he had been designer for the Vulcan 'American Moth'.

DOYN AIRCRAFT INC. • USA

This Wichita, Kansas, company, offering conversions to provide more power and performance to Cessna models 150, 170, 172, 175 and Cardinal, was taken over by Air-Mod Engineering Company of Oklahoma City. The Cessna 170 conversions were known as the Doyn Dart I; the Dart II of the mid-1960s was a refined version of the Piper Apache. Beech Travelair conversions were also completed.

DRIGGS AIRCRAFT CORPORATION • USA

Founded at Lansing, Michigan in 1927 by Ivan H. Driggs, who designed and built his first aircraft in 1915. Later worked as engineer for Dayton-Wright. In 1924, in conjunction with Johnson Airplane and Supply Company, built two Driggs-Johnson DJ-1 Bumblebee racers, followed by a second version in 1925. Developed Dart Model 1 for Air Corps research on high-lift wings in 1926. Driggs products included Dart II and Skylark III. Driggs left to work for Luscombe (q.v.) on the 1934 Phantom I, and Driggs design rights went to Phillips Aviation in 1938.

DRUINE • France

See Avions Roger Druine.

DUBNA MACHINEBUILDING PLANT JSC • Russia

Undertook manufacture and marketing of light and general-purpose aircraft designed by Typhoon Design Bureau, including Dubna-1 single-seat pleasure and agricultural ultralight (first flown 1994 and originally a homebuilt type; subsequent production in assembled form has ended), Dubna-2 two-seat variant of Dubna-1 (first flown 1996), Z-2 Selena, Z-6 Duet, Z-7 Bekas and Z-8 Stayer.

DUMOD CORPORATION • USA

Based at Opa Locka, this company produced modified Beech 18, increasing performance considerably, under the designation Dumod I. A further development, known originally as the Infinite, later as Dumod II, was produced from 1964. Rights to both acquired by Broome County Aviation in 1972.

DURUBLE, ROLAND • France

First flew in 1982 RD-03 Edelweiss 150 two/four-seat metal monoplane, made available in plans form for home construction and developed from the earlier RD-02 two-seater.

Below: Dumod Liner conversion of the Beech 18

DRAGON FLY SRL • Italy

Established 1993, produces the Dragon Fly mod 333 two-seat piston-engined light helicopter (certificated June 1996). HELIOT variant is for military and civil special operations, with a 661 lb (300 kg) useful load and is fitted with a camera and colour monitor; can carry an external module to permit unmanned remote flying; with module removed, HELIOT can be piloted.

DURAMOLD AIRCRAFT CORPORATION • USA

The Duramold F.46A, designed by Colonel V. E. Clarke and financed by Fairchild, was built in 1938 to test plastic-bonded plywood processes. It was also used by Fairchild as a test bed for their 420 hp Ranger engine. Research based on this aircraft was employed in the design of the Fairchild AT-21 Gunner.

DURANT AIRCRAFT CORPORATION • USA

Established at Oakland, California, to manufacture a two-seat biplane called the Durant-Standard J.1. This was a re-engined version of the two-seat trainer built originally by the Standard Aircraft Corporation (q.v.) and powered as the J.1 by a 200 hp Hall-Scott engine.

DURBAN AIRCRAFT CORPORATION • South Africa

Formed in 1962 to continue production of the Aeriel Mk II light aircraft, developed and built originally by Genair (q.v.) and subsequently by Southern Aircraft Construction Co and Robertson Aircraft Sales and Service.

DYKE AIRCRAFT • USA

Dyke Delta JD-2 first flew 1966 as unusual four-seat delta-wing homebuilt, still offered in plans and component forms for amateur construction. JD-2 developed from previous JD-1 flying-wing type.

DYLE ET BACALAN • France

The large naval dockyard Société Anonyme de Travaux Dyle et Bacalan formed an aeronautical company in Paris in 1925 to develop an all-metal civil and military aircraft. Built armoured fighter and bomber. Renamed Société Aérienne Bordelaise (q.v.) in 1930.

DYN'AERO SA • France

Has marketed kits to construct CR.100 two-seat aerobatic monoplane (first flown 1992) and MCR-01 Banbi (see Colomban MC-100).

E

EAC • France

Études Aéronautiques et Commerciales SARL was formed in 1960 to build modified versions of Jodel lightweight monoplanes. Also offered kits for amateur construction.

EAC • USA

Engineers Aircraft Corporation was founded at Stamford, Connecticut, to manufacture a lightweight two-seat monoplane designated EAC-1. Powered by a Wright-built version of the British Gipsy four-cylinder in-line air-cooled engine, an example was exhibited at the New York show in 1930.

EAGLE AIRCRAFT COMPANY • USA

Developed the Eagle DW-1 single-seat agricultural biplane. Agreement with Bellanca Aircraft Corporation (q.v.) of June 1979 for Bellanca to manufacture Eagle on its behalf. Eagle production lasted until early 1980s (see Bellanca Inc.).

EAGLE AIRCRAFT PTY. LTD. • Australia

Established 1985 and currently offers the Eagle 150 two-seat composites lightplane (first flown March 1988), featuring rear-mounted main wings and wide-span canards.

Below: Eagle Aircraft Company Eagle 150 kitplane

EAGLE'S PERCH INC. • USA

Founded December 1995 and offering the Eagle's Perch single-seat kit-built helicopter, first flown 1994 as the Perch Nolan 51-HJ.

EARL AVIATION CORPORATION • USA

Based at Los Angeles about 1930. Built Earl 95 two-seat lightplane with American Cirrus engine; also two-seat biplane called Earl Popular, with tandem open cockpits.

EARLY BIRD AIRCRAFT COMPANY • USA

Developed Jenny two-seat 67 per cent scale replica of the Curtiss JN biplane trainer and Spad XIII as single-seat 75 per cent scale replica of this French First World War biplane fighter, both offered for amateur construction.

EARTHSTAR AIRCRAFT INC. • USA

Has produced kits to allow construction of the Thunder Gull high-wing monoplane with pusher engine in single- and two-seat forms, with at least the two-seat Thunder Gull JT2 also available ready assembled.

EASTBOURNE AVIATION COMPANY LTD. • UK

Founded at Eastbourne, Sussex by F. B. Fowler. Built in 1913 a single-seat tractor monoplane; in 1914 two types of tractor biplane, one single-seat and one two-seat, the latter for military use. Seaplane built for 1914 Circuit of Britain had 'buried' engine driving two propellers through shafts. During war 'Circuit' seaplane was modified but then abandoned. Company built Avro 504s and B.E.2cs under contract. Firm's aerodrome near Eastbourne taken over by Royal Navy.

EAST COAST AERONAUTICS INC. • USA

Subsidiary of Barium Steel Corporation. In late 1950s made two Lockheed Shooting Stars almost entirely of magnesium. Also built Australian Jindivik pilotless target under licence for US armed services.

EASTERN AIRCRAFT DIVISION, GENERAL MOTORS • USA

Five car factories converted for Second World War production of Grumman Wildcats and Avengers. Completed 1,000th Avenger on 5 December 1943 and 2,500th Wildcat 11 April 1944. Production of new Grumman fighters planned, but Japanese surrender intervened, and plants reverted to car production.

See also under Ford on wartime conversion of American car factories.

EAST EUROPEAN MARKETS LTD. • Poland

Is marketing the J-5 Marco very light aircraft and motorglider, owned by Aviation Farm Ltd.

Ector Super Mountaineer, developed from the Cessna L-19 Bird Dog

EASTMAN AIRCRAFT CORPORATION • USA

Division of Detroit Aircraft Corporation. Made Eastman Flying Yacht four-seat flying boat or three-seat amphibian of sesquiplane configuration. Also built Eastman Sea Rover and Sea Pirate biplane flying-boats.

EBERHART AEROPLANE & MOTOR COMPANY INC. • USA

Parent company was Eberhart Steel Products Co (established 1918), making not only aircraft but bomb-carriers, bombsights, synchronising gears etc. In 1922 assembled 50 British-designed S.E.5E fighters from spare parts, 'E' suffix denoting company name and plywood-covered fuselage. Aircraft division, named as above, formed in 1925. Developed steel-construction techniques and supplied components to US aircraft industry. Experimental XFG-1 Navy fighter tested 1926/27.

ECTOR AIRCRAFT COMPANY INC. • USA

This company was formed to produce the Cessna L-19 Bird Dog, dating from 1950s, under the names of Ector Mountaineer and Super Mountaineer.

EDGLEY AIRCRAFT LTD. • UK

Founded 1974 to develop the EA7 Optica three-seat observation aeroplane, featuring a ducted propulsor powerplant to the rear of the helicopter-like bubble cockpit (first flown December 1979). Ceased trading 1985. See Optica Industries, Brooklands Aircraft Company Ltd. and FLS Aerospace Ltd.

EDGLEY SAILPLANES LTD. • UK

Produces the EA9 Optimist sport glider, the first new British glider for two decades.

EDO AIRCRAFT CORPORATION • USA

Incorporated 1925. Carried out three years of research and development in connection with seaplanes and flying-boats. From 1928 was famous for standardised float installations, and by 1947 over 300 types of aircraft had been equipped with Edo floats. During Second World War made sub-assemblies for Grumman Hellcat. First Edo-designed aircraft was the unsuccessful XSOE-1 single-seat observation floatplane. Company name changed in November 1947 to Edo Corporation. In 1962 fitted a Grumman amphibian flying-boat with experimental Gruenberg hydrofoils.

EFW • Switzerland

See Eidgenössiches Flugzeugwerke and F + W.

E.H. INDUSTRIES LTD. • International

Established 1980 by Agusta of Italy and Westland of UK (now GKN Westland, q.v.) to develop and manufacture the

EFW C-3604 ground-attack aircraft

Edo XSOE-1 single-seat observation floatplane

Experimental Edo hull on Grumman Widgeon amphibian

E.H. Industries EH 101, a joint programme by GKN Westland and Agusta

EH 101 medium multirole helicopter (first flown October 1987); offered in Naval, Utility, SAR and Civil versions. The Royal Navy is receiving (since 1997) 44 as Merlin HM Mk 1s to replace Sea Kings and the RAF is receiving 22 Merlin HC Mk 3s, while the Italian Navy wants 16 for anti-submarine/anti-ship, utility, and airborne early warning roles. First Civil variant went to the Tokyo Police in 1998.

EIDGENÖSSICHES FLUGZEUGWERKE EMMEN • Switzerland

Founded 1934 as government-run R&D organisation, with manufacturing, maintenance and upgrading capabilities. In an official specification of 1934 (see next entry) the company had designed the C-36 monoplane. Newly named EFW as above, it revived the design in 1938 and built 160 as C-3603. Of C-3604 development, only 13 were built. After the war became responsible for Swiss licence production of various foreign aircraft for Swiss Air Force, including the British Vampire, Venom and Hunter (under Hawker Siddeley contract), several versions of French Mirage and US F-5E/F combat aircraft, plus French Alouette III helicopter. Produced C-3605 as turboprop conver-

sion of wartime C-3603 fighter-bomber, used for target-towing. See F + W.

EIDGENÖSSICHE KONSTRUKTIONS WERKSTÄTTE • Switzerland

Formed at Thun early in First World War. Made aircraft to designs of A. Haefeli, who was earlier with Farman and Ago. First was DH-1 pusher (six built in 1916) showing Ago influence; DH-2 was tractor which went into produc-

tion as developed DH-3 (110 of these two-seaters built). DH-4 was fighter prototype of 1918; DH-5 (1919; 60 built) a DH-3 replacement; DH-5A a higher-powered version of 1928, with steel-tube fuselage (22 built). To a government specification of 1934 it built the C-35 multipurpose two-seat biplane as a replacement for the Fokker C.V-E, which it resembled, and which the company had produced jointly with Dornier since 1932. C-35 first flown in 1935; 80 delivered from 1937. (See also previous entry.)

EKW MA-7 single-seat fighter prototype

EKW C-35 biplane fighter

El Gavilán SA Gavilán 358 utility transport

EKIN • UK

W. H. Ekin (Engineering) Company Ltd formed at Crumlin, Co. Antrim, Northern Ireland, March 1969 to undertake production of six McCandless gyroplanes. First one flew February 1972. Extensive redesign then undertaken and new prototype flew February 1973. Modified type called WHE Airbuggy.

EKLUND ENGINEERING • USA

Has offered plans and some components to build the Thorpe T-18 single-seat metal monoplane, originally designed by John Thorpe and first flown 1964.

EKIP AVIATION CONCERN • Russia

EKIP stands for EKologia I Progress. During 1990s has been developing very unusual multipurpose transports with lifting 'saucer' configured high-volume fuselages and short outer wings, expected to provide a lift-to-drag ratio of 17-18 at high altitude and 25 during wing-in-ground-effect flight. Models flown at time of writing.

ELBIT SYSTEMS LTD. • Israel

Founded 1971 and offers modernization programmes for many combat aircraft.

EL GAVILAN SA • Colombia

Established 1991 and producing the Gavilán 358 eight-seat single piston-engined utility monoplane (formerly Aero Mercantil Gavilán), able to operate from short and unprepared airstrips (first flown April 1990, with production examples from 1997).

ELIAS, G. & BROTHERS INC. • USA

Formed in 1881 but made aircraft only after First World War, at Buffalo, NY. By 1929 had made nine experimental types for US air services and Post Office, as well as armament types for the Air Corps. In 1922 made first of seven EM/EO 'Marine Expeditionary' two-seat biplanes (wheels or floats). XNBS-3, tested August 1924, was large twin-engined bomber with steel-tube fuselage and wooden wings. Elias-Stupar was twin-engined cantilever civil biplane. EC-1 of 1927-1928 was 'convertible' light parasol monoplane; the cockpit could be open or closed.

ELICOTTERI MERIDIONALI • Italy

Formed by Agusta in 1963 as part of industrialisation programme in south Italy, operating Frosinone factory, which opened in October 1967, overhauling helicopters for Italian services. In April 1968 concluded agreement for licence production of Boeing-Vertol CH-47C Chinook for Italian Army and for Iran. Also developed Agusta-designed EMA 124 three-seat helicopter based on Agusta-Bell 47. Now known simply as Sesto Calende (VA) facility of Agusta.

ELLIOTS OF NEWBURY LTD. • UK

Formed 1895 to make furniture. Turned attention to aircraft components in 1939. During Second World War subcontracted for many types, including Airspeed Oxford, Supermarine Spitfire and de Havilland Mosquito. In August 1947 flew Eon light four-seat low wing monoplane, later altered to re-engined Eon 2. Also made gliders (Eon, Olympia etc.). Eon T.16/48 was side-by-side trainer project by Elliotts and Aviation & Engineering Projects Ltd.

ELMWOOD AVIATION • Canada

Offers plans and kits to build the Christavia Mk 1 tandem two-seat cabin monoplane and the four-seat Christavia Mk 4.

EMAIR • USA

In 1970 this division of Emroth Company began production at Harlingen, Texas, of Emair MA-1 agricultural biplane (Boeing-Stearman Model 75 derivative). Type had received FAA certification in Hawaii, though built by Air New Zealand and first flown in that country July 1969. Emair's production of 25 ended January 1976. More powerful MA-1B Diablo 1200 flew 1975 and deliveries followed. Special features included new wings and hopper forming integral part of fuselage.

Right: Emair MA-1B heavy-duty agricultural aircraft

*Above: EMBRAER
EMB-201A Ipanema
single-seat
agricultural aircraft*

*Left: The EMBRAER
EMB-121 Xingu,
Brazil's first
pressurised transport*

*Below: EMBRAER
EMB-110 Bandeirante
(Pioneer) general-
purpose aircraft*

EMIGH TROJAN AIRCRAFT COMPANY • USA

Successor to the Emigh Aircraft Corp, continuing development during 1950 of Emigh Trojan A-2 light all-metal cabin monoplane, which was built in small numbers 1948-1950. Metal fuselage was in two halves, joined on centreline. Interchangeability of components was a special feature.

EMPRESA BRASILIERA DE AERONAUTICA SA • Brazil

See EMBRAER

EMPRESA INDUSTRIAS AERONAUTICAS DEL ESTADO • Argentina

As Industrias Aeronáuticas y Mecánicas del Estado (IAME) formed 28 March 1952 to take over State activities concerning military and civil aircraft, and incorporating the Instituto Aerotécnico (formerly Fábrica Militar de Aviones). I.A.35 was twin-engined multipurpose monoplane; I.A.33 Pulqui II (first flown February 1951) a swept-wing jet fighter designed by Kurt Tank. Six Pulqui built 1955/56.

EMPRESA NACIONAL DE AERONAUTICA CHILE • Chile

Founded in 1984 from former Indaer (q.v.). ENAER's first major undertaking was production of the piston-engined T-35 Pillán basic trainer, developed with Piper assistance and using many structural components from existing Piper lightplanes, and first flown as a prototype in March 1981,

EMBRAER • Brazil

Empresa Brasiliera de Aeronáutica SA was founded in August 1969 and began operations in January 1970 to promote the Brazilian industry. In August 1974 signed cooperative agreement with Piper Aircraft Corporation, and in 1975 with Northrop. Work on Tiger II components started 1976. Successful production of the Bandeirante twin-turboprop light transport (first flown October 1968) ended in 1994. Other early production programmes included the pressurized EMB-121 Xingu transport, EMB-111A Patrulha for maritime surveillance, and Xavante (licence-built Italian Aermacchi jet trainer and attack aircraft). Privatization completed in December 1994, with the Brazilian Federal Government retaining some 15 per cent of capital. Production in 1999 included the EMB-312 Tucano turboprop trainer (first flown August 1980), EMB-314 Super Tucano (first flown May 1993) and ALX special application version, EMB-120 Brasília regional transport (first flown 1983), ERJ135 37-passenger regional jet (first flown July 1998), ERJ145 50-seat regional jet (first flown August 1995), and surveillance versions of the ERJ145. International programme is AMX combat aircraft with Aermacchi and Alenia of Italy. Divisions of EMBRAER include Indústria Aeronáutica Neiva SA (q.v.).

EMBRAER EMB-120 Brasilia operated by United Express

ERJ135 37-passenger airliner, EMBRAER's latest airliner to fly

EMBRAER RJ145 50-seat regional transport operating with Rio-Sul Linhas Aéreas

Engineering & Research Ercoupe, in 1937 an advanced lightplane

Engineering Division VCP-R racing version of VCP-1 fighter

the first production aircraft flying in 1984. The current version, the Pillán 2000 with new wings of greater span developed by Technoavia in Russia, is offered with a piston engine or a turboprop. ENAER's second industrial programme was assembly from kits and later construction of Spanish-developed CASA C-101BB and CC jets, delivered to the Chilean Air Force from 1983 as T-36 Halcón advanced jet trainers and A-36 Halcón light tactical attack aircraft respectively. From 1997 A-36s were redelivered by SAGEM of France as Halcón IIs, after avionics upgrade. In 1995 production began of the Ñamcu aerobatic, training and utility lightplane of composites construction (first flown April 1989), which is also being assembled by EuroE-NAER in the Netherlands as the Eaglet. Other current activities include aircraft modernization, maintenance and repair, component construction and satellite work.

EMSCO AIRCRAFT CORPORATION • USA

A subsidiary of the large Emsco industrial chain. First products were Emsco Challenger monoplane, with US-built Curtiss Challenger radial engine, and Emsco Cirrus with American Cirrus (British designed) in-line engine. B.3A of early 1930s was eight-seat low-wing monoplane; B.7 was two-seat sports monoplane.

ENAER • Chile

See Empresa Nacional de Aeronáutica Chile.

ENGINEERING & RESEARCH CORPORATION • USA

Established 1930. After making important components for other aircraft, designed and built the novel Ercoupe mono-

plane, developed from the original Weick 'easy-to-fly' type and first flown in October 1937. Fred E. Weick was the company's chief engineer. The type was notable for its control system, which eliminated rudder pedals, and was first marketed in 1940. Production ceased on US entry into Second World War, when company was fully engaged in defence contracts. Difficulty of obtaining duralumin led to redesigned Ercoupe of composite construction in 1941. In August 1941 one was used to demonstrate benefits of jet-assisted take-off (JATO) compared with conventionally-powered aircraft. Two examples were bought by US Army as experimental radio-controlled targets. After the war civil Ercoupe production was resumed.

ENGINEERING DIVISION, BUREAU OF AIRCRAFT PRODUCTION • USA

A division of the US War Department, created in 1918. Responsible for US developments of de Havilland designs, and 14,000 were ordered, though not delivered. Division also experimented with other types of original design. In 1920 it completed its most remarkable product, the GAX (GA-1) very large heavily armoured pusher triplane (one 37mm cannon and eight Lewis guns), of which Boeing built ten. Also made TP-1 two-seat fighter and TW-1 trainer, but a special racer was cancelled. The Bureau was later called Engineering Division, Air Service; subsequently Material Division Air Corps (1926). Moved from McCook Field (where GAX was built) to Wright Field October 1927. Numerous types and variants had associations with the Engineering Division, including Pomilio, Bristol Fighter and Packard-LePere developments. Also

Sperry-built Engineering Division R-3 racer, designed by Alfred Verville

English Electric single-seat ultra-light Wren, with 398 cc ABC engine

VCP-1 single-seat fighter, which won first Pulitzer Race (1920).

ENGINEERS AIRCRAFT CORPORATION • USA

See EAC/USA.

ENGLISH ELECTRIC COMPANY LTD. • UK

Though this company became part of British Aircraft Corporation in 1960, its origins date back to 1911 at its Coventry Works (Coventry Ordnance Works Ltd), where quantity production of other manufacturer's designs was undertaken during First World War. After the Armistice development centred on the Kingston flying-boats, following the lines of the Cork, a product of the Phoenix Dynamo Manufacturing Company Ltd., which was then also part of English Electric. Original features manifest in Ayr flying-boat and Wren ultralight monoplane (1923), but aircraft work ceased in the mid-1920s. In 1938 it was resumed, with contracts for the Handley Page Hampden (followed by the Halifax). In May 1944 an order was placed for de Havilland Vampire jet fighters. Over 1,000 Vampires built before production got under way on company's own Canberra, the first British jet bomber and the first to serve with the RAF. Canberra production continued for ten years, totalling over 1,300 examples, including 403 licence-built Martin B-57s for the USAF. Numerous variants developed, notably for reconnaissance; other countries using the type included Ecuador, France,

English Electric (later BAC) Lightning; the RAF's first Mach 2 fighter

Peru, Rhodesia, Sweden and Venezuela. Many records broken (e.g. London-Cape Town December 1953). Lightning twin-jet single-seat fighter of 1952 was RAF's first supersonic fighter (in level flight); entered service December 1959. Much development of this type was undertaken by British Aircraft Corporation, but two-seat version emanated from English Electric.

ENSTROM • USA

As R. J. Enstrom Corporation, was formed in 1959 to develop experimental helicopter, first flown November 1960. Developed type (F-28) flown May 1962; and deliveries of further-improved F-28A began in 1968. First year's production was 43 aircraft. In 1968 first tests were made with turboshaft installation. Production stopped 1970, but resumed 1971 under Enstrom Helicopter Corporation title. After intervening acquisitions, including operation as part of Pacific Airmotive Aerospace Group, 1980 purchase by Bravo Investments BVC of the Netherlands, and acquisition by US investors, resumed manufacture. By June 1977

English Electric Canberra T.17 for electronic countermeasures training

Enstrom F-28A three-seat utility helicopter

Enstrom 280FX three-seat helicopter

the 500th Enstrom helicopter had been delivered. See Spitfire Helicopter Company. Current title The Enstrom Helicopter Company, offering the piston-engined three-seat F28F (first flown December 1980 as improved F-28 type) and 280FX (available since 1985), latter based on F28F but with airframe and cabin refinements. Also offers the five-seat 480 Turbine (first flown October 1989), using an Allison turboshaft engine.

ENTLER-WERKE • Germany

Based at Wilhelmshaven. Built in 1922, in conjunction with Prof Junkers, a small two-seater cantilever biplane which had corrugated sheet-metal covering. Development was intended, and in summer 1922 an English selling price of £222 was mentioned. By 1925 the firm had ceased to exist.

ENTWICKLUNGSRING SÜD GMBH • Germany

See EWR.

EPA AIRCRAFT COMPANY LTD. • UK

Acquired Croplease (q.v.) rights 1992, but difficulties in obtaining subcontracted components from UTVA in Yugoslavia halted production of Fieldmaster Firemaster.

EQUATOR AIRCRAFT GESELLSCHAFT FÜR FLUGZEUGBAU MBH ULM • Germany

Founded 1974 out of Pöschel Aircraft GmbH (q.v.).

Enstrom 480 Turbine five-seat helicopter

ERICKSON AIR-CRANE CO LLC • USA

Founded 1972 to operate Sikorsky S-64s as heavy-lift helicopters. Developed Helitanker system for S-64 to permit firefighting role. Purchased Type Certificate and production rights for S-64 from Sikorsky in 1992, and can construct new examples to improved Erickson S-64 Aircrane standard. Also developed modifications for ex-US Army CH-54s to bring them up to Aircrane standard.

ERLA-MASCHINENWERK GMBH • Germany

Though established in 1934, the real beginnings were in 1933 as Nestler und Breitfeld of Erla. Type Erla 5 was a single-seat monoplane with an engine of 20 hp. From 1934 undertook quantity production of Arado Ar 65 and Ar 68, He 51 and Bf 109 (including early 'C' sub-type from 1937, as well as numerous later variants). Also produced assemblies for other military types.

ESHELMAN, CHESTON L., COMPANY • USA

Formed 1942. Made several experimental types, notably FW-5 ('The Wing'), having centre section built integrally with the fuselage (not to be confused with the more famous Northrop 'flying wing' of 1947), and a low-wing monoplane in which a tubular steel spar formed the fuel tank. Latter type revived after the war as E.F.100 Winglet.

ESNAULT-PELTERIE, ROBERT • France

Robert Esnault-Pelterie (1881-1957) was a pioneer in aircraft design and development, rocketry and aero-engine construction. Especially noted for tractor monoplanes and metal-tube construction. Following construction of Wright-type gliders (1904), he tested REP 1 (1907) and REP 2 (1908) powered by his own engines. Founded in 1908 Association des Industriels de la Locomotion Aérienne and merged with Chambre Syndicale des Industries Aéronautiques. Developed central-float seaplane. Vickers in England acquired licence for REP monoplanes in 1911. A few French-built REP monoplanes (including parasol type) used in First World War. After the Armistice, Esnault-Pelterie, something of a visionary, increasingly concerned himself with the problems of spaceflight.

ESPENLAUB FLUGZEUGBAU • Germany

Gottlieb Espenlaub achieved an international reputation in the 1920s building and flying gliders. Company formed at Düsseldorf early in the 1930s to build light aeroplanes as well as gliders. Types included a tailless monoplane, a two-seat high-wing monoplane and a five-seat high-wing cabin monoplane with engine of about 125 hp. During Second World War a Riga subsidiary did stress calculations for Bf 109G wooden tailplane.

One of the early classic monoplanes, the Etrich Taube

ESSEX AERO LTD. • UK

Following wide experience in aircraft-component applications of magnesium alloys, built in the late 1940s two-seat (side-by-side) Sprite low-wing monoplane of all-magnesium construction. Made ultralight components for many aircraft, including Bristol Brabazon. Also carried out repairs, modifications, furnishings etc.

ETHIOPIAN AIRLINES SC • Ethiopia

Company's Agro Aircraft Manufacturing division is producing the Ag-Cat Corporation Ag-Cat G164B Turbine under the name Eshet for distribution and operation in Ethiopia and African countries excepting Algeria, South Africa and Tunisia.

ETRICH • Austria/Germany

Austrian Igo Etrich (1879-1967) experimented in aeronautics from 1899. After working with engineer Franz Wels he made a tailless glider with backswept wings in 1907. This was intended to be powered, and led to the Etrich Taube monoplane (bird-like, with backswept warping outer wings and fan-like tail) in 1909-1910. Object was inherent stability; first flight at Wiener-Neustadt in November 1909. Small-scale production (Etrich Flieger Werke) and competitive success followed, in UK and other countries and the type was imitated frequently. Early Etrich pilots included Hellmuth Hirth. Jointly with his businessman father, Etrich had a private experimental establishment at Josefstadt. Etrich A-1 and A-2 monoplanes served with Austro-Hungarian Army before First World War. Etrich Fliegerwerke GmbH established at Liebau, Silesia, in 1912, independent of Motorluftfahrzeug Gesellschaft of Vienna and Rumpler of Berlin, each of which held a licence for the Taube. Rumpler built the type from 1911-1914, and other German makers built similar machines, as used by the German Army before and during the war. First product from Liebau was a remarkable three-seat cabin monoplane with wings of variable incidence and camber, and nosewheel landing gear. In 1914 the company was absorbed by Brandenburgische Flugzeugwerke (q.v.).

ÉTUDES AÉRONAUTIQUES ET COMMERCIALES SARL • France

See EAC.

EULER-WERKE • Germany

August Euler (1868-1957) was a pioneer pilot/builder, active in 1909-1910. In 1910 he patented a machine-gun installation for aircraft, and at the wish of the German War Department some sort of presentation of it was withdrawn from the Berlin Aeronautical Exhibition of 1912. Euler acquired a licence for Voisin aircraft, and Prince Heinrich of Prussia took his pilot's certificate on an extensively modified example of the type. At least 30 other Germans learned to fly on this aircraft. An early wartime reconnaissance type was the B II tractor biplane (built at Frankfurt in late 1914), an early version of which had tricycle landing gear; B III was a licence-built LVG; Type C a pusher of 1916; Dr 1-Dr 4 were triplanes. A quadruplane was also built (though top surfaces were really full-span ailerons), but Euler types achieved little distinction after 1916.

EURASIA DESIGN BUREAU • Russia

Is developing an advanced jet trainer and light multirole combat fighter under the name Integral, featuring a unique circular section wing root.

EUROALA • Italy

Produces Jet Fox JF 97 as two-seat microlight with piston engine carried above high-mounted wing, developed from JF 91 microlight.

EUROCOPTER GROUP • International

Founded in January 1992, Eurocopter is now said to be the first fully integrated European Aeronautical company. Up to 1997 Eurocopter Holdings SA, which owned 75 per cent of Eurocopter SA, had been owned by Aérospatiale of France and Daimler-Benz Aerospace of Germany. Since 1997 all the participants have been merged, only

Eurocopter Deutschland remaining as a Eurocopter-owned subsidiary. Several of the older helicopters originated as Aérospatiale or MBB types.

In 1998 Eurocopter delivered 216 new helicopters to customers and received orders for 272, giving the company a turnover that year of about 11.1 thousand million Francs. Its product range in 1999 includes the twin-engined civil Super Puma AS 332 (first flown September 1978) and military Cougar AS 532 variant, light multirole AS 350 Ecureuil (first flown June 1974) and military Fennec AS 550 variant, twin-engined Ecureuil AS 355 (first flown September 1979) plus similar Fennec AS 555 military version, the larger 12-passenger Dauphin AS 365 N (first flown as Panther AS 365 M in February 1984) and military Panther AS 565, new-generation EC 155 'widebody' medium-twin (first flown June 1997), BO 105 (first flown February 1967) and EC Super Five related light helicopter, EC 135/635 civil/military light multipurpose helicopters (first flown as EC 135 February 1994), and Tiger (Tigre) anti-armour, combat support, plus escort/support tandem two-seater (first flown April 1991). Eurocopter also participates in the Colibri EC 120 B light civil helicopter programme with China and Singapore (first flown June 1995), the BK 117 programme with Kawasaki of Japan (first flown June 1979), in Euromil with Mil of Russia, and in the NHIndustries NH90 (q.v.).

Above: Eurocopter Tiger in HAP escort/support form

Eurocopter Cougar AS 532, military version of Super Puma

Eurocopter EC 135 of 1994 first appearance

Eurocopter BO 105 CBS twin-engined light helicopter

Eurocopter/CATIC/ST Aero Colibri EC 120 B during its first flight

EUROCOPTER/CATIC/ST AERO • International

European collaboration with China and Singapore to develop EC 120 B five-seat light turboshaft helicopter (first flown June 1995), deliveries begun in 1997.

EUROCOPTER/KAWASAKI • International

European collaboration with Kawasaki of Japan to develop and produce BK 117 10-passenger multipurpose helicopter, first flown June 1979.

EUROENAER • Netherlands

EuroENAER formed to assemble ENAER Ñamcu lightplane in the Netherlands as the Eaglet from 1998.

EUROFAR • International

European Future Advanced Rotorcraft programme launched 1987 by Aérospatiale of France, Agusta and Alenia of Italy, DASA of Germany, CASA of Spain and Westland of the UK, to develop a civil tiltrotor transport. Agusta and CASA later withdrew. Final design not yet selected, and first flight not expected until at least 2004.

EUROFIGHTER JAGDFLUGZEUG GMBH • International

EuroFighter formed 1986 as collaboration between four nations to develop a new Mach 2 air-superiority fighter with attack and reconnaissance capabilities, known simply as Eurofighter (named Typhoon by RAF). Present shareholding DaimlerChrysler of Germany (33 per cent), Alenia of Italy (21 per cent), CASA of Spain (13 per cent) and British Aerospace (33 per cent). Powered by two Eurojet EJ200 afterburning turbofans with fully variable nozzles, has been designed for supersonic, beyond-visual-range air defence, offering also high performance and agility in subsonic close air combat. Has fly-by-wire control system and low radar cross section. First flown March 1994, and well over 700 test flights achieved by seven development aircraft by mid-1998. RAF expected to receive at least 232 from year 2002, Germany 140 air defence and 40 multirole from 2003, Italy 130 from 2002 and Spain 87 from 2003; interest from several other nations.

Eurocopter and Kawasaki unite to produce the BK 117 in latest C-1 form

EUROFLAG SRL • International

Formed 1989 by Aérospatiale of France, Deutsche Airbus of Germany, Alenia of Italy, British Aerospace and CASA of Spain to supersede FIMA in the development of the Future Large Aircraft (FLA) military freighter, since 1996 becoming the Airbus Military Company (see Airbus Industrie).

EUROFLY • Italy

Produces FireFox and simplified BasicFox tandem two-seat microlights.

EUROMIL • International

Under 1992 agreement Mil and Kazan of Russia (plus Klimov engine builder) and Eurocopter agreed to develop and manufacture jointly the Mi-38 medium multipurpose helicopter, intended to replace the Mi-8/Mi-17 series. Possible deliveries from the year 2001.

EUROPA AVIATION LTD. • UK

Markets kits to build versions of the composites Europa two seat monoplane (first flown 1992).

Above: EuroFighter DA 4, the second two-seater and final development aircraft

Left: Europa Aviation Europa kitplane, available in monowheel and tri-gear versions, with well over 500 sold

EUROPEAN AIRBUS • International

The name European Airbus was used throughout the late 1960s, predating the Airbus Industrie entry in this book. In June 1965 the first discussions were held between

Evangel 4500-300 cargo/passenger transport, designed for easy repair in the field

British and French industrial representatives concerning a collaborative project for a large-capacity short-medium range transport; almost simultaneously a study group was formed in Germany. There were talks and proposals every year until Airbus Industrie was founded in 1969.

EUROSPACE AERONAUTICAL CONSTRUCTIONS • Italy

Currently offers a series of four-seat civil and military training and touring lightplanes under the F-15-F Excalibur name (first flown October 1994), with deliveries from 1998.

EVANGEL AIRCRAFT CORPORATION • USA

Designed twin-engined STOL light passenger/cargo aircraft in 1962. Prototype Evangel 4500-300 first flew in June 1964, having rugged structure and intended for bush operations/missionary work. Manufacture ceased in 1974 after seven production aircraft were built.

Above: EWR VJ101 vertical take-off research aircraft with jet pods tilted.

Above: EWR VJ101 experimental VTOL interceptor of 1963, in horizontal flight

EVANS AIRCRAFT • USA

Developed VP-1 as single-seat open-cockpit low-wing monoplane, originally named Volksplane because of its VW engine, and two-seat VP-2, both becoming available for amateur construction from plans.

EVEKTOR LTD. • Czech Republic

See Aerotechnik CZ sro.

R.J. EVERETT ENGINEERING LTD. • UK

Developed a single-seat autogyro, first flown 1984 and sold in assembled form.

EWR • Germany

Entwicklungsring Süd GmbH was formed of a Bölkow, Heinkel and Messerschmitt design consortium on 23 February 1959 at the suggestion of the Federal German Defence Ministry, to develop a Mach 2 VTOL intercepter. By May 1963 70 flights had been made with VJ101C research aircraft, which had tilting jet-pods at wingtips. Studies were made for an entirely different VJ101D fighter. Heinkel withdrew in late 1964, and in July 1965 EWR changed from a consortium into a limited company. There was later an unsuccessful partnership with Fairchild Hiller.

EXCALIBUR AVIATION COMPANY • USA

In October 1960 acquired all rights for conversion programme (for which it already had responsibility) of Beechcraft Queen Air and Twin-Bonanza marketed by Swearingen Aircraft. Continues production at San Antonio, Texas. New company has adopted the name Queenaire 800 for former Swearingen 800.

EXPERIMENTAL AIRCRAFT • USA

Developed the Berkut as tandem two-seat composites-built canard monoplane with pusher engine, first flown 1991 and made available in kit form. See Renaissance Composites.

EXPLORER AVIATION • USA

Offers kits to build the Ellipse four-seat high-wing monoplane, first flown 1997.

EXPRESS AIRCRAFT • USA

Company re-formed 1997 to sell kits of the Express four seat composites-built cabin monoplane, previously marketed by Wheeler, Express Design and Experimental Aircraft Technologies. Also marketing kits for six-seat Loadmaster (first flown 1993 as Express Design type), Express CT, Srs 90 and Auriga.

Extra 300 L aerobatic aircraft

EXTRA FLUGZEUGBAU GMBH • Germany

Produces the Extra 200 lower-cost, two-seat and 200 hp aerobatic competition and aerobatic training monoplane (first flown 1996); Extra 300 in single-seat 300 hp aerobatic competition (300 S), tandem two-seat aerobatic and training/cross-country (300), and 300 L low-wing (instead of mid-wing) variants; Extra 330 as a derivative of Extra 300 with Textron Lycoming AEIO-580 engine; and Extra 400 pressurised high-wing six-seat touring cabin monoplane (first flown 1996).

F

FABRICA DE AVIONES ANAHUAC SA • Mexico

See Anahuac.

FABRICA DE AVIONE S.E.T. • Romania

Founded Bucharest 1923 to develop aircraft designed by Grigore C. Zamfirescu for Divisia I-a Aeriana. Designs included S.E.T. 7 biplane trainer, S.E.T. 7K reconnaissance variant, S.E.T. 10 biplane advanced trainer, S.E.T. XV biplane fighter; also made Fleet 10G trainers.

FABRICA BRASILIERA DE AVIOES • Brazil

Assumed responsibility from CNNA for continued production of M-7 Gipsy Major powered primary trainer and M-9 advanced trainer with Gipsy Six engine, designed by Lt Col A. M. Muniz. Acquired licence to build Fairchild PT-19 in 1942.

FABRICA MILITAR DE AVIONES SA • Argentina

See FMA.

FABRICA NACIONAL DE AERONAVES • Chile

Founded in June 1953 with temporary facilities at Los Cerrillos Airport, Santiago, and later moved to new premises at Rancagua. Company was dissolved in 1960. It converted PBY-6A flying-boats into 28-passenger airliners and built 50 Chincol primary trainers for the Chilean Air Force (the prototype was first flown in December 1955).

FABRICA NACIONAL DE AVIONES • Peru

State factory established at Las Palmas Airport, Lima, in May 1937 with Società Italiana Caproni (q.v.) as partner supplying plant and tooling. Twelve of contracted 25 Caproni Ca 100 trainers completed up to 1939; facilities used for general overhaul from June 1941.

Fairchild-built C-123 Provider, evolved from the Chase XG-20 cargo glider

FABRIQUE FÉDÉRALE D'AVIONS, EMMEN • Switzerland

See Eidgenössisches Flugzeugwerk.

FAIRCHILD • USA

Sherman Fairchild founded Fairchild Airplane Manufacturing Corporation in 1925. Changed to Fairchild Aviation Corporation in 1929 when The Aviation Corporation acquired controlling interest. Sherman Fairchild withdrew in 1931, retaining a subsidiary, Kreider-Reisner Corporation, Hagerstown, Maryland, which was renamed Fairchild Aircraft Corporation in 1935; became Fairchild Aircraft Division, Fairchild Engine and Airplane Corporation, in 1939; Fairchild Stratos Corporation in 1961; Fairchild Hiller Corporation in 1964 on acquisition of Hiller Aircraft Company, acquiring Republic Aviation Corporation in September 1965 and this becoming the Republic Aviation Division of Fairchild Hiller Corporation and, later, the Fairchild Republic Company division of Fairchild Industries; Fairchild Industries Inc in 1971 (acquired 90 per cent interest in Swearingen Aviation Corporation in November 1971, which became Fairchild Aircraft Corporation in 1982). Metro Aviation, with 97 per cent shareholding in Fairchild Aircraft Corporation, sold by Fairchild Industries to GMF Investments, but in 1990 Fairchild Aircraft filed for bankruptcy protection and was sold to Fairchild Acquisition Incorporated that year; name for producer of Metro, Merlin and Expediter series of twin-turboprop commuter airliner, executive transport and freighter aircraft (plus MMSA multi-

Fairchild Hiller Turbo-Porter floatplane

Fairchild Model 71, equally at home on wheels or floats

Fairchild AC-119 heavily armed gunship

Fairchild Republic A-10A, USAF's subsonic close-support aircraft

mission surveillance aircraft variant of Metro 23) became Fairchild Aircraft Incorporated. Finally, in June 1996 parent company Fairchild Aerospace bought 80 per cent of the German manufacturer Dornier Luftfahrt from Daimler-Benz Aerospace (q.v.), resulting in Fairchild Aerospace owning all of the renamed Fairchild Dornier USA Fairchild Aircraft Incorporated and 80 per cent of Fairchild Dornier Germany Dornier Luftfahrt GmbH.

Fairchild built FC-1, FC-2 and Model 71 lightplanes 1925-1931. Continued production of Kreider-Reisner Model 24C8, later supplied in four-seat version as USAAF UC-61 Forwarder and as RAF Argus. M-62 Cornell trainer introduced 1940 with variety of engines. AT-21 gunnery trainer entered production in 1942. C-82 Packet twin-boom cargo/troop transport flown September 1944; super-seded by developed C-119, first flown November 1947.

Manufactured 326 C-123 Providers 1954-1958, designed by Chase Aircraft. Licence-production of Fokker F-27/FH-227 airliner began 1957; 205 built. Hiller UH 12 and H-1100 helicopters continued in production after acquisition of Hiller company. Production of Pilatus Turbo-Porters begun June 1966; 15 of COIN version delivered to USAF as AU-23A Peacemaker, transferred to Royal Thai Air Force. In 1967 work initiated on 52 USAF AC-119 gunships.

Fairchild Aircraft Metro 23 commuter airliner

Fairchild XC-120 Packplane, which could fly with or without cargo pod

Contracts awarded after acquisition of Republic for weapons delivery enhancement of F-105 Thunderchief, subcontract assemblies for McDonnell Douglas F-4, Boeing 747. Won USAF A-X competition for close-support aircraft, prototype YA-10A flown 10 May 1972; production of A-10A Thunderbolt II ended 1984 after 713 built, and will remain in US service until the year 2028 in A-10A attack and OA-10A forward air control variants with the USAF, Air National Guard and Air Force Reserve (Lockheed Martin won contract in 1998 to provide long-term support for the fleet). Main feature of A-10A is nose-mounted GAU-8/A Avenger 30 mm seven-barrel cannon with 1,174 rounds of armour-piercing ammunition. Also manufacured wings for Merlin and Metro twin-turboprop aircraft.

FAIRCHILD AIRCRAFT LTD. • Canada

Formed 1929 with premises at Lonqueil, Quebec, parent company having withdrawn manufacturing licence from Canadian Vickers. Built 21 Model 71 seven-seaters 1930-1935, Super 71 with metal monocoque fuselage in 1934; two Super 71P photographic aircraft for RCAF in 1936; 24 Model 82s produced 1935-1938. One Model 34-42 Niska and two Model 45-80 Sikanis, first flown 1937. Wartime production of Bristol Bolingbroke for RCAF; 300 Curtiss Helldivers for US Navy 1943-1945. All-metal F-11 Husky built 1946-1948. Aircraft production stopped 1948; Husky design sold to Husky Aircraft Ltd. in 1955.

FAIRCHILD DORNIER GERMANY DORNIER LUFTFAHRT GMBH • USA/International

In June 1996 Fairchild Aerospace of USA bought 80 per cent of the German manufacturer Dornier Luftfahrt from Daimler-Benz Aerospace (q.v.), resulting in creation of Fairchild Dornier Germany Dornier Luftfahrt GmbH. Current product range comprises Fairchild Dornier 228 twin-turboprop 19-passenger commuter transport (first flown March 1981) plus special missions variant for many roles including border patrol, maritime patrol, pollution surveillance, anti-ship warfare, long-range observation etc.; Dornier 328 twin-turboprop 30-39 passenger regional transport (first flown December 1991); 328JET twin-turbofan development of 328 (first flown January 1998; 40-

Fairchild Republic T-46A Next Generation Trainer, first flown 1985 and ordered for the US Air Force as a T-37 replacement but cancelled in 1986 after one production aircraft had been completed

43 passenger version launched as 428JET, and low-wing developments are 55-passenger 528JET, 70-passenger 728JET and 90-passenger 928JET). Company also carries out subcontract work for Airbus Industrie (q.v.). See Fairchild and Daimler-Benz Aerospace.

FAIRCHILD DORNIER USA FAIRCHILD AIRCRAFT INCORPORATED • USA

See above and Fairchild and Daimler-Benz Aerospace.

FAIRCHILD REPUBLIC COMPANY • USA

See Fairchild.

Above: Fairchild Dornier 228 operated by National Cartographic Center

Left: Fairchild Dornier 328JET on roll-out

Below: Fairchild Dornier 328 turboprop transport of Afrimex

Belgian-built Fairey Fox II day bombers

FAIREY AVIATION LTD. • UK

Founded by C. R. (later Sir Richard) Fairey, initially to build 12 Short 827 seaplanes. Leased premises at Hayes, Middlesex, replaced by new factory 1917-1918. Became a public company 5 March 1929 and the following year opened new airfield at Harmondsworth, later requisitioned and incorporated in site for London's Heathrow Airport. Reorganised as holding company The Fairey Company Ltd. 31 March 1959, aircraft manufacturing subsidiary becoming Fairey Aviation Ltd. and the Stockport plant Fairey Engineering Ltd. Fairey Aviation Ltd. merged with Westland Aircraft Ltd. in 1960. Britten-Norman (Bembridge) Ltd. acquired 1972. Fairey group into liquidation 1977; engineering activities acquired by National Enterprise Board; Britten-Norman (q.v.) operated by liquidator pending sale.

Company designs included F.2 twin-engined biplane fighter; camber-changing trailing-edge flaps introduced on Hamble Baby. Fairey III series introduced 1917; final model IIIF entered production 1926 and declared obsolete 1940. Fairey Hendon (1930) was the first British cantilever monoplane heavy bomber; Long-range Monoplane

captured absolute distance record for Britain 1933. The famous Fairey Swordfish ('Stringbag') torpedo bomber entered production in 1936; 2,392 were built by Fairey and Blackburn; it was the only biplane to remain in service throughout Second World War. Other famous aircraft included Battle light bomber, Fulmar fleet fighter and Barracuda dive-bomber. Firefly name revived for Rolls-Royce Griffon-powered monoplane which entered FAA service in 1943, serving in Korea in 1950. First FAA aircraft to combine search and strike roles was the Gannet with Double Mamba coupled turbines; developed Gyrodyne convertible helicopter 1946; Jet Gyrodyne 1953; Rotodyne compound helicopter airliner 1957. Fairey Delta 2 research aircraft set world air speed record of 1,132mph (1,822kmh) on 10 March 1956.

FAIREY AVIATION COMPANY OF AUSTRALASIA PTY. LTD. • Australia

Formed in 1948 as Fairey-Clyde Aviation Co Pty. Ltd. name changed to above November 1951. Bankstown,

Sydney, factory overhauled aircraft for Royal Australian Air Force and Royal Australian Navy, converted RAN Firefly AS.5s to T.5 standard. Special Projects Division concerned with Jindivik, Meteor and Canberra drones at Woomera missile test range.

FAIREY AVIATION COMPANY OF CANADA LTD. • Canada

Incorporated November 1948 to provide overhaul and repair of aircraft for Royal Canadian Navy. Ceased operations March 1970. Converted ex RCN Avengers for agricultural and firefighting duties; Martin Mars flying-boats converted into water-bombers 1960.

FAIREY SA • Belgium

Société Anonyme Belge Avions Fairey registered 12 September 1931. Plant bombed 10 May 1940, reopened October 1946. Reorganised as Fairey SA 1964. Established originally to build Fairey Firefly II biplane fighters and Fairey Fox three-seat day bombers. Licence-production of 80 Hawker Hurricanes curtailed by bombing 1940, only two completed. Factory extended 1950-1951 when work began on Gloster Meteor F.8s for Belgian Air Force, also conversion of Meteor F.4s to T.7 standard. 240 Hawker Hunter F.4s and F.6s built 1955-1960; other activities included collaboration in multinational F-104G and Atlantic programmes. Supplied rear fuselages and nose cones for single-seat variants of Mirage V for Belgian Air Force in joint programme with SABCA. Following UK Fairey's acquisition of Britten-Norman (Bembridge) Ltd. in 1972, Islander and Trislander production was transferred to Gosselies until affected by liquidation in October 1977. See Sonaca.

FAIRTRAVEL LTD. • UK

Formed in 1962 to build Piel CP.301 Emeraude, modified to comply with British certification requirements and known originally as the Garland-Bianchi Linnet.

Fairey IIID, most of which served with the Fleet Air Arm

Fairey Rotodyne, advanced compound helicopter airliner

FALCON AIRCRAFT MANUFACTURING COMPANY • USA

Established 1958 to acquire engineering and production rights to Baumann Brigadier, re-engined with two 175 hp Continental engines to become B-350 or B-360 Falcon De Luxe Brigadier.

FALCONAR AIR ENGINEERING • Canada

Offers plans and/or components to build the Mignet HM.293 single-seat open-cockpit homebuilt, Mignet HM.360 single-seat homebuilt version of the Pou-du-Ciel and HM.380 two-seater, Cubmajor tandem two-seat cabin monoplane, Jodel F.9 single-seat monoplane and more streamlined and higher-powered F.10 variant, F.12A Cruiser side-by-side two-seat cabin monoplane, Golden Hawk ARV-1L (1996) tandem two-seat composite pusher-engined type, and two/three-seat Adam RA.14 Loisirs/Maranda designed in France by Roger Adam.

FANSTAR PARTNERS • USA

Envisaged Fanstar 200T four-seat piston-engined light aircraft with ducted fan, based on RFB Fantrainer.

FARM AVIATION LTD. • UK

Revived programme initiated by de Havilland Aircraft in 1958 to convert Chipmunk primary trainers for agricultural use. Three machines converted for the company's own use, followed by others for agricultural aircraft operators.

FARMAN • France

On 9 November 1907 Henri Farman, in a Voisin biplane, made the first powered flight in Europe to last over a minute. At a 1909 Reims meeting he flew his own Farman III, the first aircraft with effective ailerons. Brother Maurice was also a designer; the two formed Avions Henri et Maurice Farman at Billancourt, eventually nationalised in 1937, becoming part of SNCAC (q.v.).

Maurice Farman designed the MF-7 Longhorn (1913) and MF-11 Shorthorn (1914), both used as trainer and

Farman MF-7 Longhorn trainer/observation aircraft of WW1

Farman F.222 36.0 m (118 ft) span monoplane bomber

observation aircraft by the Allied forces. Farman F.20 and F.40 developed, the latter with streamlined two-seat nacelle and powered by 135 hp Renault engine. Farman F.50 night bomber followed; four-engined F.140 night bomber introduced 1925, replaced by F.221 and F.222 in 1937, the latter used subsequently by Vichy air force after June 1940 as a transport. Civil airliners included the F.60 Goliath. Twin-engined F.180 biplane, F.190 single-engined monoplane introduced 1928, three-engined F.300 in 1930.

After nationalisation, in 1939 the Farman brothers acquired the licence to manufacture the Stampe SV.4 trainer biplane. Although SNCAC was assigned manufacturing rights post-war, Farman retained licence and with Jean Stampe the Société Anonyme des Usines Farman developed Monitor I monoplane powered by 140 hp Renault engine. Variants included the II, III and IV, the latter being taken over by Stampe et Renard, Brussels.

The Farman biplane which made first flight in Japan (1910)

Farman F.40 reconnaissance, and occasionally bomber aircraft

Faucett F.19 eight-seat cabin monoplane

FFA C-3605, a turboprop conversion of the EKW C-3603

FARNER AG. FLUGZEUGBAU • Switzerland

Farner AG. was an overhaul and repair organization which produced a two-seat biplane in 1934, and in 1935 a four-seat WF.21/C4 monoplane based on the three-seat Compte AC-4 Gentleman. Prototype WF.12 two-seater built 1943, powered by Cirrus Minor located behind cabin and driving via shafts a tractor propeller mounted at wing level.

FARRINGTON AIRCRAFT CORPORATION • USA

Currently produces the tandem two-seat Model 20A Heliplane cabin autogyro as a modern development of the Air & Space (q.v.) Model 18-A. Twinstarr first flown 1991 as a kit-built two-seat sporting autogyro of much simplified form.

FAUCETT SA, CIA DE AVIACION • Peru

Aircraft operator, founded by Elmer Faucett, owning airport at Santa Cruz, Lima. Developed aircraft in 1930s for its own airline use and for Huff-Daland Dusters Inc, which it managed. Designs, based on Stinson, included F.19 eight-passenger cabin monoplane. Production discontinued 1947.

FBA • France

See Schreck FBA.

FEDERAL AIRCRAFT CORPORATION • USA

Incorporated 1928 by some workers who had helped build the Ryan monoplane for Charles Lindbergh. Known originally as Ryan Mechanics Monoplane Company. CM-1 Lone Eagle was a four-passenger cabin monoplane powered by Wright Whirlwind radial engine.

FEDERAL AIRCRAFT FACTORY • Switzerland

See Eidgenössisches Flugzeugwerk.

FEDERAL AIRCRAFT LTD. • Canada

Set up as Canadian Crown Company to co-ordinate production of Avro Anson navigation trainers for use under British Commonwealth Air Training Plan. Developed Anson II with revised hydraulically-operated undercarriage and flaps, Anson V with moulded plywood fuselage. Later assumed co-ordination responsibility for Canadian Lan-

FFA P-16 interceptor/ground attack aircraft

caster, Mosquito and other programmes. Disbanded 30 June 1946.

FEIGL & ROTTER • Hungary

Louis Rotter designed light aircraft in the 1920s, the 110 hp Le Rhone-engined Feiro I all-wood four-seater being the first post-First World War civil aircraft to be built in Hungary. Produced subsequently the improved Feiro Daru and the lightweight Feiro Dongo side-by-side two-seater.

FERGUSON AIRCRAFT INC. • USA

Offers kits to build F-2 two-seat high-wing monoplane with pusher engine.

FERRARI ULM • Italy

Offers Olimpios two-seat cabin monoplane and Tucano single-seat microlight in assembled and kit forms.

FFA • Switzerland

Founded 1948, the reorganised Swiss Dornier-Werke Alntenrhein, Flug- und Fahrzeugwerke AG. discontinued development of Morane-Saulnier piston-engined fighters after completing prototype D-3803. Awarded development contract July 1952 for P-16.04 interceptor/ground-attack aircraft with Armstrong Siddeley Sapphire, first flown 28 April 1955. Programme cancelled by Swiss Government but continued as private venture until June 1960; five aircraft built. Participated in licence-production programmes for de Havilland Vampire and Venom, Pilatus P-3, Mirage IIIRS and IIIS. Designed and manufactured Diamant glass-fibre sailplane. Currently named FFA Flugzeugwerke Altenrhein AG., continues to produce (under original agreement with SIAI-Marchetti signed in 1967) the AS-202 Bravo two-seat trainer/aerobatic aircraft (first flown 1969). FFA-2000 programme was transferred to FFT (q.v.).

FFT GESELLSCHAFT FÜR FLUGZEUG- UND FASERVERBUND-TECHNOLOGIE MBH • Germany

1989 rename of Gyroflug (q.v.), to produce SC 01 Speed Canard. Became subsidiary of Justus Dornier Group 1984. Also developed manned and unmanned surveillance

FFA AS-202 Bravo two-seat training aircraft

versions, but this programme halted. Also took over development of FFA-2000 trainer from FFA (q.v.), becoming Eurotrainer 2000A.

FFV AEROTECH • Sweden

First flew in 1988 the BA-14 Starling two-seat lightplane, designed by Björn Andreasson and a joint venture with MFI (q.v.).

FFVS • Sweden

On 1 January 1941 the Air Board of the Royal Swedish Air Force instituted Flygförvaltningens Verkstad and its own design, which became the FFVS J-22 fighter, first flown September 1942. Subcontracted programme with final assembly at Air Board Workshops, Ulvsunda; the first of more than 200 was delivered 1 September 1943.

FIAT, SOCIETA PER AZIONE • Italy

Renamed 1949 to succeed Aeronàutica d'Italia (q.v.), inheriting its plant and programme. (Fiat's Divisione Aviazione merged subsequently with Aerfer as Aeritalia (q.v.) formed 12 November 1969, fully operational 1 January 1972.)

Above: Fiat C.R.42 highly manoeuvrable biplane fighter

Below: Fiat G91Rs in Italian use as strike-reconnaissance fighters

Above: Fiat G91Y single-seat tactical reconnaissance-fighter

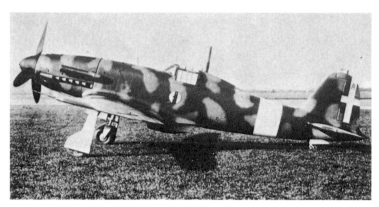

Left: Fiat G55 Centauro, a fast single-seat fighter

Fiat G49 advanced trainer flown September 1952. G80 jet trainer with de Havilland Goblin 35 engine, first flown 9 December 1951, was first post-war Italian jet aircraft. In conjunction with Macchi built 80 de Havilland Vampire FB.52As; built 221 F-86K all-weather fighters for Italy, France and West Germany, first example completed June 1955. G91 adopted as NATO light tactical fighter; prototype flown 9 August 1956 and several hundred built subsequently. Prototype of G91Y variant first flew 27 December 1966; 65 built for Italian Air Force. Licence-built 205 F-104S Starfighters for Italian Air Force. G222 twin-turboprop military transport project initiated before establishment of Aeritalia.

FIBRA AB • Sweden

Designed tandem two-seat proficiency trainer with turboprop engine driving propeller mounted in rear fuselage, ahead of tail unit.

Above: Fieseler Fi 156 Storch multi-purpose STOL aircraft

Right: Firestone lightweight helicopter, an early post-war design

FIESELER, GERHARD • Germany

Gerhard Fieseler Werke GmbH established by the aerobatic pilot in 1930. Fi 2 Tiger produced for Fieseler's own use. Fi 5R two-seat lightplane and Fi 97 four-seat cabin monoplane preceded Fi 156 Storch liaison and communications aircraft with high-lift slots and flaps. Also built Fi 167 torpedo bomber/reconnaissance biplane, designed

for carrier operation. Manufactured Messerschmitt Bf 109 fighters.

FIGHTER ESCORT WINGS • USA

Has developed kits to assemble 1+1-seat and two-thirds scale representations of P-51 Mustang and Corsair Second World War fighters.

FINAVITEC OY. • Finland

Taken over from Valmet Aviation Industries. Assembling F-18C Hornet fighters for the Finnish Air Force from kits up to the year 2000, plus their engines. Component manufacture includes tail surfaces for Saab 2000 (ending) and fuselage panels for Hornet. Also undertakes maintenance.

FINMECCANICA SPA • Italy

Holding organization for Agusta, Alenia, FIAR and other companies.

FIRESTONE AIRCRAFT COMPANY • USA

Formed in 1946 by name change from G&A Aircraft Inc, a subsidiary of Firestone Tire and Rubber Company. G&A's XR-9 single-seat helicopter developed as XR-9B tandem two-seater. Also built two-seat CA-45D. Development discontinued 1947.

Flanders B.2 biplane, served with RNAS in 1914

Fleet Model 80 Canuck two-seat lightplane

FIRMA BVL • Czech Republic

Has developed the Qualt 200L two-seat monoplane.

FISHER AERO CORPORATION • USA

Markets kits and plans to construct Avenger single-seat monoplane (appeared 1994), Celebrity tandem two-seat biplane, tandem two-seat Culex twin-engined monoplane, Horizon 2 tandem two-seat high-wing monoplane, Mariah tandem two-seat low-wing monoplane (first flown 1993), and Youngster single-seat biplane.

FISHER BODY DIVISION, GENERAL MOTORS • USA

Entered aircraft production in the 1940s with design team headed by Don Berlin, formerly of Curtiss. Developed Eagle fighter with Allison engine, prototype first flown 30 September 1943. Eight XP-75s and five P-75As were built before the programme ended.

FISHER FLYING PRODUCTS • USA

Offers kits to allow amateur construction of FP-202 Koala single-seat high-wing microlight, FP-303 single-seat low-wing microlight, FP-505 Skeeter single-seat parasol-wing microlight, FP-606 Sky Baby single-seat parasol-wing microlight, Classic tandem two-seat biplane, Dakota Hawk side-by-side two-seat cabin monoplane, R-80 Tiger Moth as tandem two-seat 80 per cent-scale representation of de Havilland D.H.82 Tiger Moth biplane, and Super Koala side-by-side two-seat high-wing monoplane.

FLAIR AVIATION COMPANY • USA

See Fletcher Aviation Company

FLANDERS, L. HOWARD LTD. • UK

First machine, F.2 single-seat monoplane, flown August 1911 then altered to two-seater as F.3. Built four F.4 two-seat monoplanes for RFC in 1912. Two-seat B.2 biplane, powered by 70 hp Gnome Rhone rotary engine, first flown 1912 and acquired by Admiralty 1914.

FLÉCHAIR SA • France

Company built experimental aircraft designed by Ing Roland Payen, who had been involved in research and development of delta-winged aircraft since 1933. Payen's Pa.49, flown 22 January 1954, was the first French jet-powered delta-wing aircraft.

FLEET AIRCRAFT INC. • USA

Established in Buffalo, NY, Fleet produced the Fleet Model 2 with Kinner engine, and built a military two-seat primary trainer for the US Army Air Service. Designated PT-6, it was an improved version of the PT series initiated by Consolidated Aircraft Corporation, of which Fleet was a subsidiary.

FLEET AIRCRAFT LTD. • Canada

A subsidiary of the US company; formed 1929 to assemble and market the Fleet trainer. Wartime production included the Fairchild Cornell PT-19. Fleet Model 80 Canuck two-seat light-plane also built in quantity 1946-1947, after which aircraft production ceased. In 1952 Fleet acquired type certificate for Super-V twin-engined Beech Bonanza conversion from Bay Aviation Services Co, Oakland, California.

FLEETWINGS DIVISION OF KAISER CARGO INC. • USA

Formed 1929 and acquired Keystone Aircraft Corporation factory in 1934. Specialised in stainless-steel structure, including wings for the Douglas Dolphin and company's own Sea Bird amphibian, the first stainless steel aircraft to receive US Approved Type Certificate. Wartime production included subcontract parts manufacture. Acquired by shipbuilder Henry J. Kaiser in March 1943 and developed Model 23 Tandem and Model 33 trainers. Designed XBTK-1 torpedo bomber in 1943; only three completed.

FLETCHER AVIATION COMPANY • USA

Began in 1941 as Fletcher Aviation Corporation, developing FBT-2 trainer and CQ-1A two-seat target-control aircraft. FL-23 two-seat observation/liaison aircraft built for 1950 USAF competition, followed in 1953 by FD-25

Fletcher FU-24 Utility agricultural aircraft

Fletcher FD-25 Defender lightweight ground support aircraft

FMA Aé.M-01 two-seat military trainer

FMA Aé.M.B.1 bomber aircraft prototype

Defender light ground-support aircraft. FU-24 utility agricultural aircraft introduced 1954, developed for New Zealand, where 100 were assembled by James Aviation Ltd. Acquired by AJ Industries in 1960 and briefly renamed Flair Aviation before assuming name as above. Introduced FU-24A six-seat passenger/cargo version. Manufacturing and sales rights for FU-24 series sold to Air Parts (NZ) Ltd. (q.v.) in 1964.

FLETTNER GMBH • Germany

Innovative aerodynamic researcher who became interested in rotary-winged flight in 1920s; Anton Flettner's first helicopter made tethered flight in 1932, blades rotated by tip-mounted engines. BMW Bramo Sh14A-powered Fl 184 two-seat gyroplane flown 1935 and, in following year, single-seat experimental Fl 185 helicopter prototype. Flettner Fl 265 with twin intermeshing rotors appeared in 1939 and six were built before production was halted in favour of the Fl 282 Kolibri, first flown in 1941. 24 were built.

FLIGHT DESIGN GMBH • Germany

Currently offers the CT two-seat very light composites cabin lightplane (first flown 1996 and produced in association with Albert Schulze-Oechterding from ASO Flugsport), hang gliders and paragliders.

FLIGHT DYNAMICS INC. • USA

Developed Flightsail VII two-seat amphibian powered by a 90 hp Continental C90. Design begun 1966; first flown October 1970.

FLIGHT ENGINEERS LTD. • New Zealand

Joint company formed by agricultural operator Barr Brothers and Marine Helicopters Ltd. to maintain own fleets, but also undertook licence-assembly of Transavia PL-12 Airtruk agricultural aircraft from 1973. T320 version powered by Continental Tiara engine introduced 1977. Production ended 1980.

FLIGHT INVERT LTD. • UK

Non-profit making organisation formed 1975 to oversee Cranfield A1 single-seat aerobatic competition monoplane programme (first flown 1976).

FLIGHTSTAR INC. • USA

Offers kits to construct Flightstar II two-seat microlight, and Spyder and Formula single-seat microlights. Two-seat

C-42 Cyclone high-wing monoplane offered in kit form and as assembled certificated aircraft in US Primary Category.

FLIGHT TEAM • Slovenia

Produces three models of the Sinus two-seat microlight/motorglider, for distribution through German agent.

FLITESTAR ANOKAGAI • Malaysia

Became Dornier Seastar (q.v.).

FLS AEROSPACE LTD. • UK

Europe's leading independent aircraft maintenance company. Rights to Optica observation aircraft and Sprint (see Orca) aerobatic primary trainer were put up for sale in 1998.

FLUGZEUG-UNION-SÜD GMBH • Germany

Joint company formed in 1956 by Ernst Heinkel GmbH and Messerschmitt AG. to manufacture Potez Air Fouga Magister jet trainers for Luftwaffe. 194 aircraft built, components being constructed by Heinkel's Speyer factory and by Messerschmitt at Augsburg with final assembly and flight-test at München-Riem. Also undertook work in Fiat G.91 combat aircraft programme and was responsible for MBB Flamingo-Trainer (first flown 1979).

FLUGZEUGWERFT LÜBECK-TRAVEMÜNDE GMBH • Germany

Founded in May 1914 at Travemünde Privall to specialise in seaplane design and construction. Aircraft included F.1, a two-seat reconnaissance aircraft, powered by a Mercedes D III engine, three of which were built. The F.2 biplane (11 built) was slightly larger, with a Mercedes D IV engine, and armed with a Parabellum machine-gun. A total of 34 armed reconnaissance patrol biplanes with Benz IV engines was built 1917-1918.

FLYGFÖRVALTNINGENS VERKSTAD • Sweden

See FFVS.

FLYGINDUSTRI, AB. • Sweden

Subsidiary of Junkers Flugzeug Werke AG., established at Linhamm, Malmö, effectively escaping restrictions on aircraft construction in Germany. Civil production included the A 20 two/three-seat mail/freight aircraft introduced in

1923, G 23/G 24 three-engined nine-passenger airliners in 1924/25 and the single-engined, six-passenger W 34 built up to 1935. Three-engined K-30C bomber built 1924 and supplied to Russia as R 42; K-37 twin-engined light bomber flown 1927; 174 built in Japan by Kawasaki and Mitsubishi. K-47 monoplane appeared 1928, used as research aircraft for dive-bombing techniques, benefiting later Ju 87 programme.

FLYING K ENTERPRISES INC. • USA

Offers kits to build Sky Raider single-seat cabin monoplane.

FLYSYNTHESIS SRL • Italy

Markets high-wing Storch two-seat cabin microlight in assembled and kit forms, plus low-wing Texan.

FMA • Argentina

Fábrica Militar de Aviones SA established at Córdoba 1927; redesignated Instituto Aerotécnico 20 October 1943, incorporated into Industrias Aeronáuticas y Mecánicas del Estado 1952, became Dirección Nacional de Fabricaciones e Investigaciones Aeronáuticas 1957, reverted to FMA in 1968. Licence-production 1927-1943 included Avro 504R, Dewoitine D.21C, Bristol F.2B, Focke-Wulf Fw 44J, Curtiss Hawk 75. Indigenous designs included Aé.C-1 three-seat monoplane, Aé.C-2 trainer of 1932, Aé.T-1 five-seater of 1933, Aé.C-3 light aircraft of 1934, and Aé.M-01 built for Argentine Army. El Boyero two-seater built 1939-1940. Production of the IA.58 Pucará twin-turboprop COIN aircraft for Argentine Air Force ended in 1986.

FMA Aé.C-2 two-seat postal and training monoplane

FMA and Vought of USA collaborated on the Pampa 2000, as a contender for the US JPATS programme

FMA IA.58A Pucará counter-insurgency aircraft

First flight of IA.63 Pampa advanced and weapon training jet trainer, also for light attack, took place in October 1984. December 1994 agreement between the Government of Argentina and Lockheed Aircraft Service Company to privatize FMA aircraft factory and maintenance depot at Córdoba, with Lockheed operating as the management organisation from July 1995. See LMAASA.

FOCKE-ACHGELIS UND CO GMBH • Germany

Formed in 1933 by Heinrich Focke, formerly of Focke-Wulf, and aerobatic pilot Gerd Achgelis. Developed world's first completely successful helicopter, Fw 61, flown as a prototype on 26 June 1936. Also designed Fw 186 Argus As10C-engined autogyro to similar requirement that had produced the Fieseler Storch. Twin-rotor Fa 223 Drache, first flown August 1940, ordered into production 1942 at Hoyenkamp factory, later at Laupheim; in 1945 a captured Drache became first helicopter to cross English Channel. Fa 330 Bachstelze rotor kite deployed operationally aboard U-boats from 1942.

FOCKE-WULF FLUGZEUGBAU GMBH • Germany

Association between Heinrich Focke and Georg Wulf formalised 1 January 1924 with formation of Focke-Wulf Flugzeugbau AG. at Bremen. Financial support followed success of A 7 Storch two-seater, flown November 1921. Wulf killed 29 September 1927 test-flying F-19 Ente

canard. In 1931 acquired licence to build Cierva C.19 Mk IV autogiro. Focke concentrated on rotary-wing activities, fixed-wing design was entrusted to Kurt Tank, formerly of BFW and of Rohrbach Metallflugzeug GmbH. Albatros Flugzeugwerke GmbH, Berlin, amalgamated with Focke-Wulf. On Focke's resignation to form Focke-Achgelis, Tank appointed technical director. Reorganised June 1936 as GmbH under control of AEG. Ceased operations 1945, reformed 1951 and combined with Weser Flugzeugbau to form Vereinigte Flugzeugtechnische Werke.

First company design was A 16 three/four-seat commercial transport, followed by the eight/nine-seat A 17, the more powerful 650 hp BMW VI-powered A 29 and the three-crew/ten-passenger A 38 airliners. S 24 Kiebitz two-seat trainer won 1931 German Aerobatic Cham-

Germany's superb Focke-Wulf Fw 190 fighter

Focke-Wulf Ta 152, Ta designation honouring designer Kurt Tank

Focke-Wulf Fw 200 Condor, civil airliner which became a potent anti-shipping aircraft

pionship flown by Gerd Achgelis, who conducted maiden flight of Fw 44 Stieglitz trainer late summer 1932, widely used by embryo Luftwaffe and in European and South American countries. First Tank design produced in any numbers (approximately 1,000) was Fw 56 Stösser fighter/dive-bomber advanced trainer, followed in 1935 by Fw 58 Weihe communications aircraft/crew trainer and in 1938 by Fw 189 reconnaissance aircraft. Fw 200 Condor airliner flown July 1937, developed into Fw 200C long-range reconnaissance aircraft. With production total of more than 19,000, Fw 190 fighter was the most notable of Focke-Wulf's designs; after the first flight on 1 June 1939, entered squadron service August 1941.

High-altitude version, with revised high aspect ratio wing, designated Ta 152.

FOKKER AEROPLANBAU GMBH • Germany

Registered originally Fokker Aviatik GmbH, on 22 February 1912, Antony Fokker's first company operated under the above name at Berlin-Johannisthal then moved to Schwerin, Mecklenberg, in 1913. Name changed later to Fokker Flugzeugwerke. Company liquidated following Fokker's return to Holland after First World War. Fokker E series monoplanes flown successfully by Boelcke, Immelmann and others 1915-1916. Introduced interrupter gear, allowing bullets from a forward-firing machine-gun to pass between the propeller blades. Fokker Dr I triplanes built 1917-18, exponents including von Richthofen and Voss. Followed into production by D VII biplane, entering service April 1918. Ensuing D VIII parasol monoplane introduced Fokker cantilever wing. Also built 400 AEG C.IV trainers. F II developed at Schwerin 1919, first of Fokker high-wing passenger aircraft.

FOKKER AIRCRAFT CORPORATION OF AMERICA • USA

Antony Fokker's Atlantic Aircraft Corporation was reorganised on 16 September 1925, inheriting premises at Hasbrouck Heights, Teterboro, and the orderbook for the Noorduyn-designed Universal. Factory at Passaic, New Jersey, opened 1927. Glendale, West Virginia, factory opened August 1928. General Motors Corporation acquired a 40 per cent holding May 1929; Fokker resigned July 1931.

Improved Super Universal six-seater introduced 1927; 123 built. Three-engined 12-passenger F.10 flown April 1927; 65 built, first three for Western Air Express, forerunner of TWA. Followed by 59 14-seat F.10As. Fokker

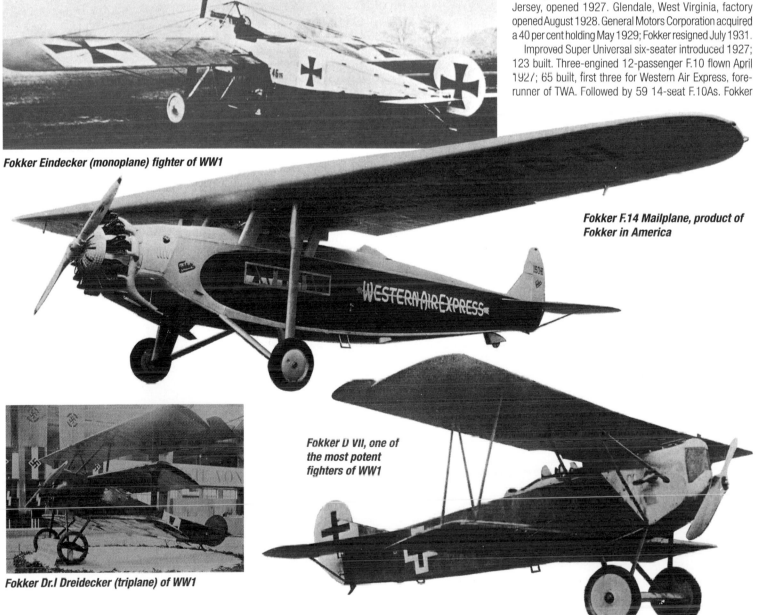

Fokker Eindecker (monoplane) fighter of WW1

Fokker Dr.I Dreidecker (triplane) of WW1

Fokker F.14 Mailplane, product of Fokker in America

Fokker D VII, one of the most potent fighters of WW1

Fokker F.VII trimotor, one of the early pioneering airliners

Fokker C.X reconnaissance/ground attack biplane

Fokker D.XXI single-seat monoplane fighter

32, first US four-engined airliner, flown 1929, having 32 seats and powered by two pairs of Pratt & Whitney Hornet engines in tandem with tractor and pusher propellers; ten built. Military designs included 1929 O-27 observation aircraft, of which 14 built.

FOKKER INDUSTRIA AERONAUTICA SA • Brazil

Initial production of 100 Fokker S-11 two-seat primary trainers, followed by 50 examples of S-12 tricycle-landing-gear version. Five S-14 Mach trainers assembled from Dutch-made components, before construction of 45 locally manufactured aircraft.

FOKKER • Netherlands

Full company name NV Koninklijke Nederlandse Vliegtuigenfabriek Fokker. Originally founded 21 July 1919 with factory at Veere, Zeeland, assembly at Amsterdam. New factory at Schiphol opened 1951. Later acquired Aviolanda (q.v.) and formed joint company with Vereinigte Flugzeugtechnische Werke in 1969. Pre-war civil airliners included eight-passenger F.VII, flown from Amsterdam to Batavia in 1924, and the F.VII-3m three-engined variant which, from 1928, was the most extensively built (116). Enlarged into 14-16-seat F.XII in 1930. F.XX tri-motor with retractable landing gear built 1933, and four-engined F.XXXVI 32-seat and F.XXII 22-seat airliners built 1934 and 1935 respectively. Principal military aircraft built 1919-1925 included C.I, C.III and C.V biplanes, used widely in Europe, China, Japan, Russia and South America. D.XXI monoplane fighter introduced 1936, flown in combat in

Second World War by Dutch and Finnish units. G.1 twin-boom twin-engined attack aircraft of 1936 also saw limited service, as did T.VIII twin-engined reconnaissance floatplanes flown to England in May 1940. Production during Occupation included Arado Ar 196 floatplanes, Bücker Bü 181 Bestmann trainers and Dornier Do 24 flying-boats.

Post-war activity included conversion of military Dakotas and Skymasters for civil use; production of S.11 and S.12 piston-engined and S.14 jet trainers between 1947 and 1955; licence-production of various types including 24 Hawker Sea Furies, 460 Hunter F.4 and F.6 fighters; final assembly and parts manufacture of 350 Lockheed F.104Gs; share in European manufacturing programme for F-16 fighter; associate member of Airbus Industrie (q.v.); production of 768 F.27 Friendship twin-turboprop airliners (first flown November 1955; figure includes those built by Fairchild in USA); and production of 241 F.28 Fellowship twin-turbofan airliners (first flown May 1967). F.27 and F.28 then replaced in production by much improved Fokker 50 (first flown December 1985) and Fokker 100

(first flown November 1986) respectively, with Fokker 60 Utility derivative of Fokker 50 first flying in November 1995 and Fokker 70 shortened derivative of Fokker 100 flying April 1993. In March 1996 company filed for bankruptcy, but Stork Group bought Fokker Aviation to continue as Fokker Aircraft BV for product support, electronic systems and components, aerostructures and special products. Several attempts to purchase the aircraft manufacturing business by foreign companies came to little, leading to the end of all aircraft production in May 1997 (latterly under trustees). See Rekkof Restart.

Fokker F.27 Friendship medium-range airliner

Fokker 60 Utility ordered by the Royal Netherlands Air Force as the only customer

Fokker 100 airliner operating with Korean Air

Fokker Maritime Enforcer Mk 2, an armed maritime variant of Fokker 50

Folland Gnat lightweight fighters

Ford Tri-Motor, known affectionately as the 'Tin Goose'

FOLLAND AIRCRAFT LTD. • UK

Formed in 1937 as reorganised British Marine Aircraft Co, Hamble; became Hamble Division, Hawker Siddeley Aviation, 1959. Undertook subcontract work on Bristol Blenheim and Beaufort, de Havilland Mosquito and Hornet, Short Sunderland and Supermarine Spitfire, among others. First original design was Fo 108 engine testbed aircraft, 12 built to Specification 43/37. Further subcontract participation in Comet, Sea Vixen, Britannia, Hunter and HS 748 programmes. Lightweight fighter designed by W. E. W. Petter flown initially as Fo 139 Midge, then as Fo 141 Gnat with Bristol Orpheus engine. Sold to Finnish and Indian Air Forces as fighter aircraft and developed as Fo 144 Gnat T.1 trainer for the RAF.

FORD MOTOR COMPANY • USA

Henry Ford provided backing for William Stout's Stout Metal Airplane Company, maker of the 2-AT single-engined eight-passenger airliner. Ford purchased Stout in 1925 and provided premises at Dearborne where Stout designed the first Ford 3-AT Tri-Motor, a modified 2-AT with three Wright J-4 engines. Howard Hicks replaced Stout and developed the 4-AT, 78 of which were built. The larger 5-AT, with three 420 hp Pratt & Whitney Wasps, was introduced in 1928, the last 'Tin Goose' being built in June 1933.

In 1941 Ford built a new factory and airfield at Willow Run, Michigan, where 5,107 Consolidated B-24E/H/J/L heavy bombers were built. A production run of 5,168 B-24Ns was cancelled at the end of the war. XC-109 bulk fuel tanker prototype converted from B-24E. A Ford factory at Iron Mountain, Michigan made 4,190 Waco CG-4A gliders.

See also Eastern Aircraft Division, General Motors, on wartime aircraft production by car manufacturers.

Fornaire F-1A Aircoupe, evolved from the Ercoupe 415

FORNAIRE AIRCRAFT COMPANY • USA

Forney Manufacturing Company acquired production rights for Engineering and Research Corporation's Ercoupe 415 two-seat light aircraft in April 1955. First production F-1 Aircoupe flew on September 1956. Offered later as Fornaire Execta, Explorer and Expediter. Rights sold in 1960 to the city of Carlsbad, New Mexico.

FOSTER WICKNER AIRCRAFT COMPANY LTD. • UK

Established in 1934 by G. N. Wickner, V. Foster and J. F. Lusty, initially at the latter's furniture factory at Bromley-by-Bow, London. Mr Wickner's earlier designs, built in Australia, included Wicko Sports Monoplane and Wicko Lion, both high-wing monoplanes on which the prototype Wicko F.W.1 was based. Of wooden construction, the F.W.1 was powered by a Ford V-8 engine, and became F.W.2 with Cirrus Minor and F.W.3 with Cirrus Major. Nine production aircraft built 1938-1939 at Southampton were designated G.M.1 with Gipsy Major engine.

FOUGA • France

Fouga's aircraft department formed 1936, subsequently building designs of M. Pierre Mauboussin who, with M. Castello, developed Castel-Mauboussin gliders and sailplanes. Operated postwar as Etablissements Fouga et Cie, becoming Air Fouga September 1956 when company was taken over, in equal shares, by Breguet, Dassault,

Above: Fouga Gemeaux two-seat twin-fuselage research aircraft

Morane-Saulnier, Sud Est and Ouest Aviation. Acquired by Henry Potez May 1958, renamed Potez Air Fouga. Early activities included production of Mauboussin 123 trainer, Castel C.25S, C.30S and C.300S gliders. Castel-Mauboussin CM.10 transport glider built for French military forces, also CM.100 powered version with two Renault engines. In the latter CM-101R Renault engines augmented by two Turbomeca Piméné turbojets. Experience with CM.8-R.9 Cyclipe and with the Gemeaux led to development of the CM.170R Magister jet trainer, first flown 23 July 1952 and subsequently built in quantity for French Air Force and overseas customers. Company operated as Potez Air Fouga until 23 September 1961, when it was completely absorbed into Etablissements Henry Potez SARL. Continued development of CM.170 Magister and CM.175 Zephyr naval version, which were first flown as production aircraft on 30 May 1959.

Above: Fouga CM.170 Magister, the world's first jet trainer

FOUND AIRCRAFT CANADA INC. • Canada

Current name for former Found Brothers Aviation (q.v.), offering the FBA-2E Bush Hawk five-seat or freight-carrying lightplane, as an improved derivative of the former FBA-2C. Testing completed in 1998.

FOUND BROTHERS AVIATION LTD. • Canada

Established at Malton, Ontario, in 1948 to build four-seat cabin monoplane designed by Captain S. R. Found. FBA-1A prototype first flown 13 July 1949. Developed version designated FBA-2A flown 11 August 1960, and FBA-2C

Above: Found Brothers FBA-2A five-seat utility transport

Found Brothers FBA-2C operating in British Columbia

five-seater on 9 May 1962. Six-seat Model 100 Centennial, with 290 hp Lycoming engine flown 7 April 1967 and superseded earlier models.

FOURNIER • France

René Fournier built RF.01 single-seat light aircraft/powered sailplane with modified Volkswagen engine, first flown 6 July 1960. Government assistance for development of improved RF-2, with 34 hp Rectimo-VW engine, subsequently produced by Alpavia (q.v.) as RF-3, with slightly uprated engine, first flown March 1963. M. Fournier designed a series of light aircraft of similar configuration for Sportavia-Putzer and Indraero. Established subsequently Avions Fournier to develop revised version of his RF-6 Sportsman, designated RF-6B; first flown 12 March 1974. Produced RF-9 motorglider 1982.

FOXJET INTERNATIONAL INC. • USA

Founded to develop Foxjet F600 four/six-seat twin-turbofan business jet.

FRAKES AVIATION INC. • USA

Specialists in turbine conversions of piston-engined aircraft, including Grumman Mallard with two Pratt & Whitney turboprop engines, and Grumman Ag-Cat which with a similar engine becomes Turbo-cat. Under contract to Mohawk Air Services, Frakes modified and obtained certification for the Mohawk 298, an updated Nord 262 with two 1174 shp turboprop engines for use by Allegheny Commuter airlines system.

FREEBIRD SPORT AIRCRAFT • USA

Markets kits to construct Freebird two-seat microlight.

FREEDOM LITE INC. • Canada

Markets kits to build the SkyWatch SS-11 tandem two-seat microlight.

FREEWING AIRCRAFT • USA

Offers plans to construct Freebird Mk V, a two-seat monoplane with pivoting main wing.

FRIEDRICHSCHAFEN GMBH • Germany

Flugzeugbau Friedrichshafen established with factory at Mansell, later at Warnemünde, producing many seaplane designs for German Navy. FF 29 twin-float reconnaissance seaplane introduced November 1914 for coastal patrol and fighter versions. Replaced by FF 49, with more pow-

Fournier RF-8 two-seat trainer built by Indraéro SA

Frake's turboprop conversion of Grumman Mallard

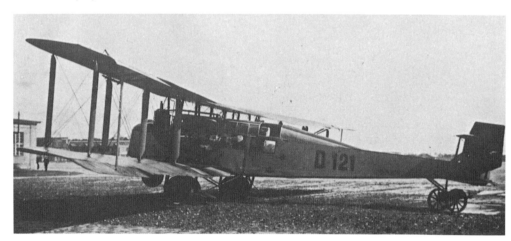

Friedrichshafen G IIIa twin-engined long-range bomber converted for use as an airliner

erful Benz Bz IV engine, introduced in May 1917. Also built land-based aircraft, including G III long-range bomber with two Mercedes D IV engines, used on Western Front in 1917.

FRONTIER AIRCRAFT • USA

First flown in 1995, the MD-11 two-seat high-wing cabin monoplane can be built from kits.

FUJI JUKOGYO KABUSHIKI KAISHA • Japan

Successor to Nakajima Aircraft Company, established 15 July 1953 with factory at Utsunomiya City. Built Cessna L-19E Bird Dog observation aircraft under licence. Concluded agreement with Beech in November 1953 to manufacture Beech B45 Mentor trainers; total of 124 built, deliveries commencing August 1954. From Mentor Fuji developed LM-1 Nikko four-seat liaison aircraft, first flown

Fuji FA-200 Aero Sabaru four-seat lightplane

Fuji T-1F2, Japan's first post-war jet aircraft

Fuji KM-2B tandem two-seat primary trainer

Funk B.2 lightweight two-seat monoplane

June 1955. Similar two-seat KM-2 developed. KM-2B with widened fuselage and tandem seating for two selected as JASDF primary trainer in August 1975. Fuji assembled or built more than 120 Bell 204B/B2 helicopters from 1962.

Fuji T-1 two-seat jet trainer was first post-war Japanese jet aircraft. Forty T-1As built with Bristol Orpheus engines, and 20 T-1Bs with Japanese engines. FA 200 Aero Subaru four-seat light aircraft first flown 12 August 1965 (nearly 300 built). Work on FA-300 twin-engined light transport began 1971, continued as joint venture with Rockwell International, USA, following agreement signed 28 June 1974, as Rockwell Commander 700; prototype first flown in Japan on 13 November 1974 and 30 delivered before co-operation ended in 1980 (also development of the higher-powered FA-300/Commander 710 then ended). Current programmes include production of the T-5 primary/basic trainer for the JMSDF (as turboprop devel-

opment of the KM-2, with KM-2Kai prototype flying in April 1988) AH-1S attack helicopter, 205B/UH-1J general-purpose helicopters (205Bs from 1995, military UH-1Js from 1993), participation in the Mitsubishi F-2 programme, subcontract work on the Mitsubishi F-15J and Kawasaki P-3C and T-4, manufacture of assemblies for a range of Boeing airliners, production of UAVs, and participation in space programmes.

FUNK AIRCRAFT COMPANY • USA

Formed 1941 at Coffeyville, Kansas, successor to Akron Aircraft Inc., to market Funk Bros. Model B two-seat monoplane. Production resumed after Second World War, aircraft redesignated B-85-C Bee, with Continental C-85 engine. Manufacturing rights acquired in 1962 by Thomas H. McLish of Sharon, Pennsylvania.

FUNK, D.D., AVIATION COMPANY • USA

Founded in 1950 at Salina, Kansas, by Don D. Funk; produced F 23 agricultural aircraft in two versions, F-23A with 240 hp Continental W-670 engine and F-23B with 275 hp Jacobs R-755.

F + W • Switzerland

See Eidgenössiches Flugzeugwerke (Federal Aircraft Factory) for early history. Adopted F + W title in 1972 from former EFW and two other used names. Subsequent work has included assembly of Hawk trainers, Hornet fighters, component production for Airbus and McDonnell Douglas airliners, manufacture of missiles, and more. See SF.

Below: Fuji-built Bell AH-1S attack helicopter (JGSDF)

GABARDINI SA • Italy

Manufactured a 80 hp rotary-engined two-seat mono-plane at Novara in 1913, used for a non-stop flight between Milan and Venice. Company subsequently opened factory at Cameri in 1914 to build a military version of this mono-plane, powered by a smaller engine. Also built biplane trainers. Nothing more heard of company until it produced a two-seat light cabin monoplane, the Lictor 90, in 1935.

GABRIEL BROTHERS • Poland

A small company which produced the P.5 single-seat para-sol monoplane in the 1920s.

GAC • USA

Situated on Long Island, New York, General Aircraft Corporation produced the Skyfarer two-seat cabin monoplane with simplified controls in 1941, but sold manufacturing rights to Grand Rapids Industries Inc (q.v.) in 1943. GAC built Waco CG-4A gliders for the USAAF in the Second World War. A company with the same name, but based at El Segundo, California, announced plans in 1969 for a 36-seat STOL transport, the GAC-100, powered by four Pratt & Whitney PT6A-40 turboprop engines.

GAC • USA

General Airplanes Corporation founded in June 1928 at Buffalo; by 1930 had produced GAC 101 Surveyor three-seat twin-engine high-wing cabin monoplane, GAC 102A Aristocrat three-seat high-wing cabin monoplane and the GAC Mailplane sesquiplane.

GAF • Australia

See Government Aircraft Factories.

Gail Model 202A Golduster agricultural aircraft

GAIL AIRCRAFT ENGINEERING COMPANY • USA

Based at Sacramento, California. Built agricultural aircraft, including the Model 202 Mantis, first flown May 1956 with 190 hp Lycoming engine.

GALAXY AEROSPACE • USA

New company, founded 1997 and partly owned by Israel Aircraft Industries, to promote the IAI Astra SPX and pro-mote and fit-out the 8-18 passenger Galaxy widebody intercontinental business jet developed by IAI (first flown December 1997).

GALLAUDET ENGINEERING COMPANY • USA

Built seaplanes during First World War at New York factory. A twin-engine biplane seaplane built for US Navy featured a four-bladed pusher propeller which revolved around the fuselage behind the wings. Later built 5-seat biplane tourer, the Liberty Tourist, and rebuilt 25 DH-4s for US Army. Company dissolved 1923 and factory acquired by Consolidated Aircraft Corporation (q.v.).

GALLEAO • Brazil

Former naval workshops which built aircraft for Brazilian Air Force, including Focke-Wulf Fw 44 primary trainers

Above: Gallaudet Chummy Flyabout two-seat monoplane

Below: GAC 102A Aristocrat, used by Richard Byrd's expedition to the Antarctic

Gallaudet D-4 seaplane with mid-fuselage mounted pusher propeller

and Fw 58 twin-engined advanced trainers. In 1946 a batch of Fairchild PT-19 trainers was built under a licence agreement.

GALLINARI • Italy

This shipbuilding company built seaplanes during the First World War, and tested them at the Marina di Pisa.

G AND A AIRCRAFT INC. • USA

Formerly the AGA Aviation Corporation (q.v.), G and A Aircraft succeeded the Pitcairn-Larsen Autogiro Co Inc. (q.v.), which itself took over the Pitcairn Autogiro Company (q.v.) in 1940. In 1943 G and A was acquired by the Firestone Aircraft Company (q.v.) of Akron, Ohio, together with almost 200 patents concerned with rotary-wing aircraft. G and A built gliders and experimental autogiros in the Second World War, and carried out subcontract manufacture.

GANNET AIRCRAFT • USA

Formed at Sun Valley, California, in late 1950s to produce modified version of Grumman Widgeon amphibian known as Super Widgeon and powered by two 300 hp Lycoming engines. Company used SCAN 30 airframes (licence-built in France) for initial conversions.

GANZAVIA KFT • Hungary

Founded by Ganz Machinery Works Holding Ltd. to develop the GAK-22 Dino.

Below: GanzAVIA GAK-22 Dino negative-staggered biplane

Gardan GY-80 Horizon four-seat lightplane

GARDAN • France

Light aircraft designer responsible for the CAB Minicab, Supercab and Sipa 200 and 300. Designed four-seat, all-metal lightplane, the GY-80 Horizon, which flew in July 1960 with 150 hp Lycoming engine. Horizon subsequently entered quantity production with Sud Aviation (q.v.) under an agreement signed in 1962.

GARLAND-BIANCHI AIRCRAFT COMPANY • UK

Formed in 1955 by P. A. T. Garland and D. E. Bianchi to licence-build the Piel CP.301 Emeraude two-seat light aircraft, subsequently renamed Linnet. Built two aircraft before a new company, Fairtravel Ltd. (q.v.), was formed by AVM Don Bennett to take over production. Fairtravel Ltd. built three more Linnets, the last being delivered in 1965

GARRETT, RICHARD, & SONS • UK

Built 60 RAF F.E.2bs under subcontract in 1918. A contract for a further 100 was cancelled at end of the First World War.

GASHULYAK, YAROSLAV • USSR

Designed the G-1, a single-seat helicopter powered by Irbit two-cylinder motorcycle engine, in the spring of 1961. The aircraft is said to have gone into production for flying clubs following successful tests at Kirovograd in the Ukraine.

GATARD • France

M. Albert Gatard designed and built several light monoplanes in mid-1950s with a new control system using a variable-incidence large-area tailplane. AG 01 Alouette was a two-seater, AG 02 Poussin a single-seater and AG 03 Hirondelle two-seat side-by-side. Development of all three aircraft continued into the 1970s.

GATES AIRCRAFT CORPORATION • USA

Established 1929 by Ivan R. Gates. Acquired manufacturing rights for Belgian Stampe and Vertongen RSV.18-100 and 26-100 aircraft. No details found of numbers built, if any.

GATES LEARJET CORPORATION • USA

William P. Lear founded the Swiss American Aviation Corporation (q.v.) in 1960 to build a twin-jet executive aircraft, originally designated SAAC-23 and later named Learjet. Tooling was completed in Europe but moved to Wichita, Kansas, in 1962, when the company became known as Lear Jet Corporation. In 1967 Bill Lear sold his 60 per cent interest in the company to Gates Rubber Cor-

poration, and in 1970 the name was changed to Gates Learjet Corporation. Became Learjet Inc (q.v.) in 1987.

GAZUIT-VALLADEAU • France

Known mainly as light aircraft maintenance company. Gazuit was formerly a designer with Morane-Saulnier, and Valladeau had been a subcontractor for some Wassmer aircraft. The company produced a 2/3-seat light aircraft, the GV 103L, which first flew on 1 May 1969. Subsequently built a second example with the intention of finding a sponsor for production of the type, but this did not materialise.

GEE BEE • USA

See Granville Brothers Aircraft Co.

GEEST FLUGZEUGBAU GMBH • Germany

Formed in 1915 at Berlin-Oberschöneweide with capital of 80,000 marks. Built number of allegedly inherently stable monoplanes during First World War.

Below: Gates Learjet 25 ten-seat twin-jet executive transport

Gates Learjet 24D eight-seat twin-jet light executive transport

GENAIR • South Africa

Durban-based (General Aircraft (Pty.) Ltd.) built the Piel Emeraude two-seat light aircraft under the name Aeriel Mk II. First prototype flown in October 1959, and first production aircraft in February 1960. Aeriel was subsequently built by Southern Aircraft Construction and Robertson Aircraft Sales, but in September 1962 Durban Aircraft Corporation (q.v.) was formed to continue its construction.

GENAIRCO • Australia

General Aircraft Company Ltd. formed in 1929 at Sydney/Mascot Aerodrome. Built large factory, initially carried out overhauls, but by 1930 had designed a three-seat biplane, the Genairco, powered by Cirrus Hermes engine. Subsequently produced a four-seat version. Company thought to be inactive by about 1934.

GENERAL AEROPLANE COMPANY • USA

Based at Detroit, Michigan; built three types of aircraft during First World War and operated a flying school. The aircraft were Gamma S biplane with floats; Gamma L, similar but with wheels; and the Beta flying-boat. All had engine installations driving pusher propellers.

GENERAL AIRCRAFT COMPANY LTD. • Australia

See GENAIRCO

GENERAL AIRCRAFT CORPORATION • USA

See GAC.

GENERAL AIRCRAFT LTD. • UK

Established 1931 at Croydon Airport. Chief designer was Swiss H. J. Stieger. Acquired world rights from Monospar Company for its system of construction for aircraft up to 3,000 lb (1,360 kg) laden weight. First type was ST-3 three-seat enclosed cabin monoplane with two 45 hp Salmson radial engines. Later built series of light twins; GAL 41 Monospar of 1939 was first British aircraft with pressurised cabin. Single-engined pre-Second World War Cygnet monoplane (see C. W. Aircraft) was first light all-metal stressed-skin civil aircraft in UK; also an experimental open-cockpit version, the Owlet. Took over premises of British Aircraft Manufacturing Company in 1938. Built Hotspur training gliders and later Hamilcar assault gliders during Second World War. Post-war work included conversion of Mosquitoes as target tugs and design of GAL-60 Universal Freighter, built as the Beverley after General Aircraft merged with Blackburn in January 1949.

GENERAL AIRCRAFT (PTY.) LTD. • South Africa

See Genair.

GENERAL AIRPLANES CORPORATION • USA

See GAC.

GENERAL AIRPLANE SERVICE • USA

Fixed-base operator at Sheridan, Wyoming, in early 1950s. Converted Piper J-3s, PA-11s and PA-12s for agricultural work by installation of bigger engines. Company's Model II ag-plane was a mixture of Piper parts with a 200 hp Ranger engine from Fairchild PT-19 and a new lower wing to make it a biplane; first flight 12 October 1953.

GENERAL AVIA • Italy

Established in 1970 by Dott Ing Stelio Frati, designer of a series of light aircraft from the Ambrosini F.4 to F.250 (subsequently developed as the SIAI SF.260), to develop aircraft of Frati design for mostly manufacture by other concerns. First was the F.20 Pegaso light twin; two prototypes built (first flown 1971) and an agreement was reached for production aircraft to be manufactured by Italair (q.v.). Also designed the Canguro transport (developed by SIAI-Marchetti but became a VulcanAir type; q.v.) and the Jet Squalus (see Promavia and Alberta Aerospace). Currently produces F.22 Pinguino two-seat aerobatic lightplane and trainer in several versions with retractable or fixed undercarriages (first flown June 1989), the F.22 Bupp variant with only fixed undercarriage and other changes, plus the F.220 Airone four-seat development.

GENERAL AVIATION MANUFACTURING CORPORATION • USA

Incorporated in May 1930, with W. H. Miller as chief engineer. The Fokker Aircraft Corporation, in which General Motors Corporation held 41 per cent interest, was taken over by General Aviation Manufacturing Corporation in summer 1931. In 1933 merger concluded between GAC and North American Aviation Inc (q.v.). GA built F-15 twin-engine pusher monoplane flying-boat for USCG and GA.43 ten-passenger single-engine cabin monoplane, which later became known as Clark GA.43.

GÉNÉRAL AÉRONAUTIQUE • France

Formed in February 1930 by a number of the most important French aircraft manufacturers, and one engine manufacturer, as a result of a concentration and rationalisation of policy proposed by the French Air Minister. Companies were Lorraine-Hanriot, Chantiers Aéro-Maritimes de la Seine, Nieuport-Delage, Société Aérienne Bordelaise, Société d'Emboutissage et de Constructions Aéronautiques, Latham, and Société Lorraine (all q.v.).

Below: General Aircraft GAL 58 Hamilcar X powered assault glider, intended for operation in the Pacific theatre of war

Above: General Dynamics F-16 single-seat advanced combat fighter

GENERAL DYNAMICS CORPORATION • USA

A major reorganisation in 1961 resulted in General Dynamics' 12 operating divisions being divided into two major groups. On the aerospace side, the Western Group contained components of the Convair division, which itself had originated in 1923 as the Consolidated Aircraft Corporation (q.v.), merging in 1943 with Vultee Aircraft Inc to form Consolidated Vultee Aircraft Corporation (both q.v.). Before this, Consolidated had taken over two other aircraft companies, Thomas Morse and Hall Aluminium (q.v.). In 1954 Consolidated Vultee merged with the General Dynamics Corporation to become the Convair Division, at which time the CV-880 and -990 jet transports were in production, together with F-102 and F-106 fighters, and the B-58 Hustler was at an advanced stage to provide the USAF with its first supersonic bomber (first flown November 1956). Two USAF wings eventually flew B-58As.

In December 1964 the first flight took place of the F-111, a variable-geometry tactical fighter-bomber which entered USAF operational service from 1968, followed by the FB-111A strategic bomber variant which replaced B-58As from 1970. In January (officially February) 1974 the first flight took place of the F-16 lightweight fighter for the USAF; selected for engineering and manufacturing development in 1975, but with ground-attack options and provision for radar and navigation avionics suited to all-weather operations. Chosen also for service by European air forces, with European assembly, F-16 deliveries began 1979 (nearly 4,000 delivered by 1999 to many forces worldwide). Light aircraft manufacturer Cessna bought in 1985, but sold to Textron in 1992. The Tactical Military Aircraft division of General Dynamics was bought by Lockheed Corporation in March 1993, becoming Lockheed Fort Worth Company; taking over programmes including F-16 and the General Dynamics share in the F-22 (previously a programme of three manufacturers: General Dynamics, Lockheed and Boeing).

Right: General Dynamics F-111C Aardvark of the RAAF, the only remaining operator of the F-111

GENERAL DYNAMICS CORPORATION, FORT WORTH DIVISION • USA

Became separate division of General Dynamics after June 1974, before which it was a part of Convair division. Became responsible for F-111/FB-111 variable-geometry combat aircraft and General Dynamics F-16 air-superiority fighter. See previous entry.

GENERAL MOTORS (EASTERN AIRCRAFT DIVISION) • USA

A division of the General Motors Corporation, formed in January 1942 for aircraft production in five of the Corporation's US eastern seaboard factories. Built Grumman Wildcats under designation FM-1 (first flew 1 September 1942), and Avengers as TBM-1.

GENERAL WESTERN AERO CORPORATION • USA

Built Meteor two-seat light monoplane in early 1930s, powered by 100 hp Kinner engine.

GÉRIN • France

Jacques Gérin developed a biplane with variable wing area, the Varivol. Wing trailing edges could be wound in and out by electric motor. Full-scale tests in windtunnel at Chalais Meudon followed by flying tests in March 1936. Pilot M. Demimuid killed in Varivol crash on 29 November 1936, but this was not attributable to variable-wing mechanism, which was intact.

GERMAN BIANCO SA • Argentina

Large industrial company which formed division in 1944 for glider production and aircraft repair. Began licence-production of Italian Macchi M.B.308, flying the first in February 1959. Production was completed in the late 1960s.

GERMANIA FLUGZEUGWERKE GMBH • Germany

Formed at Leipzig during First World War to produce aircraft under subcontract. Also operated a flying school using company-designed aircraft. Closed at time of Versailles Peace Treaty.

GERNER GMBH • Germany

Foundation date not known, but by 1931 had built a two-seat all-steel light aircraft, the G.II.R, powered by BMW or Salmson engine. Later version was G.II.R6 with Hirth H.M.60 engine. Completely taken over in 1934 by specially formed new company, Adlerwerke GmbH of Frankfurt (q.v.).

GERONIMO CONVERSIONS CORPORATION • USA

Successor to Vecto Instrument Corp and Vecto Aircraft Engineering Division (q.v.), having acquired the assets of both companies on their owner's death in 1965. Based at San Antonio, Texas, Geronimo carried out Vecto-designed conversions on the Piper Apache, fitting bigger engines

Above: Gippsland GA-200 Fatman agricultural aircraft

Left: Gippsland GA-8 Airvan utility transport

Right top: GKN Westland Lynx Mk 21As operated by Brazilian Navy

Right bottom: GKN Westland Lynx Mk 9 light battlefield helicopter with the British Army

and improving the aircraft's internal and external appearance. Company name changed to Seguin Aviation (q.v.) in late 1960s.

GEVERS AIRCRAFT INC. • USA

Established 1988 to develop the unique Genesis six-seat twin piston-engined monoplane, featuring telescopic wings and a multi-configurational undercarriage to permit operations from land, water or snow. Construction of prototype began 1998.

GIDROPLAN LTD. • Russia

Name of former Redan (q.v.) since 1995. Producing Che-22 three-seat amphibious flying-boat (first flown 1992), developed from the single example of the Boris Chernov Che-20 two-seat homebuilt prototype that was tested

1989-1992. Che-25 four-seat derivative of Che-22 first flown 1996 but not selected for further production. Has also developed the Tsykada twin-engined very light agricultural monoplane.

GILLIS AIRCRAFT CORPORATION • USA

Incorporated in 1927 at Battle Creek, Michigan, Gillis made its debut at the 1928 Detroit Air Show with the Crusader four-seat commercial cabin biplane, powered by a 125 hp Ryan Siemens engine.

GIPPSLAND AERONAUTICS PTY. LTD. • Australia

Approved manufacture and maintenance facility established in 1971. Also developed and offers piston-engined GA-200 Fatman single/two-seat agricultural aircraft with

an 800-litre hopper (first flown March 1991) and the AG-Trainer as dual-control training model, plus latest GA-8 Airvan piston-engined 8/9-seat general-purpose utility monoplane suited to operations from unprepared and short airstrips (first flown March 1995).

GKN WESTLAND LTD. • UK

Current name for former Westland Helicopters Ltd. (q.v.). Operates three divisions as: GKN Westland Aerospace Ltd. with activities including manufacture of structures (airframe or nacelles) for Lynx and EH 101 helicopters, and many airliners including Airbus A330/A340, Boeing 737/747/767/MD-11/C-17, Saab 2000, Fairchild Dornier 328, Bombardier Dash 8 and Global Express, Lockheed Martin C-130J, and IPTN N250, plus helicopter and engine transmissions; GKN Westland Helicopters Ltd., manufacturing Boeing Apache Longbow as WAH-64 for British Army,

Global Huey800 conversion for UH-1H

EH 101 (company has 50 per cent holding with Agusta of Italy), and operates GKN Westland Heliport; and GKN Westland Technologies Ltd. Lynx general-purpose army and naval twin-turboshaft helicopter first flown March 1971 as joint programme with Aérospatiale of France, and continues in production (some 400 built). Sea King first flown May 1969 as medium multirole type, derived from Sikorsky S-61, and 326 delivered up to end of production in late 1990s (including Commando tactical assault derivative).

GLASFASER ITALIANA SRL • Italy

Constructed prototype T-30 Katana. See Pietro Terzi.

GLASSIC COMPOSITES LLC • USA

Markets kits to construct SQ.2000 composites-built four-seat canard monoplane with pusher engine, available in several versions.

GLENNY & HENDERSON • UK

Company at Byfleet, Surrey, which built two Henderson-Glenny HSF.II Gadfly single-seat light monoplanes in 1929, one with an ABC Scorpion II engine, the other with a Salmson AD.9 radial.

GLOBAL HELICOPTER TECHNOLOGY INC. • USA

Founded 1987, offers the Huey800 as a retrofit installation for the Bell UH-1H helicopter, based on a replacement LHTEC T801 turboshaft engine, offering much-extended range.

GLOBE AIRCRAFT CORPORATION • USA

Formed originally as the Bennett Aircraft Corporation to manufacture aircraft from Duraloid, a new type of bonded plywood. Produced twin-engine eight-seat monoplane, the BTC-1, about 1940. Company reorganised and renamed Globe Aircraft Corporation in 1941. First design under new name was the GC-1 Swift, a two-seat light monoplane with retractable landing gear and Continental engine. Development stopped by war, but produced post-war from 1945. Company built also Beech 18s for US Government during Second World War.

GLOSTER AIRCRAFT COMPANY LTD. • UK

Formed in 1917 as the Gloucestershire Aircraft Company Ltd. to take over subcontract work from the Aircraft Manufacturing Company and H. H. Martyn & Co Ltd. of Cheltenham. D.H.4 and D.H.6 fuselages had been built by Martyn, and by the end of the war the company had supplied 461 Bristol Fighters and 165 RAF F.E.2bs, as well as Nieuport Nighthawks and other fuselages.

Fifty Nighthawks, renamed Sparrowhawks, built for Japan to a 1920 order, were shortly followed by the first true Gloucester aircraft, the Bamel single-seat racing biplane, designed and built in less than four weeks. Its designer, H. P. Folland, joined the company soon after the Bamel's completion. A line of biplane fighters followed, the Grebe and Gamecock being notable successes, and in 1926 the company was renamed Gloster Aircraft Company Ltd. moving its main factory to Hucclecote, Gloucester.

Joining the Hawker Siddeley Group (q.v.) in 1934, Gloster continued fighter production with the Gauntlet and Gladiator, the latter being the RAF's last biplane fighter. During the Second World War Gloster built 2,750 Hurricanes and 3,330 Typhoons, and produced Britain's first jet aircraft to specification E.28/39, the first of two single-jet prototypes flying in 1941 and leading to the twin-jet Meteor of 1944. A total of 3,545 Meteors was produced by Gloster and Armstrong Whitworth. Gloster's final production aircraft was the twin-jet delta-wing Javelin all-weather interceptor, flown in 1951, of which 435 were produced for the RAF. Gloster ceased aircraft production in 1956.

Globe GC-1 Swift two-seat lightweight cabin monoplane

Gloster Meteors, the first RAF jet fighters

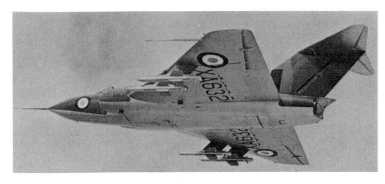

Gloster Javelin twin-jet delta-winged fighter

Gloster Gauntlet, last open cockpit biplane in RAF service

GOEDECKER FLUGZEUGBAU • Germany

Small company at Niederwalluf-on-Rhine, built several Taube-type monoplanes pre-war and Goedecker B trainer prototype in 1915. Also ran flying school. Closed at time of Versailles Peace Treaty.

GOETZE • Germany

Commandit Gesellschaft Richard Goetze founded in First World War with four factories in the Berlin area. Reputed to have built Otto biplanes.

GOLDEN CIRCLE AIR INC. • USA

Offers kits to build single-seat T-Bird I, two-seat T-Bird Side by Side, two-seat T-Bird Tandem and three-seat T-Bird III microlights.

GOLDEN EAGLE AIRCRAFT CORPORATION • USA

Incorporated in 1929 at Inglewood, California, with F. M. Smith as chief engineer. Built Golden Eagle Chief high-wing two-seat training monoplane at that time. Three versions built with engines from 60-100 hp.

GOODYEAR AIRCRAFT CORPORATION • USA

Formed 1940 to take over the Goodyear Zeppelin Corporation. Served as aircraft manufacturer and subcontractor to numerous companies during Second World War, including complete construction of the FG-1 Corsair, a Chance Vought design. Reverted to lighter-than-air craft post-war, but built a few GA-2 Duck three-seat experimental amphibians in 1947-8. GA-400R light single-seat helicopter flown in May 1954. Produced the Goodyear Inflatable Aircraft with an inflatable wing in mid-1950s.

GOSPORT AIRCRAFT CO LTD. • UK

Formed in early part of First World War at Gosport, Hants. Built flying-boats, mainly Norman Thompson FBAs plus some Porte/Felixstowe F.5s.

Above: Goupy experimental triplane

Right: Gotha G.III twin-engined heavy bomber of WW1

GOTAVERKEN • Sweden

Shipbuilding company, opened an aircraft department for licence-construction of Hawker aircraft for Swedish government. Received order for Hart biplanes powered by Swedish-built Pegasus engines in 1935. Subsequently built a few light aircraft of its own design, most notably the GV.38 high-wing monoplane.

GOTHAER WAGGONFABRIK AG. • Germany

Operated aircraft works and flying school at Gotha and seaplane school at Warnemünde in First World War. Manufactured large quantities of aircraft during the war, including seaplanes and twin-engine bombers. Closed by Versailles Peace Treaty. Reopened in mid-1930s with two-seat training biplane, Go 145. In Second World War built Bf 109 fighter and Do 172 bomber, also Go 242 glider and a powered version designated Go 244.

GOUPY • France

Company engaged largely in experimental work but built a few biplanes of its own design from around 1913.

GOURDOU ET LESEURRE • France

Joint designers of a parasol-wing monoplane in 1918. Few built. Developed into C.1 fighter of 1922 with retractable landing-gear and Gnome-Bristol Jupiter engine. In 1925 became associated with the French dockyard Ateliers et Chantiers de la Loire, with change of name to Loire-

Goodyear GA-2 Duck three-seat amphibian

Right: Gourdou et Leseurre Type A parasol-wing monoplane fighter

Above: GAF Nomad Search Master, a maritime version of this STOL utility aircraft

Gourdou-Leseurre. In 1929 disassociated with LGL and returned to original title.

GOVERNMENT AIRCRAFT FACTORIES • Australia

Aircraft production at Australian Government-owned factories began during Second World War with Bristol Beauforts and Beaufighters, and later included Lancasters and Lincolns (see Department of Aircraft production). Designed and produced Jindivik target aircraft, flown in 1952, after a piloted version, Pika, had flown in 1950. Built Mirage fighters and trainers for the RAAF in 1960s-1970s. Produced Nomad twin-engine STOL transport, first flown in July 1971. See AeroSpace Technologies of Australia (ASTA).

HANS GRADE FLIEGER WERKE • Germany

Hans Grade was the first German to fly in a triplane of his own design and with his own engine. Before First World War Grade had a civil flying school at Bork. His aircraft, mostly high-wing monoplanes, were not adopted by the military. First German looping flights made in a Grade monoplane with landing gear both above and below wing! Sold factory to Aviatik (q.v.) during First World War.

GRAHAME-WHITE AVIATION COMPANY LTD. • UK

Founded by Claude Grahame-White in 1909, company began operations with flying school at Pau, France. Moved

Gee-Bee Sportster, one of the highly successful Granville Brothers racers

to England, acquired Hendon Aerodrome in 1911 and built factory. Acquired agency in 1913 for Morane-Saulnier monoplanes and built these for War Office. Also built own design pusher biplane in 1914, adopted by Admiralty as standard school machine. Three-engine Ganymede bomber of 1918 had two tractor and one pusher propeller with twin fuselages. Company stopped producing aircraft in 1919.

GRAND RAPIDS INDUSTRIES INC. • USA

Furniture manufacturer which built wooden parts for aircraft and gliders in Second World War. Acquired manu-

facturing rights of Skyfarer two-seat light cabin monoplane from General Aircraft Corporation (q.v.) in 1943. Aircraft had simplified control system and was the second aircraft to be certificated by the US Civil Aeronautics Board as characteristically incapable of spinning. Design was shelved because of war; licence transferred to Le Mars Manufacturing Company in 1944.

GRANVILLE BROTHERS AIRCRAFT INC. • USA

Based at Springfield, Massachusetts, Granville became known for the 1930-1933 series of Gee Bee racers, first

Grahame-White Type 10 Charabanc five-seat biplane

Grahame-White Type 11 Warplane, with pusher engine, built in 1914

of which came second in the 1930 All-America Air Derby round the USA. In September 1932 Gee Bee R-1 Super Sportster set new world landplane speed record of 294.417mph (473.820kmh). Company succeeded by Granville, Miller and de Lackner in 1934. Built Granville R6H Cyclone-engined monoplane for England-Australia race, but aircraft only reached Bucharest.

GREAT LAKES AIRCRAFT CORPORATION • USA

Established in 1929 at Cleveland, Ohio. Built aircraft for US Army and Navy, plus a series of single and two-seat biplanes, beginning with the 2T-1A single-seater and including also the TG-1 Torpedo bomber. Company reappeared in mid-1960s to build scaled-down kit version of Great Lakes Sport Trainer known as Baby Great Lakes.

GREAT PLAINS AIRCRAFT • USA

Markets kits and plans to construct single-seat Sonerai I monoplane and tandem two-seat Sonerai II in various subversions. Sonerai I originally designed by John Monnett and first flown 1971.

GREEK NATIONAL AIRCRAFT FACTORY • Greece

British company Blackburn Aeroplane & Motor Co developed aircraft factory at Phaleron, Athens, following a 1925 agreement with Greek Government. Subsequently built there Blackburn Velos torpedo-bombers, Avro 504 variants and Breguet 19s.

GREEN SKY ADVENTURES INC. • USA

Sells plans and kits to construct Micro Mong single seat biplane and plans for the Zippy Sport single-seat monoplane.

GREGA, JOHN • USA

Developed a modernised version of the 1920's Pietenpol Aircamper two-seat parasol-wing monoplane, first flown 1963 and available in plans form (plus some components) as the GN-1 Aircamper.

GRENCHEN, FLUGZEUGBAU • Switzerland

A small scale builder of the WF.21/C4 four-seat monoplane designed and also built by Farner AG (q.v.).

GRIFFON AEROSPACE INC. • USA

First flew in 1997 the seven-seat, reverse-stagger Lionheart cabin biplane, offered as a kit.

Great Lakes Sport Trainer, a two-seat sporting biplane

GRIGOROVICH, D. P. • USSR

Russian designer of the P.I.1 four-seat high-wing commercial monoplane, built by a State factory at Leningrad in mid-1920s, powered by 100 hp Bristol Lucifer engine.

GRINVALDS • France

Orion four-seat composites monoplane, with pusher propeller aft of tail, produced by Jean Grinvalds 1982. Plans and access to moulds later made available from Club Orion.

GROB • Germany

See Burkhart Grob Luft- und Raumfahrt GmbH & Co KG.

GROEN BROTHERS AVIATION INC. • USA

Has developed the three-seat Hawk III multipurpose cabin gyroplane, first flown February 1997 in H2X prototype form, capable of vertical (jump) take off. Initial 200 ordered by Shanghai Energy and Chemical Company (SECC) in China for corporate transport and air taxi applications. Five-seat Hawk V, eight-seat Hawk VIII and 30+ seat Commuter Hawk proposed, SECC having ordered up to 100 Hawk Vs and 180 Hawk VIIIs in 1998.

GROPPIUS • USSR

Two-seat commercial biplane designed by E. E. Groppius and built in late 1924 by a State factory in Moscow. Powered by 300 hp Hispano-Suiza engine.

GRULICH • Germany

Deutscher Aero-Lloyd, the air transport company, built a high-wing training monoplane designed by Dr Ing K. Grulich in 1925. Designated S.1, it could have either 75 hp or 100 hp Siemens engine.

GRUMMAN AEROSPACE • USA

See below.

GRUMMAN AIRCRAFT ENGINEERING CORPORATION • USA

Incorporated 1929 at Farmingdale, New York. Contractor to US Navy and Coast Guard. Built FF-1 (first flown 1931) and SF-1 two-seat biplane fighters with retractable landing gear, followed by single-seat F2F (first flown October 1933) and F3F (delivered 1936), plus all metal amphibian as the JF-1 (first flown May 1933), later known as the Duck. Subsequent production, mainly for the US Navy and Marine Corps, included F4F Wildcat fighter (first Grumman monoplane, first flown September 1937), TBM Avenger torpedo-bomber (first flown August 1941), F6F Hellcat fighter (delivered from 1943), F7F Tigercat twin-

Grumman Avenger torpedo-bomber of 1941 (Grumman)

engined carrier fighter-bomber (first flown December 1943) and F8F Bearcat fighter (first flown August 1944) during Second World War, plus Widgeon and Goose (delivered from 1939) amphibians. Post-war aircraft included the anti-submarine Guardian (first flown December 1945), Albatross amphibian (first flown October 1947), F9F Panther as its first jet fighter (first flown November 1947), and F11F Tiger day jet fighter (first flown July 1954 in original F9F-9 form).

Grumman's entry into specialized electronic warfare aircraft began in December 1952 with the first flight of its S2F Tracker (later S-2), though this was a carrierborne anti-submarine aircraft. From Tracker were developed variants for carrier transport operations; the C-1 Trader and, more importantly, the WF (later E-1) for airborne early-warning, with an over-fuselage radome (first flown March 1957) and based on the S-2A. Such was the success of the E-1 concept that the much improved E-2 Hawkeye was developed, which first flew in October 1960 (originally as W2F-1) and remains in production in 1999 by Northrop Grumman (q.v.), itself leading to the C-2 Greyhound transport derivative (first flown November 1964). Grumman also developed the OV-1 Mohawk for the US Army for observation, first flown April 1959 and also using the successful twin-turboprop engine layout.

In April 1960 Grumman flew the A2F-1, which in production form became the A-6 Intruder twin-jet carrierborne long-range and low-level strike aircraft, finally withdrawn

Grumman F9F-6 was named Cougar, basically a swept-wing development of Panther

Above: Grumman-developed OV-1D Mohawk observation aircraft used by the US Army

Right: Grumman Albatross, modified in early 1980s to civil G-111 configuration for use by Chalks International, the commuter airline of Resorts International

Above: Grumman won a contract in 1975 to produce EF-111A Raven tactical radar jamming aircraft from F-111As

Right: Grumman Tomcat was finally produced in F-14D 'Super Tomcat' form, by conversion plus by manufacture of 37 new aircraft up to 1992

from service in the late 1990s. Intruder itself spawned an electronic warfare variant, the EA-6 Prowler, first flown May 1968 and still in service in 1999. The final fighter to carry the Grumman name was the F-14 Tomcat, designed as a carrier based variable-geometry long-range type armed with super-long-range Phoenix air-to-air missiles (first flown December 1970, entering service with the US Navy from 1972 and exported to Iran for land-based operations from 1976). By the time Tomcat had flown company had been divided (1969) into Grumman Aerospace and other individual corporations via the Grumman Corporation holding company. American Aviation Corporation (see AAC) became part of Grumman American Aviation Corporation (q.v.) in 1973. In May 1994 Grumman and Northrop merged to form Northrop Grumman (q.v.).

GRUMMAN AMERICAN AVIATION CORPORATION • USA

Part of Grumman Corporation, with merger of American Aviation Corporation in 1973 (see AAC). Produced the Gulfstream 2 executive transport and the Lynx, Cheetah, Tiger, Cougar and T-cat family of light aircraft. Also marketed the Super AgCat cropduster, built for Grumman by Schweizer Aircraft. Company sold to American Jet Industries (AJI) in 1978, becoming Gulfstream American (q.v.) in 1979.

Above: Grumman-developed A-6E/TRAM Intruder carrier strike aircraft

Gulfstream Aerospace Gulfstream V global business jet

GUANGZHOU ORLANDO HELICOPTERS LTD. • China

Joint Chinese/US company formed 1985 to assemble Panda, as Chinese version of Orlando OHA-S-55 Bearcat. See Orlando Helicopter Airways.

GUERCHAIS • France

Located at St Cloud, company formed in mid-1920s and built several light monoplanes of its own design, first being Guerchais-Hanriot. Built T-9 light cabin monoplane with 120 hp Renault engine in 1930. See also Roche Aviation.

GUILLEMIN • France

M. J. Guillemin designed a high-wing single-engine light postal or ambulance monoplane, the J. G. 40, shown on the Blériot Aéronautique stand at the 1930 Paris Air Show. The latter company acquired the licence to build aircraft designed by M. Guillemin. A two-seat light aircraft, the J.G.10, competed in the French Air Ministry Light Aeroplane Competition of 1931, but retired with engine trouble.

GUIZHOU AVIATION INDUSTRY CORPORATION • China

Continues to develop tandem two-seat supersonic lead-in/fighter conversion trainer versions of the Chengdu J-7, as the JJ-7 or FT-7 for export. First JJ-7 flew in July 1985, and latest lengthened FT-7P variant entered service with Pakistan in 1996.

GULDENTOPS • Belgium

Operators of the Belgian National Aviation Schools founded in 1936 at Brussels, Kiewit and Gosselies. M. Guldentops designed and built several light aircraft, and after he took over the Société Bulte a training biplane known as the Bulte-Guldentops appeared in 1938, powered by a Cirrus Hermes engine.

GULFSTREAM AEROSPACE CORPORATION • USA

Current name for former Gulfstream American Corporation (q.v.). As Gulfstream Aerospace Corporation, sold to Chrysler Corporation 1985 but repurchased March 1990. Rights to light aircraft range sold to American General Aircraft Corporation (q.v.) 1989. Gulfstream IV twin-turbofan long-range business jet first flown September 1985 and remains in production, together with various special-purpose variants including the SRA-4 for mainly military roles including electronic warfare, search and rescue, anti-submarine/ship, and communications. New Gulfstream V global business jet first flew November 1995; also forms the platform for an ASTOR contender under Lockheed Martin leadership.

GULFSTREAM AEROSPACE OKLAHOMA OPERATIONS • USA

Founded by Gulfstream American chairman Allen Paulson after purchase of former Rockwell Commander aircraft series. Programme ended 1985.

GULFSTREAM AMERICAN CORPORATION • USA

Founded 1979 at Savannah in Georgia, following 1978 purchase of Grumman American Aviation Corporation (q.v.) by AJI (q.v.). Put twin-turboprop Grumman Gulfstream I executive aircraft back into production as Gulfstream I-C commuter airliner, and offered retrofit programme for existing twin-turbofan Gulfstream IIs, to have Gulfstream III wings fitted (becoming Gulfstream II-B). Gulfstream III twin-turbofan executive transport development completed by Grumman under Gulfstream contract; first flight December 1979. Acquired Rockwell International's general aviation types, thereafter continuing marketing Commander Jetprop series. See Gulfstream Aerospace Corporation.

GULFSTREAM AMERICAN CORPORATION OF CALIFORNIA • USA

See AJI.

GV • Sweden

See Gotaverken.

GWINN AIRCAR COMPANY INC. • USA

Formed at Buffalo in 1935 by Joseph M. Gwinn Jnr, a former chief engineer with Consolidated Aircraft Corporation (q.v.). First product, in 1937, was Gwinn Aircar, a two-seat cabin biplane with tricycle landing gear, claimed to be stall- and spin-proof.

Gyrodyne G.C.A.2C with co-axial rotors

GYRODYNE COMPANY OF AMERICA INC. • USA

Known originally as P. C. Helicopter Corporation, the Gyrodyne Company was incorporated in New York in August 1946 for the development of advanced rotary-wing aircraft. Bought a five-seat coaxial design from defunct Helicopters Inc., and developed it into the G.C.A.2. Projected G.C.A.7 Helidyne with stub wings and two engines with pusher propellers mounted above wings. One man portable helicopter, XRON-1 Rotocycle, developed for US Navy Bureau of Aeronautics in mid-1950s, plus some ground-cushion vehicles.

GYROFLIGHT LTD. • UK

Formed in 1969 to develop gyroplanes designed by Ernest Brooks, who was killed when his ultralight Mosquito gyroplane crashed. Gyroflight produced a small number of Hornet single-seat gyroplanes and gyrogliders in the early 1970s.

GYROFLUG INGENIEURSGESELLSCHAFT MBH • Germany

Founded 1978 to develop Speed Canard as full production aircraft based on US Rutan VariEze. See FFT.

Above: Gulfstream Aerospace Gulfstream IV-SP entered operations 1992

GYROPLANE • France

Produced the G-20 two-seat light observation and liaison helicopter immediately following Second World War.

Gulfstream Aerospace Gulfstream SRA-4, used by Swedish Air Force as S 102B for sigint and Tp 102 for communications

HAL • India

See Hindustan Aeronautics Ltd.

HALBERSTÄDTER FLUGZEUGWERKE GMBH • Germany

Halberstädt's first aircraft, the C.I reconnaissance biplane, first flew in May 1916, and together with more powerful C.III and C.V developments, was produced in large numbers in the First World War. The CL class two-seat escort fighters were particularly successful in ground-strafing roles during the campaigns of autumn 1917. Halberstädt's D-class single-seater scouts were strong and manoeuvrable, but inferior to Allied fighters in speed. A number of D.II and D.III scouts were built by Hannoversche Waggonfabrik AG (q.v.). The Halberstädt D.V, the company's final scout design, appeared in early 1917.

HALL ALUMINUM COMPANY • USA

Founded 1927 to develop a prototype naval flying-boat based on the hull design of Britain's Felixstowe F.5 for the US Naval Aircraft Factory (q.v.). The twin-engined Hall PH-1 was superseded by PH-2 and PH-3 variants which served in small numbers with the US Coast Guard during the Second World War. In 1936 Hall flew the XP2H-1 four-engined patrol bomber, largest American-built flying-boat at that time.

HAMBURGER FLUGZEUGBAU GMBH • Germany

Formed originally by Blohm und Voss in 1933 (see Bv). Aircraft production resumed 1956 with licence manufacture of Nord Noratlas for Luftwaffe. Co-operated in licence-production of Luftwaffe Lockheed F-104Gs and assisted with design work of Fokker F28 and Dornier Do 31E V/STOL project. HFB 320 Hansa Jet 6/11-seat business jet first flew 1964. Merged with Messerschmitt-Bölkow in 1969 to form MBB.

HAMC • China

See Harbin Aircraft Manufacturing Corporation.

HAMILTON AEROSPACE • USA

HX-321 sporting two-seater appeared 1987. Work followed on H-1 and HT-2 turboprop/turbofan derivatives.

Above: Hamilton Nomair T-28-R1 two-seat military trainer

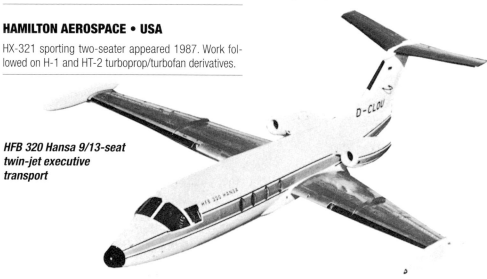

HFB 320 Hansa 9/13-seat twin-jet executive transport

Halberstadt CL.II two-seat fighter-escort

Hall XFH-1 Fighter, single-seat naval aircraft

Hamilton Westwind, a turboprop-powered conversion of the Beech 18

HAMILTON AIRCRAFT COMPANY INC. • USA

Overhauled surplus military aircraft for overseas disposal. Reworked ex-USAF North American T-28 trainers as Hamilton Nomair for civil and military customers. A Beech 18 conversion, the Hamilton Little Liner, superseded by turboprop Hamilton Westwind II and III, and a lengthened fuselage Westwind IV put under development but halted, by which time company had become Hamilton Aviation.

HAMILTON METALPLANE DIVISION OF BOEING • USA

Manufactured propellers and metal flying-boat hulls under subcontract in 1920s, before developing the all-metal, cantilever-winged Hamilton Metalplane in 1926. An airliner version followed in 1928, serving chiefly with Northwest Airways. Hamilton steel propellers were the company's major innovation before merging with Boeing and United Aircraft Corporation in late 1928.

HAMMOND AIRCRAFT CORPORATION • USA

Formed 1931 to take over production of Ryan Speedster biplane from Detroit Aircraft Corporation (q.v.). A prototype twin-boom two-seat lightplane, the Hammond Model Y, was built in 1934. Redesignated Stearman-Hammond Y-1S, it was produced in small numbers until 1938.

HANDASYDE AIRCRAFT COMPANY LTD. • UK

A former partner in Martin & Handasyde Ltd. (q.v.), George Handasyde set up his own company at war's end and constructed a glider for the *Daily Mail*'s 1922 Itford Meeting. For the Lympne Motor Glider Competition in 1923 he produced a small powered monoplane which was built by the Air Navigation & Engineering Company. In 1929 Handasyde joined the Desoutter Aircraft Company as general manager.

HANDLEY PAGE LTD. • UK

In June 1909 Frederick Handley Page (later Sir) established this company, building a series of monoplanes with crescent-shaped wings inspired by the Austrian designer Josc Weiss. In the First World War the company became well-known through its O/400 and V/1500 heavy bombers, the former leading to the W8 airliner of 1920, which entered service with Handley Page Air Transport. The Handley Page HP.42 airliner, which served with Imperial Airways from 1931, set new standards of comfort and safety on British

Handley Page E (H.P.5) the first really successful design by Frederick Handley Page

Handley Page V/1500 long-range bomber, Britain's biggest aeroplane of WW1

Above: Handley Page HPR 7 Herald 214 operated in later life by British Air Ferries

Empire routes. Military bombers were also produced: the Hinaidi, Hyderabad, Heyford and, early in the Second World War, the twin-engined Hampden. Best known was the four-engined Halifax, which shared Bomber Command's offensive against Germany with the Lancaster. After the war the Hastings military transport and its civilian Hermes counterpart went into production, and Handley Page created the crescent-winged Victor 'V' bomber. The company's last project before its liquidation in 1970 was the Jetstream twin-turboprop executive transport/feederliner, which was taken over by Scottish Aviation.

HANDLEY PAGE (READING) LTD. • UK

In June 1948 Handley Page took over the former Miles Aircraft Ltd. (q.v.) of Woodley, Reading, and with it the Miles Marathon four-engined feederliner. Handley Page (Reading) produced the aircraft as a navigational trainer for the RAF and also as a short-haul airliner. The Reading-based company was also responsible for development of the HPR.3 Herald airliner, which flew initially with four piston engines in 1955, and was subsequently manufactured with two Rolls-Royce turbines as the Dart Herald.

HANNAFORD AIRCRAFT COMPANY • USA

After acquiring in 1948 the manufacturing and marketing rights to the pre-war Rose Parakeet single-seat sports biplane from Rose Aeroplane & Motor Company (q.v.), Hannaford offered production versions of the aeroplane with 40-85 hp engines.

Handley Page Victors, the last of the British 'V' bombers to enter service

Handley Page Victor, finally serving with RAF as a flight refuelling tanker

HANNOVERSCHE WAGGONFABRIK AG. • Germany

Hannover, a manufacturer of railway rolling stock, began licence production of Aviatik C.1, Rumpler C.1A and Halberstädt scouts in 1915 before proposing a compact two-seat escort fighter to German High Command. The biplane-tailed CL.II entered service in late 1917, and was succeeded by the CL.III and CL.IIIa, also built under licence by Luftfahrzeug Gesellschaft (q.v.) as CL.IIa. Small numbers of the enlarged C.IV and CL.V were constructed, plus experimental CL.IIIs with various engine and airframe changes. The company's fighters were known popularly as 'Hannoveraners'.

HANRIOT • France

Aeroplanes Hanriot et Cie was founded during the First World War. Its first design was the Le Rhone-engined HD1 sesquiplane fighter, rejected by the French services but subsequently used very successfully by Italian and Belgian pilots. An HD2 floatplane version and more-powerful HD3 two-seat reconnaissance/escort fighter were also built. After the war Hanriot licence-manufactured British Sopwith aircraft and produced the H43 advanced biplane trainer, H46 Styx liaison and ambulance monoplane and the H131 low-wing racing monoplane, which won the 1931 Coupé Michelin. In 1930 the company became a division of Société Général Aéronautique (SNCAC), manufacturing aircraft under the Lorraine-Hanriot name (both q.v.).

HANSA UND BRANDENBURGISCHE FLEGZEUGWERKE GMBH • Germany

With Ernst Heinkel as chief designer, this company produced the most important German seaplanes of the First World War, commencing with the KDW single-seater developed from the D1 landplane, followed by the W.12 with characteristic Hansa upswept fuselage and 'upside-down' tail arrangement. The W.29 monoplane set the pattern for Heinkel's later designs, outperforming Allied aircraft in combat from introduction in April 1918. The larger W.33

Above: Hanriot HD1 fighter, used by the Belgian and Italian air forces

Hanriot H182 braced high-wing monoplane

Harbin Y-12 (IV) 19-seat transport

Harbin Z-9A Haitun twin-turboshaft helicopter

was delivered before the Armistice, and continued in production in Finland and Norway as the A-22 until the mid-1920s, as did the W.29 in Denmark.

HANSEATISCHE FLUGZEUGWERKE KARL CASPAR AG. • Germany

Founded as the Zentrale für Aviatik at Hamburg-Fuhlsbüttel in late 1911; began by building Etrich/Rumpler Taube monoplanes. In 1913 renamed Hansa-Flugzeugwerke, merging shortly before the First World War with Brandenburgische Flugzeugwerke of Igo Etrich, becoming the Hansa and Brandenburgische Flugzeugwerke (q.v.). This partnership dissolved in 1916, the Hamburg factory being renamed Hanseatische Flugzeugwerke Karl Caspar AG. Next two years spent mainly in licence-building other companies' aircraft, though an interesting cannon-armed twin-engined fighter prototype by Caspar appeared in late 1918. Before end of First World War company acquired the ex-Fokker factory at Travemünde, eventually closing the Hamburg works and transferring its activities there. Here, in 1921, the Caspar Werke AG (q.v.) was formed.

HARBIN AIRCRAFT MANUFACTURING CORPORATION • China

Created in 1952 from the Mansyu Hikoki Seizo Kabushiki Kaisha of Manchuria (q.v.). Began the H-6 bomber programme in 1957, initially assembling two Tu-16s from Soviet-supplied components, the first flying in September 1959, but in 1961 this programme was transferred to Xi'an (q.v.). Manufactured the H-5 jet bomber from 1966 to the 1980s, based on the Soviet Ilyushin Il-28. Developed and still produces the Y-11 (first flown about 1975) and Y-12 (first flown June 1984) general-purpose transports and Z-9 Haitun twin-turboshaft helicopter as licence-produced Eurocopter Dauphin 2. Was pursuing development of a new helicopter in 1999, and is a partner in the Colibri EC 120 B helicopter programme. Also produced two prototype (one static) and five production SH-5 anti-submarine amphibians (one civil, tested as a firebomber).

HARLOW ENGINEERING CORPORATION • USA

Formed 1938 to develop the Harlow PJC-2 four-seat all-metal cabin monoplane, which remained in production until December 1941. Four were delivered to the USAAF as UC-80s. A PC-5A two-seat trainer version was developed in 1939 and assembled under licence 1941-1942 by Hindustan Aeronautics Ltd. (q.v.). After America's entry into Second World War, Harlow Engineering undertook military contract work.

D & J HARMON COMPANY INC. • USA

Offers components to convert Van's RV-4 into high-performance Rocket two-seater.

Hawker Fury II single-seat interceptor fighter

Hawker Osprey taking-off from an aircraft carrier

Hawker Sea Fury single-seat carrier-based fighter-bomber

HARRIS & SHELDON LTD. • UK

Birmingham-based company which, in 1918, subcontracted to build a batch of 100 Bristol F.2B Fighters with Sunbeam Arab engines.

HAWK AIRCRAFT DEVELOPMENT CORPORATION • USA

Intended to produce Hawk 72 as variant of Cessna 172P.

HAWKER AIRCRAFT LTD. • UK

Following reorganisation in 1933, the Hawker company concentrated on fighters, and the first production Hurricane, a monoplane development of the Fury, first entered service in late 1937. This fighter achieved significant success in the Battle of Britain. The Typhoon, initially none too successful, proved effective as a fighter-bomber and saw the peak of its development in the Tempest, Fury and Sea Fury which served with RAF and Fleet Air Arm during late 1940s and early 1950s, and with foreign air arms well

Hawker Hurricane, the RAF's first eight-gun fighters

Hawker Hunter interceptor fighters

Hawker Siddeley Harrier VTOL/VSTOL jet fighter, developed from the P.1127 Kestrel

Hawker Siddeley HS 748 of Austrian Airlines

into the 1960s. In early post-war period Hawker developed the Sea Hawk shipboard fighter, progressing to the Hunter, the single Mk 3 version of which, produced by modification of the original prototype, gained the world speed record at 727.6mph (1,170.96kmh) in 1953. Such was the success of the Hunter that refurbished aircraft were later exported. Hawker's greatest innovation was in the field of VTOL fighters, first with the experimental P.1127 Kestrel, which led to the Hawker Siddeley Harrier (see Hawker Siddeley).

HAWKER DE HAVILLAND LTD. • Australia

Produces aerostructures for Airbus and Boeing, supports RAAF F-111 and P-3 improvement programmes, and is a team member under Raytheon Systems Company proposing the Airbus A310 for the RAAF's AEW&C requirement. Previously, in 1980s, having bought Australian Aircraft Consortium and formed it into the Trainer Aircraft Division of HDH, continued development for short time of A10B turboprop-powered two-seat basic trainer.

HAWKER ENGINEERING CO LTD. • UK

In 1921 former Sopwith test pilot Harry Hawker took over the premises of the former Sopwith Aviation Company (q.v.). Although he died that same year in a crash, the re-established company began building a series of military aircraft, beginning with a single Duiker monoplane, followed by the Woodcock fighter. Under the design leadership of Sydney Camm (later Sir), produced such aircraft as the Tomtit trainer biplane and the Horsley bomber/torpedo-bomber, Mk 1 versions of which were the last all-wooden aircraft built by the company. Best known of all H. G. Hawker products were the Hart/Demon/Audax/Osprey two-seaters and the beautiful Fury single-seat fighter; all had entered production before the company name was changed to Hawker Aircraft Ltd. (q.v.) in 1933.

HAWKER SIDDELEY AVIATION LTD. • UK

In mid-1963 the Hawker Siddeley Group incorporated the Hawker, de Havilland, Avro, Armstrong Whitworth, Folland and Blackburn companies into Hawker Siddeley Aviation, the aircraft products of each company becoming known as Hawker Siddeley aircraft. Merged into British Aerospace (q.v.) in April 1977. Final products under its own name were the HS 125 corporate jet (first flown August 1962; see Raytheon Aircraft Company), HS 748 turboprop airliner (first flown June 1960), Trident short/medium-range airliner (first flown January 1962), Harrier and Sea Harrier (see British Aerospace), Buccaneer (former Blackburn), Nimrod maritime patrol jet (first flown May 1967), and Hawk jet trainer (see British Aerospace).

HAWK INTERNATIONAL • USA

Developed GafHawk freighter under original aircraft division of Hawk Industries Inc. See Ameco-Hawk.

HAYDEN AIRCRAFT CORPORATION • USA

Formed 1955 to build the Stout Bushmaster 15-AT, a modern development of the Ford Tri-Motor transport. Initial pre-production series of three aircraft planned with financial support from Air-Craft & Hydro Forming Inc.

Above: Heath Parasol ultra light monoplane

Right: Heinkel He 112 single-seat fighters

HAYES AIRCRAFT CORPORATION • USA

Specialist military conversion company, which adapted 137 North American TB-25L/N Mitchell bombers for pilot training and from 1958 developed and manufactured KB-50J/K jet-boosted tanker conversion of the Boeing B-50 Superfortress for USAF.

HB-AIRCRAFT INDUSTRIES LUFTFAHRZEUG AG. • Austria

Developed HB-23 Hobbyliner two-seat light aircraft/motor-glider and Scanliner surveillance/observation/patrol variant, principally produced in 1980s. Company renamed HB Flugtechnik 1992, but halted production. Aircraft currently produced by HB Aviation International (q.v.).

HB AVIATION INTERNATIONAL • Netherlands

Hobbyliner and Scanliner in production in the Netherlands; see HB-Aircraft Industries for more details.

HEATH AIRCRAFT COMPANY • USA

Formed in 1926 by Ed Heath, whose 1928 Baby Bullet mid-wing monoplane racer exceeded 100mph (160kmh) on only 32 hp. Heath Super Soarer biplane glider, built 1930, was first unpowered aircraft to loop-the-loop. Heath Parasol of 1931, designed to be powered by a converted motorcycle engine, sold in large numbers to amateur builders.

HEINKEL • Germany

Ernst Heinkel established his own company shortly after the liquidation of Hansa Brandenburg (q.v.), building a series of single-engined seaplanes (He 1 to He 8) in Sweden to circumvent the ban on the construction of military aircraft in Germany. The He 51 biplane fighter went into production for the Luftwaffe in the 1930s and served with the Condor Legion in Spain. When the Heinkel He 70 passenger/mailplane appeared in 1932, ostensibly for Deutsche Lufthansa, it was the most advanced aerodynamic design then seen in Europe. A natural outgrowth of

Above: Heinkel He 111, an extensively-used multi-purpose bomber of the Luftwaffe

this design was the Heinkel He 111 twin-engined bomber which served with the Luftwaffe throughout the Second World War. A Rolls-Royce Merlin-engined version of the He 111 was built by CASA in Spain, and served with the Spanish Air Force until the late 1960s. Heinkel also produced late in the war the He 162 Volksjäger (People's Fighter), a lightweight turbojet fighter constructed almost entirely of wood. Heinkel had designed, built and flown the world's first jet aircraft, the He 178, in 1939. Other significant Heinkel projects included the He 177 Greif heavy bomber and the He 219 Uhu nightfighter.

Right: Heinkel He 162 Salamander jet fighter

HELI-AIR • USA

Became Jaffe Helicopter Incorporated (q.v.).

HELIBRAS • Brazil

See Helicópteros do Brasol SA.

HELICOM INC. • USA

Founded in 1954 as Helicopter Engineering Research Corporation by Harold E. Emigh, designer of the Emigh Trojan lightplane, to develop and market a single-seat personal helicopter. Known as the Helicom Commuter Jr Model H-1A, the prototype first flew in 1960, and was sold both in ready-to-fly form and as a kit for assembly by amateur constructors. A ground trainer version was developed also,

mounted via a gimbal to a castoring base which was too heavy for the helicopter to lift from the ground.

HELICOP-JET • Canada

Based in Canada for project management, but with French connections in helicopter development; first flew in France in 1976 and 1984 two prototypes of a four-seat helicopter with rotor driven by cold-air tip jets. Programme later halted.

HELICOPTEROS DO BRASIL SA • Brazil

Founded 1978, with partial Aérospatiale of France shareholding, to assemble Aérospatiale SA 315B Lama and AS 350B Ecureuil helicopters, known locally as HB 315B Gavião and HB 350B Esquilo respectively. Current programmes encompass continued assembly of Esquilo plus the military AS 550 Fennec version, and AS 365 Dauphin and military AS 565 Panther (all Eurocopter types).

HELICOPTER TECHNIK MÜNCHEN GMBH • Germany

Founded to produce the Skytrac two-seat lightweight multipurpose helicopter, designed originally by Wagner Helicopter Technik (q.v.). The HTM FJ-Skytrac received both German and FAA certification, and the company developed a kit to convert the Skytrac into a four-seat light helicopter known as the HTM Skyrider. Production terminated owing to lack of capital.

HELIO • USA

Founded 1948 as Helio Aircraft Corporation to develop the two-seat Koppen-Bollinger lightplane. Four-seat STOL derivative Helio Courier entered production 1954. Superseded by the H-391B, H-395 and H-395A Super Couriers introduced from 1958. Helio H-250 and H-295 six-seat utility aircraft flew in 1964 and 1965 respectively, and were produced for both civil and military use; Super Couriers in USAF service designated U-10. The H-550A Stallion with turboprop engine followed. Helio was acquired by General Aircraft Corporation (q.v.) in 1969 and renamed Helio Aircraft Company, but the assets later acquired by Helio Courier Ltd. (which produced H-295 Super and HT-295 Trigear Couriers), Helio Precision Products and, in 1976, Helio Aircraft Ltd. In 1984 company bought by Aerospace Technology Industries and in 1989 by Aircraft Acquisition Corporation; the latter re-formed company as Helio Aircraft Corporation to produce Couriers and turboprop H-550A Stallion, plus develop new piston-engined Courier

Helio Model H-550A Stallion ten-seat utility aircraft

Helio Super Courier light STOL monoplane

700 and turboprop-engined Super Courier, which did not take place.

HELIOPOLIS AIR WORKS • Egypt

Formed 1950 to manufacture a local version of the German Bücker Bü 181D Bestmann as the Gomhouria trainer for Egypt, Jordan, Libya, Saudi Arabia, Somalia and the Sudan.

HELITEC CORPORATION • USA

Aviation Specialties Inc. (q.v.) developed a turbine-engined conversion for surplus military Sikorsky S-55 helicopters, first certificated in the USA in 1971. Helitec Corporation was founded subsequently to continue the conversion and marketing of the S-55 for sale in the USA, Canada, Europe and South America.

HELLENIC AEROSPACE INDUSTRY LTD. • Greece

Established 1975. Undertakes maintenance and modification of military and commercial aircraft, engines, avionics and equipment. 1907 contract to extend the life of Hellenic F-4 Phantoms by structural work.

HELWAN AIR WORKS • Egypt

Inaugurated by President Nasser in 1962, Helwan's first project was licence-manufacture of the Spanish Hispano HA-200 Saeta jet trainer, known in Egypt as Al Kahira. German designer Willy Messerschmitt led a Helwan team to develop the HA-300 supersonic fighter, first flown in prototype form in March 1964.

HENDERSON SCOTTISH AVIATION FACTORY • UK

Subcontractor in First World War, built a batch of 100 Avro 504K trainers.

HENDY AIRCRAFT COMPANY • UK

This company's first design was the Hendy 281 Hobo, a small single-seater using Basil Henderson's patented wing construction. A tandem-two-seat derivative, the Hendy 302, was built by George Parnall and Co (with whom Hendy amalgamated in 1935) and was entered in the 1930 King's Cup Air Race. The 1934 Hendy 3308 Heck was an advanced three-seater constructed by Westland Aircraft for Whitney Straight.

HENSCHEL FLUGZEUGWERKE AG. • Germany

Henschel's Hs 123 biplane dive bomber was tested during the Spanish Civil War and, though obsolescent, served with the Luftwaffe until 1942 in close-support roles, particularly on the Russian Front. The Hs 126 parasol-wing,

Helwan Al Kahira, licence-built version of the Hispano HA-200

Helwan HA-300 single-seat delta-wing lightweight fighter

Henschel Hs 123A, the Luftwaffe's last biplane aircraft

Heston Aircraft twin-boom Air Observation Post

Heston Phoenix five-seat cabin monoplane

two-seat observation/liaison aircraft first entered Luftwaffe service in 1938. A twin-engined single-seat close-support and ground-attack aircraft, the Hs 129, was produced in some numbers and used to good effect on the Eastern Front, particularly as a tank-buster. The final Hs 129B-2/R-4 version was armed with a 75 mm cannon. A prototype jet dive-bomber, the Hs 132, was completed but did not fly before the end of the war. The company also experimented with a number of wire-, radio- and even television-guided missiles.

HESTON AIRCRAFT CO LTD. • UK

Founded 1934 to take over the assets of Comper Aircraft Company Ltd. (q.v.). Developed the Heston Type 1 Phoenix in 1935, a five-seat cabin monoplane with retractable landing gear, the first on a British high-wing aircraft. Also produced the 2,300 hp Napier Sabre-powered Heston Type 5 racer. Sponsored by Lord Nuffield for a British attempt on the world speed record, it crashed on maiden flight in June 1940. A second was never completed.

HIGGINS AIRCRAFT INC. • USA

This New Orleans-based company was subcontracted by Curtiss-Wright in 1942 to manufacture 500 Curtiss C-46 Commando military transports. Only two had been built by Higgins when the contract was cancelled.

HIGGINS INDUSTRIES INC. HELICOPTER DIVISION • USA

Under the direction of Enea Bossi, this subsidiary of the Andrew Higgins shipbuilding concern was developing a twin-engined, four-passenger helicopter and a two-seat experimental helicopter when the parent company's military contracts terminated and all aircraft work was suspended.

HIGHER PLANES INC. • USA

Markets kits for the single-seat Mitchell Wing A-10 microlight with pusher engine, and T-10 two-seater.

HIGHLANDER AIRCRAFT CORPORATION • USA

Offers Highlander two-seat monoplane in kit form, but originally designed in the UK by Richard Noble as the ARV Super2, then becoming Island Aircraft ARV-1 Super2 and Aviation Scotland ARV-1 Super2. Also certificated in Sweden as Opus 280 (see ASL Hagfors).

HILLBERG HELICOPTERS • USA

In addition to helicopter maintenance and modification, offers the RotorMouse EH 1-01 as a single-seat turbine experimental-category helicopter for construction from a kit (first flown August 1993), RotorMouse EH 1-02 tandem two-seat version, and RotorMouse (Baby Huey) four-seater. Also built the T-4 Turbine as a four-seat turbine helicopter (not in production at time of writing), and produces a retrofit kit for the RotorWay Exec to provide a turbine engine (first flown 1997).

Hillberg Helicopters RotorMouse EH 1-01

Hillberg Helicopters Turbine Exec retrofit of RotorWay Exec

HILLER AIRCRAFT • USA

Formed 1942 as a division of Hiller Industries. Name changed to Hiller Helicopters (q.v.) in 1948.

Below: Hiller Aircraft Corporation UH-12E5 five-seat helicopter

HILLER AIRCRAFT CORPORATION • USA

Founded 1994 by Jeffrey Hiller (son of the founder of the original Hiller Aircraft company) and a consortium, to repurchase assets from Rogerson Hiller Corporation (q.v.). First flight January 1995 of the UH-12E5 five-seat helicopter, and June 1995 for first newly built UH-12E3. Current pro-duction is believed to centre on the piston-engined UH-12E3 three-seater and the UH-12E3T turboshaft variant.

HILLER AVIATION INC. • USA

Formed in 1973 after acquiring the design rights, tooling and spares for Hiller 12E light helicopters from Fairchild Industries (q.v.). The company provided support for operators of Hiller helicopters and produced three-seat UH-12E and four-seat UH-12E-4 turbine conversions of the UH-12E, developed in conjunction with Soloy Conversions. Also introduced former Fairchild Hiller FH-1100 in 1984 (later as RH-1100). Became subsidiary of Rogerson Aircraft in 1984, reviving first the name Hiller Helicopters and later becoming Rogerson Hiller Corporation (q.v.).

Hiller Model 12E-4 four-seat helicopter

Hiller X-18 tilt-wing VTOL research aircraft

Hillson Bi-Mono experimental Slip-Wing byplane/monoplane

HILLER HELICOPTERS • USA

In 1948 Hiller Helicopters produced the Hiller UH-12, subsequently supplying it to civilian operators and, as the H-23B and OH-23C/D Raven, to the US Army and to foreign air arms under the MDAP programme. Three-seat UH-12E (first flown 1958) and four-seat UH-12E4 variants also developed. The Hiller HOE-1 Hornet ramjet ultralight helicopter and 'Flying Platform' were two military experimental types devised by the company. After amalgamation with Fairchild Industries (q.v.), the Hiller FH-1100 turbine transport helicopter was produced for the expanding executive transport market. See Hiller Aviation for second use of name Hiller Helicopters.

HILLMAN HELICOPTER ASSOCIATES • USA

After Douglas Hillman developed WankelBee helicopter with rotary combustion engine (first flown 1975) and two-seat Hornet (first flown 1978), Hillman Helicopter designed Model 360 as three-seat utility helicopter of very modern design, which first flew 1981.

HILLS & SONS • UK

Manchester-based woodworking firm which acquired a licence to produce the Czechoslovakian Praga E.114 Air Baby two-seat lightplane. Thirty manufactured from 1936, known as Hillson Pragas. A single Hillson Helvellyn two-seat, mid-wing lightplane was built and flown in 1939 and one Hillson Pennine was produced, but not flown before the outbreak of war. During Second World War the company was involved in contract work for the Air Ministry, and developed an experimental 'slip-wing' conversion of the Hawker Hurricane to enable the aircraft to take off at

greater than normal gross weight, releasing the upper wing in flight.

Below: Hinchman H-1 Racer autogyro   *Above: Hindustan Aeronautics Ltd. Advanced Light Helicopter*

HINCHMAN AIRCRAFT COMPANY • USA

First flew in 1987 the original version of its H-1 Racer single-seat autogyro. Plans and kits available for the Racer in latest form.

HINDUSTAN AERONAUTICS LTD. • India

Hindustan Aircraft Ltd. (formed in 1940) was amalgamated with Aeronautics India Ltd. (formed 1963) to establish Hindustan Aeronautics Ltd. in October 1964. Hindustan Aircraft designed and built the first indigenous Indian aircraft, the Hindustan HT-2 two-seat trainer, which first flew in 1951 and was produced for the Indian Air Force and civilian flying clubs. The HUL-26 Pushpak high-wing lightplane, based on the American Aeronca Chief, entered production in 1959, the HAOP-27 Krishak derivation being manufactured as a liaison aircraft for the Indian Air Force and Army. Deliveries of the HAL HJT-16 Kiran two-seat jet trainer began in 1966. The HF-24 Marut single-seat fighter was designed by a team led by Kurt Tank, and deliveries

HAL HAOP-27 Krishak liaison aircraft

HAL HF-24 Marut single-seat fighter

of the Ajeet lightweight jet fighter, developed from the Folland/Hawker Siddeley Gnat which HAL licence-produced, began to the Indian Air Force in 1976. HAL also built the HA-31 Basant agricultural aircraft.

Assembly of Soviet MiG-21 fighters began 1966, with full manufacture from 1970 (production ended). Assembly/production of Soviet MiG-27M began 1984 (production ended 1994). Assembly/production of the SEPECAT Jaguar International as the Shamsher (first flown March 1982) ended 1998. HPT-32 Deepak two-seat ab initio and basic piston-engined trainer first flown 1977; 134 built for Indian Air Force and eight for Navy to replace HT-2s. Licence-manufactured SA-315B Lama and SA-316B Alouette III helicopters as Cheetah and Chetak respectively up to 1998, when production gave way to the indigenously

developed Advanced Light Helicopter (first flown August 1992). HAL responsible for manufacture of the ADA Light Combat Aircraft. New HJT-36 turbofan trainer and HTT-38 turboprop trainer announced for development in 1998. Continuing work on AWACS aircraft. Other work includes overhaul of all Indian Air Force aircraft, together with component manufacture in connection with international aircraft programmes and India's space research programme.

HIPP'S SUPERBIRD INC. • USA

Offers plans and kits to construct J-3 Kitten single-seat high-wing microlight and higher-powered J-5 Super Kitten, plans and kits for J-4 Sportster single-seat parasol-wing microlight and more-powerful Super Sportster, and kits

HAL licence-built HS 748 transport

for Reliant single-seat high-wing microlight and more-powerful Reliant SX.

Hindustan Aeronautics Ltd. Cheetah light helicopter

Hispano licence-built Airco D.H.6

Hispano HS-42 advanced trainer

Hispano HA-220 Super Saeta

HIRO NAVAL AIR ARSENAL • Japan

Hiro's Navy Type 90-1 three-engined flying-boat, built in the early 1930s, had Japanese-built Hispano-Suiza engines and bore a close resemblance to the German Rohrbach flying-boats. In 1932 the company started work on a twin-engined land-based attack bomber, Hiro G2H1, which went into production in 1935 as Navy Type 95. Only eight were built, two by Mitsubishi, which subsequently developed a long-range reconnaissance version which influenced the design of the successful Mitsubishi G3M bomber.

HIRT AIRCRAFT • USA

Expected to market plans and kits for the composites-built Trio two-seat monoplane with forward swept wings.

HIRTENBERGER • Austria

Hirtenberger Patronen Zündhutchen und Metallwarenfabrik AG began aircraft manufacture in 1935 after taking over Flugzeugbau Hopfner (q.v.). Only the Hirtenberger HS-9 parasol-wing training/touring monoplane was produced. An open-cockpit tandem two-seater, it had either a 125 hp Siemens or 120 hp de Havilland Gipsy Major engine, the latter variant being designated HS-9A.

HIRTH • Germany

Wolf Hirth GmbH, a pre-war manufacturer of sailplanes, made wooden subassemblies for Messerschmitt projects during the Second World War, including a high-speed glider-trainer for Me 163 Komet pilots, and components for the Me 321 and Me 323 Gigants. The re-established company, owned largely by Messerschmitt-Bölkow-Blohm (q.v.), built Arnold Wagner's Acrostar competition aerobatic aircraft in small numbers, and supported the Bölkow BO 107, 207, 208 and 209 lightplanes.

HISPANO AVIACION • Spain

La Hispano Aviación SA manufactured the Fiat CR.32 biplane fighter as the HA-132-1 Chirri between 1938-1942. In 1943 the company received a contract to build the Messerschmitt Bf 109G under licence for the Spanish Air Force. Designated Hispano HA-1109, it was powered initially by a Hispano-Suiza HS-12Z engine and later, in HA-1109/1110 Buchon variants, by the Rolls-Royce Merlin. An indigenous HA-43D-1 advanced two-seat military trainer went into production for the Spanish Air Force in 1947, followed in 1953 by the HA-100EI replacement, with tricycle landing gear, designed by Willy Messerschmitt. Messerschmitt also supervised design of the HA-200 Saeta jet trainer, which first flew in 1955 and which was later developed as the HA-220 Super Saeta single-seat light ground-attack aircraft. Hispano merged with Construcciones Aeronáuticas SA (q.v.) in 1972.

HISTORICAL AIRCRAFT CORPORATION • USA

Offers kits to build a range of 60 per cent scale single-seat fighter representations, including P-51D, Corsair, PZL P.11c and P-40 Tomahawk, plus an 85 per cent scale representation of Ryan STA.

HITACHI KOKUKI KABUSHIKI KAISHA • Japan

Founded in 1939, this company produced the Hitachi T-2 two-seat sesquiplane trainer of wood and metal construction.

HK AIRCRAFT TECHNOLOGY AG IG • Germany

Currently offers the Wega two-seat and composites constructed very light aircraft, promoted by the European Union and the Bavarian Ministry of Economics, Transport and Technology.

HOAC-AUSTRIA, FLUGZEUGWERK WIENER NEUSTADT GESELLSCHAFT MBH • Austria

Now Diamond Aircraft Industries GmbH (q.v.).

HOCKADAY AIRCRAFT CORPORATION • USA

Formed in 1937. Design work on the CV-139 Comet two-seat high-wing cabin monoplane, but was suspended in 1940 to make way for military contract work for other aircraft companies. The project was resumed in 1944, when the sole prototype was test flown.

HOFFMANN FLUGZEUGBAU-FRIESACH GESMBH • Austria

Founded 1981. Now Diamond Aircraft Industries GmbH (q.v.).

HOLLANDAIR TB • Netherlands

Formed as an aeronautical trading concern in 1956 specialising in the overhaul of aircraft and engines. One example only of the Hollandair HA-001 Libel (Dragonfly) single-seat agricultural aircraft was built in 1957.

HOLSTE • France

Max Holste's first designs were the MH.52 two-seat lightweight sporting aircraft with tricycle landing gear and the MH.53 Cadet trainer variant, characterised by a twin-fin tail which reappeared on the MH.1521M Broussard utility transport and liaison aircraft, produced in quantity for the French Air Force and Army. A twin-engined development, the MH.260 Super Broussard, was redesignated Nord 262 when Max Holste became incorporated with Nord Aviation (q.v.) in 1961. A small remaining private sector of the company is now part of Reims Aviation (q.v.), which builds Cessna aircraft under licence for European distribution.

Holste Broussard transport and liaison aircraft

Holste MH.250 Super Broussard transport

HONGDU AVIATION INDUSTRY (GROUP) CORPORATION LTD. • China

New name (since March 1998) for Nanchang Aircraft Manufacturing Company (q.v.). Currently produces the Q-5/A-5 attack aircraft, CJ-6A piston trainer, N-5A agricultural aircraft and K-8J Karakorum jet trainer.

HÖNNINGSTAD • Norway

Established 1936, Hönningstad designed and built the Norge Model A light transport aircraft in 1938. Designed a twin-engined, 12-passenger amphibian built by Norsk Flyindustri AS (q.v.), as the Finnmark 5A, intended specifically for operation in the Northern and Arctic regions; only one prototype was completed. The Hönningstad Polar C5 bush-plane was built in 1948 by Wideröes Flyveselskap OG Polarfly (q.v.).

HOOPER & COMPANY • UK

This Chelsea-based coachbuilder was a First World War subcontractor, building Sopwith-Strutters, Camels, Ship's Camels and Dolphins.

HOPFNER • Austria

This was the first Austrian company to manufacture an aeroplane after the First World War; the Hopfner S.1 three-seat monoplane. A developed version with Gipsy Major engine was designated HS-1033. Hopfner also produced the HA-1133 four-seat twin-engined amphibian before being taken over in 1935 by Hirtenberger Patronen, Zundhutchen und Metallwarenfabrik AG (q.v.).

HOPPI-COPTERS • USA

The Pentecost Hoppi-Copter was a 90 lb (41 kg) personal helicopter pack designed to be strapped to an infantryman's back to make it possible for him to surmount terrain obstacles. It first flew in 1945, but landing shock problems proved insurmountable. A second version with seat and landing gear was tested later, and two were acquired in 1948 for evaluation by the British Ministry of Supply. Capital Helicopter Corporation (q.v.) took over the patents in 1954 and flew a Hoppi-Copter with rotor blade-mounted pulse jets.

HORTEN GEBRÜDER • Germany

The Horten brothers conducted flying-wing experiments pre-war, building a series of tailless high-performance gliders. The Horten Ho V and Ho VI were both powered aircraft, leading to the turbojet-powered Ho IX flown in the summer of 1944. Before being destroyed in a landing accident after only a few hours flight, it had been flown at a speed of 497 mph (800 kmh). This was developed by Gothaer Waggonfabrik (q.v.) as the Gotha Go 229 V3 single-seat fighter, but the Gothaer works were captured by advancing US forces before this prototype was completed.

HOWARD AERO INC. • USA

Formed in 1947 as a modification, repair and maintenance organisation. In 1963 Howard combined with Alamo Aero Service, specialising in the conversion of ex-military Lockheed PV-1 Venturas and civilian Lockheed Lodestars to high-speed executive transports known as Howard 250s, 350s and 500s, according to configuration and powerplant. A three-engined version of the Beech Travel Air twin was also flown experimentally.

Right: Howard DGA-15 five-seat floatplane

Below: Howard Aero Model 500, a conversion of the Lockheed Lodestar

HOWARD AIRCRAFT CORPORATION • USA

Benjamin Howard built his first aeroplane, the DGA-1 ('Damn Good Airplane'), in 1923, while working for the Curtiss company. His DGA-3 *Pete* racer, built for the 1930 US National Air Races, was succeeded by DGA-4 *Ike* and DGS-5 *Mike*. With DGA-6 *Mister Mulligan* Howard won all three major American racing titles in 1935, and this design was developed through several models into the Howard DGA-15 five-seat cabin monoplane which served with the US Navy in transport, instrument trainer and ambulance roles during the Second World War. The Howard DGA-18K two-seat primary trainer was produced in quantity during 1940-1942 for the US Government's Civilian Pilot Training Programme.

HOWARD HUGHES ENGINEERING PTY. LTD. • Australia

Markets completed examples or kits of the Australian Light Wing PR tandem two-seat cabin monoplane and Australian Light Wing GR-912 side-by-side two-seat cabin monoplane.

HTM • Germany

See Helicopter Technik München GmbH.

Hughes Hercules, the world's largest flying-boat, and the aeroplane with the largest wing span ever to have flown

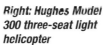

Left: Hughes YAH-64 advanced attack helicopter prototypes

Right: Hughes Model 300 three-seat light helicopter

HUFF-DALAND AIRPLANES INC. • USA

Produced a number of single-engined military biplanes in the early 1920s, when James McDonnell (later of the McDonnell Douglas Company) was chief engineer. The XLB-1 three-seat, single-engine light bomber was tested in 1923 and was developed as the twin-engined XLB-3, with a crew of five. In 1924 Huff-Daland was reorganised as Keystone Aircraft Corporation (q.v.) and the production bomber aircraft was known by this latter company name.

HUFFER • Germany

Flugzeugbau Dr Georg Huffer produced a civilian version of the First World War Fokker D.VII fighter, known as the Huffer H.9. It was an open-cockpit training/sporting two-seater powered by a Mercedes engine. A parasol wing monoplane, the HB.28, was also designed and built by the company in the late 1920s.

HUGHES AIRCRAFT COMPANY • USA

Founded in 1935 by businessman/film magnate Howard Hughes to produce the Hughes H-1 racing aeroplane, in which Hughes established a world landplane speed

record of 352.46mph (567.23kmh). The Hughes XF-11 experimental twin-engined, twin-boom photo-reconnaissance aircraft, which had contrarotating propellers, crashed on its maiden flight, seriously injuring Hughes. He then sponsored the massive Hughes H-4 Hercules. Made entirely of wood, this eight-engined flying-boat had the greatest wingspan (320 ft; 97.54 m) of any aircraft built to date. It made its one and only flight on 2 November, 1947 with Howard Hughes at the controls. Between 1949-1952 the Hughes Aircraft Company built and tested the XH-1 heavylift helicopter, designed as a 'flying crane' for the USAF.

HUGHES HELICOPTERS • USA

Known formerly as the Hughes Tool Company, became a Division of the Summa Corporation in the early 1970s. Hughes first two-seat light helicopter, the Model 260, first flew in 1955. It continued in production, though much-modified, as the Hughes 300. Production of the OH-6A Cayuse turbine helicopter for the US Army and other military forces led to the commercial Model 500 one/seven-seat light helicopter, with military variants in the Defender

series. Hughes won the US Army's competition for an Advanced Attack Helicopter (AAH) with its Model 77, a twin-turbine design which first flew in September 1975, and which received the Army designation YAH-64 Apache. Also developed the unique NOTAR (no tail rotor) anti-torque system, initially tested on a converted OH-6A in December 1981. Company taken over by McDonnell Douglas January 1984.

HUMBER • UK

The Humber Motor Company Ltd. manufactured a British version of the Blériot XI in 1910, known as the Humber-Blériot Monoplane. At the 1910 Olympia Aero Show Humber exhibited a single-seat monoplane designed by aviator Hubert Le Blon. Powered by a three-cylinder Humber engine, it had variable-camber wings and a small-diameter tapering wooden boom served as the fuselage. Two further Blériot modifications were built to the design of Captain T. T. Lovelace, and two Roger Sommer biplanes were completed towards the end of 1910. One of the latter carried the first official air mail in India.

Left: Original AH-64A version of Hughes-developed Apache attack helicopter, live firing a 70-mm rocket

ETS HUMBERT • France

Offers Moto-du-Ciel as two-seat open microlight, available as plans or kits, and Le Tetras as two-seat cabin monoplane in kit form.

HUMMEL, MORRY • USA

Offers plans to complete the single-seat Bird low-wing monoplane, as modified Watson Windwagon, first flown 1981. Also offers plans for CA-2 single-seat microlight.

HUNTING AIRCRAFT LTD. • UK

In 1957 the Hunting-Percival Company (q.v.) was renamed Hunting Aircraft and continued with production of the Provost, Jet Provost, Prince, Pembroke and Sea Prince before being absorbed by the British Aircraft Corporation (q.v.). BAC had a controlling interest in the company on its formation in 1960, and acquired the remaining shares in 1964.

HUNTING FIRECRACKER AIRCRAFT LTD. • UK

Founded 1984 to propose to RAF a turboprop version of Firecracker trainer, with company formed by Hunting Associated Industries plc, Firecracker Ltd. and Guinness Mahon bankers. See The Norman Aeroplane Company.

HUNTING-PERCIVAL AIRCRAFT LTD. • UK

The Percival light aircraft manufacturing company became part of the Canadian-owned Hunting Group in 1954. Production was undertaken of the Percival P.56 Provost trainer for the RAF and several overseas forces. A turbine powered derivative, the P.84 Jet Provost, flew shortly after the merger and was delivered to the RAF subsequently as its standard basic jet trainer. This eventually continued in production in much-modified form as the BAC Strikemaster. The Percival P.50 Prince twin-engined light transport was manufactured for civilian operators, as the Pembroke C.1 for the RAF, Swedish Air Force, Luftwaffe, and several other air arms, and as the Sea Prince for the Fleet Air Arm. An executive President variant was manufactured in small numbers after the company became Hunting Aircraft Ltd. (q.v.) in 1957.

HUNTINGDON AIRCRAFT CORPORATION • USA

Incorporated in 1928 at Bridgeport, Connecticut, this company developed two aeroplanes, the Huntingdon II two-seat landplane, powered by a Wright-built Gipsy, and the Huntingdon 12, a four/six-seat amphibian with a Pratt & Whitney Wasp engine.

HUREL-DUBOIS • France

Formed to develop Maurice Hurel's theories on high-aspect-ratio wings. His first design, the Hurel-Dubois HD-10 single-engined research aircraft, flew in 1948 and led to a twin-engined derivative, the HD-31. Production versions included the HD-32 transport, HD-33 freighter and HD-34 photo-survey aircraft for the Institut Géographique National. While still active in the French aviation industry, the company is no longer an aircraft constructor.

HUSKY AIRCRAFT LTD. • Canada

Formed 1955 to re-establish a production line for the Fairchild F-11 Husky bush-plane which first flew in 1946. Production models were offered in land or floatplane versions, designated F-11-2 Leonides Husky and F-11-3/4 Super Husky.

HYNES HELICOPTER • USA

See Brantly-Hynes.

HY-TEK • USA

Offers kits to construct Hurricane single-seat microlight, Ultra 103, Clipwing and Hauler.

Hunting Percival Pembroke

Hunting Percival Provost two-seat trainer

Hurel-Dubois HD-32 transport aircraft

Hurel-Dubois HD-10 research aircraft

IA • Argentina

See Fábrica Militar de Aviones.

IABSA • Brazil

Indústria Aeronáutica Brasileira SA produced in the late 1960s a two-seat lightweight primary trainer/sporting aircraft under the designation IABSA Premier 64-01. A single-seat aerobatic biplane, the IABSA Aerobatic 65-02, was under development.

IAI • Israel

See Israel Aircraft Industries.

IAME • Argentina

See Empresa Industrias Aeronáuticas y Meccánicas del Estado.

IAR • Romania

Formed in 1925 as the state-owned Societate Anonima Industria Aeronautica Romania to build aircraft and aero engines. Aircraft built under licence included the Potez 25, Morane-Saulnier 35, Fleet 10-G, PZL 11c and XXIV. Indigenous designs included the IAR.15 single-seat fighter monoplane. Renamed Regia Autonoma Industria Aeronautica Romana (q.v.) in 1940, but still using IAR for types. Came under joint Soviet/Romanian control as Sovromtractor (q.v.) from 1946, with Brasov works known as URMV-3 (q.v.) during 1950s. Renamed ICA Brasov (q.v.) 1968 and changed again to IAR-SA Brasov (q.v.) in 1991.

IAR-SA BRASOV • Romania

Current name (since 1991) for re-equipped IAR works at Brasov, created from ICA Brasov and with lineage also in URMV-3, Sovromtractor, and Regia Autonoma Industria Aeronautica Romana (q.v. all). Has built Aérospatiale Alouette helicopter as IAR 316B (280), Russian Ka-126 helicopter and French Puma helicopter (as IAR 330L Puma) under licence, with Puma 2000 upgraded IAR 330L model currently offered with more engine power, Hellfire anti-armour missiles and advanced avionics among changes. Has agreement with Eurocopter to construct up to 80 AS 350BA and AS 355N helicopters. Made agreement with Bell Helicopter Textron of USA to licence build 96 AH-1W SuperCobra attack helicopters for the Romanian armed forces as AH-1RO Draculas, with Bell taking a majority shareholding in the privatising company as part of the agreement. Kraiova works to licence-manufacture Russian Beriev Be-32K. Own products include IAR 46 two-seat lightplane (first flown 1993), IAR-35 glider and IS-28 series of gliders/motorgliders.

IAv BACAU • Romania

Founded 1953 as a repair factory. First flew its version of the Soviet Yakovlev Yak-52 trainer in 1978, and assisted in other Romanian programmes, plus aero engines. Became Aerostar SA (q.v.) in 1991.

IAv BUCURESTI • Romania

Name for IRMA (q.v.) from 1980, until renamed Romaero SA (q.v.).

IAv CRAIOVA • Romania

Intreprinderea de Avioane Craiova founded February 1972 to develop the IAR-93/J-22 Orao attack aircraft with SOKO of Yugoslavia (first flown October 1974). Renamed S.C. Avioane SA Craiova (q.v.) in 1991.

IBERAVIA • Spain

This company, established in 1946, began the development of aircraft in 1948. A two-seat training glider, the IP-2, was designed, but construction was undertaken by AISA (q.v.). Designed and built in 1950 the I-11 two-seat lightweight training/sporting aircraft, followed by the I-115 basic trainer. Was involved in helicopter design when the company was taken over by AISA.

IBIS AEROSPACE LTD. • International

Founded in 1997 as a joint venture by Aero Vodochody of Czech Republic and AIDC of Taiwan to develop and manufacture the Ae 270 Ibis ten-seat or utility shorthaul turboprop transport designed by Aero Vodochody and first flown in 1999.

ICA BRASOV • Romania

Intreprinderea de Constructii Aeronàutice was the Brasov unit of the Centrala Industriala Aeronautica Romana (q.v.), formed by reorganisation of the national aircraft industry in 1968. Undertook repair and overhaul of light aircraft; built aircraft of its own design, such as the IAR-824 six-seat general-purpose light aircraft and IS-28/IS-29 sailplanes, manufactured Aérospatiale SA 316B Alouette

Below: ICA-Brasov IAR-827 agricultural aircraft (Arth Mihai Andrei/Romaero/Aero Design Srl)

III helicopters under licence, participated in licence-construction of the Britten-Norman BN-2A Islander and carried out series production of nationally-designed aircraft. Name changed to IAR-SA Brasov (q.v.) In 1991.

ICAR LTD. • Ukraine

Established 1995 and offering the AP-23M Enei two-seat light recreational and utility braced monoplane (first flown November 1995).

IKARUS AD • Yugoslavia

Formed at Novi Sad in 1923, Ikarus was one of the country's largest aircraft manufacturers. Initial production centred on a number of S.M. training flying-boats, followed by a military type I.O. In 1926 the company acquired a licence to build the Potez 25 biplane, and established a new factory at Zemun for its production.

IKARUS COMCO • Germany

Markets C.22 side-by-side two-seat microlight.

IKARUSFLUG GBR LEICHTFLUGZEUGBAU • Germany

Offers the Eurofox two-seat, STOL, very light, braced high-wing cabin monoplane (certificated 1996), which is available in assembled or kit forms. Variant of the Czech Aerotechnik Aeropro/Evektor Fox (which see for design and manufacturing details).

Below: Ilyushin II-62 four-turbofan long-range commercial transport

ILYUSHIN • Russia

During the early 1920s Sergei Vladimirovich Ilyushin (died 1977) was a student at the Zhukovskii Military Air Academy, and began glider design. From 1935 one of the most successful Soviet aircraft designers, beginning with II-4 (DB-3) bomber developed from TsKB-26 design, of which nearly 7,000 built. Founded own OKB just before Second World War, though 1933 generally attributed as starting point for Ilyushin designs. Most famous wartime aircraft was II-2 Shturmovik armoured ground-attack aircraft, a vital weapon in the defeat of the German invasion of Russia, and of which more than 36,000 were built.

Post-Second World War developed II-12 and II-14 transports which established Aeroflot's civil airline network. II-28 bomber of 1948 (in class of British Canberra) was first Soviet jet bomber, remaining in large-scale use for many years. II-18 civil transport, which entered service with Aeroflot in 1959, was nation's first turboprop airliner. II-38 anti-submarine/maritime patrol aircraft developed from II-18 and first flown 1961. II-20 reconnaissance, electronic intelligence and communications relay aircraft also

Above: Ilyushin II-76MDK, used for cosmonaut weightlessness training (Piotr Butowski)

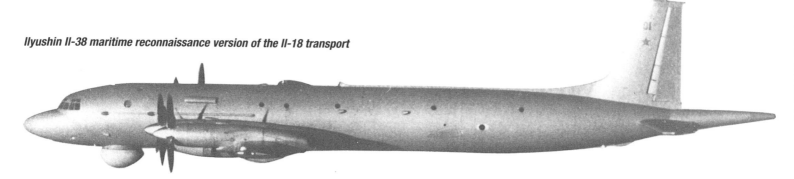

Ilyushin Il-38 maritime reconnaissance version of the Il-18 transport

Above: Ilyushin Il-114 short-haul airliner

developed from Il-18, with Il-24 civil variant. Il-62 114/186-seat turbofan-powered transport, which inaugurated Aeroflot's Moscow-New York service in July 1968, was Soviet Union's first long-range jet airliner.

Il-76T four-turbofan medium/long-range freight transport first flew 1971 and over 900 built, with in-flight refuelling tanker derivative first flown 1983 as Il-78, and communications relay variant as Il-82. Il-86 widebody transport first flew 22 December 1976; 103 built before production ended. Strategic-command-post version became Il-80 *Maxdome*. Follow-on Il-96 widebody airliner first flew December 1988 and remains in production. Il-98 proposed as twin-engined derivative of Il-96. Il-106 heavy military transport and Il-112 shorthaul regional airliner projected. Il-114 twin-turboprop transport first flew March 1990 and ordered, with production and marketing by Uzbekistan-Russian consortium. Special electronic versions of Il-114 developed for 'Open Skies' missions and Russian Federal Border Guard patrol. Il-103 4/5-seat lightplane first flown May 1994 and manufactured by MAPO 'MiG'. Current name Ilyushin Aviation Complex, or Aviatsionnyi Kompleks imeni S.V. Ilyushina.

IMAM • Italy

See Meridionali.

IMCO • USA

Intermountain Manufacturing Company acquired at public auction the former Callair Inc (q.v.), developing from the well-known Callair series of agricultural aircraft an improved model designated IMCO Callair A-9. A scaled-up version, the B-1, first flew on 15 January 1966. IMCO sold the Callair assets to Rockwell-Standard Corporation (q.v.) in December 1966, which continued production of these aircraft at Afton, Wyoming, under the banner of Aero Commander (q.v.).

IMPA • Argentina

Industria Metalúrgica e Plástica SA, a munitions factory, opened an aircraft department in September 1941. A new factory opened at Quilmes Airport, Buenos Aires, in December 1944. Products included prototypes of RR-11 two-seat low-wing cabin monoplane (1942) and Chorlito light single-seat trainer (1943). Only production aircraft was the Tu-Sa (or LF-1), of which 25 were built 1943-1944.

INALET COMPANY • Russia

Formerly known as VIST and founded 1990, is developing a range of turboshaft-powered transport aircraft with vertical take-off and landing/air-cushion capability, by virtue of engine power being switched between conventional propellers and a large horizontal fan occupying the centre fuselage. Also developing a 32-passenger regional airliner as the Inalet-32, featuring an aerodynamically shaped fuselage and stub wings, plus the more conventional Inalet-60 62/68-passenger regional airliner and freighter with twin turbofan engines mounted at the rear of the fuselage.

INDAER • Chile

Industria Aeronáutica established 1980 by military FAdeC to assemble/manufacture Piper and CASA aircraft, and co-develop Pillán trainer. Became Empresa Nacional de Aeronáutica Chile (q.v.) in 1984.

INDÚSTRIA AERONAUTICA BRASILEIRA SA • Brazil

See IABSA.

IMCO Call Air A-9, a trend-setting agricultural aircraft

INDÚSTRIA AERONAUTICA DEL PERU SA • Peru

Originally intended to assemble Aermacchi MB-339A jet trainers, but instead put into production Chuspi two-seat sporting, training and agricultural lightplane (first flown 1987). Later planned to build Aero Boero lightplanes and Pilatus Turbo Porter types.

INDÚSTRIA AERONAUTICA NEIVA SA • Brazil

Formerly Sociedade Construtora Aeronáutica Neiva Ltda, and since March 1980 a subsidiary of EMBRAER, when all work on the EMBRAER/Piper series of light aircraft and production of the EMB-202 Ipanema agricultural aircraft were transferred (over 780 built). Including earlier company, Neiva has produced over 3,200 aircraft since 1956, many under licence from Piper and including Ipanemas, Urupema gliders, Cariocas, Coriscos, Tupis, Minuanos, Sertanejos, Senecas/Cuestas, Navajos and Carajas.

INDÚSTRIA METALURGICA DEL NORTE LTDA • Chile

See Indústrias Cardoen Ltda.

INDÚSTRIA METALURGICA E PLASTICA SA • Argentina

See IMPA

INDÚSTRIA PARANAENSE DE ESTRUTURAS LTDA. • Brazil

Developed IPE 06 Curucaca very light tandem two-seat monoplane (first flown 1990).

INDUSTRIA VALTION LENTOKONETEHDAS • Finland

See IVL.

INDUSTRIAS CARDOEN LTDA. • Chile

Following demise of programme to develop single-seat attack helicopter from BO 105, company developed C206L-III multipurpose helicopter from Bell LongRanger (first flown 1989), featuring pilot only in cockpit behind flat-plate glazing, plus cabin accommodation. Took new name Indústria Metalúrgica del Norte Ltda 1992.

INDUSTRIE MECCANICHE E AERONAUTICHE MERIDIONALI • Italy

See Meridionali entries.

INDUSTRIGRUPPEN JAS AB • Sweden

Established 1981 by Swedish companies concerned with development and production of the Gripen fighter, namely Saab, Volvo Aero Corporation, Ericsson Radar Electronics (now Ericsson Microwave Systems) and FFV Aerotech; Ericsson-Saab since joined. Continues to act as contractor on Gripen programme for FMV, but fighter is developed and manufactured by Saab AS Gripen, a business unit of Saab AB division of Saab Group (q.v.).

INIZIATIVE INDUSTRIALI ITALIANE SPA • Italy

III offers the composites-built Sky Arrow tandem two-seat monoplane in two versions, the 450T microlight in assembled and kit forms and certificated 650T/TC.

INLAND AVIATION COMPANY • USA

Founded in the late 1920s, this company built a two-seat monoplane of braced parasol wing configuration, known as the Inland Sport. The more powerful Super Sport, with an 110 hp Warner Scarab engine, established an American altitude record on 25 October 1929, and a world speed record for light aircraft on 12 February 1930.

Right: III Sky Arrow 650TC two-seat lightplane

*Right: IPT FG-8
Guanabara executive
transport*

INNOVATION ENGINEERING INC. • USA

Provides kits to construct the two-seat Genesis high-wing microlight and a twin-engined version known as Skyquest.

INSTITUTO AEROTÉCNICO • Argentina

See Fábrica Militar de Aviones.

INSTITUTO DE PESIQUAS TECHNOLOGICAS • Brazil

See IPT.

INSTYTUT LOTNICTWA • Poland

Origins in 1926. Undertakes research, development and testing of aircraft, aero engines, materials and instruments/avionics. Proposed the Kobra 2000 in 1993 for air-to-ground combat operations in the next century, but abandoned. Flew the prototype I-23 four-seat lightplane in October 1998, for deliveries from 1999, and was expected to fly its new IS-2 two-seat light helicopter prototype in 1999.

INTEGRATED SYSTEMS AERO ENGINEERING INC. • USA

Markets the Omega II tandem two-seat piston-engined aerobatic lightplane, developed from the Streak 90 Palomino. Originally offered as kit, but currently only as a more-powerful certificated aircraft.

INTER-AIR • USA

International Aircraft Manufacturing Inc established at Alexandria, Minnesota, from Downer (q.v.), to build a new version of the Bellanca Model 14-19-3A four-seat light aircraft designed originally by G. M. Bellanca (see Bellanca Aircraft Corp).

INTERAVIA JSC • Russia

Produced SL-90 Leshiy (first flown 1991) as patrol lightplane for forestry service, partly developed by Aviotechnica (joint Russian and Bulgarian company) and manufactured in 1992 (see also NPP Alpha-M); developed into current I-1 two-seat lightplane (first flown 1992) for pleasure flying and various other roles including training, survey and agriculture. I-3 is single-seat unlimited aerobatic monoplane (first flown 1993), easily converted into a tandem two-seater by use of an interchangeable modular cockpit unit (see Technoavia SP-91). See Technoavia for I-5 project development as SM-92 Finist, the latter which is also being developed by Interavia as I-12.

INTERCEPTOR COMPANY • USA

Original company, Interceptor Corporation, established 18 November 1968. First aircraft produced was Interceptor 400, a turbine-engined development of the Myers 200C built as the Model 200D by Aero Commander Inc (q.v.), from whom Interceptor Corporation acquired all rights and tooling. Prototype Interceptor 400 first flew 27 June 1969. Was sold and subsequently repurchased by current Interceptor Company, which acquired Type Certificate at end of 1974. The interceptor 400 was an advanced four-seat cabin monoplane with a pressurised cabin, which was an

Interavia I-1L two-seat lightplane (Piotr Butowski)

unusual feature for this class of aircraft. It was powered by a 665 shp Garrett-AirResearch turboprop engine. See Prop-Jets Inc.

INTERCITY AIRLINES COMPANY • Canada

Formed in 1947 to construct and develop a three-seat helicopter, designed by American engineers Bernard Sznycer and Selina Gottlieb, designated SG VI-D. This was a conventional single rotor/anti-torque tail rotor type, with a 165 hp Franklin engine.

INTECO • Czech Republic

Produced the VM-23 Variant as a four-seat cabin monoplane.

INTERMOUNTAIN MANUFACTURING COMPANY • USA

See IMCO.

INTERNATIONAL AEROMARINE CORPORATION • USA

Founded 1982, partly owned by David Thurston, to produce TA16 Seafire amphibian. See Teal and Thurston Aeromarine Corporation.

INTERNATIONAL AIRCRAFT CORPORATION • USA

Founded at Cincinnati, Ohio, the company was Incorporated in 1928. Production included the International F-17 Sportsman, a three-seat open cockpit biplane, and the F-18 Air Coach, a six-seat enclosed cabin biplane.

INTERNATIONAL AIRCRAFT MANUFACTURING INC. • USA

See Inter-Air.

INTERNATIONAL AVIATION CORPORATION • USA

Founded 1982 to licence produce British Pilatus Britten-Norman Trislanders, initially from UK parts.

INTERPLANE LTD. • Czech Republic

Produces the Griffon and Skyboy ultralights.

INTERSTATE AIRCRAFT & ENGINEERING CORPORATION • USA

Founded in April 1937, this company was originally a manufacturer of hydraulic and other precision components for the US aircraft industry. Produced in 1940 the Cadet two-

Intora-Firebird tip-jet helicopter in one-man variant

seat light cabin monoplane which, after US entry into the Second World War, was developed as a light liaison and observation aircraft for the US Army. Designed and built a number of drone aircraft prototypes for both US Army and Navy. All were pilotless radio-controlled weapon carriers.

INTER WORK • Czech Republic

Produced the TL-32 Typhoon and TL-132 Condor two-seaters in assembled and kit forms, joined by TL-96 Star, TL-232 Condor and TL-532 Fresh two-seaters under the later company name TL Ultralight.

INTORA-FIREBIRD PLC • UK

Offers the Firebird open-frame single-seat helicopter, also available in UAV form, and the enclosed-fuselage Atlas Firebird two-seater.

INTREPRINDEREA DE CONSTRUCTII AERONAUTICE • Romania

See ICA.

INTREPRINDEREA DE REPARAT MATERIAL AERONAUTICE • Romania

see IRMA.

INVINCIBLE AIRCRAFT CORPORATION • USA

In the late 1920s the Invincible Metal Furniture Company of Manitowoc, Wisconsin, formed an aircraft division to build a four-seat cabin monoplane. The fuselage and tail unit were welded steel-tube structures, the wing of wooden construction. Access to the cabin was by a completely circular door on the starboard side of the fuselage.

Israel Aircraft Industries Astra SP business jet

IPT • Brazil

Instituto de Pesiquas Technólogicas (National Institute of Technical Research) was concerned primarily with research into materials suitable for use by the national aircraft industry. Was also responsible for the construction of a small number of lightweight cabin monoplanes.

IPTN • Indonesia

See PT Industri Pesawat Terbang Nusantara.

IRAN AIRCRAFT INDUSTRIES • Iran

Developed the Fajr two-seat lightplane, first flown 1988.

IRELAND AIRCRAFT INC. • USA

One-time sales representative of the Curtiss Aeroplane and Motor Co, G. S. Ireland founded his company to manufacture an aircraft known as the Ireland Comet, which combined surplus Curtiss Oriole fuselages with new wings and tail unit. Incorporated in 1926, the company began production of the Ireland Neptune, a five-seat amphibian flying-boat.

IRMA • Romania

Intreprinderea de Reparat Material Aeronautice was the Bucharest unit of the Centrala Industriala Aeronautica Romana (q.v.), formed by reorganisation of the national aircraft industry in 1968. Specialised in the repair and overhaul of aircraft and engines for Tarom and other airlines, and manufactured under licence the Britten-Norman BN-2A Islander. Became IAv Bucuresti (q.v.).

IRWIN AIRCRAFT COMPANY • USA

In 1916 J. F. Irwin designed a small single-seat monoplane, designated M-T, powered by a motorcycle engine. After the First World War the company built an improved version, the M-T-2, powered by a 20 hp Meteor engine.

ISAACS, JOHN • UK

Markets plans to build Fury II single-seat biplane, a 70 per cent representation of pre-war Hawker Fury, and Spitfire as 60 per cent representation of Supermarine Spitfire, first flown 1963 and 1975 respectively.

ISHIDA CORPORATION • Japan

Financed TW-68 programme for the development in the USA of a tilt-rotor passenger and utility aircraft during 1990s.

ISLAND AIRCRAFT • UK

Founded 1988 to continue development of ARV Super2 lightplane. See Aviation Scotland and Highlander.

ISRAEL AIRCRAFT INDUSTRIES • Israel

Established April 1967 from former Bedek Aircraft Company (founded 1953), as a repair and maintenance organisation. Bedek manufactured Slingsby sailplanes under licence from 1957, and also initiated licence production of the French Fouga Magister. IAI now composed of several operating groups and subsidiaries, including Bedek Aviation Group (for aircraft maintenance and modification/upgrading, engine work, overhaul and modification of

components and subsystems, and manufacture of manned and unmanned ground equipment, boats and aircraft structures), Commercial Aircraft Group (work includes Westwind, Astra and Galaxy business jets, manufacture of subassemblies for Boeing, and much more), Military Aircraft Group (overhaul, repair and modification of combat aircraft, design and manufacture of UAVs, and helicopter work), and Electronics Group.

Built Nesher fighter 1969, an Israeli-designed interim modified version of the French Mirage III. Developed a more-capable version as the Kfir, which first flew in 1973 and went through several progressively improved variants by manufacture and modification. Designed light STOL transport known as Arava, prototype of which first flew 27 November 1969, and produced civil and military versions. Acquired in 1967 all rights of Rockwell-Standard Corporation's Jet Commander twin-turbojet business transport and developed this into the improved twin-turbofan IAI 1124 Westwind, which entered production in 1976. Developed the IAI 1125 Astra (first flown March 1984), which remains available in 1999 in latest SPX form.

Shareholder in Galaxy Aerospace (q.v.) in USA, which promotes the Astra SPX and promotes and fits-out the new Galaxy widebody bizjet developed by IAI. Developed the Phalcon airborne early warning and intelligence aircraft, using the conformal Phalcon radar system developed in co-operation with Elta Electronics Industries of IAI's Electronics Group, which can also be installed on aircraft other than the original modified Boeing 707 type (first B707/Phalcon flew May 1993; other platforms being proposed include Airbus A310, Boeing 767 and Ilyushin Il-76).

Above: Israel Aircraft Industries Arava STOL transport

Below: Israel Aircraft Industries Kfir combat aircraft

Bedek Aviation Group maintenance and repair of F-16s and F-4s

IAI modified Grumman Tracker for the Argentine Navy as S-2E/UP, with changes including new TPE331-15 turboprop engines and a starboard-wing searchlight

ISRAVIATION LTD. • Israel

Developed the ST-50 pusher-engined business aircraft, first flown December 1994. Stopped trading in September 1997.

ISSOIRE AVIATION • France

Société Issoire Aviation formed 1978 following bankruptcy of Wassmer Aviation (q.v.) by President/General Director of Siren SA (q.v.). In addition to subcontract work for the French aircraft industry and construction of sailplanes, offered IA 80 Piranha as two-seat lightplane.

ITALAIR SPA • Italy

Founded 1974 and intended to produce the General Avia F.20 Pegaso, but all rights returned to General Avia the following year.

ITOH CHU KOKU SEIBI KABUSHIKI KAISHA • Japan

See Shin Nihon Koku Seibi Kabushiki Kaisha.

IVL • Finland

Founded in 1921 at Sveaborg, near Helsinki, to manufacture aircraft for the Finnish Air Force. First production was the A-22 seaplane, a licence-built version of the Hansa-Brandenburg W.33. A neat biplane reconnaissance/bombing aircraft, the Korka, was in production in the mid-1920s. Only one nationally-designed combat aircraft saw service in Second World War, the Myrsky single-seat monoplane fighter.

Right: Israviation ST-50 pusher-engined prototype

JABIRU AIRCRAFT PTY. LTD. • Australia

Manufactures Jabiru two-seat composites lightplane in LSA ultralight, new SK assembled or kit, and ST general aviation assembled or kit forms (first flown 1989, as LSA). Also produces its Jabiru 2200 engine, as used in its aircraft.

JACKAROO AIRCRAFT LTD. • UK

Formed late 1950s at Thruxton, Hampshire, to produce the Thruxton Jackaroo widened-fuselage four-seat version of the de Havilland Tiger Moth. First 'production' conversion flew on 15 April 1957, and quite a number of Tiger Moths were converted subsequently to Jackaroos. Company also designed a four-seat low-wing lightplane called the Paragon, being re-formed in early 1960s as Paragon Aircraft Ltd. (q.v.) to produce it under new name of Paladin.

Above: Jackaroo 'wide-body' version of the Tiger Moth

Jabiru lightplane, marketed in UK by ST Aviation

Jodel D.9 Bébé single-seat lightplane

JAFFE • USA

Jaffe Aircraft Inc. intended to manufacture the Swearin-gen-developed SA-32T Turbo Trainer, but abandoned the programme. Jaffe Helicopter Inc. at same San Antonio address marketed the 222SP as an upgrade of the Bell 222.

JAMIESON CORPORATION • USA

Formed late 1940s as Jamieson Aircraft Company Inc. to develop and produce the J-2-L1 Jupiter, a small, three-seat low-wing monoplane with retractable landing gear and a vee tail. Name changed in middle/late 1950s, and in December 1958 flew prototype of a four-seat, single-tailed development of Jupiter known as the Take 1. This was certificated in mid-1963 and limited production of an improved model, the Jamieson 'J', soon began.

JANOX • USA

Manufacturer of reflector landing systems which, in about 1970, acquired Navion Aircraft Corporation (q.v.). Intended to continue production of Navion Model H in new factory at Coshocton, Ohio; instead, Navion Aircraft Corporation

was purchased in late 1972 by Mr Cedric Kotowicz, who moved all assets to a new plant at Wharton, Texas, sub-sequently setting up the Navion Rangemaster Aircraft Company (q.v.).

JAVELIN AIRCRAFT COMPANY INC. • USA

Plans are available to construct Wichawk biplane, first flown 1971 and offering side-by-side seating plus optional third seat. Also offers plans for V6 STOL, a four-seat high-wing cabin monoplane which uses Piper PA-22 Tri-Pacer components.

JCC AVIATION • France

Offered kit to construct J.300 two-seat cabin microlight.

JDM • France

Founded late 1940s by Jean Dabos to market Roitelet (Wren) single-seat ultra-light monoplane. Poinsard-engined prototype flew successfully, but lack of suitable produc-tion engine prevented manufacture and by 1951 company had been dissolved.

Left: Jamieson 'J' four-seat cabin monoplane

JETCRAFTERS INCORPORATED • USA

Founded by Ed Swearingen to offer Taurus perfor-mance/operating cost improvement for Beech King Air 90

JETCRAFT USA INC. • USA

Planned to market twin-boom executive jet aircraft based on newly-built components of de Havilland Vampire T Mk 11 fighter type. Initial Jetcraft Executive Mark I prototype built.

JETSTREAM • UK

Company formed September 1970 to continue develop-ment/construction and production of H.P.137 Jetstream twin-turboprop transport after closure that year of Hand-ley Page Aircraft Ltd. (q.v.). Initial production line laid down at Northampton late 1970 for Jetstream Series 200, but manufacture taken over early 1970s by Scottish Aviation (q.v.) before any aircraft had been built. With Scottish Avi-ation part of British Aerospace from 1977, Jetstream air-craft became BAe types. Jetstream Aircraft Ltd. founded January 1993 as part of British Aerospace's Regional Air-craft division reorganisation, briefly becoming part of Aero International (Regional) before recent placing under British Aerospace Regional Aircraft Ltd. (BARAL) for engineering management support to former Jetstream customers (Jet-stream aircraft now out of production).

JIM KIMBALL ENTERPRISES INC. • USA

Offers kits and plans to build the Pitts Model 12 tandem two-seat sporting biplane, an original Curtis Pitt's design and having been occasionally known as Macho Stinker.

JINGDEZHEN HELICOPTER CORPORATION • China

New name from 1998 for Changhe Aircraft Industries Corporation (q.v.).

JODEL • France

Established at Beaune in March 1946, by Jean Delemontez and Edouard Joly, the former as business and technical manager, latter as test pilot. Initial activities concerned with repair of gliders and light aircraft of Service d'Avia-tion Légère et Sportive on behalf of French government.

In parallel, Jodel designed and built C.9 Bébé single-seat light monoplane, first flown January 1948. After official tests with D.9, French government ordered two prototypes of two-seat D.11 (Salmson engine) and D.111 (Minie engine). Followed by D.112, and D.140 Mousquetaire. All built for private use in France and other countries. Licence-built by other French companies including Alpavia, Société Aéronautique Normande and Wassmer (all q.v.). Licences for building in Germany, Italy, Spain and other continental countries also granted. Delemontez left to join Pierre Robin at Centre Est Aéronautique (CEA, q.v.) in 1957. Various wood/fabric Jodel models remain available through supply of plans and/or kits/components via SAB in Beaune (also D.9 Bebe via Falconar in Canada, q.v.), including D.9 Bebe single-seater, D.11 two-seater, D.18 two-seater (developed from Delemontez-Cauchy DC-01 and first flown 1984), D.19 nosewheel version of D.18, D.20 Jubilee two-seater of 1997 and the first SAB aircraft offered as a complete kitplane, and D.150 Mascaret two-seater (formerly commercially built by SAN in France).

JOHNSON AIRCRAFT INC. • USA

In 1945 developed at Fort Worth, Texas, the Rocket 140 and 185 retractable-gear low-wing cabin monoplanes. Reorganised 1947 as Johnson Aircraft Corporation, developing from the Rocket the four-seat Bullet 125. This was built under licence by Texas Aircraft Manufacturing Company (q.v.), later being acquired by that company and renamed Texas Bullet.

JOHNSON AIRPLANE & SUPPLY COMPANY INC. • USA

Dayton, Ohio, firm supplying aeronautical equipment and rebuilding surplus military aircraft. Expanded in 1926, rebuilding DH-4s and also producing the Canary, a single-engined three-seat biplane. Last product (first flown December 1936) was the Twin-60, a twin-pusher-engined two-seat open-cockpit biplane with 30 hp Cherub engines.

JOINT EUROPEAN HELICOPTER SRL • International

Founded 1986 by Agusta of Italy, Fokker of Netherlands, CASA of Spain and Westland of UK to develop Tonal light attack helicopter, based on Agusta A 129 Mangusta. Project halted 1990.

JONES AIRCRAFT CORPORATION • USA

Formed 1935 by Ben Jones after acquiring rights in D-25 biplane previously built by the New Standard Aircraft Company (q.v.). Jones built 10 of these in 1938, in factory at Schenectady, New York. In 1937 it introduced the S-125 and S-150 two-seat light cabin monoplanes, powered by Menasco engines.

Right: Jodel D.117 two-seat cabin monoplane

Right: Jovair J-2 two-seat light autogyro

Right: Jovair Sedan 4E tandem-rotor helicopter

JORA SPOL • Czech Republic

Produced the Jora side-by-side two-seat cabin monoplane in kit form, constructed of composites and wood.

JOUCQUES AVIATION • UK

First World War subcontractor for RAF B.E.2b at Willesden, London. Taken over 1917 by British Aerial Transport Company (BAT, q.v.).

JOVAIR • USA

New name from middle/late 1950s of D. K. Jovanovitch's Helicopter Engineering and Research Corporation (q.v.), continuing development of the little JOV-3 tandem-rotor helicopter. From 1949 this had been entrusted to Aircraft Division of McCulloch Motors Corporation, which developed a slightly larger model, the MC-4C. In February 1953 this became the first US tandem-rotor helicopter to receive commercial certification. Jovair Corporation was formed some years later and took the design a stage further, resulting in the Sedan 4E (certificated 1963), of which limited production began in 1965. In June 1962 Jovair flew the prototype J-2 two-seat light autogyro; both programmes were taken over 1969-1970 by McCulloch Aircraft Corporation (q.v.).

Junkers Ju 87 Stuka dive-bomber

Junkers Ju 88 used in a variety of roles

JUNKERS FLUGZEUG UND MOTORENWERKE AG • Germany

Professor Hugo Junkers (1859-1935) became enthusiastically interested in aircraft development and worked for several aero-engine manufacturers. Convinced that all-metal structure was the ultimate answer to successful aircraft design, he produced the experimental J1 'Blechesel' ('tin donkey') cantilever monoplane which flew on 12 December 1915, giving unexpectedly stable performance. Then teamed briefly with Anthony Fokker (see Junkers-Fokker-Werke). Junkers Flugzeug Werke AG formed at Dessau 24 April 1919, first concentrating on all-metal civilian transports such as F 13 four-passenger monoplane (more than 350 built). In 1923 received concession from Soviet government to build aircraft in old Russo-Baltic factory at Fili, near Moscow; established Swedish subsidiary, AB Flygindustri (q.v.), near Malmö, and formed Junkers Motorenbau GmbH for production of aero engines. After death of Hugo Junkers the company became state-owned and, amalgamating with the aero-engine firm, became Junkers Flugzeug und Motorenwerke AG in 1936, then the largest aviation company in the world. For German rearmament programme, Junkers built factories in many other parts of Germany, and in Czechoslovakia and France.

Major types produced included G24 and G31 airliners of 1925/1926: W33 and W34 cargo transports, used also as trainers by Luftwaffe; the G38 'flying wing' of 1928 (prototype flew 6 November 1929; production models carried 34 passengers plus seven crew). Some used as military transports in early stages of Second World War. On 13 October 1930 came first flight of famous Ju 52 cargo transport. Three-engined Ju 52/3m based on latter used in wide variety of roles before and during Second World War, production totalling more than 4,850. Pre-war production continued with Ju 60 and Ju 160 airliners, Ju 86 bomber, transport and trainer, and Ju 87 dive-bomber in many versions. Followed by Ju 88/188/388 family of twin-engined bombers. The Ju 90/290/390 family began as four-engined 38/40-seat airliners, converted as heavy

transport/reconnaissance types in Second World War. Junkers was among first companies to produce military jet aircraft; two prototypes of its Ju 287 with forward-swept wings were captured by Russians in 1945. After Second World War aircraft production ended, and with absorption of small aero-engine plant by Messerschmitt group (q.v.) in 1975, the Junkers name disappeared entirely.

JUNKERS-FOKKER-WERKE AG. • Germany

Prof Hugo Junkers built his J 1 aircraft in 1915 to exemplify his 1910 patent for a cantilever all-metal wing. Six J 2s were then built, but when J 4 ground-attack biplane was ordered for German Army he was not geared for mass production. Thus, Junkers-Fokker-Werke was formed at Dessau on 20 October 1917, with equal shares held by Junkers and Anthony Fokker. Conflicts of personality caused Fokker and Junkers to separate in 1918, and the Junkers re-formed following April as Junkers Flugzeugwerke AG (see above).

JUNKERS • Spain

Avions Metalicos Junkers was founded at Madrid in 1923 to provide facilities for the construction of Junkers aircraft

in Spain. A two-seat all-metal monoplane was in production in 1924.

JUNQUA-DIFFUSION INTERNATIONALE • France

Developed RJ.03 Ibis and tandem two-seat canard monoplane, first flown 1991 and offered in plans form for home construction; Ibis developed from RJ.02 Volucelle.

JURCA, MARCEL • France

Developed a very extensive range of light aircraft, many remaining available for home construction from plans. These include MJ.2 Tempete single-seat wood/fabric aerobatic monoplane (first flown 1956), MJ.5 Sirocco tandem two-seat aerobatic monoplane (first flown 1962), MJ.8 as 75 per cent scale replica of Fw 190 fighter, MJ.9 as 75 per cent scale replica of Bf 109 fighter, MJ.10 Spitfire as 75 per cent scale wooden replica of Supermarine fighter, MJ.12 as 75 per cent scale replica of P-40 fighter, MJ.53 Autan side-by-side two-seater (first flown 1991), MJ.77 Gnatsum as 75 per cent scale wooden replica of P-51 Mustang fighter, and a range of full-size replicas of Second World War fighters, including MJ.80/Fw-190, MJ.90/Bf-109 and MJ.100/Spitfire).

Junkers G38 inter-war civil transport

Junkers Ju 52/3m, numbered among the most famous civil/military transports

KABES, Dr AERO TOVARNA LETADEL • Czechoslovakia

See Aero Tovarna.

KAISER FLUGZEUGBAU • Germany

Has developed and is marketing the Kaiser Magic single-seat biplane with a choice of 125 hp or 200 hp PZL-Franklin piston engine. Displayed at ILA Berlin in 1998.

KAISER-HUGHES INC. • USA

Henry J. Kaiser was a world leader in shipbuilding, associated primarily with the prefabricated Liberty Ship of Second World War. In 1942 Kaiser proposed construction of 5,000 transport flying-boats for troop carrying. Lacking aviation experience, he formed a joint company with Hughes Aircraft (q.v), Hughes to undertake design and Kaiser construction of the Hughes-Kaiser HK-1, the world's largest aircraft. In November 1942 a contract was signed for three aircraft, one for static test and two for flight. By 1944 construction of the first was still at the preliminary stage, and the US Army and Navy withdrew technical assistance. The contract was reduced to one aircraft; Kaiser withdrew, and thereafter the design was called the Hughes H-4 Hercules.

KALININ • USSR

Konstantin Alexievich Kalinin patented a wing of elliptical form in 1923, and in 1925 built the K-1 (RBZ-6), a small high-wing monoplane. Most notable developments were the K-4 (22 built) and the scaled-up K-5 (260 built, 1930-1934). K-5, typically an eight-seater, made a significant contribution to Russian civil aviation. K-7 was an exceptionally large experimental bomber of 1933, having two faired underslung tandem-wheel landing-gear units and six engines. K-12 and K-13 were also bombers. In all, Kalinin designed 16 types before his bureau was disbanded in 1938.

KAMAN • USA

Formed in 1945 by Charles H. Kaman as Kaman Aircraft Corporation to develop a special servo-flap control system for helicopter rotors and 'synchropter' intermeshing twin-rotor system, with aim of eliminating anti-torque tail rotor. K-125A built in 1947; K-190 in 1948; K-225 built in small numbers as YH-22 from 1949. HOK-1 delivered in quantity to US Navy and Marines during 1950s; HTK-1 to Navy as trainer/ambulance, and also adopted as remote-controlled drone. By late 1960s well over 200 H-43 Huskie turbine-powered rescue helicopters were serving with the USAF. H-2 Seasprite naval rescue and utility helicopter first flown July 1959, retaining servo-flap system, though on a conventional main rotor. Seasprite developed in many versions, early production models using a single turboshaft engine and later models with twin turboshafts; experi-

Kaiser-Fleetwings XBTK-1 bomber-torpedo prototype

ments included stub wings serving as sponsons and gunship version with Minigun chin turret among other weapons.

In the late 1960s much subcontracting undertaken, together with development of Rotorchute and allied devices. Became Kaman Group in 1965 with extended activities, with Aerospace subsidiary subsequently taking

Kaman Huskie helicopter

Kaman Seasprite utility helicopter

*Right: Kaman K-MAX
'Aerial Truck'*

*Below: Kaman SH-2G
Super Seasprite
upgrade of SH-2F*

Kamov Ka-25Ts target acquisition and over-the-horizon guidance for ship-to-ship missiles helicopter (Piotr Butowski)

the present name Kaman Aerospace Corporation as part of Kaman Group. Current programmes include producing upgraded SH-2Fs as SH-2G Super Seasprites for anti-submarine/anti-shipping, over-the-horizon targeting, SAR, mine countermeasures, vertrep and other roles, for delivery to Royal Australian Navy, Royal New Zealand Navy, Egypt and US Navy Reserve; production of K-MAX 'Aerial Truck' single-seat, turboshaft-powered and twin inter-meshing rotor external-lift helicopter (first flown December 1991); and subcontract work on Boeing airliners and for various military aircraft including AH-1, C-17, Comanche, F-22 and V-22.

KAMAN AIRCRAFT OF CANADA LTD. • Canada

Formed in the mid-1950s to study possible Canadian market for Kaman helicopters.

KAMERTON-N LTD. • Russia

Developed the Ratnik two-seat multipurpose light auto-gyro, flight tested from 1995.

KAMOV • USSR/Russia

Nikolai Ilych Kamov studied design of autogyros and heli-copters from 1929. He gained distinction for lightweight single-seat helicopters after Second World War, including Ka-8 of 1947. Design bureau formed 1948, followed by single-seat Ka-10 of 1950 appearance as piston-engined helicopter for shipborne observation duties, with two con-trarotating rotors and therefore no anti-torque tail rotor; these rotor design features were to be found in most sub-sequent Kamov helicopters. Ka-15 two-seater of 1950s used for agricultual work in addition to naval anti-subma-rine and other roles, and Ka-18 four-seat development flown 1957 and widely operated on varied civil tasks. Ka-22 Vintokryl was very large twin-turboprop convertiplane, first seen in 1961; established many world records. Very important twin-turboshaft powered Ka-25 first flown April 1961 and deployed by Soviet Navy as shipborne anti-sub-marine-warfare helicopter, also for target acquisition, join-ing Navy from 1972 and manufactured up to 1977.

Much more capable Ka-27 first flown August 1973 and joined Soviet Navy from 1981, with Ka-28 as export ver-

Kamov Ka-26 twin-engined helicopter

sion; related Ka-29 first flown July 1976 as shipborne assault and transport variant plus Ka-33 export model without weapons, Ka-31 flown October 1987 as shipborne AEW&C variant, and Ka-32 first flown October 1980 as civil model for transport, flying-crane, rescue, offshore support, patrol, firefighting and other uses, with Ka-327 as maritime patrol version of Ka-32. Piston-engined civil

Kamov Ka-50 Black Shark single-seat combat helicopter (Piotr Butowski)

Ka-26 first flew 1965 (some military use), with modern Ka-126 (first flown October 1987) and Ka-128 turboshaft developments, all having pod-and-boom fuselages to allow attachment of modules aft of cockpit for various cargoes (from passenger carrying to agricultural equipment) or left open for flying-crane duties; new twin-turbine development is Ka-226 (first flown September 1997). Ka-50 first flown June 1982 as important single-seat combat helicopter, with Ka-50N Black Shark night-attack version flying March 1997, while side-by-side two-seat derivative became Ka-50 Alligator (first flown June 1997). New military multipurpose twin-turboshaft helicopter is Ka-60 for 10 equipped troops (rolled out July 1998), with 16-passenger civil version as Ka-62. Light single-turboshaft Ka-115 to fly 1999, carrying pilot and up to four passengers. In 1996, Kamov became a member of MIG MAPO-M (q.v.).

KAPPA SPOL • Czech Republic

Produces the KP-2U Sova two-seat low-wing lightplane, first flown May 1996.

KARHUMÄKI • Finland

Veljekset Karhumäki OY founded in 1924. In the 1930s the Viri single-seat light monoplane was built, design by Finnish Club of Aeronautical Engineers. In 1939-1941 a new factory was built, near Halli airfield, where trainers for Finnish Air Force were built; also the Karhu 48-seat strut-braced high-wing cabin monoplane with skis, wheels or floats.

KARI-KEEN AIRCRAFT INC • USA

Formed in June 1928 as a subsidiary of Kari-Keen Manufacturing Company Inc, which made automobile accessories. Built Kari-Keen 90 high-wing side-by-side two-seat light cabin monoplane.

KARO AVIACIJOS TIEKIMO SKYRIUS • Lithuania

The Lithuanian Army's aircraft factory, responsible for the construction of the Anbo 41, a two-seat day/night obser-

vation aircraft, and the Anbo 51 two-seat trainer, both monoplanes.

KAWANISHI KOKUKI KOGYO KABUSHIKI KAISHA • Japan

In July 1924 A Kawanishi biplane seaplane made a round-Japan flight in nine days. Company formed as above in November 1928, taking over works and windtunnel (at Kobe) of Kawanishi Machine Works. Held Short Bros licence and was Rolls-Royce agent. At the time of formation was supplying aircraft, components and accessories to Japanese Navy. Early types included a single-seat biplane fighter and a two-seat long-range high wing monoplane. At the end of 1930 moved to new works at Narao. In February 1933 flew new three-seat reconnaissance floatplane (E7K) adopted by Japanese Naval Service. Short and Rolls-Royce connections manifested in Navy type 90-2 (K.F.1) flying-boat, built in England, assembled in Japan. Built from 1936 a highly successful long-range maritime reconnaissance/bomber/transport flying-boat, the strut-braced H6K. Subsequent H8K had deep hull and cantilever wing. N1K

Kawanishi H6K4 ('Mavis') maritime patrol flying-boat

Kawanishi K-6 biplane

single-seat fighter monoplane of 1942 originated as float-plane but was developed into outstanding landplane. Projects included suicide aircraft based on German V-1. In 1949 the company re-emerged as ShinMaywa (q.v.).

KAWASAKI JUKOGYO KABUSHIKI KAISHA • Japan

See below.

KAWASAKI KOKUKI KOGYO KABUSHIKI KAISHA • Japan

Formed in 1918 as subsidiary of heavy-industrial complex Kawasaki Jukogyo to build aircraft and aero engines. Based at Kobe, in the early 1930s built Salmson biplanes and engines as well as own designs. Had Dornier licence for all-metal construction, and in December 1924 the first Kawasaki-Dornier Wal flying-boat made a notable flight with a German pilot. Thereafter made aircraft mainly for the Japanese Army. A designer of Kawasaki landplanes was German Dr Richard Vogt, with the company 1923-1933. Vogt designs were Type 88 reconnaissance biplane

Kawanishi H8K flying-boat

(1927), Type 92 single-seat biplane fighter (1930), and Ki-3 single-engined biplane bomber. Japanese-designed were Ki-10 single-seat fighter biplane (1935), Ki-32 single-engined monoplane bomber (1937), Ki-45 fast and widely used twin-engined fighter (1939), Ki-48 twin-engined light bomber (1939), Ki-61 single-seat fighter (liquid-cooled engine and showing German influence (1941), Ki-100 radial-engined development (1944) and Ki-102 twin-engined fighter (1944).

Kawasaki Ki-61 single-seat fighter

After the war, in March 1954, a new company of the same name was founded by the merger of Kabushiki Kaisha Kawasaki Gifu Seisakusho and Kawasaki Kikai Kogyo Kabushiki Kaisha. The Kawasaki KAL-1 (July 1953) was the first post-war all-metal aircraft of Japanese design. Early production covered 210 Lockheed T-33 jet trainers, 48 Lockheed P-2H Neptunes and 239 Bell Model 47 helicopters, all built under licence from the USA. Also made major components for the NAMC YS-11 turboprop transport.

Company reorganised in April 1969 as Kawasaki Jukogyo Kabushiki Kaisha. In November 1970 flew C-1 twin-turbofan military transport, production aircraft later going to the JASDF. Went on to complete 82 P-2Js (derived from Neptune), 211 KH-4 helicopters (derived from the Model 47), 160 KV107 helicopters (derived from the Boeing Vertol 107 Model II), and many Hughes/McDonnell Douglas Model 500D and OH-6DA helicopters (production continued through 1998). Produced the Lockheed Martin P-3C Orion for the JMSDF; 101st and final aircraft delivered in 1997, when four EP-3/UP-3D electronic intelligence/training variants remained to be delivered up to the year 2000. Also produced 16 CH-47J examples of Boeing Chinook for the JASDF and is completing delivery of 52 CH-47JAs

Kawasaki KH-4 light helicopter

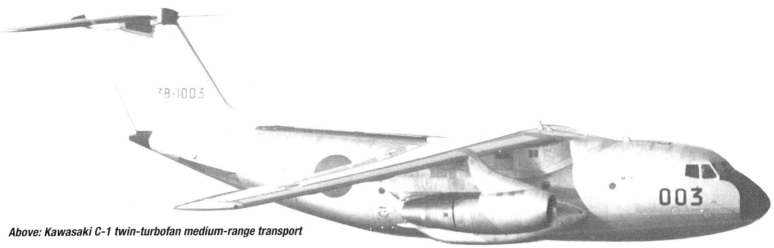

Above: Kawasaki C-1 twin-turbofan medium-range transport

to the JGSDF. Is prime contractor on the new OH- I Kogata Kansoku armed scout, observation and attack helicopter (first flown August 1996), and had almost completed manufacture of some 200 T-4 intermediate jet trainers and liaison aircraft for the JASDF by 1998. Also constructs components and assemblies for the the F-15J and various Airbus and Boeing airliners. Is teamed with Eurocopter on the BK 117 helicopter, and has engine and space programmes.

Below: Kawasaki OH-1 Kogata Kansoku armed scout, observation and attack helicopter, first flown in 1996

Above: Kawasaki P-2J anti-submarine patrol aircraft

Kayaba Heliplane autogyro

KAYABA • Japan

In 1939 a US-built Kellett KD-1A autogiro was exported to Japan. K. K. Kayaba Seisakusho developed Ka-1 along similar lines for Japanese Navy; used for observation, anti-submarine patrol (incl. shipborne), and for testing rocket-augmented rotors. Ka-2 was re-engined.

KAZAN HELICOPTER PLANT • Russia

Founded 1939, and since 1951 has manufactured Mil helicopters. Holds 25 per cent shareholding in Euromil (q.v.).

Own designs are Ansat twin-turboshaft light multipurpose helicopter (first flown 1998) for up to 10 persons, and Aktay three-seat piston helicopter (to fly about year 2000).

KB MAI • Russia

Design Bureau of Moscow Aviation Institute (see Aviatika). Current aircraft are Aviatika-MAI-890 single-seat very light multipurpose pusher monoplane (first flown in 1990 as MAI-89 prototype), also available in autogyro and training glider forms, Aviatika-MAI-900 Acrobat single-seat aerobatic competition monoplane (first flown 1993), and Aviatika-MAI 910 two-seat recreational and utility cabin lightplane (first flown 1995), with 960 development having a thicker tailboom.

KELLETT AUTOGIRO CORPORATION • USA

Under Pitcairn-Cierva licence developed and built autogiros at Philadelphia from 1929. A K-3 was taken to the Antarctic by Admiral Byrd on his second expedition in 1933, piloted by William S. McCormick. K-4 had two side-by-side seats with demountable enclosure but retained wings. KD-1 of 1934 had tandem seats but was wingless and had direct-control rotor. In 1938 US Army Air Corps bought

seven Kellett autogiros for experimental use. From 6 July 1939 a Kellett KD-1B of Eastern Airlines operated the first scheduled mail service by a rotary-wing aircraft, from the roof of the Philadelphia Post Office and the Camden airport. In 1939 Kellett exported an autogiro to Japan (see Kayaba). YG-1 was developed into XR-2 and XR-3 for the US Army. XR-8 and XR-8A of 1943/1945 had twin side-by-side rotors. As Kellett Aircraft Corporation the company later undertook research and development contracts and subcontracting. Built its own KH-15 single-seat research helicopter (1954), the world's first rocket-driven helicopter. In late 1950s attempted unsuccessfully to resume production of pre-war KD-1A direct-control autogiro.

KELLNER-BÉCHEREAU • France

Avions Kellner-Béchereau was founded at Billancourt in 1933. Kellner had built car bodies; also SPAD fighters under contract from 1916. Béchereau was experienced in aircraft design (Deperdussin and SPAD types) and had patented new kinds of wooden construction, using moulds. During the 1930s the company made 60 fuselages for recently-ordered SPAD 510 fighter biplanes, using Béchereau system. Built monoplane with Delage inverted engine for Coupe Deutsch de la Meurthe. In 1936 built a

Kazan-built Mil Mi-8

single-seat lightplane using Béchereau-patented 'double wing' (divided laterally, with rear parts hinged differentially to act as slotted flaps or ailerons), and in 1937 two side-by-side-seater developments were built, one of metal and one of wood. With low-powered Train engine, aircraft of this type (E-1 single-seater) established class records. Company's aeronautical activities ceased in 1941.

KELLY, DUDLEY • USA

Markets plans to build Kelly-D and Hatz CB-1 tandem two-seat biplanes, the latter originally designed by John Hatz and first flown 1968.

KELOWNA FLIGHTCRAFT GROUP • Canada

Offers the CV5800 as an extensively reworked, modernised and lengthened Convair CV580 (first flown February 1992), with improvements including a 'glass' cockpit using display screens and adoption of turboprop engines; CV340 and CV440 can be similarly upgraded. Operates an extensive fleet of aircraft under its Kelowna Flightcraft Air Charter division, and undertakes repairs, modifications and maintenance.

KEMMERIES AVIATION • USA

Has produced since 1987 plans and kits to build Tukan single-seat or 1+1-seat microlight with Rogallo wing and trike.

KEN BROCK MANUFACTURING INC. • USA

Produces kits to build the KB-2 Freedom Machine single-seat autogyro and KB-3 single-seat ultralight autogyro.

KENNEDY AEROPLANES LTD. • UK

Founded early in First World War by Chessborough J. H. Mackenzie-Kennedy, with offices in South Kensington, London, following establishment of the Kennedy Aeronautic Company in Russia in 1909. In 1911 the founder met Igor Sikorsky and shared enthusiasm for large aircraft. Was associated in the English company with T. W. K. Clarke, well known in British aeronautics. With War Office permission, construction started on the Kennedy Giant by the Gramophone Company Ltd. Late in 1916 components were sent to Northolt Aerodrome for erection in the open. In 1917 attempts to fly the underpowered machine resulted in a 'hop'. Building of a bomber was started at Newcastle-on-Tyne, but financial failure came in 1920.

V. KENSGAILA AIRCRAFT ENTERPRIZE • Lithuania

First flew in 1989 the VK-8 Ausra two-seat agricultural aircraft.

KENTUCKY AIRCRAFT CORPORATION • USA

Founded in 1926 to manufacture a three-seat biplane named the Kentucky Cardinal. The two aircraft completed were of welded steel tube construction and powered by Curtiss OX-5 engines. Company went into liquidation in 1927 following death of the principal.

KERR, DICK, & COMPANY LTD. • UK

Based at Lytham St Annes, near Preston, Lancs., where late in First World War Felixstowe F.3 twin-engined flying-boats were built to Government contract. Fairey subcontracted the first of three N.4 four-engined flying-boats to the company. Dick Kerr built the superstructure, though the hull was made by May, Harden & May Ltd. and transported by road in 1919. In 1921 the flying-boat was dismantled and taken by road to the Isle of Grain, where it first flew 4 July 1923.

Kelowna Flightcraft CV5800 modernised Convair CV580

Keystone Y1B-4 bomber prototype

Keystone Patrician civil transport

KESTREL AIRCRAFT COMPANY • USA

Produces a series of four-seat high-wing lightplanes of mainly carbonfibre construction, with fixed or retractable undercarriages and piston engines ranging from 160 hp to 250 hp, plus the K-325 six-seat or utility variant with 325 hp engine.

KEUTHAN AIRCRAFT • USA

Kits are available to allow amateur construction of the Buccaneer high-wing amphibian in single- and two-seat versions, Sabre high-wing pusher-engined monoplane in single- and two-seat versions, and Zephyr two-seat high-wing monoplane.

KEYSTONE AIRCRAFT CORPORATION • USA

Originally Huff-Daland; became Keystone March 1927, still centred at Bristol, Pennsylvania. Later absorbed Loening, becoming Keystone-Loening, and then became part of Curtiss-Wright. Keystone was main supplier of twin-engined bombers to US Army from 1927 to 1932. LB-5A (25 delivered in 1928) was first true Keystone bomber. Largest USAAC bomber order in a decade was for 63 LB-10A (all converted to B-3A and B-5A on change of Army categories). Last production contracts for bombers placed 1931 (for 25 B-4A and 39 B-6A). Pathfinder was three-engined civil transport; NK a biplane trainer for a 1928 competition (19 built); PK a twin-engined flying-boat based on NAF design (18 delivered in 1931). Patrician was three-engined 20-passenger low-wing monoplane. Other types were characteristically Loening, including the OL-8 biplane amphibian; the Air Yacht civil amphibian; and the Commuter four-seat cabin amphiblan.

KINGSBURY AVIATION COMPANY • UK

Built Airco D.H.6 trainer biplanes under subcontract from 1917. Late in 1917 began construction of three triplane seaplanes, to carry Davis recoilless gun, but contract cancelled January 1918.

THE KING'S ENGINEERING FELLOWSHIP • USA

See Angel Aircraft Corporation.

KINGSFORD SMITH AVIATION SERVICE PTY. LTD. • Australia

Formed in 1946 from Kingsford Smith Air Service. Undertook sales, servicing and overhaul of light and medium aircraft, and in 1955 began design of special agricultural type which materialised as PL-7 Tanker biplane. Fuselage was mild-steel tank, tail carried on tubular booms, tricycle landing gear. Flew September 1956. Later Cropmaster was entirely different low-wing monoplane, and special Auster conversions were offered. To these were added (1959/1960) E.P.9 conversion, details of which were supplied to Lancashire Aircraft. Company sold out in 1963 to Victa Ltd. of Milperra, Sydney.

KINNER AIRPLANE & MOTOR CORPORATION • USA

Formed in 1919. Known chiefly for its air-cooled radial engines. Aircraft designed by the company round its own engines included Courier two-seat parasol monoplane of late 1920s. In 1930s was producing Sportster strut-braced low-wing monoplane with open side-by-side seats. Sportwing was refined version, Playboy was wire-braced and enclosed and Envoy was scaled-up Playboy seating four. Three Envoys acquired by US Navy as XRK-1 were not experimental, but staff transports. During 1937 company still offered six types of engine and was working on twin-engined Invader, but in 1938 was in receiver's hands, though continuing operations under control of a trustee.

KIRKHAM, CHAS. B. • USA

Kirkham (1882-1969) was a friend and collaborator of Glenn Curtiss. He made motorcycle engines from about 1900, and in 1910 an aero engine. In 1915 he joined Curtiss in engine work and is chiefly known in connection with the famous D-12. Wanting a fighter worthy of his K-12 engine, with its small frontal area, Kirkham planned a two-seat triplane with excellent streamlining, first flown 5 July 1918. To this record-breaker the name Kirkham Fighter, 18-T or Curtiss-Kirkham was applied, though the Curtiss name alone was later used for land and sea versions. US Army had 18-B biplane equivalent, also sometimes called Curtiss-Kirkham. Navy's two 18-Ts were later adapted for racing. In 1920s Kirkham's company Kirkham Products designed aircraft to special order.

KITAIR • France

Offers kits to build Helios-5-TR and Hermes side-by-side two-seat wood/composites monoplanes.

KITZ KOPTERS INC • USA

In mid-1960s developed conversion scheme for increasing payload of Bell Model 47 helicopter, primarily for agricultural work. Also repaired, modified and operated Bell helicopters.

KJELLER FLYFABRIKK • Norway

The Norwegian Army Aircraft Factory, located at Kjeller. Built under licence during the 1930s Fokker C.V and de Havilland Gipsy Moth and Tiger Moth. Also did repair and overhaul of military-aircraft equipment, and experimental work.

KLEMM, HANNS • Germany

Dr Ing Hanns Klemm (1885-1961) was an eminent pioneer in the development of light aircraft. During the First World War he worked with Zeppelin, Dornier and Hansa und Brandenburgische Flugzeugwerke, and later with Daimler, for whom he designed biplanes and monoplanes, including fighters. After the war he concentrated on light and economical aircraft, sometimes called Daimler-Klemm. L 15 of 1919 was originally a glider, though later powered, but had high wing. True precursor of the classic Klemm low-powered two-seat line of low-wing monoplanes was L20 of 1924. In December 1926 Leichtflugzeugbau Klemm GmbH was formed (notably associated with Böblingen), and L 25 was produced from 1927 with many types of engine, consolidating Klemm's reputation. K 131 and K 132 of early 1930s were cabin types. Company renamed Hans Klemm

Flugzeugbau August 1938, and was then making K 135 cranked-wing tourer/trainer series for Luftwaffe and export. In new type-number series built Kl 105-107. During Second World War contributed to military-aircraft production, afterwards Klemm revived Kl 107 three-seat cabin model. Production ended November 1957.

KLEYER • Germany

Adlerwerke vorm Heinrich Kleyer AG. was formed at Frankfurt am Main in 1934 to take over Frankfurter Flugzeugbau Max Gerner GmbH. Made low-cost, low-powered all-metal light aircraft with Gerner engines.

KNOLL AIRCRAFT CORPORATION • USA

Formed to build aircraft to designs of Felix Knoll, formerly with Rohrbach and Heinkel in Germany. KN-1 of 1928 was a four-seat cabin biplane with forward stagger.

KOCHERGIN • USSR

A design team under the general supervision of V. P. Yatsenko designed in the early 1930s an unusually compact two-seat fighter biplane, called DI-6 or TsKB-11. Production began at the end of 1935.

KOENIG ENGINEERING • France

Offers kit to construct AK.09 Faucon two-seat composites monoplane, also available from Germany as Junkers Ultima.

KOLB COMPANY INC. • USA

Markets kits to build a series of single- and two-seat microlights of differing designs in the Firestar, Slingshot and Flyer range.

KONDOR FLUGZEUG-WERKE GMBH • Germany

Designed and built military aircraft in First World War, including D I and D 7 single-seat fighter biplanes (1918 and 1917 respectively), and E III parasol monoplane.

KONINKLIJKE MAATSCHAPPIJ 'DE SCHELDE' • Netherlands

The aircraft department of a dockyard; opened in 1935, employing technicians from Pander. Built S.12 four-seat cabin monoplane, Scheldmusche light single-seat pusher biplane; best known for Scheldmeeuw single-seat flyingboat, which was built in all-metal and composite versions. From 1939 made wings for Dornier Do 24 flying-boats, Aviolanda building the hulls.

KOOLHOVEN, FREDERICK • Netherlands

Koolhoven (1886-1945) designed, built and flew his first aircraft in 1910, but was later well known in the UK for his Deperdussin, Armstrong Whitworth and BAT associations. After the Armistice he returned to the Netherlands, and for the NV Nationale Vliegtuigindustrie designed the F.K.31 two-seat fighter-reconnaissance monoplane (1922). In 1926 he became a consultant engineer at The Hague; then designed several aircraft, including the F.K.41 three-seat cabin monoplane. In 1934 the NV Koolhoven Vliegtuigen was formed, by which time it was claimed that 51 F.K. types had been produced. More followed, including the F.K.52, an outstanding two-seat fighter biplane with cantilever undercarriage, and the F.K.58 single-seat fighter monoplane, ordered in quantity by France.

KOREAN AIR • South Korea

Aerospace division of the commercial airline, Korean Air Lines, founded 1976. Has built more than 300 McDonnell Douglas (now Boeing) MD 500 helicopters, and is now constructing Sikorsky UH-60Ps for the nation's armed forces. In addition to developing its own four-seat lightplane as the Chang-Gong 91 (first flown 1991), it is currently working on its Multi-Purpose Helicopter (KMH) with Sikorsky assistance (to be flown in about the year 2000). Other activities include maintenance, upgrading, and production of components for US and European airliners.

KREIDER-REISNER AIRCRAFT COMPANY INC. • USA

Built the Midget in 1926, which did well in that year's National Air Races. In 1927 built the Challenger three-seat open-cockpit biplane using the cheap Curtiss OX-5 (or other) engine. Smaller two-seater also made. In April 1929 company was bought by the Fairchild Airplane Manufacturing Corp and the Kreider-Reisner types were added to the Fairchild series, the Challengers then being known as Fairchild KR biplanes (Challenger C-6 was KR-21; C-4 was KR-34). As a division of Fairchild Aviation Corporation in the mid-1930s Kreider-Reisner built the Fairchild 22 two-seat open-cockpit monoplane and the Fairchild 24 cabin type, also producing the Fairchild 71 amphibian.

KREUTZER, JOSEPH, CORPORATION • USA

In 1928 made the Air Coach six-seat high-wing monoplane with 90 hp nose engine and two 65 hp units outboard.

OKB KRILYA • Russia

Has been developing the Yrbis six-seat executive transport and the turboprop two-seat Orka.

KRONFELD LTD. • UK

Formerly The British Aircraft Co (1935) Ltd of London Air Park, Feltham, Middlesex. Renamed as above in 1936, in which year 20 Drone ultralight monoplanes were built, one model becoming known as Kronfeld Super Drone. The Kronfeld Monoplane of 1937, likewise a pusher, was intended as a Drone successor, but only one was built.

KHRUNICHEV STATE SPACE RESEARCH CENTRE • Russia

The Aviation Department of this organisation was founded in 1994, and is affiliated to Aeroprogress Inc (q.v.).

KYLE-SMITH AIRCRAFT COMPANY • USA

Founded at Wheeling, West Virginia, to manufacture a two-seat biplane intended for sport and training, powered by a radial engine. It was reported in 1919 that the company was also building to official specification, presumably under subcontract.

Koolhoven F.K.43 four-seat cabin monoplanes

Klemm L 35 lightplane

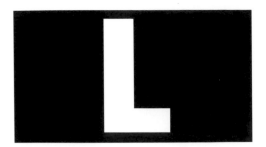

LAGG • USSR

See Lavochkin.

LAIRD AIRPLANE COMPANY • USA

Emil Matthew 'Mattie' Laird built his first Model S aircraft in 1919. Commercial activity at Chicago began in 1920 with the Swallow, a redesigned Curtiss JN-4, claimed as first US commercial aircraft. Design sold to Lloyd Stearman's Swallow Aeroplane Manufacturing Company as the New Swallow. Built the first LC (Laird Commercial) 1924. Also designed Super Swallow, an improved New Swallow. Laird concentrated subsequently on custom-built sporting and racing aircraft, such as LC-DW Solution, the only biplane to win the Thomson Trophy. In 1931 Super Solution Jimmy Doolittle set US coast-to-coast records. With same aircraft set record of 293.193mph (471.8kmh) at 1932 National Air Races. Production continued of three-seat Speedwing biplane. Last project was in 1936, redesigning and completing ex-Lawrence Brown racer for Colonel Roscoe Turner, as LTR 14 Meteor.

LAIRD, CHARLES • USA

Charles Laird of Wichita, Kansas, built the Whippoorwill cabin biplane and changed company name in 1927 to avoid confusion with his brother 'Mattie' of E. M. Laird Airplane Company (above).

LAKE AIRCRAFT DIVISION, CONSOLIDATED AERONAUTICS • USA

Formed at Sandford, Maine, and purchased manufacturing rights to Colonial Skimmer in 1959, marketed initially as Lake Skimmer. Merged with Consolidated Aeronautics (q.v.) 1962, continuing production as Lake LA-4A amphibian, the first under the Lake name appearing in 1960. 1978 production model was LA-4 200 Buccaneer. One LA-4 used by Bell Aerospace (q.v.) to test Air Cushion Landing System (ACLS) 1963-1968. Company became Lake Amphibian Inc. in 1983 and Lake Aircraft Inc. in 1987 (q.v.).

LAKE AIRCRAFT INC. • USA

Current name for Lake Amphibian Inc. Markets six-seat Renegade amphibian (first flown 1983), four-seat Turbo-Renegade with turbocharged piston engine, Seafury and Turbo Seafury as variants for salt water operations, and military Seawolf with underwing NATO pylons for stores. Over 1,300 amphibians manufactured by all Lake companies, past and present.

LAKES FLYING COMPANY • UK

Formed in 1911 by Captain E. W. Wakefield. Built the first successful British seaplane (designed by A. V. Roe) at Cockshott, Windermere. In 1912 built interesting seaplane with

Above: Lake amphibian, originally based on colonial skimmer

Lancashire Aircraft Prospector utility aircraft

central float, designed by Oscar T. Gnosspelius. Renamed Northern Aircraft Company (q.v.).

LAMBERT AIRCRAFT CORPORATION • USA

A Robertson, Missouri, company founded in 1934 by J. P. Wooster Lambert, of the Lambert Engine and Machine Company, to take over and continue production of aircraft designed by Mono Aircraft Corporation (q.v.) of Moline, Illinois, part of Allied Aviation Corporation (q.v.).

Latécoère L.521 six-engined commercial flying-boat

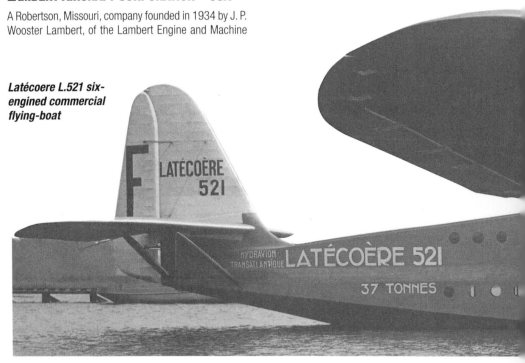

LA MOUETTE • France

Produces Ghost Rogallo-type wings for microlights, Topless hang glider, Paramotor series of single-seat powered ram-air parachutes, and La Mouette/ULM Cosmos Phase II two-seat Rogallo-wing microlight.

LAMSON AIRCRAFT COMPANY INC. • USA

Manufacturer at Seattle, Washington, of the Model L.101 Air Tractor, a 1953 agricultural aircraft designed by Central-Lamson. Production ceased in 1955.

LANCAIR INTERNATIONAL INC. • USA

The original Lancair 200 composites monoplane, designed by Lance Niebaur, first flew in 1984. From the subsequent Lancair 320 evolved the current Lancair 320 Mk II two-seat monoplane that is available in kit form, together with kits for the four-seat Lancair IV, IVP with pressurised cabin and Tigress as a two-seat variant of IV. Four-seat Lancair Super ES has also given rise to the Columbia 300 for certification, the latter being a joint venture programme with a Malaysian organisation.

LANCASHIRE AIRCRAFT COMPANY LTD. • UK

Formed from Samlesbury Engineering, Ltd., 1960, which had bought Edgar Percival Aircraft Ltd in 1959. Continued production of E.P.9 general-purpose aircraft as the Lancashire Aircraft Prospector at Squire's Gate, Lancashire.

Right: Latécoere L.290 torpedo-bomber floatplane

LANDGRAF HELICOPTER COMPANY • USA

Incorporated 1943 at Los Angeles by Fred Landgraf, after several years development of H-2 twin-rotor light helicopter, which first flew in 1944. US Army development contract 1945. Retractable tricycle landing gear, and overlapping synchronised rotors. UK licence held by Firth Helicopters of London, but parent company inactive by 1949.

LANIER AIRCRAFT CORPORATION • USA

E. H. Lanier formed company at Newark, New Jersey, in 1943, to continue research work on semi-flying-wing STOL aircraft. Six research models were followed by single-seat Paraplane I, II and Commuter 110. Capable of sustained level flight at speeds as low as 19mph (31kmh). The two-seat Commuter 120 was planned in 1961.

LANZIUS AIRCRAFT COMPANY • USA

A New York company, formed to design and build biplanes with variable-incidence wings. Built aircraft to government contract 1917-1918.

LARKIN/LASCO • Australia

Formed as the Larkin-Sopwith Aviation Company of Australasia, which began operation in 1919 and became Lasco, at Melbourne, in 1921. Built 32 de Havilland Gipsy Moths under licence for the government. In 1930 built one- and three-engined transports, known as the Lascoter, Lascowl and Lasconder. At least one de Havilland

D.H.50 constructed. Withdrawal of government subsidy and economic depression caused close-down.

LARKIN-SOPWITH AVIATION COMPANY OF AUSTRALASIA

See Larkin/Lasco.

LARON AVIATION TECHNOLOGIES INC. • USA

Offers kits to build the two-seat Shadow and Streak Shadow under licence from CFM of the UK. Also offers kits for Star Streak two-seat monoplane, two-seat Tundra and single-seat version as 1/2 Tun microlight, and Wizard two-seater (formerly Dong In type q.v.).

LARSON AERO DEVELOPMENT • USA

Based at Concord, California, produced the D.1. agricultural aircraft in 1959 and the F-2 Baby ultralight single-seat biplane in 1960.

LAS • USA

See Lockheed Aircraft Service Company.

ETS D. LASCAUD • France

Markets kit to construct Bifly single-seat wooden microlight.

LATÉCOERE • France

The Forges et Ateliers de Construction Latécoère began its interest in aviation in 1917, showed an aircraft at the 1919 Paris Salon, and another two, the LAT 4 airliner and LAT 6 bomber, in 1921. The Société Industrielle d'Aviation was formed in 1922. From 1925 Latécoère developed an airline to South America and built a series of commercial aircraft for this route. Part of the Toulouse factory went to SNCAM (q.v.) in 1936. Developed a series of bomber aircraft (L.28, L.29) and torpedo-carrying floatplanes, the L.290 and L.298, the latter in service in 1939-1940. Some LeO flying-boats also built. In the 1930s developed a number of two- and four-engined

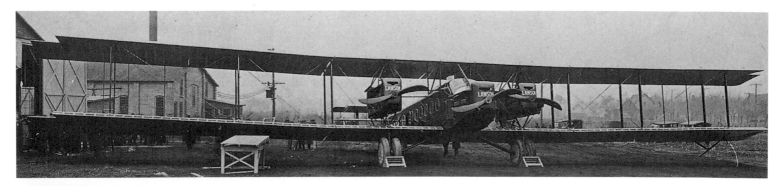

Above: Lawson L-4 three-engined civil airliner

Left: Latham 42 flying-boat patrol bomber

commercial flying-boats, culminating in the six-engined L.521 *Lieutenant de Vaisseau Paris* of 1938 and L.631 of 1939. Construction of the latter was interrupted by the war, but four were eventually completed by Breguet (q.v.) and used on commercial routes in the Mediterranean until 1948. The firm was sequestered in 1945 under the name of Ateliers Aéronautiques de Toulouse, but returned to the original owners and name in 1947.

LATHAM • France

Jean Latham built flying-boats during the First World War. After the war became Latham et Cie Société Industrielle de Caudebec, later Hydravions Latham, continuing the design and construction of single- and multi-engined flying-boats. In 1920 built the Gastambide-Levasseur variable-incidence biplane. Explorer Raoul Amundsen was lost on the Latham 47-2 searching for the crew of the airship *Italia* in 1925. In 1929 company amalgamated with Société d'Emboutissage et de Constructions Méchaniques, later Amiot, (both q.v.).

LAVERDA SPA • Italy

Formerly Aeromere SpA (q.v.), taken over by Dr Laverda in 1964 to continue manufacture of the Super Falco under licence from Aviamilano Costruzioni Aeronàutiche (q.v.).

LAVOCHKIN • USSR

Semyon Alexse'evich Lavochkin headed a design bureau formed for fighter production under the 1938 programme. The first aircraft, the I-22, flew in 1939; also called LAGG-

1 (Lavochkin, Gorbunov, Gudkov). Alterations on the production line 1940-1941 resulted in LAGG-3. Wood construction, with phenoformaldehyde impregnated fuselage. Superseded by La-5 with radial engine in 1942. Followed by 1943 La-7, 1945 La-9, 1946 La-11. This latter all-metal aircraft was the last piston-engined fighter in Soviet Air Force. Bureau later produced La-17, the first Soviet turbojet fighter with reheat, but was disbanded on Lavochkin's death in 1960.

LAWSON AIRCRAFT CORPORATION • USA

A. W. Lawson of Wisconsin designed a pursuit aircraft in 1918; not built. Followed by two-seat training biplane, and the twin-engined L-2 of 1920, built for the Lawson Airline Company. The L-4 three-engined airliner of 1922-1923 had sleeper berths and a shower.

LAZAROW, CWIETAN • Bulgaria

Worked for DAR before Second World War. From 1946 built the LAZ-7M; LAZ-8 four-seat taxi; LAZ-11 ambulance version of -8; and LAZ-12 single-seat aerobatic aircraft. All except the LAZ-7 sporting monoplane were built in prototype form only. The LAZ-10H light helicopter was abandoned before completion. All powered aircraft production in Bulgaria ceased in 1961.

LEARAVIA CORPORATION • USA

Founded at Reno to develop Lear Fan 2100 twin-turboshaft business aircraft with tail-mounted propeller, designed by William Lear. See Lear Fan Ltd.

LEAR FAN LTD. • UK/USA

Founded 1980 by Learavia (q.v.) and British Government to produce Lear Fan 2100 twin-turboprop business aircraft (first flown 1981). Ownership passed 1982 to Fan Holdings Inc. of USA, but with production in Northern Ireland. Production moved to USA 1983 but programme halted 1985.

LEAR INC. • USA

Founded as an electrical company at Santa Monica, California, in 1930. An aircraft engineering division produced the Learstar, a high-speed, long-range transport based on the Lockheed Lodestar, in 1953. First delivered in 1955; production taken over by PacAero Engineering Corporation (q.v.) in 1957.

LEARJET INC. • USA

Founded 1987 from former Gates Learjet Corporation (q.v.), becoming division of Bombardier in 1990. Currently offered business jets are 11-seat light Learjet 31A (first flown May 1987), 11-seat mid-size Learjet 45 (first flown October 1995), and 12-seat transcontinental Learjet 60 (first flown October 1990).

LEAR JET INDUSTRIES INC. • USA

Originally the Swiss-American Aviation Corporation (q.v.), founded by William Lear in 1960 to build a fast twin-jet executive aircraft. Versions built in some numbers. Acquired Brantly Helicopters, itself acquired by Gates Rubber Company of Denver, Colorado, becoming Gates Learjet (q.v.).

LEAVEN BROTHERS • Canada

Limited re-production of 1945 Fleet Model 80 Canuck, 1965-1966.

LEBEDEF • USSR

Established at Petrograd in 1912, during First World War built numbers of aircraft of British and French origin. The original two-seat reconaissance Lebed' 12 was built until early 1919.

Learjet 31s operated by Singapore Airlines

Learjet 60 transcontinental business jet

Lebedef Lebed' 12 reconnaissance aircraft

Leduc 0.22 experimental ramjet-powered interceptor

LEDUC FILS • France

Leduc began designing athodyds (ramjets) in 1929 at Argenteuil, as well as experimental aircraft in which to test them. The L.010-1, started 1937 and completed 1945, was first purely athodyd-powered manned aircraft to fly. Followed by L.010-2 and similar L.016-1 in 1951. All air-launched from Languedoc mother plane. In 1953-1954 appeared the L.021-01 and -02, and plans existed for a swept-wing aircraft with Atar 101 turbojet engine for independent take-off and an 0.22 supersonic fighter.

LEFEBVRE • France

Robert Lefebvre markets plans to construct the MP.205 Busard single-seat racing monoplane (first flown 1975), developed from Max Plan MP.204 of 1952.

LEGERS BOURGOIS • France

Exhibited its first aircraft, the A.T.-35 two-seat parasol-wing monoplane powered by an Anzani 3-cylinder engine, at the 1928 Paris Salon. Subsequently produced the B.T. three-seat low-wing monoplane with 100 hp Michel engine.

LEICHTFLUGZEUG GMBH & CO KG • Germany

Offers in assembled or kit form the Sky Walker tandem two-seat very light aircraft.

LEICHTFLUGZEUGE-ENTWICKLUNGEN DIPL ING HERMANN MYLIUS • Germany

Developed series of related light sporting aircraft, but only MY 102 Tornado single-seater flown (1973). Others were to be MY 103 Mistral two-seater and MY 104 Passat four-seater.

LENART AIRCRAFT COMPANY • USA

Founded by W. Lenart of Dowagiac, Michigan, who built his first biplane in 1919. Produced a two-seat all-metal biplane in 1930.

LeO • France

See Lioré et Olivier.

LETALSKI INSTITUT 'BRANKO IVANUS' SLOVENIJA • Yugoslavia

The former Letalski Konstrukcijski Biro (q.v.) and Institut LZS 'Branko Ivanus', which combined in about 1968. Built L-200D under licence.

LETALSKI KONSTRUKCIJSKI BIRO • Yugoslavia

Lubljana aircraft design office founded in 1947 on an amateur basis by students of the Higher Technical School. Designed KB-6 Matajur, two-seat trainer and tourer, in production in the 1950s.

LET AS • Czech Republic

Current name for former Letecky Narodni Podnik (q.v.), via Let Koncernovy Podnik. L 410 19-passenger STOL short-haul commuter transport first flown April 1969 and remaining in production in L 410 UVP-E form; higher-powered L 420 variant first flew November 1993, and lengthened model proposed as L 430. Forty-passenger L 610 regional airliner first flew December 1988 and current L 610G version followed in December 1992.

LETECKÉ OPRAVNY KBELY (LOK) • Czech Republic

State-owned repair works that in mid-1990s had anticipated privatisation and development of the Family Air light-plane.

LETECKY NARODNI PODNIK • Czechoslavakia

Produced a large number of successful aircraft before Second World War under the name of Aero (q.v.). Established at Kunovice in 1950, initially for licence production of the Soviet Yak-11 and the Z-37 Cmelák, Aero 45 and L-200D Morava. See Let AS.

LET MONT SRO • Czech Republic

Offers the Tulak two-seat cabin monoplane in assembled and kit forms.

LETORD • France

This company built bombers to designs of the Section Technique de l'Aéronautique, 1916-1918, as the Establissements Letord at Chalais-Meudon. The last of these

Left: LETL-410 Turbolet twin-turboprop transport

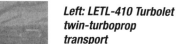

Left: LIBIS 160 three-seat light sporting monoplane

Let L 410 UVP-E commuter transport

Let L 610G 40-passenger commuter airliner

Letord 7 twin-engined night bomber

aircraft to be developed was intended as a night bomber. It was in the same class as the Handley Page bombers, with a wingspan of 85 ft (25.91 m). In 1923 Letord built an experimental aircraft for the government, which was evolved by Becherau, designer of the pre-war Deper-dussins. In 1925 part of the works was let to Villiers (q.v.), which built racing aircraft and the small Albert biplane produced under licence of Tellier-Duhamel.

LETOV • Czechoslovakia

See Vojenská.

LETOV AS • Czech Republic

First flew in May 1997 the L-11 side-by-side two-seat basic trainer and glider-towing lightplane, but in 1998 was in financial difficulties and required investor to complete development. Then also offering LK-2 Sluka single-seat

microlight (first flown 1991), LK-3 Nova two-seat microlight/homebuilt (first flown 1993), and ST-4 Aztek two-seat microlight (1996 type), all three in assembled or kit forms.

LEVASSEUR, PIERRE • France

Levasseur completed his first aircraft in 1911. Specialised subsequently in marine aircraft, largely for the French Navy. The Levasseur PL-8 was built specially for a transatlantic

Letov LK-2 Sluka microlight

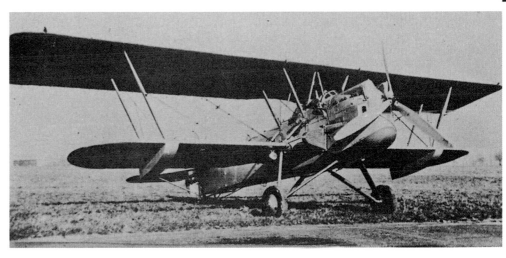

flight from Paris to New York, in 1927, but was lost at sea. Company had ceased operations by mid-1930s.

LEVY • France

In 1915 Marcel Besson designed his first flying-boat, the development work and later production being carried out in the aircraft factory of Georges Levallois, a financier (Hydravions Georges Levallois et Levy). During First World War flying-boats and bombers were produced for the French Navy by Levy-Besson, the latter setting up in his own name after the war. Twelve Levy-Lepen HB-2 reconnaissance flying-boats were operated in France by the US Navy, and three were taken to USA. Levy-Biche marine aircraft were built for French Navy to 1927, when production was taken over by Levasseur.

LEWIS AND VOUGHT CORPORATION • USA

This Long Island, New York, company built training aircraft in 1918 to designs of Chance M. Vought, for US Army. Later designs appeared under name of Vought.

LEXICON AVIATION • USA

Has produced the RS-1 Shrike single-seat turbojet-powered monoplane, first seen in 1996

LEZA LOCKWOOD • USA

Offers kits to construct light twin-engined Air Cam tandem two-seat monoplane, designed originally for National Geographic aerial survey.

LFG • Germany

See Luftfahrzeug GmbH.

LIBIS • Yugoslavia

See Letalski Institut 'Branko Ivanus' Slovenija.

LIGHT MINIATURE AIRCRAFT • USA

Provides plans and kits to build the LM-1 as single-seat scale representation of Piper J-3, LM-2 as single- and two-seat 75 per cent-scale representations of Taylorcraft cabin monoplanes, single-seat LM-3 as 75 per cent-scale representation of Aeronca, and LM-5 as Super Cub representation.

LIGHT'S AMERICAN SPORTSCOPTER INC. • Taiwan

Established 1990, offers Ultrasport 254 single-seat ultralight kit-built helicopter, Ultrasport 331 Experimental category version, and Ultrasport 496 two-seater (Ultrasport 254 first flew July 1993). Subsidiary is American Sports-Copter Inc.

Above: Levasseur PL-7 carrier-based torpedo-bomber

Right: Levasseur PL-14 seaplane torpedo-bomber

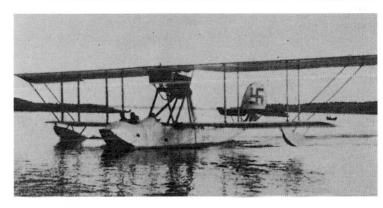

Right: Levy GL 40 flying-boat patrol bomber

Below: Light's American SportsCopter Ultrasport 496

LTV Aerospace A-7E Corsair II carrier-based attack bomber

LILIENTHAL JSC • Ukraine

Formed 1975 and marketing hang gliders, motorgliders and the X-32 Bekas tandem two-seat ultralight suited to recreational, training and agricultural uses (first flown 1993).

LINCOLN AIRCRAFT COMPANY INC. • USA

Official name of Lincoln-Page (see next entry) from 1929, but both names used indiscriminately.

LINCOLN-PAGE AIRCRAFT COMPANY • USA

Ray A. Page began construction at Lincoln, Nebraska, in 1922 as the Nebraska Aircraft Corporation (q.v.) with the five-seat Air Coach. Between 1923 and 1925 offered the Lincoln-Standard Tourabout, a three-seat rework of the Standard J.1 of 1916. Also produced the Sport Lightweight biplane. Page acquired the rights to the New Swallow and redesigned this as the three-seater Lincoln-Page LP-3 in 1928, an attempt to catch up with developments in light aircraft design. In 1929 produced a two-seat trainer known

as the Lincoln-Page Trainer. Last design was the parasol-wing Lincoln Playboy of 1931. Firm was now the Lincoln Airplane and Flying School.

LING-TEMCO-VOUGHT INC. • USA

Formed from the 1917 Chance Vought Aircraft Company Inc. by merging with Ling-Temco Electronics in 1961, with a new Chance Vought Corporation as its aerospace division. First aircraft was a continuation and development of the F-8 Crusader supersonic carrierborne air-superiority fighter of 1955. Developed into the LTV A-7A in 1966. Rationalisation in 1963 produced LTV Incorporated, which includes LTV Aerospace Corporation, of which Vought Aeronautics Division is a part. Corsair II production under the name of the Vought Corporation (q.v.). In 1964 in combination with Hiller-Ryan developed the XC-142A VTOL transport with swivelling wings. LTV Electro-systems developed the L450F quiet reconnaissance aircraft in 1970. Became Vought Corporation 1976 (q.v.), LTV Aircraft Products Group 1986 and LTV Aerospace and Defense Company 1990. Undertook considerable subcontract work, including on B-

LTV-Hiller-Ryan XC-142A tilt-wing VTOL transport

Right: LTV F-8 Crusader for US Navy featured variable incidence wings, to keep fuselage level while increasing wing angle-of-attack to reduce speed. French Navy received F-8E(FN)s, one seen here attempting to land on USS Dwight D. Eisenhower in 1983 (US Navy)

2 and many transport aircraft. Teamed with Argentina to propose Pampa 2000 for JPATS programme, but not selected. Took name Vought once again in 1992.

LINKE-HOFMANN WERKE • Germany

Railway engineering company of Hundsfeld, Breslau, which entered aviation in 1916 by repairing and building under licence Roland and Albatros aircraft. In 1917 completed its first R-plane (R = *Riesenflugzeug*; giant aircraft) contract. The R.I. rebuild later crashed on test. The R.II was the largest single-propeller aircraft ever built.

Right: LTV Aerospace F-8 Crusader carrier-based fighters

LeO 20 twin-engined three-seat night bomber

LIORÉ ET OLIVIER • France

Etablissments LeO of Levallois-Perret was founded by Henri Olivier and Fernand Lioré. Established as agricultural and industrial engineers in 1906, entered aviation 1908. Lioré worked with Witzig-Lioré-Dutheuil in 1912. Firm built Morane-Saulnier types before and during First World War, producing over 2,000. From 1916 built Sopwith 1-Strutter. In 1921 started up airline Aeronavale (Société Maritime de Transport Aériens), and in 1922 began design and construction of civil and military flying-boats and bombers. An airliner derived from the 1924 bomber served Air Union. Four engined flying-boats developed up to Second World War. Cierva autogiros built under licence. LeO 451, built 1939-1940, was best French bomber of period and used for research after war. The Argenteuil factory became part of SNCASE and the Rochefort plant part of SNCASO (both q.v.) in 1936.

LeO 451, only modern bomber in French service at beginning of WW2

LIPNUR • Indonesia

See Departemen Angkaten Udara Republik Indonesia, Lembaga Industri Penerbangan Nurtanio.

LISUNOV • USSR

Boris Lisunov was sent to the USA to study the Douglas DC-3 and prepare for production in the Soviet Union. Production under designation PS-84 began in 1939, entering service in the same year. In 1942 the PS-84 became known as the Li-2. The only Soviet wartime transport, it was used post-war by Aeroflot.

LITHUANIAN ARMY AIRCRAFT FACTORY • Lithuania

Based at Kaunas, Kovno, and building its own-design light aircraft from 1922. After the death of the designer, Lieutenant Dobkevicius, the company built training and reconnaissance aircraft for the army.

LITTLE WING AUTOGYROS INC. • USA

Offers single- and two-seat versions of its Roto-Pup kit autogyro.

LKB • Yugoslavia

See Letalski Konstrukcijski Biro.

Lloyd reconnaissance biplane of WW1

Lockheed Constellation
four-engined transport

LLOYD FLUGZEUGWERKE GMBH • Hungary

Built 400-500 bomber, reconnaissance and fighter aircraft for the Austro-Hungarian Air Service in the First World War. Called originally Ungarische Lloyd Flugzeug unde Motoren Fabrik, built DFW types under licence at Budapest.

LMAASA • USA

Lockheed Martin Aircraft Argentina SA began management of FMA on 1 July 1995, under the Argentine Government's privatization programme. Contracts with LMAASA covered management of the aircraft factory, a 25-year concession on the maintenance depot at Córdoba, the refurbishment and modernization of 36 ex-US Navy A-4M Skyhawks into A-4AR Fightinghawks, and aircraft maintenance for the Argentine Air Force for five years.

LMSC • USA

See Lockheed Missiles and Space Company.

LOCKHEED AIRCRAFT CORPORATION • USA

In September 1977 Lockheed Aircraft Corporation took new name Lockheed Corporation. See Lockheed Martin Corporation for all Lockheed company history.

LOCKHEED MARTIN AIRCRAFT ARGENTINA SA • USA

See LMAASA.

LOCKHEED MARTIN CORPORATION • USA

Allan and Malcolm Loughead built their first aircraft, the Model G seaplane, in 1913. Formed the Loughead Aircraft Manufacturing Company at Santa Barbara, California, in 1916. Built F-1 twin-engined flying-boat 1918, S-1 monocoque-fuselage biplane 1919. Company liquidated 1921. The Lockheed Aircraft Company of Hollywood was formed in 1926. Built the Northrop-designed high-wing Vega from 1925, a fast two-seater intended for airline work; 141

were built between 1925 and 1932. Company moved to Burbank 1928. Vega gave rise to low-wing series of transports, the Altair/Orion/Sirius, differing in seating arrangements. Many records and notable flights performed on these aircraft.

In 1929 Lockheed became part of the Detroit Aircraft Corporation, a multi-company body that went bankrupt in 1931. Lockheed brothers left the company, formed Lockheed Brothers Aircraft Corporation (q.v.) Company purchased by Robert E. Cross and Lloyd Stearman for a consortium, resumed trading under old name. Launched a new series of twin-engined transports, starting with the Lockheed 10A Electra. In 1937 the L-14 Super Electra appeared, a smaller executive version of the L-10A. RAF bought 250 bomber variants of 14, called Hudson, in 1938. L-18 Lodestar flew 1939, a lengthened and more powerful Model 14. Ventura of 1941 was a bomber variant of Model 18. Naval PV-1 came in 1942 and the torpedo-carrying PV-2 Harpoon in 1943. Success of the Harpoon led to long-range Neptune, main equipment of patrol squadrons 1947-1962.

In 1939 TWA formulated a requirement for a long-range transport and C. L. Johnson designed the 347mph (558kmh) Constellation, which first flew in 1943. First 22 requisitioned as military transports. Built up to 1958 in increasingly powerful, larger-capacity and longer-range versions. First flight August 1954 of C-130 Hercules tactical military turboprop transport, later also produced in commercial form; delivered from 1956 and remaining in production in 1999 in latest C-130J form with fully integrated digital avionics, advanced engines and propellers, and other improvements (well over 2,200 Hercules transports built). C-130 followed by much larger strategic C-141 StarLifter transport (first flown December 1963) and C-5A Galaxy (first flown June 1968) which, at 769,000 lb (348,810 kg) gross weight and with a span of 222 ft 8 in (67.88 m), was then the world's largest operational aircraft; C-5B followed for USAF and two C-5As modified to carry outsized space cargoes as C-5Cs. Company also produced the four-turboprop Electra airliner (first flown December 1957) and derived P-3 Orion long-range maritime patrol/reconnaissance aircraft (first flown August

Lockheed Model 10 Electra

Lockheed P-38 Lightning night fighter

1958, and remaining in production in the USA until 1995, although Japanese Kawasaki-built examples continued in production).

The Lockheed P-38 Lightning of 1939, introduced as a high-altitude interceptor, had worldwide use, mainly as ground-attack and fighter-bomber aircraft. First US jet fighter was Lockheed P-80 Shooting Star (first flown January 1944), which later saw service in Korea. F-104 of 1954 was smallest-span-ever American service aircraft (wings spanned 21 ft 11 in; 6.7 m) and first fighter capable of sustained Mach 2.0. Saw widespread service as part of US offshore arms and aid deals. Subsequent activities included CP-140 Aurora for Canada as a development of the Orion; S-3 Viking carrierborne anti-submarine aircraft (first flown January 1972 and later also used by the US Navy in ES-3A electronic reconnaissance and signals/communications intelligence, and US-3A carrier on-board delivery variants); and L-1011 TriStar widebodied airliner (first flown November 1970).

Secret 'Skunk Works' at Palmdale, California, was responsible for the military U-2 Dragon Lady spyplane (first flown August 1955), A-12 Mach 3.6 strategic reconnaissance aircraft sponsored by the CIA (first flown April 1962) and developed into the YF-12 interceptor and fully operational SR-71A Mach 3+ strategic reconnaissance aircraft for the USAF, and more recently the F-117A stealth fighter for subsonic night attack on priority targets (first flown June 1981; see below), among other types.

In September 1977 Lockheed Aircraft Corporation took new name Lockheed Corporation. The Tactical Military Aircraft division of General Dynamics bought by Lockheed Corporation in March 1993, becoming Lockheed Fort

Lockheed Electra prop-jet of 1957

Lockheed Constellations as C-121 military transports

Lockheed WV-2 Warning Star airborne early warning aircraft of 1950s delivery, based on Constellation airframe

Lockheed F-104C Starfighter was the first US Air Force fighter capable of sustained Mach 2

Lockheed P-3K Orion maritime patrol aircraft with the RNZAF (RNZAF)

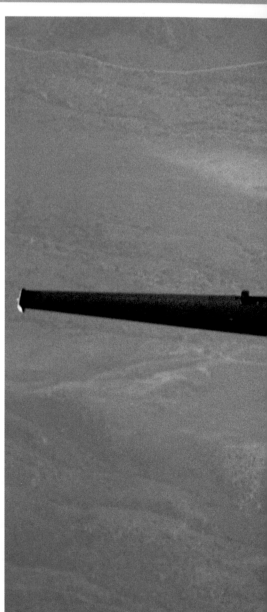

Lockheed Martin C-130J-30 Hercules for the RAF, seen just before delivery in late 1998

*Left: Lockheed Martin
F-16C Block 50D*

*Right: Lockheed Martin
S-3A Viking carrier-borne
anti-submarine aircraft*

*Below: Lockheed U-2
Dragon Lady spy-plane
first flew August 1955,
and remains in service.
U-2Rs (illustrated) have
now been re-engined as
U-2Ss*

Worth Company. In March 1995 Lockheed Corporation merged with Martin Marietta (q.v.) to form present Lockheed Martin Corporation. Intended merger with Northrop Grumman, announced in July 1997, did not take place. Present company set-up includes Lockheed Martin Tactical Aircraft Systems in charge of F-16 production and updates and part of the F-22 programme; Lockheed Martin Aeronautical Systems tasked with F-22, military transport and maritime patrol aircraft work, plus production and support of C-130 and P-3; and Lockheed Martin Skunk Works which undertakes advanced, secret and innovative design/development, present work including support and improvement of F-117A, U-2, X-33 reusable launch vehicle and more. There are many other divisions.

Current Lockheed Martin programmes include continued production of the F-16 fighter and C-130 transport,

Above: Lockheed Martin F-117A Nighthawk stealth fighters

Below: Lockheed Martin F-22 Raptor is destined for service in the 21st century

Left: The remarkable Lockheed SR-71A Mach 3+ strategic reconnaissance aircraft

Above: Lockheed Martin Joint Strike Fighter, being developed in association with Northrop Grumman and BAe, seen in Royal Navy variant

Above: A prototype Lockheed Martin F-22 Raptor advanced tactical fighter takes on fuel from a USAF KC-135 tanker, escorted by a two-seat example of one of the world's most important current warplanes, the General Dynamics F-16.

development and production of the F-22 Raptor air dominance fighter (first flown September 1990, with first flight of an engineering and manufacturing development aircraft September 1997, and deliveries of full production to start to USAF in 2002 to allow initial operational capability in 2005); and development in association with Northrop Grumman and BAe of Joint Strike Fighter for US forces.

LOCKHEED AIRCRAFT SERVICE COMPANY • USA

Was division of Lockheed Aircraft Corporation. Designed and fitted major modifications to Boeing KC-135 including Airborne Light Optical Tracking System (ALOTS), C-133, C-130, C-121 Airborne TV and radio transmitting station/studio for Vietnam, and cargo Electra. Later worked on A-4S Skyhawk and C-130 conversions, among other programmes.

LOCKHEED AND INDUSTRIAS KAISER • Argentina

Formed in 1960 for production of the AL-60 (see Lockheed-Azcarate SA).

LOCKHEED-AZCARATE SA • Mexico

Formed by Juan F. Azcarate in 1957 with Lockheed, to design an aircraft specifically to suit Central American conditions. Built the LASA-60 4/6-seat utility aircraft in 1959.

Construction undertaken by Lockheed-Azcarate, Macchi (q.v.) and Aviones Lockheed-Kaiser. Lockheed acquired a substantial holding in Aermacchi 1959.

LOCKHEED BROTHERS AIRCRAFT CORPORATION • USA

The Lockheed Brothers left the Company after the Detroit merger and set up the Airover Company, later called Alcor, to build the Uni-twin, with two Menasco engines side-by-side in the nose, driving two propellers. The name of the company was changed to Lockheed Vega when it became a subsidiary of the revived parent organisation. The Lockheed Vega Twin then named Olympic Duo-4, crashed 1938. Firm also built low-wing Starliner and NA-35 trainer. With Boeing and Douglas during Second World War, as the BVD pool, built B-17s. Allan Lockheed, during Alcor period, was associated with Alhambra Airport and Air Transport Company.

LOCKHEED MISSILES AND SPACE COMPANY INC. • USA

Entered the aviation field with Q-Star, developed from the QT-2 (Quiet Thrust) two-seater. Q-Star designed for night sensory missions in Vietnam. The 1967 X-26/QT-2PC quiet reconnaissance aircraft was based on a strengthened Schweizer SGS-2-32 glider, with silenced 180 hp Wankel engine. Saw limited service after the 1968 Tet offensive. Claimed to have operated undetected at 100 ft (30 m). A

much modified version of this silent reconnaissance aircraft was developed in 1968 as the YO-3A.

LOCKSPEISER AIRCRAFT LTD. • UK

David Lockspeiser attempted to develop LDA (land development aircraft) general utility aircraft over two decades up to mid-1980s, with rear-mounted main wings and large canards, and rear-mounted engine with pusher propeller. A 70 per cent-scale prototype flew 1971 as LDA-01, and intended full-size LDA-500 Boxer and larger LDA-1000 Boxer were designed.

LOCKWOOD AVIATION SUPPLY INC. • USA

New versions of former Maxair Drifter are offered in kit form, in single- and two-seat models.

LOEHLE AIRCRAFT CORPORATION • USA

Produces kits to build the very light 5151 Mustang as an approximately 75 per cent-scale representation of the P-51 Mustang fighter in both fixed- and retractable-undercarriage versions, a similar representation of the P-40, and the Sport Parasol single-seat microlight.

LOENING AERONAUTICAL ENGINEERING COMPANY • USA

Grover C. Loening built a monoplane flying-boat in 1911.

Loening M-8 high-wing monoplane fighter

Loening amphibian, first to serve with US Coast Guard

Formed company in 1918, and built his first Air Yacht (based on pre-war design). A two-seat monoplane fighter with very advanced features was ordered by the Government, but contract for 2,000 cancelled at war's end. Produced very popular line of single-float, biplane flying-boats based on Air Yacht for civil and naval use. Merged with Keystone Aircraft Corporation (q.v.) in 1928. Built monoplane and biplane pursuits for the Army. After takeover by Keystone, Loening set up the Grover-Loening Aircraft Company at Garden City, New York, as consultant, and built small amphibian flying-boat XS2L for US Navy in 1931. Delivered XSL-2 experimental submarine-borne version in 1933.

LO-FLUGGERÄTEBAU GMBH • Germany

Markets kits to build LO-120 tandem two-seat very light aircraft, with smaller LO-120 Bausatz I also offered.

LOHNER • Austria-Hungary

Built one-, two-, and three-seat reconnaissance flying-boats during First World War, which were very successful. Early Macchi (q.v.) designs were copies of Lohner flying-boats

LOHNER-DAIMLER • Germany

Formed 1911, producing Arrow biplanes. One sold to Austro-Hungarian Army, 1911. Amalgamated with Etrich (q.v.) in 1912.

LOIRE • France

Shipbuilder of St Nazaire and la Baule which entered aviation on acquiring Gourdou and Leseurre (q.v.) in 1925 to become Loire-Gourdou-Leseurre. The latter left in 1929 and Loire started their own aviation department. The first original design appeared in 1931. In 1933, Nieuport-Delage (see Nieuport) merged with Loire to become the Groupe Loire-Nieuport. They built single and multi-engined flying-boats, both civil and military, and fighters for the navy. Also constructed Bloch 200 and Dewoitine 500 for the Armée de l'Air. In 1936 became part of SNCAO (q.v.).

LOMBARDA (AERONAUTICA) SA • Italy

Succeeded Aeronàutica Vittorio Bonomi (q.v.) in 1931, building light aeroplanes and gliders. After the Abyssinian War turned to military aircraft production. During Second World War built Heinkel He 111 and Loire 130.

LOMBARDI & CIE • Italy

This Vercelli company took over in 1947 from the 1939 Avia (Azionaria Vercellese Industrie Aeronautiche) (q.v.), continuing production of the light FL-3 and building an experimental attack glider. Also subcontract work on Fiat G-50. Post-war resumed production of FL-3 and small number of the LM-5 Aviastar, and 1949 LM-7. This latter was a prototype only; company then ceased aeronautical work and production taken over in 1953 by Meteor SpA (q.v.).

LONDON AND PROVINCIAL AVIATION COMPANY LTD. • UK

Based in Edgware and opened a flying school at Hendon in 1914. Built some Caudron trainers for the school and two trainers designed in 1916 by A. A. Fletcher, formerly with Martinsyde (q.v.). Moved to aerodrome at Edgware. Small numbers of the Fletcher design were used, some in civil use after the war.

LONGREN AIRCRAFT INC. • USA

A Topeka, Kansas, company which in 1921 pioneered vulcanised moulded fibre fuselages on small folding-wing light aircraft. Built an experimental aircraft for the US Navy in 1922. Liquidated in 1924, re-formed about 1933 to build experimental metal monocoque fuselage.

LOPRESTI FLIGHT CONCEPTS • USA

Founded 1991 to take over development of SwiftFury two-seat aerobatic lightplane (first flown 1989 as Lopresti Piper development of Globe/Temco Swift).

LOPRESTI PIPER AIRCRAFT ENGINEERING COMPANY • USA

Founded 1987 as subsidiary of Piper (q.v.), but ceased operations December 1990.

LORING, DR JORGE • Spain

Founded in Madrid by Dr Loring of the Compañía Española de Tráfico Aereo. Received order for 20 Fokker C.IV for Spanish Army Air Corps in 1924. First indigenous design was the R.1 for the army. Further reconnaissance types followed, and light aircraft. Built Cierva Autogiro under licence.

LORRAINE-HANRIOT • France

Operated at Argenteuil as Aeroplanes Hanriot et Cie (q.v.) to 1930, when it became Lorraine-Hanriot, a division of Société Générale Aéronautique. When this organisation broke up in 1933 the company became known as Compagnie des Avions Hanriot.

LOUGHEAD BROS • USA

See Lockheed Aircraft Corporation.

LOUIS-CLÉMENT • France

Based in Boulogne-sur-Mer. Produced a gullwing monoplane racer at the 1919-1920 Paris Salon and an ultralight single-seat triplane.

Loire 46-C1 four-gun monoplane fighter

Lombardi Avia CM-3 lightweight monoplane

LOVAUX LTD. • UK

Subsidiary of FLS Aerospace for aircraft maintenance. Took over Optica Scout observation aircraft from Brooklands (q.v.) and marketed Optica and Scoutmaster derivative for electronic surveillance. Also purchased SAH-1 from Orca Aircraft Ltd. See FLS Aerospace for fate of Optica.

LTV • USA

See Ling-Temco-Vought Inc.

LUALDI & CIE SPA • Italy

Established at Rome in 1953, and built an experimental helicopter, the ES53, incorporating the Hiller Rotormatic system. Became Hiller agent. Designed the L.55, L.57, L.59, each larger and developed from original. L.59 built at the Aermacchi works in 1961, was delivered to the Army Department of the Ministry of Defence.

LÜBECK-TRAVEMÜNDE • Germany

A subsidiary of DFW (q.v.) founded at Travemünde in 1914. Designed and built a small number of large, single-engined seaplanes for the German Navy 1917-1918.

LUBELSKA WYTWORNIA SAMOLOTOW • Poland

Formed at Lublin in 1936 to take over operations of the bankrupt company of E. Plage and T. Laskiewicz (q.v.). Took over some designs and began work on their own twin-engined bomber and a single-engined air ambulance.

LUCAS • France

Offers plans and some components to construct L.5 side-by-side two-seat (or 3/4-seat) low-wing monoplane (first flown 1976) and L.6 tandem two-seat low-wing monoplane (first flown 1991).

LUCCHINI & C • Italy

Markets Speedy single-seat microlight in assembled and kit forms.

LUFTFARHZEUG GMBH • Germany

Founded by Krupp from the Flugmaschine Wright GmbH (originally Motorluftschiff Studiengesellschaft, 1906). Adopted Roland as trade name. Built Albatros B and C types under licence at Charlottenberg until their own Roland C.II of 1915. Built a series of 12 fighter designs, of which only the D.II was built in quantity. Produced the V-19 Stralsund, the first aircraft designed for carriage by submarines. After the war converted and built civil aircraft until 1925, including single-engined landplanes and seaplanes for civil airlines. Operated a number of shorthaul routes around the Baltic. Went into liquidation 1928.

LUFT TORPEDO GMBH • Germany

Based at Johannisberg and engaged in experimental seaplane fighter design in 1918. A small number were built for test purposes.

LUFTVERKEHRS GMBH • Germany

Based at Johannisthal, Berlin; one of the largest German aircraft companies during First World War. Built Farmans under licence, its own first design being the B.1 of 1913. An efficient aircraft remaining in service for observation and training for some years, it was the forerunner of all German two-seat observation aircraft of 1914-1918. Developed lengthy series, including very popular C.V and C.VI as well as prototype fighters and bombers. Converted several post-war for service with civil airlines.

LUKHOVITSY MACHINE BUILDING PLANT • Russia

Founded 1953 as division of GAZ-30 factory (now MAPO), with assembly of aircraft since 1968. In addition to constructing the MiG-29 and other aircraft, built five SL-39WM 'Terminator' two-seat lightplanes from Interavia I-1 components before assembling Interavia I-1Ls.

LUSCOMBE AIRCRAFT LTD. • UK

Produced designs for light recreational aircraft with rear-mounted wings and engines, starting with Vitality of 1971, from which Valiant ultralight and Rattler single-seat military versions developed. Other types included Viper and Ranger, Super Ranger and Twin Ranger, latter three types later further developed by United Aerospace Technologies (q.v.).

Lualdi L.59 light helicopter

L.W.S.4 Zubr twin-engined monoplane bomber

Above: LWF Butterfly ultra-light monoplane

LWF Model H Owl triplane bomber prototype

LUSCOMBE AIRPLANE CORPORATION • USA

Don A. Luscombe's first aircraft, the Monocoupe, was built by the Central States Aero Company (q.v.) of Davenport, Ohio. Became in 1928 the Mono Aircraft Corporation (q.v.) of Moline, Illinois, with Luscombe as President and chief engineer. He left in 1933 and next year set up the Luscombe Aircraft Engineering Company of Kansas City, producing the Phantom I, the first US metal light aircraft and a very successful design developed by Ivan Driggs from the Monocoupe D-145; 125 were built. Fabrication of parts was farmed out, reducing overhead costs on the production line. Production ceased during Second World War because of metal shortage, but was resumed in 1949. Following the L-4 Model 90 four seater of 1934 came the 1937-1938 Model 8a, of which 1,100 were built, and the 1940 Silvaire, of which production had reached 6,000 by 1961. The Skybaby and two other low-powered versions were built. The post war company, based at Dallas, Texas, went bankrupt in 1949, but was revived with finance from Texas Engineering and Manufacturing Company Inc (q.v.) under the old name. The emergency of the 1950s caused suspension of production and the company was bought by Temco Aircraft Corporation (q.v.), which sold manufacturing rights of the Silvaire Model 8 in 1955 to the Silvaire Aircraft Company (q.v.).

LVG • Germany

See Luftverkehrs GmbH.

LWF ENGINEERING CORPORATION INC. • USA

Formed 1915 at College Point, Long Island, by Joseph Lowe, Charles F. Willard and Robert G. Fowler. Patented Willard's laminated wooden monocoque fuselage, but all three left in 1916, after which name assumed to mean Laminated Wooden Fuselage. Converted twelve DH-4s to single-seaters for US Post Office, and built experimental twin-engined version. Built series of its own designs, including trainers V-1, -2 and -3 of 1918-1919 for the Army. Constructed also Curtiss HS-2L and Douglas DT-2 for Navy, Martin NBS-1 for Army. In 1919 built ultralight Butterfly and a three-engined triplane, Model H Owl, based on Caproni design. This was offered to the Army but was not accepted. Built Model T-3 for Army, 1923-1924, designed but did not build experimental XNBS-2. Company ceased production in 1924.

LWS • Poland

See Lubelska Wytornia Samolotow.

LVG C.II reconnaissance/bomber aircraft

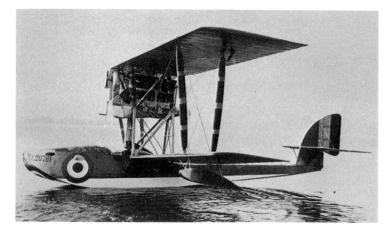

Macchi M-7 flying-boat fighter

Macchi M-8 flying-boat patrol bomber

MACCHI • Italy

Founded in 1912 at Varese as Società Anonima Nieuport-Macchi, specialising in marine aircraft. During First World War built L-1 licence-manufactured Lohner L-40 flying-boats, M-3 fighter and M-5 biplane flying-boat, developed into M-7 which won 1921 Schneider Trophy, an achievement repeated by M-39 in 1926. MC.72 floatplane set world airspeed record of 440.67mph (709.19kmh) on 23 October 1933. Pre-Second World War commercial flying-boats included 12-seat MC.94 and 26-seat MC.100. MC.200 Saetta fighters produced from 1937, developed into MC.202 Falgore, and MC.205 Veltro. Post-war developments included MB.308 two/three-seat cabin mono-plane, also built in Argentina by German Bianco SA (q.v.), MB.320 six-seat light twin and 150 M.416 licence-built Fokker S.11 trainers. Joint programme with Fiat to build Vampire FB.52As, followed by MB.326 jet trainer, first flown 10 December 1957 and later produced also in two-seat and single-seat armed strike trainer forms. Lockheed of USA acquired shareholding in Aermacchi in 1959. Became known as Aermacchi in 1961 (q.v.).

MACDONALD BROS AIRCRAFT LTD. • Canada

Formed maintenance organisation 1930, opened factory at Stevenson's Airport, Winnipeg, after outbreak of war, manufacturing components for Anson trainers, also a final assembly centre for Anson Vs built under scheme supervised by Federal Aircraft.

MACHEN INC. • USA

Converted Ted Smith (Piper) Aerostars to improved Superstars.

MAEFIN • Italy

Markets quick-build kit for TopFun two-seat monoplane.

MAESTRANZA CENTRAL DE AVIACION • Chile

Chilean Air Force Central Workshops; in 1947 built Tri-colo-Experimental two-seat cabin monoplane designed by Alfredo Ferrer; first indigenous Chilean aircraft. In early 1950s Captain H. Fuentes designed H.F.XX-02 trainer, built at El Bosque Air Base.

Above: Macchi C.205N-1 Orione (Orion) interceptor prototype

MAGNI-AVIAZIONE • Italy

Founded by Piero Magni in 1919, primarily research and development organisation but manufactured aircraft for other designers, including Jona J-6 tilting-wing sesqui-plane and the conventional-winged J-6S military trainer.

Magni Vittoile high-speed sporting monoplane

Above: MAPO 'MiG' MiG-29s operated by the German Luftwaffe

Magni's own aircraft included PM-3-4 Vale 1937 single-seat aerobatic aircraft and the derived PM-4-1 Supervale.

MAHONEY-RYAN AIRCRAFT CORPORATION • USA

Incorporated 1922 at St Louis, Missouri, known originally as Ryan Airlines. Developed Ryan M-1 mailplane from which, in 1927, was derived *Spirit of St Louis*, built for Charles Lindbergh's New York-Paris flight; commercial development produced as Ryan Brougham. Company merged with Detroit Aircraft Corporation 24 May 1929.

MAINAIR SPORTS LTD. • UK

Markets Blade tandem two-seat flex-wing microlight in assembled form, Mercury single- or two-seat flex-wing monoplane in assembled or kit forms, and (from 1997) Rapier tandem two-seat flex-wing microlight in assembled or kit forms.

MAINTENANCE COMMAND DEVELOPMENT CENTRE • India

See MMPL.

Manzolini Libellula III light helicopter

MAKINA VE KIMYA ENDUSTRISI KURUMU • Turkey

See MKEK.

MALDEN AG-CRAFT INC. • USA

See Ag-Cat Corporation.

MALMÖ FLYGINDUSTRI • Sweden

See MFI.

MALMÖ FORSKNINGS & INNOVATIONS AB. • Sweden

See MFI.

MANN AND GRIMMER • UK

Seventeen-year old R. Mann designed M.1 two-seat fighter-reconnaissance biplane, built with assistance of R. P. Grimmer and test-flown at Hendon 19 February 1915. Conventional radial engine, nose-mounted, but facing aft so that propeller shaft extending through fuselage drove interplane strut-mounted twin pusher propellers via chain drives. Wrecked 16 November 1915, development discontinued.

MANN, EGERTON & COMPANY LTD. • UK

At its Norwich factory built 12 Short 184 or Mann, Egerton Type A seaplanes, and from this developed own Type B seaplane powered by Sunbeam engine. Built own design H.1 and H.2 shipboard fighters 1917. Subcontract production of Airco D.H.9/9A, D.H.10/10A, Sopwith 1 strutters, Short Bombers and SPAD 7s

MANSYU HIKOKI SEIZO KABUSHIKI KAISHA • Manchuria

Established by Imperial Ordnance issued June 1938, incorporating aircraft manufacturing facilities of Manchuria Aviation Company at Harbin which developed Hayabusa six-passenger cabin monoplane airliner, powered by Nakajima Kotobuki radial. Acquired Tachikawa Hikoki Kabushiki Kaisha (q.v.) in 1940. Produced wartime combat aircraft and trainers.

MANZOLINI DI CAMPOLEONE • Italy

Designed Libellula coaxial single-seat light helicopter, first flown 7 January 1952, later developed as Libellula II with Walter Minor engine and certificated on 15 October 1962; Libellula III two-seater followed with Walter M332 engine.

MAPO • Russia

Voenno-Promyshlennyi Komplex Moscow Aviation Production Organisation can trace its lineage to 1893 and the original factory in Moscow. Constructed French Nieuports and Farmans during First World War, and in 1918 was named State Aircraft Works No 1. Retitled MAPO in 1991 and in 1996 became MIG 'MAPO' (Military Industrial Group 'MAPO') as state-owned concern comprising MAPO 'MiG' (see Mikoyan and Gurevich entry), Kamov (q.v.) and several other important Russian aviation-related companies and organisations. In 1997 Myasishchev Design Bureau was added, giving rise to latest MIG 'MAPO-M' title. In addition to combat aircraft production and development of transports, also manufactures smaller civil aircraft such as Aviatika-890, T-101 Grach, I-1L and and Il-103 for others, plus maintenance and servicing.

MAPO 'MiG' • Russia

Current name (since 1995) for constructor of Mikoyan aircraft, comprising MAPO production factory and ANPK 'MiG' named after A.I. Mikoyan Aviation Scientific-Production Complex (see Mikoyan & Gurevich entry). Part of larger MIG 'MAPO-M' organisation (see MIG 'MAPO'). Currently producing MiG-21 upgrade as MiG-21-93, MiG-29 *Ful-*

crum lightweight close-air-combat fighter (first flown October 1977 and over 1,500 built, serving since 1983), improved MiG-29M (first flown April 1986) and MiG-33 export version, MiG-29K shipborne fighter prototype (first flown July 1988, first landing on aircraft carrier *Admiral Kuznetsov* November 1989, and development restarted in 1996 after earlier programme halt), MiG-35 multirole fighter (first flight 1999?), MiG 1-44 uniquely configured new-generation combat aircraft (first seen February 1999), and MiG-AT/UTS/AC series of advanced and combat trainers. MiG-301/321 are reported hypersonic reconnaissance aircraft, thought to be under development. Also developing MiG-110 light multipurpose transport and MiG-115 and MiG-125 transports.

MAPO 'MYASISHCHEV' • Russia

Part of the MIG 'MAPO-M' (q.v.) organisation since June 1997. See also Myasishchev.

MARANDA AIRCRAFT COMPANY LTD. • Canada

Formed in Montreal by Bernard C. Maranda to develop and manufacture ultralight aircraft, acquiring world-wide licence for Adam RA-14 and RA-17 high-wing monoplanes from French designer Roger Adam in 1957. These marketed as RA 14BM1 and BM3. Also developed Hawk BM4, based on Bearn Minicab, and Lark BM6 single-seat aerobatic biplane.

MARENDAZ AIRCRAFT LTD. • UK

D. M. K. Marendaz designed the four-seat Mk III cabin monoplane, two built by International Aircraft & Engineering Ltd. at Maidenhead 1937/1938. Marendaz company,

Maranda Super Loisir two-seat cabin monoplane

at Barton-in-the-Clay, Bedfordshire, built prototype Marendaz Trainer two-seat monoplane which first flew December 1939.

MARINAVIA FARINA SRL • Italy

Founded in 1946 by industrial designer Domenico Farina with headquarters in Milan. Designed and built several gliders and sailplanes, and prototype QR.14 Levriero four-seat touring aircraft, powered by two de Havilland Gipsy Major 10 engines, first flown 1947, in which year it won Coppa dell'Aria at Milan.

MARINENS FLYVEBATFABRIKK • Norway

Naval Flying-Boat Factory established at Horten in 1915 to build aircraft for Royal Norwegian Navy, including early Farman designs, Hansa Brandenburg W.33 twin-float fighter reconnaissance aircraft and, during 1920s, a small number of Douglas DT-2B and DT-2C torpedo carriers. Breda Ba 28 trainer seaplane also built under licence. Indigenous seaplanes included M.F.8 biplane trainer, M.F.9 single-seat fighter, M.F.10 advanced trainer and M.F.11 three-seat reconnaissance aircraft.

MARK ABTEILUNG FLUGZEUGBAU • Germany

Engineering company, based at Breslau, which built 3- and 5-cylinder Baer radial engines and Reiseler sports monoplanes.

MARQUART, EDWARD • USA

Designed the MA-4 Lancer single-seat biplane and MA-5 Charger two-seat aerobatic biplane, made available in plans form.

MARSHALL & SONS • UK

Based at Gainsborough, Lincolnshire, during First World War; manufactured under subcontract Bristol F.2B with Sunbeam Arab engines.

MARSHALL AEROSPACE • UK

Known as Marshall's Flying Schools Ltd. until 1962, becoming Marshall of Cambridge (Engineering) Ltd., developed major engineering, overhaul and conversion organisation at Cambridge. During 1958-1960 produced much-modified Auster T.7 designated Marshall MA.4, a boundary layer research aircraft built under Ministry of Aviation contract for Cambridge University. Undertook the lengthening of 29 RAF Hercules transports as C.Mk 3s up to 1985, plus conversion of other RAF Hercules C.Mk 1s into flight refuelling tankers, and conversion of ex-airline TriStars into tankers for the RAF. Known as Marshall of Cambridge Aerospace Ltd. since 1992. Offers design, modification, maintenance, support and specialist manufacturing for aircraft, while other programmes include association with Lockheed Martin of the USA on the RAF/British Army's proposed airborne stand-off radar (ASTOR) proposals using a modified Gulfstream V as the core platform.

MARSH AVIATION COMPANY • USA

Based at Mesa, Arizona, developed conversion of Rockwell S2R Thrush Commander with AiResearch TPE 331 turboprop engine; first S2R-T Turbo Thrush delivered 1976. Also developed Schweizer Super Ag-Cat conversion, Beech T-34 turboprop conversion to Turbo Mentor, and produced TS-2F Turbo Tracker as re-engined Grumman S-2 Tracker for maritime work and firefighting.

Marshall (Lockheed) Hercules W.Mk.2 conversion for the RAF's Meteorological Research Flight

Martin MB-2 short-range night bomber

Martin PBM-5A Mariner anti-submarine amphibian

MARTIN • USA

After withdrawal from Wright Martin Aircraft Corporation (q.v.), Glenn L. Martin formed his own company at Cleveland, Ohio, in 1917, occupying a new factory at Baltimore, Maryland, in 1929. During Second World War operated US government plant at Omaha, Nebraska. Aircraft production ceased 20 December 1960 when the last P5M-2 Marlin was handed over to US Navy. MB-1 twin-engined biplane bomber first flown 17 August 1918, followed by improved MB-2. Other inter-war military aircraft included MO-1 three-seat observation aircraft, PM-1 and PM-2 flying-boats for the US Navy and the B-10 and B-12 bombers. Latter developed into Model 167, supplied to RAF from 1940 as Maryland, and Model 187 which RAF used as Baltimore. B-26 Marauder bomber, first flown 25 November 1940, ordered from drawing board, of which total production exceeded 4,700. US Navy flying-boats included five Mars transports, Mariner and Marlin patrol flying-boats, and XP6M-1 Seamaster four-jet flying-boat flown 14 July 1955. US Navy acquired AM-1 Mauler car-

Above: Martin Baltimore light bomber for the RAF

rier-attack and P4M Mercator patrol aircraft, USAF ordered English Electric Canberras licence-built as Martin B-57 from 1953. Civil production comprised Martin 130 26-seat flying-boats for Pan American 1934-1935, and Model 2-0-2 and 103 Model 4-0-4 airliners from 1947.

In the form of the Martin Marietta Corporation, Martin

returned to piloted aircraft production in 1965 with SV-5 piloted lifting body research vehicle, built as SV-5J with J-85 or J-60 jet engine and as SV-5P or X-24A with XLR-11 rocket engine. Vehicle was launched from Boeing

Martin Marietta X-24A lifting-body research aircraft

Martin Marietta X-24B lifting-body research aircraft

Martin 130 Clipper 26-seat flying-boat transport

Early attempt by Martin to produce a large jet bomber came with the six-jet XB-48, first flown in 1947 but not selected for production

English Electric licensed Martin to build a variant of Canberra for the US Air Force, as B-57 with tandem cockpits for the two-man crew. Here a B-57 releases 750-lb bombs over Vietnam in 1967

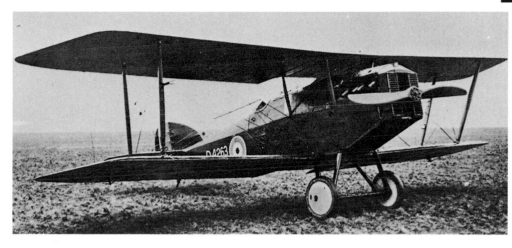

Martin & Handasyde F.4 Buzzard single-seat fighter

B-52 mother plane. In March 1995 Martin Marietta merged with Lockheed Corporation to form present Lockheed Martin Corporation (q.v.).

MARTIN & HANDASYDE; MARTINSYDE LTD. • UK

Based at Woking, Surrey, with premises at Brooklands, partnership of H. P. Martin and G. H. Handasyde built series of monoplanes from 1908 to 1914. Martinsyde Ltd. registered in 1915. undertook subcontract production of RAF B.E.2c and S.E.5A. First original wartime design was S.1 single-seat scout, built 1914-October 1915. G.100, a large single-seat fighter with Beardmore engine, appeared in late 1915. Later examples with more powerful Beardmore engine designated G.102; both known colloquially as Elephant, derived from their size. Six prototypes of F.3 fighter ordered 1917, developed into F.4 Buzzard which was ordered in quantity although only 52 had been delivered by Armistice in 1918, Some civil use in developed forms, some sold to overseas air forces. Company went into liquidation 1921.

Above: Martin-Baker F.18/39 (MB.3) six-cannon fighter prototype

MARTIN-BAKER AIRCRAFT COMPANY LTD. • UK

Formed in 1934 by James Martin, who had evolved a method of steel-tube construction. Currently leading manufacturer of ejection seats, having made first live firing on 11 May 1945. Built experimental MB.1 two-seat light aircraft to demonstrate construction system, flown March 1935. Private venture MB.2 eight-gun fighter with Napier Dagger engine flown 3 August 1938. MB.3 experimental fighter with Napier Sabre first flown 31 August 1942, followed by MB.5 with Rolls-Royce Griffon 83 driving contrarotating propellers, which made maiden flight 23 May 1944.

Right: Martin-Baker F.5/34 (MB.2) single-seat fighter prototype

MARYLAND PRESSED STEEL COMPANY • USA

Aircraft department at Hagerstown, Maryland, built designs of Joseph Bellanca, who in 1919 developed single-seat biplane powered by 35 hp Anzani engine; also CE two-seat biplane. Activity ceased and Bellanca joined Omaha Aircraft Corporation in Autumn 1921.

MASARYKOVA LETECKA LIGA • Czechoslovakia

See Zlin.

MASQUITO AIRCRAFT NV • Belgium

Developed and first flew in May 1996 the M58 two-seat ultralight helicopter. Improved M80 version with more powerful 80 hp Jabiru 2200 piston engine followed, intended for sale in assembled and certificated form, and as a kit of parts.

MATTLEY AIRPLANE & MOTOR COMPANY INC. • USA

Established at St Bruno, California, built a single-seat cabin monoplane known as the Fliver Plane. In 1933 had in production a lightweight one/two-seat parasol-wing monoplane named the Mattley Fliver, powered by a 40 hp Continental engine.

MAUBOUSSIN • France

Pierre Mauboussin established design office and factory at Puteaux, Seine, developing Corsair light aircraft which was built as Corsair 120 and Corsair Minor. Production licence for all Mauboussin aircraft acquired by Société des Etablissements Fouga (q.v.) in 1936. Mauboussin 123,

development of Corsair, built 1937-1938, and as M 129 1947-1948.

MAULE AIR INC. • USA

Maule Aircraft Corporation formed by B. D. Maule at Jackson, Michigan, to manufacture M-4 four-seat light aircraft; production transferred to Moultrie, Georgia, September 1968. Prototype flown 8 September 1961, produced as M-4 with 145 hp Continental engine, as M-4 Rocket with 210 hp Continental. M-4 Strata-Rocket with Franklin engine led to M-5-220C Lunar Rocket, flown 1 November 1971, while M-4 Rocket became M-5-210C; M-5-235 with 235 hp Lycoming O-540 engine also built. Current name Maule Air Inc., offering large range of four-

Maule M-4 four-seat light aircraft

and five-seat lightplanes for recreational and business uses in the M-7, MT-7 and MXT-7 series. Over 2,000 Maule aircraft built since 1961.

MAY, HARDEN & MAY LTD. • UK

Southampton-based subsidiary of Aircraft Manufacturing Company (q.v.) which built hulls for a number of flying-boats designed by other companies. These included 12 Porte Babies, two Phoenix P.5 Cork I/II, and 80 Felixstowe F.2A/F.5.

MAYO COMPOSITE AIRCRAFT COMPANY LTD. • UK

Formed 1935 to develop Major R. H. Mayo's concept of composite aircraft. A heavily-laden long-range upper component, too heavy to become airborne under its own power, was carried aloft on the back of a short-range aircraft whose function was simply to effect take-off. Ordered by Air Ministry for experimental operation by Imperial Airways, the two components of the Short-Mayo Composite were built by Short Bros at Rochester, and comprised S.20 *Mercury* floatplane as upper component and S.21 *Maia* as the lower. Components completed 1937, first separation in flight 6 February 1938. On 21 July 1938 *Mercury* carried a 1,000 lb (454 kg) payload non-stop 2,900 miles (4,667 km) from Foynes, Eire, to Montreal and on to New York, a total distance of 3,240 miles (5,214 km) in 22 hr 31 min flying time.

Right: Short/Mayo Mercury/Maia composite aircraft

MBB • Germany

See Messerschmitt-Bölkow-Blohm GmbH.

MBB/KAWASAKI • International

Formed to jointly develop BK 117 8-12 seat multipurpose helicopter under agreement signed 25 February 1977, MBB to design main and tail rotors, tail unit and hydraulic systems and Kawasaki responsible for fuselage, landing gear and transmission. Now a Eurocopter/Kawasaki programme.

McCANDLESS (AVIATION) LTD. • UK

Founded by Rex McCandless at Newtownards, County Down, to develop single-seat gyroplane built originally as M-2 in 1962. Developed later as M-4 with original Triumph motorcycle engine replaced by 1500cc Volkswagen engine. Production M-4 built by W. H. Ekin (Engineering) Ltd. (q.v.).

McCARTHY AIRCRAFT COMPANY • USA

Established May 1925 at Grand Rapids, Michigan, as McCarthy Aeronautical Engineering Company, building Air Scout two-seat cabin monoplane with Anzani radial engine.

McCULLOCH AIRCRAFT CORPORATION • USA

In 1949 Helicopter Division of McCulloch Motors Corporation appointed as chief designer D. K. Jovanovich, formerly of Helicopter Engineering and Research Corporation (q.v.), who developed his JOV-3 as McCulloch MC-4 tandem rotor two-seat helicopter, first flown Los Angeles 20 March 1951. Four-seat version developed as MC-4E. Later initiated quantity production of Jovanovich's J-2 two-seat gyroplane, first flown June 1962.

McDONALD BROTHERS AIRCRAFT • Canada

Founded in 1930. See Bristol Aerospace Ltd.

McDONNELL AIRCRAFT CORPORATION • USA

Incorporated 6 July 1939 at St Louis, Missouri, merged with Douglas Aircraft Corporation Inc. (q.v.) 28 April 1967. Built Fairchild AT-21 gunnery trainers at Memphis, Tennessee, plant and designed XP-67 experimental twin-engined fighter in 1942. Developed first US Navy twin-jet fighter, FH-1 Phantom I, which was first flown 26 January 1945. Enlarged version was F2H Banshee, flown 11 January 1947. F3H Demon single-engined jet fighter, maiden flight 7 August 1951. XF-88 jet fighter for USAF cancelled 1950 but developed later as F-101 Voodoo, flown 29 September 1954. F-4 Phantom II twin-engined missile-armed attack fighter flown 27 May 1958, subsequently standard USAF, USN and USMC fighter, built also for reconnaissance and anti-radar roles and widely exported; 5,057 built in USA up to June 1979, and production by Mitsubishi in Japan continued until 1981. See below for 1967 merger with Douglas.

McDONNELL DOUGLAS CORPORATION • USA

Created 28 April 1967 by merger of Douglas and McDonnell (both q.v.). Continued development and production of F-4 at St Louis (until 1979). On 23 December 1969 received contract for F-15 Eagle air-superiority fighter, first flown 27 July 1972; still in production by Boeing (q.v.), with latest dual-role F-15E two-seater (first production F-15E flown December 1986) suited to both air superiority and long-range interdiction. Evolved F/A-18 Hornet multi-mission carrierborne and land-based combat aircraft suited to fighter and attack missions (first flown November 1978, with the latest F/A-18E and F Super Hornet variants, first flown November 1995, recently placed into production by

McCulloch MC-4 tandem-rotor helicopter

Boeing), STOVL AV-8B Harrier II and II Plus with British Aerospace for US Marine Corps (first flights November 1981 and September 1992 respectively; see British Aerospace and Boeing), and T-45 Goshawk naval jet trainer (first flown April 1988; see Boeing) from British Hawk.

Long Beach and Palmdale factories continued production of A-4 Skyhawk attack aircraft until 1979, DC-8 four-jet airliner (until the early 1970s, and in the 1980s instituted a re-engine programme) and DC-9 twin-jet airliner (first

McDonnell Goblin parasite jet interceptor   *McDonnell XV-1 experimental convertiplane*

McDonnell Douglas (now Boeing) MD-83 operated by Crossair

*McDonnell Douglas A-4E
Skyhawk attack-bomber*

flown February 1965 and produced until the end of the 1970s, when the new designation MD-80 was adopted for developed models), and developed widebody triple-engined DC-10 (first flown 29 August 1970 and the last delivered in 1989, when replaced by the MD-11; see Boeing). Purchased Hughes Helicopters January 1984, taking over that company's range that included small helicopters and the AH-64 Apache, plus the NOTAR (no tail rotor) anti-torque system. Merger of McDonnell Douglas with Boeing announced in December 1996, and from August 1997 the combined company began operating as a single unit under the collective name The Boeing Company (q.v.).

Below: McDonnell Douglas (now Boeing) MD-11 operated by Delta Air Lines (Delta Air Lines)

Above: McDonnell F3H-2N Demon all-weather fighters

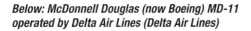

McDonnell Douglas MD 520N NOTAR helicopter, now a Boeing type since merger, but offered for sale

McDonnell F-101 Voodoo interceptor fighter and tactical fighter-bomber

Left: McDonnell FD/FH Phantom carrier-based fighters

Right: Early example of a McDonnell Douglas F-15 Eagle fighter

Above: McDonnell Douglas AH-64D Apache Longbow attack helicopter, now a Boeing product

Below: McDonnell Douglas KC-10A Extender tanker (based on DC-10) refuelling Lockheed C-5 Galaxy

Right: 5,000th McDonnell Douglas F-4 Phantom
built in 1978

McKinnon Turbo-Goose amphibian conversion

Meridionali-built Chinook transport helicopter

McKINNIE AIRCRAFT COMPANY INC. • USA

Transocean Air Lines subsidiary, formed in 1947 at Fargo, North Dakota, developed all-metal two-seat McKinnie 165 with Franklin engine, first flown 10 August 1952.

McKINNON ENTERPRISES INC. • USA

Conversion specialists at Sandy, Oregon, having entered field in 1953 with Grumman Widgeon with wingtip floats and Lycoming engines replacing the original Rangers. Grumman Goose also converted, as McKinnon G-21C with four Lycoming engines, and as Turbo Goose with two turboprops. Became McKinnon-Viking Enterprises 1978, then producing G-21G Turbo Goose, and Super Widgeon.

MDB FLUGTECHNIK AG. • Switzerland

Founded 1991 to continue development of the MD3-160, as begun by MDC Max Dätwyler AG, which is currently being manufactured in Malaysia by SME Aviation (q.v.) as the AeroTiga.

MDC MAX DÄTWYLER AG. • Switzerland

See under D.

MECAVIA • France

Markets kit to construct tandem two-seat composites-built Onyx Biplace, developed from single-seat Piel CP.150 Onyx and featuring rear-mounted wings and high canard.

MELBOURNE AIRCRAFT CORPORATION • Australia

Developed MA-2 Mamba two-seat light aircraft (first flown 1989). See Aviation Industries of Australia.

Meridionali EMA 124 three-seat light helicopter

MELEX USA INC. • USA

Subsidiary of PZL of Poland to market and support its agricultural aircraft in the West. Developed T45 Turbine Dromader as turboprop modification of M-18 Dromader, plus a waterbomber.

MERCKLE FLUGZEUGWERKE GMBH • Germany

Established at Oedheim, acquired from Dr Winter of Brunswick Technical College licence to build Kiebitz two-seat STOL monoplane. In 1956 began development of SM-67 Turboméca Artouste-powered five-seat helicopter, initially as private venture and later to government contract.

MERCURY AIRCRAFT INC. • USA

Formed at Menominee, Michigan, developed B-100 four-seat cabin monoplane with Allied Monsoon (licence-built

Regnier) engine, and BT-120 two-seat trainer biplane suitable for engines of 95-150 hp.

MERIDIONALI-AERFER SPA • Italy

Succeeded Società Anïnima Industrie Aeronautiche Romeo (q.v.), which had been formed in 1934 to absorb Officine Ferroviarie Meridionali's aviation activities; became part of Società Italiana Ernesto Breda (q.v.) group. Developed Ro.37 two-seat reconnaissance biplane which served October 1936 with Italian Aviacion Legionaria during Spanish Civil War and equipped Italian Air Force reconnaissance units during Second World War. Also used operationally were Ro.43 two-seat, single-float catapult seaplane and single-seat fighter version, Ro.44.

MERLIN AIRCRAFT INC. • USA

Made kits available to construct the Merlin GT-582 two-seat monoplane, originally developed in Canada as the Macair Merlin.

Meridionali (IMAM) Ro.37 reconnaissance biplane

Meridionali (IMAM) Ro.57 single-seat fighter

Messerschmitt Me 109G (Bf 109G), the famous single-seat fighter of WW2

MERVILLE • France

Propeller manufacturer established in 1919, began aircraft production 1959 with SM.30 single-seat sailplane; improved SM.31 prototype flown 11 January 1960. Also developed D.63 two-seat light aircraft based on Druine Condor, first flown 23 March 1962, with tricycle landing gear and Potez 4 E-20 engine.

MESSERSCHMITT GMBH • Germany

Founded by Willi Messerschmitt at Bamberg in 1923 as Messerschmitt Flugzeugbau; became GmbH 28 April 1926. Merged with Bayerische Flugzeugwerke (q.v.) 8 September 1927, but reconstituted June 1931 when BFW collapsed. BFW reformed 1933 and renamed Messerschmitt AG 11 July 1938. Amalgamated with Bölkow (q.v.) as Messerschmitt Bölkow GmbH 1968 and then with Hamburger Flugzeugbau (q.v.) to form Messerschmitt-Bölkow-Blohm (q.v.) 14 May 1969. S-16 powered glider flown 1924; M-18 three-passenger, single-engined airliners built for Nordbayerische Verkehrsflug AG and others 1925. Developed into M-20 and M-20b built for Lufthansa 1928. Highly successful M-23 two-seat sporting monoplane introduced 1929.

After being renamed in 1938 continued production of BFW's Bf 108 and of Bf 109 fighter, Bf 110 twin-engined long-range fighter. Rocket-powered Me 163 fighter first flown August 1941, and first of Me 262 twin-jet fighters on 18 July 1942. Bf 110 developed into Me 210 fighter-bomber first flown 2 September 1939, built up to 1944, and re-engined Me 410, which made maiden flight in late

Messerschmitt Me 163, the world's first manned rocket-powered interceptor

1942. Me 321 Gigant troop carrier/cargo glider (180 ft; 54.68 m wingspan) introduced 1941; 175 built together with 201 of Me 323 powered version with six Gnome-Rhone radial engines.

Reconstituted post-war company formed Flugzeug-Union Süd (q.v.) with Heinkel in August 1956, building Fouga Magister under licence and later taking part in programmes for Fiat G.91, Lockheed F-104G, Transall C.160 and Bell UH-1D.

MESSERSCHMITT-BÖLKOW-BLOHM GMBH • Germany

Formed 14 May 1969 as merger of Messerschmitt-Bölkow GmbH and Hamburger Flugzeugbau GmbH (q.v.), headquarters at Ottobrun, Munich. Inherited its forebears' production programmes, including Bölkow's 208C Junior, 209 Monsun and 223 Flamingo light aircraft and BO 105 helicopter, also HFB's Hansa executive jet. Produced BO 105 and Tornado, latter by virtue of its 42.5 per cent holding

Messerschmitt Me 110 twin-engined fighter

Messerschmitt Me 410 fighter-bomber

MBB BO 105C five-seat light helicopter

MBB BO 209 Monsun two-seat lightplane

in Panavia, and participated in Airbus, Transall, and Fokker F-28 programmes; took over VFW January 1981. Became part of Deutsche Aerospace AG (q.v.) in 1989.

METALAIR CORPORATION • USA

See Pittsburgh Metal Airplane Co.

METEOR SPA COSTRUZIONI AERONAUTICHE • Italy

Established in 1947, initially manufactured series of gliders and sailplanes, turning to powered aircraft in 1953 when company acquired assets of Francis Lombardi & Cie (q.v.), further developing FL.3 light aircraft, FL.53 two-seater, three-seat FL.54, and FL.55 four-seater. Own 110 hp Alfa 2 and 220 hp Alfa 4 engines powered two-seat Meteor Bis and four-seat Meteor Super.

METROPOLITAN WAGGON COMPANY • UK

Subcontractor for Handley Page O/400 bomber, of which 100 manufactured at Birmingham factory with Rolls-Royce Eagle VIII engines.

MEYERS AIRCRAFT COMPANY • USA

Formed 1936 at Tecumseh, Michigan. Developed OTW-160 biplane trainer and MEW-165W monoplane trainer for US schools within CAA War Training scheme. Post-war production included MAC 125 and MAC 145 two-seat cabin monoplanes with Continental engines. Meyers 200 four-seat cabin monoplane flown 8 September 1953, deliveries began 1959. Acquired by Rockwell-Standard Corporation (q.v.) 12 July 1965, and marketed Model 200 as Aero Commander 200. Manufacturing rights in this model were acquired in 1977 by Meyers Aircraft Manufacturing Company of Broomfield, Colorado, to build the Meyers 200D.

MFI • Sweden

Founded 1959 as AB Malmö Flygindustri as subsidiary of Trellborgs Gummifabric AB, with Björn Andreasson as designer. His independently-designed BA-7 developed as MFI-9 two-seat light aircraft, production prototype flown 17 May 1961, licence production by Bölkow (q.v.) as 208C Junior. MFI-10 Vipan short-field four-seater flown 25 February 1961. Company acquired by Saab-Scandia (q.v.) in 1961 and evolved MFI-15 multipurpose two/three-seat military aircraft, flown 11 July 1969, later renamed Safari

and then further developed into MFI-17 Supporter armed ground-support version, first flown 6 July 1972.

MFI • Sweden

Malmö Forsknings & Innovations AB founded by Björn Andreasson after original MFI (see previous entry). Produced MFI-18. Intended to put MFI-11 lightplane into production (first flown 1992) as modern version of MFI-9B, but programme halted. Production of BA-14B lightplane (first flown 1988) was also then delayed.

MIAMI AIRCRAFT CORPORATION • USA

Established at Hieleah, Florida, in February 1929; designed and built Miami Maid five-seat amphibian monoplane with Menasco-Salmson radial, production aircraft powered by 300 hp Wright J-6 engine.

MICROJET SA • France

Subsidiary of engine-manufacturer Microturbo SA, Microjet founded to develop and assemble Microjet 200 B two-seat very light trainer powered by two Microturbo turbojet engines (first flown 1980). Many components built by

Meteor FL.55 four-seat lightplane

MFI-15 (Saab) three-seat military aircraft

MFI-10 four-seat cabin monoplane

Mikoyan MiG-21 single-seat multi-role fighter

Mikoyan MiG-1 single-seat fighter of WW2

Mikoyan MiG-15, Russia's first swept-wing jet-fighter

Marmande Aéronautique, later building complete pre-production aircraft.

MID-CONTINENT AIRCRAFT CORPORATION • USA

Originated 1949, markets the King-Cat agricultural biplane as a Schweizer/Ag-Cat Corporation Ag-Cat C converted with a 1,200 hp radial piston engine, new three-blade propeller and 1,893-litre or 2,271-litre hopper.

MiG • USSR/Russia

See Mikoyan & Gurevich.

Mikoyan MiG-21bis fighters in Polish markings (Piotr Butowski)

MIG 'MAPO-M' • Russia

See MAPO 'MIG'.

MIGNET • France

See Société d'Exploitation des Aéronefs Henri Mignet.

MIGNET DO BRASIL • Brazil

Formed early 1950s to build Mignet H.M.310 Estafette two-seat modernised version of the designer's earlier Pou-du-Ciel light aircraft; new development flown 1951 with Continental A90 engine.

MIKE SMITH AIRCRAFT INC. • USA

Produced Super Interceptor two-seat turboprop lightplane, expected to be followed by six-seat Lightning Model 400 with turboprop driving tail-mounted propeller, but instead followed by XP-99 Prop-Jet as conventionally-configured, pressurised six-seater with nose turboprop (first flown 1982).

A.I. MIKOYAN AVIATION SCIENTIFIC-PRODUCTION COMPLEX • Russia

See Mikoyan & Gurevich.

MIKOYAN & GUREVICH • USSR/Russia

A. Mikoyan and G. Gurevich design bureau established December 1939; still operating as MAPO 'MiG' (q.v.) as part of MIG 'MAPO-M' organisation (q.v.), although Gurevich retired in early 1960s and Mikoyan died 9 December 1970. MiG-1 fighters with AM-35 engine produced 1940-1941; developed MiG-3 produced until 1942. First jet aircraft built in quantity was MiG-9 with twin RD-20 (BMW 003A) engines, flown 24 April 1946. Swept-wing MiG-15 with Russian copy of Rolls-Royce Nene introduced 1947, built under licence in Czechoslovakia and Poland. Followed by approximately 9,000 of derived MiG-17, with redesigned wing, manufactured 1950-1957. Twin Mikulin AM-5-powered MiG-19 flown September 1953, built under licence in Czechoslovakia, Poland and China. Superseded by delta-winged MiG-21, in service in the USSR from 1959 and, when built in India, was first Russian aircraft manufactured in non-communist country.

As ANPK 'MiG' named after A.I. Mikoyan Aviation Scientific-Production Complex, produced MiG-23 (4,278 constructed 1969-1985; also built in India) and MiG-27 (over

Mil Mi-10K flying-crane helicopter

Mil Mi-12 (V-12) world's largest helicopter

Mil Mi-1 general-purpose helicopter

900 between 1973 and 1983) related variable-geometry fighter and ground-attack aircraft, MiG-25 Mach 2.8+ reconnaissance aircraft and interceptor (some 1,200 built up to 1985), and MiG-31 long-range interceptor (about 400, operational from 1983). See MAPO 'MiG' for latest aircraft.

MIL • USSR/Russia

Mil helicopter design bureau established March 1947 by Mikhail Leontyevich Mil (died January 1970), who began developing helicopters and autogyros in 1929. Mi-1 first flown 1948, also manufactured by PZL-Swidnik (q.v.) in Poland 1956-1965. Mi-2 first flown in Soviet Union but production transferred to Poland. Enlarged Mi-4 introduced 1952, also built in China. Mi-6 with detachable wings to provide up to 20 per cent of required lift in cruise flight first flown June 1957, then world's largest helicopter, and 864 built at Rostov-on-Don (now Rostvertol) factory 1959-80, plus 50 at Moscow-Fili 1960-62. Mi-6 formed basis for Mi-22 airborne command post. Mi-8 first flown June 1961, becoming much produced medium civil and military helicopter (well over 7,000 built since 1965 and continuing), as turbine replacement for Mi-4; Mi-8 derivatives include Mi-9 tactical airborne command post (first flown 1977) and Mi-19 variant for use by commanders of tactical rocket units, Mi-17 (first flown August 1975) with change of engines and other modifications and Mi-171/Mi-172 export models, and lengthened Mi-173. Mi-10 flying crane development of Mi-6 first flown 1960, produced up to 1971. Two Mi-6 rotor/power packages used on giant

Mil Mi-14PS search and rescue helicopter in Polish service, with floats inflated (Piotr Butowski)

Mil Mi-26 very-heavy-lift helicopter

Mi-12 with an overall rotors span of 219 ft 10 in (67 m), then the largest helicopter in world. Mi-14 became shore-based amphibious anti-submarine, SAR and mine-countermeasures helicopter (first flown August 1967).

Mi-26 first flown December 1977 as very heavy lift helicopter with two powerful turboshaft engines and single eight-blade main rotor, with Mi-27 as airborne-command-post derivative. Series of helicopter gunships began with Mi-24 (first flown September 1969) and joining Soviet armed forces from 1970s, with Mi-25 as export version of Mi-24D tandem-cockpit variant and Mi-35 as second and improved export variant based on upgraded versions of Mi-24; most of over 2,500 built between 1970 and 1989, though small-scale production up to 1996. Latest attack helicopter from Mil is Mi-28, first flown November 1982 but yet to join armed forces at time of writing. Mi-34 first flown November 1986 as piston-engined lightweight sporting and training four-seat helicopter. Proposed new types include Mi-40 eight-troop armoured and armed assault helicopter, Mi-46 heavy transport helicopter, Mi-52 three-seat light piston helicopter, Mi-54 utility helicopter, Mi-58 medium civil helicopter, and

Mil Mi-28 attack helicopter

Mi-60MAI two-seat light training helicopter. Approximately 25,000 Mil helicopters have been built. Current name Mil Moscow Helicopter Plant. Has 25 per cent shareholding in Euromil (q.v.).

MILES AIRCRAFT LTD. • UK

Formed in October 1943, successor to Phillips & Powis Aircraft Ltd. (q.v.) at Woodley, Reading. Into liquidation November 1947, aircraft interests acquired by Handley Page (Reading) Ltd. (q.v.). Developed M.33 Monitor target tug. Manufacture included M.38 Messengers, some at Newtownards, Northern Ireland; M.57 Aerovan light freighters, M.65 Gemini light twins. Also developed M.68 Boxcar, with detachable freight container; M.71 Merchantman, which was enlarged four-engined Aerovan, and M.60 Marathon feederliner, later produced by Handley Page.

F. G. MILES LTD. • UK

Formed 1951 at Redhill, Surrey; transferred to Shoreham, Sussex, 1952. Acquired by British Executive and General Aviation (q.v.) February 1961. Developed M.75 derivative of Gemini with Cirrus Major engines; M.77 Sparrowjet conversion of M.5 Sparrowhawk prototype; M.100 Student jet trainer, first flown 15 May 1957; H.D.M.105 aerodynamic test vehicle, which had Aerovan fuselage with Hurel-Dubois high-aspect ratio wing, flown 31 March 1957.

MILLER AIRCRAFT CORPORATION • USA

Formed 1937 at Springfield, Massachusetts, to market Zeta series of two-seat light aircraft; Z-1 with 95 hp Menasco B-4; Z-2 with 125 hp Menasco C-4; and Z-3 with 150 hp Menasco C-4S.

MILLET-LAGARDE • France

Formed by Mm. Millet and Lagarde to exploit latter's ML-10 twin-boom, heavily-staggered biplane four-seater, powered by 180 hp Regnier engine and first flown 1949.

MINTY • Australia

Ted Minty designed Skyhook single-seat light autogyro, first flown 1978.

MIRAGE AIRCRAFT INC. • USA

Made plans and some components available for the construction of the Celerity two-seat monoplane, originally designed by Larry Burton and first flown in 1985.

MITSUBISHI AIRCRAFT INTERNATIONAL INC. • USA

Founded 1965 as a subsidiary of Mitsubishi of Japan to assemble the MU-2 turboprop transport, followed by the

Miles M.3 Falcon three-seat cabin monoplane

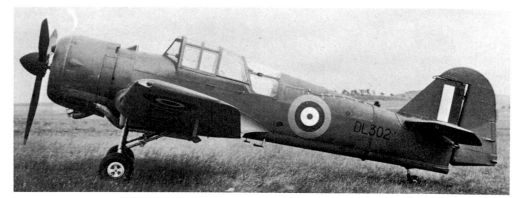

Miles Master two-seat advanced trainer

basically similar Solitaire and Marquise with different Garrett TPE331 engines and variations in fuel capacity. Subsequently assembled and marketed Mitsubishi Diamond business jets, but in December 1985 the Diamond II was acquired by the Beech Aircraft Corporation, becoming the Model 400 Beechjet, and in 1986 all US general aviation work by MAI ended.

MITSUBISHI JUKOGYO KABUSHIKI KAISHA • Japan

Mitsubishi Heavy Industries Ltd. formed 11 April 1934, merger of Mitsubishi Shipbuilding and Engineering Co Ltd. and Mitsubishi Aircraft Co Ltd. Long association with Japanese Navy, commencing with Type 10, operational 1922. Most notable aircraft were 1937 A5M4 'Claude'; 1942 J2M3 'Jack'; 1939 A6M3 'Zeke' (Zero), which were all fighters; 1941 Ki-46 'Dinah' reconnaissance aircraft; 1940 G3M1 'Nell' and 1941 G4M1 'Betty' medium bombers; 1940 Ki-21 'Sally' heavy bomber; and its replacement, 1944 Ki-67 'Peggy'.

Post-war built North American F-86F Sabres, Sikorsky S-55s, S-62As, and S-61s, and Lockheed F-104J Starfighters with Kawasaki, with which company it also manufactured McDonnell Douglas F-4EJ Phantoms. Produced 90 T-2 supersonic jet trainers, the first Japanese-developed supersonic aircraft (first flown 1971 and all delivered by 1988) and 77 F-1 single-seat close-air-support derivatives (all delivered by 1987). Developed MU-2

Miles Aerovan transport

Mitsubishi A5M2 fighter

turboprop executive aircraft (first flown 1963), built in Japan and assembled and marketed in USA by subsidiary Mitsubishi Aircraft International (q.v.), followed by the MU-300 Diamond (first flown 1978), which later became the Beech Model 400 Beechjet.

Produced 213 McDonnell Douglas (now Boeing) F-15J/DJ fighters for JASDF by 1998, and in October 1995

Mitsubishi Ki-21, Type 97 heavy bomber

Mitsubishi A6M Zero-Sen, Japan's most famous fighter

Mitsubishi RP1, recently flown only as a twin-turboshaft technology demonstrator

Mitsubishi MU-21 twin-turboprop light transport

Mitsubishi T-2 two-seat jet-trainer

Mitsubishi F-1 close support fighters

Mitsubishi-built F-4EJKai, as upgraded F-4EJ

Prototype Mitsubishi F-2 fighter support aircraft

first flew new Japanese-developed F-2 fighter support aircraft, intended to replace F-1 and based on F-16 but incorporating new technologies. Currently modernizing F-4EJ fleet, is a partner in the Bombardier Global Express programme, has a 20 per cent share in the Kawasaki OH-1 helicopter programme, constructs Sikorsky S-70B-3 helicopters for the JMSDF as SH-60Js (the first flew 1991) plus UH-60Js for SAR with JMSDF and JASDF and UH-60JAs for JGSDF, has developed the new MH2000 twin-turbine multipurpose helicopter (first flown July 1996), and constructs components for the Dash 8, various Boeing airliners and Sikorsky S-92. Also has engine and space activities.

MKEK • Turkey

Full name Makina ve Kimya Endustrisi Kurumu. In 1952 MKEK took over THK factory at Ankara, together with existing designs. THK-15 became the MKEK Model 1, THK-16 the Model 2, THK-5 and 5A the Models 5 and 5A, THK-

Mitsubishi UH-60JA, built for JGSDF for combat SAR role and based on US Sikorsky S-70B-3

MK Helicopter MKII in ultralight form

14 the Model 6 and THK-2 the Model 7. Developed Model 4 Ugur tandem two-seat primary trainer for Turkish Air Force, three presented to Royal Jordanian Air Force.

MK HELICOPTER GMBH • Germany

Produced the MKII two-seat helicopter in ultralight form, first flown 1996 and offered ready-assembled. Ultralight since withdrawn, giving way to new and improved certificated version.

MMPL • India

For the Maintenance Command Development Centre, Air-Vice Marshal Harjinder Singh of the Indian Air Force designed Kanpur I four-seat light aircraft, prototype built at MCDC in 132 days. Kanpur II with 250 hp Lycoming engine, first flown October 1961.

M.M. Super Rotor LTDA. • Brazil

AC.4 single-seat autogyro dated from 1970s as a design of Altair Coelho. Marketed by this company after purchase of rights and many sold in assembled and kit forms.

MOHAWK AIRCRAFT CORPORATION • USA

Formed at Minneapolis in 1927, developing Spurwing two-seat monoplane with Warner Scarab engine and similar three-seater Redskin.

MOHAWK AIR SERVICES • USA

Subsidiary of Allegheny Airlines Inc., Washington D.C., formed to control conversion programme for Mohawk 298, UACL PT-6A-45-powered Nord 262 airliner, being undertaken by Frakes Aviation Inc. (q.v.). First example flew 7 January 1975.

MÖLLER FLUGZEUGBAU • Germany

Founded at Bremen late 1930s, built Stomo 3 single-seat cabin monoplane powered by 18 hp Kroeber M.4 engine. Similar Möller Sturmer had a 53 hp Zundapp engine.

MOLLER INTERNATIONAL • USA

Established 1983 to develop circular VTOL 'power-lift' aircraft named Volantor M200X, which flew more than 150 times. Thereafter designed M200 and M400 Skycar two- and four-seat VTOL lightplanes of very unusual configuration, with Mollar rotary engines and computer-reconfigured variable-lift vanes to provide thrust, and futuristic

Moller M400 Skycar before fitting of engines

Mooney Mk.22 Mustang four-seat light aircraft

Mooney M-10 Cadet two-seat lightplane

airframes with only small fixed lifting surfaces. Moller M400 prototype built in mid-1990s.

MOYES MICROLIGHTS PTY. LTD. • Australia

Markets kits for the Dragonfly tandem two-seat microlight.

NPO MOLNIYA • USSR/Russia

Created 1976 to develop the Buran, Russia's first reusable spacecraft. With less work on Buran in later years, began developing civil aircraft. First to fly was six-seat Molniya-1 general-purpose transport with twin booms and pusher engine (first flown December 1992); Allison turboprop-powered version proposed as Molniya-3. Projects include twin-engined Aist general-purpose transport in six- and nine-seat versions; Lagoda 10-seat amphibian; Molniya-

100 19-passenger transport; Molniya-300 6/15-passenger high-performance business/commuter transport; Molniya-400 combi transport or freighter with twin turbofans, in combi configuration carrying 250 passengers on upper deck and freight containers on lower deck; Molniya-1000 Heracles twin-fuselage super-heavy freighter with a 450-tonne payload (or possible 1,200-seat passenger capsule) and 6-10 engines; and Vityaz smaller variant of Heracles.

MONO AIRCRAFT CORPORATION • USA

Formed at Moline, Illinois, manufacturing a series of two-seat, high-wing cabin monoplanes during 1920s and 1930s, including Monocoupe 70 with Velie radial engine and Monocoupe 110 powered by Warner Scarab. Company acquired by Lambert Aircraft Corporation (q.v.) July 1934. In a succession of acquisitions and amalgamations

the Mono identity disappeared, but the Monocoupe configuration influenced many later designs.

MONOCOUPE AIRCRAFT OF FLORIDA • USA

Successor to Monocoupe Airplane and Engine Corporation of Melbourne, Florida, developed Meteor four/five-seat cabin monoplane with two Lycoming O-320 engines.

MONTANA COYOTE INC. • USA

Made kits available for the Mountain Eagle two-seat cabin monoplane, a 1994 revision of a 1991 design.

MONTEE AIRCRAFT COMPANY • USA

Formed by Kenneth W. Montee at Santa Monica, California, in early 1920s. Montee designed four-seat open cockpit monoplane, with Hall-Scott L-4 engine, in which he won second prize in 'On to New York' race at 1925 National Air Races; he died in December 1926 while engaged on a mapping operation.

MOONEY AIRCRAFT CORPORATION • USA

Mooney Aircraft formed July 1946 at Wichita, Kansas, and merged with Alon Inc. (q.v.) October 1967. Became Aerostar Aircraft Corporation (q.v.) on 1 July 1970, renamed Mooney Aircraft Corporation October 1973. Developed M-18 Mite single-seat light aircraft with Crosley engine; became M-18 Wee Scotsman with Lycoming engine. M-20 four-seat version first flown 10 August 1953 with Lycoming O-320 engine, superseded by O-360-A-powered M-20A and by all-metal M-20C Mark 21 in 1961. Square windows introduced 1967 for O-360-AID-powered Ranger and Executive, and M20J or Model 201, both of which had Lycoming IO-360-A1B6D engines. Mooney's 10,000th aircraft built 1994. Four-seat Allegro (former M20J) production ended 1998, and Encore (M20K) now only built in batch orders. Bravo (M20M) four-seater has

Prototype Molniya-1 general-purpose transport

turbocharged TIO-540-AF1A and was previously known as TLS (first appeared 1989), while Ovation (M20R) first flew May 1994 and has Teledyne Continental IO-550-G5B engine.

MORANE-SAULNIER • France

Formed 1911 at Puteaux, Seine, by brothers Robert and Léon Morane with Raymond Saulnier, as Aéroplanes Morane-Saulnier. Acquired by Potez Group in 1963 and became Société d'Exploitation Etablissements Morane-Saulnier, reorganised as Gérance des Etablissements Morane-Saulnier 20 May 1965, subsidiary of Sud Aviation (q.v.). Developed series of parasol-winged fighters and training aircraft, beginning with 1913 Type L or MS.3; principal production aircraft throughout 1920s and 1930s included MS.130, MS.230 and MS.315 two-seat trainers. Series of single-seat monoplane fighters introduced from 1935, including MS.406s built for French Air Force up to Occupation; development of basic design continued by Morane-Saulnier design bureau and derived MS.450 built by Dornier Werke AG in Switzerland as D-3802A. Also built Fieseler Storch for Germans as MS.500 Criquet. After liberation developed MS.470 series of advanced trainers, several light aircraft and then MS.733 Alcyon basic trainer. MS.760 Paris introduced into French Air Force service in 1958. MS.880 Rallye touring aircraft first flown 10 June 1959; see SOCATA.

MORAVAN INC. • Czech Republic

In 1949 Zlinská Letecká Akciová Spolenost (see Zlin) changed its name to Moravan Národni Podnik, although its products retained the Zlin title. The current name for the company is Moravan Inc. The Zlin 26 all-wood two-seat tandem trainer was superseded by the metal Zlin 126 Trener, which went into production in 1953. The basic design was developed subsequently through Z 226, Z 326, Z 526 and Z 726 models in both Trener (two-seat) and Akrobat (single-seat competition aircraft) variants with retractable landing gear and a variety of engines. As one of the world's foremost aerobatic aircraft, the Zlin was also widely exported outside the Eastern bloc. Production thereafter included Zlin 42 M two-seat light training and touring aircraft, Z 50 L and later Z 50 LS aerobatic aircraft (first flown 1975 in original Z 50 L version) and Z 726 trainer. An agricultural and firefighting monoplane was the Z 137 T (first flown 1981). Currently produced are the Z 142 two-seat basic and advanced civil/military piston-engined trainer (first flown December 1978), Z 242 variant of Z 142 with a US Textron Lycoming engine in place of the LOM Prague type, and Z 143 L four-seat lightplane with Textron Lycoming engine (first flown April 1992).

MORAVAN NARODNI PODNIK • Czechoslovakia

See MORAVAN INC.

Morane-Saulnier 'Bullet' scout of WW1

Morane-Saulnier MS.406 single-seat fighter

Morane-Saulnier MS.225 fighter

Moravan Zlin Z 50 LS aerobatic monoplane (Tána Vesela/Moravan)

Moravan Zlin Z 242 Ls (Tána Vesela/Moravan)

Moravan Z 137 T agricultural and fire-fighting aircraft (Tána Vesela/Moravan)

MORAVKO-SLEZKA VAZOVKA TATRA • Czechoslovakia

Founded in 1935 as part of the Ringhoff-Tatra combine. Obtained licences to build the Avro 626 as T.126, and the Bücker Bü 131 Jungmann as the T.131. Produced also an own-design two-seat trainer under the designation T.1. Ceased production at the outbreak of Second World War.

MORELAND AIRCRAFT INC. • USA

Founded by G. E. Moreland in the late 1920s at Inglewood, California, to produce the Moreland M-1 three-seat biplane powered by a 225 hp Wright engine.

MORGAN & COMPANY • UK

Factory at Leighton Buzzard, Bedfordshire; during First World War built Sopwith 1-strutters, Airco D.H.6s, Avro 504Ks and Vickers Vimy bombers under subcontract.

MORRISEY AIRCRAFT COMPANY • USA

Founded in 1949 by William J. Morrisey at Long Beach, California, to market Model 1000 Nifty tandem two-seater first flown 1948. Initially flown with Continental A65 and later with Continental C90. Reorganised as Morrisey Aviation Inc. at Santa Ana, California, and in 1958 began

delivery of series production aircraft as Morrisey 2150 with 150 hp Lycoming engine. Rights in 2150 acquired by Shinn Engineering and later Varga Aircraft, which produced its Kachina version. Morrisey Aircraft Company re-established in Las Vegas, producing single-seat Bravo in 1981 for construction from plans, and more recently has offered Morrisey 2000 two-seater in certificated and kit forms as modern development of Nifty.

MORROW AIRCRAFT CORPORATION • USA

Formed at San Bernardino County Airport, California, by Howard Morrow, factory completed 1 April 1941. Developed Model 1-L tandem two-seat trainer for Civil Pilot Training Program. Employed plastic-bonded plywood construction and was powered by a Lycoming 0-435A engine.

MORSE AIRCRAFT CORPORATION • USA

Established at Ithaca, New York, in January 1917. Thomas brothers, backed by Morse Chain Company, built 100 S-4B single-seat biplane advanced trainers developed from Thomas S-4 prototype fighter, followed by 497 improved S-4Cs. 200 Morse MB-3A fighters built by Boeing (q.v.) 1921-1922, in addition to 50 built by Thomas-Morse. 0-19 two-seat observation aircraft built 1928-1931.

Below: Morrisey Nifty two-seat lightplane

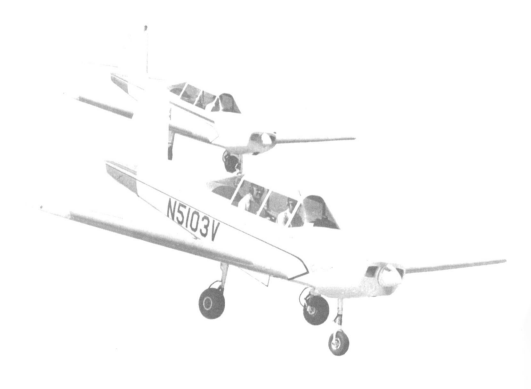

Mosca MB bis, Russian fighter of WW1

Mureaux 113 fighter/reconnaissance aircraft

MOSHIER TECHNOLOGIES CORPORATION • USA

Founded 1986 to develop Aurora 400-C four-seat VTOL aircraft of very unusual configuration.

MOSKOVSKIY AVIATSIONNI ZAVOD MOSCA • USSR

The Mosca Moscow Aviation Works was first established in Russia by F. E. Mosca, Savoia's designer. By late 1916 this factory was building about five aircraft per month, these being Nieuport and Morane types built under licence. First original design was the Mosca MB, first flown in July 1915, a single-seat high-wing monoplane fighter evolved from the Morane J. Followed by MBbis with forward-firing synchronised machine-gun.

MOSS BROTHERS AIRCRAFT LTD. • UK

Formed in 1936 at Chorley, Lancashire, where prototype M.A.1 two-seat cabin monoplane was built 1937. Powered by Pobjoy Niagara III engine, it was converted to open cockpit configuration 1938. Following year open-cockpit M.A.2 completed, powered by Cirrus Minor, and later converted to cabin version.

MOTH AIRCRAFT CORPORATION • USA

Formed at Lowell, Mass., in 1926 to manufacture de Havilland Moths under licence. Built 18 D.H.60G and 161 D.H.60M biplanes.

MOTORLUFTFAHRZEUG GESELLSCHAFT • Austria

Established in Vienna, was one of the early builders of heavier-than-air craft. Produced both the Etrich Dove and the Loehner Arrow.

MOUNTAIN TRIKES • USA

Markets kits to construct two-seat Mountaineer Dual 175 and single-seat Mountaineer Mite Lite microlights with trikes.

MPC-75 GMBH • International

Founded by MBB of Germany and CATIC of China to develop 80-passenger MPC 75 twin-propfan airliner following agreement of 1985. Project later abandoned.

MSP AIR SPOL SRO • Czech Republic

First flew in March 1995 its WK 94 two-seat lightplane, which is available in production form.

MUDRY ET COMPAGNIE • France

Established 1958 by M. Auguste Mudry in former SAN factory at Bernay, Normandy. Built CAARP-developed CAP 10 two-seat and CAP 20 single-seat aerobatic aircraft. Merged in early 1978 with CAARP (q.v.). Became known as Avions Mudry et Cie until assets purchased by AeroTech Europe (q.v.).

MUEYETEMI SPORTREPULO EGYESULET • Hungary

Sport Flying Association of Technical University, Budapest. Designed and built light aircraft throughout 1920s and 1930s, including Gerle 13 with Armstrong Siddeley Genet Major engine, M.19 tandem two-seat cabin monoplane powered by Gipsy Major and M.21 single-seat aerobatic biplane.

MULLER • Germany

Brothers Jacob and Philipp Muller formed Boots und Flugzeugbau Gebr Muller at Darmstadt in 1908, manufacturing parts for Voisin aircraft being built under licence by August Euler. After First World War developed several light aircraft, including GMG V two-seat cabin monoplane with Argus As.16 or BMW Xa engine.

MUNIZ, CASSIO • Brazil

Established at Sao Paulo; developed Casmuniz 52, first all-metal twin built in Brazil. Designed for short-field, limited-maintenance operations, with two Continental L100 engines. The four/five-seat Casmuniz 52 was first flown in April 1952 and subsequently taken over for flight test and production by Oficina de Mantencao e Recuperacao de Avioes Ltda

MUREAUX • France

Les Ateliers de Construction du Nord de la France et des Mureaux, headquartered at Mureaux, Seine-et-Oise, absorbed into SNCAN 1 March 1937. Before this had developed a number of military prototypes including Mureaux 115.R2 two-seat fighter and Mureaux 200.A3 two/three-seat reconnaissance derivative, both with Hispano-Suiza 12Y engine; also Mureaux 190 single-seat fighter.

MURPHY AIRCRAFT MANUFACTURING LTD. • Canada

Offers kits to build Maverick side-by-side two-seat cabin monoplane, Rebel and Rebel Elite three-seat STOL cabin monoplane, plans and kits for the Renegade II tandem two-seat open-cockpit microlight biplane and heavier Renegade Spirit, and kit for the SR-2500 Super Rebel four-seat cabin monoplane.

MUSTANG AERONAUTICS • USA

Produces plans and kits for the single-seat Midget Mustang and two-seat Mustang II low-wing monoplanes.

Above: Myasishchev M-101T Gzhel turboprop transport (Piotr Butowski)

MYASISHCHEV • USSR/Russia

Vladimir Myasishchev's design career included association with the ANT-16 and ANT-29 before work began, in 1940, on prototype DVB-102 twin-engined bomber. New bureau established 1951 to develop four-jet long-range heavy bomber, which became Mya-4 Molot (NATO code-name: *Bison*), first flown January 1953; also served as maritime research aircraft and finally as tanker and heavylift transport. Designed M-52 *Bounder* four-jet delta-winged strategic bomber seen at 1961 Soviet Aviation Day display, but not put into production. Produced Il-22 airborne command post, as converted Ilyushin Il-18 airliner. Important M-17 first flew in May 1982, having been designed originally in early 1970s as high-altitude reconnaissance balloon interceptor but developed into M-17/M-55 high-altitude reconnaissance and ecological monitoring aircraft. Small civil aircraft include pressurized and single turboprop eight-seat M-101 Gzhel (first flown 1995) and M-201 Sokol twin-engined version, with projects covering M-202PW Olen enlarged development of the Indian Saras, M-203PW Barsuk radial-engined general-purpose transport, and M-500 piston-engined agricultural monoplane suited also to other roles.

MYLIUS FLUGZEUGWERK GMBH & CO KG. • Germany

Currently marketing the single-seat MY-102 aerobatic and towing aircraft, two-seat MY-103 in Standard and Basic Trainer variants, and four-seat MY-104 for touring, IFR training and other uses. All are low-wing monoplanes based on a common modular design, with interchangeable sub-structures. See Leichtflugzeuge-Entwicklungen Dipl Ing Hermann Mylius.

Right: Myasishchev M-55.2 Geophysica, recently used on an international Polar experiment

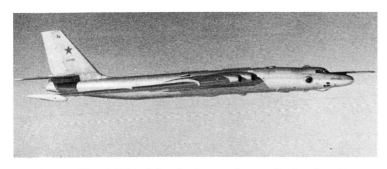

Myasishchev Mya-4 ('Bison') bomber/reconnaissance/tanker aircraft

Myasishchev 'Bounder' strategic bomber

NAGLER HELICOPTER COMPANY INC. • USA

Nagler's Model NH-160 single-seat helicopter first flew in 1955. The VG-1 Vertigyro developed later comprised a Piper Colt aircraft fuselage with conventional engine. Its rotor system was driven by a turbine engine, enabling the craft to be flown as a gyroplane, a helicopter, or a combination of both.

NAKAJIMA HIKOKI KABUSHIKI KAISHA • Japan

Nakajima's Ki-27 ('Nate'), the Imperial Japanese Army's first monoplane low-wing fighter, entered service in 1936 and outnumbered all other Japanese fighters at the time of Pearl Harbor. The B5N ('Kate') carrier-based torpedo bomber played a major role in that attack, and was largely responsible for sinking the US aircraft carriers during the Battle of Midway. Nakajima's Ki-43 Hyabusa ('Oscar') interceptor fighter, though deficient in firepower, was the mount of most Japanese fighter aces. The much less manoeuvrable Ki-44 Shoki ('Tojo') was used primarily as a home-defence fighter. Other significant Nakajima aircraft included the B6N Tenzan ('Jill') torpedo-bomber, the J1N1 Gekko ('Irving') three-seat reconnaissance/nightfighter; the Ki-49 Donryu ('Helen') heavy bomber; and the Ki-84 Hayate ('Frank'), a good all-round fighter, though relatively unproven in battle. Nakajima developed also a floatplane version of the Zero fighter as the A6M-2 ('Rufe').

NAMC • China

See Nanchang Aircraft Manufacturing Company.

NAMC • Japan

see Nihon Kokuki Seizo Kabushiki Kaisha.

NANCHANG AIRCRAFT MANUFACTURING COMPANY • China

Formed in 1951; produced a variant of the Soviet Yakovlev Yak-18 trainer known locally as the CJ-5, the improved CJ-6A still being built in the late 1990s in very low volume for the same radial piston-engined primary training role. Also co-produced (with Shenyang) a Soviet MiG-19 fighter variant known as the J-6, and licence-built the Antonov An-2 general-purpose biplane as the Y5 before this was taken over by the Shijiazhuang Aircraft Manufacturing Corporation (q.v.). Very important programme to develop the Q-5 dedicated attack aircraft from J-6 technology was begun at Shenyang in 1958 but transferred to Nanchang. June 1965 saw first flight of a Q-5 *Fantan* prototype, featuring an area ruled fuselage for minimum transonic drag, cockpit armour protection, a 'solid' nose and a weapon bay (for early test and production aircraft, but omitted from improved production versions). Entered Chinese service in 1970 and also exported from 1983 as upgraded A-5. Also developed the N-5A agricultural aircraft (first

flown December 1989) and partnered Pakistan Aeronautical Complex in development of the K-8 Karakorum jet trainer (first flown November 1990). Name changed to Hongdu Aviation Industry (Group) Corporation Ltd in March 1998 (q.v.).

NAPIER AND MILLER LTD. • UK

Built RAF B.E.2c and B.E.2e under subcontract during First World War.

Nakajima B5N1, Type 97 bomber

Nakajima Ki-4, Type 94 reconnaissance

Nakajima P-1 night mailplane

Nanchang-developed A-5C export version of Q-5, now marketed by Hongdu

NAPIER & SONS LTD. • UK

This well-known manufacturer of motor car and aero engines built large numbers of RAF R.E.8s and Sopwith Snipes under First World War subcontracts at its Acton, London works.

NARDI SA PER COSTRUZIONI AERONAUTICHE • Italy

Established in Milan in 1933 by three brothers. Nardi's first aircraft was the F.N.305 tandem two-seat lightplane, which flew in 1935 and was intended as a fighter trainer. A 1938 successor, the F.N.315, was exported to six countries, and a light-attack version was flown experimentally. The first post-war product was the F.N.333 amphibian, a three/four-seat twin-boom design later acquired by SIAI-Marchetti (q.v.) and marketed from 1962 as the Riviera, and in America as the North Star amphibian

NASH AIRCRAFT LTD. • UK

Developed the Petrel two-seat touring, training and glider tug lightplane, first flown 1980.

NATIONAL AERO MANUFACTURING CORPORATION • Philippines

Until 1982 a subsidiary of the Philippines Aerospace Development Corporation (q.v.), which began assembly and licence-manufacture of MBB (q.v.) BO 105 helicopters in 1974. Later that year a contract was signed with Britten-Norman (q.v.) for the assembly and eventual manufacture of the BN-2A Islander, and for the development and marketing of an amphibious version. Assembly of Islanders began in 1976 from sets of parts from the UK. In 1978 a four-seat utility aircraft was developed in conjunction with the Philippine Government's National Sciences Development Board. 1982 closure.

NATIONAL AERONAUTICS COMPANY • USA

Produces kits and plans to allow amateur construction of the Cassutt IIIM single-seat monoplane racer, originally designed/built by Captain Tom Cassutt in 1954

NATIONAL AEROSPACE LABORATORIES • India

Developed the Hansa (see Taneja). Is developing the Saras 14-passenger transport and multipurpose aircraft with rear-mounted turbine engines driving six-blade pusher propellers, originally as a joint venture programme with Myasishchev of Russia (withdrew 1997). First flight imminent.

NATIONAL AIRCRAFT DIVISION OF AMERICAN AIRMOTIVE CORPORATION • USA

Established in 1956 to remanufacture Boeing-Stearman PT-13/17 Kaydet trainers as the NA-75 agricultural aircraft. Modifications included new high-lift wings of all-metal construction. The NA-75 was offered either in completed form or as a conversion.

NATIONAL AIRCRAFT FACTORIES • UK

Three factories established by the UK Ministry of Munitions in First World War to increase the productive capacity of Britain's aircraft industry. No 1 at Waddon, Surrey, built Airco D.H.9s; No 2 at Heaton Chapel, near Stockport, Airco D.H.9s and de Havilland D.H.10s; and No 3 at Aintree, Lancs., built about 125 Bristol Fighters.

NATIONAL AIRWAYS SYSTEM • USA

In 1926 this company designed and produced the three/four-seat open-cockpit Air King commercial/touring biplane. Alternative engines offered included the Curtiss OX-5, Hispano-Suiza and Wright Whirlwind.

NATIONAL DYNAMICS (PTY) LTD. • South Africa

Formed 1975 after acquiring the prototype and all production rights of the Patchen Explorer/Observer four-seat cabin lightplane conceived originally by Thurston Aviation Corporation (q.v.) in the USA, as a landplane development of the Teal amphibian. Also offered Schweizer Aircraft Corporation products and the Air Nova Falcon aerobatic sailplane, and redesigned the Reed Rooivalk single-seat aerobatic biplane as Falcon.

NATIONALE VLIEGTUIGINDUSTRIE • Netherlands

Established after First World War at 's-Gravenhage, this new company acquired as designer the well-known Frederick Koolhoven (q.v.). His designs for the company included the F.K.23A, a single-seat biplane fighter; F.K.29 three-seat commercial biplane; and F.K.31 two-seat high-wing monoplane which served in the pursuit, interception and army observation roles.

NATIONAL STEEL CAR CORPORATION LTD. • Canada

In 1938 this company entered into an agreement with Westland Aircraft of Great Britain (q.v.) to manufacture Westland Lysanders for the Canadian Government and later for the RAF. Under a similar arrangement National Steel Car also made North American Harvards, and contracted to build Yale trainers for Canada after the fall of France.

NAVAL AIRCRAFT FACTORY • USA

The US Naval Aircraft Factory at Philadelphia, Pennsylvania, was authorised in 1917 and established in early 1918. Its first, and major, task was the construction of 150 Curtiss H-16 patrol flying-boats. Built improved H-16s as F-

National Dynamics built Explorer/Observer

5L, as well as Hanriot seaplanes and Loening two-seat monoplanes. Original designs of NAF include the PT-1/2 torpedo seaplanes of 1922; TS-1/3 carrier-based biplane fighters of 1922; and extensively-built N3N-1/3 primary trainer biplanes, which originated in 1934 and remained in service for 27 years. Production in Second World War included 300 Vought-designed OS2 N-1 observation/scout monoplanes, and 156 Consolidated PBN Nomads (better known as the PBY Catalina).

NAVAL AIR ESTABLISHMENT • China

First established in 1918, this organisation was relocated to Shanghai in 1931. Two principal aircraft types were built: the Chiang Hung two/three-seat touring seaplane, which first flew in July 1931, and the Chiang Gae'n two-seat reconnaissance biplane or advanced military trainer.

NAVION AIRCRAFT COMPANY • USA

Founded in 1965 by the American Navion Society to provide spares and support for owners of Ryan/North Amer-

ican Navion lightplanes. All rights to the aircraft were acquired and a developed version, the five-seat Navion Rangemaster H, was produced before the company was liquidated and taken over by the Navion Rangemaster Aircraft Company (q.v.).

NAVION RANGEMASTER AIRCRAFT COMPANY • USA

In 1972 Navion Rangemaster purchased the assets of the bankrupt Navion Aircraft Company (q.v.), including jigs, machine tools and spare parts to support Ryan/North American Navion lightplanes. In 1973 production of the Navion Rangemaster restarted, the first aircraft flying late the following year. Consolidated Holding Incorporated acquired control of the company in 1975 and announced plans to manufacture the Rangemaster H at the rate of one per week.

Navion Rangemaster five-seat cabin monoplane

NAF N3N-3 primary training aircraft

Above: NH1-H3 Kolibrie helicopter

Right: Neiva N621 Universal (Brazilian AF T-25) trainers

NDN AIRCRAFT LTD. • UK

Established 1976 by N. D. Norman, formerly of Fairey Britten-Norman, to develop the NDN-1 Firecracker two-seat trainer/sport aircraft. The first piston-engined prototype flew in May 1977; turboprop variant of Firecracker first known as NDN 1T Turbo Firecracker (see The Norman Aeroplane Company). Also developed Fieldmaster agricultural aircraft (first flown 1981) and Freelance four-seat utility lightplane (first flown 1984).

NEBRASKA AIRCRAFT CORPORATION • USA

Established at Lincoln, Nebraska, during First World War, was a builder of the Lincoln Standard biplane, and also built aircraft under subcontract to the US government.

NEDERLANDSE HELICOPTER INDUSTRIE NV • Netherlands

This company designed and built the NH-H3 Kolibrie light helicopter which first flew in May 1956. For propulsion the Kolibrie employed ramjets mounted at the tips of its rotor blades. Ten helicopters were built before production rights were handed over to Aviolanda Maatschappij voor Vliegtuigbouw (q.v.), which subsequently abandoned it.

NEIVA • Brazil

See Sociedade Construtora Aeronáutica Neiva Ltda.

Neiva Regente 360C four-seat utility aircraft

New Piper PA32R-301 Saratoga

New Piper PA46-350P Malibu Mirage

NESTLER LTD. • UK

Became established in the British aircraft industry before First World War by obtaining an agency for Sanchez-Besa aircraft. Subcontractor for components in war. Built one example of the Monosoupape Gnome-powered Nestler Scout to the design of Monsieur Boudot. It was destroyed at Hendon in 1917 and no further aircraft were constructed.

NESTLER UND BREITFELD • Germany

see Erma Maschinenwerk GmbH.

THE NEW PIPER AIRCRAFT INC. • USA

Established July 1997 as subsidiary of Newco Pac Inc, taking over assets of Piper Aircraft Corporation. Production of PA18-150 Super Cub ended 1995, and production ended of PA28-236 Dakota. Currently marketed are 160 hp PA28-161 Warrior III four-seat lightplane (first flown 1976, as development of original 1972 Warrior), 180 hp PA28-181 Archer III four-seat lightplane, 200 hp PA28-201 Arrow four-seat lightplane (first flown 1975), 300 hp PA32R-301 Saratoga five/six-seat lightplane, PA34-220T Seneca V five/six-seat twin 220 hp-engined

Piper PA34-220T Seneca

lightplane (unveiled 1997), PA44-180 Seminole four-seat twin 180 hp-engined lightplane (first flown 1976), and 350 hp PA46-350P Malibu Mirage (first flown 1983) and turboprop-powered Malibu Meridian (first flown 1998) six-seat and single-engined business aircraft.

NEW STANDARD AIRCRAFT CORPORATION • USA

In 1928 the Gates-Day Aircraft Corporation (q.v.) became New Standard Aircraft Corporation, and the following year produced the White New Standard D-25 tandem, open-cockpit four-seat biplane, developed from the Gates-Day GD-24. The two-seat D-26, D-27 mailplanes and D-28 floatplane followed.

NEW TECHNIK INC. • USA

Founded 1990 by Aircraft Acquisition Corporation to produce lightplanes based on Taylorcraft models, as two-seat L-2M Tech 2 and four-seat Model 20 Tech 4, plus the twin-engined Twin Tech.

NEW ZEALAND AEROSPACE INDUSTRIES LTD. • New Zealand

Aero Engine Services Ltd and Air Parts (NZ) Ltd amalgamated in 1973 to form New Zealand Aerospace Industries. Production of the Fletcher FU-24 agricultural aircraft and the AESL Airtrainer CT4 was integrated, and examples were delivered to Australia, Bangladesh, Iraq, Pakistan, Thailand and Uruguay. The Airtrainer CT4 was delivered to the air forces of Thailand, Australia and New Zealand, but went out of production. Company assets were purchased by Pacific Aerospace Corporation Ltd (q.v.).

NHINDUSTRIES • International

NHIndustries founded 1992 by Agusta of Italy, Eurocopter Deutschland of Germany, Eurocopter and Fokker to develop and produce the twin-turboshaft NH90 tactical transport (TTH) and multirole NATO frigate helicopter (NFH). First flown December 1995, production deliveries are expected to begin in the year 2003, first to the Netherlands (navy). Planned orders are for France to receive between 68 and 133 TTHs and 27 NFHs, Germany 205 TTHs and 38 NFHs, Italy 160 TTHs and 64 NFHs, and the Netherlands 20 NFHs.

NIAT JSC • Russia

National Institute of Aviation Technologies. Developing NIAT-2.5SI Freighty amphibious transport, to operate in remote areas; initial design phase completed 1995

NICHII KOKU KABUSHIKI KAISHA • Japan

Established at Kyoto in October 1939, by Kanegafuchi Cotton Mill and the Italian Fiat Company (q.v.), to produce Fiat aircraft and engines under licence.

NHIndustries NH90 in NFH form

Left: Nieuport IIG light monoplane of 1912

Right: Nieuport XVII biplane fighter of WW1

Left: Nieuport-Delage 629 monoplane fighters

NICHOLAS-BEAZLEY AIRPLANE COMPANY INC • USA

Established in Missouri in 1921 to supply aircraft materials and accessories. Two aircraft designs were built: the NB-4 three-seat open-cockpit low-wing monoplane, which was offered with Lambert, Warner or Armstrong Siddeley engines; and the NB-8 two-seat parasol-wing lightplane, powered by a Szekely engine.

NICK D'APUZZO AIRPLANE DESIGNS • USA

Markets plans and components to construct D-201 Sportwing two-seat open-cockpit sporting biplane, developed from previous PJ-260 Senior Aero Sport.

NIELSEN AND WINTHER AS • Denmark

During First World War built Nieuport types under licence, and put into small-scale production a biplane of its own design.

NIEUPORT • France

Designer Gustave Delage made the Nieuport company famous with his series of fighters. The sesquiplane Nieuport XI and XVII served with British, French, Belgian, Russian, Italian, Dutch, Finnish and American services during the First World War. The improved Nieuport 28 biplane which appeared in 1917 was less successful, but best known for its exploits with the American 94th Aero Squadron ('Hat-in-Ring') in the hands of Eddie Rickenbacker and Raoul Lufbery. Nieuport aircraft were manufactured under licence in Britain and Italy.

Société Anonyme des Établissements Nieuport amalgamated with the Astra airship company, but all construction of airships was abandoned and the company name changed again to SA Nieuport-Delage. This new company's next project was the design and construction of two racing seaplanes for the 1929 Schneider Trophy races, but these were not finished in time to compete. The Nieuport-Delage 62-C1 was a single-seat sesquiplane fighter of partial wood construction, with monocoque fuselage, powered by a Lorraine or Hispano-Suiza engine. The 82-C1 was an all-metal version. Other projects included the N-D 481 single-seat, high-wing aerobatic or sporting monoplane; the N-D 641 mailplane; and the N-D 540 all-metal long-range passenger aircraft, which had jettisonable long-range fuel tanks.

NIEUPORT & GENERAL AIRCRAFT • UK

Formed to licence-manufacture Nieuport fighter designs for the Royal Flying Corps and Royal Naval Air Service. Sopwith Camels and Snipes were also built under subcontract. In 1917 H. P. Folland joined the firm's Cricklewood-based design team and produced the BN.1 fighter, followed by the Nieuport Nighthawk in 1919, which was produced by the Gloster Company (q.v.) when Nieuport & General closed down in 1920.

NIEUPORT-MACCHI • Italy

First became established in the aircraft industry in 1912, building Nieuport designs under licence. During First World War built Nieuport XIs under the designation Nieuport 110 or 11000, as well as Nieuport XVII, Nieuport 27 and 29. Also undertook the manufacture of the French Hanriot HD1 sesquiplane fighter at its Varese plant during 1915.

NIEUSCHLOSS-SICHTIG AEROPLANE WORKS • Hungary

Established at Albertfalva, was building aircraft in 1923 to the design of Bela Oravecz and George Szebeny, including a side-by-side two-seat monoplane evolved by both designers, and a tandem two-seat monoplane.

NIHON HIKOKI KABUSHIKI KAISHA • Japan

Best known as Nippi, original Yokohama works date from 1935. Atsugi works followed for maintenance and repair of Japanese aircraft and of US Navy aircraft in region. Yokohama manufactures components/assemblies for Japanese aircraft and Boeing airliners. Has carried out YS-11EA ECM conversions (first flown 1991).

Nihon NAMC YS-11 twin-turboprop airliner

Left: Nipper Mk.III
single-seat lightplane

NIHON KOKUKI SEIZO KABUSHIKI KAISHA • Japan

Following the decision made in 1956 to develop a medium-sized passenger airliner in Japan, a Transport Aircraft Development Association was established in May 1957, and succeeded in June 1959 by Nihon (better remembered as NAMC), responsible for the development and manufacture of the NAMC YS-11 twin-turboprop airliner (first flown 1962), which was delivered to airlines in the USA, Europe and the Far East, and to the Japanese Air Self Defence Force; for the latter Nihon converted aircraft as electronic countermeasures (ECM) YS-11E.

NIPPER AIRCRAFT LTD. • UK

In 1966 Nipper Aircraft acquired world marketing rights for the Fairey/Tipsy Nipper ultralight aeroplane, which it supplied in completed or kit form. After liquidation in May 1971 Nipper Kits and Components Ltd was formed to support existing aircraft, and continues to market the aircraft in Mk III form as plans and some components.

NIPPI • Japan

See Nihon Hikoki Kabushiki Kaisha.

NIPPON KOKUSAI KOKUKI KOGYU KABUSHIKI KAISHA • Japan

Formed in June 1941 by the amalgamation of Nippon Koku Kogyu KK and Kokusai Kokuki KK, this small manufacturer produced sub components and built the Kokusai Ki 86 biplane trainer, a version of the German Bücker Bü 131 Jungmann.

NOORDUYN AVIATION LTD. • Canada

Designed and manufactured the Norseman eight/ten-seat cargo-transport aircraft, which first flew in 1935 and was delivered to the RCAF and the USAF; with the latter ser-

vice it was designated C-64A. Norsemans were especially popular as bushplanes in the northern regions of Canada and with civilian operators in northern Europe. The Canadian Car & Foundry Company (q.v.) acquired Noorduyn's assets in 1946 and produced an improved Norseman Mark V until 1950. Noorduyn licence-manufactured North American Harvard trainers during Second World War for both the RCAF and RAF.

NORD-AVIATION • France

Nord-Aviation produced a version of the Messerschmitt Bf 108 Taifun, known as the Nord 1002 Pingouin, for the French military service immediately after the Second World War. A tricycle landing gear variant, the Nord 1101 Noralpha, and a redesigned civilian four-seat derivative, the Nord 1203 Norécrin, were also produced in quantity, together with Nord NC-853/856 Norvigie liaison/trainer aircraft delivered to the French army and to aero clubs in the mid-1950s. A batch of N.1402 Noroit twin-engined amphibians were built for the French navy; and the N.2501 Noratlas twin-boom, twin-engined transport, first flown 1952, was subsequently produced in France and Germany. Nord took over the Max Holste Super Broussard twin engined transport design and developed it as the Nord 262 airliner, delivered to European and US airlines and to the French navy by Aérospatiale (q.v.).

Above: Nord 3202 trainer of the French Army

Left: Nord N.2501 Noratlas
twin-engined transport

Below: Nord 262 twin-engine
pressurised light transport

Noorduyn Norseman eight/ten-seat cargo/transport floatplane

NORD GMBH • Germany

Three German aircraft manufacturers, Hamburger Flugzeugbau, Siebel-Werke ATG GmbH and Weser Flugzeugbau GmbH (all q.v.), formed this company to licence-manufacture Nord N.2501 Noratlas transports for the Luftwaffe, the first flying in August 1958.

THE NORMAN AEROPLANE COMPANY LTD. • UK

New name for NDN Aircraft Ltd (q.v.) after 1985 move of factory to Wales. Continued development of Firecracker tandem two-seat turboprop trainer (first flown 1983) that had been proposed for the RAF by Hunting Firecracker Aircraft Ltd (q.v.). Also continued development of Fieldmaster agricultural aircraft and Freelance. See Croplease.

NORMAN AVIATION • Canada

Markets kit for the Karatoo J-6 two-seat monoplane (version of Anglin Karatoo), kit and plans for the two-seat Nordic II cabin monoplane, kit for the Nordic VI-912 two-seater, and kit for single-seat Nordic VII cabin monoplane.

NORSK FLYINDUSTRI AS • Norway

Formed in 1947 to produce the Finnmark 5A amphibian designed by Birger Honningstad (q.v.), which did not progress beyond the prototype stage. Norsk also manufactured metal floats for a variety of aircraft.

North American XB-70 Valkyrie supersonic bomber, used only for research purposes after bomber programme cancellation

North American Vigilante carrier-borne bomber/reconnaissance jet

NORTH AMERICAN AVIATION INC. • USA

Formed originally as a holding company in 1928, North American's first product was the O-47 Army observation aircraft of 1937. The NA-16 Yale two-seat military trainer followed, being developed through fixed- and retractable-landing-gear variants into the T-6 Texan/Harvard trainer which continued in production in Canada until 1954 and served with virtually every non-Communist air arm in the world. North American's best-known aircraft was the P-51 Mustang fighter, one of the best fighter aircraft of the Second World War. Most Mustangs served in Europe, flying escort duties for US Eighth Air Force bombers. Significant aircraft evolved by North American include the B-25 Mitchell twin-engined medium bomber; the B-45 Tornado, the first American four-jet bomber; the F-86 Sabre, the USAF's first swept-wing fighter; the F-100 Super Sabre, the world's first operational fighter capable of supersonic speed in level flight; the T-28 Trojan/Fennec trainer and light ground-attack aircraft which succeeded the T-6; the A-5 Vigilante carrier-based jet bomber/reconnaissance aircraft; the XB-70 Valkyrie supersonic bomber with Mach 3 speed capability; and the X-15 rocket research craft, which attained an altitude of 354,200 ft (107,960 m) in 1963 and was flown at a speed of 4,534mph (7,298km/h) in 1967. In the same year North American merged with the Rockwell Standard Corporation to form North American Rockwell (both q.v.).

Below: North American F-86 Sabre

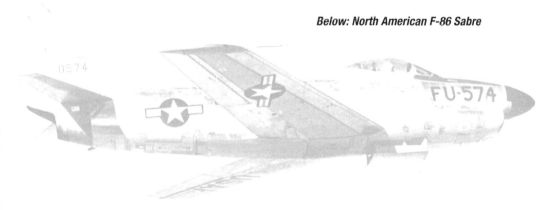

Below: North American Harvard (AT-6 Texan) trainers

North American X-15 hypersonic research aircraft

North American B-25 Mitchell light bomber

North American P-51 Mustang long-range escort/fighter

NORTH AMERICAN ROCKWELL CORPORATION • USA

Following company reorganisation, the former Aero Commander division of Rockwell became part of NAR, and its Shrike, Commander 685 and Turbo Hawk Commander twin-engined business aircraft were marketed under the new company name, together with Quail, Sparrow, Snipe and Thrush Commander agricultural aircraft and the Darter and Lark Commander single-engined lightplanes. The Model 112 Commander lightplane and B-1 swing-wing supersonic bomber projects were started before the company name was changed to Rockwell International in 1973.

NORTHERN AIRCRAFT COMPANY • UK

Known formerly as the Lakes Flying Company (q.v.), operated a seaplane training school at Cockshott, Lake Windermere, and built the Lakes Waterhen and Seabird aircraft.

NORTHERN AIRCRAFT INC. • USA

Purchased from Bellanca all rights, jigs and tooling for the Bellanca 14-19 Cruisemaster four-seat lightplane. The Bellanca Model 14 was one of the classic lightplane designs, since built by several manufacturers. First production of the Northern Cruisemaster started in October 1956. Northern also supplied spares, support and modification kits for Republic Seabee amphibians after a merger with the American Aviation Corporation (see AAC). Became Downer Aircraft Industries Inc (q.v.).

North American P-51D Mustangs on escort duty over Europe in WW2 (US Air Force)

North American F-82 Twin Mustang was develped from 1944 as a long-range bomber escort for the Pacific Theatre of operations and was still active in the Korean war.

NORTHROP • USA

Company had its foundations in California in 1929, when John K. Northrop formed Northrop Aircraft Corporation as a division of United Aircraft and Transport Corporation and built the Alpha (first flown 1930), first all-metal stressed-skin aeroplane, followed by the Beta 300 hp aircraft of 1931, first to exceed 200mph (322kmh). New Northrop Corporation founded after split with United Aircraft and Transport Corporation, with Douglas Aircraft holding a majority shareholding. Producing the Gamma high-speed mailplane in 1933 and other types. Northrop Corporation absorbed into Douglas 1937, and new independent Northrop Aircraft Inc established 1939 to concentrate on military projects, including the A-17 attack-bomber and P-61 Black Widow three-seat, twin-boom nightfighter, first aircraft in this category to be ordered by USAAF. Northrop experiments with the tailless XP-56 interceptor led to a number of post-war flying-wing projects, culminating in eight jet-engined YB-49 flying-wing bomber of 1947. The F-89 Scorpion all-weather fighter entered production two years later, serving USAF and Air National Guard Units until 1963. Extending its activities into other fields, the company changed its name to Northrop Corporation in the year 1959. In May 1994 Grumman (q.v.) and Northrop merged to form Northrop Grumman Corporation (q.v.).

Northrop F-89 Scorpion two-seat fighter

Northrop YB-49 flying-wing bomber

Northrop's final pre-merger production aircraft included the F-5E/F Tiger II lightweight tactical jet fighter/fighter trainer, developed with US Government funding mainly for export as International Fighter Aircraft (first F-5E flown August 1972), derived from the 1959 N-156 prototype and early production F-5A/B Freedom Fighters built for supply under Military Assistance Programmes. The T-38 Talon two-seat advanced trainer variant of N-156 for the USAF (first flown April 1959) went out of production in 1972 after 1,187 had been built, but these are being modernised to T-38C standard for redelivery from 1999 by Northrop Grumman. Northrop developed the YF-17 Cobra for competition against the Lockheed YF-16 for the USAF's Lightweight Fighter Programme, but lost and became principal subcontractor to McDonnell Douglas on a proposed carrierborne naval fighter derivative. This eventually entered production as the carrier- and land-based F/A-18 Hornet (see McDonnell Douglas and Boeing). Finally developed the B-2 Spirit subsonic strategic stealth bomber (first flown July 1989) for the USAF (see Northrop Grumman Corporation).

NORTHROP GRUMMAN • USA

In May 1994 Grumman (q.v.) and Northrop (q.v.) merged to form Northrop Grumman Corporation. Two of the five main divisions are Commercial Aircraft, to construct aerostructures and components for the commercial aircraft of other companies and engines, and Military Aircraft Systems, working on B-2 and all other Northrop Grumman aircraft production and modernisation programmes,

and principal subcontractor to Boeing on Hornet. Delivered 21 B-2A Spirit stealth bombers, achieving initial operational capability with the USAF in April 1997 and full capability with the 715th Bomb Squadron in 1999. Undertakes F-5/T-38 modernisation, F-14 work, EA-6B Prowler remanufacturing, production of E-2C Hawkeye in latest

Hawkeye 2000 form (first flown April 1998; see Grumman entry for earlier development and production of E-2), and production of E-8C Joint STARS as joint USAF and US Army co-operation programme for an airborne surveillance and target acquisition system (first flown August 1995 for first production E-8C).

Northrop P-61 Black Widow night fighter, with Curtis P-40K Warhawk behind

Northrop Delta 8-passenger high-speed transport

Northrop T-38 Talon fighters

Northrop Grumman B-2A Spirit stealth bomber

NUD • Turkey

Established in 1937 at Istanbul, NUD built gliders under licence and produced the two-seat NU D.36 training biplane and a prototype NU D.38 high-wing, twin-engined six-pasenger airliner.

NURI DEMIRAG TAYYARE FABRIKASI • Turkey

see NUD.

NV NEDERLANDSCHE VLIEGTUIGENFABRIEK

see NV Koninklijke Nederlanse Vliegtuigenfabriek Fokker.

NYGE-AERO • Sweden

Produced VLA-1 Sparrow in 1984 as very light two-seat monoplane with pusher propeller.

Northrop Grumman E-8C Joint STARS airborne surveillance and target acquisition system

Northrop Grumman E-2C Hawkeye AEW&C aircraft in US Navy service

OAKLAND AIRMOTIVE • USA

California-based company specialised in civilian executive transport conversions of surplus US Navy Lockheed PV-2 Harpoon patrol bombers. The resultant Oakland Centaurus seated 8/14 passengers and was offered as a high-speed corporate transport in the late 1950s and early 1960s. A twin-engined conversion of the Beechcraft Bonanza was also completed to order, and renamed Oakland Super V.

OAKLEY LTD. • UK

Oakley controlled the Ilford Aeroplane Works, which undertook the installation of Curtiss engines in 1916. In 1917 the company was contracted to build a batch of 25 Sopwith Triplanes, but only three were completed before the aircraft became obsolescent. Also undertook component manufacture and aircraft repair work during First World War.

OBERLERCHNER, JOSEPH • Austria

A former manufacturer of sailplanes, Oberlerchner flew a prototype all-wood two-seat JOB 5 lightplane in 1958. The developed JOB 15 four-seater, which had metal/wood/glassfibre construction, entered production in 1961, powered by a Lycoming engine. It remains in service with Austrian and other European aero clubs, especially as a glider tug.

OEFFAG • Austria

Oesterreichische Flugzeug-Fabrik AG was a subcontractor in the First World War to the German Albatros-Werke (q.v.) producing its Albatros D.II, D.III and D.V series scouts, together with licence-manufactured Austro-Daimler engines.

OERTZ-WERKE GMBH • Germany

Max Oertz, an established builder of yachts, entered the aircraft business in 1911. The company produced three examples of the mid-wing M1911-12 monoplane and a single developed M1912-13 model.

OESTERREICHISCHE-UNGARISCHE FLUGZEUGFABRIK • Austria

A subsidiary of the German Aviatik company (q.v.), this manufacturer built Aviatik B.I and B.II two-seat reconnaissance aircraft for the Austro-Hungarian Flying Service and worked on a single-seat scout version of the Aviatik C.I. This aeroplane, the D.I. Berg-Scout, was at first prone to wing failures under load, but eventually ran to 11 production batches.

Oakland Airmotive conversion of the Beechcraft Bonanza

OGDEN • USA

Established in 1929, Ogden's only product was the trimotor Osprey cabin monoplane, offered in three versions: the Model C, which carried two crew and four passengers (seven passengers if the lavatory was removed), the Model PB with Menasco B4 engines, and the Model PC with Menasco Pirate engines.

OGMA • Portugal

Founded in 1918 as a department of the Portuguese Air Force, Oficinas Gerais de Material Aeronáutico has been responsible for the licence-production or assembly of many military aircraft types, including the Vickers Valparaiso, Avro 626 Cadet, de Havilland Tiger Moth, Morane-Saulnier MS.233, de Havilland Chipmunk, Auster D.4 and D.6 and Dornier Do 27. Made components for Aérospatiale SA-315B Lama and SA-318 Puma helicopters. Offers maintenance and repair facilities for aircraft, avionics and engines.

OKAMURA • Japan

This branch of Nihon aircraft works built the N52 two-seat lightplane in 1952, and collaborated with Tokyo University students in the design and construction of a two-seat sailplane.

OK FLY SRO • Czech Republic

Producer of hang glider skins and windsurfer sails. Also expected to put its Lesus side-by-side two-seat monoplane into production.

OMAC INC • USA

Established at Reno in 1977 to produce OMAC 1 business aircraft with pusher turboprop engine (first flown 1981). Second prototype served as testbed for improved Laser 300 version; production prototype flew July 1988, but further development halted soon after owing to funding difficulties.

Oberlerchner JOB 15-150 four-seat lightplane

Omega BS-12D four-seat twin-engined helicopter

OMAREAL • Brazil

Oficina de Manutenco e Recuperaceo de Avioes Ltda, the Brazilian maintenance and overhaul facility based at Sao Paulo, acquired manufacturing rights to the Casmuniz 52 twin-engined five-seat lightplane in 1955. Designed and built by Cassio Muniz SA (q.v.), the Casmuniz 52 was intended for easy construction from single-curvature metal to facilitate field repair in bush operations. OMAREAL took over the flight testing of the sole prototype, but no production ensued.

OMEGA AIRCRAFT CORPORATION • USA

Founded 1953 as a subsidiary of Allied Aero Industries for further development of the Sznycer-Gottlieb SG VI helicopter. The Omega BS-12 four-seat, twin-engined heli-

copter flew in 1956, and was succeeded by the BS-12D with more powerful engines and the 1963 BS-12D3S supercharged version. Production was to have started in 1964, when all development was suspended after completion of four prototypes.

O'NEILL AIRPLANE COMPANY INC. • USA

Formed 1962 to develop the Waco Model W Aristocrat design, for which all rights were acquired. Two versions were evolved, the Model W Winner, which was to have been a serious production machine, and the Aristocrat II for amateur construction. The O'Neill Pea Pod canard design was proposed also, but all activity on the Aristocraft terminated in 1974. Designed eight-seat Model J Magnum with unusual four-wheel undercarriage in 1980s. Further developed Magnum V8 six-seater, featuring swing tail for

loading cargo, which can be built from plans and some available components.

ONG AIRCRAFT CORPORATION • USA

This Kansas City-based company manufactured the Ong Model M-32W high-wing monoplane, powered by a Warner Super Scarab engine, before America's entry into the Second World War.

ON MARK ENGINEERING COMPANY • USA

Formed 1954 as a specialist maintenance and modification contractor for Douglas B-26 Invader bombers, developing high-speed executive transport and heavily-armed counterinsurgency versions. The On Mark Marketeer was a six/eight-seat corporate transport based on the B-26 air-

On Mark Marksman pressurised light transport

Orenco Model `D' single-seat biplane fighter

frame. The externally similar Marksman had a pressurised cabin. A B-26K Counter Invader was developed for the USAF's Tactical Air Command. In 1962 Mark was responsible for the first Pregnant Guppy conversions of the Boeing Stratocruiser, on behalf of Aero Spacelines Inc (q.v.), for the transportation of space rockets and other bulky cargo.

OPTICA INDUSTRIES LTD • UK

Took over Optica observation aircraft from Edgley (q.v.) following purchase from receiver by A. Haikney of Aero-Docks in 1985 and formation of this company to restart production in 1986. Fire of January 1987 destroyed seven finished Opticas and hangar. Company renamed Brooklands Aircraft Company Ltd (q.v.).

ORCA AIRCRAFT LTD • UK

Purchased SAH-1 trainer from Trago Mills but went into administration 1989. SAH-1 became Sprint when purchased by Lovaux/FLS Aerospace (q.v.).

ORENCO • USA

Ordnance Engineering Corporation's Model 'D' single-seat biplane fighter was the first such aircraft of all-American design. Four wooden prototypes powered by 300 hp Wright-Hispano engines were built, followed by 50 production aircraft manufactured under licence by the Curtiss company.

ORLANDO HELICOPTER AIRWAYS INC • USA

Founded 1964 and undertook remanufacture of Sikorsky S-55 and S-58 helicopters into range of new models for civil/military uses.

ORLOGSVAERFTET • Denmark

The Royal Danish Naval Dockyard (Orlogsvaerftet) constructed 12 Hawker Danecocks under licence in 1927/1928. A single-seat biplane fighter derived from the Hawker Woodcock, the Danecock was armed with two 7.7 mm Madsen machine-guns. It remained in service until

Left: Orenco F-4 four-seat tourer or mailplane

1937 with the Royal Danish Air Force, which designated it the L.B.II Dankok.

OSPREY AIRCRAFT • USA

The original Osprey amphibian was designed by George Pereira; current Osprey 2 two-seat amphibian first flew 1973 and plans and kits are available to allow amateur construction. Also marketed as plans and kits is the Osprey GP-4, a two-seat monoplane first flown in 1984.

OSRODEK KONSTRUCKCJI LOTNICZYCH • Poland

Formed 1957 by the Polish Minister of Heavy Industry, to take over all design activities formerly conducted by the Polish Aviation Institute. First design was the MD-12 four-engined feederliner/photo-survey aircraft, which flew in 1962. A developed version of Russian Yak-12, known as the PZL-101 Gawron (Rook), has been produced in quantity for agricultural and air-ambulance duties. Now superseded by the PZL-104 Wilga (Thrush), which is offered for agricultural, air-ambulance, transport, glider-tug and parachute roles, and has been widely exported. Licence production is under way in Indonesia. Deliveries of the TS-11 Iskra (Spark) two-seat aerobatic jet trainer to the Polish Air Force began in 1963. (See also Panstwowe Zaklady Lotnicze.)

OTTAWA CAR AND AIRCRAFT LTD • Canada

This pre-war manufacturer of street-cars entered the aircraft industry as Canadian agent for Armstrong Whitworth, Avro and Armstrong Siddeley, and built Avro Tutor and Prefect trainers and Armstrong Whitworth Atlas and Siskin fighters for the RCAF. During Second World War parts for Hampden bombers, Hawker Hurricanes and Avro Ansons

Above: Osprey GP.4 prototype

were manufactured, and Anson airframes shipped from England were assembled.

OTTO WERKE • Germany

Gustav Otto Flugmaschinenwerke built six M1912 two-seat biplane observation aircraft for the German Army in 1912. The aircraft was broadly similar to the French Caudron G series.

OUEST AVIATION • France

Formed in 1936, incorporating factories of Marcel Bloch, Blériot and Loiré et Olivier, subsequently merging with SNCASO (all q.v.) and changing name to Ouest Aviation in 1956. Original designs included S.O.94R twin-engined trainer; S.O.95 Corse and S.O.30 Bretagne military transports; S.O.4050 Vautour twin-jet bomber; and the S.O.9000 Trident. The S.O.1221 Djinn two-seat helicopter was produced, and Vertol H-21 helicopters were manu-

factured under licence for the French Army. Ouest became part of Aérospatiale (q.v.).

Right: Ouest Aviation S.O.4050 Vautour

PACIFIC AEROSPACE CORPORATION LTD. • New Zealand

Established 1982, following the purchase of the assets of New Zealand Aerospace Industries (q.v.). Currently markets the CT/4E Airtrainer two/three-seat training lightplane (first flown 1972 in original form, and 1991 in present CT/4E form); piston-engined FU24-954 Fletcher suited to agricultural, firefighting and many other utility roles, or for carrying six/eight passengers when using optional pas-

senger kit, or two stretchers and two sitting casualties in an air-ambulance role (first flown 1954); and CR-750 Cresco turboprop development of the FU24 (first flown 1979). Company also manufactures components/assemblies for Airbus and Boeing aircraft.

PAC • USA

see Pacific Airmotive Corporation.

PACAERO • USA

Formed in 1957 at Santa Monica, California, as a subsidiary of Pacific Airmotive Corporation (q.v.) to continue manufacture of the Learstar Executive transport, with two Wright Cyclone engines. PacAero also carried out modifications to other types, including conversion of North American T-28 trainers to Nomad standard with a bigger engine. Dissolved and merged with Pacific Airmotive Corporation's Aircraft Division in early 1960s.

Pacific Airmotive Tradewind, a conversion of the Beech 18

Pacific Aerospace Corporation CR-750 Cresco for agricultural work

Packard-Le Pére LUSAC-11 fighter

PACIFIC AEROSYSTEM INC. • USA

Markets kits for the Sky Arrow two-seat high-wing monoplane, also produced in Italy by III.

PACIFIC AIRMOTIVE CORPORATION • USA

This company continued the work of PacAero (q.v.). It also produced a conversion of the Beech 18 known as the Tradewind, with single fin and rudder, tricycle landing gear and improved avionics. PAC also has considerable agency agreements and is heavily involved in modification, repair and maintenance contracts, and in 1968 took over the R.J. Enstrom Corporation (q.v.), manufacturer of light helicopters. Helicopter production was stopped in 1970 when the Purex Corporation, owner of Pacific Airmotive Corporation, began to reduce its aviation commitments.

PACIFIC AIRPLANE & SUPPLY CO. • USA

Company founded in early 1920s at Los Angeles, California. First product was the Hawk six-seat twin-engined commercial biplane. Built Model C-1 single-seat racing monoplane in 1921, with 90 hp Curtiss OX-5 engine.

PACKARD-LE PERE • USA

Captain Le Père of the French Aviation mission to the USA designed a two-seat fighter, the LUSAC-11 (Le Père United States Army Combat), which was built by the Packard Motor Car Company in 1918. Thirty LUSAC-11s with Liberty engines and three LUSAC-21s with Bugatti engines were built, but contracts for quantity production were cancelled at end of First World War.

PAKISTAN AERONAUTICAL COMPLEX • Pakistan

Established 1978. Comprises four factories: Aircraft Manufacturing Factory constructs the Saab MFI 17 Safari Supporter under licence as the Mushshak and Super Mushshak, and is partnered with Hongdu and AVIC of China in developing and producing the K-8 Karakorum jet trainer and light attack aircraft. Other factories are Kamra Avionics and Radar Factory, Mirage Rebuild Factory and F-6 Rebuild Factory (the last being the oldest factory of the group), for manufacturing components and overhauling Pakistan's Chinese-supplied combat aircraft.

Pakistan Aeronautical Complex Mushshak with canopy lifted

Early example of K-8 Karakorum jet, developed by China/Pakistan

PANAVIA AIRCRAFT GMBH • International

Until delivery of the final aircraft in 1998, Panavia's Tornado Mach 2+ two-seat variable-geometry multirole combat aircraft was Europe's most important military aircraft programme. Originally a joint venture by British Aerospace (UK), MBB (West Germany) and Aeritalia (Italy) (all q.v.) – now Alenia of Italy (15 per cent), Daimler-Benz Aerospace (42.5 per cent) and British Aerospace (42.5 per cent) – the project has been managed by the specially formed Panavia Aircraft GmbH, based in Germany. Orders covered 781 production IDS Tornadoes for interdictor strike and ECRs for electronic combat and reconnaissance, as 228 IDSs for the RAF, 210 IDS and 35 ECR for the Luftwaffe, 112 IDSs for the German Navy, 99 IDSs for the Italian Air Force, and 96 IDSs for Saudi Arabia.

The first prototype flew 14 August 1974, and deliveries began June 1979, with a Trinational Tornado Training Establishment being opened in 1981 to train crews from all participating countries. An air defence variant (ADV) of Tornado first flew in October 1979, developed specifically for the RAF as a long-range air defence interceptor, changes including GEC-Marconi Foxhunter multimode radar in place of the IDS's ground-mapping radar and terrain-following radar, although some 80 per cent commonality was achieved between the types. RAF received 170 ADVs, of which 152 were in current F.Mk 3 improved form. Saudi Arabia was the only other customer, having 24.

Panavia Tornado IDS in latest RAF GR. Mk 4 form, as upgrade of Mk 1

RAF Panavia Tornado F Mk 3 air defence variant flying over River Kwai

Pander & Zonen EH-120 Luxe two-seat sesquiplane

PANDER & ZONEN • Netherlands

Woodworking company which took up aircraft construction in early 1920s, with Model D single-seat monoplane and Model E two-seat sesquiplane. Concentrated on special designs rather than mass production, but Pander aircraft were adopted by Dutch flying clubs. Built Postjager tri-motor low-wing mailplane in 1934.

PANEK/MATTLENER • Germany

Offers kits to construct PUL 10 two-seat flying-wing monoplane, derived from Canadian Ultraflight Lazair and PUL 9 and formerly known as Nike Aerdelta PUL 10 in Italy.

PANSTWOWE ZAKLADY LOTNICZE • Poland

Founded January 1928. As Poland's National Aircraft Establishment, built the P.1 single-seat fighter monoplane with Hispano-Suiza engine in 1929-1930, and subsequently the famous P.11 single-seat fighter and P.19 cabin monoplane. The PZL Los medium bomber of 1937 was followed by the Wojk twin-engined fighter, Sum light

PZL P.11 fighter, which fought a grim defensive action in WW2

bomber and Mewa reconnaissance monoplane by the beginning of Second World War. Factories at Warsaw-Okecie (original) and Mielec, latter used by occupying Germans as forced-labour Heinkel factory 1940-44. See PZL.

PZL P.37 Loś monoplane bomber prototype

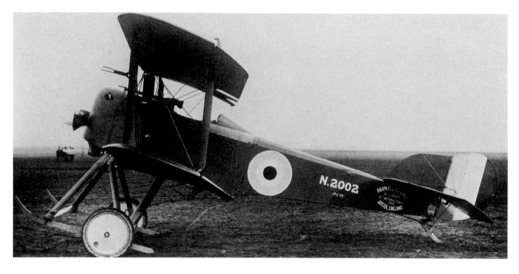

Parnall P.1, a Parnall-built version of the Fairey Hamble Baby

Parnall Prawn experimental flying-boat

PAPA 51 INC. • USA

Has produced kits to build Thunder Mustang two-seat 75 per cent-scale representation of P-51 fighter, first flown 1996.

PARAGON • UK

Formed early 1960s at Thruxton Aerodrome near Andover, Hampshire, from the earlier Jackaroo Aircraft Ltd (q.v.), for conversion of standard two-seat Tiger Moth biplanes to four-seat configuration by inserting a new wider centre fuselage and extending the top wing centre section. 18 Jackaroo conversions were carried out by the company, which also designed a light monoplane, the Paragon (subsequently Paladin), but this was not built. Assets acquired 1964 by Hampshire School of Flying.

PARAMOUNT AIRCRAFT CORPORATION • USA

Founded in 1928 at Saginaw, Michigan. Built Cabinaire four-seat cabin biplane with 165 hp Wright Whirlwind engine.

PARAPLANE CORPORATION • USA

Produces kits for single-seat powered parachutes with trikes, with single and twin engine arrangements.

PARASCENDER TECHNOLOGIES INC. • USA

Offers kits for its single- and two-seat powered parachutes with trikes, including an agricultural spraying version.

PARKER, CALVIN • USA

Offers plans and raw material kits to construct the Teenie Two single-seat monoplane.

PARKS AIRCRAFT INC. • USA

A division of the Detroit Aircraft Corporation (q.v.) by 1930, Parks had built training aircraft for its own companies, Parks Air College and Parks Air Lines. After the Detroit takeover, Parks aircraft were built by Ryan (q.v.). Following Ryan's demise the Park name was revived for the P-1H biplane built by Hammond (q.v.).

Parnall Plover single-seat carrier-based fighter

PARNALL & SONS • UK

Woodworking firm in Bristol which built seaplanes in First World War to War Office specifications. Subsequently taken over by W. T. Avery and abandoned aircraft production (but see next entry).

PARNALL, GEORGE, & CO. • UK

After the take-over of Parnall & Sons (q.v.) by W. T. Avery, George Parnall founded his own company with personnel from the former aircraft division of Parnall & Sons to continue aircraft manufacture under government contract. First product was the Puffin, a military central-float amphibian with a single Napier engine. It was followed by a wide variety of types including the Possum twin-engine triplane, Plover fighter, Pixie ultralight, Peto submarine-borne scout and Elf light biplane. Built Hendy 302 monoplane for Henderson Aircraft Company (q.v.) in 1930. Parnall Aircraft Ltd formed in 1935 to take over aircraft business and acquire patents, rights, etc. of aircraft armament firm Nash & Thompson Ltd and similar patents and rights of Hendy. Concerned with turrets and aircraft armament in Second World War; no longer produced aircraft.

PARQUE DE AERONAUTICA • Brazil

The works at Rio de Janeiro's military air base built Waco biplanes for Brazilian Air Force mail services in late 1930s, plus Muniz two-seat training monoplane.

PARTENAVIA COSTRUZIONI AERONAUTICHE SPA • Italy

A Naples company formed in 1949 to build series of light aircraft. First to enter production was the P-57 Fachiro of 1957, a four-seat high-wing monoplane with Lycoming engine. This was followed by various developments includ-

Partenavia Observer, modified from the standard P.68

ing the P.64 Oscar (first flown April 1965), also produced in South Africa under licence as the RSA.200 by AFIC (Pty) Ltd (q.v.), and the P.66 Charlie. Partenavia's first twin was the P.68 six-seat light transport, first flown in May 1970. It was subsequently placed into production in several forms, including the Observer 2 for observation and patrol. AP.68 TP-600 Viator 11-seat transport followed in March 1985. New projects in the early 1990s included PD.93 Idea four-seat trainer and utility monoplane, but in March 1998 Partenavia ceased work and its P.68 series was bought via auction by VulcanAir SpA (q.v.).

PASOTTI SpA • Italy

In early 1950s built four-seat F.6 Airone cabin monoplane with two Lycoming engines, followed by a single-engine version, the F-9 Sparviero, with Hirth engine.

PASPED AIRCRAFT COMPANY • USA

Based at Glendale, California. Built Skylark two-seat light cabin monoplane in mid-1930s, with 125 hp Warner Scarab engine; there was no further development.

PAYEN • France

Engineer engaged in delta-wing aircraft research; built two deltas before Second World War, and in 1954 flew PA-49 all-wood delta research aircraft powered by one Turboméca Pallas gas turbine. Built several more experimental aircraft in early 1970s.

Partenavia P.68 Victor six-seat light transport

Partenavia P.59 Jolly high-wing monoplane

Below: Partenavia aircraft outside factory, showing P.68s, Oscars and Observer

Pazmany PL-1 sportsplane, built subsequently as military trainer

Pemberton-Billing P.B.9 single-seat scout biplane

PAXMAN'S NORTHERN LITE • Canada

Offers plans and kit to build Aerocraft Viper two-seat cabin monoplane.

PAZMANY AIRCRAFT CORPORATION • USA

Founded as L. Pazmany & Associates at San Diego, California; produced the PL-1 two-seat light aircraft with Continental engine in 1962. A production version, the PL-2, had a higher-powered engine. A number of PL-1s built by the Chinese Nationalist Air Force as basic trainers, and examples of the PL-2 by the air forces of Indonesia, Korea, Thailand and Vietnam. PL-2 two-seater remains available in plans form, as are the single-seat PL-4A (first flown 1972), which has been built by air cadets in Argentina and Canada, and PL-9 Stork two-seater (represents Second World War Fieseler Storch).

PC FLIGHT • Germany

Offers kits to construct Pretty Flight two-seat high-wing cabin microlight.

P.C. HELICOPTER CORPORATION • USA

see Gyrodyne.

PEGAS • Russia

Undertaking development of the Chirok three-seat light amphibian, featuring twin piston engines and a 'joined' inverted-vee tail unit.

PEGASE AERO ENR • Canada

Offers plans and kits to build Pegazaire-100 STOL side-by-side two-seat cabin monoplane.

PEGASUS AVIATION • UK

Markets the AX2000 two-seat very light monoplane and several flex-wing microlights as the single-seat Chaser-S, two-seat Quantum Sport and Supersport, two-seat Quantum LITE Basic 503TC and two-seat Quasar.

PEGLER & COMPANY LTD. • UK

Doncaster, Yorkshire, company which built Sopwith Cuckoo torpedo-bombers under subcontract in 1918.

PEGNA & BONMARTINI • Italy

Formed in early 1920s in Rome to take over aeronautical work of Pegna-Rossi-Bastianelli, comprising the P.R.B. flying-boat and a small sporting monoplane. Company taken over by Piaggio (q.v.).

PEMBERTON-BILLING LTD. • UK

Noel Pemberton Billing began aeronautical experiments in 1908 with a primitive monoplane. Acquiring a factory at Woolston, Southampton, in 1913, he began to design and build marine aircraft, his P.B.1 biplane flying-boat being exhibited at the 1914 Olympia Show, but not flown. Company registered June 1914. At outbreak of First World War in 1914 designed, built and flew P.B.9 single-seat scout biplane in nine days. The P.B.29E night patrol quadruplane of 1915, built in seven weeks from beginning of design, paved the way for the improved version, the P.B.31E Nighthawk. By the time this had flown the company had been renamed Supermarine Aviation Works (q.v.).

PENA, LOUIS • France

Louis Pena offers plans to construct Bilouis 01 tandem two-seat aerobatic monoplane, Bilouis Dahu four-seat tourer and Capena 01 single-seat aerobatic monoplane.

PENNSYLVANIA AIRCRAFT SYNDICATE • USA

Formed in early 1930s to develop a rotary-wing aircraft, designed in Germany in 1926 by Walter Rieseler and Walter Kreiser, and further developed in the USA by E. Burke Wilford. The Wilford Gyroplane, powered by a Kinner R-5 engine, accumulated a considerable amount of test flying.

PERCH INC. • USA

Produced the Perch Nolan 51-HJ single-seat homebuilt helicopter, now developed into the Eagle's Perch (q.v.).

PERCIVAL AIRCRAFT LTD. • UK

Formed in 1932 by E. W. Percival and E. W. B. Leake at Gravesend, Kent, moving to Luton, Bedfordshire, in 1937. Built series of successful light aircraft beginning with the single-engine Gull and later twin-engine Q-6 six/seven-seat cabin monoplane. Percival Gulls were used for a number of record-breaking flights, and the type was developed into the Proctor light communications aircraft. Several Mew Gull racers were built in the late 1930s. After Second World War, production of the Proctor continued for civilian customers, while a new three-seat trainer, the Pren-

Percival Mew Gull single-seat racing monoplane

Percival Proctor I communications aircraft

tice, appeared in 1946 and was built in quantity for the RAF and several overseas air forces. It was followed by the Provost trainer, ordered for the RAF in 1951. Following the experimental Merganser light transport of 1946, a larger version, the Prince, flew in 1948 and was produced in civil and military versions. The company's name was changed in 1954 to Hunting Percival Aircraft (q.v.).

PEREGRINE FLIGHT INTERNATIONAL • USA

Rights to BD-10 jet purchased from Bede Jet Corporation 1995, with redesignated factory-production BD-10 used as PJ-1 prototype (first flown November 1994) and PJ-2 version for certification flying June 1995. See Vortex Aircraft Company.

PERFORMANCE AIRCRAFT • USA

First flew in 1996 the Legend two-seat composites monoplane, available in kit form.

PERFORMANCE ENGINEERING • USA

Offers kits to build Mountain Goat two-seat bush plane.

PETLYAKOV, V.M. • USSR

Russian designer who headed a bureau before and during Second World War. Notable designs were the PE-2 light bomber and PE-8 four-engined heavy bomber, the latter a development of the 1936 ANT-42 with more powerful engines. The PE-8 entered service in 1941.

PETROLINI • Argentine

Took over production of El Boyero two-seat light monoplane from the Instituto Aerotécnico in late 1940s, and built 160 to government contracts for flying clubs and schools.

PETTERS LTD. • UK

Yeovil engineering company which started producing Short seaplanes to Admiralty contract in 1915 at its new factory, known as the Westland Aircraft Works. The company was renamed Westland Aircraft (q.v.) in 1935.

PEYRET, LOUSE • France

Louis Peyret began aircraft construction with a tandem-wing glider, winning a *Daily Mail* £1,000 prize in 1922. Following year he produced a light aeroplane, which subsequently crashed, and later a light seaplane for M. Le Prieur, the Albessard monoplane and the Mauboussin P.M.4 single-seat monoplane. Peyret became technical manager of Avions Mauboussin (q.v.).

PFALZ FLUGZEUGWERKE GMBH • Germany

Founded at Speyer-am-Rhein in 1913, company built the Otto biplane with Rapp engine in First World War, and subsequently obtained a licence to build Morane parasol monoplanes. Later built a series of single-seat biplane fighters, most notably the D.III and D.XII. Pfalz aircraft manufacture came to an end when the Armistice was signed.

PHALANX ORGANIZATION INC. • USA

Founded to develop MP-18 Dragon small-size and turbofan-powered combat aircraft of very unusual and futuristic design, capable of VTOL flight using vectoring nozzles. Prototype was under construction in mid-1980s, but no flight is known.

Pfalz D.III, this company's first single-seat fighter

Petlyakov PE-8 four-engined heavy bomber

Phillips & Powis/Miles Mohawk built for Charles Lindbergh

Phillips & Powis/Miles Master trainer prototype

PHEASANT AIRCRAFT COMPANY • USA

Founded 1927 at Fond du Lac, Wisconsin, company's first product in mid-1920s was Pheasant three-seat commercial biplane with 90 hp Curtiss OX-5 engine, followed by Traveler single-seat cabin monoplane.

PHANTOM SPORT AIRPLANE CORPORATION • USA

Offers kits to build single- and two-seat versions of the Phantom microlight.

PHILIPPINE AIRCRAFT COMPANY INC. • Philippines

Constructed version of Denny Kitfox as Skyfox for marketing in Western Pacific region.

PHILIPPINE AEROSPACE DEVELOPMENT CORPORATION • Philippines

Government corporation established in 1973 to promote development of a Philippines aerospace industry. Aircraft manufacture was undertaken until 1982 by a subsidiary company, National Aero Manufacturing Corporation (q.v.). Assembled 44 MBB BO 105 helicopters and 67 Britten-Norman Islanders. A four-seat utility high-wing monoplane powered by a 300 hp Textron Lycoming engine was designed (see National Aero Manufacturing Corporation entry). Assembled 24 SIAI-Marchetti S211 jet trainers, 18 SF.260TP turboprop trainers and eight Lancair lightplanes. Became partner in Eurocopter Philippines to assemble Eurocopter helicopters from kits (plus sales and maintenance). Philippine Helicopter Services Inc subsidiary maintains BO 105s and MD 500s.

PHILIPPINE AIR FORCE • Philippines

Self Reliance Development Wing built prototype of Lycoming powered three-seat primary trainer, the XT-001.

Very similar to Italian SIAI SF.260, of which 32 were bought for the PAF. The SRDW also acquired prototype of American Jet Industries' Super Pinto COIN aircraft.

PHILLIPS & POWIS AIRCRAFT LTD. • UK

Formed in 1935 to take over aircraft manufacturing business operated by Phillips & Powis Aircraft (Reading) Ltd, which had produced the initial Miles Hawk series of light aircraft. Name changed 1943 to Miles Aircraft (q.v.).

PHILLIPS AVIATION CO. • USA

Founded at end of 1930s in Los Angeles, California, to continue development of light two-seat monoplane, the Phillips I-B, designed originally by Aero Engineering Corporation. Also built CT-1 two-seat biplane.

PHOENIX DYNAMO • UK

Bradford company which became Admiralty contractor in First World War for construction of Short 184 seaplanes, Short landplane bombers, Maurice Farman Longhorns and a pair of Armstrong Whitworth F.K.10 quadraplanes. Later built Felixstowe F.3 and F.5 flying-boats and two Phoenix P.5 Cork flying-boats. Phoenix became part of the English Electric Co Ltd (q.v.) in 1918 and continued development of flying-boats, initially the P.5 Kingston.

PHÖNIX-AVIATECHNICA LTD. • International

Founded 1991 as joint Bulgarian/Russian company to develop LKhS twin-engined light utility biplane.

PHÖNIX FLUGZEUGWERFT GMBH • Austria

This company manufactured a series of Phönix single-seat fighter aircraft powered by Austro-Daimler engines. The DI and DII were flown during First World War by the Austro-Hungarian Flying Service, a few being fitted with cameras for high-speed aerial photo-reconnaissance work. Seventeen of the final batch of 122 Phönix DIIs were completed as improved DIII variants and transferred to the Swedish Army Air Service after the war.

PIAGGIO, RINALDO • Italy

SA Piaggio & Co, an engineering and shipbuilding company, produced some Caproni aircraft and parts during the First World War, but subsequently abandoned aircraft manufacture until it took over Pegna & Bonmartini (q.v.) in 1923. First product was the Piaggio-Pegna pursuit monoplane with Hispano-Suiza engine. Later was associated with Società di Costruzioni Meccaniche Aeronàutiche in licence-construction of Dornier Wal flying-boats. Built P.32 twin-engined heavy bomber at end of 1930s and several four-engined P.108 heavy bombers during Second World War.

Resumed aeronautical work in late 1946 with conversion of Dakotas for airline service. Built P.136 five-seat

Piaggio P.108B, Italy's only heavy bomber of WW2

Piasecki VZ-8P VTOL test rig

twin-engined amphibian, prototype flying in 1948, followed by a series of trainers for the Italian Air Force; the P.149 was also licence-built by Focke-Wulf in Germany. Produced the P.166 executive transport in 1957, with two Lycoming engines and pusher propellers, as with the P.136; P.166-DL3 turboprop variant later developed and produced, with final P.166-DL3-SEM Maritime variant for search and surveillance, coastal patrol and other roles still available in 1998, but only to special order. Signed agreement with US Douglas company (q.v.) in 1961 for joint development of light utility aircraft, first flown in 1964. Designated PD.808 and powered by two Bristol Siddeley Viper turbojets, only a small number was built.

The present Rinaldo Piaggio company was formed in February 1964 as a separate concern, but in 1994 was put under insolvency protection; 51 per cent shareholding in the company was purchased by Tushav, a Turkish holding company, in mid-1998, and protection was there-after lifted. P.180 Avanti twin-pusher turboprop business aircraft flown September 1986, but only 43 production aircraft ordered; turbofan derivative may be developed. Has manufactured components for Aeritalia/Alenia, AMX International, Dassault and Panavia.

PIASECKI AIRCRAFT CORPORATION • USA

Formed June 1955 by Frank Piasecki, who was concerned in development of vertical-lift aircraft and flew the Model 59K Sky-Car flying jeep with an Artouste turboshaft engine in 1958 under a US Army contract. Technical interchange agreements signed with Breguet Aviation (q.v.) in 1957 included sales rights for that company's STOL transports in the USA and Canada, but these were dropped in 1962. Also provided engineering assistance to Agusta from 1960 for the AZ-101G and AZ-105 helicopters. Built prototype of PiAC 16H-1C Pathfinder compound helicopter in 1962, continuing development under a US Navy contract, but no

Piaggio P.166C 13-seat light transport

Piaggio P.166-DL3-SEM Maritime

Above: Piasecki Heli-Stat during roll-out in 1985

production followed. Researched the possibility of linking helicopter and aerostat principles with the proposed Heli-Stat. Recent work includes developing vectored-thrust ducted propeller system for attack helicopters under US Army contract, definition of a possible US Marine Corps medium-lift replacement type, and marketing the PZL-Swidnik W-3A in the Americas and Pacific Rim regions.

PIASECKI HELICOPTER CORPORATION • USA

Formed in 1946 from the P-V Engineering Forum which had completed several rotary-wing contracts for NACA and the US Navy. The latter ordered an XHRP-1 helicopter which flew in 1945; following successful tests it was placed in production. Further orders followed for XHJP-1 tandem-rotor helicopters for USN shipboard operations and the large XH-16, which had a fuselage of DC-4 size. In 1956 the company became Vertol Aircraft Corporation (q.v.).

PIDEK INDUSTRIES • Canada

Former Polish Air Force pilot Joseph Pidek designed and built J.P.2B two-seat ultralight helicopter at Vancouver in 1962. The aircraft was not developed beyond prototype stage.

PIEL AVIATION SA • France

See Avions Claude Piel.

Piasecki PiAC 16H-1 Pathfinder compound helicopter

Piasecki PV-3/US Navy HRP-1

Piasecki HUP-2 Retreiver, delivered to US Navy in early 1950s for plane guard and utility work

PIETENPOL, DON • USA

Offers plans for the well known two-seat Aircamper and single-seat parasol-wing Sky Scout.

PIK • Finland

see Polyteknikkojen Ilmailukerho.

PILATUS BRITTEN-NORMAN LTD. • UK

The name for Britten-Norman Ltd (q.v.) after the 1979 takeover by Pilatus Aircraft Ltd of Switzerland, but before the July 1998 buyout.

PILATUS AIRCRAFT LTD. • Switzerland

Formed as Pilatus Flugzeugwerke AG in 1939, as a subsidiary of the Oerlikon armaments company. First aircraft was SB-2 Pelican six-seat light transport of 1944, but prototype only built. Followed by P-2 advanced trainer, produced in quantity for the Swiss Air Force in late 1940s, and the P-3 advanced trainer from 1953. Series production of the P-3 followed for the Swiss Air Force, and six went to the Brazilian Navy. In May 1959 Pilatus flew the first PC-6 Porter STOL monoplane with a Lycoming piston engine; this type has been in continuous production ever since, later developments using Astazou, Garrett, and most recently Pratt & Whitney Canada PT6A turboprop engine as the PC-6/B2-H4 Turbo Porter. Pilatus also signed a licence agreement for production of Turbo Porters by Fairchild-Hiller (q.v.) in USA. Also undertook Mirage production and maintenance work for the Swiss Air Force.

Now known as Pilatus Aircraft Ltd. Company's current

Pilatus PC-12 utility and business turboprop transport

Pilatus PC-6/B2-H4 Turbo Porter prior to delivery to Tyrolean Jet Service

Pilatus PC-9s before delivery to Burma

Pilatus PC-7 Turbo Trainers, used by Malaysian aerobatic team

product range encompasses the PC-7 Turbo Trainer (first flown August 1978 in production form), PC-7 Mk II (M) Turbo Trainer (first flown September 1992) with new features including stepped cockpits for improved vision, advanced electronic cockpit displays and more powerful engine, the PC-9 (M) Advanced Turbo Trainer (first flown May 1984) with the highest engine power of the range and also selected in 1995 for US military service as the Raytheon/Beech (q.v.) T-6A Texan II, and the PC-12 util-

ity and business turboprop transport (first flown May 1991 and also available in military form). Also, in 1979 Pilatus took control of the UK's Britten-Norman Ltd (q.v.) company, becoming Pilatus Britten-Norman, but sold this company in July 1998.

PINTSCH, JULIUS AG • Austria

This engineering company started an aircraft department in mid-1930s to manufacture Raab Schwalbe II and Tigerschwalbe II general-purpose biplanes for the Austrian Air Force.

Piper Cherokee Six 6/7-seat cabin monoplane

Piper Aztec E six-seat cabin monoplane

PIPER • USA

Formed originally as Taylor Aircraft Company (q.v.), reorganised as Piper Aircraft Corporation in 1937 at Lock Haven, Pennsylvania, with W. T. Piper as President. Initial production type was the Cub two-seat high-wing monoplane, of which 10,000 had been completed before the end of 1941. In 1948 Piper took over the Stinson Division of Consolidated Vultee Aircraft Corporation (q.v.) and acquired the Stinson Voyager production rights, but production of this type was soon halted. Piper's first twin was the four-seat Apache, which entered production in 1954. The later four-seat single-engine Comanche first flew in 1956. A whole line of light aircraft has followed the original Cub, from the Pacer/Tri-Pacer/Colt series of high-wing monoplanes to their successors, the Cherokee low-wing series, first of which flew in 1960. Piper produced the specialised Pawnee agricultural monoplane in 1959. Series of twins developed from the Apache to Aztec, Twin Comanche, Seneca and Navajo, plus other aircraft such as single-engined PA-38 Tomahawk. Company became subsidiary of Bangor Punta Corporation, then Lear Siegler Inc (1984), and later Romeo Charlie Inc (1987), finally with only Cheyenne and Malibu Mirage offered, but became insolvent early 1990s, though reduced-rate production continued while buyer sought. See The New Piper Aircraft Inc.

Piper Navajo, company's first corporate/commuter transport

Piper Tri-Pacer high-wing lightplane

Piper's famous Cub, of which more than 40,000 have been built

Plage I Laskiewicz-built Hanriot biplane with experimental butterfly tail

PIPER NORTH CORPORATION • USA

Founded 1989 at Lock Haven as subsidiary of Romeo Charlie Inc to produce Navajo Chieftain and possibly other aircraft, but closed soon after.

PIPPART-NOLL FLUGZEUGBAU • Germany

Based in Mannheim, built several Taube monoplanes in 1914 using steel cables below the wings in place of the normal bracing structure.

PITCAIRN • USA

Established in mid-1920s in Philadelphia, Pennsylvania, Pitcairn Aviation Inc built series of biplanes including PA-5 Mailwing high-performance single-seat mailplane used on US Air Mail routes. Turned to autogiro construction with PAA-1 of 1931. Name changed to Pitcairn Autogiro Company in early 1930s. Sold number of PA-18 and -19 autogiros, including a military version of the PA-34 two-seater to the USAAC. Plant and contracts taken over in 1940 by Pitcairn-Larsen Autogiro Company, in turn succeeded very shortly afterwards by Aga Aviation Corporation (q.v.).

PITTS AEROBATICS • USA

Pitts Aviation Enterprises founded at Florida to market plans for the Curtis Pitts biplane. New company formed as Pitts Aerobatics in 1977 at Afton, Wyoming, to continue sales and engineering of the Pitts aerobatic biplane at the same location by Aerotek Inc, which formerly built the Pitts S-2 for Pitts Aviation Enterprises. Aerotek continued to produce the S-2 for Pitts Aerobatics and the single-seat Pitts S-15 for pilots who did not wish to build their own. See Christen Industries.

PITTSBURGH METAL AIRPLANE CO • USA

Formed in 1929 to take over the San Francisco-based Thaden Metal Aircraft Company, which had built the Thaden T-4 four-seat all-metal monoplane, powered by a Wright Whirlwind engine. Company name changed in 1931 to the Metalair Corporation (q.v.) when it became a Division of the General Aviation Corporation.

PLAGE I LASKIEWICZ • Poland

Engineering firm which formed an aviation department in 1920. Poland's first aircraft manufacturer, it was based at Lublin and built the Ansaldo Ballila, A-300 and Potez 25 under licence. Subsequently built series of indigenous designs such as the Lublin R-VIII reconnaissance biplane, R-XI five-passenger monoplane. Ceased production following German occupation in 1940.

PLANET AIRCRAFT LTD. • UK

Built Satellite three-seat light aircraft with vee tail and pusher propeller in 1949. The first aeroplane constructed entirely of magnesium sheet, it was powered by a Gipsy Queen engine, but did not fly and was subsequently broken up. Fuselage of the second prototype was used in the Firth helicopter.

PLATT LE PAGE AIRCRAFT CO. • USA

The Platt Le Page Aircraft Company was formed about 1940 for development and production of rotary-wing aircraft to US Government contract. Various types were under development by 1946, but little was subsequently heard of the company.

POBJOY • UK

Founded 1930 as Pobjoy Airmotors Ltd, engine manufacturer. In 1935 became public company and enlarged scope to include aircraft manufacture. Chairman Oswald Short, managing director Arthur Gouge. Built Pirate high-wing monoplane 1935, but performance disappointing. Acquired licence to build Short Scion and Scion Senior light transports. Short Bros took over all Pobjoy's issued shares in 1938. Company was subcontractor for aircraft parts in Second World War.

PODLASKA WYTWORNIA SAMOLOTOW • Poland

Established in 1923; produced own civil and military designs in quantity, and also engaged in licence production. Built wide variety of civil types in early 1930s, mainly for military, but included PWS 24T four-passenger cabin monoplane. Ceased production following German occupation in 1940.

POLIKARPOV, N. N. • USSR

Designer of fighter aircraft in early 1930s, such as the I-16, first monoplane fighter with enclosed cockpit and retractable landing gear, but most famous design was the 1927 Po-2 biplane, built in thousands.

Pitts S-2A aerobatic biplane

PWS 10 single-seat fighter

Portsmouth Aerocar Major

boom high-wing six-seat aircraft, flown in 1947; not put into production.

PÖSCHEL AIRCRAFT GMBH • Germany

Small company which built P-300 Equator six-seat STOL amphibian (first flown 1970). Its single Lycoming engine drove a pusher propeller at the end of the fuselage, behind the T-tail. A turboprop version, the P.400 Turbo Equator, suffered an accident during tests in 1977, by which time company had already been renamed Equator (q.v.), and work continued into 1980s.

POTEZ, HENRY • France

Founded during First World War as Société d'Etudes Aéronautiques (q.v.) at Aubevillers. Built a two-seat tractor biplane, the Type 4C.2. Post-war the company became known as Henry Potez and established itself as a major French aircraft manufacturer with a long series of civil and military aircraft. In 1937 Potez became part of the nationalised French aircraft industry in the SNCAN group. At that time it was producing the 56 twin-engine light transport, the 63 fighter-bomber and the Potez-CAMS 141 four-engine reconnaissance flying-boat, together with prototypes of the 661 12-passenger four-engine monoplane and the Potez-CAMS 160 six engine flying-boat, a scale model of the proposed Type 161 transatlantic flying-boat.

For 16 years the company was not involved in aviation, but in 1953 produced the Potez 75 single-engine twin-

Polikarpov Po-2 utility biplane, built for more than 25 years

POLYTEKNIKKOJEN ILMAILUKERHO • Finland

The Flying Club of the Finnish Institute of Technology was founded in 1932 and built a series of gliders; the PIK-20 high-performance sailplane is still in production. PIK has also built several low-wing single-engine monoplanes, the PIK-11 in 1953, the PIK 15 glider tug in 1964, and the PIK-19 glider tug and two-seat trainer in 1972.

POMILIO • Italy

Company founded during First World War which built biplanes powered by Fiat engines.

PONNIER • France

Former Director of the Hanriot factory at Rheims, Ponnier founded his own company around 1912 and built a monoplane which Emile Vedrines flew into second place in the 1913 Coupé Internationale d'Aviation at Reims, achieving 123mph (198 km/h).

PONY JSC • Russia

See REDA-MDT Ltd.

POP'S PROPS • USA

Markets kits to build Cloudster single-seat parasol-wing monoplane, plus Pinocchio and Zing.

POPULAR FLYING ASSOCIATION • UK

Markets plans for Currie Wot single-seat biplane (first flown 1937) and single-seat Luton LA.4 Minor parasol wing monoplane (first flown 1936).

PORTERFIELD AIRCRAFT CORPORATION • USA

Formed in 1934 by E. E. Porterfield, former President of American Eagle Aircraft Corporation. Built two-seat light

cabin monoplane which entered production in 1935. Suspended civil production when America entered Second World War.

PORTHOLME AERODROME LTD. • UK

Huntingdon, Cambridgeshire, company which built aircraft under subcontract during First World War, including Sopwith Camels and Snipes, and Wight Type 840 seaplanes.

PORTSMOUTH AVIATION LTD. • UK

Founded in 1932 as Wight Aviation Ltd (q.v.) to operate air services to the Isle of Wight. Repaired military aircraft during Second World War. Built prototype of Aerocar twin-

Potez 63-II three-seat reconnaissance aircraft

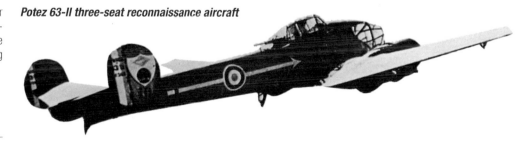

Potez 25 two-seat reconnaissance aircraft

Procaer Picchio lightplane

boom ground-attack aircraft, built by SNCAN. A contract for 500 for the French Army was awarded in 1956, but was cancelled later because of military cutbacks. Took over Air-Fouga (see Fouga) in 1958, and continued production of that company's Magister jet trainer. Built two prototype turboprop transports, Potez 840, flying first in 1961. Proposed versions were 841 with PT6A engines and 842 with Astazou Xs, but production did not proceed beyond six aircraft. Also built Paris III twin-jet executive aircraft developed by Morane-Saulnier. Potez was absorbed by Sud Aviation (q.v.) in 1967, which in turn became part of Aérospatiale (q.v.) in 1970.

POTTIER, JEAN • France

Markets plans and some components to construct a wide range of light aircraft, including P.50 Bouvreuil single-seat monoplane (first flown 1979), P.60 Minacro single-seat aerobatic biplane, P.70S single-seat monoplane, P.80S single-seat monoplane, P.100TS two/three-seat monoplane (first flown 1980), P.110TS three-seat monoplane, P.170S tandem two-seat monoplane, P.180S side-by-side two-seat monoplane, P.190S Castor side-by-side two-seat monoplane as wooden version of metal P.180S, P.210S Coati single-seat monoplane, P.220S Koala side-by-side two-seat version of Coati, P.230S Panda three-seat monoplane, P.240S Saiga four-seat version of Panda, and P.300 Ara three-seat monoplane (kits anticipated).

PRECEPTOR AIRCRAFT CORPORATION • USA

Markets plans and kits to build the N-3 Pup single-seat microlight representation of a Piper Cub, the Sport as a lighter version of Pup, the L-4 Super Pup as a more-powerful version of Pup, and the two-seat Ultra Pup, and kits for the Stinger single-seat parasol-wing monoplane (first flown 1995). Also produced the Storch Replica.

PREDAPPIO SA • Italy

Division of the Caproni Group (q.v.) which produced two trainers in the late 1930s, the Ca.602 two-seat biplane and a single-seat aerobatic version, the Ca.603, both powered by Alfa-Romeo in-line engines.

PROCAER • Italy

see Progetti,

PROFESSIONAL AVIATION SERVICES (PTY) LTD. • South Africa

Has undertaken major modification of DC-3 and offers aircraft charter services.

PROGETTI COSTRUZIONI AERONAUTICHE SPA • Italy

Based in Milan, Procaer built several aircraft to the design of Stelio Frati, the first being the Lycoming engined F15 Picchio, three-seat aerobatic monoplane, which flew in 1959. Cobra 400 two-seat light jet aircraft with Marbore engine was flown in 1960 but not developed. Late developments concerned the F15 and the F15F version built for Procaer by General Avia (q.v.).

PROGRESSIVE AERODYNE INC. • USA

Offers kits to build the SeaRey two-seat high-wing amphibian and the single-seat Sting Ray variant.

PROMAVIA SA • Belgium

Established 1984 to develop the Jet Squalus side-by-side two-seat jet trainer with other potential uses. Also began collaborating with Mikoyan of Russia on the ATTA/MiG 815 advanced jet trainer. Jet Squalus first flew 1987, but by 1998 company had ceased trading. See Alberta Aerospace Corporation.

Below: Promavia Jet Squalus side-by-side two-seat jet trainer

IPTN N-250 prototype during an early test flight

PROP-JETS INC. • USA

Founded to continue development of Interceptor 400 turboprop-powered four-seat light aircraft, as 400A. See Interceptor Company.

PROSTAR AIRCRAFT INC. • USA

Has produced kits to build the PT.2C two-seat high-wing cabin monoplane.

PROVENCE-AVIATION • France

The aircraft branch of Chantiers de Provence, a large naval dockyard in the mid-1920s. Produced the C.P.A.1 twin-engine military monoplane with two Lorraine-Dietrich engines.

PROWLER AVIATION INC. • USA

Kits have been made available to construct the Jaguar tandem two-seat, 300mph (480kmh) low-wing monoplane, derived from the Prowler of 1985 designed by George Morse.

PRUDDEN-SAN DIEGO AIRPLANE COMPANY • USA

Incorporated at San Diego, California, in 1927, to manufacture the TM-1 tri-motor high-wing monoplane seating six passengers and powered by Siemens-Halske engines. Super TM-1 had Ryan-Siemens wing engines and a Wright J-5c in the nose position.

PRVA SRPSKA FABRIKA AEROPLANA • Yugoslavia

First aircraft factory in Yugoslavia, established in 1925 for construction of military types under licence. PSFA produced indigenous Rogozarski two-seat reconnaissance biplane in early 1930s, powered by Walter Castor engine. Series of aircraft for Yugoslav Air Force followed, but the Rogozarski factory was destroyed in Second World War. In 1946 the remnants of the Rogozarski, Ikarus and Zmaj companies were brought into the government aircraft factories and resumed production.

PSFA • Yugoslavia

see Prva Srpska.

PT CIPTA RESTU SARANA SVAHA • Indonesia

Took over assets of Aerodis America (q.v.) 1991, and also planned to distribute in Asia the FFT Speed Canard.

PT INDUSTRI PESAWAT TERBANG NUSANTARA • Indonsia

IPTN created August 1976. Partner with CASA of Spain in the Airtech CN 235 regional transport programme, plus CN 295. Developed N-250 50/68-passenger twin-turboprop regional airliner (first flown August 1995), and has proposed the 70-passenger N-270 variant. N2130 expected to fly in the year 2002 as a 132-passenger medium-range airliner. Produces NC-212 version of CASA C-212, NBO-105 version of Eurocopter BO 105, NSA-332 version of Eurocopter Super Puma, and various Bell helicopters as NBell types. Subcontract work includes parts for Lockheed Martin F-16 fighter and Boeing 737/767 airliners.

PUGET PACIFIC PLANES INC. • USA

Formed after Second World War at Tacoma, Washington, to build Wheelair IIIA four-seat twin-boom light aircraft, powered by Lycoming engine. Believed not to have entered production.

PÜTZER • Germany

Alfons Pützer KG known primarily as sailplane manufacturer; produced an improved motorised version of the Doppelraab sailplane, known as the Elster in 1957. Small batch produced for German club use. Alfons Pützer and Comte Antoine d'Assche, director of the French company Alpavia SA (q.v.), formed a new company in 1966, Sportavia-Pützer (q.v.), to produce the Fournier series of light aircraft.

P-V ENGINEERING FORUM INC. • USA

see Piasecki Helicopter Corporation

PWS • Poland

see Podlaska Wytwornia Samolotow SA.

PZL • Poland

See Panstwowe Zaklady Lotnicze for pre-1945 history. Under political reorganisation in 1956, the Polish aircraft industry was revived with production of Soviet aircraft and

Pützer Elster B lightplane

PZL-Swidnik Mi-2Ch with smokescreen-laying gear (Piotr Butowski)

some indigenous types. In foreign markets most Polish aircraft subsequently appeared under the PZL title, such as the PZL-101 Gawron and PZL-104 Wilga utility aircraft of 1960 and 1962 respectively, the first being a development of the Yak-12. The Gawron was used extensively as an agricultural aircraft, along with the PZL-built An-2 biplane, but later purpose-built dusters and sprayers were built. Today, PZL types are produced under three separate organisations: PZL 'Warszawa-Okecie' SA (q.v.), WSK 'PZL-Mielec' SA (q.v.), and PZL-Swidnik SA (q.v.).

PZL-SWIDNIK SA • Poland

One of three separate PZL organisations, currently undertaking helicopter production and development. Origins in 1951, manufacturing components for LiM-1 fighters (Polish version of MiG-15). First helicopter production was SM-1 (Mil Mi-1), of which huge numbers were completed, followed by SM-2. Mil Mi-2 was first flown in Soviet Union in September 1961 as twin-turboshaft helicopter, but all production transferred to Poland in 1964, allowing first Polish-built Mi-2 to fly in November 1965; production lasted until 1996, after 5,450 had been built in a large number of variants for civil and military roles. Kania first flown June 1979 as modernised development of Mi-2 using US Allison turboshaft engines and AlliedSignal Bendix/King avionics, but only some 13 built to date. W-3 Sokól first flown November 1979 as 12-passenger civil/military intermediate multipurpose helicopter with twin turboshafts, of which well over 100 built to date and some exported; many variants, Polish armed forces versions including W-3RM Anakonda for air/sea rescue, and W-3W Sokól and similar W-3WA each with 23 mm cannon and outriggers for missiles, rockets and other weapons; SW-5 is anticipated development of W-3 using French avion-

ics. S-1W Huzar anti-armour and attack helicopter expected to fly 1999 and be built for the Polish armed forces; based on W-3 design. Four/five-seat SW-4 light utility single-turboshaft helicopter first flew October 1996.

PZL 'WARSZAWA-OKECIE' SA • Poland

Current name for the original 1928 factory. In 1995 became a stock company owned by the Polish Ministry of Industry and Trade. Most activities centre on agricultural aircraft and lightplanes, but production includes the PZL-130 Orlik aerobatic trainer which first flew in October 1984 and is used by the Polish Air Force. Short take-off PZL-104 Wilga (first flown 1962) remains in production in several versions, including the Wilga 35, Wilga 80, and latest

and refined PZL-104M Wilga 2000 with modified wings, new fuel tanks, increased take-off weight, US avionics and, as for Wilga 80-550, a US instead of Polish engine. PZL-105L Flaming first flew in 1989 as a Wilga replacement with a larger cabin and other improvements, but development has been halted at present in favour of Wilga 2000. PZL-106 Kruk agricultural aircraft first flew in 1973, with the current PZL-106BT Turbo-Kruk appearing in 1985. A new agricultural aircraft and waterbomber, the PZL-240 Pelikan biplane, is being developed. Also produces the PZL-110 (first flown 1978) and PZL-111 Koliber lightplanes originally based on the Socata Rallye, and has most recently developed the PZL-112 Koliber Junior side-by-side two-seat trainer (first flight expected 1999).

PZL "Warszawa-Okëcie" PZL-110 Koliber 150A

PZL 'Warszawa-Okëcie' PZL-130TC-1 Orlik trainers

PZL 'Warszawa-Okëcie' PZL-104 Wilga 80

PZL 'Warszawa-Okëcie' PZL-105L Flaming

QANTAS • Australia

The well-known airline Queensland and Northern Territory Aerial Services Ltd, founded in 1922 to operate airline route Charleville-Cloncurry-Camooweal. Secured manufacturing rights of de Havilland D.H.50 biplane in 1926 and built several.

QUAD CITY AIRCRAFT CORPORATION • USA

Developed kits to construct a range of single- and two-seat high-wing monoplanes in the Challenger series.

QUESTAIR INC. • USA

Has marketed kits to build the metal Venture side by-side two-seat low-wing monoplane with retractable undercarriage, first flown in 1987, and the Spirit derivative with fixed undercarriage.

QUICKSILVER ENTERPRISES INC. • USA

Successor to Eipper, and has offered kits to construct a range of trike microlights in the MX Sprint and Sport series, plus the single-seat GT 400 pod-and-boom microlight and two-seat GT 500, the latter having become the

first homebuilt to be certificated under new FAA regulations in the USA.

QUICK FLIGHT • USA

Has produced kits to build Quiet Bird single-seat microlight, made available from the Flight Shack in Lakeport.

QUIKKIT CORPORATION • USA

Developed the composites-constructed Glass Goose two-seat amphibious biplane (introduced in kit form in 1992) from the former Aero Composites Sea Hawker of 1982 first flight.

R

RAAB FLUGZEUGBAU GMBH • Germany

Formed in 1959; took over the Italian plant of Colonel Mario de Bernardi, with plans to build his Aeroscooter ultralight aircraft in Germany. Raab Flugzeugbau also acquired rights to licence-produce Ambrosini Rondone four-seat monoplane.

RAAB FLEUGZEUGBAU GMBH • Greece

Formed at Riga in 1934, but moved to Athens in 1935 as Société Anonyme pour la Fabrication et l'Exploitation des Avions Raab.

RAAB-KATZENSTEIN FLUGZEUGWERKE • Germany

Formed in 1925 by Raab & Katzenstein, formerly with Dietrich Flugzeugwerke (q.v.). First product was Schwalbe two-seat training biplane with Siemens engine. Built several other light aircraft before company name changed to Rheinische Luftfahrt Industrie (Rheinland), continuing manufacture of an improved Schwalbe, the FR-2.

RACA • Argentina

see Representaciones Aero Comerciales Argentinas SA.

RACEAIR • USA

Has offered plans to build the Skylite single-seat parasol-wing microlight.

RADWAN LTD. • Poland

Founded 1989, offers the KR-2PM Swift two-seat monoplane in two versions.

RAE • UK

see Royal Aircraft Establishment.

RAGWING AVIATION • USA

Developed plans and kits to allow construction of single-seat RW.2 Special biplane, available as a homebuilt or microlight, and single- and two-seat parasol-wing monoplanes designed as representations of the Pietenpol Aircamper, known as RW.1 Ultra-Piet and RW.3 Trainer PT2T respectively. Also offers other types up to RW.11.

RAJ HAMSA ALTRALIGHTS PVT LTD. • India

Markets kits to construct X'Air two-seat microlight.

RAMOR FLUGZEUGWERKE • Austria

Built KE-14 four-seat light cabin monoplane of own design in early 1930s; powered by de Havilland Gipsy 1 engine.

RAND-ROBINSON ENGINEERING INC. • USA

Produces plans and kits to construct KR-1 composites and wood single-seat monoplane (first flown 1972) and KR-2 two-seater (first flown 1974); KR-2S is enlarged development.

RANKIN AIRCRAFT • USA

Founded to market improved version of pre-war Porterfield CP-65, as Collegiate two-seat lightplane.

RANS COMPANY • USA

Markets kits for a very extensive range of aircraft, including S-4 and S-5 Coyote single-seat high-wing monoplanes, S-6 Coyote II two-seater, S-7 Courier tandem two-seat high-wing monoplane, S-9 Chaos single-seat mid-wing monoplane, S-10 Sakota two-seat variant, S-12 and S-14 Airaile two-seat and single-seat high-wing monoplanes, and S-16 Shekari two-seat aerobatic monoplane.

RANSOMES, SIMS & JEFFERIES • UK

Ipswich, Suffolk, company building aircraft under subcontract in First World War, including Airco D.H.6s and RAF F.E.2bs.

RAWDON BROTHERS AIRCRAFT INC. • USA

Flying school operator which designed and built a Lycoming engined two-seat monoplane, the T-1, in 1949.

RAYTHEON AIRCRAFT COMPANY • USA

Founded in 1994 as a division of Raytheon International Inc, bringing together the activities of the Beech Aircraft Corporation and Raytheon Corporate Jets, the latter having been British Aerospace Corporate Jets, producing Hawker bizjets, before the August 1993 acquisition. Continues to market a range of Beech lightplanes (including Bonanza A36 and B36TC, Baron 58, King Air C90, and Super King Air B200 and 350), Beechjet 400A business aircraft and the 1900 Airliner (current 1900D Airliner version first flown March 1990), plus Hawker 800XP corporate jet (Hawker 1000 production ended in 1998), while its latest bizjet to fly is the Premier I (December 1998), and the Hawker Horizon will follow in 1999. Also manufactures a variant of the Swiss Pilatus PC-9 as the Beech PC-9 Mk II, which is being produced for the USAF and US Navy as the T-6A Texan II primary undergraduate flight trainer and undergraduate navigator trainer. Other activities include the production of missile targets.

Raytheon/Beech PC-9 Mk II, based on Swiss Pilatus PC-9

Raytheon/Beech Baron 58 high-performance twin

Raytheon/Beech King Air 350 pressurised transport

Raytheon Beechjet 400A destined for Chinese customer

Raytheon Hawker 800XP corporate jet

Raytheon/Beech Bonanza B36TC, seen on the 50th anniversary of Bonanza appearance

Raytheon/Beech 1900D Airliner

RAYTHEON CORPORATE JETS • USA

The name for British Aerospace Corporate Jets following its acquisition by Raytheon in August 1993 acquisition (see above).

RAYTHEON SYSTEMS COMPANY • USA

Founded December 1997 as a division of the Raytheon Company, following its merger with Hughes Defense. Also incorporates Raytheon Electronic Systems, Raytheon TI Systems, and Raytheon E-Systems. Wide range of diverse programmes include development of the HISAR integrated surveillance and reconnaissance system, as first demonstrated on a Beech King Air B200T, and an airborne early warning and control aircraft based on the Airbus A310 using Israeli Phalcon electronically-scanned phased arrays housed in a non-rotating over-fuselage radome.

RAYTHEON SYSTEMS LTD. • UK

Founded December 1997 as a division of the US Raytheon Company, currently heading a team involved in developing an airborne stand-off radar (ASTOR) contender for the British forces, based on a Bombardier Global Express aircraft.

Above: Latest Raytheon business jet, the Premier I

REARWIN AIRPLANES INC. • USA

Based at Kansas City, produced Junior two-seat light monoplane in 1931, followed by Speedster with American Cirrus engine. Taken over in 1935 by partnership called Rearwin Airplanes. In 1937 bought assets of Le Blond Aircraft Corporation.

REDA-MDT LTD. • Russia

Established 1991. Developed the two-seat Pony amphibian (first flown 1994), produced by Pony JSC (q.v.). Four-seat Prize, based on Pony but with twin engines, under development.

REDAN • Russia

Founded 1992 but known as Gidroplan since 1995 (q.v.).

REDFERN, WALTER • USA

Has sold well over 5,000 sets of plans to build replica of First World War Fokker Dr I triplane fighter. Also offers plans for Airco D.H.2, Nieuport 17 and 24.

REDWING AIRCRAFT LTD. • UK

Founded 1929 by P. G. Robinson as Robinson Aircraft Company; produced Redwing two-seat light biplane with Armstrong Siddeley Genet engine. Works at Croydon, Surrey, was transferred to Colchester, Essex, in December 1930, and in April 1931 name was changed to Redwing Aircraft Ltd. In June 1932 Redwing bought Gatwick Aerodrome and formed a school of flying and aeronautical engineering, and in 1934 company moved back to Croydon. A total of 12 Redwings was built, last being delivered in 1933.

REFLEX FIBREGLASS WORKS INC. • USA

Kits for the Lightning Bug single-seat composites-built monoplane, and White Lightning WLAC-1 four-seat composites monoplane, are available via RFW

REGENT CARRIAGE CO. LTD. • UK

London (Fulham) company which built Avro 504Bs under subcontract during First World War.

REGGIANE SA • Italy

Built Caproni aircraft during First World War, but closed its aircraft department after the war. Resumed aircraft manufacture in mid-1930s, producing the Ca.405 Procellaria high-performance twin-engine bomber in 1937. Re 2000 Falco I fighter appeared in 1940 with Fiat radial engine, and other versions followed. By 1946 the company had ceased aircraft manufacture and was building railway coaches.

Redwing II side-by-side two-seat biplane

Reggiane Re 2000 Falco I single-seat fighter

Regia IAR.821 agricultural aircraft

REGIA AUTONOMA INDUSTRIA AERONAUTICA ROMANA • Romania

1940-45 name for IAR (q.v.), state-owned under the Ministries of War and Marine, but becoming part of Sovromtractor (q.v.) under partial Soviet control from 1946.

REID AIRCRAFT CO. • Canada

Formed 1928 by W. T. Reid to build biplane of his own design; merged with Curtiss Aeroplane & Motor Company of New York.

REID & SIGRIST LTD. • UK

Instrument manufacturer which opened an aircraft department in 1939 and built a twin-engined advanced trainer

Reims Rocket, a licence-built Cessna 172

popularly known as the Snargasher, of which only a prototype was built. Subcontract work during Second World War included production of Boulton-Paul Defiant two-seat fighters and modification of B-25 Mitchells for the RAF. Another trainer prototype, the R.S.3 Desford, was built in 1945.

REIMS AVIATION SA • France

Known as Société Nouvelle des Avions Max Holste (q.v.) until 1960, when the US Cessna company took over a 49 per cent holding and company was renamed. Reims acquired licence-manufacturing rights for several Cessna types such as the Model 150, 172, 177, 182 and 337, for sale in European and African markets. Currently manufacturers and customises the twin-turboprop F 406 Caravan II (first flown 1983) unpressurised utility transport,

with a range of Vigilant derivatives offered for maritime surveillance, calibration, electronic warfare, border surveillance, survey, pollution control and other roles, and can be lightly armed. Plans to reintroduce the F172 and F182 versions of Cessna lightplanes was halted in 1998. Subcontract activities include work on Airbus, ATR and various Dassault Aviation programmes.

REKKOF RESTART • Netherlands

Company formed with intention of restarting production of the Fokker 50 and 100, having bought tooling and rented the production factory in 1998. See Fokker.

REMINGTON-BURNELLI • USA

Was producing in 1924 the BR-2 Freighter, an all-metal biplane freighter designed specifically for cargo carrying. Typical of Junkers-inspired design, it combined the Burnelli lifting fuselage with corrugated light alloy skins.

REMOS AIRCRAFT GMBH • Germany

Established 1987. Has produced the Gemini and Gemini Ultra two-seat monoplanes, now only built to order, and currently markets the G-3 Mirage as a composites-built very light high-wing monoplane (first flown 1997). US version of Gemini Ultra is Micro-Viper, distributed by Akro-Viper Inc.

Remos Aircraft G-3 Mirage composites monoplane (Frank Herzog)

Republic P-47 Thunderbolt, single-seat fighter/fighter-bomber

Republic F-105 Thunderchief supersonic tactical fighter-bomber

RENAISSANCE COMPOSITES • USA

Offers kits to build former Experimental Aircraft (q.v.) Berkut tandem two-seat composites pusher monoplane with canard.

RENARD • Belgium

Société Anonyme Avions et Moteurs Renard established 1927 as aero-engine manufacturer; produced the Epervier all-metal single-seat fighter in 1928-1929 with Sabca Jupiter engine designed by Alfred Renard. Constructions Aéronautiques G. Renard founded about 1929 to build commercial aircraft designed by Renard. First two types were R.17-100 four-seat single-engine cabin monoplane and R-30-300 tri-motor five-passenger cabin monoplane. R-31 reconnaissance and R-33 training monoplanes appeared in 1932-1933; advanced low-wing single-seat fighter R-36 with Hispano-Suiza engine exhibited at 1937 Brussels Aero Show. Company was inactive during Second World War, but began to reorganise in 1945.

Republic Seabee four-seat light amphibian

ers. The larger and heavier F-105 Thunderchief followed in 1955, and in 1965 the company became the Republic Aviation Division of Fairchild Hiller Corporation (q.v.).

Below: Republic F-84 Thunderstreak jet fighter

REP • France

see Esnault-Pelterie, Robert.

REPLICA PLANS • Canada

Markets plans to construct the S.E.5A as an 85 per cent scale replica of the First World War fighter.

REPRESENTACIONES AERO COMERCIALES ARGENTINAS SA • Argentina

RACA began assembly of Hughes 500C helicopters in 1975 under licence. A minimum of 120 helicopters are to be built.

REPUBLIC AVIATION CORPORATION • USA

Founded as Seversky Aircraft Corporation (q.v.) at Long Island, New York, in 1931; name changed to Republic Aviation Corporation in 1939. Secured $56.5 million contract for fighter from the USAAC in 1940, largest single fighter order ever placed until then by US Government. Built P-35, P-44 and P-43 Lancers for USAAC plus some EP-1s, based on P-35, for Swedish Government. Lancer design developed further into P-47 Thunderbolt for USAAF, of which 15,329 were built during Second World War. Immediate post-war designs included the Seabee single-engine amphibian, the XF-12 high-altitude long-range four-engine photo-reconnaissance aircraft prototype, and the F-84 Thunderjet/Thunderstreak/Thunderflash series of jet fight-

Revolution Mini-500 Bravo

REVOLUTION HELICOPTER CORP. INC. • USA

Established January 1990, manufacturing the Mini-500 Bravo single-seat kit-built helicopter (first flown 1992) and the new two-seat Voyager-500.

REX FLUGMASCHINE GMBH • Germany

An aircraft works and flying school formed early in First World War by Dr Friedrich Hansen for construction of aircraft, chiefly Bristol and Morane monoplanes.

REY, FRANÇOIS • France

Built experimental R-1 twin-engine monoplane with variable-incidence wings, first flown with normal wings in 1949, and with articulated wings in 1951. Original patents taken out in 1938 and an aircraft built in 1940, but was destroyed during the war.

RFB • Germany

See below.

RHEIN-FLUGZEUGBAU GMBH • Germany

Founded in 1957, RFB obtained licence from Rhein-West Flug (q.v.) to build the RW-3 Multoplane in 1957, flying first production aircraft in 1958 and following with a small batch. Built and flew RF1 six-seat STOL transport in 1960; with two Lycoming engines geared to drive single pusher propeller in a wide-chord duct. In 1968, VFW-Fokker (q.v.) acquired 65 per cent of shares in RFB, and in 1969 RFB acquired a percentage holding in Sportavia company (q.v.). Company became busy with military contracts for overhaul, and target towing for some years, and built in collaboration with Grumman-American (q.v.) the Fanliner two-seat light aircraft with Wankel rotary engine, first flown in 1973. It was re-engined in 1976 with a Dowty Rotol ducted propulsor. Based on the Fanliner's promise, the Federal German Government awarded a contract for two Fantrainer prototypes with ducted fan engines, first flown in 1977 and 1978. Production Fantrainer 400s and 600s were ordered only by Thailand, the first (a 600) flying in 1984 and most assembled in Thailand from kits. Projected Fantrainer 800 did not enter production; neither did the proposed Tiro-Trainer with a turbofan engine. Company ceased trading in 1997.

Below: RFB AW1-2 Fantrainer with ducted-fan propulsion

Rey 01 experimental monoplane

RFB RF1 six-seat STOL transport

Rhein-Flugzeugbau X-114 ground-effect craft, continuing earlier work with the X-113 Aerofoil Boat that had first flown in 1970

RHEINISCHE LUFTFAHRT INDUSTRIE GMBH • Germany

see Raab-Katzenstein.

RHEIN-WEST FLUG • Germany

RWF formed at Porz-Westhoven, near Cologne, in early 1950s to develop a new light aircraft, the RW 3 Multoplane, basically a powered sailplane with Porsche engine driving a propeller mounted between the fin and rudder, and under the tailplane. The production licence was subsequently transferred to Rhein-Flugzeugbau GmbH (q.v.).

RICCI BROTHERS • Italy

Shipbuilding company which began aircraft manufacture in First World War. Post-war, the R.6 single-seat and R.9 two-seat sports triplanes were built around 1920, plus the large three-engine twin-hull R.I.B. flying-boat. Company closed down in about 1925.

RICHMOND AIRWAYS INC. • USA

Based at Staten Island, New York, for private hire and pleasure flights. This company built a Sea Hawk five-seat flying-boat in 1928, with Curtiss C-6 engine driving pusher propeller.

RIDDLE AIRLINES INC. • USA

Operator of a large fleet of Curtiss C-46 twin-engine transports, Riddle produced a modification kit in the mid-1950s which added 40mph (64kmh) to cruising speed and 2,204 lb (1,000 kg) to the payload. The improved model was

designated C-46R, and Riddle subsequently converted its own fleet of 32 to have 2,100 hp Pratt & Whitney engines.

RIESELER, SPORTFLUGZEUGBAU • Germany

Established at Berlin/Johannisthal Aerodrome after First World War, Sportflugzeugbau Rieseler built a single-engine single-seat light sporting parasol monoplane with a two cylinder Haacke engine which was put into production by Stahlwerk Mark (q.v.) at Breslau. A two-seat version, the R.IV/23, was subsequently developed.

RILEY AIRCRAFT CO. • USA

Based at Fort Lauderdale, Texas, company specialised in conversions of existing types to improve performance. In 1953 converted Ryan Navion to twin-engine configuration as the Twin Navion with Lycoming engines, and by 1961

was producing a conversion of the Cessna 310 known as the Riley 65 Rocket. Later aircraft which received Riley conversions included the D.H. Dove and Heron, the Cessna 340 and 414, and, in 1975, the Handley Page built Jetstream. Became Riley Turbo Sales Corporation, and Riley Turbostream Corporation in 1970 and Riley Aircraft Corporation 1979. Purchase by Advanced Aircraft Corporation in 1983. Subsequently, Riley International Corporation formed to continue Riley conversions.

RINGHOFFER-TATRA AS • Czechoslavakia

Aviation department of the Ringhoffer-Tatra combine was formed in 1935. Built the Bücker Jungmann trainer under licence as the Tatra T.131, the T.1 two-seat cabin monoplane and the T.126 biplane trainer. Production was stopped by Second World War.

Riley turboprop conversion of the Handley Page Jetstream

RNAS Experimental Eastchurch Kitten, intended as ship-based fighter

RNAS EXPERIMENTAL CONSTRUCTION DEPOT, PORT VICTORIA • UK

Commissioned early in 1915 on the Isle of Grain as the RN Aeroplane Repair Depot, and named Port Victoria to distinguish it from the original air station. Experimental Armament Section set up alongside, followed in 1916 by the Seaplane Test Flight. Began construction in 1916 with the P.V.1, a Sopwith Baby fuselage with modified wings and enlarged floats. There followed a series of seaplane prototypes, the Grain Kitten and Eastchurch Kitten land-planes and the final type to be built by the ECD, the Grain Griffin, a converted Sopwith B.1 single-seat bomber. The Depot was subsequently renamed the Marine Experimental Aircraft Depot.

ROBEY & CO. LTD. • UK

Engineering company in Lincoln, Lincolnshire, which built Sopwith Gunbus and Farman Longhorn biplanes and Short 184 seaplanes to Admiralty orders in First World War, and also designed and built its own single-seat scout and two prototypes of a 'Fighting Machine' with two manned gun positions in upper wing .

ROBIN • France

Formed in 1957 as Centre Est Aéronautique to produce light aircraft; name changed to Avions Pierre Robin in 1969 and currently known simply as Avions Robin. Pierre Robin founded company in collaboration with Jean Delemontez, the engineer responsible for the Jodel series of light aircraft. First Centre Est type was the DR.100 three-seater, and the basic design was constantly refined through a number of variants. Current aircraft from Avions Robin are Robin 200 two-seat lightplane and trainer (first flown 1971); DR 400 (first flown May 1972) that was offered in two-seat and 112 hp DR 400/100 Cadet form during 1980s but now only in 118 hp DR 400/120 Dauphin 2+2 two-plus-two seating form, 160 hp DR 400/140 B Dauphin 4 four-seat form, 160 hp DR 400/160 Major four-seat form with extra fuel capacity and increased wing area, 180 hp DR 400/180 Regent four-seat form, 180 hp 400/180 R Remo 180 four-seat form for glider towing and with reduced fuel, 200 hp DR 400/200 R Remo 200 four-seat form for glider towing, and latest 200 hp DR 400/200i President four/five-seat form with larger fuselage to offer increased cabin space; Robin 2160 two-seat aerobatic lightplane (certificated 1978); and Robin 3000 four-seat lightplane with T-tail (first flown 1988 in current 3000/160 form). Robin 1180 Aiglon had first flown in 1976 as metal

Robin (Centre Est) DR 253 Régent lightplane

Robin HR.100/200 Royale four-seat lightplane

Robinson R22 Beta light helicopters

Robin DR400/140 B Dauphin 4 four-seat lightplane

four-seater, but expected production of improved Aiglon II had not taken place at time of writing.

ROBINSON HELICOPTER COMPANY • USA

Formed 1971 to design and build a low-cost, piston-engined, two-seat lightweight helicopter as the R22, which first flew in August 1975. Deliveries started 1979 and over 2,700 since sold in several versions, including improved R22 Alpha and Beta, Mariner with floats, IFR Trainer for instrument training, Law Enforcement and Agricultural. Four-seat development first flown March 1990 as R44 Astro, with deliveries from 1993; variants include IRF Trainer, Newscopter for media operations, and Police Helicopter.

ROCHE AVIATION • France

Company formed after Second World War, with M. Guerchais as chief engineer; connection with prewar Avions Guerchais not known. Guerchais Roche produced several two-seat light aircraft from about 1946, the Types 35 with Renault engine, the 39 with Mathis radial engine, and the 30 with Ford V-8 engine, as well as the type 107 single-seat glider.

ROCK SEGELFLUGZEUGBAU • Germany

Mainly sailplane manufacturer, but built Krähe single-seat powered sailplane in 1957, with 18 hp Zink-Brändl engine.

ROCKET AIRCRAFT CORPORATION • USA

Formed in 1946 by take-over of Johnson Aircraft Inc. (q.v.) of Fort Worth, Texas. Johnson had designed the Rocket cabin monoplane in 1941, with moulded plastic plywood construction and Lycoming engine. The Rocket 185 received its Approved Type Certificate in April 1946.

ROCKWELL INTERNATIONAL CORPORATION • USA

Formed by merger of North American Aviation (q.v.) and Rockwell Standard Corporation in 1967. In 1973 North American Rockwell and Rockwell Manufacturing Company merged to become Rockwell International Corporation. Air-

Robinson R44 Newscopter with CCD camera

craft production after the 1967 merger included the Aero Commander line of single and twin-engine aircraft, the turboprop OV-10 Bronco armed reconnaissance aircraft, T-2 Buckeye jet trainer, B-1B Lancer supersonic swing-wing bomber, and the Sabreliner executive and light jet transport. Company's aerospace and defence units purchased by The Boeing Company (q.v.) on 6 December 1996, becoming Boeing North American. Similarly, Rockwell Australia became Boeing Australia Ltd.

Above: Rockwell B-1

Right: Rockwell International B-1B Lancer, first used in action in 1999

Rockwell T-2E Buckeye used by Greece

ROE, A.V. • UK

In 1906 A. V. Roe began aircraft design, and on in July 1909 was the first Briton to make tentative flights in an all-British aircraft, namely his Roe I triplane. Two years later, in 1911, the renowned Avro Company was established. First aircraft to enter quantity production was the 504 trainer, built in large numbers and several versions. Then followed a long line of Avro biplanes including the Tutor, Cadet and Avian. In 1928 Avro acquired a licence to build the Fokker F.VIIB/3M as the Avro 618 Ten: it carried eight passengers and two crew, and orders included five for Australian National Airways. Rivalling the success of the 504 was the twin-engined Anson trainer and coastal patrol monoplane, flown as the Avro 652 civil transport for Imperial Airways in 1935. More than 10,000 Ansons were built in Britain and Canada between 1935 and 1952. The twin-engined Manchester bomber of 1939, with the unproven Rolls-Royce Vulture engines, was not a success, but led to the superb four-engined

Rockwell Ranger 2000 primary jet trainer, developed for the USAF/USN JPATS competition and first flown 1993, but not selected

Avro 504s, one of the most famous trainers to enter RAF service

Avro Lancaster, the RAF's most successful heavy bomber of WW2

Right: Avro Shackleton MR Mk 2 was an airborne early warning aircraft, the last Shackleton version in RAF service and its final piston-engined front-line aircraft

ROE, A.V. • Canada

In 1945 UK company A. V. Roe acquired Victory Aircraft Ltd (q.v.) factory at Toronto/Malton Airport, where Lancasters, Lincolns, Ansons and a York were built during Second World War. New company named Avro Canada, and it produced the first Canadian-designed jet fighter, the twin-engined CF-100. Prototype flew in 1950; 639 were built for the RCAF and 53 for the Belgian Air Force. Flew prototype C-102 Jetliner in 1949, but no production order was received. Avro Canada became a member of the Hawker Siddeley Group in 1955, and in 1962 became Hawker Siddeley Canada Ltd. (q.v.). CF-105 Arrow delta twin-jet all-weather fighter prototype flew in 1958. Only five CF-105s were built before the project was cancelled in favour of Bomarc surface-to-air missiles. An interesting project was the Avrocar VTOL aircraft developed under a US Department of Defense contract and flown in 1959 in California. In its prototype form it was circular; a flying saucer!

ROGERSON HILLER CORPORATION • USA

New name for Hiller Helicopters (see Hiller Aviation) before 1994 buy-out by Hiller Aircraft Corporation (q.v.).

ROHR AIRCRAFT CORPORATION • USA

Based at Chula Vista, California, was aircraft component subcontractor in Second World War. Built M.O.1 two-seat tail-first (canard) monoplane in 1946. No further aircraft production known.

Lancaster, of which 7,374 were built during Second World War. The York transport derivative mated the same wings and tail, plus a central fin, with an entirely new fuselage seating 12 passengers. The Lincoln bomber was built as a replacement for the Lancaster, entering RAF service soon after VJ-day. Avro's post-war Tudor transport was not a success, and the company's last piston-engined aircraft was the Shackleton four-engined maritime reconnaissance aircraft. Following production of four Avro 707 delta research aircraft, the company produced the four-jet delta-wing Vulcan bomber, which began to enter RAF service in 1956. Avro's last design before being restyled the Avro Whitworth Division of Hawker Siddeley Aviation, in 1963, was the Avro 748 twin-turboprop transport (first flown in 1960).

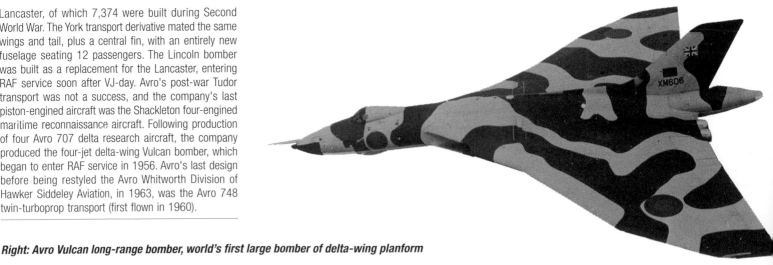

Right: Avro Vulcan long-range bomber, world's first large bomber of delta-wing planform

Avro Anson, the RAF's `Faithful Annie' trainer/transport

Avro Canada CF-100 Canadian-designed jet fighter

Rohrbach Rocco 10-passenger commercial flying-boat

Roland D.II single-seat fighter, built also by Pfalz

ROHRBACH METALL FLUGZEUGBAU GMBH • Germany

Founded 1922 by Dr Ing Rohrbach to continue construction and development of all-metal aircraft designed by him when working previously with the Zeppelin company. Associated company, Rohrbach-Metall-Aeroplane Co A/S, formed in Copenhagen to avoid limitations imposed on construction in Germany. Built ten Ro-II seaplanes for Japanese Navy and Ro-IIIA for Turkey, followed by Rodra twin-engine flying-boat and Rofix single-seat fighter. Copenhagen plant closed in late 1920s when restrictions on German manufacture were lifted. German factory continued flying-boat and landplane construction, including Roland three-engined 10-passenger monoplane. In April 1934 Weser Flugzeugbau GmbH (q.v.) took over the company and Dr Rohrbach became technical director of Weser.

ROLAND LUFT FAHRZEUG GMBH • Germany

Pre-First World War manufacturer of Parseval airships at Adlershof, subsequently built two-seat fighter and the Roland D.II single-seat fighter biplane during First World War. Production ceased at end of war.

ROLLASON AIRCRAFT AND ENGINES LTD. • UK

Initially an aircraft sales and service organisation. Began aircraft construction in 1957 with Druine Turbulent single-seat light monoplane powered by a Rollason-converted Ardem motor car engine. In 1961 built two-seat Druine Condor with 75 hp Continental engine. Later versions used more powerful Continental engines. Rollason also rebuilt a number of Tiger Moths and other aircraft, and carried out seaplane conversions of the Tiger Moth and Turbulent.

ROMAERO • Romania

With a lineage that can be traced to 1920 (via companies including IRMA and IAv Bucuresti), this company assembled from British-supplied kits nine BAC One-Eleven airliners as 1-11s, the first appearing in 1982. Current work, in 1999, includes the manufacture of Britten-Norman BN2 Islanders (some 500 produced over 30 years) and the production of subassembles for Boeing and Galaxy Aerospace. In January 1999 Britten-Norman of the UK received approval from the Board of Directors of Romania's State Ownership Fund for its tender offer to acquire Romaero.

ROMANO, E. • France

Built R-3 seaplane with Hispano-Suiza engine in early 1920s to carry out research on seaplane floats. Subsequently produced series of aircraft from the R-5 all-metal flying-boat to R-16 general-purpose tri-motor monoplane.

Rollason (Druine) Turbulent ultra-light monoplane

Rollason (Druine) D62 Condor lightplane

Romaero-built BAC One-Eleven, as 1-11

Taken over to form part of the nationalised French aircraft industry in 1937, becoming part of the SNCASE group (q.v.).

ROMEO • Italy

As Officine Ferroviarie Meridionali in 1925, obtained rights to build Fokker aircraft under licence, including the C.V., which was fitted with an Italian-built Jupiter engine and known as the Ro.1. Also built Fiat biplanes. In 1934 Società Anïnima Industrie Aeronàutiche Romeo was formed to take over the aeronautical activities of Meridionali (q.v.), but within two years there was another change of name to Società Anònima Industrie Meccàniche e Aeronàutiche Meridionali (SAIMAM), and indigenous types of aircraft were produced including the Ro.37 and 45 reconnaissance biplanes, the Ro.41 single-seat fighter, and the Ro.43 two-seat fighter seaplane. By 1936 SIAMAM had become part of Breda.

RONCHETTI, RAZZETTI AVIACION SA • Argentina

Builder of J-1 Martin Fierro single-seat agricultural monoplane with 300 hp Lycoming engine. Prototype first flew in 1975 and a small batch produced.

RRA J-1 Martin Fierro

ROOS, VICTOR H. AIRCRAFT CO. • USA

Succeeded American Eagle-Lincoln Aircraft Corporation (q.v.) in mid-1930s, and continued to produce American Eaglet light monoplane with 45 hp Szekely engine.

ROOS-BELLANCA AIRPLANE CO. • USA

Established 1922 at Omaha, Nebraska, to produce aeroplanes designed by Professor G. Bellanca, first being the Bellanca C.F. high-wing monoplane of about 1924, powered by an Anzani engine. Prof Bellanca left the partnership in 1925 and joined the Wright Aeronautical Corporation (q.v.) the following year. Wright built several Bellanca monoplanes, the last of which established a world endurance record, remaining in the air for more than 51 hours (see also Bellanca).

RotorWay Exec homebuilt helicopter

Royal Aircraft Factory S.E.5a

ROOTES SECURITIES LTD. • UK

Managed the factory at Speke, Liverpool, established under the British Government's 1936 scheme to create 'shadow' factories to augment the productive capacity of the aviation industry. This scheme brought the British motor car industry, which had some experience of quantity production, to aid the aircraft builders. Rootes' factory at Speke built Bristol Blenheim I and IV aircraft, and Beaufighters VIF and X came from their Blythe Bridge, Staffordshire, factory.

ROSE AEROPLANE & MOTOR • USA

Founded in Chicago by J. W. Rose in mid-1930s as Rose Airplane Corporation. Produced Parakeet light single-seat biplane with 40 hp Continental engine.

ROSS AIRCRAFT CORPORATION • USA

Company established in New York which built RS-1 light monoplane in 1940; war stopped production plans. A new model, the RS-2L two-seater, powered by a Lycoming engine, was built in 1942.

ROTARY AIR FORCE MARKETING INC. • Canada

Offers single- and two-seat autogyros for home assembly using kits.

ROTOCRAFT LTD. • UK

Formed jointly by Mitchell Engineering Group and Servotec Ltd to develop the Grasshopper twin-engined light helicopter designed by Jacob Shapiro. Powered by two Walter Minor engines, this was first flown in 1962. A second example was built, but the type did not enter production.

ROTOCRAFT SA (PTY) LTD. • South Africa

Founded in 1953 to develop the Minicopter single-seat light autogyro, prototype of which was designed and built by Mr L. L. Strydom and flown in 1962. Several were built for South African customers.

ROTOR-CRAFT CORPORATION • USA

Company engaged in helicopter development immediately after Second World War. Built two-seat helicopter for US Army under designation XR-11. Little more heard until the mid-1950s, when the RH-1 Pinwheel 'strap-on' personal helicopter appeared in 1954.

ROTORWAY INTERNATIONAL • USA

RotorWay Aircraft Inc founded 1970 to market in plans and kit forms the Scorpion single-seat helicopter, developed from the Schramm (q.v.) Javelin. Followed by the two-seat Scorpion Too, subsequently known as Scorpion 133 and using a RotorWay RW-145 piston engine. Exec two-seat helicopter appeared 1980 to supplement and eventually replace Scorpion 133, currently offered in its latest kit-built Exec 162F form (available since 1994) using a 150 hp RotorWay RI 162F engine; over 500 Exec 90 and latest Exec 162F kits delivered since 1990, in which year company became RotorWay International.

ROTOR-WINGS & FLYING MACHINES • USA

Offers plans to build former Flaglor Scooter single-seat high-wing monoplane, first flown 1967.

ROYAL AIRCRAFT ESTABLISHMENT • UK

Known originally as the Royal Aircraft Factory, Farnborough, and was involved in dirigible construction and repair before First World War. It was renamed Royal Aircraft Establishment during the war and initiated biplane designs for the Royal Flying Corps, including the B.E.2 and F.E.2 series, F.E.8, R.E.8 and finally the S.E.5 fighter.

ROYAL ARMY AIRCRAFT FACTORY • Denmark

Formed in 1914 to undertake aircraft construction and repair work for the Royal Army Flying Corps. Built foreign aircraft under licence before Second World War, including the Fokker C.VE reconnaissance biplane, and Gloster Gauntlet and Fokker D.XXI fighters.

ROYAL ARMY AIRCRAFT FACTORY • Sweden

Built series of indigenous designs for the Swedish Air Force from the mid-1920s. Early biplane types were the Tumeliten single-seat trainer and J.24B single-seat fighter, followed by S.21H.L reconnaissance biplane.

ROYAL NAVAL DOCKYARD • Denmark

Built seaplanes and flying-boats for the Danish Navy from 1914, comprising both original designs and licence-built types such as Hawker Danecock (Dankok).

RTAF • Thailand

Royal Thai Air Force office of aeronautical engineering founded 1975. Produced RTAF-5 twin-boom and turbo-prop-powered forward-air-control aircraft (first flown 1984). Later undertook life extension programme for Airtrainers and assembled Fantrainers for RTAF.

RUFFY, ARNELL & BAUMANN AVIATION • UK

Italian Felix Ruffy and Swiss Edouard Baumann founded flying school at Hendon in 1915 and subsequently built several training aircraft of their own design. Company became part of the Alliance Aeroplane Company Ltd (q.v.) when the latter expanded in 1918.

RUMPLER GMBH • Germany

Founded before First World War as E. Rumpler Luftfahrzeugbau, with the company's works and flying school based at Berlin/Johannisthal aerodrome, and with a military flying school at Monchelberg. Began production with licence construction of Etrich Taube monoplane, but subsequently became famous for a series of armed biplane reconnaissance aircraft in First World War, including the C.I, C.IV and C.VII. Went into liquidation about 1919 owing to lack of work.

RUSCHMEYER AIRCRAFT PRODUCTION KG • Germany

Established 1987, developed the R90 four-seat touring and IFR training monoplane of composites construction,

Rumpler (Etrich) Taube monoplane

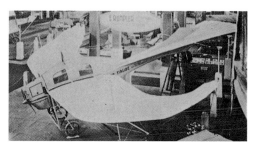

Rumpler Taube `Airliner'

Rumpler C.I. reconnaissance aircraft

Russo-Baltic Il'ya Muromets

Ryan PT-22 two-seat primary trainers

Ryan X-13 Vertijet experimental tail-sitting VTOL aircraft

first flown in 1991 and certificated 1992. Original R90-230 RG version with 230 hp engine and retractable undercarriage is to be joined by the R90-180 RG with a 180 hp engine and retractable undercarriage, the R90-230 FG with 230 hp engine and fixed undercarriage, and R90-300 T-RG with a supercharged 300 hp engine and retractable undercarriage. The R90-420 AT is a turboprop proof-of-concept model, first flown 1993 and used at present only as a factory aircraft.

RUSSO-BALTIC WAGGON WORKS • Russia

This large Russian engineering company based at St Petersburg, was only partly concerned with aircraft production. It was responsible, however, for the construction of the Il'ya Muromets series of four-engined bombers, designed by Igor Sikorsky, which equipped Russia's Eskadra Vozduchnykh Korablei (Squadron of Flying Ships) in First World War. Largest of the series was the Type IM-Ye2, with a wingspan of 113 ft 2 in (34.50 m) and a gross weight of 15,432 lb (7,000 kg). The Sikorsky S-16 reconnaissance biplane was also built.

RUSTON PROCTOR & COMPANY • UK

Engineering company based at Lincoln, Lincolnshire, which constructed RAF B.E.2s, Sopwith Camels and Snipes under subcontract during First World War.

RUTAN AIRCRAFT FACTORY • USA

Founded 1969, first flew VariViggen two/four-seat canard monoplane for construction by amateur builders from plans in 1972. Other aircraft followed, including VariEze two-seater (first flown 1974), Defiant four-seater (first flown 1978), Grizzly joined-wing/canard STOL transport (first flown 1982), and Voyager (q.v.).

RYAN • USA

Founded 1928 at St Louis, Missouri, as Mahoney-Ryan Aircraft Corporation (q.v.), deriving from Ryan Airlines, which began operations on US West Coast in 1922, and in 1926 began manufacture of Ryan M-1 mailplane from which Charles Lindbergh's transatlantic Ryan NYP *Spirit of St Louis* was developed in 1927. Commercial version

of the latter, Ryan Brougham, was built in quantity. Ryan merged with Detroit Aircraft Corporation (q.v.) in 1929, but DAC did not survive the slump in 1930-1931. T. Claude Ryan formed Ryan Aeronautical Company in 1933-1934 and produced the S-T training monoplane, forerunner of a series of successful Ryan trainers. The YO-51 Dragonfly of 1940 was observation monoplane built for the USAAC. A new fighter for the US Navy in 1943 reflected a 'belt and braces' outlook on the new gas turbine engine, having a mixed powerplant comprising a conventional piston engine and rear-fuselage jet. Known as the FR-1 Fireball, it was too late to see operational service in Second World War. Acquired design and manufacturing rights of Navion four-seat all-metal monoplane from North American Aviation (q.v.) in 1947 and put it into quantity production. Ryan developed to a mid-1950s USAF contract the X-13 Vertijet, a delta-wing vertical-take-off jet with Rolls-Royce Avon engine. A flex-wing research aircraft was built in 1961, and the XV-5A lift-fan research aircraft followed in 1964. Development of the 'fan-in-wing' VTOL principle continued with two prototype aircraft, later restyled XV-5B.

Ruschmeyer R90-230 FG lightplane

SAAB GROUP • Sweden

Svenska Aeroplane AB founded at Trollhätan 1937 to develop and build military aircraft. In 1939 amalgamated with Aircraft Division of Svenska Järnvägsverkstäderna (q.v.) and moved main establishment to Linköping. From 1950 acquired other important facilities, including underground factory at Linköping. Name changed to Saab Aktiebolag May 1965; Malmö Flygindustri (q.v.) became a subsidiary in 1967; in 1968 merged with Scania-Vabis group to became Saab-Scania. Current name Saab Group, comprising five main divisions: Saab AB, Saab Dynamics AB for guided weapons and electronics, Saab Training Systems AB, Saab Aircraft AB for marketing and supporting commercial aircraft, and Saab Combitech AB. Saab AB parent division established January 1997 to combine activities of previous Saab Military Aircraft, Saab Aircraft and

Saab Service Partner, and develops and manufactures military and commercial aircraft within business units known as Gripen, General Military Aircraft, Future Products and Technology, Operations Commercial Aircraft, and Collaborative Programmes.

First aeroplanes were licence-built Junkers Ju 86K twin-engined bombers, Northrop-Douglas dive-bombers and North American trainers. First own-design production aircraft was Saab 17 dive-bomber of 1940, used widely and 60 delivered to Ethiopia from 1947. Saab 18 was twin-engined bomber of 1942, some late examples of which had ejection seats. Saab 21A of 1943 was piston-engined single-seat fighter, and 21-R was jet development of the same aircraft. Saab 29 was the so-called 'flying barrel' swept-wing jet fighter, in production until 1956, while Saab 32 Lansen of 1952 was swept-wing fighter/attack/recon-

naissance two-seater. Saab 35 Draken 'double-delta' fighter appeared in 1955, and a squadron remained active as interceptors until 1999. Saab 105 of 1963, a twin-jet light side-by-side two-seater armed multipurpose aircraft, still in use as a trainer in 1999; Swedish Air Force aircraft have just undergone an upgrade with new engines and thus redesignated Sk 60W. Saab 37 Viggen multirole combat aircraft, first flown February 1967, has foreplane and delta wings, and with its STOL capability remains a very potent weapon system. Produced for service between 1971 and 1990, it has been continuously upgraded; redelivered in latest upgraded form 1998 for continued service in JA 37 interceptor and AJS 37 attack/interceptor/maritime-reconnaissance variants. Latest combat aircraft is Saab AB Gripen JAS 39 Gripen, first flown December 1988 and taken into Swedish Air

Saab J 29F Tunnan fighters (J. Thurrsson)

Saab Sk 60W re-engined jet trainer in Swedish service (J. Lindahl)

Force service from 1996. Grippen is the world's first combat aircraft of the new-generation type and the first to combine the roles of interceptor, attack and reconnaissance in a single aircraft (all as primary roles) by the adoption of push-button control to select the required function in the computer programmes of the totally integrated avionics suite.

Civil types have included Saab 90 Scandia twin-engined 32-passenger transport (first flown November 1946); Saab 91 Safir all-metal 3/4-seater (first flown November 1945); two/three-seat high-wing Safari (first flown in July 1969) and its military Supporter development (first flown 1972). In production until 1999 has been the Saab 340 turboprop regional transport (first flown January 1983, and finally produced in 340B and BPlus variants with accommodation for up to 37 passengers) and the Saab 2000 50/58-seat turboprop regional airliner (first flown March 1992). Saab has also developed an airborne early warning and control variant of the 340B airliner as the S 100B Argus (first flight of AEW&C prototype with overfucolage radar July 1994), plus a search-and-rescue variant for the Japanese Maritime Safety Agency as the SAR 200 (delivered 1997).

Saab J35 Draken (Saab/H.O. Arpfors)

Saab JA37 Viggen interceptors with F4 Wing of Swedish Air Force (Peter Modigh/Swedish Defence Images)

American Airlines ordered more than 140 Saab 340s

Saab 2000 airliner operated by Crossair

Saab S 100B Argus AEW&C aircraft based on 340B airliner

Saab Safari was developed into military armed Supporter

Saab J35 Draken (Saab/H.O. Arpfors)

Saab AB Gripen JAS 39 Gripen, Sweden's latest combat aircraft, using road as runway (Johnny Lindahl)

SAAC • Switzerland

See Swiss-American Aviation Corporation.

SÄÄSKI, OSAKEYHTIÖ • Finland

Founded 1928. Built two-seat biplane for wheels, skis or floats which was convertible for ambulance work and was developed into cabin type.

SABCA • Belgium

See Société Anonyme Belge de Constructions Aéronautiques.

SABLATNIG FLUGZEUGBAU GMBH • Germany

Austrian Josef Sablatnig experimented and flew before First World War. Moved to Germany and in 1913 became a director of Union Flugzeugwerke GmbH (q.v.), where he did technical work and flying. When Union company went into liquidation (1915) founded above-named company in Berlin, famous for seaplanes used by German Navy but built other types also. SF1 floatplane (1915) developed into very successful SF2 (licence-built by LFG and LVG; q.v.); SF4 was single-seat fighter floatplane, built both as biplane and triplane; SF5 was widely used SF2 replacement; SF8 was last Sablatnig floatplane built in numbers (trainer of 1918). Landplanes included trainers, single-engined night bombers and a monoplane. N1 was two-seat land fighter used at Kiel. After war developed civil types, including P1 four-passenger biplane and P3 six-passenger high-wing monoplane. One light sports type built, but aircraft work ceased 1921.

SABRE AIRCRAFT INC. • USA

Offers kits to build Sabre single- or two-seat microlight with Rogallo wing and trike.

SABRELINER CORPORATION • USA

Founded 1983, following purchase of Rockwell International's Sabreliner Division by Wolsey & Company, to support Sabreliners in use, upgrade Lockheed T-33 series aircraft, and other work. Won contract in 1989 to undertake life extension programme on USAF T-37s.

SADLER AIRCRAFT CORPORATION • USA

Previously known as American Microlight Inc and Sadler Aircraft Company, developed A-22 Piranha lightly armed surveillance version of its microlight, now also being developed by TUSAS (q.v.) in Turkey as Bat.

SAFA • France

see Société Anonyme Française Aéronautique.

SAGE, FREDERICK & COMPANY LTD. • UK

Company engaged originally in fine woodwork. In early 1915 was asked by Admiralty to build aircraft, and was first concerned with airships. In June 1915 received order for Short 184 floatplanes, and carried out modifications to, and built, Avro 504K trainers. Built own-design Sage Type II, two-seat biplane fighter, with enclosed crew and gunnery arrangements (flown 1916); Type III was trainer for Admiralty (flew 1917); Types 4a, b and c were patrol and trainer floatplanes; none entered production.

SAIMAN • Italy

See Società Anònima Industrie Meccàniche Aeronàutiche Navali.

ST CROIX AIRCRAFT • USA

Offers plans to build Pietenpol Aerial as biplane development of Pietenpol Aircamper, plus Excelsior Ultralight and replica of First World War Sopwith Triplane.

ST LOUIS AIRCRAFT CORPORATION • USA

Formed at St Louis, Missouri, as a subsidiary (later a division) of the St Louis Car Company. At 1929 Detroit Aircraft Show exhibited the Cardinal high-wing monoplane, the company's first aeroplane. Cardinal Senior which followed had more power. In mid/late 1930s made components but in 1940 delivered small batch of PT-15 biplane trainers to US Army. During Second World War made Fairchild PT-23 under subcontract.

Above: Sablatnig Luftdroschke monoplane

Right: Salmson 2A2 two-seat reconnaissance biplane

SALMSON • France

Founded 1912 at Billancourt, Seine, by Emile Salmson (1859-1917) to develop radial type watercooled engines jointly designed by Canton and Unné as installed in French, British and Russian aircraft. In late 1915 turned to aeroplane construction. First was unorthodox Salmson-Moineau SM-1 of 1916, designed by René Moineau, with 'buried' engine and twin tractor propellers. The Type 2 conventional two-seat reconnaissance tractor biplane was tested early 1917, with Salmson (Canton-Unné) engine. As the 2A2 it served with French and US squadrons and 2,300 were built. At Armistice 2A2 converted to Limousine, used by several European airlines. In mid-1930s turned to light aircraft, producing D6 Cricri parasol monoplane with small Salmson air-cooled radial engine (see Société Franáaise d'Aviation Nouvelle).

SAMSUNG HEAVY INDUSTRIES • South Korea

Founded 1938, and Samsung Aerospace Industries Co Ltd division established 1977, originally to undertake aeroengine work (which continues). Prime contractor among South Korean companies involved in producing F-16 fighters for the Republic of Korea Air Force under the Korean Fighter Programme (120 to be delivered by 1999), is heading development of the KTX-2 lead-in fighter trainer/light combat aircraft (with Lockheed Martin of the USA as a partner since 1997; expected to fly in 2001), is developing the Kari eight-seat business aircraft, heads a South Korean consortium developing airliners, assembles and markets the Russian Mil Mi-26 helicopter, collaborates on the Bell 427 helicopter, and produces components for Bell Canada helicopters, Boeing airliners and the Canadian Dash 8 airliner.

SAN • France

See Société Aéronautique Normande.

SANDERSON, ANGUS & COMPANY • UK

Engineering company of Newcastle-upon-Tyne, Northumberland, which built aircraft under subcontract during First World War, including Armstrong Whitworth F.K.8, Armstrong Whitworth Quadruplanes and Bristol Fighters.

Impression of Samsung KTX-2 supersonic trainers, being developed with Lockheed Martin

SANDS, RON • USA

Offers plans to construct full-size replicas, as Fokker Dr 1, Fokker D VIII and 1929 Primary Glider.

SÃO CARLOS ENGINEERING SCHOOL • Brazil

Engineering School of University of São Paulo took over former IPT (Instituto de Pesquisas Technologicas research institute) 1975. Produced prototypes. First flight of IPAI-26 Tuca two-seat aerobatic lightplane 1979. Other aircraft included IPAI-27 Jipe Voador (former SP-18 Onça), IPAI-28 Super Surubim, IPAI-29 Tira Prosa and IPAI-30.

SARGENT-FLETCHER COMPANY • USA

See Fletcher Aviation Company.

SASEBO NAVAL AIR ARSENAL • Japan

During Second World War built in quantity the Mitsubishi-designed F1M2 shipboard spotter/reconnaissance central-float seaplane, last operational biplane to serve with Japanese Navy.

SASO • France

See Société Aéronautique du Sud-Ouest.

SATIC • International

Special Aircraft Transport International Company GIE, formed October 1991 as joint venture between Aérospatiale of France and Daimler-Benz Aerospace Airbus of Germany to develop a successor to the Super Guppy outsized freighter used to carry large Airbus airliner assemblies between factories in Europe. Resulting A300-600ST Super Transporter, known also as Beluga, based on A300-600R but with many important modifications including a completely new upper fuselage section to provide a freight hold of 24 ft 3 in (7.4 m) cross-section, with access via the largest door ever installed on an aircraft (upward-opening); cockpit moved forward and below cargo deck; new tailplane with endfins. First Beluga flown September 1994 and four of five ordered now in service (last for delivery in 2001); also used for charters when not engaged on main work.

SAU SCIENTIFIC-PRODUCTION CORPORATION • Russia

Samoloty-Amfibii Universalnye established 1993 to develop and manufacture twin piston-engined R-50 Robert six-seat light amphibian (first six were to be built by Dubna); single-engined technology demonstrators were R-01 and R-02 (first flown 1989 and 1996 respectively).

SAUNDERS AIRCRAFT CORPORATION LTD. • Canada

Formed 1968 to design and manufacture ST-27 conversion of British de Havilland Heron light transport. Major changes included turboprop power. Was working on successor (ST-28) when financial support ended 1976.

SAUNDERS, S. E. LTD. • UK

Based at Cowed, Isle of Wight. Originally built boats, and later hulls for fast motor boats and some of earliest flying-boats (e.g. Sopwith Bat Boat). Especially famous for 'Consuta' copper-sewn plywood construction. In 1913 received

Below: SATIC A300-600ST Super Transporter, known also as Beluga, during test flying

Above: Saunders-Roe Princess flying-boat

Right: Saunders ST-27, a de Havilland Heron conversion

order for B.E. biplanes. During First World War built under subcontract Avro 504 landplanes, Short 184 floatplanes and Norman Thompson and Felixstowe F.2A and F.5 flying-boats. Began own design, first of which was T.1 two-seater (1917) with detachable wings for ship-board stowage. Aircraft built post-war included the Kittiwake seven-passenger twin-engined wooden amphibian of 1920 with camber-changing gear on wing leading and trailing edges; Medina ten-passenger twin-engined wooden flying-boat of 1926; and Valkyrie three-engined military flying-boat of 1927 with developed form of Linton-Hope hull.

SAUNDERS-ROE LTD. • UK

In 1928 pioneer pilot/constructor A. V. Roe (later Sir) acquired an interest in S. E. Saunders Ltd (q.v.) and firm was reconstituted as above. First new product was Cutty Sark flying-boat, with Fokker-type wing, built in small numbers; also larger Cloud (1931) of which RAF had 16. Most successful product was twin-engined London biplane flying-boat of 1934 which served with RAF until 1941. Shrimp two-seat four-engined aircraft was built to serve as research vehicle for larger types. Company built the Supermarine Walrus and Sea Otter in quantity. SR/A1 of 1947 was world's first jet-propelled flying-boat fighter, but was not ordered into service. Princess ten-turboprop commercial flying-boat of 1952 was a great technical achievement, but never entered service. SR.53, first flown in 1957, was experimental turbojet/rocket interceptor which demonstrated climb of about 50,000 ft (15,240 m)/min. Promising SR.177 development was abandoned despite international interest. Company entered helicopter field in early 1950s with small Skeeter (originally Cierva), though in 1928 S.E. Saunders had made Isaaco Hellcogyre (which never flew) for the Air Ministry. Five-seat P.531 built 1958, but in 1959 company was acquired by Westland Aircraft (q.v.), which developed the P.531 as the Wasp/Scout.

SAVAGES LTD. • UK

An old-established engineering and woodworking company of Kings Lynn, Norfolk, which built under subcontract during First World War Airco 1/1A, D.H.6 and Avro 504K.

Savary pre-WW1 biplane

SAVARY • France

Founded at Chartres by Robert Savary. Was building biplanes in 1910. Won order for three aircraft after military trials in 1911. In February 1913 Joseph Frantz established time-to-height record on Savary biplane with Salmson engine, carrying five passengers, but pre-war output was ten machines only. In 1915 Robert Savary was associated with Henri de la Fresnaye in forming a joint company to build Nieuport fighters. No aircraft built after First World War.

SAVIAT JSC • Russia

Formed 1990 to develop a series of composite passenger aircraft, each featuring rhomboidal wings with the slightly swept lower wings joined to forward-swept upper wings via fins; engine with ducted pusher propeller. Five-seat E-1 shown in mock-up form but development halted 1995-96, when restarted with MiG 'MAPO-M' assistance; 16-seat E-5 proposed.

SCALED COMPOSITES, INC. • USA

Founded 1980 by Burt Rutan as a research-and-development company, offering its services to those requiring specialist help in developing advanced aircraft projects. Undertook work on the NASA AD-1 oblique-wing research aircraft, a sub-scale demonstrator of the Fairchild NGT trainer (flown September 1981), a sub-scale demonstrator of the Beech Starship 1 business aircraft (at which time company bought by Beech, 1985, but sold back 1988), plus several other uniquely configured aircraft that included the Rutan 151 ARES agile response effective support combat jet (first flown February 1990). Latest aircraft is Proteus multipurpose, high-altitude and long-duration sensor platform, first flown as a proof-of-concept prototype in July 1998 and featuring rear-mounted main wings, large-span canards, twin tail booms and a slender fuselage. Initial application is to be for Angel Technologies Corporation, which requires many for communications relay use.

SCAN • France

See Société de Constructions Aéro Navales de Port-Neuf

S.C. AVIOANE SA CRAIOVA • Romania

New name from 1991 for IAv Craiova (q.v.). Work on IAR-93 stopped. IAR 99 Soim (first flown 1985) and improved IAR 109 Swift jet trainers, lead-in fighter trainers and light attack aircraft superseded by New IAR 99 Soim that first flew in May 1997.

SCENIC AIR LINES • USA

In 1977 acquired from American Jet Industries (q.v.) engineering and manufacturing rights for turboprop conversions of Cessna Models 402 and 414, now known as Turbo Star 402 and Turbo Star Pressurised 414. Converted Twin Otters to have low-noise propellers and large windows in 1991.

SCHAFER AIRCRAFT MODIFICATIONS INC. • USA

Founded 1977, and from 1979 developed modifications for other aircraft, including installing turboprop engines to Piper Navajo as Schafer Comanchero, turboprop engines to Piper Chieftain as Comanchero 500, installing higher-rated turboprops to Piper Cheyenne II as Comanchero 750, and developing turboprop conversion and fuselage stretch for DC-3 as DC-3-65TP Cargomaster.

SCHAPEL AIRCRAFT COMPANY • USA

Founded 1973. Produced S-525 Super Swat twin boom and turboprop-powered agricultural aircraft 1980, followed by design of S-325 Mini-Swat conventionally-configured agricultural aircraft, SA-882 Flying Wing tailless research aircraft 1985, and design for S-185 as lightweight single-seat attack aircraft.

Scheibe SF-40-C-Allround

SCHEIBE-FLUGZEUGBAU GMBH • Germany

Formed at Dachau, near Munich, in 1951 by Egon Scheibe, who at first built gliders designed by Scheibe in Austria. His Sperling two-seat light high-wing monoplane first flew August 1955, and was developed with new wing and tail as SF-23A and built in numbers until 1963. SF-24A Motorspatz built from 1959. SF-25 Motorfalke license-built from 1970 by Slingsby Sailplanes Ltd. (q.v.) in U.K.

as Type 61 Falke. SF-28A Tandem-Falke tandem two-seat motorglider no longer offered. Currently available are the SF-25C Falke 2000 and Rotax-Falke two-seat motorgliders, and the SF-40 two-seat lightplane (first flown 1994), the latter originally offered in A and B versions with tail-wheel undercarriages, but the latest version is the SF-40-C-Allround with a nosewheel undercarriage. SF-34B Delphin now produced in France as the S.N. Centrair

Alliance 34 two-seat glider, while the SF-36 R two-seat motorglider is also expected to go into production in France.

SCHELLER, BERNHARD • Germany

In early 1930s built cantilever low-wing two-seat mono-plane with continuous head-fairing. Steel-tube con-struction.

Scheibe Motorfalke powered glider

SCHEMPP-HIRTH FLUGZEUGBAU GMBH • Germany

In 1935 at Göppingen, near Stuttgart, Wolf Hirth (q.v.) founded company named Sportflugzeugbau Schempp-Hirth to build sailplanes. In 1960s company renamed and built the Milan G56 light tourer, also French Piel Emeraude under license. During early 1960s production of powered aircraft ceased, license rights for Emeraude being transferred to Binder Aviatik AG (q.v.). Currently builds large series of gliders and motorgliders in Discus, Janus, Nimbus and Ventus forms.

SCHEUTZOW HELICOPTER CORPORATION • U.S.A.

Formed early 1960s by Webb Scheutzow to build light helicopter with special rotorhead (blades carried on rubber bushings). Bee side-by-side two-seater flew 1966. Ceased development 1977.

SCHRAMM AIRCRAFT COMPANY • U.S.A.

Founded 1968 by D J Schramm to market the Javelin single-seat helicopter in assembled and component forms (first flown 1965). See RotorWay.

SCHRECK, HYDRAVIONS FBA • France

Louis Schreck, South American representative for Delaunay-Belleville automobiles, returned to France in 1909. Joined Hanriot at Juvissey and in 1911, jointly with engi-

Scheutzow Model B helicopter

neer named Gaudard, designed D'Artois flying-boat. Formed Hydravions Schreck FBA, and aided by British capital acquired Donnet-Lévêque/Denhaut flying-boat patents, and was associated with that company until it was acquired by Bernard (q.v.) in 1934. FBA 16 was side by-side two-seat flying-boat; FBA 17 a utility type which established a seaplane height record in December 1923. A development was brought by U.S. Coast Guard in 1931. In the later 1930s Schreck was carrying out flying-boat repairs and subcontract work.

SCHÜTTE-LANZ, LUFTFAHRZEUGBAU • Germany

In 1909 the well-known company Luftschifflan Schütte-Lanz was established to build airships. This company's Luftfahrzeugbau was founded in 1915 at Zeesen, near Königswusterhausen, Brandenburg, in recognition of the fact that airships must be supplemented by airplanes. The

Schweizer-built Grumman Ag-Cat

C-1 of 1915 had an unconventional engine installation; D-III built in 1916 was a single-seat fighter. Company built the Ago-Flugzeugwerke (q.v.) two-seat C-IV in quantity. Had studied "giant" aircraft and was included in 1916 R-plane "giant" program. Contract awarded for six Staaken bombers. R.27-29 delivered late 1917 and became operational; three other Staaken machines (R.84-86) unfinished at Armistice. Company also made special equipment (e.g. bomb gear and engine-room telegraphs) for other builders of giants, but own ambitious twin-boom project of 1917 remained unrealized. After aircraft work ended company remained as plywood manufacturer.

SCHWEIZER AIRCRAFT CORPORATION • U.S.A.

Primarily designers and makers of sailplanes, one of which (SGS 2-32) fitted with piston engine was tested by Lockheed Aircraft Corporation (q.v.) as Q-Star for "quiet recon-

Schweizer RU-38A Twin Condor, first flown 1995

Schweizer SA 2-37A surveillance aircraft

YO-3A, using Schweizer wings and tail, new fuselage and muffled engine. Company also built for Grumman (q.v.) the Ag-Cat agricultural biplane, later for Gulfstream, before acquiring rights in 1981 (Ag-Cat subsequently produced by Ag-Cat Corporation; q.v.). In 1972 acquired rights for Teal light amphibian, but in 1976 sold them to Teal Aircraft Corporation (q.v.). Makes fuselage assemblies for Piper Aircraft Corporation and structures for Bell Helicopters (both q.v.). Became licence-holder for Hughes 300 helicopter in 1983, producing piston-engined three-seat Model 300C from 1984 to present day and developing new 3/4-seat Model 330 turboshaft-powered helicopter (first flown June 1988); also supports Hughes Model 269s. In 1986 flew the SA 2-37A low-noise special-missions aircraft suited to surveillance and other roles, followed in May 1995 by a radical twin-boom SA 2-37A conversion known as SA 2-38A, two joining the US Coast Guard as RU-38A Twin Condors for covert patrol and surveillance (one by conversion, one built as new).

SCHWEIZERISCHE FLUGZEUGFABRIK •
Germany

See Flugzeughau A. Comte.

Right: Schweizer Model 300C three-seat helicopter

SCIM • France

See Société Générale des Constructions Industrielles et Mécaniques.

SCINTEX-AVIATION SA • France

A division of Scintex SA, a mechanical and electrical equipment manufacturer, held an exclusive licence to build improved versions of the Piel Emeraude. Built the CP301C, also in C1, C2 and C3 versions; the two-seat Super Emeraude with fixed landing gear as the CP1310/CP1315; and the 4/5 seat ML 250 Rubis, with retractable landing gear, which first flew on June 1962.

SCOTTISH AVIATION LTD. • UK

Formed 1935, but for several years was concerned mainly with aircraft repair work and management of flying school and airport (Prestwick, Scotland). First aircraft produced was Prestwick Pioneer single-engined five-seat STOL monoplane, first flown 1950. Twin Pioneer of 1957 first appeared as 16-passenger civil type, but was used also by RAF. Company re-engaged in important repair, maintenance and modification work, involving Lockheed aircraft, and made freighter conversion of Vickers Viscount. Has made large components for Lockheed Hercules over long period. Final aircraft under its own name were Bulldog (flown originally in 1968 as military trainer version of Beagle Pup); Bullfinch with retractable landing gear, first flown August 1976; and twin-turboprop Jetstream, developed 1966-1970 by Handley Page (q.v.) and continued by BAe. Merged into British Aerospace (q.v.) in April 1977; as a British Aerospace company offered support facilities for Beagle Pup, B.206 and Basset.

SEA • France

See Société d'Etudes Aéronautiques.

SEABIRD AVIATION AUSTRALIA PTY LTD. • Australia

Currently offers the Seeker SB7L two-seat monoplane (first flown October 1989), featuring a pod-and-boom fuselage with heavily glazed cabin, braced high-mounted wings with two hardpoints for attaching 264 lb (120 kg) of stores, and a piston engine with pusher propeller. Uses include agriculture, surveillance, patrol, photographic, search and rescue, training, media.

SEAPLANE EXPERIMENTAL STATION • UK

Located at Felixstowe, Suffolk, its products being identified by initial F. Particularly associated with Squadron Commander J. C. Porte, RNAS, who assumed command of the Felixstowe station in September 1915. Porte had started aeronautical work in 1909; his interest in flying-boats led him to join Curtiss, in USA, during 1914. Before taking

Scottish Aviation Bulldog military trainer

command at Felixstowe had flown Curtiss flying-boats on operations, and set out to improve them. Felixstowe F.1 had wings and tail of Curtiss H.4 but Porte hull. F.2 was comparable development of H.12, and further improved as F.2A and used extensively from late 1917. Porte Baby was early 3-engined type, from one of which a Bristol Scout was air-launched in May 1916. F.3 was larger than F.2A, but though built in quantity was less highly regarded. Some were built in Malta Dockyard, others by British contractors. Some completed as further developed F.5, a type also used by US Navy and Japan. Felixstowe Fury was very large 5-engined type, flown (and wrecked) after Armistice.

SEAWIND/SNA INC. • USA

Markets kits to construct Seawind 3000 four-seat composites amphibian, developed from the former Canadian Seawind 2000.

SECAN • France

See Société d'Études et de Constructions Aéro-Navales.

SECAT • France

See Société d'Études et de Construction d'Avions de Tourisme.

Scottish Aviation Twin Pioneer STOL monoplane

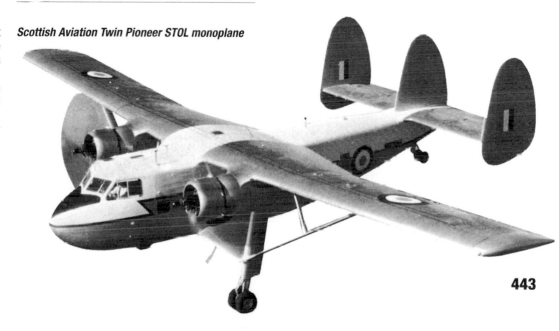

SECM • France

See Société d'Emboutissage et de Constructions Mécaniques.

SECURITY AIRCRAFT CORPORATION • USA

As Security National Aircraft Corporation was established by W. B. Kinner, founder of Kinner Airplane & Motor Corporation (q.v.). Type SI-A was almost identical to Kinner Sportster. Taken over February 1937 by company named as above. New factory then built at Long Beach, California, to make Airster 2-seat monoplane and Security 5-cylinder radial.

SEEMS • France

See Société d'Exploitation des Etablissements Morane-Saulnier.

SEGUIN AVIATION • USA

Company established 1967 to produce a conversion of the Piper (q.v.) twin-engined Apache. Known as the Seguin/Piper Geronimo, it had more powerful engines, and many refinements to the original structure and equipment.

Seversky P-35 single-seat fighter

SEIBEL HELICOPTER COMPANY • USA

Established early 1948. Seibel had worked with Bell Helicopters, but joined the Boeing company (both q.v.) in 1946. With two collaborators built in 1947 S-3 light helicopter (lateral and longitudinal control effected by changing centre of gravity). S-4A of 1948 had special blade-attachment system patented for S-3. Followed by S-4B with more powerful engine and side-by-side seats. In March 1952 company taken over by Cessna (q.v.).

SELLET-PELLETIER HÉLICOPTERE • France

First flew in 1987 the Grillon 120 single/two-seat light helicopter.

SEPECAT • International

See Société Européene de Production de l'Avion Ecole de Combat et d'Appui Tactique.

SEQUOIA AIRCRAFT CORPORATION • USA

Markets in plans and kit forms a homebuilt version of the Italian Stelio Frati F.8L Falco wooden two-seat monoplane, plus the metal 300 Sequoia.

SERV-AERO ENGINEERING INC. • USA

At Municipal Airport, Salina, California, converted to turbine power standard types of agricultural aircraft powered formerly by Pratt & Whitney radial piston-engines, including Rockwell Thrush Commander. Other conversions, including those of Grumman Ag-Cat biplanes, involved fitting the British Alvis Leonides engine.

SERVICE AVIATION COMPANY • USA

Was based at Wabash, Indiana, trading as Sattco. In summer of 1922 built Liberty-engined transport largely from D.H.4 parts. Pilot sat behind cabin in ply-covered fuselage.

SERVICIOS AEREAS DE AMERICA SA • Mexico

In 1960s serviced and repaired aircraft and engines, but undertook licence-manufacture of higher-powered Maule

Seversky BT-8 basic trainer

M-4, developed specially for Mexican conditions and called Cuauhtemoc M-1.

SET • Romania

Established at Bucharest 1923. SET X was single-seat fighter/trainer biplane; SET XV single-seat fighter biplane with enclosed cockpit, built in small numbers for Romanian Air Force during early 1930s; SET 7 was a specially equipped trainer; SET 7K a re-engined observation derivative ordered in series by Romanian Government. Later SET 31 also adopted officially.

SEVERSKY AIRCRAFT CORPORATION • USA

Incorporated February 1931 by Russian-born Alexander P. Seversky (or De Seversky), First World War military pilot who became US citizen 1927. A test pilot and consulting engineer, he established the Seversky Aero Corporation in 1922. Developed novel amphibious landing gear, promoted by Seversky Aircraft Corporation for fast all-metal fighter-type aircraft. Aircraft design owed much to Alexander Kartveli, who developed landplane fighters with retractable landing gear. In 1935 Seversky established new speed record for amphibious aircraft, and land-fighter development culminated in order for 77 single-seaters for USAAC, designated P-35. In 1939-1940, following orders for amphibians from USSR and landplanes from Japan, Sweden contracted for 120 export versions of P-35. Several fighter, multipurpose and trainer variants developed, and BT-8 (first purpose-built machine of its class) adopted in USA. Seversky Executive (2 passengers in cabin behind pilot) won 1937 Bendix Trophy race. In 1939 company offered USAAC XP-41 single-seat fighter, but in October 1939 company was reorganised as Republic Aviation Corporation (q.v.). Special supercharger evolution for late Seversky fighters led to the famous Republic P-47 Thunderbolt long-range escort fighter/bomber.

SEYEDO SHOHADA • Iran

Seyedo Shohada project was for the conversion of Bell 206A JetRanger into a tandem two-seat gunship helicopter or an agricultural helicopter.

SF • Switzerland

Schweizerische Unternehmung für Flugzeuge und Systeme Entreprise Suisse d'Aeronautique et de Systemes

Impresa Svizzera d'Aeronautica e Sistemi (Swiss Aircraft and System Company), founded 1996 from amalgamation of former F + W and industrial division of Swiss Air Force Logistics Command and various departments of Federal Ordnance Office. Continues work on Hornet and Airbus programmes, plus Boeing 717 and MD-80, Rafale auxiliary tanks, Ariane rocket nose fairings, and more.

SFAN • France

See Société Française d'Aviation Nouvelle.

SFCA • France

See Société Française de Constructions Aéronautiques.

SG AVIATION (INDUSTRIA AERONAUTICA ITALIANA) • Italy

Markets two- and three-seat versions of the Storm monoplane in assembled and kit forms.

SGP • Austria

See Simmering-Graz-Pauker AG.

SHAANXI AIRCRAFT COMPANY • China

First flew in December 1974 a Chinese derivative of the Antonov An-12B freighter, as the Y8, of which some 60 have gone into military and civil use. Maritime surveillance prototype also flown with Litton radar.

SHADIN COMPANY LTD. • USA

Formed to produce developed version of Bücker Bü 181 Bestmann, as S-10 Aeropony.

SHANGHAI AVIATION INDUSTRIAL CORPORATION • China

Assembled and then manufactured 35 McDonnell Douglas (now Boeing) MD-80 series airliners, the first flying in July 1987 and entering commercial service that same month. Delivery of the first of 20 follow-on MD-90-30 Trunkliners began 1998.

SHCHERBAKOV, A. Y. • USSR

Leader of a design group which developed the twin-engined high-wing monoplane Shch-2 light transport, used for such duties as liaison, transport and supply of partisan forces late in Second World War. After war adopted by Aeroflot. Robust structure, with fixed landing gear and large double freight doors, made the Shch-2 adaptable for a wide variety of transport duties.

SHCHETININ • USSR

In 1909 the first Russian aeronautical company, named Pervoe Rossikoe Tovarishchestvo Vozdukhoplana Vaniya

Shaanxi Y8C pressurised version of Y8, first flown 1990

Shchetinin M-5 flying-boat trainer

S.S. Shchetinin after its principal founder, was established in St Petersburg. A collaborator in the enterprise was another pioneer, the designer Y. M. Hakkel, and about 1912-1913 the company was joined by the later-renowned D. P. Grigorovich. First built Farman and Blériot-type aircraft, but after Grigorovich joined began to specialise in marine aircraft. First was the M-1 flying-boat of 1913, generally of Donnet-Lévêque type. M-5 of 1915 was a trainer and reconnaissance type built for the Imperial Navy. About 500 examples of the larger and higher-powered M-9 of 1915-1916 were built. Later construction included the M-11 single-seat fighter flying-boat; and the larger M-15 and M-20 reconnaissance aircraft.

SHENYANG AIRCRAFT CORPORATION • China

This important manufacturer has constructed the majority of Chinese fighters, fighter-bombers and jet trainers since the 1950s, including the JJ-2 two-seat jet trainer variant of the Soviet MiG-15UTI, J-5 variants of the MiG-17F and PF from 1956 to 1959, J-6 variants of MiG-19, JJ-6 trainers, and an enlarged and twin-engined development of the Chengdu J-7 known as J-8 *Finback* (first flown July 1969), which was still being developed in improved versions in the latter 1990s. Undertakes Chinese assembly of the Russian Sukhoi Su-27 fighter, for Chinese service as the J-11, and produces components for Airbus, Boeing, de Havilland and LockheedMartin transports.

SHENYANG SAILPLANE AND LIGHTPLANE CO. LTD. • China

Produces the HY 650 (HU2) three/four-seat braced-wing cabin lightplane (first flown 1996 in current C and D versions).

SHERPA AIRCRAFT MANUFACTURING COMPANY • USA

Markets the Sherpa five-seat utility cabin monoplane (first flown 1994).

Right: Shenyang J-8 II multirole fighter in PLA Air Force service

ShinMaywa search-and-rescue aircraft

SHERWOOD AMERICA AVIATION • USA

Markets the Sherwood Ranger XP biplane (see TCD).

SHIJIAZHUANG AIRCRAFT MANUFACTURING CORPORATION • China

Established 1970 and currently manufacturing the Y5 as a licence-built version of the Antonov An-2 general-purpose biplane (Chinese manufacture of An-2 began in 1957), plus several very light aircraft in the W5A, W5B and W6 Dragonfly range.

SHINMAYWA INDUSTRIES LTD. • Japan

ShinMaywa became the title of the Kawanishi company after re-establishment in October 1949 as overhaul centre for Japanese and US aircraft. Also made components for other constructors, developed re-engined de Havilland Heron, but after contract in January 1966 directed attention especially to new marine aircraft. Rebuilt a Grumman Albatross as a dynamically similar flying model for projected very large STOL ASW flying-boat for Japanese Maritime Self Defence Force. The latter type developed as four-turboprop PS-1, but later also as US-1 amphibious search-and-rescue aircraft. PS-1 flew October 1967; US-1 October 1974. First prototype PS-1 converted later as waterbombing test vehicle. Basic type remarkable for low take-off and landing speeds, achieved by boundary-layer control system and large flaps for slipstream deflection. Company also carries out major subcontract work for advanced Mitsubishi and Kawasaki aircraft (both q.v.), and manufactures components for Boeing 717/757/767/777 and Gulfstream bizjets.

SHINN ENGINEERING INC. • USA

During early 1960s produced, as Shinn Model 2150-A, about 50 Morrisey (q.v.) 2150 utility two-seat lightplanes.

SHIN NIHON KOKU SEIBI KABUSHIKI KAISHA • Japan

Established December 1952 as Itoh Chu Koku Seibi Kabushiki Kaisha to maintain and repair light aircraft. In

Right: ShinMaywa US-1A STOL amphibian for search and rescue and other roles

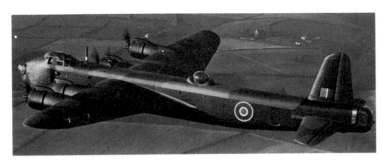

Left: Short Stirling, the RAF's first four-engined monoplane bomber

Left: Short G-Class long-range flying-boat

Left: Short Skyvan light utility transport

1960 produced the N-58 Cygnet light cabin monoplane designed by students at Nihon University. Aided in development of, and produced, N-62 Eaglet four-seater also designed at Nihon University. Late in 1968 converted a number of North American T-6 Texan trainers to represent Nakajima BSN torpedo-bombers for film *Tora! Tora! Tora!*. Adopted above company name on 29 May 1970, thereafter concentrating on manufacture of aircraft equipment.

SHIRL DICKEY ENTERPRISES • USA

Sells plans to construct E-Racer two-seat canard monoplane of composites construction.

SHORT & HARLAND LTD. • UK

In June 1936 Short Bros Ltd (see following entry) collaborated with shipbuilders Harland & Wolff to form above-named company. In Second World War built and had built under subcontract Short Stirling four-engined bombers and Sunderland flying-boats; also Handley Page Here-fords. In 1947 Short & Harland joined Short Brothers (Rochester & Bedford) Ltd and altered name to Short Brothers and Harland Ltd, concentrating activities at Belfast, Northern Ireland. Sealand twin-engined amphibian flying-boat of 1948 was produced in small numbers. Sandringham and Solent flying-boats used by BOAC stemmed from the Sunderland. Of great technical significance was the SC.1 VTOL (jet-lift) research programme, which followed exploratory research by Rolls-Royce. First free vertical take-off made 25 October 1958. Company became heavily involved in production of English Electric Canberra and Bristol Britannia. From 1963 built Belfast heavy transports (four turboprops) and many Skyvan light piston-engined transports (first flown January 1963). Twin-turboprop Shorts 330 30-passenger regional airliner flown August 1974, with Sherpa offered as freighter derivative. Much important manufacture and modification work carried out for leading international constructors and operators under subcontract. Name Short Brothers Ltd readopted June 1977 (see next entry).

SHORT BROTHERS PLC • UK

Founded by brothers Horace, Eustace and Oswald Short in November 1908 as Short Brothers Ltd, though Eustace and Oswald had made balloons since 1898. At Leysdown, Isle of Sheppey, completed first biplane, construction of which had begun at Battersea, London, in 1909. Received order for six Wright biplanes, in one of which Hon. C. S. Rolls made first return crossing of English Channel. Company pioneered multi-engine and multi-propeller types,

Above: Shorts Belfast heavy freighter, built for the RAF but later used commercially by HeavyLift Cargo Airlines

and tractor biplanes with folding wings for naval use. Did more to aid development of early naval flying than any other British firm. New works at Rochester, Kent, started 1914. Most famous type was 184 torpedo-bomber, which was used at Battle of Jutland and was also the first to sink a ship at sea. During First World War established airship works at Cardington, Bedfordshire. After First World War

developed Cromarty flying-boat but diversified in other fields. Gave special attention to all-metal aircraft (Silver Streak of 1920 and derivatives) and concentrated later on large civil and military flying-boats (Singapore biplane series for RAF from 1926; Calcutta and Kent for Imperial Airways). Six-engined Sarafand of 1936 was then largest British flying-boat. Wing form developed for Scion and

Scion Senior monoplanes used for famous fleet of Empire flying-boats in 1936, for equally-famous Sunderland military development; also on Short-Mayo composite aircraft and Stirling four-engined monoplane bomber.

Jointly established Short and Harland Ltd in 1936 with shipbuilder Harland & Wolff (see previous entry); became British Government run 1943, leading to integration of

Short Brothers (Rochester & Bedford) Ltd and Short and Harland into Short Brothers and Harland Ltd in 1947 (see entry above). Name Short Brothers Ltd readopted June 1977, but current name Short Brothers PLC, as part of Bombardier Aerospace Group since 1989 (see Bombardier Inc) and operating three principal business units, as Aero-space producing aircraft components and engine nacelles, Missile Systems, and Belfast City Airport. Shorts 360 36-passenger transport (first flown June 1981) followed Shorts 330/Sherpa, with final complete aircraft built by Shorts becoming the Tucano for the RAF, a variant of the EMBRAER turboprop trainer.

Above: EMBRAER Tucano variant for the RAF was the final complete aircraft produced by Shorts

Far right: SIAI-Marchetti SF260 is now marketed by Aermacchi; seen here are two Turkish SF260Ds, as previously delivered by SIAI-Marchetti

SIAI-Marchetti SM.1019 two-seat STOL lightplane

SIAT Flamingo two/four-seat light aircraft

SHOWA HIKOKI KOGYO KABUSHIKI KAISHA • Japan

Before and during Second World War built the Douglas DC-3 under licence. After war was first Japanese aircraft manufacturing company to resume operations, under US Government contracts. Aided in manufacture of NAMC YS-11 Japanese-designed transport.

SIAI • Italy

See Società Idrovolanti Alta Italia.

SIAI-MARCHETTI SOCIETÁ PER AZIONI • Italy

The former Savoia Marchetti company (see Società Idrovolanti Alta Italia), the history of which it shares. Since 1946 engaged in overhaul and repair work and developed new aircraft. Types have included SA.202 Bravo trainer produced jointly with FFA (q.v.) in Switzerland; S.205 four-seater and S.208 development. First flew SF.250 aerobatic trainer in July 1964; became highly successful SF.260 production aircraft for civil and military use

(initials in SF.260 denoted design by Stelio Frati). In 1968 company formed a Vertical Flight Division, but increasing helicopter work became associated with Agusta and Elicotteri Meridionale. SM.1019 light multipurpose high-wing monoplane followed 1969, SF.600 Canguro transport 1979 (recently taken over by VulcanAir, q.v.), and S211 jet trainer and light attack aircraft 1981. Company taken over by Aermacchi January 1997.

SIAT • Germany

See Siebelwerke-ATG GmbH.

SIBNIA NAMED AFTER CHAPLYGIN • Russia

Siberian aeronautical research institute founded in 1940s as reserve organisation in war for TsAGI. In addition to aerodynamics testing and other work has developed (with Rastr Scientific-Technical Centre) the Dzhinn two-seat lightplane and builds replicas of the Polikarpov I-16 and I-153 fighters of the 1930s.

SIDDELEY-DEASY MOTOR CAR COMPANY LTD. • UK

Based at Coventry, Warwickshire; was concerned in production of RAF R.E.7 and R.E.8 and Airco D.H.10 during First World War. Own experimental types included R.T.1 of 1917-1918, a redesigned R.E.8; S.R.2 Siskin, developed from ideas of Major F. M. Green and precursor of famous Armstrong Whitworth line of fighters; and Sinaia twin-engined bomber, completed 1921, also associated with Armstrong Whitworth. In 1919 Armstrong Whitworth and Siddeley-Deasy combined to form in 1920 Sir W. G. Armstrong Whitworth Aircraft Ltd (q.v.).

SIEBELWERKE-ATG GMBH • Germany

Name was that of F. W. Siebel (1891-1954), associated with early sport-flying in Germany and who helped form the Klemm company (q.v.), for which he took charge of new works at Halle (Saale). In 1937 Siebel established own company as Flugzeugwerke Halle GmbH (q.v.), later renamed as above. First aircraft was Fh 104 5-passenger monoplane of 1937. Si 201 was experimental military

Left: Sikorsky S-58 in US Navy service

Left: Sikorsky S-64 flying-crane helicopter

Right: Sikorsky CH-53E Super Stallion in US Marine Corps service

reconnaissance aircraft; Si 202 Hummel of 1938 a side-by-side 2-seater. In Second World War Siebel contributed to production of standard German military types; also built own Si 204 communications aircraft, though this was mainly built by SNCAC (q.v.) in France. After war produced Si 222 Super-Hummel and 3-seat Si 308. As member of Nordflug group helped with Noratlas.

SIEMENS-SCHUCKERT WERKE GMBH • Germany

Began airship construction in 1907. In 1909 manufactured aeroplanes, but poor results stopped work in 1911. Aeroplane department reopened 1914. In October started design of four-engined aircraft similar to that of Sikorsky in Russia. As entirely new venture company sponsored designs by two Steffen brothers leading to giants R.I-VII of 1915-1917. R.VIII, which did not fly, was then world's largest aeroplane with span of 158 ft (48.16 m), and had experimental rotating gun-turret. Other advanced projects included steam-turbine monoplane and wire-guided flying bombs. Company also made E-I monoplane single-seat fighter and D-I copy of Nieuport. D-III and D-IV also built in quantity. Fighters were technically very advanced.

SIEMETZKI, ALFONS • Germany

Known also as Asro, and from Asro T-3 prototype single-seat turbine-powered helicopter (first flown December 1961) Siemetzki developed Asro 4 turbine-powered two-seater, ground tests of which began May 1964.

SIKORSKY AIRCRAFT • USA

Igor Sikorsky (1889-1972) founded company as Sikorsky Aero Engineering Corporation 5 March 1923. As young Russian built first helicopter in 1909, but no flight achieved. In 1912 was appointed to technical post with Russo-Baltic Waggon Works. Pioneered very large four-engined aircraft and continued development during First World War. After forming US company built large twin-engined S-29A. Numerous experimental and production aeroplanes in late 1920s and 1930s, and in October 1928 Sikorsky Aviation Corporation founded, becoming in 1929 a division of United Technologies Corporation (so remaining). Name Sikorsky

Sikorsky S-69 two-seat research helicopter

Sikorsky CH-53E heavy-lift helicopter

Sikorsky S-70 assault helicopter prototype

truly re-established by flying-boats and amphibians. S-38 twin-engined amphibian preceded S-40 four-engined flying-boat of 1931. S-42 had full-length hull, set new records and pioneered trans-ocean commercial flying.

Sikorsky still lured by helicopter idea, and on 14 September 1939 flew his VS-300 in controlled flight. VS-300 much modified in development. XR-4 of 1942 was first practical US military helicopter. Later types immensely varied, including: S-51 (first flown August 1943 as proto-

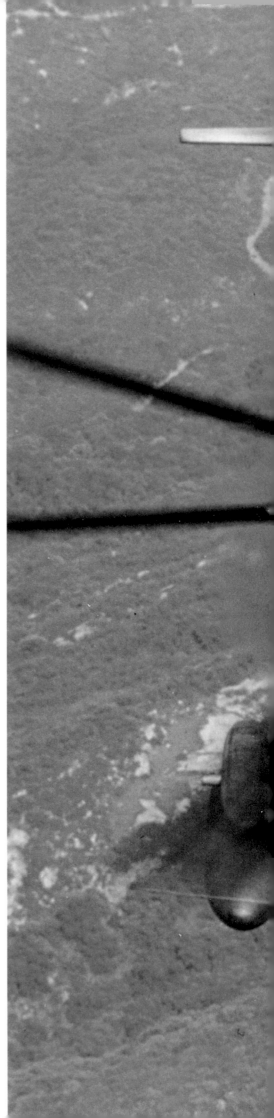

*Sikorsky S-70 Black Hawk with
External Stores Support System
for carrying weapons*

Sikorsky S-70B Seahawk naval helicopter for Greece

Sikorsky S-76C+ with increased engine power

Sikorsky SH-3 Sea King, operated by Canadian Forces as CH-124, seen overflying two destroyers (Canadian Forces/Ken Matherson)

type for military tandem two-seat R-5, later also going into production in four-seat S-51 commercial form), two-seat S-52 (first flown 1947 and developed into three/four-seat model), S-55 (first flown November 1949 and with the engine in the fuselage nose to keep the main cabin clear for 12 troops or passengers) and S-58 (first flown March 1954), all establishing world fame for Sikorsky helicopters, while S-61 (first flown March 1959) formed the basis for many of the western world's most important amphibious anti-submarine helicopters in the SH-3 Sea King series.

Currently specialises in intermediate/heavy helicopters,

although jointly developing the RAH-66 Comanche tandem two-seat multirole battlefield helicopter with Boeing (first flown January 1996) for US Army service from the year 2006. Current range includes S-70/H-60 Black Hawk (first flown October 1974) as military assault helicopter for 11 14 equipped troops, with variants for electronic warfare, combat rescue, special operation and more, with optional armament via external stores support system stub-wings; SH-60 Seahawk naval anti-submarine and anti-ship derivative of Black Hawk, also capable of transport, medevac, communications, search and rescue, and more (first flown

December 1979) and with its own variants including Jay-hawk medium-range recovery multi-mission helicopter for the US Coast Guard; S-76 civil and military 14-seat twin-turboshaft helicopter (first flown March 1977); H-76 Eagle armed multirole and naval variant of S-76; triple-turboshaft CH-53E Super Stallion heavy transport and amphibious assault helicopter (first flown March 1974), with MH-53E Sea Dragon US Navy airborne mine-countermeasures variant, and S-80 export model; and latest S-92 Helibus of 1998 first appearance as a civil/military medium twin-tur-boshaft helicopter for up to 22 passengers.

459

Boeing and Sikorsky are teamed to produce the RAH 66 Comanche multirole battlefield helicopter for the US Army

Silvercraft SH-4 light helicopter

SILVAIRE AIRCRAFT COMPANY • USA

At end of Second World War production tooling for Model 8 Silvaire was moved by Luscombe Airplane Corporation (q.v.) to Dallas, Texas. In 1949 Luscombe company was brought by Temco Aircraft Corporation (q.v.) which built about 50 Silvaires. In 1955 the above-named company acquired rights and equipment for Model 8 Silvaire, inaugurated production at Fort Collins, Colorado, and flew first aircraft off line September 1956.

SILVERCRAFT SPA • Italy

Formed early 1962. In October 1963 flew XY prototype light helicopter, further developed with financial and technical assistance of shareholder SIAI-Marchetti. SH-4 (flown 1963 in XY prototype form and 1965 as SH-4) was first helicopter of all-Italian design and construction to receive both Italian and US certification. By late 1960s serious production had begun as SIAI-Marchetti/Silvercraft SH-4, but under name Silvercraft alone deliveries began 1970. Production ceased 1977, as single example of SH-200 two-seater first appeared.

SIMB • France

See Société Industrielle des Métaux et du Bois.

SIMERA • South Africa

Previously a separate division of Denel (Pty) Ltd's Aerospace Group, undertaking civil activities that included maintenance, refurbishment and upgrade of aircraft, engines and components. Agreement of 1994 with Deutsche Airbus covered conversion of A300s and A310s into freighters. Merged with Atlas Aviation division in April 1996 under new name Denel Aviation (q.v.)

SIMMERING-GRAZ PAUKER AG. • Austria

A well-known engineering company which, in early 1960s, planned production of its four-seat twin-engined SGP-222, which had first flown May 1959. Plans abandoned by mid-1960s, though several prototypes built.

SGP-222 lightplane prototype

SIMMONDS AIRCRAFT LTD. • UK

Formed September 1928, in which year O. E. (later Sir Oliver) Simmonds designed and built the Spartan two-seat biplane. Outwardly conventional, but planned for 'Spartan' economy (e.g. interchangeable wings and ailerons, and rudder interchangeable with elevator). At Southampton, Hampshire, produced 49 examples, mostly for export, but some for National Flying Services Ltd. One made many Arctic flights. (See Spartan Aircraft Ltd.)

SIMPLEX • France

In early 1920s built tailless monoplanes to design of M. Arnoux, one of which was entered for 1922 Coupe Deutsch race. Wing was built in one piece.

SIMPLEX AIRCRAFT CORPORATION • USA

Founded 1928 at Defiance, Ohio. Built Red Arrow two-seat mid-wing monoplane, with optional cockpit enclosure. It was of wooden construction. A monoplane called the Kite was developed in 1931.

SINGAPORE TECHNOLOGIES AEROSPACE LTD. • Singapore

Founded in 1975 as Singapore Aerospace, adding 'Technologies' into its name in March 1995; aerospace branch of Singapore Technologies Pte Ltd and restructured in 1998, since when often referred to as ST Aero. Modified Singapore's A-4S/S-1 Skyhawk attack jets into A-4SU Super Skyhawks by installation of new engine, minor structural modifications, substantial avionics upgrade and provision to launch Maverick missile, with initial oprational capability achieved 1992. Offers Northrop-Grumman F-5 Tiger II upgrade, has a shareholding in the Eurocopter EC 120 helicopter programme, produces Boeing 777 nosewheel doors, and offers aircraft and engine maintenance and repair, and more.

SINO SWEARINGEN COMPANY • USA

Founded 1995 as partnership between Swearingen Aircraft Incorporated and Sino-Aerospace International Incorporated, to develop and market the SJ30-2 six/seven-seat entry level executive business jet (first flown 1996), developed from Swearingen SJ30.

Sino Swearingen SJ30-2 entry level executive business jet

SIOUX AIRCRAFT CORPORATION • USA

Known earlier as Simplex Aircraft Corporation (q.v.); was incorporated at Defiance, Ohio, in 1928. Built aircraft under the name Sioux Red Arrow and Sioux Kite.

SIPA • France

See Société Industrielle Pour l'Aéronautique.

SITAR • France

See Société Industrielle de Tolerie pour l'Aéronautique et Matériel.

SIVEL SRL • Italy

Established 1990. SD-27 Corriedale two-seat touring and training lightplane offered for sale since 1998 (first flown 1992), and SD-28 Trittico more-powerful two-seat aerobatic and sporting aircraft to fly 1999.

SIX-CHUTER INC. • USA

Markets kits to build Skye-Ryder Aerochute and Aerochute 2 single- and two-seat microlights comprising ram-air parachutes and powered trikes.

SKANDINAVISK AERO INDUSTRI AS. • Denmark

Founded 1937 to build light aircraft. Financed by a large Danish industrial concern; took over aircraft business formerly conducted by Kramme & Zeuthen, builders of KZI light single-seat monoplane. Prefix KZ retained for KZII two-seat trainer, supplied to Danish Air Force; KZIII and VII four-seat cabin monoplanes; KZVIII aerobatic monoplane, and KZX artillery observation type. In mid-1950s turned increasingly to repair and maintenance of military aircraft, and aircraft production had ended by late 1950s.

SKODA-KAUBA FLUGZEUGBAU • Czechoslovakia

Founded spring 1942 at Cakowitz, near Prague. Worked for Germans. Experimental types included Sk-V4 light fighter-trainer with German Argus engine. SK257 development received German production order; five completed before Russians captured factory.

SKYCRAFT PTY LTD. • Australia

Produced Scout single-seat microlight, first flown 1974 and built in large numbers.

SKYFOX AVIATION LTD. • Australia

Founded as a public company in 1996 but originating in 1991. Offers the Skyfox STOL two-seat braced high-wing

Below: Sivel SD-27 Corriedale two-seat lightplane   *Right: Skyfox CA22 STOL lightplane*

cabin monoplane (first flown September 1989) for pleasure, training, surveillance and other roles, in CA22 ultralight, CA25 tailwheel general aviation and CA25N
nosewheel general-aviation versions.

SKY SPORTS INTERNATIONAL • USA

Founded 1980 to market Humbug single-seat ultralight.

SKYSTAR AIRCRAFT CORPORATION INC. • USA

Markets kits for developed versions of the original Denny
Kitfox (first flown 1984), as the Kitfox Classic IV side-by-

side two-seat high-wing cabin lightplane, Kitfox Series 5,
long-wing Kitfox Speedster, and Kitfox Vixen with nosewheel undercarriage. Also offers kits for Pulsar II composites-built low-wing monoplane (as two-seat
development of original Star-Lite), and Pulsar XP with more
engine power.

SKYTRADER CORPORATION • USA

Founded 1984 to develop former Dominion Aircraft Skytrader 800 but with some changes. Planned Skytrader
ST1700 Conestoga and military ST1700 MD Evader but
company ceased trading 1989.

SLINGSBY AVIATION LTD. • UK

In 1938, at Kirbymoorside, Yorkshire, Slingsby Sailplanes
Ltd built Kirby Kitten single-seat monoplane, designed by
F. N. Slingsby. Chiefly famous for gliders. Motor Tutor of
1948 was Slingsby Tutor glider with engine and landing
gear. Slingsby/Osbourne Twin Cadet of 1969 had two small
engines outboard. Other conversions made, but Type 61
Falke was basically German Scheibe. Also built replicas of
Sopwith Camel, Rumpler, etc. Name changed, and in 1969
Slingsby Aircraft Company Ltd was acquired by Vickers
Ltd (q.v.), resuming construction of gliders. Current Slingsby
Aviation Ltd is member of ML Holdings PLC group and
offers professional pilot training and subcontract compo-
nent building, in addition to sales of the T67 Firefly side-

Slingsby Hengist I 15-seat transport glider

Slingsby T67M260 Firefly trainer, used by the US Air Force as T-3A Enhanced Flight Screener

SME MD3-160 AeroTiga

by-side two-seat civil/military piston-engined trainer and private aerobatic-capable lightplane (first flown May 1981, as licence-built Fournier RF6B).

SLOANE AIRCRAFT COMPANY INC. • USA

Established in New York shortly before USA became involved in First World War. Built a military biplane with unusual back-swept wings. Believed to have built aircraft under subcontract for the US government.

SME AVIATION SDN. BHD. • Malaysia

Founded 1993 and currently manufacturing the MD3-160 AeroTiga two-seat pleasure and training lightplane (designed and developed in Switzerland by MDB Flugtechnik AG and first flown 1983, with first Malaysian-built example in 1995).

L. B. SMITH AIRCRAFT CORPORATION • USA

Established at Miami 1947. Operated manufacturing, conversion and servicing facilities for numerous types of aircraft, but also built its own Tempo II pressurised executive transport based on Douglas B-26 bomber, which first flew in 1959.

SMITH, TED, AIRCRAFT COMPANY INC. • USA

In 1967 began production of Aerostar series of twin-engined business aircraft. Occupied new factory at Van Nuys, California, 1968. Airframe concerned claimed to have only about 50 per cent of components used in comparable types, with loads carried by unstiffened sections of metal skin. Some vertical and horizontal surfaces interchangeable. In 1972 became Ted R. Smith and Associates Inc, further developing Aerostar range, with distinctive mid-set wing.

SNCAC • France

See Société Nationale de Constructions Aéronautiques du Centre.

SNCAM • France

See Société Nationale de Constructions Aéronautiques du Midi.

SNCAN • France

See Société Nationale de Constructions Aéronautiques du Nord.

SNCAO • France

See Société Nationale de Constructions Aéronautiques de l'Ouest.

Smith Super 46C conversion of the Curtiss C-46 Commando

Smith Tempo II executive transport

SNCASE • France

See Société Nationale de Constructions Aéronautiques du Sud-Est.

SNCASO • France

See Société Nationale de Constructions Aéronautiques du Sud-Ouest.

SNIPE AIRCRAFT DEVELOPMENTS LTD. • UK

Was developing in mid-1980s the Lapwing low-cost two-seat lightplane.

SNOBIRD AIRCRAFT INC. • USA

Offered kit-built single- and two-seat autogyros in Adventurer, Charger, Exciter and Stealth Charger forms.

SNOW AERONAUTICAL CORPORATION • USA

Founded 1955 by Leland Snow to make agricultural aircraft of own design. Incorporated 1961; expanded 1963. Original Snow S-2B, a low-wing single-seat monoplane of metal construction, with fixed landing gear, received

Ted Smith Aerostar business aircraft

FAA Type Approval July 1958. By end of February 1965 260 aircraft of basic S-2 series delivered to 19 US states and 11 foreign countries. Corporation acquired by Rockwell-Standard 1965 and known as Aero Commander (q.v.), Olney Division.

SNOW AVIATION INTERNATIONAL INC. • USA

Founded 1990 to develop twin-turboprop commercial SA-204C STOL passenger/cargo transport and military SA-210AT derivative.

SOCATA GROUP AEROSPATIALE • France

See Société de Construction d'Avions de Tourisme et d'Affaires.

SOCIEDADE CONSTRUTORA AERONAUTICA NEIVA LTDA • Brazil

Neiva produced Model N621/T-25 Universal trainers for the Brazilian Air Force and a series of lightplanes. In March 1980 it was renamed Indústria Aeronáutica Neiva S.A (q.v.), as a subsidiary of EMBRAER.

SOCIETA ANÓNIMA INDUSTRIE MECCANICHE

Snow S-2C agricultural monoplane

AERONAUTICHE NAVALI • Italy

Founded 1929, SAIMAN specialised in repair and maintenance of marine aircraft and boats. In 1932 built experimental C.10 monoplane with variable-incidence wing. During 1934-1938 made SAIMAN 200 two-seat trainer biplane and 201 and 202 two-seat touring monoplanes. SAIMAN 204 of 1939 was an experimental derivative, but LB.4 made by the company in 1938 was a very different twin-boom airframe with tricycle landing gear.

SIAI S.M.72 three-engined bomber

SOCIETÁ ANONIMA NIEUPORT-MACCHI • Italy

See Macchi.

SOCIETÁ DI COSTRUZIONI MECCANICHE DI PISA • Italy

Established 1922 to build Dornier types under licence. In that year built six Wal and two Delphin. Wal developed as special military type for Spanish Navy, with Rolls-Royce Eagle engines. In 1926 a machine of this type flew South Atlantic.

SIAI S-55X twin-hulled flying-boat

SIAI S.M.79 transport/bomber

SOCIETÁ IDROVOLANTI ALTA ITALIA • Italy

Forerunner of present Siai-Marchetti organisation (see Siai-Marchetti Società Per Azioni). Founded 1915 by Luigi Cape at Sesto Calende, with a seaplane base on Lake Maggiore. As Idrovolanti Savoia built FBA flying-boats under licence. Name 'Savoia' had a geographical and historical connotation (House of Savoy), and after the war new flying-boats were known by the name Idrovolanti Savoia, or Savoia. These achieved early distinction, notably in the 1920 Schneider Trophy contest. Names Savoia and Marchetti were linked in 1922, when Alessandro Marchetti became technical director of company renamed Società Idrovolanti Alta Italia--Savoia-Marchetti. In 1925 the company gained publicity when an S.16*ter* was flown to Australia and Tokyo and back to Italy by Francesco De Pinedo. Famous types included the twin-hulled S-55 which, though first flown in 1924, is remembered chiefly for General Balbo's mass-formation flights of 1930 and 1933. Special long-range landplane S-64 broke world's duration and distance records in June 1930. Initials S. M. for type numbers were not commonly applied until later, and then particularly in association with fast 3-engined civil and military types. Most famous was S.M.79 bomber and torpedo bomber of Second World War. Civil types included the record-breaking S.M.75 of 1939. Last Second World War aircraft was S.M.91 twin-boom fighter-bomber, but S.M.84 bomber served as transport until 1948.

SIAI S.8, a classic flying-boat

designed by Umberto Savoia and Rodolfo Verduzio. Structural weakness attributed to both, and Type 9 was rejected by Italian Army on this account, though accepted by Navy.

SOCIÉTÉ AÉRONAUTIQUE DU SUD-OUEST • France

Formed 1935 at Bordeaux-Merignac by the Potez group (q.v.) when it took over the Société Aérienne Bordelaise (q.v.). Was intended as a decentralised production source for Potez and Bloch aircraft. Incorporated in SNCASO (q.v.) 1936.

SOCIÉTÉ AÉRONAUTIQUE FRANÇAISE • France

New name of Société des Avions Dewoitine (q.v.), conferred after Dewoitine's return to France from Switzerland. Dewoitine fighters were eventually responsibility of SNCAM. Meanwhile, D.37 series of parasol-wing monoplane fight-

SOCIETA ITALIANO AVIAZIONE • Italy

Had close Fiat links (like Ansaldo and several other Italian companies), and its S.I.A.7 and 9 series of two-seat reconnaissance-bomber biplanes, dating from 1917, were

ers was developed by Lioré et Olivier (q.v.), though name Dewoitine was sustained in fighter field primarily by the low-wing D.500 series, many of which were built by Lioré et Olivier. Société Aeronautique Française gained greatest publicity with record-breaking D.332 Emeraude, first flown 1933, and with D.338 as used extensively by Air France in late 1930s. This latter aircraft was, perhaps, the finest 3-engined airliner in service before Second World War, and continued in use after fall of France.

S.I.A.-9B reconnaissance/bomber aircraft

SOCIÉTÉ AÉRONAUTIQUE NORMANDE • France

Formed 1948. First prototype of the SAN-101 two-seat high-wing monoplane flew 1949. Built other light aircraft, notably Jodel D.150 Mascaret; 4/5-seat Jodel D.140 Mousquetaire; and D.140R, for use as glider tug and in mountainous areas. The products were known as SAN Jodel and attained considerable success, but company went into liquidation early in 1969.

SOCIÉTÉ ANONYME BELGE DE CONSTRUCTIONS AÉRONAUTIQUES • Belgium

Formed December 1920. Had close SABENA associations and that airline used SABCA's only S.2 single-engined monoplane transport. Built Handley Page 3-engined airliners for SABENA Belgian Congo service; also Poncelet ultralight monoplane and other private-owner prototypes. Held Breguet and Avia licences, and from 1927 directed attention to metal construction. Outcome was S-XI 20-passenger monoplane with three 500 hp engines, as well as similar S-XII 4-passenger monoplane with three 120 hp engines. Built under licence Renard R.31 reconnaissance monoplane and Savoia-Marchetti S.73 transport. Built S.47 2-seat low-wing monoplane fighter of 1937 in collaboration with Caproni (q.v.). Company revived in 1950s. In 1960s assembled, maintained and repaired Republic F-84; also collaborated with Avions Fairey on Hawker Hunter and made Vautour components for Sud Aviation. Much work of various kinds on Lockheed Starfighter, Dassault Mirage and Breguet Atlantic; also missile and space activities. Dassault Aviation took 53 per cent shareholding, while in 1998 Fokker's shareholding was then reportedly being sold. Recent work has included weapon system integration, development of the cockpit front panel, final assembly and flight testing of Belgian Army A-109 helicopters; update of F-5s; production and upgrading of F-16s; upgrade of Mirage 5s and F1s; production of servo actuators; and construction of sub assemblies for Dassault, Boeing, Airbus and Fokker aircraft.

SOCIÉTÉ ANONYME DES ATELIERS D'AVIATION LOUIS BREGUET • France

see Breguet Aviation.

SOCIÉTÉ ANONYME FRANÇAISE AÉRONAUTIQUE • France

In early 1930s licenced to build Netherlands-designed Koolhoven F.K.43 four-seat high-wing monoplane as SAFA F.K.43.

SOCIÉTÉ ANONYME POUR LA FABRICATION ET L'EXPLOITATION DES AVIONS RAAB •

SCAN 30 version of Grumman Widgeon

Greece

Formed at Athens in 1935, when Herr Raab transferred his aircraft manufacture from Riga (see Raab Flugzeugbau).

SOCIÉTÉ ANONYME POUR LA RÉALISATION D'AVIONS PROTOTYPES • France

Established at Billancourt in 1926 to build aircraft to the design of Louis Bécherau, formerly with Deperdussin and SPAD (q.v.). First production design was the C.2, a two-seat monoplane powered by a 500 hp Salmson engine.

SOCIÉTÉ ANONYME POUR L'AVIATION ET SES DÉRIVES • France

See SPAD.

SOCIÉTÉ ANONYME POUR LES APPAREILS DEPERDUSSIN • France

See SPAD.

SABCA-built Dassault Mirage 5 (rear aircraft)

SOCIÉTÉ BULTE • France

See Guldentops.

SOCIÉTÉ DE CONSTRUCTIONS AÉRO NAVALES DE PORT-NEUF • France

Light monoplane flying-boat designated SCAN 20, built secretly 1941. Tested October 1945. Delivery of 23 to French Navy under way 1951. Also built Grumman Widgeon for French Navy as SCAN 30.

SOCIÉTÉ DE CONSTRUCTION D'AVIONS DE TOURISME ET D'AFFAIRES • France

Formed 1966 as subsidiary of Sud-Aviation (q.v.), to develop and produce group's light sporting and business aircraft. Currently subsidiary of Aérospatiale (q.v.) and known as Socata Groupe Aérospatiale, products including the TB30 Epsilon tandem two-seat piston-engined trainer (first flown December 1979), Rallye lightplane in four-seat 235F form, TB9 Tampico Club 4/5-seat lightplane (first flown March 1979), TB10 and more powerful TB200 Tobago 4/5-seat lightplanes for basic/instrument flight training and cross-country flying among their many uses (first flown February 1977 and March 1991 respec-

SOCATA TB 30 Epsilon

SOCATA Omega tandem two-seat turboprop military trainer

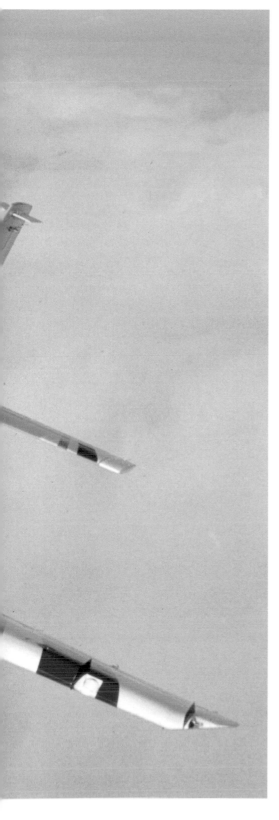

SOCATA TB20 Trinidad test flown in 1998 with the new Morane Renault engine

SOCATA TBM 700s operated by Armée de l'Air

tively), TB20 and TB21 Trinidad 4/5-seat lightplanes with higher-powered piston engines for advanced instrument training among other roles, TBM 700 pressurised and turboprop-powered business aircraft (first flown July 1988), Omega tandem two-seat turboprop military trainer (first flown April 1989), TB360 Tangara twin piston-engined lightplane (first flown February 1997) based on US Gulfstream American GA-7 Cougar, new MS 180 Morane and MS 250 Morane 4/5-seat lightplanes expected to fly in the year 2000 and featuring newly developed SMA MR turbocharged piston engines, tandem two-seat MS 300 Epsilon Mk 2 turboprop-powered basic and primary military trainer that is expected to fly in year 2000, and HALE high-altitude long-endurance communications and electronic intelligence platform, based on TBM 700 but with 157 ft 6 in (48 m) wingspan (expected to fly in year 2004). Company made components under subcontract for wide variety of aircraft, including Magister and Concorde, and

SOCATA TB200 Tobago XL four/five-seat lightplane

current work includes components for Eurocopter helicopters, Airbus and ATR airliners, Dassault Falcon bizjets, Lockheed Martin Hercules freighter, and CFM56 engine.

SOCIÉTÉ D'EMBOUTISSAGE ET DE CONSTRUCTIONS MÉCANIQUES • France

Founded 1916 by Félix Amiot. During First World War built Morane, Breguet and Sopwith types. After war repaired Breguets, and from 1921 helped in construction of early Dewoitine monoplane fighters. Specialised in metal stamping and press-work. Lutàce of 1921 was side-by-side two-seater biplane using special form of steel-tube construction of SECM design. SECM 12 was two-seat single-engined night bomber (developed as SECM-Amiot 120B.N.2); 22 was trainer for French competition of 1923; 23 was 3-seat tourer; 24 an elementary trainer. Firm also made Lorraine-Dietrich aero engines, as fitted in Amiot-SECM (or Amiot) 122 series of late 1920s.

SOCATA Rallye lightplanes

SOCIÉTÉ DE RECHERCHES ET DE CONSTRUCTIONS MÉCANIQUES • France

Originally a specialist in aircraft hydraulic systems, began small-scale construction of aircraft for other small manufacturers. After failing to obtain a licence to build the CAB Supercab, designed a new lightplane known as the SRCM-153 Joigny, which first flew in March 1960. This was a

three/four-seat monoplane with rectractable landing gear, powered by a Lycoming engine.

SOCIÉTÉ D'ÉTUDES AÉRONAUTIQUES • France

Formed 1916. Forerunner of Potez (q.v.) concerns. Made series of two-seat biplanes, notably SEA 4 reconnaissance aircraft and SEA 7, the latter a 'limousine' first flown December 1919.

SRCM-153 Joigny lightplane

SECAT S.4 high-wing monoplane

SECAN Courlis twin-boom monoplane

SEEMS MS760 Paris light jet

SOCIÉTÉ D'ÉTUDES ET DE CONSTRUCTIONS AÉRO NAVALES • France

Subsidiary of Usines Chausson of automotive industry. After Second World War undertook to produce all-metal light aircraft. Resulted in Courlis twin-boom monoplane of 1946, with tricycle landing gear and special loading arrangements. After 1950 concentrated on components, including Speedpak freight container for Lockheed Constellation, and external tanks for fast aircraft.

SOCIÉTÉ D'ÉTUDES ET DE CONSTRUCTIONS D'AVIONS DE TOURISME • France

Established in 1938, produced the RG-60 single-seat biplane, RG-75 two-seat cabin monoplane and S.5 two-seat high-wing cantilever monoplane. Production ended at outbreak of Second World War.

SOCIÉTÉ D'EXPLOITATION DES AÉRONEFS HENRI MIGNET • France

Early aircraft from Henri Mignet was HM.14, popularly known as the Flying Flea (first flown 1933). Founded Mignet do Brasil (q.v.) post-war but later returned to native France to produce series of new aircraft. Available in assembled or kit form is HM.1000 Balerit microlight, a tandem-wing two-seat Pou-du-Ciel type; customers include the French Armée de l'Air, for surveillance.

SOCIÉTÉ D'EXPLOITATION DES ÉTABLISSEMENTS MORANE-SAULNIER • France

Provisional name for the Morane-Saulnier company (q.v.) after it had been acquired in 1963 by the Potez Group (q.v.). MS760 Paris jet-propelled communications aircraft

was developed further into 6-seat Paris III of 1964. Production also included Rallye-Club, Super-Rallye and Rallye Commodore, the latter first flown in February 1964 after formation of SEEMS.

SOCIÉTÉ EUROPÉENE DE PRODUCTION DE L'AVION ÉCOLE DE COMBAT ET D'APPUI TACTIQUE • International

An Anglo-French company, SEPECAT formed May 1966 by Breguet Aviation and British Aircraft Corporation to design and produce the high-subsonic Jaguar twin-jet strike fighter/trainer; current operating companies are British Aerospace (q.v.) and Dassault Aviation (q.v.). Prototype first flew September 1968 and production Jaguars began equipping the French Armée de l'Air in 1972, followed by the RAF in 1974. Versions became Jaguar A as

SEPECAT Jaguar International, used by the Indian Air Force as Shamsher and many built by HAL

RAF SEPECAT Jaguar on a lo-level training exercise

SIPA S.12/121 two-seat advanced trainer

the French single-seat tactical support aircraft; Jaguar B as the British two-seat operational trainer (original RAF designation Jaguar T. Mk 2); Jaguar E as the French two-seat trainer; Jaguar S as the RAF single-seat tactical support aircraft; and Jaguar International as the more-powerful export version. Production ended in Europe in 1985 after delivery of 12 Internationals to Ecuador, 200 to France, 40 Internationals to India, 18 Internationals to Nigeria, 24 Internationals to Oman, and 203 to the RAF. In addition, International was also put into assembly/production by HAL in India as the Shamsher, 91 being delivered to the Indian Air Force for various roles, including maritime strike, by close of production in 1998.

SOCIÉTÉ FRANÇAISE D'AVIATION NOUVELLE • France

Formed 1935 by M. Chasseris, a director of Nieuport (q.v.) for 25 years. Made light aeroplanes and gliders. Licenced for British BAC Drone 1935; modified to suit French requirements as SFAN 2. Larger two-seat model to same formula was SFAN 4.

SOCIÉTÉ FRANÇAISE DE CONSTRUCTIONS AÉRONAUTIQUES • France

Formed July 1934 to build light aircraft. First production model was SFCA Maillet 20, an unusual 3-seat cabin monoplane of very clean design, though with raised pilot's cockpit. SFCA Lignel 20 was 1/2-seat light monoplane with retractable landing gear. Company also had licence for Peyret 'tandem monoplane', renamed and developed as Taupin.

SOCIÉTÉ GÉNÉRALE DES CONSTRUCTIONS INDUSTRIELLES ET MÉCANIQUES • France

Known originally as Etablissements Borel (see Borel), denoting origin in 1909 by pioneer constructor Gabriel

Borel. To designs of Paul Bocaccio built two-seat fighter after First World War.

SOCIÉTÉ INDUSTRIELLE DES MÉTAUX ET DU BOIS • France

Formed 1922 and best known by name Bernard, Adolphe Bernard built SPADs from 1917, original designs materialising only after Armistice. In December 1924 SIMB V2 (or Bernard) racing monoplane raised world speed record to 278.48mph (448.17kmh). Type 12C.1 was a low-wing all-metal monoplane fighter; 14C.1 was wooden sesquiplane fighter. In June 1929 special Type 190 (191GR) carried Assolant and Lefèvre on west-east North Atlantic crossing. A number of experimental aircraft built before closure in 1935.

SOCIÉTÉ INDUSTRIELLE DE TOLERIE POUR L'AÉRONAUTIQUE ET MATÉRIEL ROULANT • France

Produced, like a number of French contemporaries, designs by Yves Gardan. In late 1960s these included the GY90, 100 and 110. GY100 was four-seat tourer or

SNCAC NC853 two-seat lightplane

aerobatic two-seater, production of which began September 1968.

SOCIÉTÉ INDUSTRIELLE POUR L'AÉRONAUTIQUE • France

Formed 1938 and until 1940 was manufacturing parts under subcontract for Lioré et Olivier, Amiot and Morane types and overhauling Mureaux aircraft. First post-war production aircraft was S.10 (French version of Arado 396, for which the company had wartime responsibility). Developed versions were built in quantity. SIPA 901 (derived

SFECMAS 1402 Gerfaut delta-wing research aircraft

SNCAN 1101 Noralpha cabin monoplane

SNCAN 1500 Griffon turbo-ramjet research aircraft

from S90 of 1947) flew 1948 and ordered by Government for Service de l'Aviation Légère et Sportive. Minijet, flown in 1952, was world's first all-metal 2-seat light jet; SIPA 300 was more conventional jet trainer. Later trainers and light aircraft included Coccinelle 2-seater, and 5-seat turboprop Antilope. Company was associated with production of Caravelle, Mirage, Alouette and Concorde, and specialised in furnishing and equipping airliners. Taken over by subsidiary of Aérospatiale (q.v.).

SOCIÉTÉ NATIONALE DE CONSTRUCTIONS AÉRONAUTIQUES DE L'OUEST • France

Formed January 1937, incorporating Breguet and Loire-Nieuport establishments. Made series of Loire 46 gull-wing single-seat fighters, some of which went to Spain and fought in Civil War; also Loire-Nieuport LN 41 single-seat cranked-wing dive-bombers, a few of which saw action against advancing Germans in 1940. New company had associations also with Loire 210 central-float fighter seaplane of 1939; Loire 130 flying-boat for shipboard catapult launch; and Loire 70 three-engined reconnaissance flying-boat.

SOCIÉTÉ NATIONALE DE CONSTRUCTIONS AÉRONAUTIQUES DU CENTRE • France

Formed February 1937. Incorporated Farman and Hanriot establishments. Played part in final development of Farman line of four-engined heavy bombers which had engines in tandem underslung pairs, derived from F.211 of 1931. One converted Atlantic mailplane of this form was first Allied aircraft to bomb Berlin. Of Hanriot origin

SNCASE SE.200 six-engined commercial flying-boat

was the NC600 (derived from H.220) twin-engined fighter prototype flown in 1939, though abandoned when the SNCAC former Hanriot factory at Bourges was chosen to build Breguet 696. After German withdrawal SNAC built 64 Focke-Wulf Fw 190 as NC900. Company dissolved 1949.

SOCIÉTÉ NATIONALE DE CONSTRUCTIONS AÉRONAUTIQUES DU MIDI • France

Formed February 1937, occupied Dewoitine (q.v.) factory at Toulouse. Designed and produced D.520 monoplane fighter, first flown 1938, of which about 400 delivered and 180 more ordered later under Franco-German Armistice authorisation. The second mentioned batch was built by SNCASE (q.v.) which by 1941 had absorbed SNCAM. D.750, first flown 1940, was unusual twin-engined multipurpose folding-wing monoplane for operation from planned aircraft carriers.

SOCIÉTÉ NATIONALE DE CONSTRUCTIONS AÉRONAUTIQUES DU NORD • France

Formed early 1937. Incorporated elements of Potez, Amiot, Breguet, CAMS and Mureaux (all q.v.). Dominant concern was production of Potez 630 series of twin-engined multipurpose aircraft. Peak output reached in May 1940. Development of basic type (e.g. Potez 671 specialised fighter with elliptical wing) was also SNCAN concern. In 1949 took over part of liquidated SNCAC. In 1954, when company flew prototypes of trainers later built in quantity, amalgamated with Société Française d'Études et de Constructions de Matériels Aéronautiques Spéciaux (SFEC-MAS, formerly Arsenal de l'Aéronautique) (both q.v.). From January 1958 called Nord-Aviation. Under new name continued development of Nord/SFECMAS Gerfaut delta-wing fighter; also Griffon, with fuselage forming outer casing of very large ramjet with turbojet in centre for take-off and to ignite ramjet. Noratlas twin-boom transport, though first flown September 1949, continued in production and development under new name, achieving wide success. Nord

SNCASE Grognard twin-jet attack aircraft

SNCASE Baroudeur skid-landing strike aircraft

SNCASO Bretagne transport

SNCASO SO.1310 Farfadet convertiplane

SNCASO SO.1221 Djinn helicopter

name was emphasised in Noroit flying-boat and Noréclair shipboard aircraft.

SOCIÉTÉ NATIONALE DE CONSTRUCTIONS AÉRONAUTIQUES DU SUD EST • France

Formed December 1936. Incorporated elements of Lioré et Olivier, Potez, Romano and SPCA (all q.v.). Company thus became responsible for development and production of Le045 twin-engined bomber, first flown January 1937, outstanding in many points of design and much used and adapted during and after Second World War. Built also Romano trainers and Le043 catapult floatplane, of type first flown December 1934. In 1941 the company absorbed SNCAM (q.v.). Early post-Second World War products included Languedoc four-engined airliner, developed from Bloch 161 of 1939, which entered service between Paris and Algiers in 1946, and was ordered additionally for military use. Military types in development included Grognard twin-jet attack aircraft of 1950; the unique trolley-launched skid-landing Baroudeur strike aircraft of 1953; and Mistral and Aquilon developments of the British de Havilland Vampire and Sea Venom. Especially notable original developments were the Alouette helicopter series first flown in 1951, and the rear-engined twin-jet Caravelle in 1955. Became part of Sud-Aviation (q.v.).

SOCIÉTÉ NATIONALE DE CONSTRUCTIONS AÉRONAUTIQUES DU SUD OUEST • France

Formed November 1936. Incorporated elements of Marcel Bloch, Lioré et Olivier, Blériot and SASO. A prime responsibility was development and production of Bloch types, especially single-seat fighters derived from MB150 of 1936. Redesign facilitated production and improved performance, resulting in MB151 and 152. By June 1940

production totalled about 600, involving five plants. MB175 twin-engined bomber was in production and was revived after Second World War as torpedo aircraft. Several other prototypes built, including four-engined bomber. In 1941 company was merged into SNCAO (q.v.). In 1942 completed forerunner of Bretagne twin-engined transport, though not flown until 1945; then used commercially and experimentally. Numerous and varied post-Second World War types included distinctly unusual forms of rotary-wing aircraft. Aeriel (1948) and Djinn (1953) with tip jets, and Farfadet convertiplane (1953). The eminently successful Vautour multipurpose twin-jet flew 1952, and was much developed thereafter. High-speed research types were swept-wing Espadon and, of special technical interest, straight-wing mixed-power Trident, first flown 1953 (well before formation of Ouest-Aviation in 1957).

SOCIÉTÉ PROVENÇALE DE CONSTRUCTIONS AÉRONAUTIQUES • France

The aircraft branch of the Société Provençale de Constructions Navales and the Messageries Maritimes. In March 1925 acquired sole rights for construction of Météore aircraft from Compagnie Générale de Constructions Aéronautiques. Built Météore 63 three-engined flying-boat. Under Paulhan-Pillard licence-built E.5 three-engined monoplane flying-boat and T3-BN.4 twin-engined twin-float coast-defence floatplane. SPCA 30-M.4 was big multi-seat landplane fighter with two fuselages and central nacelle. Type 40T was three-engined all-metal airliner which gave good service in early 1930s. In 1936 company's Marseilles works were leased by Government for SNCASE (q.v.).

SOKO • Yugoslavia

Founded October 1950, and produced licence-built Westland Whirlwind helicopters. Designed the G-2A Galeb two-seat armed jet basic trainer (first flown 1961), produced for the Yugoslav Air Force and for export; the J-1/RJ-1 Jastreb attack and reconnaissance versions of Galeb; the P-2 Kraguj piston-engined counterinsurgency aircraft (first flown 1966); the G-4 Super Galeb jet trainer (first flown July 1978); built the Aérospatiale/Westland (q.v.) Gazelle

Right: SOKO J-22 Orao attack aircraft, develped with Romania

SOKO G2 Galeb basic jet trainer

helicopter under licence in several versions, including Partizan, GAMA anti-armour model and HERA reconnaissance model; and joined IAv Craiova (q.v.) of Romania in development/production of J-22 Orao/IAR-93 attack aircraft (first flown 1974 but out of production before all deliveries made, due to regional conflict). Privatised 1991, at which time extensive subcontract work included components/assemblies for Airbus, ATR, Dassault, de Havilland, EMBRAER, Eurocopter, McDonnell Douglas and Tupolev commercial aircraft. Did not go out of business during regional conflict that followed, but had short periods of inactivity during the worst of the troubles. See Soko Air Ltd for 1998 restructure.

SOKO AIR LTD. • Bosnia-Herzegovina

Following 1998 restructure of Soko company (q.v.) and its division into several smaller concerns under Soko Holding Co, Soko Air Ltd was created at the Mostar-Rodoc factory to undertake its aviation programmes. They include the Soko 2 two-seat very light monoplane (first flown November 1996) and LH1 two/three-seat light helicopter, which was at an advanced stage of design at time of writing. Other work includes civil aircraft component production for international customers, and design of four- and six-seat lightplanes.

Below: SOKO Super Galeb jet trainer

Solar XRON-1 experimental helicopter

SOLAR AIRCRAFT COMPANY • USA

In 1931-1932 at Lindbergh Field, San Diego, California, built Solar MS-2 sesquiplane all-metal ten-passenger transport aircraft. Was also a manufacturer of aircraft components.

SOMMER, ROGER • France

First began aeronautical work in 1904. Special Sommer biplane of 1911 lifted 13 persons. After a dormant period the company resumed aircraft construction 1915, and at the Armistice the Sommer works was claimed to have been producing up to 200 aircraft per month under subcontract.

SONACA SA • Belgium

Founded 1978 from Falrey SA, and undertakes varied aerospace activities that includes manufacture of components for Airbus, EMBRAER RJ145, Dassault Atlantique and Agusta A 109/A 119.

SOPWITH AVIATION COMPANY LTD. • UK

T. O. M. Sopwith was pioneer sportsman/pilot. Rebuilt early aircraft before First World War, began development of own types and formed important associations with F. Sigrist (engineer and largely responsible for future success) and H. G. Hawker (pilot). Company registered March 1914. Became world famous for fighter aircraft, built in great numbers by many companies, though Bat Boat of 1913 was notable flying-boat and Tabloid landplane of same

year gained renown as floatplane by winning 1914 Schneider Trophy. Wartime developments were Schneider and Baby floatplanes. First landplane fighter built in great numbers was two-seat 1½-Strutter. Pup was smaller single-seater, and both types made major contributions to ship-flying. Triplane of 1916 excelled in climb. Two gun Camel, in service 1917, excelled in manoeuvrability; shipboard version had detachable rear fuselage. Cuckoo of 1917 was world's first deck-landing torpedo-bomber. Snipe was intended to succeed Camel late in war, and remained in RAF service until 1926: Salamander was similar but armoured for ground attack. In 1920 the Sopwith Aviation Company was succeeded by the Hawker Engineering Company (q.v.). The Sopwith fighters sacrificed stability for manoeuvrability, and became the most famous British aircraft of First World War.

SORRELL AIRCRAFT COMPANY LTD. • USA

Markets kits to build SNS-7 Hiperbipe as two-seat aerobatic biplane with reverse-stagger wings.

SOUTHERN AIRCRAFT CORPORATION • USA

At Garland, Texas, in 1940, built prototype biplane trainer. In new works made components for Consolidated B-24, Grumman Hellcat and Avenger.

SOUTHERN AIRCRAFT LTD. • UK

Associated with Shoreham Aerodrome, Sussex, and F. G. Miles, who developed the Avro Baby into Martlet and Metal Martlet light aerobatic and sporting types. Last example flew 1931.

SOVROMTRACTOR • Romania

Name for IAR/Regia (q.v. both) from 1946 while under Soviet occupation. Brasov works (known as URMV 3 Brasov between 1950 and 1959; q.v.) demilitarized and put under joint Sovict/Romanian management, mainly for production of agricultural equipment. Aircraft development at Brasov by mid-1956 included IAR 811 piston trainer (first flown 1949), IAR 813 two-seat lightplane, IAR 814 twin-engined transport of 1953 and IAR 817 single-engined general-purpose light transport of 1955. Aircraft from LFIL factory at Reghin included RG-6 tandem two-seat sports and training monoplane.

SPAD • France

Silk merchant Armand Deperdussin (1867-1924) was associated from 1910 with a series of notable monoplanes. Built precursor in 1909 for show in a Paris store. By 1914 monoplanes bearing Deperdussin name were used not only privately but by several military authorities. Designed

Sopwith Camel single-seat biplane fighter

Sopwith Triplane fighter

Sopwith Snipe fighter

Sopwith Pup fighter

SPAD XIII, extensively-built French fighter

SPAD 81, a post First World War fighter of the French AF

by Louis Béchereau, these aircraft were especially noted for speed performances in 1912-1913, and in some instances for monocoque construction. Deperdussin, a great promoter, became involved in financial difficulties and in 1915 the company as named above was declared bankrupt. The Deperdussin name had links with several companies, including the British Deperdussin Company with which John Porte (see Seaplane Experimental Station) was connected. Initials SPAD were also ascribed to Société Provisoire des Aéroplanes Deperdussin and Société Parisienne des Avions Deperdussin, as well as Société des Productions Armand Deperdussin.

After Deperdussin was arrested for embezzlement the company was renamed Société Pour l'Aviation et ses Dérives in 1915, thus retaining these initials. Chief technician was at first Béchereau, later André Herbemont. Company became world famous for SPAD single-seat fighters and fast reconnaissance adaptations. More than 2,000 fighters built at Suresnes factory alone; great numbers under licence in France and elsewhere. Classic tractor single-seat biplane flown late 1915 as SPAD V: developed into SPAD VII of 1916, thus establishing company's name in aviation history. Characteristic design feature was two-bay wing cellule with special form of bracing. Combination with Hispano-Suiza 8-cylinder vee engine was major factor in success. SPAD XII had a 37 mm engine-mounted gun. From May 1917 improved two machine-gun type XIII replaced VII. Large numbers ordered by US. SPAD XX of late 1918 was two-seat fighter to Herbemont design and precursor of new Blériot-SPAD line of single-strut monocoque-fuselage biplane fighters, built after Blériot (q.v.) took over SPAD company in 1921.

SPARMANN'S FLYGPLANVERKSTAD • Sweden

In 1936 built S-1 single-seat low-wing monoplane trainer. Several delivered to Swedish Air Force.

SPARTAN AIRCRAFT COMPANY • USA

Early in 1927 Spartan G-3 three-seat open-cockpit biplane was built by Mid-Continent Aircraft Company. Company

as above established 1928 at Tulsa, Oklahoma. Built C-3 with Ryan-Siemens engine. Continued to build biplanes but by 1931 was producing series of 4/5-seat cabin monoplanes; also low-wing side-by-side 2-seaters, further developed as C2-60. Spartan Executive 4/5-seat all-metal monoplane of 1936 converted in 1938 to Zeus 2-seat military type; a few of which supplied to China and Mexico. In 1940 US Navy ordered 201 Spartan NP-1 biplane trainers for new Naval Reserve schools.

SPARTAN AIRCRAFT LTD. • UK

Early in 1930 Simmonds Aircraft Ltd, which had made the Spartan biplane, was reconstituted under the above name. Made altered version of Simmonds Spartan called Spartan Arrow. Spartan Three-Seater built at East Cowes, Isle of Wight, where company moved early 1931. Spartan Cruiser was development of Saro-Percival (later Spartan)

Spartan Zeus light bomber

Mailplane of 1931, and the refined Cruiser III ended production in May 1935.

SPCA • France

See Société Provençale de Constructions Aéronautiques.

SPECIAL AIRCRAFT TRANSPORT INTERNATIONAL COMPANY GIE • International

See SATIC.

SPECIALIZED AIRCRAFT COMPANY • USA

Produced Tri Turbo-3 as triple-turboprop conversion of DC-3.

Spartan Arrow floatplane

Spartan Cruiser II eight-seat light transport

SPECTRUM AIRCRAFT CORPORATION • USA

Produced SA-550 Spectrum-One as modified Cessna Sky-master, with changes including lengthened fuselage and rear-mounted turboprop engine (first flown 1983).

SPEEDTWIN DEVELOPMENTS LTD. • UK

Markets kits for the Speedtwin Mk I and Mk II tandem two-seat and twin-engined aerobatic monoplane.

SPENCER AIRCRAFT INC. • USA

Offers plans and kits to construct the Amphibian Air Car four-seat pusher-engined amphibian, originally patented in 1950 and thereafter marketed until 1988 by Spencer Amphibian Air Car Inc.

SPENCER-LARSEN AIRCRAFT CORPORATION • USA

Formed 1937 by P. H. Spencer (formerly of Amphibions Inc, q.v.) and V. A. Larsen (previously with Fokker, Standard and Sikorsky) to develop two-seat amphibian with remotely-driven pusher propeller.

SPERRY, LAWRENCE, AIRCRAFT COMPANY • USA

Lawrence Sperry was son of Elmer Sperry (Sperry Gyroscope Co). Worked on aeroplanes from 1911; company as named founded 1919. In 1920 made cantilever monoplane wing for Curtiss JN, and built experimental triplane amphibian. From 1921 tiny Messenger single-seat biplane (designed by Engineering Division, US Air Service, and called also Verville-Sperry) was in production. Also to official designs built Verville-Sperry Racers. A Messenger brought to England by Lawrence Sperry in 1923 came down in the Channel and Sperry lost his life, after which the company closed.

SPITFIRE HELICOPTER COMPANY • USA

Based at Media, Pennsylvania. In January 1975 began design of Spitfire Mark I light helicopter, developed from Enstrom F-28A but with turbine powerplant. Other projects included Spitfire Mark II helicopter with additional cabin space and more engine power, and Spitfire Mark IV with auxiliary propulsion engines at tips of stub wings.

SPORT AIRCRAFT INC. • USA

Sells plans and kits to construct the S-18 side-by-side two-seat low-wing monoplane, formerly sold by Sunderland Aircraft and based on the original Thorpe T-18 Tiger.

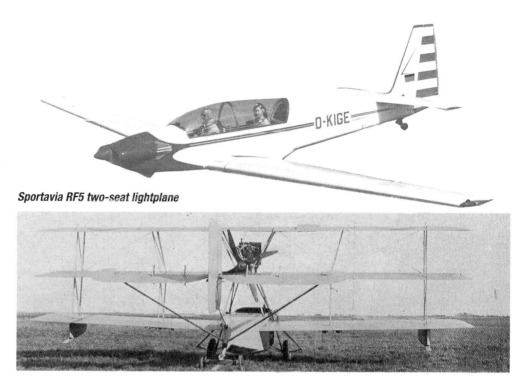

Sportavia RF5 two-seat lightplane

Sperry experimental triplane amphibian

SPORTAVIA-PUTZER GMBH U CO KG • Germany

Formed 1966 to take over from Alpavia SA (q.v.) manufacture of Avion-Planeur series designed by René Fournier. By spring 1969 had delivered 150 RF4D single-seaters. Two-seat RF5 flew 1968, followed by RF6 and RS180 Sportsman four-seat lightplane. Became entirely owned by Rhein-Flugzeugbau GmbH 1977 and lost name 1001.

SPORT COPTER INC. • USA

Offers single-seat kit-built ultralight Lightning and kit-built Vortex autogyros, plus two-seat Sport Copter II autogyro.

SPORT RACER INC. • USA

Offers plans to build a tandem two-seat mid-wing monoplane suited to racing and aerobatics.

SRCM • France

See Société des Recherches et de Constructions Mécaniques.

ST AERO • Singapore

See Singapore Technologies Aerospace Ltd.

STAMPE ET RENARD SA • Belgium

Formed after Second World War by merger of Constructions Aéronautiques G. Renard and Stampe et Vertongen (both q.v.) Overhauled and modified highly successful S.V.4 series of trainer biplanes, as used by Belgian and French Air Forces. Developed modernised S.V.4D; also, as a collaborative venture with Farman (q.v.), new monoplane called Minitor using fuselage components of S.V.4. By 1970 had ceased aeronautical work.

STAMPE ET VERTONGEN • Belgium

Established 1922. Specialised in trainer aircraft. Early type designations signified that Alfred Renard was chief designer. In April 1923 flew RSV.32-90 and developed several biplane types and parasol monoplanes. Greatest success was S.V.4 series of two-seat trainer biplanes, built from 1933 and famed for manoeuvrability and strength. Type was also built by SNCAN (q.v.) in France. S.V.5 was military multi-purpose type; S.V.7 a bomber/reconnaissance biplane; S.V.10 a two-seat twin-engined military multipurpose type for Belgian Government. Although the company's Antwerp factory was destroyed in Second World War the name lives on in aerobatic flying.

STANDARD AIRCRAFT CORPORATION • USA

Anticipating eventual entry of USA into First World War, was formed in 1916, with factories in New Jersey. Made to own designs SJ trainers; E-1 single-seat fighters, used for advanced training; H-3 landplane reconnaissance biplanes and H-4-H floatplanes. Also built 80 Curtiss HS

Stampe aerobatic biplane

Standard Aircraft Mailplane

single-engined flying-boats and began quantity production of Handley Page and Caproni large bombers. Also built about 140 DH-4s; total wartime output was over 1,000 aircraft.

STANDARD MOTOR COMPANY LTD. • UK

Established at Coventry, Warwickshire, built aircraft to government contracts during First World War, including RAF B.E.12 and R.E.8 and Sopwith Pups.

Standard E-1 fighter/trainer

STAR AIRCRAFT COMPANY • USA

Formed in late 1920s, directors having connections with Phillips Petroleum Company. In early 1930s built Star Cavalier two-seat high-wing cabin monoplane.

STAR AVIATION INC. • USA

Offered LoneStar Sport Helicopter as kit-built single-seater.

STARFIRE AVIATION INC. • USA

Offers plans to build the Firebolt two-seat aerobatic biplane, based on the Steen Skybolt and having good cross-country performance.

STARK IBÉRICA SA • Spain

Successor to Stark Flugzeugbau AG of Minden/Westf, Germany. In late 1960s was continuing development and production of Stark version of Druine Turbulent and Stamo engine.

STAR KRAFT INC. • USA

First flew in 1994 the all-composites Star Kraft 700 eight/nine-seat pressurised business aircraft with nose and tail piston engines. Projected variants are the 700-SE with one engine and fixed undercarriage, 1100 12-seat lengthened version, and 500 five-passenger single-engined model.

Star Kraft 700 pressurised business aircraft

STARLIGHT ENGINEERING • USA

First flew in 1997 the Warp 1-A single-seat pusher-engined monoplane, now offered in kit form.

STARLING BURGESS COMPANY • USA

William Starling Burgess was yacht and boat builder. Made an aeroplane 1909/10. Built Wright biplanes under licence as Burgess-Wright. Also developed twin-engined type, tractor type and flying-boat. From 1913 under licence from Britain's J. W. Dunne, made Burgess-Dunne tailless float-planes, Burgess developing the single main float. Two such seaplanes bought by US Navy 1916, and one used for gunnery trials. Navy also bought tractor floatplanes and UK bought 36 landplanes developed by the Burgess company.

STATES AIRCRAFT CORPORATION • USA

In very early 1930s built, at Chicago Heights, Illinois, B-3 parasol monoplane, with two tandem seats.

STAUDACHER AIRCRAFT INC. • USA

Custom-built aerobatic aircraft.

STEARMAN • USA

Originally Stearman Aircraft Company, formed at Venice, California, by Lloyd Stearman in 1927. Stearman was already known in connection with Laird, Swallow and Travel Air; the new company was formed by consolidating Lyle-Hoyt Aircraft Corporation (formerly West Coast distributor of Travel Air) and technical ability of Stearman. Factory soon moved to Wichita, Kansas, building private and commercial aircraft and becoming part of United Aircraft and Transport Corporation. Types built included three-seaters, trainers and mailplanes. On break-up of United combine

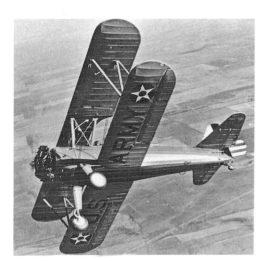

Stearman 75, a classic trainer

Steward-Davis Jet Packet, a jet-augmented version of the Fairchild C-82

in 1934, Stearman became a Boeing subsidiary and in 1939 the Wichita Division of Boeing. Nevertheless, biplane trainers built throughout Second World War were persistently called Stearman. Basic type was Model 75, dating from 1936 and having numerous service designations; production totalled about 10,000. Name Kaydet (originally Canadian) not favoured in USA, where Army models had PT and Navy models NS designations. Some versions had enclosed cockpits. After Second World War some 4,000 of Model 75 converted for cropdusting.

STEARMAN-HAMMOND AIRCRAFT CORPORATION • USA

Formed 1936, after Dean B. Hammond and Lloyd Stearman (see Hammond and Stearman entries) had spent two years developing the Hammond Model Y two seat twin-boom pusher monoplane and the type had been granted an Approved Type Certificate. Aircraft had been redesigned for production as Y-1S and a few built before work was abandoned in 1938.

STEEN AERO LAB • USA

Offers plans to construct the very-well-known Skybolt tandem two-seat sporting biplane, the Knight Twister hiplane, and plans for the Pitts Special biplane.

STELUX AIRCRAFT CORPORATION • USA

Designed the Trenzo two-seat lightplane with rear mounted wings and pusher propeller from 1984. Not known to have flown.

STERN, RENÉ • France

Markets plans for the Stern/Mallick SM-01 Vega side by-side two-seat monoplane (first flown 1992) and ST-87 Europlane side-by-side two-seat monoplane developed from single-seat ST-80 Balade and first flown 1991.

STEWARD-DAVIS INC. • USA

Under name Steward-Davis/Jet-Packet made and promoted modernised commercial version of Fairchild C-82 with turbojet mounted above fuselage for augmented power. In 1961 adapted C-119 in similar manner as Jet-Pak.

STEWART 51 INC. • USA

Markets kits to build S-51D Mustang tandem two-seat 70 per cent-scale representation of Second World War P-51 fighter.

STINSON AIRCRAFT DIVISION OF VULTEE AIRCRAFT INC. • USA

In 1926 the Stinson Aeroplane Syndicate, West Detroit, Michigan, founded by E. A. Stinson, made Detroiter four-passenger biplane designed jointly by Stinson and F. Verville. Name Detroiter was confusingly retained for later monoplanes. Three Detroiter biplanes acquired in 1926 by Northwest Airways Inc, at which time manufacturing company renamed Stinson Airplane Corporation. Detroiters of several forms used widely by commercial and private operators; e.g. flew first regular air mail service in China. Detroiter monoplanes much developed, though general type was claimed as first US aircraft with soundproofed

Stinson L-5B light ambulance

Stinson Reliant four/five-seat cabin monoplane

and heated cabin, engine starter and wheelbrakes. Detroiter Junior of 1928 was scaled-down version for private and executive work. Detroiters established several records, including 174 hr airborne, July 1929. About 1933 new tapered wing form adopted for Reliant single-engined series, which succeeded Detroiter line. Reliant series was especially successful and built in great quantities, 500 being transferred to Royal Navy under Lend-Lease. Voyager was later two-seat high-wing monoplane. Sentinel liaison type very widely used under Vultee name, the Stinson company having undergone several corporate and nominal changes to become a Vultee division in 1940.

STODDARD-HAMILTON AIRCRAFT INC. • USA

Produces kits to construct the very popular Glasair two-seat low-wing monoplane in various models (first flown 1979 and thought to have been the first pre-moulded composite kitplane), plus kits for the GlaStar two-seat high-wing cabin monoplane (first flown 1994 and many hundreds sold). Other aircraft have included the Turbine 250/III turboprop two-seater, and T-9 Stalker two-seat turboprop variant of Glasair III as trainer (first flown 1988).

STOLP STARDUSTER CORPORATION • USA

Markets plans and kits to build a range of very well-known aircraft, as the SA-101 Starduster single-seat biplane, SA-300 Starduster Too tandem two-seat biplane (first flown 1957), SA-500 Starlet single-seat high-wing monoplane (first flown 1969), SA-750 Acroduster Too tandem two-seat aerobatic biplane (first flown 1973), and aerobatic SA-900 V-Star (single-seat biplane development of Starlet).

STOUT METAL AIRPLANE COMPANY • USA

In 1919 W. B. Stout (former aeronautical writer and engineer) formed Stout Engineering Laboratories Inc at Detroit, Michigan. Built Batwing cantilever monoplane, hoping for US Navy and civil orders. In 1920/1922 built and flew large twin-engined coast-defence torpedo-carrier monoplane for Navy. In 1922 established Stout Metal Airplane Company with himself as chief designer and Edsel Ford as a director. Specialised in metal construction. Seven-passenger Stout Air Pullman of 1924 had corrugated metal skin. In August 1925 the company was bought by Henry Ford and joint publicity was gained when Stout Mail Plane marked 'Ford' operated on Detroit-Cleveland route. AT-4 of 1926 established famous Tri-Motor line, associated with name Ford. In 1931 Stout Engineering Laboratories exhibited Sky Car two-seat monoplane at Detroit.

STREAMLINE WELDING • Canada

Markets kits to construct single- and two-seat aerobatic/competition biplanes in the Ultimate series.

STROUKOFF AIRCRAFT CORPORATION • USA

Formed at West Trenton, New Jersey, by Michael Stroukoff, responsible for design of Chase C-123 military transport, after controlling interest in the Chase Aircraft Company Inc, of which Stroukoff was vice-president, had been acquired by the Kaiser-Frazer Corporation. New Stroukoff corporation developed design of C-123. Experimental model with boundary-layer control flown December 1954. Stroukoff also developed for amphibious aircraft of this class 'pantobase' landing gear (retractable land/water skis and wingtip floats).

STUDENTS DESIGN BUREAU SKB • Russia

Founded 1955 at Samara State Aerospace University. Most recent aircraft are A-16 single-seat composites lightplane, Che-15 two-seat open ultralight floatplane (optional wheels or skis), and S-202 two-seat amphibious flying-boat (first flown 1994). Re-winged S-302 and four-seat S-400 projected.

Stroukoff YC-134 transport prototype

Stout Sedan commercial transport

Stout Air Pullman seven-passenger transport

Sud-Aviation Alouette helicopter

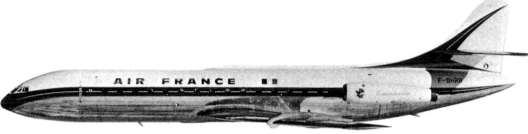

Sud-Aviation S.E.210 Caravelle jet transport

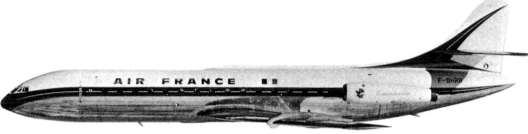

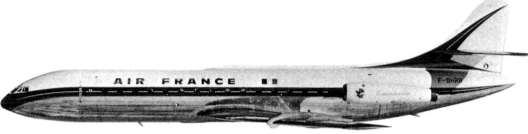

STURTEVANT AEROPLANE COMPANY • USA

Formed 1915 at Boston, Massachusetts. Derived from B. F. Sturtevant Company which made steel products, including engines. From 1916 built steel-framed tractor seaplanes for US Navy and generally similar landplanes for US Army Signal Corps. Also built Curtiss JN and DH-4 aircraft under subcontract. No production of aircraft after First World War.

SUD-AVIATION • France

Formed 1 March 1957 by amalgamation of Ouest-Aviation and Sud-Est Aviation, known until 1 September 1956 respectively as SNCASO and SNCASE (both q.v.). Main responsibility was further development and marketing of highly successful S.E.210 Caravelle twin-jet airliner, first flown in 1955, and Alouette series of helicopters. Continued also development of S.E.5000 Baroudeur, S.O.9050 mixed-power interceptor and widely used S.O.4050 Vautour twin-jet multipurpose aircraft. Frelon series of large turbine-powered helicopters developed after first flight in February 1959, and Super Frelon flew December 1962, setting new world records. Design leadership in A300 European Airbus assumed and diversification into non-aeronautical fields undertaken. Jointly with Nord-Aviation (q.v.) made Corvette light rear-engined jet transport. In 1970 became major component of Aérospatiale (q.v.).

SUD-EST AVIATION • France

Until 1 September 1956 known as Société Nationale de Constructions Aéronautiques du Sud-Est (SNCASE) (q.v.). On 1 March 1957 amalgamated with Ouest-Aviation into Sud-Aviation (both q.v.).

SUKHOI DESIGN BUREAU • USSR/Russia

P.O. Sukhoi was engaged in design long before Second World War, and in 1932 was working with a team under A. N. Tupolev on ANT-25 long-range record-breaker. Sukhoi Design Bureau founded 1939, using previous Bureau Osovikh Konstruktsii (q.v.) offices. In Second World War Sukhoi's own name was especially associated with Su-2

Sukhoi Su-27SK export version

Su-30MK version of Sukhoi Su-30 features improved radar, canards and engine thrust vectoring

*Left: Sukhoi Su-29 and
Su-31 (lower) aerobatic
aircraft*

Sukhoi Su-7 close-support and ground-attack fighter

light bomber and attack aircraft. He was responsible for twin jet Su-7 of 1947. The later and unrelated Su-7 of his second jet series became a swept-wing attack aircraft first seen 1956. Su-9, operational from 1959, and Su-11 were single-seat all-weather fighters with delta wings. The operational and large-size Su-15 twin-jet delta-wing all-weather interceptor was also tested in prototype *Flagon-B* STOL form in July 1967. Su-17 first flew August 1966 as very much improved variable-geometry fighter developed from Su-7, and was followed by Su-20 and Su-22 for export. Su-24 is a currently used variable-geometry attack type, seating two crew side by side and has been in service since February 1975. A nuclear strike bomber, reconnaissance and electronic warfare aircraft, Su-24 was designed to penetrate enemy defences for five minutes at 870mph (1,400kmh) and 650 ft (200 m) altitude, as a supersonic replacement for the Il-28 and Yak-28. In total, about 1,200 Su-24s were built during 1972-92, finally giving way on the production line to the Su-27IB.

Sukhoi died in September 1975, but subsequent Sukhoi designs continue to honour his name. These include Su-25/Su-28 and Su-39 related subsonic close-air support and tank-busting jets (first Su-25 flew February 1975 and became operational in 1981), the much praised Su-27 *Flanker* long-range air-supriority fighter (first flown May 1977 and in production since 1982 for home use and export, latter including J-11s assembled in China), the tandem two-seat Su-30 multirole fighter and attack variant of Su-27 that carries further avionics to allow it to command a group of Su-27s (first flown December 1989 and users including India), the side-by-side two-seat Su-32FN maritime strike aircraft and Su-27IB or Su-34 tactical interdictor developed from Su-27, the Su-33 or Su-27K carrierborne fighter Su-27 derivative (first flown August 1987 and first deployed on board *Admiral Kuznetsov* in 1995), Su-35 advanced air-superiority fighter (first flown June 1988) and Su-37 variant with thrust-vectoring nozzles, again Su-27 developments.

A fifth-generation tactical fighter, approximately equivalent to the US F-22, is the S-37, first flown in Septem-

ber 1997 and featuring swept-forward wings and eventually to have thrust-vectoring engine nozzles. S-54 and S-55 are newly designed lightweight jets for multirole combat and training uses, T-60S is a projected strike bomber of very stealthy appearance and S-80 is a new transport with patrol and surveillance variants. An interesting programme in 1999 is the development of the KR-860, a super-large 860-seat airliner. General-aviation programmes include Su-26, Su-29 and Su-31 single- and two-seat aerobatic competition aircraft (first flown 1984, 1991 and 1992 respectively) and Su-49 tandem two-seat primary trainer, while projects are for S-16 twin turboprop transport for 16 passengers or cargo, S-21 10-passenger supersonic business jet (with projected 68-passenger S-51), S-38 single-seat agricultural monoplane, and S-96 twin-propfan 8-passenger executive transport.

SULLIVAN AIRCRAFT MANUFACTURING COMPANY • USA

In 1930 built a low-wing cabin monoplane which was developed as the K-3.

SUMMIT AERONAUTICAL CORPORATION • USA

In 1941 was testing and developing HM-5 two-seat cabin monoplane built by Vidal process (moulding under fluid pressure), for which company held licence from Aircraft Research Corporation. War production of other items then supervened.

SUMMIT AVIATION INC. • USA

Developed Sentry O2-337 as armed military version of Cessna T337, with Thailand among operators.

SUNBEAM MOTOR CAR COMPANY LTD. • UK

Famous for aero engines to designs of Frenchman Louis

Coatalen. Built aeroplanes in quantity under subcontract during First World War, including Short types and Avro 504s. In 1917 the Sunbeam Bomber, a fairly large single-seat biplane with cockpit very far aft and machine-gun very far forward, was evolved; probably one only built.

SUPER 580 AIRCRAFT COMPANY • USA

Produced remanufactured and turboprop-engined conversion of Convair 340, 440 and 580 series transports, as Super 580.

SUPERDRONE AVIATION INC. • USA

Made kits available to construct the two-seat Little Bear, as a Piper Cub representation.

SUPERIOR AIRCRAFT COMPANY • USA

A division of the Priestly Hunt Aircraft Corporation was formed in mid-1956 at Culver City, California, to acquire the assets of Culver Aircraft Corporation (q.v.) which became bankrupt in 1946. Put into production the Superior Satellite, a two-seat low-wing cabin monoplane, derived from the Culver Model V.

SUPERMARINE AVIATION WORKS LTD. • UK

Founded 1912 by Noel Pemberton Billing (see Pemberton-Billing Ltd). In 1915 designed Night Hawk anti-airship fighter with many ingenious features, including searchlight and recoilless gun. Other designs were a twin-float seaplane and Baby single-seat fighter flying-boat, the latter flying in February 1918. Company's post war Schneider Trophy Sea Lion racing flying-boats were developed from Baby, but advanced S.4 racer of 1925 was a twin-float seaplane, though still of wooden construction. The S.5 and S.6 seaplanes, which followed, were renowned for race-winning and record-breaking, but especially as forerunners of Second World War Spitfire, designed by Reginald

Supermarine S.6B racing seaplane on display at Horse Guards in London

Supermarine's historic Spitfire, designed by R.J. Mitchell

Mitchell (1895-1937), who had joined company in 1916. Well-known maritime aircraft included the Admiralty (AD) type built by Supermarine (and Pemberton-Billing) in First World War, and Seal/Seagull/Scarab/Sheldrake series developed during 1920s and 1930s.

When the company was absorbed by Vickers in 1928 it was already famous for large multi-engined flying-boats, particularly Southampton, distinguished in RAF service from 1925, especially for long cruises. Successors were much-refined Scapa of 1932 and Stranraer of 1935, and the Walrus and Sea Otter earned their place in FAA history during Second World War. The Supermarine Spitfire first flew 5 March 1936. Well over 20,000 were built by various makers. Basic change came when the Rolls-Royce was replaced by the Griffon engine. Seafire was naval development (over 2,500 built). Spiteful and Seafang were late piston-engined types with new wing, from which the jet-propelled Attacker was developed to enter service in 1951. Swept-wing Swift was unsuccessful as fighter, and twin-jet Scimitar of 1958 concluded fighter line.

M.M. SUPER ROTOR INDÚSTRIA AERONAUTICA LTDA. • Brazil

Developed AC-4 Andorinha single-seat autogyro (first flown 1972) and M-1 Montalvá two-seat autogyro (first flown 1985).

SUPER STINKER INC. • USA

Established to market kit-built single-seat aerobatic aircraft of Pitts design.

SVENSKA AERO AKTIEBOLAGET • Sweden

From 1921 built aircraft at Lidingö to Heinkel design; sometimes called Svenska Aero Aktiebolaget (Heinkel). S.1 was typical Heinkel (Brandenburg) twin-float seaplane, variously powered; S.11 was development; H.D.14 was torpedo-bomber biplane; H.D.17 fighter-reconnaissance biplane. Of Swedish design were Pirat two-seat multipurpose biplane, Falken trainer and Jaktfalk single-seat biplane fighter. In 1931 company liquidated and effects taken over by AB Svenska Järnvägsverkstädern (q.v.) which company brought Jaktfalk production to 18.

SVENSKA AEROPLAN AB. • Sweden

See SAAB.

SVENSKA JÄRNVÄGSVERKSTÄDERNA, AB. • Sweden

In early/mid-1930s, at Linköping, built Viking three-seat cabin monoplane with wheel or float landing gear, developed later into Viking II four-seater; also Type 2 light multipurpose aircraft; and produced under licence Raab-Katzenstein Tigerschwalbe trainers for Swedish Air Force. In 1939 company's Aircraft Division amalgamated with Svenska Aeroplan AB, helping to form SAAB (q.v.).

SWALLOW AIRCRAFT COMPANY INC. • USA

As Swallow Airplane Manufacturing Company of Wichita, Kansas, was successor to E. M. Laird Company (q.v.). First product was Model 1924 Swallow Commercial three-seater (a refined Laird Swallow). Type was successful, especially in Middle West, and improved progressively. On 6 April 1926 a Swallow biplane (modified New Swallow type, called Swallow Mail plane) made inaugural flight for Varney Air Lines (later part of United Air Lines) marking significant advance in US air transport. Swallow Commercial of 1928 offered with various engines; Swallow Special 3-seater had Axelson engine. In 1930s company developed Swallow Coupé light cabin monoplane. As Swallow Aircraft Company Inc was developing two-seat low-wing types in 1941, but their production inhibited by Second World War.

SWANSON AIRPLANE COMPANY INC. • USA

S. S. Swanson was an amateur constructor, and in 1923 co-producer of Swanson-Freeman light biplane. Later worked with Lincoln-Standard Aircraft Corporation. Company named above incorporated 1930, and developed Swanson coupé two-seat high-wing cabin monoplane.

SWEARINGEN AIRCRAFT CORPORATION • USA

Founded 1953, and for some years before 1966, when its Merlin series of twin-turboprop executive aircraft reached production, this company had built prototypes for other makers, including Piper Twin Comanche. By late 1960s was building Merlin IIB eight-seater as successor to IIA (33 built) and 22-seat Metro commuter airliner. Also offered improved versions of Beechcraft types. Merlin III was 8/10-seat executive type; Merlin IV a corporate version of Metro. In 1971 the company became a subsidiary of Fairchild Industries, becoming Swearingen Aviation Corporation, but later renamed Fairchild Aircraft Corporation (q.v.).

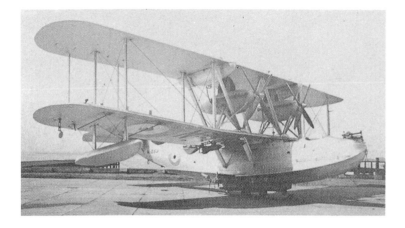

Supermarine Southampton reconnaissance flying-boat

Swearingen Merlin III 8/10-seat transport

SWEARINGEN AIRCRAFT INCORPORATED • USA

Established 1982 by Ed Swearingen. Manufactured aircraft components and offered aircraft modifications, plus developed and marketed as SX300 a two-seat kitplane (see Airight Inc). Also produced SA-32T Turbo Trainer prototype for Jaffe Aircraft (first flown 1989), and developed SJ30 entry level business jet (first flown 1991); see Sino Swearingen Company.

SWICK AIRCRAFT • USA

Made plans available for the Swick T two-seat cabin monoplane.

Swearingen Metro commuter airliner

SWING SPOL SRO • Czech Republic

Former name for BTA Top-Air sro (q.v.).

SWISS-AMERICAN AVIATION CORPORATION • Switzerland

Formed 1960 by Mr William P. Lear, former chairman of Lear Inc of USA, to make fast executive aircraft known as Lear Jet (Lear Jet Model 23=SAAC 23). By 1964 all work had been transferred to USA.

SYNAIRGIE • France

Offers kits to construct SkyRanger, Skylight and Jet Ranger two-seat microlights.

SZEKELY CORPORATION • USA

In 1930, at Holland, Michigan, made small single-seat low-wing cantilever monoplane called Flying Dutchman.

Right: Swearingen Merlin IVC corporate transport

TAAL • India

See Taneja Aerospace and Aviation Ltd/India

TACHIKAWA • Japan

New name from 1936 of Ishikawajima Aircraft Company Ltd (q.v.). Built for Japanese Army Air Force the Ki-9 and Ki-17 two-seat biplane trainers from 1935-1942 and 1935-1944 respectively; Ki-36 Army co-operation monoplane and its trainer derivative, the Ki-55 (1938-1944 and 1939-1943); the twin-engined Ki-54 multipurpose trainer-transport (1940-1945) and, under licence as the army Type LO, 64 examples of the Lockheed Model 14 twin-engined transport. Other ventures included the Ki-74 long-range pressurised twin-engined reconaissance-bomber of 1944-1945 and prototypes of the twin-engined reconaissance Ki-70, Ki-77 and Ki-94 high-altitude 'heavy' fighter. Company re-formed November 1949 as Shin Tachikawa Kokuki Kabushiki Kaisha. Built prototypes of the R-52 lightplane (first all-Japanese post-war aircraft) and R-53 in 1950s.

JSC TAGANROG AVIATION SCIENTIFIC-TECHNICAL COMPLEX NAMED AFTER G.M. BERIEV • USSR•Russia

See Beriev.

TALLERES GENERALES DE AERONAUTICA MILITAR • Mexico

See next entry.

TALLERES NACIONALES DE CONSTRUCCIONES AERONÁUTICAS • Mexico

National Aircraft Manufacturing Workshops, established November 1915 at Valbuena, near Mexico City. Began by building Blériot, Morane-Saulnier and other foreign types under licence. Own first products were the Microplane Veloz single-seat fighter biplane of 1918 and the Series A two-seat general-purpose biplane. Followed in late 1920s by the Azcarate-E training and reconnaissance sesquiplane. Aircraft design halted by Government 1930, but shortly afterwards built Chance Vought 02U Corsairs under licence. Later products included Teziutlan primary trainers in 1942 and, in late 1940s, the prototype TTS-5 six-seat twin-engined general-purpose transport.

TAMPIER, RENÉ • France

Exhibited a folding-wing roadable biplane at the 1921 Paris Salon. This had an auxiliary engine to drive the landing wheels, which could be used also as a self-starter for the main engine. When driven on the road it travelled tail first. He developed also for the French Army a two-seat reconnaissance aircraft designated T.4, which also featured a two-cylinder auxiliary engine. This was not only

Tarrant Tabor long-range bomber prototype

intended for main engine starting, but was also used to power a generator in flight to provide essential electrical services, and in particular to make possible the use of early air-to-ground communication equipment.

TANDEM AIRCRAFT KG. • Germany

Markets Sunny two-seat biplane microlight, plus kits for single-seat version.

TANEJA AEROSPACE AND AVIATION LTD. • India

Based in Bangalore and with production facilities at Hosur in Tamilnadu, TAAL undertakes aircraft production, servicing and maintenance, and runs a Flying Training Academy. It was licensed by the former Partenavia of Italy (now VulcanAir) to assemble versions of the P 68/Observer/Viator series, and also manufacturers the Hansa 3 lightplane developed by National Aerospace Laboratories (q.v.).

TARRANT, W. G. • UK

Building contractor of Byfleet, near Brooklands, Surrey, which undertook aircraft component manufacture during First World War. Only aircraft produced was Tabor long-range bomber, designed with collaboration from Royal Aircraft Establishment; this six-engined triplane nosed-over and was wrecked in its first attempt to take off in May 1919.

TAYLOR • UK

John F. Taylor designed JT.1 Monoplane single-seat monoplane and JT.2 Titch single-seat racing monoplane, first flown 1959 and 1967 respectively. Plans for both aircraft remain available from Mrs T. Taylor.

TAYLOR AIRCRAFT COMPANY INC. • USA

Formed 1929 by C. G. Taylor and brother as Taylor Brothers Aircraft Corporation to market the Chummy side-by-side two-seat lightplane. Became Taylor Aircraft Company Inc founded in 1931 by C. G. Taylor to market the Cub, small tandem two-seat cabin monoplane, in Models E-2 and F-2. Company ran into financial difficulties; rights to Cub acquired by its secretary/treasurer, W. T. Piper, in 1935, who in 1937 formed Piper Aircraft Corporation (q.v.). Taylor formed the Taylorcraft Aviation Company (q.v.) in 1936.

TAYLOR BROTHERS AIRCRAFT CORPORATION • USA

See Taylor Aircraft Company Inc.

TAYLORCRAFT AEROPLANES (ENGLAND) LTD. • UK

Created November 1938 at Thurmaston, Leicester, to build US Taylorcraft cabin monoplanes in UK under name Auster. Became Auster Aircraft Ltd (q.v.) on 7 March 1946, by which time it had built more than 1,600 Taylorcraft C, Plus C, Plus D and Auster I, II, III, IV and V, as well as early Auster J-1 Autocrats and prototype of J-2 Arrow.

Taylorcraft Plus D two-seat lightplane

TAYLORCRAFT AVIATION CORPORATION • USA

Successor to Taylor Aircraft Company Inc (q.v.) formed 1936 at Alliance, Ohio by C. G. Taylor as the Taylorcraft Aviation Company. Renamed Taylor-Young Airplane Company later that year, and Taylorcraft Aviation Corporation in 1940. Main pre-war lightplanes were Models B, C and D, of which C and D formed basis for formation of Taylorcraft Aeroplanes (England) Ltd (q.v.). During Second World War built over 1,900 similar L-2 Grasshoppers for USAAF, TG-6 training gliders based on L-2, and components for Consolidated PBY, Curtiss C-46 and Douglas A-26. Built some 2,800 Model B-12Bs in 1945-1946; went bankrupt in 1946, but then re-formed in 1947 as Taylorcraft Inc, producing models BC-12D, Ace, Traveler, Topper, Ranch, Wagon, Tourist, Sportsman and Special de Luxe. The factory moved to Pittsburgh in 1954 but then ceased manufacture four years later. It was re-formed again in April 1968 as Taylorcraft Aviation Corporation, and from 1973 resumed production of an updated two-seat Sportsman 100. Company ceased trading 1986, and in 1989 was purchased by Aircraft Acquisition Corporation, developed a series of two/three-seat lightplanes under the F22 designation. From 1992 operated independently of AAC and took name of Taylorcraft Aircraft.

TBM SA. • International

Founded by Mooney in USA and Socata in France to launch in 1987 development of TBM 700 pressurized business aircraft (first flown July 1988 and now marketed by Socata).

TECH'AERO • France

Markets kit to construct TR.200 Cobra tandem two-seat aerobatic monoplane.

TCD LTD. • UK

Markets kits for the Sherwood Ranger ST single- or tandem two-seat biplane.

TEAL AIRCRAFT CORPORATION • Canada/USA

From 1976 this company held manufacturing and tooling rights for the Thurston (q.v.) Teal, which was previously owned by Schweizer Aircraft Corporation (q.v.). Plans to restore the Teal to production in 1978, as the TSC-1A3 Marlin, did not take materialize.

TEAM INC. • USA

Tennessee Engineering and Manufacturing. Markets plans and/or kits to build a range of aircraft, including Air-Bike single-seat and open-frame microlight, Hi-MAX single-seat cabin monoplane, and miniMAX single-seat mid-wing monoplane.

Teal (formerly Thurston Teal) amphibian

TECHNICAL CENTRE, CIVIL AVIATION DEPARTMENT • India

Basically a research and development centre in Delhi. Produced nine types of gliders from 1950, as well as the Revathi two/three-seat trainer.

SCF TECHNOAVIA • Russia

Established 1991 and in 1992 put four-seat Yak-18T into production. Produces SM-92 Finist as six-passenger or seven-paratroop light STOL transport (first flown December 1993; can be armed), SM-94 six-seat multipurpose development of Yak-18T, and SP-95 aerobatic competi-

Technoavia SM-92 Finist STOL transport

Technoavia SP-91 prototype of SP-95 aerobatic aircraft

tion aircraft with interchangeable single- and two-seat cockpit. SS-98 is projected agricultural monoplane, SM-95 is under development as a twin-engined version of Finist for patrol, Miniakro is a projected aerobatic ultra-light, and Ronata is a four-seat wing-in-ground-effect aircraft.

TECHSPACE AERO • Belgium

Celebrating its 50th anniversary in 1999, produces components for various aero engines, plus maintenance, repair and testing.

TECNAM • Italy

See Costruzioni Aeronautiche Tecnam srl.

TELLIER • France

Motorboat builder Alphonse Tellier (one of his craft towed Voisin's float glider in 1905) built his first aircraft, for Emile Dubonnet, in 1909-1910, but went into liquidation in 1911.

Re-formed upon outbreak of First World War, Tellier's company built floats and hulls for other marine aircraft before flying prototype of T2 flying-boat in June 1916. This soon crashed, but with new funds from Dubonnet Tellier evolved the T3 two-seat bomber flying-boat of 1917 and its

cannon-armed derivative, the TC6. Most were built by Nieuport and other manufacturers. Final products were the unsuccessful twin-engined T5 flying-boat and tri-motor T7. In August 1918 the company was absorbed by Nieuport (q.v.), with Tellier as its marine aircraft designer.

Tellier TC6 cannon-armed bomber flying-boat

Temco Swift two-seat cabin monoplane

Temco TT-1 Pinto jet primary trainer

TEMCO AIRCRAFT CORPORATION • USA

Title from about 1950 of Texas Engineering & Manufacturing Company Inc (q.v.). Three TE-1A Buckaroo primary trainers (development of Globe Swift) evaluated by USAF 1951, leading in 1953 to civil Model 33 Plebe (no production) and military Model TE-1B. Temco also converted Navions to Twin Navions and Boeing C-97s into ambulance aircraft. Absorbed Luscombe (q.v.) in 1953, and in December that year acquired Riley Twin Navion programme. Major subcontractor in 1950s for Bell, Boeing, Convair, Douglas, Lockheed, Martin and McDonnell military aircraft. Last own product was TT-1 Pinto two-seat jet primary trainer, flown March 1956. The company became Temco Electronics about 1960, and reappeared in the aviation industry as part of Ling-Temco-Vought (q.v.).

Temco T-35 trainer prototype

PIETRO TERZI SRL • Italy

Product range encompasses T-9 Stiletto two-seat lightplane (first flown 1990) for club and private flying, train-

Pietro Terzi T-9 Stiletto lightplane

z

499

Pietro Terzi T-30C Katana aerobatic aircraft

ing, surveillance and more; T-30 Katana single-seat aerobatic/competition monoplane (first flown 1991); and Windspider inflatable sailing craft.

TEXAS AIRCRAFT MANUFACTURING COMPANY • USA

Based at Stewart Airport, Tyler, Texas. Acquired in early 1950s from Johnson Aircraft Corporation (q.v.) the Bullet light aircraft, produced as Texas Bullet.

TEXAS AIRPLANE MANUFACTURING COMPANY INC. • USA

Dallas-based company which in mid-1970s acquired assets of Carstedt Inc (q.v.) and is continuing marketing of latter's Jetliner 600 lengthened-fuselage turboprop conversion of de Havilland Dove as the CJ600.

TEXAS ENGINEERING & MANUFACTURING COMPANY INC. • USA

This company built 329 Globe Swifts under licence before Globe (q.v.) went bankrupt in 1947, when it acquired rights in this aircraft. It was renamed Temco (q.v.) about 1950.

TEXAS HELICOPTER CORPORATION • USA

Developed M74 Wasp (certification 1976) and M79T Jet Wasp II (first flown 1979 with piston engine) as single-seat piston-engined agricultural/utility and two-seat turboshaft-powered modifications of Bell 47G/TH-13T helicopters respectively. Assets bought by Aerodyne (q.v.) 1985.

THK • Turkey

See Turk Hava Kurumu Ucak Fabrikasi.

THOMAS BROTHERS AEROPLANE COMPANY • USA

Founded at Bath, New York, 1912 by William and Oliver Thomas, who built their first aircraft in Winter 1909-1910.

Thomas Brothers T-2 pre-First World War biplane

Thomas-Morse MB-7 racing monoplane

Products included T-2 biplane (similar to Curtiss J) and D-5 two-seat observation biplane, of which two evaluated by US Army. Merged January 1917 with Morse Chain Company to form Thomas-Morse Aircraft Corporation (q.v.).

THOMAS-MORSE AIRCRAFT CORPORATION • USA

Formed January 1917 at Ithaca, New York, from merger of Thomas Brothers Aeroplane Company (q.v.) and Morse Chain Company. Principal products during and after First World War were S-4 single-seat advanced training biplane and its S-5 seaplane version; MB-3 single-seat fighter; R-2 and R-5 Pulitzer Trophy racers of 1921-1922 and their unsuccessful MB-9 and MB-10 pursuit/training derivatives. Last aircraft produced were O-19 two-seat observation biplane and O-19-derived XO-932 sesquiplane of 1932. Development/production of these two continued after Thomas-Morse had been acquired in 1929 by Consolidated Aircraft Corporation (q.v.).

THOMPSON, NORMAN, FLIGHT COMPANY LTD. • UK

Seaplane manufacturer of Bognor, Sussex, formed October 1915 to succeed White and Thompson Ltd (q.v.). Prod-

ucts included N.1B two-seat flying-boat fighter, N.T.2B two-seat flying-boat trainer, also built by Supermarine and S.E. Saunders Ltd (both q.v.), and N.T.4 and 4A four-seat anti-submarine and training flying-boats. One N.T.2B was shipped to Canada to make forestry patrols from Lake St John, Quebec. The N.T.4s were similar to Curtiss H.4s and known as Americas, but there was no connection between the two companies.

THORP AIRCRAFT COMPANY • USA

Formed about 1949-1950 at Pacoima, California by John W. Thorp to develop his Sky Skooter two-seat light aircraft, first flown August 1946, itself developed from Lockheed Little Dipper. Built three of T-111 model; introduced T-211 in 1953, production of which undertaken by Tubular Aircraft Products Company (q.v.). Currently Thorp Engineering markets plans for T-18 Tiger homebuilt.

THRUSTER AIRCRAFT SERVICES LTD. • UK

Markets T.300 side-by-side two-seat open microlight, T.500 derivative with enclosed rear fuselage, and T.600 Nova two-seat microlight developed from T.300, all in completed and kit forms.

THRUSTER AIRCRAFT (AUSTRALIA) PTY. LTD. • Australia

Marketed the T.300 side-by-side two-seat open microlight in completed or kit forms (see previous entry).

THULINS, ENOCH, AB AEROPLANFABRIC • Sweden

Title from 1914 of the former AVIS (Aeroplanvarvet i Skane) company formed 1913 by Dr Enoch Thulin and Oskar Ask. Models A, B, C and D were respectively Swedish versions of the Blériot monoplane, Morane-Saulnier monoplane, Albatros B.II and Morane-Saulnier parasol. Thulin designs included the Type E, FA, G, GA, H, K, L, LA, N and NA. Total factory output was 99 aircraft, of which 32 produced in 1918. Dr Thulin died in flying accident in 1919. AB Thulinverken, a company which was formed a year later, is not connected with aviation.

THUNDERBIRD AIRCRAFT INC. • USA

The Thunderbird Aircraft Company was established in November 1927 at Glendale, California, to build and develop the Thunderbird biplane, designed by Theodore A. Woolsey, and first flown in June 1926. The production W-14 was a three-seat open-cockpit biplane powered by a Curtiss OX-5 engine.

THURSTON AEROMARINE CORPORATION • USA

Superseded International Aeromarine (q.v.); initially to produce two-seat Teal III amphibian (delivered from 1995), then expected to be followed by Seafire four-seat amphibian. Also then anticipated was eight-seat Seamaster with two turboprop engines.

THURSTON AIRCRAFT CORPORATION • USA

This company was organized in July 1966 by David B. Thurston to develop marine aircraft. It designed and manufactured the TSC-1A1 Teal two/three-seat light amphibian later acquired by Schweizer and later Teal Aircraft Corporation (q.v.).

TIB • Czech Republic

Produces the Caprice 21 tandem two-seat very light monoplane.

TIME WARP • USA

Produces a Supermarine Spitfire representation.

TIMM AIRCRAFT CORPORATION • USA

Formed at Van Nuys, California; was inactive in aircraft manufacture for several years, but in late 1930s produced prototype T-840 twin-engined six-seat transport. Then it developed a plastic-bonded plywood Aeromold, applying this first to the S-160-K two-seat primary trainer of 1940, which was built in Second World War as N2T-1 trainer for US Navy. Timm also built 434 Waco CG-4A cargo gliders, and did wartime subcontract work for Harlow, Lockheed, Vultee and other companies.

TIMMINS AVIATION LTD. • Canada

Transport aircraft repair and overhaul works at Montreal International Airport which in early/mid-1960s produced a 'general aviation' conversion of the Catalina amphibian. Aircraft and Texaco Sky Service Divisions merged on 1 January 1967 with Atlantic Aviation of Wilmington, Delaware, USA.

TIPSY • Belgium

Formed in late 1930s together with Tipsy Aircraft Company Ltd in UK (q.v.) to build ultralight aircraft designed by E. O. Tips and previously manufactured by Avions Fairey (q.v.). Pre-war products at Gosselies were single-seat S2 and two-seat B or B-2 (open cockpits) and BC (enclosed cabin). B-2 revived post-war as Tipsy Trainer, and BC as Belfair (from Belgian Fairey), together with new design of Junior in 1946 and Nipper in 1957. Production of Nipper taken over by Cobelavia in 1961, and by Nipper Aircraft Ltd in 1966 (both q.v.)

Transland Ag-2 agricultural aircraft

TIPSY AIRCRAFT COMPANY LTD. • UK

Formed 1937 at Hanworth Air Park. Middlesex, to licence-build Anglo-Belgian lightplanes of E. O. Tips. Continued production post-war but closed down in 1952.

TITAN AIRCRAFT • USA

Offers kits to construct the Tornado Sport single-seat monoplane, Tornado UL 103 microlight version, and Tornado II Trainer two-seater.

TL ULTRALIGHT • Czech Republic

See Interwork.

TOWLE AIRCRAFT COMPANY INC. • USA

Incorporated in 1928 at Detroit, Michigan, to build the Towle TA-3 eight-passenger amphibian flying-boat. A high-wing cantilever monoplane, it was powered by twin radial engines mounted on multi-strut pylons on the wing upper surface.

TRADEWIND TURBINES • USA

Produced Prop-Jet Bonanza as turboprop conversion of Beech A36 Bonanza, originally developed by Allison Gas Turbine Division and Soloy Conversions Ltd.

TRAGO MILLS LTD. • UK

Aviation division built prototype SAH-1 two-seat aerobatic lightplane (first flown August 1983) but sold to Orca Aircraft Ltd (q.v.).

TRANSALL • International

Arbeitsgemeinschaft Transall group founded 1959 by France and Germany to develop C-160 twin-turboprop freighter, first flown 1963 and 169 production aircraft delivered to France, Germany, South Africa and Turkey. Small second series built for France, first aircraft flying 1981.

TRANSAVIA CORPORATION PTY. LTD. • Australia

Established 1964 as division of Transfield Construction Pty Ltd, and first flew in 1965 original PL-12 Airtruk, very unusual twin-boom agricultural aircraft, put into production and service. Later developed into Skyfarmer T-300A.

TRANSLAND AIRCRAFT • USA

A Division of Hi-Shear Rivet Tool Company, and manufacturer since early 1950s of equipment for agricultural aviation. Built Ag-1 agricultural research aircraft in about 1953, followed 1956 by Ag-2, using components from Vultee BT-13. Plans to build five Ag-2s in late 1950s thwarted. Revived in 1965, but still none produced.

TRAVEL AIR MANUFACTURING COMPANY • USA

Noted chiefly for its Model 2000/3000/4000/8000/9000 family of commercial and training biplanes of the mid/late 1920s, following its formation in 1924 by Walter H. Beech (later of Beechcraft, q.v.) and others. Travelair Model R 'Mystery Ships' came first in 1929 Thompson Trophy race and 2nd in 1930, easily beating best US Army and Navy entries. Company purchased by Curtiss-Wright Corporation (q.v.) in 1930.

TRECKER AIRCRAFT CORPORATION • USA

Division of Kearney & Trecker Corporation which in early/mid-1960s assembled at Milwaukee, Wisconsin, Italian Piaggio P.136L-1s and L-2s under names Trecker Gull and Super Gull.

TRELLA AIRCRAFT SYNDICATE • USA

Established in 1921 at Detroit, Michigan, to produce the Trella Speedster two-seat lightweight biplane, powered by a 65 hp Le Blond radial engine.

Tridair Gemini ST helicopter

TRIDAIR HELICOPTERS INC. • USA

Established 1980. Offers modification of Bell LongRanger into twin-engined Gemini ST (first flown January 1991), with two Allison 250-C20R engines; modification also incorporates other changes.

TRIDENT AIRCRAFT LTD. • Canada

Established in early 1970s to develop Trigull-320 six-seat light amphibian, first flown August 1973 and eventually becoming TR-1 Trigull. Turbo Trigull offered with turbocharged engines.

TRI-R TECHNOLOGIES INC. • USA

Markets kits to build the KIS (Keep It Simple) side-by-side two-seat composites monoplane (first flown 1991), plus the four-seat TR-4 Cruiser (first flown 1994).

TSENTRALNYI AERO-GIDRODINAMICHESKII INSTITUT • USSR

See ANT.

TUBULAR AIRCRAFT PRODUCTS COMPANY INC. • USA

Builds under licence from Thorp Aircraft Company (q.v.) the Model 211, a developed version of the Thorp Sky Skooter lightplane. Eight built by Spring 1965; suspended 1966.

TUGAN AIRCRAFT LTD. • Australia

Built in 1936 six examples of the Gannet twin-engined, high-wing monoplane for cartographic survey/ambulance duties for the RAAF, designed by Wg Cdr L. J. Wackett. Taken over 1936 by Commonwealth Aircraft Corporation (q.v.).

TUPOLEV JOINT STOCK COMPANY • USSR/Russia

Doyen of Soviet aircraft designers, A. N. Tupolev (1888-1972) studied under great Soviet aviation pioneer N. E. Zhukovskii and during First World War worked at Duks factory in Moscow. In 1918 assisted Zhukovskii to found ANT (q.v.) becoming head of design department 1920 and president of commission to design and build all-metal aircraft 1922. Initially followed Junkers formula, using corrugated metal skins; first to appear were ANT-1 and ANT-2 (A. N. Tupolev) cantilever monoplanes. Became head of AGOS department of the Moscow TsAGI in 1922; during 1920-1936 most designs bore ANT designations although some emanated from his design team leaders, chief deputy A. A. Archangelskii, W. M. Petlyakov and P. O. Sukhoi (e.g. Sukhoi designed ANT-25 and 37). Tupolev's first major design was ANT-4 (TB-1) heavy bomber of 1925, forerunner of several very large machines including ANT-6 (TB-3) bomber; ANT-9 commercial passenger transport and huge ANT-20 *Maxim Gorkii* propaganda aircraft of 1934. Also designed ANT-40 (SB-2) twin-engined medium bomber.

In 1936 Tupolev was arrested during Stalin's purges for 'revolutionary activities' and condemned to death, but sentence commuted and after some five years' imprisonment was released and restored to favour (ostensibly in recognition of Tu-2 medium bomber, designed while in prison) and given his own design bureau. After Second World War continued to place emphasis on large aircraft; Tu-4 copy of Boeing B-29 Superfortress helped win him a Stalin Prize in 1948.

Main early post-war products included Tu-14 twin-jet naval medium bomber; Tu-16 intermediate-range twin-jet bomber (first flown April 1952; also produced in China

Right: Tupolev Tu-95 Bear-B maritime reconnaissance bomber

as the Xi'an H-6); and a quartet of four-turboprop swept-wing giants: the Tu-95 long-range strategic bomber (first flown November 1952 and built up to 1992), Tu-142 naval variant for long-range anti-submarine warfare and communications relay (first flown June 1968 and still in use today), Tu-114 200-passenger transport based on Tu-95 (first flown November 1957) and Tu-126 AWACS aircraft (first flown 1962). Later military types included the twin-jet Tu-22, the first Soviet supersonic bomber that first flew in 1959, and the Tu-128 very large all-weather interceptor (first flown March 1961). Most recent military aircraft include the variable-geometry wing Tu-22M *Backfire* intermediate-range Mach 1.8 bomber and missile launcher (first flown August 1969 and 514 built during 1971-90) and the variable-geometry wing Tu-160 *Blackjack* heavy missile bomber with a speed of Mach 2.05 and range of over 7,590 miles (12,215 km) without in-flight refuelling (first flown December 1981 and entered Soviet service from 1987), while projects include the Tu-204P maritime patrol derivative of the Tu-204 airliner, Tu-2000 hypersonic bomber, and a subsonic strealth bomber.

Early turbojet and turbofan powered transport aircraft included twin-jet Tu-104 (based on Tu-16 and first flown June 1955); Tu-124 (first flown March 1960); Tu-134 (first flown July 1963) and tri-jet Tu-154 (first flown October 1968). Tu-144 became, in December 1968, the first supersonic airliner in the world to fly. It exceeded Mach 2 for the first time in May 1970 and was the first of its type to enter regular service when, in December 1975, it began freighting for Aeroflot prior to initial passenger services in 1977. However, Tu-144 was not a success and services were terminated in June 1978; in November 1996 a converted Tu-144D flew again as the Tu-144LL, used thereafter for an international High-Speed Civil Transport research programme to assist in the development of a next-generation supersonic transport.

Most recent Tupolev commercial transports, programmes and projects include the convertible cargo/passenger Tu-130 (to fly on standard and liquid natural gas in the 21st century), Tu-136 projected light passenger/cargo transport with twin Pratt & Whitney turboprop engines, Tu-155/Tu-156 conversions of Tu-154 to use cryogenic fuel engines (Tu-155 for research flew 1988), Tu-204 medium-range airliner for typically 214 passengers (first flown January 1989) and its projected Tu-206 cryogenic fuel derivative, Tu-214 and Tu-224 airliners based on Tu-204 but featuring increased take-off weights and longer range (first flight of Tu-214 March 1996), Tu-230 projected light/medium freighter, 166-passenger Tu-234 airliner as a short-length variant of Tu-204, Tu-244 projected supersonic airliner, Tu-304 and Tu-306 (cryogenic fuel variant) projected long-range airliners for up to 392 passengers (to fly 2001?), projected Tu-324 regional and business transport, Tu-330 and liquid-gas Tu-338 freighters, Tu-334 medium-range airliner for typically 102 passengers (first flown February 1999) and its Tu-336 cryogenic fuel derivative, Tu-404 projected giant 850-seat airliner, and Tu-414 projected 70-passenger regional jet.

Tupolev general-aviation projects include Tu-34 pressurized five/seven-seat STOL transport with twin turboprop engines and pusher propellers, Tu-54 single-seat agricultural monoplane, Tu-400 eight/ten-seat business jet with regional airliner potential, and Tu 4X4 four/seven-seat business jet as smallest aircraft in the Tu-324/400/414 range.

TURBAY SA. • Argentina

First design by Ing Alfredo Turbay was the T-1 Tucan parasol-wing lightplane, first flown April 1943. Six Tucans ordered from Sfreddo & Paolini (q.v.) were halted when the latter firm was seized and nationalized by the government and plans to revive production in 1963 were also thwarted. The T-2 five-seat twin-engined monoplane was destroyed by fire in early 1949 before it had flown; thus

Tupolev Tu-95 long-range bomber

the next design to fly was the T-3A six-passenger light transport in December 1964. Turbay SA was formed in January 1961 to build the proposed T-3B production version and a lengthened fuselage development, the T-4, but no production was achieved.

TURK HAVA KURUMU UCAK FABRIKASI • Turkey

Aircraft factory of the Turkish Air League formed 1941 at Etimesgut, near Ankara. Built several gliders, including the

Tupolev Tu-154 medium/long-range transport

Tupolev ANT-4 (TB-1) heavy bomber

*Tupolev Tu-16 twin-jet
medium bomber*

Above:Turbay T-3A light transport

TURNER AIRCRAFT INC. • USA

Offers plans to build T-40A side by-side two-seat wooden low-wing monoplane, plus Super T-40 with increased wingspan and more engine power.

TUSAS AEROSPACE INDUSTRIES INC. • Turkey

TUSAS Havacilik ve Uzay Sanayii AS, founded May 1984 as a joint-venture company with Turkish Armed Forces Foundation and Turkish Air League (2 per cent shareholding), Lockheed Martin of Turkey (42 per cent) and General Electric (7 per cent). TAI currently manufactures Lockheed Martin F-16C/D Block 50Ds for the Turkish Air Force under the US Peace Onyx II programme plus wings and fuselages for US production lines under Peace Onyx I, assembles Airtech CN 235M transport for air force, assembles UH-60L Black Hawks for army, co-manufactures Eurocopter Cougar Mk Is for air force, and contributes to Airbus FLA, Eurocopter EC 135 and Sikorsky S-76 pro-

grammes. Other work includes UAVs and aircraft modernization, development of the TG-X1 Bat very light single-seat attack-surveillance aircraft (first flown February 1997, based on US Sadler A-22 Piranha), and development of the HD-XX twin-turbofan regional transport.

TWIN CAT CORPORATION • USA

Founded 1979 to offer kits to convert Gulfstream American Ag-Cat agricultural aircraft to twin-engined configuration.

TWO WINGS AVIATION • USA

Markets kits for the Mariner single- or two-seat amphibious biplane, plus the Mariner Mono monoplane variant.

TYPHOON DESIGN BUREAU • Russia

Now merged into Dubna Machinebuilding Plant JSC (q.v.).

THK-1 12-seat troop transport glider, and five types of light aircraft: the THK-2 single-seat aerobatic trainer; THK-5/5A twin-engined light transport/ambulance; THK-11 three-seat pusher-engined twin-boom light tourer; THK-15 tandem two-seat primary trainer; and THK-16 twin-jet trainer. Also built about 100 Miles M.14s under licence. Turkish Air League control ceased 1952; renamed Makina ve Kimya Endustrisi Kurumu (see MKEK).

Right: TUSAS TG-X1 Bat very light attack-surveillance monoplane

Uetz U2V two-seat lightplane

UAC • USA

See United Aircraft Corporation.

UDET FLUGZEUGBAU GMBH • Germany

German First World War air ace Ernst Udet lent his name to this company, established near Munich in 1921 by American William Pohl. The Udet U-1 single-seat lightplane of 1922 was followed by a two-seat U-2; more powerful U-4; cabin monoplane U-5; another ultralight two-seat U-6; parasol-winged single-seat U-7 Kolibri; small airliner U-8; and an 11-seat high-wing transport U-11 Kondor. Udet left the company in 1925, after agreeing to production of a light training biplane, the Udet U-12 Flamingo, destined to become the company's best-known aircraft. A two-seat open-cockpit biplane of wooden construction, it was demonstrated throughout the world by Udet. Although the company went out of business in 1925, Flamingo production continued as Bayerische Flugzeugwerke AG (q.v.) in Germany, as well as in Austria, Hungary and Latvia. It served in many roles, notably as a trainer with the German civil flying clubs and at clandestine Luftwaffe pilot training centres.

UETZ FLUGZEUGBAU • Switzerland

This company developed an improved version of the French Jodel D119 two-seat lightplane known as the Uetz U2V, first flown 1962. Series production began in 1964. In that year a redesigned four-seater, the U4M Pelikan, also went into production.

UKROVOZDUKHPUT • USSR

This company (The Ukranian Air Transport Co) was one of the most important aviation companies in Russia in the 1920s. Besides operating several airlines, Ukrovozdukhput manufactured aircraft to the designs of K. A. Kalinin, who patented the elliptical wing planform in 1923. One of his best-known designs was the 1928 Kalinin K-4 single-engined cabin monoplane, produced as a transport or air ambulance.

ULTIMATE AEROBATICS LTD. • Canada

Put on to market in 1980s kits to modify Pitts Special aerobatic biplane to improve performance.

Umbaugh Model 18 autogyro

ULTIMATE AIRCRAFT CORPORATION • Canada

Founded 1990 to market modified Pitts Special aerobatic biplane in plans, kits and assembled forms, plus series of aerobatic/competition biplanes as 10 Dash 100, 10 Dash 200, 10 Dash 300 single-seaters, and two-seat 20 Dash 300.

ULTRAVIA AERO INC. • Canada

Offers kits to construct the side-by-side two-seat Pelican Club series of cabin monoplanes.

UMBAUGH AIRCRAFT CORPORATION • USA

Developed the Umbaugh Model 18 two-seat, jump-start autogyro which first flew in 1959. Limited production followed, including five aircraft assembled and tested by the Fairchild Corporation (q.v.) in 1960. In 1965 production of the U-18 was taken over by Air & Space Manufacturing (q.v.) and the aircraft was redesignated Air & Space U-18A.

UMBRA SA. • Italy

Founded in 1935 by Muzio Macchi, Umbra built Savoia-Marchetti S.M.79 torpedo-bombers under licence. Postwar production comprised aircraft and systems components until work was begun, in 1968, on the AUM-903 three-engined STOL light transport project. Current production is concentrated on licence manufacture of the Scheibe SF-25B Motorfalke motor glider for the Italian and North African markets.

UNGARISCHE FLUGZEUGBAU AG. • Hungary

Founded by Baron Skoda, proprietor of the Skoda Gun Works, in association with a group of Hungarian banks, to build Loehner aircraft immediately after First World War.

UNIKOMTRANS • Russia

Has developed a four-seat light amphibian as the Unikomtrans 11 (displayed 1995, but not known to have flown by 1998).

United biplane trainer

UNION FLUGZEUGWERKE GMBH • Germany

Founded in 1956 by Ernst Heinkel Flugzeugbau and Messerschmitt AG (both q.v.) as a joint enterprise to manufacture under licence French Fouga-Potez Magister jet trainers for the Luftwaffe, production of 210 being completed in 1963. Later activities included the procurement of spares for German military aircraft and preparing technical manuals.

UNIS, OBCHODNI SPOL, SRO • Czech Republic

Has developed and flown the NA 40-Bongo two-seat and twin-turboshaft light helicopter without a tail rotor. Deliveries expected 1999.

UNITED AEROSPACE TECHNOLOGIES LTD. • UK

Put under development the two-seat composites-built Ranger lightplane, the four-seat Super Ranger, and six-seat and twin-engined Twin Ranger, all with rear-mounted wings, canards and pusher propellers, and all former Luscombe (q.v.) designs.

UNITED AIRCRAFT CORPORATION • USA

This conglomorate was founded in 1934 to group together the activities of Pratt & Whitney Aircraft and Engines, Hamilton-Standard (formerly Hamilton Metalplane), United Airports and Vought-Sikorsky, each company retaining its separate identity.

UNITED EASTERN AEROPLANE CORPORATION • USA

Established in New York; built three trainer biplanes for use in own Eastern School of Aviation. During Second World War built aircraft under contract.

UNITED HELICOPTER INC. • USA

This company succeeded the Aircraft Division of Hiller Industries, established in 1942 to develop and produce helicopters with twin coaxial rotors. A two-seat C4 Commuter prototype was flown, together with the United J-5, the first US-built helicopter to employ jet torque conversion.

UNITED STATES AIRCRAFT CORPORATION • USA

Undertook aircraft conversions, including Turbo Express lengthened and turboprop conversion of DC-3.

UNITED STATES ARMY ENGINEERING DIVISION • USA

Established at McCook Field, Ohio, the US Army Engineering Division was concerned with the design, development and manufacture of aircraft for the US Army. These included the FVL-8 and BVL-12, biplane fighter and bomber respectively, designed by Italian Ottorino Pomilio; USD-9 version of the British Airco D.H.9; XB-1 version of the Bristol F.2B Fighter; M-1 and MAT communications aircraft designed by Alfred Verville and built by the Sperry Aircraft Company (q.v.); three R-3 low-wing monoplane racing aircraft by the same Verville/Sperry combination; VCP-1 (Verville-Clark Pursuit) of 1918; NBL-1 'Barling' bomber designed by Briton Walter Barling and built by Witteman-Lewis Aircraft Corporation (q.v.); and GA-1, or G.A.X. (Ground Attack Experimental), built by the Boeing Company (q.v.). With establishment of the USAAC in 1926, the Engineering Division was replaced at McCook Field by the Matériel Division.

UNIVERSAL DYNAMICS RESEARCH AND DEVELOPMENT • Philippines

Developed piston-engined Defiant 300 wooden two-seat lightplane (first flown 1988) and later turboprop-engined Defiant 500 metal lightplane.

UNIVAIR AIRCRAFT CORPORATION • USA

Founded in 1946 to manufacture propellers and components for light aircraft. Acquired type certificates and production rights for a number of post-war American lightplanes, including the Globe Swift, Ercoupe and Mooney Mite. Built to order updated version of the Stinson 108 Voyager, as 108-5.

UPPERCU-BURNELLI AIRCRAFT CORPORATION • USA

Formed 1930 to develop the theories of Vincent Burnelli on aerofoil-shaped fuselage structures; occupied the former Aeromarine Plane & Motor Company (q.v.) plant at New Jersey. First project was Model 101 high-speed twin-engined transport developed from earlier Remington-Burnelli Airliner projects, the 1920 RB-2, 1927 CU-16 and 1929 UB-20. Subsequently became the Burnelli Aircraft Corporation (q.v.).

URBAN AVIATION SRO • Czech Republic

Markets its UFM 11 and UFM 13 Lambáda composites-built two-seat monoplanes in completed and kit forms.

Utva 56 four-seat lightplane

URDANETA Y GALVEZ LTDA. • Colombia

Established 1950. Since 1961 this company has been South American distributor for the products of the Cessna Aircraft Company (q.v.), assembling and part-manufacturing certain Cessna types such as the Model A188 AgWagon agricultural aircraft. It is planned that the company will eventually undertake licence manufacture of complete airframes from the Cessna range.

URMV-3 • Romania

See Sovromtractor for pre 1950 set-up of former IAR/Regia under Soviet occupation. Further products under URMV-3 title included the IAR 821 single-seat agricultural/utility aircraft, and the IAR 823 STOL utility transport. See also IAR and IAR-SA Brasov.

US AVIATION • USA

Markets kits to allow construction of Cumulus single-seat microlight/motorglider, developed from the Cloud Dancer. Also offers SuperFloater kit glider.

Utva 65 agricultural aircraft

US LIGHT AIRCRAFT CORPORATION • USA

Offers kits to build Hornet tandem two-seat high-wing microlight.

UTVA, FABRICA AVIONA • Yugoslavia/Serbia

Utva produced light utility aircraft, including the Utva 56 four-seater, first flown in 1956, and thereafter developed through a number of U60 air-taxi/tourer/freight/agricultural/ambulance and floatplane versions. The Utva 65 was originally an agricultural aircraft, developed as the U66 to serve various utility roles and including the armed U66V version. The Utva 75 two-seat trainer/glider-tug/agricultural aircraft entered production in late 1970s. Lasta 1 tandem two-seat piston-engined trainer first flew September 1985 but was superseded before production by the design of the refined Lasta 2. Development started of Utva 95 agricultural aircraft, probably based on Utva 75. Formerly fabricated components for the IAR-93/J-22 Orao and Super Galeb programmes, and produced items for various Boeing airliners.

UNIS NA 40-Bongo light helicopter

VALENTIN FLUGZEUGBAU GMBH • Germany

Best known for its gliders/motorgliders, developed Taifun 12E as two-seat lightplane (first flown 1985), further developed into Taifun 11S four-seater of 1988.

VALMET AVIATION INDUSTRIES • Finland

Followed on from Valmet OY (see below) before the latest change to Finavitec OY (q.v.). Manufactured the L-90TP RediGO turboprop trainer before being sold to Aermacchi of Italy in 1996. Began assembly of 57 F-18C Hornet fighters for the Finnish Air Force from kits, and manufactured parts, plus their engines.

Valmet Leko-70 Vinka light trainer

Valmet L-90TP RediGO turboprop trainer before being sold to Aermacchi of Italy

VALMET OY KUOREVEDEN TEHDAS • Finland

Valmet Oy was shortened title from 1958 of state-owned group (Valtion Metallitehtaat Lentokonetehdas, q.v.) consisting of several metalworking factories. Kuoreveden Tehdas (Kuorevesi Works) was formerly part of factory group Valmet Oy Tampere, from which it separated in 1974, and became the largest aircraft factory in Finland. Foreign aircraft produced under licence included Potez (Air Fouga) Magister jet trainers and 12 Saab Draken fighters. Own-designed Leko-70 Vinka two-seat piston-engined trainer evolved by new design group created September 1970, followed in 1985 by the two/four-seat L-80 TP turboprop version. Also flew prototypes of the PIK-23 Towmaster. Valmet also assembled 46 of the 50 BAe Hawk jet trainers for Finnish Air Force. Other activities included overhaul and repair of military and civil aircraft and piston aero engines. The other aviation member of group was Valmet Oy Linnavuoren Tehdas, at Siuro, concerned mainly with overhaul and repair of jet aero engines. See Valmet Aviation Industries.

VALSTS ELEKTROTECHNISKA FABRIKA • Latvia

(Government Electrotechnical Factory) at Riga. Aviation division established 1935 under Karlis Irbitis, pioneer aircraft designer/builder in Latvia since mid-1920s. First production was I-11 (Irbitis's 11th design), two-seat low-wing monoplane, built 1936. A year later came improved I-12. Single examples followed of small series of small, lightweight fighter/trainers and, in 1939, the 300mph (483kmh) I-16 two/four-gun single-seat light fighter. VEF built I-17 two-seat primary trainer for Latvian Air Force in 1940, and two I-18 two-seaters developed from earlier Pulins/Irbitis I-8. When Latvia was invaded on 17 June 1940, VEF had 380-400mph (612-644kmh) I-19 fighter on drawing board.

VALTION LENTOKONETEHDAS • Finland

Finnish State Aircraft Factory, created February 1928 from former IVL (Ilmailuvoimien Lentokonetehdas = Aviation Force Aircraft Factory) which, from its formation near Helsinki in 1921, had built Hansa-Brandenburg W.33 seaplanes and Caudron C 60 trainers under licence for Finnish Air Force, plus the Finnish-designed Kotka maritime reconnaissance/bomber biplane. First VL product was the Sääski two-seat trainer, followed by licence production of de Havilland Moths and Blackburn Ripons. After producing the Vima light trainer and Tuisku advanced training/reconnaissance biplanes, the VL was reorganised in 1936 and moved to Tampere, where it produced Pyry monoplane trainers, Fokker C.X. biplanes, Fokker D.XXI fighters and Bristol Blenheim bombers under licence. Next indigenous product was single-seat Myrsky fighter of 1942-1945. Became part of Valtion (next entry) after Second World War.

VALTION METALLITEHTAAT LENTOKONETEHDAS • Finland

Soon after Second World War Valtion Lentokonetehdas (q.v.) was integrated into this larger group (State Metal Works, Aircraft Factory) with other nationally-owned metalworking factories. Works were at Tampere (main plant), Linnavuori (aero engines) and Kuorevesi (aircraft repairs). First post-war product was the Vihuri two-seat advanced trainer, built for Finnish Air Force. Known from 1958 by shortened title of Valmet Oy (q.v.).

VANCOUVER AIRCRAFT • Canada

The temporary name in 1938 of Boeing Aircraft of Canada Ltd (q.v.). When it became wholly Canadian owned it soon reverted to the earlier title.

VAN'S AIRCRAFT INC. • USA

Offers plans and kits for the RV-3 single-seat low-wing monoplane, RV-4 tandem two-seat low-wing monoplane, RV-6/6A side-by-side two-seat low-wing monoplane (commercially built in Nigeria as Air Beetle), and RV-8 tandem two-seat low-wing monoplane.

VARDAX CORPORATION • USA

Produces turboprop conversion of de Havilland Canada DHC-3 Otter, as Vazar Dash 3 Turbine Otter.

VARGA AIRCRAFT CORPORATION • USA

In 1965 this company acquired from Shinn Engineering Inc (q.v.) full manufacturing rights, tooling and spares for Shinn Model 2150A. Put into production by Varga in 1977 as Model 2150A Kachina. Design originated from Morrisey Nifty of 1957, built by a former Douglas test pilot.

VECTO INSTRUMENT CORPORATION • USA

Since early 1960s has marketed Vecto Geronimo, an uprated-engine and refined airframe/equipment version of standard Piper Apache. About 31 conversions completed by spring 1965; after death of Vecto's owner later that year, assets purchased by Geronimo (q.v.).

VEETOL HELICOPTERS PTY. LTD. • Australia

Predecessor of VTOL Aircraft (q.v.), developing Phillicopter.

VEGA AIRCRAFT CORPORATION • USA

Title from 1941 of Vega Airplane Company (q.v.); continued production of Lockheed Vega B-34 Ventura twin-engined medium bomber for USAAF/USN/RAF and Boeing B-17 Flying Fortress for USAAF between 1941 and 1944. Absorbed into Lockheed Aircraft Corporation (q.v.) 30 November 1943; name Vega abandoned; Vega plant

Vecto Geronimo version of the Piper Apache

became Lockheed's Factory A. Ventura B-34 production ended 1943; PV-1 naval version and Boeing B-17 manufacture continued until 1944 under responsibility of Lockheed.

VEGA AIRPLANE COMPANY • USA

Known formerly as Airover Company, formed at Burbank, California, as associated company of Lockheed Aircraft Corporation (q.v.) in 1937. Began research/development experiments with light aircraft, devising (with Menasco) a unit called Unitwin; two small engines coupled side-by-side to drive single propeller flight-tested in Lockheed Altair in 1938. Then designed five/six-seat Starliner twin-tailed low-wing cabin monoplane using similar powerplant. Small batch of radio-controlled targets built in 1939. Factory expanded 1940, and mid-year received contract to build large numbers of Lockheed Ventura bombers for RAF. Then, in conjunction with Boeing and Douglas (q.v.), mass produced Boeing B-17 Flying Fortress bombers; became wholly-owned subsidiary of Lockheed in 1941 as Vega Aircraft Corporation (q.v.).

VELOCITY AIRCRAFT • USA

Markets kits to build various models of the composites four-seat Velocity monoplane, with pusher engine and canards.

VENDOME, RAOUL, & COMPANY • France

Designed or built several novel prototypes between 1906-1914, and after outbreak of First World War produced small number of single-seat monoplanes for artillery spotting for French Army. Last known design was 1916 experimental military biplane with two Gnome engines mounted laterally.

VENGA AEROSPACE SYSTEMS INC. • Canada

Signed agreement in 1994 with Baoshan Iron & Steel Complex in China to develop Timberwolf turboprop-powered sporting aircraft plus a jet trainer based on the Venga TG-10 Bushfire.

VERCELLESE INDUSTRIE AERONAUTICHE • Italy

Formed at Vercelli about 1940 to produce F.L.3 light tourer. Little known of company activities during Second World War; possibly subcontractor for military aircraft. In 1946-1947 was renamed AVIA (Azionaria Vercellese Industrie Aeronàutiche, q.v.), continuing to develop F.L.3.

VEREINIGTE FLUGTECHNISCHE WERKE-FOKKER GMBH • Germany

Established late 1963 as Vereinigte Flugtechnische Werke GmbH (VFW), from merger of Focke-Wulf GmbH and Weser Flugzeugbau GmbH, joined in 1964 by Ernst Heinkel Flugzeugbau (all q.v.). During 1968-1969, acquired 65 per cent holding in Rhein-Flugzeugbau GmbH (q.v.), later becoming 100 per cent owner of RFB. From 1 January 1969 became joint partner with Fokker of the Netherlands (q.v.), mainly for marketing purposes, renamed VFW-Fokker GmbH, partnership lasting until 1980. Programmes in late 1960s/early 1970s included VAK-191B V/STOL and VJ 101 tilt-engine research prototypes, H2 (autogyro) and H3 (compound helicopter) experimental rotorcraft. VFW was involved in major licence production of Lockheed F-104G Starfighters (with Fokker), Sikorsky CH-53Gs (with Dornier and MBB) and Bell UH-1D helicopters, and was overall programme manager for Transall C-160 heavy military transport (built with Nord/Aérospatiale and HFB/MBB). Was involved in design/construction of Dornier Do 31E VTOL transport; built major components for Fokker Followship, Airbus A300B and Panavia Tornado; was major overhaul facility for several important military and civil aircraft; also member of European Spacelab consortium. Principal late aircraft programme was VFW 614 twin-turbofan short-haul transport (first flown July 1971), but production of this halted 1978. Taken over by MBB 1981.

VERILITE AIRCRAFT COMPANY INC. • USA

Founded 1983 by De Vore Aviation Corporation. Produced Model 100 Sunbird as pusher-engined two-seat lightplane (first flown 1987).

VERTECH • USA

Offered the G-1B single-seat ultralight helicopter (plans or kit), Kestrel single-seat pressure-jet helicopter (plans or kit), MEG-2XH strap-on pressure-jet helicopter (plans or kit), Shadow two-seat autogyro (kit), and Skylark I single-seat helicopter (kit).

VERTIDYNAMICS CORPORATION • USA

Founded March 1970 by Bruno Nagler to build Vertigiro VG-2, single-rotor combined autogyro/helicopter based on 1936 Nagler VG-1. VG-2P prototype and VG-2C production model were never manufactured, but in March

VFW 614 twin-turbofan short-range transport

VFW VAK 191B V/STOL research aircraft

1971 Nagler formed Nagler Aircraft Corporation (q.v.), starting on completely new projects.

VERTICAL AVIATION TECHNOLOGIES INC. • USA

Founded 1988. Undertakes repair of Sikorsky and Orlando helicopters; modifies Sikorsky S-55 helicopters for various uses including agricultural, passenger carrying, assault, heavylift, camping, computerised aerial advertising, and training (latter Aggressor, reconfigured to appear as a Russian Mi-24); and offers a modernized version of the four-seat Sikorsky S-52-3 helicopter, known as Hummingbird and sold in kit form.

VERTOL AIRCRAFT COMPANY • Canada

A wholly-owned subsidiary of Vertol Aircraft Corporation (q.v.), the Canadian Company was operated as completely independent. It was formed in February 1954, on former RCAF airfield at Arnprior, Ontario, initially to service and overhaul helicopters. Entered production

with the Model 42A, a modified version of the Piasecki (Vertol) H-21 helicopter. A tandem-rotor general-purpose helicopter, it accommodated a crew of 1/2 and 18 passengers.

VERTOL AIRCRAFT CORPORATION • USA

Title from March 1956 of former Piasecki Helicopter Corporation of Morton, Pennsylvania (q.v.). Helicopter products included Model 107 (civil), and CH-46 Sea Knight for naval supply. The latter was built by Kawasaki (q.v.) in Japan in 1978 as KV-107/II. Nearly 600 Vertol H-21 Work Horse military transport helicopters, Model 43 (military export version) and Model 44 (commercial transport based on H-21) were completed. Tilt-wing Model 76 VTOL research aircraft evaluated by USAF as VZ-2. Model 114/CH-47 Chinook heavylift military helicopter begun by Vertol, but primary development and production by Boeing Vertol. Company became Vertol Division of The Boeing Company (q.v.) on 31 March 1960, later known as Boeing Vertol Company (q.v.).

Vertol Model 76 tilt-wing VTOL research aircraft, tested as the VZ-2A from 1957

Vertol HUP-1 Retriever tandem-rotor helicopter

VERVILLE AIRCRAFT COMPANY • USA

Alfred V. Verville was formerly a designer with Engineering Division of US Army Air Service, producing his first (unsuccessful) aeroplane in 1915. He is best known for his later Verville-Packard and Verville-Sperry racing aircraft of the early 1920s. In 1925-1927 he produced the Buhl-Verville Airster two-seat biplane, first civil aircraft to be certificated in US (March 1927).

VIBERTI • Italy

Formed shortly after Second World War by Dr Angelo Viberti to build light aircraft. First product, Musca 1 two-seat tourer/trainer low-wing monoplane, first flown 1948; slightly modified Musca 1 *bis* appeared in 1949. There were designs for Musca 2 three-seat cabin monoplane and Musca 4 high-wing version of 1, and floatplane variant, but doubtful if they were built. Probably dissolved about 1950-1951.

VICKERS (AVIATION) LTD. • UK

Famous shipbuilding/engineering/armaments group of Vickers Ltd formed an Aviation Department on 28 March 1911, under Capt H. F. Wood. Production rights for Esnault-Pelterie REP tractor monoplane obtained in same year; several variants built before First World War. In 1912 Vickers produced Type 18 Destroyer for Admiralty; pusher-engined gun-carrying fighter from which evolved, via successive E.F.B. (Experimental Fighting Biplane) prototypes, the F.B.5 and F.B.9 'Gunbus' fighters of First World War. Later front-gunned tractor-engined F.19 was less successful. During war also built RAF B.E.2 series, B.E.8, F.E.8 and S.E.5a and Sopwith 1½-Strutters under licence. Vickers Vimy of 1917 remained standard RAF bomber throughout 1920s: one used by Alcock and Brown for first non-stop Atlantic crossing by aeroplane on 14/15 June 1919. Vimy Commercial was 11-passenger airliner with enlarged fuselage; Vernon troop transport developed from this. Vimy and Vernon succeeded respectively by Virginia and Victoria in mid-1920s, followed by Pegasus engined development, the Valentia.

In July 1928 company renamed as Vickers (Aviation) Ltd, and four months later took over Supermarine Aviation Works (q.v.), specialist in marine aircraft. Vickers' own products continued in early 1930s with Vildebeest torpedo-bomber and Vincent general-purpose biplane. June 1935 saw first flight of Pegasus engined long-range Wellesley bomber, first RAF aircraft to use system of geodetic construction devised by Dr B. N. (later Sir Barnes) Wallis, who remained head of research until early 1970s. Subcontract production included Armstrong Whitworth Siskin IIIAs (1929-1930), Hawker Harts (1932-1934) and Hart Trainers (1936). In March 1936 the prototype was flown of R. J. Mitchell's supreme design, the Supermarine Spitfire; and in June 1936 prototype of Vickers Wellington twin-engined bomber.

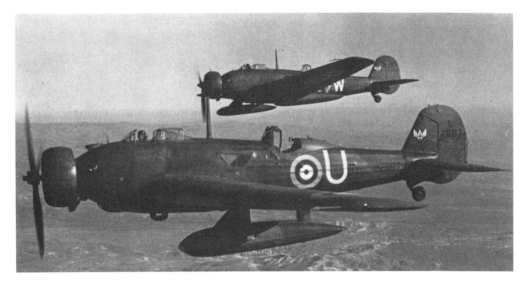

Vickers Wellesley long-range bombers

Vickers Vildebeest torpedo-bomber

Vickers (Supermarine) carrier-based Scimitar

Vickers (Supermarine) Attacker carrier-based fighter

VICKERS-ARMSTRONGS LTD. • UK

Vickers-Armstrongs Ltd took over in October 1938 the former Vickers (Aviation) Ltd and Supermarine Aviation Works (Vickers) Ltd; each, however, retained the separate identity of its products, the latter becoming Vickers-Armstrongs Ltd (Supermarine Division). Vickers' main concern up to and during Second World War was production of Wellington bomber and Avro Lancaster; Wellington replaced at end of war and early post-war by its non-geodetic successor, the Warwick. In August 1946 came first flight of VC1 Viking, first post-war British transport to enter airline service. Subsequent products included four-jet Valiant (first British V-bomber); world's first turboprop airliner to enter production/service, the Viscount; and in 1959 the four-turboprop Vanguard airliner.

New subsidiary entitled Vickers-Armstrongs (Aircraft) Ltd created from 1 January 1955 to continue all Vickers and Supermarine work under one management. In 1960 Vickers merged with Bristol Aeroplane Company and English Electric Company (q.v.) to form British Aircraft Corporation (q.v.).

Below: Vickers Viscount 802/806 type operated by British Air Ferries (E.T.W. Dennis & Sons Ltd/British Air Ferries)

Vickers Viscount Srs 800 turboprop airliner

VICTA LTD. • Australia

Initially producer of 2-stroke engines and lawnmowers; Aviation Division established September 1959 to manufacture Airtourer, two-seat aerobatic lightplane designed by Henry Millicer, chief aerodynamicist of Government Aircraft Factories (q.v.). Prototype built by Air Tourer group of Australian Ultra Light Aircraft Association and first flew March 1959; production deliveries began mid-1962. Also that year produced prototype Victa 67A two-seat autogyro. Aviation Division closed 2 January 1967; manufac-

Above: Victa Airtourer lightplane

turing rights in Air tourer and later Aircruiser obtained by Aero Engine Services Ltd (q.v.) of New Zealand.

VICTOR AIRCRAFT CORPORATION • USA

This company built at Freeport, Long Island, New York, in 1917-1918, radial-engined scouting/advanced training biplanes designed by A. S. Heinrich.

VICTORY AIRCRAFT LTD. • Canada

Originated 1942 at Malton, Ontario, under Canadian Ministry of Munitions and Supply, to take over and manage Malton aircraft factory of National Steel Car Corporation to speed production of Avro Lancaster bombers. First Victory-built Lancaster delivered to RAF in August 1943. Total production 430, including seven unarmed mailplanes for transatlantic government service operated by Trans-Canada Air Lines; these were forerunners of the Lancastrian post-war transport version of the Lancaster. One Avro Lincoln Mk XV bomber built 1945. Company acquired from Canadian government in July 1945 by Hawker Siddeley Aircraft Company Ltd, becoming A. V. Roe (Canada) (q.v.) and subsequently designing first Canadian jet fighter.

VIKING AIRCRAFT LTD. • USA

Offers plans and kits to construct Dragonfly two-seat composites monoplane of unusual design, with mid-mounted wings and canards, plus kits for Cygnet two-seat monoplane (originally the Sisler SF-2 Whistler).

VIKING AVIATION • USA

Bought some assets of Bellanca Aircraft Corporation (q.v.) 1982, and initially provided product support for Bellanca Viking, thereafter intending to put Viking back into production. Company became known as Bellanca Inc (q.v.).

VIKING FLYING BOAT COMPANY • USA

Built in 1936, at New Haven, Connecticut, five OO-1 single-pusher-engined flying-boats for US Coast Guard, based on French Schreck FBA 17HT-4.

VILLIERS • France

Founded late 1924 at Meudon. Products included Type 2 AMC2 fighter, and two prototypes of Type 4 HBA2 twin-float biplane for armed reconnaissance; Type 24 night-fighters for Aéronautique Maritime; last design was Type 26 twin-float cabin monoplane. Company closed down in 1930; factory taken over following year by Potez (q.v.).

VINOT ET DEGUINAND • France

Long established as a manufacturer of motor cars, Vinot et Deguinand turned to the construction of aircraft after

Classic Voisin biplane of 1909

First World War, carrying out subcontract work for the French government. The company constructed the Pescara helicopter.

VISIONAIRE CORPORATION • USA

Founded 1988 and developing the six-seat, single-turbofan VA-10 Vantage, said by the manufacturer to be the world's first composite business jet. Proof-of-concept prototype built by Scaled Composites (q.v.) and first flown November 1996. Development prototypes now flying.

VOISIN • France

First European commercial manufacturer of aircraft, formed by brothers Gabriel (1880-1973) and Charles (1888-1912) Voisin at Billancourt (Seine). Dominant partner was Gabriel, one of aviation's earliest pioneers who had built gliders (with varying success) for Archdeacon, Blériot and others from 1904. When Blériot formed his own company in February 1907 the AA Les Frères Voisin was formed in new premises at Lyons, and from spring 1907 began building series of boxkite biplanes (Hargrave-based) for Delagrange, Paulhan, Farman, Moore-Brabazon and others; by end of 1909 had built nearly 20, though by then this type had been separately much improved by Henry Farman. First 'gunbus' biplane appeared 1910, a canard oddity in 1911, and the large Icare seaplane in 1913; but Voisin chiefly

Voisin VIII LAP night bomber

known for extensive series of successful military bombers of 1914-1918. Primitive but strong, these Voisin 'chicken-coops' appeared in many variants, principal being Types 3, 4, 5, 8, and 10 of which, collectively, nearly 3,400 were built. Although reliable, their design had progressed little by 1918, and in 1919 Gabriel Voisin left the aviation industry and subsequently entered the automobile industry.

VOJENSKÁ • Czechoslovakia

Vojenská továrna na letadla Letov created 1923, initially building the designs of Alois Smolik. Major output centred on S-1/S-2 reconnaissance/light bomber biplanes; S-4 fighter of 1922; S-6 bomber; S-10 trainer (licensed from Hansa-Brandenburg); S-16 long-range reconnaissance biplane, built late 1920s/early 1930s for Czechoslovakia, Latvia and Turkey; S-18 trainer; S-19 four-passenger civil

Vojenská S-16 reconnaissance biplane

Vojenská S-528 reconnaissance/bomber

Volmer VJ-24W SunFun microlight

transport; S-20 biplane fighter; S-21 trainer version of S-20; S-32 five-passenger high-wing tri-motor; and the S-328/528 series of reconnaissance/light bomber biplanes. Also undertook licence production of Tupolev SB-2 twin-engined monoplane bomber. Built Arado and Junkers types during German occupation 1940-1945.

VOLAIRCRAFT INC. • USA

Only product was Volaire Model 10, certificated 1961. Limited production at Aliquippa, Pennsylvania, as Model 1050 four-seat high-wing monoplane before, in mid-1965, becoming a division of Aero Commander Inc (q.v.); aircraft renamed Aero Commander 100.

VOLKSEIGENER BETRIEB • Germany

East German State aircraft factory; enjoyed brief existence in 1950s, with plants at Pirna/Elbe (Entwicklungsbau Pirna) and Dresden/Klotzsche. Established 1954 to licence-build Soviet Ilyushin Il-14 twin-engined passenger transport and a variety of gliders. In 1956 was selected to develop BB-152 four-jet, swept-wing civil transport (Pirna turbojets), originally joint project from Prof Dipl Ing Brunolf Baade (deputy director of VEB) and Soviet designer Dr Bronin. Three twin-jet prototypes developed as Type 150 at Podberezje in USSR, themselves derived from Junkers Ju 287 bomber. Twenty-two BB-152s laid down, but only five prototypes completed; first flight in December 1960. Programme was closed down and state aircraft manufacture in East Germany ended in 1961.

VOLMER AIRCRAFT • USA

Produces plans to construct VJ-22 Sportsman two seat amphibian (first flown 1958) and VJ-24W SunFun single-seat open microlight (earlier VJ-23 Swingwing is recognised as having been the first modern microlight).

VOLPAR INC. • USA

Volpar Inc formed in 1960. Volpar marketed tricycle landing-gear kit for Beechcraft Model 18. Following merger with Volitan Aviation Inc, kits produced to convert Model 18 to turboprop power, designated Turbo 18. Lengthened-fuselage versions followed, Turboliner and Turboliner II; then came 'Packaged Power' units for Beech 18, de Havilland Dove and Beaver, Grumman Goose. Larger premises acquired February 1975 to increase production of Turboliner II. From 1976 collaborated with Century Aircraft Corporation (q.v.) in producing turboprop conversions for Handley Page Jetstream. Produced programmes to upgrade T-33 as T-33V and Falcon 20 as PW300-F20. As Volpar Aircraft Corporation, was acquired by Gaylord Holdings of Switzerland 1990.

VORTEX AIRCRAFT COMPANY LLC • USA

Founded 1997 and developing the PhoenixJet-TJ tandem two-seat military primary jet and electronic warfare trainer, also suited to other military tasks and for use as a civil sporting aircraft. Developed from the Bede Jet Corporation (q.v.) BD-10 prototype first flown July 1992, via the later Peregrine Flight International (q.v.) Peregrine PJ-2. Major design review undertaken, with original supersonic wing replaced by subsonic and simpler wing of greater strength and carrying more fuel.

VOUGHT CORPORATION • USA

Ling-Temco Vought operated under the above title after 1 January 1976; for previous history, see the various

Vought A-7E Corsair II of US Navy

Vought OS2U-1 Kingfisher observation aircraft

entries under Lewis & Vought, Chance Vought, Vought-Sikorsky, Ling-Temco-Vought and LTV Aerospace Corporation. Manufacture and product support of the A-7 Corsair II tactical fighter/attack aircraft. Became LTV Aircraft Products Group in 1986 (see Ling-Temco-Vought). Following 1992 sale of 49 per cent stock in LTV to Northrop and Carlyle Group, became Vought Aircraft Company, finally merging as a division of Northrop Grumman in 1994 after remaining stock purchased, becoming Northrop Grumman's headquarters for its Commercial Aircraft Division.

VOUGHT-SIKORSKY • USA

Chance Vought and Sikorsky Aircraft Division of United Aircraft Corporation formed as result of April 1939 reorganisation within UAC, upon which Chance Vought moved headquarters to Stratford, Connectictut. From 1936 concentrated primarily upon manufacture for the US Navy, major programmes including the SB2U Vindicator scout-bomber, OS2U Kingfisher observation aircraft, and F4U Corsair single-seat naval fighter. Of the massive production of the wartime Corsair, which continued until 1952, Vought alone built more than 7,700. Vought-Sikorsky products at this time included the Sikorsky designed VS-43 and VS-44 flying-boats and the historic VS-300, the world's first fully practical helicopter, from which the production R-4 and R-5 and later designs were developed. Vought and Sikorsky were reconstituted in January 1943 as separate manufacturing divisions of UAC, so that Sikorsky could concentrate on helicopter development and Vought on combat aircraft, primarily the F4U and OS2U. After the war, Chance Vought Aircraft Division moved to Dallas, Texas, in 1948-1949, and produced its first jet fighter for the US Navy, the F6U Pirate. On 1 July 1954 the company became independent of UAC, under the new name of Chance Vought Aircraft Inc (q.v.)

USMC version (AU-1) of the Vought Corsair

VOYAGER AIRCRAFT INC. • USA

Founded 1981 by Richard 'Dick' Rutan and Jeana Yeager to develop Voyager two-crew, twin piston-engined trimaran aircraft of very unusual configuration to make first-ever non-stop and unrefuelled flight around the world. Voyager first flew June 1984 and achieved world flight December 1986. Designer was Burt Rutan and aircraft built at Rutan Aircraft Factory.

VSTOL AIRCRAFT CORPORATION • USA

US agent for the Pairadigm tandem two-seat kit-built monoplane developed in Venezuela, and the single-seat Super Solution 2000.

VTI • Yugoslavia

Vazduhoplovno-Tehnici Institut undertook design work on the Romanian/Yugoslav IAR-93/J-22 Orao attack aircraft programme.

VTOL AIRCRAFT PTY. LTD. • Australia

Formed 1971 by D. A. Phillips to develop Phillicopter two-seat light helicopter. Design had began 1962, prototype first flew 1971, and the current improved model appeared 1992.

VULCAN AIRCRAFT COMPANY • USA

Incorporated in 1928, the Vulcan Aircraft Company was established at Portsmouth, Ohio, to produce the American Moth two-seat lightweight sporting aircraft.

VULCAN • UK

Based at Crossens, Southport, Lancashire; built under sub-contract during First World War Airco D.H.4, D.H.9 and D.H.9A and RAF B.E.2c, d and e.

VULCANAIR SPA • Italy

Established 1989, and in 1996 was purchased by a new holding group to develop aircraft manufacturing, maintenance, air transport and other aviation related tasks, plus a flying school for commercial crews. Has taken over the SF600A Canguro multipurpose transport from SIAI-Marchetti (first flown 1978) and in 1998 purchased rights and tooling for former Partenavia's P 68 series of transport aircraft (P 68, Observer 2 and Viator).

VULTEE • USA

Vultee entered aircraft manufacturing in mid-1930s, having formed in 1932 the Airplane Development Corporation (q.v.), which two years later was acquired by the Aviation Manufacturing Corporation. A Vultee Aircraft Division of the latter company was formed in 1936, becoming Vultee Aircraft Inc when it acquired the parent corporation's assets in 1939. First product was the V-1 eight-passenger monoplane, but became better known for its military aircraft, of which most notable were the V-11 two/three-seat attack monoplane, built for Brazil, China and Turkey, and a licence sold to the USSR; the improved V-12 for China; more than 11,000 BT-13/BT-15 and SNV Valiant two-seat basic train-

VulcanAir P 68 C, taken over from Partenavia in 1998

VulcanAir Observer 2 observation and patrol version of P 68

ers for the USAAF and USN between 1940-1944; V-48 Vanguard single-seat fighters for China and USAAF; and V-72 Vengeance dive-bombers for the RAF, USAAF and Brazil between 1941-1942. Vultee purchased the Stinson Aircraft Division (q.v.) of the Aviation Manufacturing Corporation in 1940, producing Stinson Model 74s for the USAAF as L-1 Vigilant during Second World War. In December 1941 Vultee bought a 34 per cent controlling interest in another subsidiary of The Aviation Corporation, Consolidated Aircraft Inc (q.v.), with which it merged in 1943 to form the Consolidated Vultee Aircraft Corporation (q.v.).

Vultee Vanguard single-seat fighter

Vultee Vengeance dive-bomber which served with USAAF and RAF

WACO AIRCRAFT COMPANY • USA

Started by George 'Buck' Weaver in 1919 at Loraine, Ohio, as the Weaver Aircraft Company ('Waco' trademark), and built Cootie parasol-wing aircraft. Reorganized as Advance Aircraft Company in 1923 at Troy, Ohio. Waco became official name 1929. First really successful venture was three-seat Model 9 of 1924. Developed long and successful line of cabin biplanes, sporting, racing, and military aeroplanes. By 1936 was largest constructor of commercial aircraft in USA. Wartime production of own-design cargo and troop carrying assault glider, CG-4A Hadrian. After war developed a new monoplane, the Aristocraft (see O'Neill), but abandoned it in 1947. Company went out of business.

WACO AIRCRAFT COMPANY • USA

Founded 1966 to build Savoia-Marchetti S.205 (as Waco Vela II) plus turbosupercharged Taurus derivative, SF.260 (as Waco Meteor), and Socata Rallye Commodore (as Waco Minerva). Became Waco Aircraft Division of Allied Aero Industries. Ceased work 1971.

WAG-AERO INC. • USA

Markets plans and kits to construct two-seat Sport Trainer high-wing monoplane, four-seat Sportsman 2 + 2, and two-seat Wag-A-Bond, all modern representations of Piper types.

WAGENER, FLUGZEUGBAU • Germany

Hans Wagener of Hamburg produced his first aircraft, the HW4A, in 1933. Used as test-bed for experimental two-stroke engine.

WAGNER, HELICOPTER TECHNIK • Germany

Joseph Wagner of Friedrichshafen began developing a helicopter in 1960, as a basic, torque-free vehicle to which specialised equipment and accommodation could be added. Rotorcar III was roadable; main development vehicle was Sky-trac. Aerocar and three Sky-trac 1s completed in mid-1960s.

WAITOMO AIRCRAFT LTD. • New Zealand

Formerly Bennett Aviation Ltd (q.v.) of Te Kuiti. Designed first commercial aircraft built in New Zealand, the Airtruk, which flew 1960. Small-scale production. Design based on Luigi Pellarini Transavia Airtruk.

WALLACE AIRCRAFT COMPANY • USA

Formed 1928 at Chicago, Illinois, to manufacture the B.330 Touroplane, shown at Detroit Aero Show. Stanley Wallace had been concerned with aircraft designs since 1915. Acquired 1929 by American Eagle Aircraft Corporation

Waco VKS-7 4-seat cabin biplane

Wallis WA-116 light autogyro

Waco CG-4A Hadrian troop carrying assault glider

Waitomo Airtruk light aircraft

(q.v.), under E. E. Porterfield, who continued production of Touroplane B.

WALLIS AUTOGYROS LTD. • UK

The first light autogyro developed by Wg Cdr Ken Wallis flew in 1961. The original WA-116 appeared in various guises, including four Beagle-built military prototypes and a two-seater. Holds Class E3/E3a records for height 15,220 ft (4,639 m) and speed 111.225mph (179kmh). Rolls-Royce powered WA-117 appeared 1965 and WA-118 Meteorite, WA-120 followed 1970. WA-121 (first flown 1972) became smallest and lightest of the range, followed by WA-122/R-R two-seat trainer (first flown 1980) and WA-201 twin-engined research autogyro.

WALRAVEN • Netherlands

L. W. Walraven began designing and building light aircraft at Bandoeng, Java, in spare time as chief engineer to Netherlands East Indies Army Air Force, from 1922. Completed W.4 1938, which was ordered as trainer by Netherlands East Indies flying clubs.

WALTZ SA. • Mexico

Franciso J. Waltz, Mexico City, was distributor for Aero Commander. Produced in 1959 a high-altitude conversion of de Havilland Heron with 340 hp Lycoming engine for Mexican use under name Super Heron.

WARING AND GILLOW LTD. • UK

Undertook contract from government to build 500 Airco D.H.9s in First World War. Subcontracted 50 to Wells Aviation Company Ltd (q.v.). May have assembled some Handley Page O/400s in 1918, including some built in the USA.

WARNER AEROCRAFT INC. • USA

Made available plans and kits to build single-seat Revolution 1 and two-seat Revolution II low-wing monoplanes, based on former Country Air Space-Walker.

WARRIOR (AERO-MARINE) LTD. • UK

Has been developing the Centaur six-seat amphibian, unveiled in 1998 as a project. Scale model tested, and prototype is expected to be built by CMC, allowing early production deliveries in about the year 2002 if programme fully funded.

WASHINGTON AEROPROGRESS INC. • USA

Associated to Aeroprogress in Russia, initially to market T 411 Wolverine kits.

WASSMER • France

Founded 1905 by Benjamin Wassmer. Up to Second World War was repair and overhaul organization. Started aircraft production at Issoire in 1945, building Jodel D.112 under licence. Opened own design department 1955. First production aircraft Jodel-Wassmer D.120 Paris-Nice. In 1959 built WA.40 Super Sancey, followed by Baladou and 1966 WA.52 Europa, one of the first aircraft extensively constructed from glassfibre. WA.54 Atlantic appeared 1973 and WA.80 Piranha in 1975. Formed in 1971 with Siren SA company named CERVA (q.v.) to develop an all-metal four/six-seat light aircraft.

WATANABE TEKKOSHO KABUSHIKI KAISHA • Japan

The Watanabe Iron Works (K. K. Watanabe Tekkosho) began making aircraft parts during 1920s, building trainers from 1931. Ki-51 Army Type 99 still serving 1941, but obsolete. Developed seaplanes (E13A, E14Y) during Second World War; fighters (A5M and J7W); K10W1 trainer, copied from North American NA-16, built in 1941; production after first 26 given to Nippon (q.v.). Built K11W1 bomber-crew trainer in 1940, and copy of Bücker Bü 131 Jungmann. In 1942 produced Q14 Tokai three-seat long-range naval patrol aircraft. Reorganized as Kyushu Hikoki K.K. in 1943 and products known retrospectively under that name.

WATERHOUSE AIRCRAFT INC. • USA

Established at Glendale, California, incorporated 1926. Began by building a 3-seat Cruzair monoplane with a 200 hp Wright radial engine.

WATERMAN AIRPLANE CORP. • USA

Waldo D. Waterman of Santa Monica, California, produced in 1934 design for a two-seat tailless monoplane as a simple private aircraft. Corporation formed 1935 to develop roadable aircraft with detachable wings and motor-car engine driving propeller by vee belts. In 1967 produced the W-11 Chevvy Bird, his 11th design, as test bed for Chevrolet Corvair motor car engine.

Wassmer D.120 Paris-Nice lightplane

Wassmer WA.52 Europa lightplane

Wassmer WA.41 Baladou four-seat cabin monoplane

WATSON • USA

Offers plans for the Windwagon, a small single-seat metal monoplane (first flown 1977).

W.D. FLUGZEUGLEICHTBAU GMBH • Germany

Markets in completed and kit forms the Dallach Sunrise II tandem two-seat microlight in monoplane or biplane configurations, plus D.3 Sunwheel tandem two-seat biplane and D.4 Fascination side-by-side two-seat monoplane.

WEATHERLEY AVIATION COMPANY INC • USA

John C. Weatherley operated the Weatherley Campbell Aircraft Company as a fixed-base operator, at Dallas, Texas.

Weatherley 201 agricultural aircraft

Acquired plans of the Colt 4-seater from Luscombe Airplane Corporation (q.v.). Weatherley Aviation Company established at Hollister, California. Built WM 62C agricultural aircraft 1961-1965, a converted Fairchild 62. Developed W.201, a much-improved agricultural aircraft in 1967; followed by 201A in 1970 and 201C in 1975. In production in 1998 were the 600 and 600 BTG single-seat agricultural aircraft, the latter a turboprop version.

WEAVER AIRCRAFT COMPANY • USA

See Waco Aircraft Company.

WEEDHOPPER INC. • USA

Has marketed kits for the DeLuxe Ultralight single-seat open-frame microlight.

WEIR, G. & J. LTD. • UK

This engineering firm of Cathcart, Glasgow, built Airco D.H.9 and RAF B.E.2c, B.F.2e and F.E.2b aircraft under subcontract during First World War. In 1930s built Autogiros under Cierva licence; C.28/W-1 in 1933, W-2 in 1934, W-3 and W-4 in 1936. In 1937-38 built and flew W-5 twin-rotor helicopter under Focke licence, followed by W-6 of 1938-39, world's first helicopter to carry a passenger. Outbreak of war ended development.

WEISER UND SOHN • Austria

During First World War built Aviatik (q.v.) military types under subcontract.

WEISS, MANFRED, FLUGZEUG UND MOTORENFABRIK AG. • Hungary

One of Hungary's largest industrial organisations; opened an aircraft department at Budapest 1928, beginning with licence-production of Fokker F.VIII and C.V and Bristol Jupiter engine. Built first of its own designs 1931; produced two-seat biplane 1936.

WELCH AIRCRAFT INDUSTRIES • USA

Fixed-base operator Orin Welch built aircraft for his West Virginia Flying School in late 1920s. Introduced his aircraft Falcon OW-5 in 1931, of which about 65 built, at South Bend, Indiana, between 1935-1940.

WELLS AVIATION LTD. • UK

London company based at Whiteheads Grove, Chelsea. Built 50 Airco D.H.9s under contract to Waring and Gillow (q.v.), plus 100 Sopwith 1½-Strutters. In 1915 designed and built the Reo, a small single-seat biplane. Went into liquidation 1917, but production continued under Sir Samuel Waring.

WELSH, GEORGE • USA

Produced examples of Model A Welsh Rabbit single-seat lightplane (first flown 1965) and two-seat Model B (first flown 1968).

WENDT • USA

Formed in New York by George W. Constant in 1939 to build the W.2 two-seat monoplane.

WERFTE WARNEMÜNDE • Germany

Established in early 1917 as a subsidiary of Flugzeugbau Friedrichshafen; in 1933 Werfte Warnemünde became known as Arado Flugzeugwerke (q.v.).

WESER FLUGZEUGBAU AG. • Germany

Formed, as Weser Flugzeugbau GmbH, aviation department of Deutsche Schiff- und Maschinenbau 'Weser' AG in 1934. Took over Rohrbach Metallflugzeugbau GmbH (q.v.). Undertook contract manufacture during First World War for other manufacturers. Reconstituted in 1956 as the Finanz-und-Wervaltungs GmbH, reverting to Weser

Westland Lysander two-seat army co-operation aircraft

Westland Wapiti two-seat general purpose biplane

Flugzeugbau 1959. The company then built the Nord Noratlas under licence from 1960, with Hamburger Flugzeugbau and Siebelwerke-ATG (q.v.), under the name of Flugzeugbau Nord GmbH at Hamburg. In 1958, with Hamburger, Nord Aviation (q.v.), and Dipl Ing Prof Walter Blume Leichtbau-und-Flugtechnik, it formed Arbeitsgemeinschaft Transall. Finally the company combined with Focke-Wulf Flugzeugbau (q.v.) in 1963, losing its individual identity entirely.

WEST AUSTRALIAN AIRWAYS LTD. • Australia

Formed at Perth in 1921 to operate Geraldton-Derby airline and licensed to build the de Havilland D.H.50 in Australia. Produced first aircraft in 1926.

WESTERN AIRCRAFT SUPPLIES • Canada

Markets plans and some components to construct the PGK-1 Hirondelle two-seat monoplane.

WESTERN AIRPLANE CORPORATION • USA

Formed at Chicago, Illinois, to build a three-seat biplane powered by a 90 hp Curtiss OX-5 engine.

WESTERN PACIFIC AVIATION CORPORATION • Philippines

Manufactures to order a version of the Skystar Kitfox, known as Skyfox.

WEST VIRGINIA AIRCRAFT COMPANY • USA

This company was established at Wheeling, West Virginia, and produced a three-seat triplane during 1919-1920.

WESTLAND AIRCRAFT LTD. • UK

Petters Ltd, an engineering company founded 1910, undertook government aircraft construction in 1915 as Westland Aviation Works at Westland Farm, Yeovil, Somerset. Produced Short 184, Short 166, Sopwith 1½-Strutter, Airco D.H.4 and D.H.9 biplanes; adapted the last for Liberty engine as D.H.9A. Also built Vickers Vimy. First of its own designs were the single-seat N.1b scout and Wagtall and the two seat Weasel, but the war's end prevented production. First civil aircraft, the four-seat cabin Limousine, was followed by a naval D.H.9A development, the Walrus, and the 1923 Dreadnought, a very advanced but unsuccessful monoplane based on Woyevodsky's flying-wing theory. The Woodpigeon and Widgeon I and II that followed were Westland's only attempt to enter light-aircraft market. Apart from Westland IV/Wessex three-engined airliners of 1929-1931, the rest of the designs from Yeovil were military fighters or general-purpose aircraft. Wapiti, built from 1927, was basically a modernisation of the D.H.9A and was followed in 1931 by an improved version, the Wallace. The Westland P.V.3 private prototype for the Wallace was used on the Houston Everest expedition of 1933. From the P.V.7 monoplane, the last general-purpose type, the army co-operation Lysander was developed, the best-known company design of Second World War. Company became Westland Aircraft Ltd in July 1935. Westland fighters included the twin-engined Whirlwind, which saw limited squadron service in Second World War, followed by the high-altitude Welkin, which did not enter service. Following the war, four naval strike squadrons

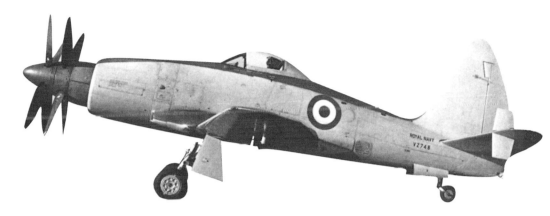

Westland Wyvern single-seat carrier-based strike aircraft

Westland Belvedere hauling a Bloodhound surface-to-air missile

Five-seat Westland Widgeon was developed from Dragonfly and first flew 1955, with most examples produced as conversions of Dragonfly helicopters

were equipped with the turboprop Wyvern, the last fixed-wing aircraft built by the company.

In the 1930s Westland had built two autogiros for Juan de la Cierva, and in 1946, with declining sales of fixed-wing aircraft, decided to concentrate on rotary-wing designs. Negotiated with Sikorsky (q.v.) a licence to build a modified version of the four-seat Sikorsky S-51. Re-engined and altered in detail, it was produced as the Dragonfly in 1948. Followed by the S-55 Whirlwind and in 1959 Westland's first turbine-powered helicopter, the Gnome-engined Whirlwind. In the reorganisation of Britain's aircraft industry Westland acquired the helicopter interest of Bristol Aircraft (1960), Fairey Aviation (1960), and Saunders-Roe (1959) (all q.v.). From this came production contracts for the army Belvedere and Scout and Royal Navy Wasp, while the Sikorsky designs, enhanced increasingly by Westland improvements, resulted in the S-58 Wessex. Beginning in 1966 the company was known as Westland Helicopters Ltd (see next entry).

WESTLAND HELICOPTERS LTD. • UK

Activities included production of the Sea King, developed from the Sikorsky S-61 to Royal Navy requirements; Commando army version of Sea King; and Gazelle and Lynx, which formed part of the Anglo-French helicopter co-operation programme with Aérospatiale (q.v.). Gazelle production started in 1971 and Lynx in 1975 (naval, military and

Westland Sea King all-weather anti-submarine helicopter

Westland/Aérospatiale Lynx multipurpose helicopter in naval service

British Army Westland SA 341 Gazelle

Latest British Army Lynx AH Mk 9, first army variant to have a wheeled undercarriage

civil versions constructed). Following the construction of 40 Aérospatiale/Westland Pumas for the RAF, the company continued to produce Puma component for French assembly lines. (See GKN Westland Ltd.)

WEYMANN • France

Charles Weymann designed and built in 1916 an all-metal biplane with conventional fuselage. In 1929 joined with lePère, and Weymann-lePère was formed from the remains of a separate company called Avimeta (q.v.) which had closed in 1928. Weymann-lePère held a Cierva licence; when lePère left in 1930 Weymann reverted to original name.

W.H. EKIN (ENGINEERING) CO. LTD. • UK

WHE founded 1969 to produce McCandless Mk IV Gyroplanes. Redesign produced Airbuggy single-seat autogyro, first flown 1973.

WHITE AIRCRAFT COMPANY LTD. • USA

Burd S. and Harold L. White, of Des Moines, Indiana, did general aircraft rebuilding work 1918-1926. Designed and produced their own private and commercial aircraft, Humming Bird, in 1926.

WHITE AIRCRAFT INC. • USA

Donald G. White of Buffalo, New York, formed a company in 1939 to continue production, in modified form, of the Pirate amphibian designed and built previously by Argonaut Aircraft Inc (q.v.).

WHITE AND THOMPSON LTD. • UK

Based at Bognor, Sussex. Acquired UK rights to products of Curtiss Aeroplane Company (q.v.). Built Short S.38 trainers under subcontract in 1914. About 1910 had designed and built an unsuccessful aircraft with wings covered in sheet aluminium. Registered 1912 as private company; designed and built one- and two-engined flying-boats for the Admiralty in 1914.

WHITE, J. SAMUEL, & COMPANY LTD. • UK

Boatbuilding company at Cowes, Isle of Wight, which in 1914 constructed to the design of Harris Booth, of the Air Department, the largest aeroplane then built in Britain, the AD 1000 three-engined torpedo-bomber. Also built Short 184s under subcontract and designed and built aircraft under name of Wight Aviation. (q.v.).

WHITEHEAD AIRCRAFT LTD. • UK

Established at Richmond, Surrey, built Airco D.H.9 and RAF B.E.2a and B.E.2b under subcontract during First

Wibault-Penhöet 282T-12 transport

World War. Was a major supplier of Sopwith Pups. Built a prototype only of own-design Comet single-seat scout.

WHITTAKER, MIKE • UK

Markets plans to build MW.5 Sorcerer single-seat monoplane, MW.6 Merlin two-seat monoplane, MW.7 single-seat aerobatic monoplane, and MW.8 single-seat monoplane with enclosed cockpit.

WHITTLESEY MANUFACTURING COMPANY INC. • USA

Formed 1929 at Bridgeport, Connecticut, by H. Newton Whittlesey, with exclusive US rights to manufacture the Avro Avian.

WIBAULT, MICHEL • France

Established in Paris. Wibault's first aircraft, a single-seat fighter, appeared too late to see service in First World War. Subsequently designed night bombers and fighters for the Armée de l'Air, as well as civil aircraft. Produced an all-metal aircraft in 1921 and changed from biplane to monoplane configuration 1923. In 1924 flew the prototype of a monoplane fighter, the Wibault 7, produced from 1925 and built under licence by PZL (q.v.) and Vickers (q.v.).

WIBAULT-PENHÖET • France

A new company formed in 1931 by a merger of Avions Michel Wibault with Chantiers de St Nazaire Penhöet, which built a number of single- and multi-engined airliners in the 1930s. Taken over by Breguet (q.v.).

WICKO • Australia

Wickner Aircraft of Australia, formed by Geoffrey Wickner in 1929 to build the high-wing Wizard monoplane and light single-seat Lion monoplane. Rebuilt several Avro Avians before helping to form Foster Wickner (q.v.).

WIDERÖES FLYVESELSKAP AS. • Norway

The oldest flying company in Norway, established in 1933 a repair department for aircraft and engines. In 1945 built

the C.5 Polar monoplane, a five-seat general-purpose or ambulance aircraft which took part in the Norwegian-British-Swedish Antarctic expedition of 1951.

WIENER KARROSERIE FABRIK • Austria

Built an experimental fighter in 1918, but no details found of subsequent products.

WIENER-NEUSTADTER • Germany

Originally Wiener-Neustadter Flughafen Betriebs GmbH, after the Anschluss of 1938 was amalgamated with Hirtenberg, whose manufacturing department it absorbed under the name Wiener-Neustadter Flugzeugwerk GmbH. Light two-seat biplane in production 1937, later undertook subcontracts on Bf 109. In 1943-1944 built the world's first tip-jet helicopter, designed by team under Friedrich von Doblhoff. Four built and tested. Conventional piston-engine provided compressed air which, mixed with fuel, was fed to tip-mounted combustion chambers through rotor blades. System adopted by other designers.

WIGHT AVIATION LTD. • UK

Aviation department of J. Samuel White (q.v.) under Howard T. Wright, who joined company in 1912. Employed double-cambered aerofoils on early designs. Built training and operational seaplanes for Admiralty, a twin-engined torpedo bomber in 1915 and an experimental single-seat quadruplane.

WILDEN, HELMUT • Germany

Formed 1974 at Hennef-Sieg. Designed VoWi 8 two-seat lightweight sporting aircraft which first flew in 1974, followed by ultralight single-seat, very simple VoWi 10, which was being built under subcontract in 1977.

WILEY POST AIRCRAFT CORPORATION • USA

Founded in Oklahoma City in 1935 to build Model A, cheap two-seat aircraft. Powered by converted Model A Ford engine, the first example was built by Straughan Aircraft. Wiley Post acquired rights to Straughan assets 1935, and transferred production to Oklahoma City. Thirteen Model As built before company liquidated after Wiley Post's death.

WILLIAMS, GEO. AIRPLANE AND MANUFACTURING COMPANY • USA

George W. Williams designed and built his first aircraft, a light monoplane, about 1908 and started operations at Temple, Texas, as the Texas Aero Manufacturing Company. With George Carroll was credited with development of first full monocoque cantilever wing (not flown). Only. production aircraft Texas-Temple of 1928-1929. On Williams's death in 1929 company reorganised as the Texas Aero Corporation.

WILLIAMS INTERNATIONAL • USA

In addition to engine manufacture, has developed the V-Jet II as an engine demonstration aircraft as part of a joint NASA/industry General Aviation Propulsion Program, intended to assist the US light aircraft industry through turbofan technology. V-Jet II first flew April 1997 as a five-seat jet of composites construction.

WINDECKER RESEARCH INC. • USA

Became Windecker Industries. Held licence from Dow Chemicals for a reinforced plastic aircraft developed by Dr Leo Windecker, Midland, Texas. Flight tested 1967. First production Windecker AC-7 Eagle I, mainly Fibraloy reinforced plastic, flown 1969. See Composite Aircraft Corporation. Also produced single example of YE-5 for USAF.

WING AIRCRAFT COMPANY • USA

Subsidiary of Hi Shear Corporation, Torrance, California. George S. Wing formed company 1960 to develop and market sporting twin-engined executive Wing Derringer. Company became independent 1966.

WINGS UNLIMITED • USA

Provides plans to build the Kingfisher and Super Kingfisher two-seat amphibian; Kingfisher was originally the Anderson Kingfisher, first flown 1969, subsequently marketed by Richard Warner Aviation.

WITTEMAN-LEWIS AIRCRAFT CORPORATION • USA

Aeronautical construction engineers of Newark, New Jersey. Rebuilt Airco D.H.4s to DH-4B standard for US Army. During 1922-1923 built the Barling six-engined triplane bomber to Walter Barling's design. Had produced own-design mail carrier in 1920, when firm moved to Teterboro. Built twin-engined Sundstedt-Hannevig seaplane 1923, for transatlantic attempt by Capt Sundstedt. Firm acquired by Fokker 1923-1924.

Wing Derringer high-performance lightplane

Witteman-Lewis-built Barling bomber of 1923

Witteman-Lewis floatplane

WKF • Austria

see Wiener Karroserie Fabrik.

WNF • Germany

see Wiener Neustadter Flugzeugwerke.

WOLF, DONALD • USA

Markets plans for the W-11 Boredom Fighter single-seat biplane styled as a First World War fighter (first flown 1979).

WOLSELEY MOTORS LTD. • UK

Motor car manufacturer of Birmingham, Warwickshire, which produced under subcontract during First World War RAF B.E.2c and S.E.5a aircraft. Also built improved Hispano-Suiza 200 hp engine as Wolseley Viper.

WOMBAT GYROCOPTERS • UK

Developed the Wombat Gyrocopter single-seat autogyro in the 1990s.

WOODSON AIRCRAFT CORPORATION • USA

Entered aviation at Bryan, Ohio, in 1926, producing a convertible cargo/passenger two-seat biplane, the 'Foto'.

WREN AIRCRAFT CORPORATION • USA

Fort Worth, Texas. Built James L. Robertson's Wren 460, STOL-configured Cessna 182, first flew 1963. Additions included foreplanes, wing spoilers and double-slotted flaps. Produced in small numbers.

WRIGHT AERONAUTICAL COMPANY • USA

The Wright brothers built first successful aircraft in the world, 1903; first practical model 1905. Sold first military

Wren 460 STOL lightplane

aircraft in world to US Army Signal Corps 1908. Continued producing same basic and outdated type though later, from Model I tractor biplane, aircraft were more conventional. Sold a few aircraft to US Navy 1914. Became Wright-Martin Aircraft Corporation (q.v.) 1916.

WRIGHT AERONAUTICAL CORPORATION • USA

Mainly an engine manufacturing company. After Wilbur's death, 1912, Orville continued at Dayton plant as independent experimenter. Built to official designs and produced Hispano-Suiza engines during the First World War. Giuseppe Bellanca joined 1924 and Wright-Bellanca monoplane and Apache shipboard fighter produced in 1925. Bellanca left 1927 to re-form his own company (see Bellanca Aircraft Corporation). Wright became part of Curtiss-Wright (q.v.) 1929.

WRIGHT FLUGMASCHINE • Germany

Based at Adlershof, Berlin, built redesigned Wright models for military use during 1912-13. One was armoured.

WRIGHT, HOWARD & WARWICK • UK

Howard and Warwick Wright set up small aircraft factory in Battersea and exhibited a monoplane at the 1910 Olympia show. Designed and built helicopters, ornithopter, biplanes, and series of monoplanes, including five Avis. In 1910 T. O. M. Sopwith achieved the longest all-British flight to date with a Howard Wright 1910 biplane, a distance of 169 miles (272 km).

WRIGHT-MARTIN AIRCRAFT CORPORATION • USA

Formed in 1916 at Los Angeles, California, by merger of Glenn L. Martin Company, Simplex Automobile Company, General Aeronautical Company and Wright Aeronautical Company. Current Martin designs of 1917 produced under Wright-Martin name; 1920 Pulitzer racer built to designs of Loening, but then reverted to Martin name.

WSK 'PZL-MIELEC' SA. • Poland

Full name is Wytwórnia Sprzetu Komunikacyjnego 'PZL-Mielec' SA. The Transport Equipment Manufacturing Centre (WSK) at Mielec was the largest of the Polish pre-Second World War aircraft factories, having been founded in 1938. Post-war, it built Soviet MiG-15 fighters under licence until 1959. Decline in fighter orders led to development of the TS-8 Bies two-seat aerobatic trainer (first flown 1955) and the TS-11 Iskra jet trainer (1960). Nearly 12,000 Russian (now Ukrainian) Antonov-designed An-2 biplane transports built in several versions since 1960. Design office formed for M-15 Belphegor three-seat and turbofan-powered agricultural aircraft (1973) and M-17

Wright-Martin Type V two-seat biplane

Wright Model HS two-seat biplane

WSK-Swidnik built Mil Mi-2 helicopter

two/three-seat light aircraft. I-22 Iryda advanced jet trainer and light attack aircraft first flew March 1985, and small number joined Polish Air Force, along with several M-93K derivatives, but production terminated in 1997; upgrade to modified M-96 standard was planned. Production of M18 Dromader agricultural aircraft continues, with some 700 production aircraft built in several versions since 1979. Production also continues of the M20 Mewa, first flown 1979 as development of US Piper PA-34-200T Seneca II. Antonov An-28 transport built since 1984, more recently in M28 Skytruck form; larger development expected to be certificated in 1999 as M28.03 or 04 Skytruck Plus. M26 Iskierka piston trainer first flew in 1986 and entered production in 1995. Tampico Club TB 9 built under Socata contract. See also PZL.

WSK-SWIDNIK • Poland

Produced jet fighters up to 1951, when defence cuts were made; then turned to Mi-1/SM-1 helicopter production and a helicopter design office was formed. Initially, Polish aircraft, licence-built or native, were produced under name of PZL: Polskie Zaklady Lotnicze (q.v.). In 1957 WSK renamed WSK im Zygmunta Pulawskiego. Production of SM-1 ended late 1960s and Mi-2 production began1965 See PZL - Swidnik

Below: WSK PZL-Mielec example of the Antonov An-2

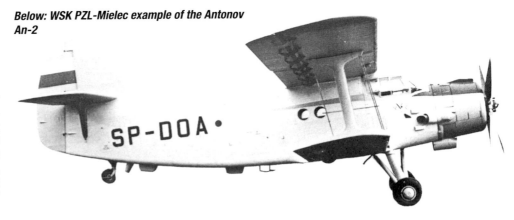

WSK 'PZL-Mielec' M20 Mewa

WSK 'PZL-Mielec' An-28 transport

WSK 'PZL-Mielec' M26 Iskierka

WSK 'PZL-Mielec' M18A Dromader agricultural aircraft

WSK MD-12F four-engined light commercial transport

WTA INC. • USA

Received from Piper rights to PA-18-150 Super Cub light-plane and PA-36 Brave agricultural aircraft; 250 Super Cubs built before becoming once again Piper type, while PA-36 produced as New Brave.

XIAMEN AD LIGHT AIRCRAFT COMPANY • China

Produces the AD 100 single/two-seat lightplane and Nan-jing University of Aeronautics and Astronautics FT-300 three-seat derivative, both pusher-engined types of com-posites construction and with rear-mounted wings and canards.

XI'AN AIRCRAFT COMPANY • China

This major aircraft company was established in 1958. In 1961 it took over from Harbin production of the H-6, a Chinese version of the Soviet Tupolev Tu-16 *Badger* bomber, and also developed the H-6D as a cruise missile carrier. Produced the Y7 short/medium-range transport based on the Soviet An-24, the first flying in December 1970, and improved versions continue in production. Y7H and Y7H-500 are current military and civil versions of the An-26. A supersonic strike aircraft first flew in 1989 as the JH-7, which might have entered service in small num-bers with the PLA Naval Aviation for maritime strike duties from 1994. An export version of JH-7 was revealed in November 1998 as the FBC-1 Flying Leopard.

Xi'an Y7-100 short/medium-range passenger transport

YZ

Yakovlev Yak-36 VTOL combat aircraft

YAKOVLEV JOINT STOCK COMPANY — A.S. YAKOVLEV DESIGN BUREAU/YAK AIRCRAFT CORPORATION • USSR/Russia

Aleksandr Sergievich Yakovlev won a design competition for lightplanes even before entering an engineering academy in 1927. His design bureau was established 1935, and first military design was the Yak-4 twin-engined fighter, completed 1939. The Yak-1/3/9 series of single-seat fighters served the Soviet Union well in combat during Second World War and were built in larger numbers than any other Soviet wartime fighter. A Yak-3 airframe was modified to produce the Yak-15 jet fighter in 1945, developed subsequently as the Yak-17. The Yak-23 of 1947 was a complete redesign, resembling the earlier fighters only in fuselage configuration.

Other post-war Yakovlev designs included the Yak-12 high-wing utility aircraft, produced also in Poland and China, Yak-11 and Yak-18 trainers, Yak-28 twin-jet bomber and reconnaissance aircraft (production began 1960) and related Yak-28P radar-equipped all-weather interceptor (first flown 1960), and Yak-40 (first flown October 1966) and Yak-42 (first flown March 1975 and still in production) short-range transports. The important Yak-38 operational VTOL combat aircraft (first flown January 1971 but now withdrawn from Russian naval use) was followed by a new VTOL prototype known as the Yak-41 (first flown March 1987) which was subsequently abandoned, as was the projected next-generation STOVL Yak-43 and the Yak-44 shipborne AEW&C aircraft. The Yak-142 transport is a new variant of Yak-42D, featuring mostly US digital avionics and other improvements. Projected airliners include the short-range twin-turbofan Yak-46-1 for 126 passengers, short-range Yak-46-2 with propfan engines, and Yak-242 138-180 passenger short-range airliner.

In the field of general aviation, Yakovlev developed the Yak-18T 4-seat multipurpose lightplane development of Yak-18 (first flown 1967 and still available), Yak-50 aerobatic sporting aircraft (first flown 1972), Yak-52 tandem

Right: Yakovlev Yak-58 and Yak-112, with Beriev Be-32K beyond and abandoned Yak-141 VTOL supersonic fighter behind (Piotr Butowski)

two-seat piston trainer (first flown 1974 and still built in Romania), Yak-54 two-seat aerobatic trainer (first flown December 1993), Yak-55M single-seat aerobatic aircraft (first flown 1989), Yak-58 six-seat business transport with a pusher piston engine (first flown April 1994), and Yak-112 four-seat light aircraft (first flown October 1992). General-aviation projects include Yak-48, thought to be derived from the Israeli-designed Galaxy, Yak-56 piston-engined primary trainer and Yak-57 single-seat aerobatic competition aircraft. Yakovlev is also a partner with Aermacchi of Italy in the Yak/Aem-130 and Yak-131 jet trainer and light combat aircraft programme. In total, Yakovlev has pro-

Yakovlev Yak-40 three-turbofan transport aircraft

Below: Yakovlev Yak-130D demonstrator for the Yak/Aem-130

Yokosuka B4Y1 carrier-based attack aircraft

Yokosuka MXY-7 Ohka piloted and air-launched suicide aircraft

duced over 70,000 aircraft of more than 100 types since 1927, and the present Design Bureau is joined by the Saratov and Smolensk manufacturing facilities under Yak Aircraft Corporation.

YEOMAN AIRCRAFT (PTY.) LTD. • Australia

Formed 1958 as an associate of Kingsford-Smith Aviation Service to specialise in development of agricultural aircraft. First prototype Yeoman UA-1 conversion of Commonwealth CA 6 Wackett trainer flew in 1960, followed by production versions: KS.3 Cropmaster 250 and Fieldmaster 285.

YERMOLAEV • USSR

On Stalin's orders Vladimir Gregorovich Yermolaev began design work on a long-range bomber, the DB-240 prototype of which first flew in 1940. This twin diesel-engined low-wing monoplane was based on the design of R. L. Bartini's Stal' 7 and had the same distinctive inverted-gull wings. Designated Yer-2, more than 400 were built 1940-1944 and used principally as long-range night bombers. A Yer-20N special-purpose long-range transport version, which carried 18 passengers, was developed from the bomber.

YOKOSUKA NAVAL AIR DEPOT • Japan

Yokosuka's B3Y1 Navy Type 32 carrier biplane first flew in 1932. Some 200 B4Y1 attack aircraft followed, those remaining in service Second World War known as 'Jean' to the Allies. The D4Y Suisei ('Judy') two-seat carrier dive-bomber was in service by the Battle of Midway in 1942 and appeared also in D4Y2-S nightfighter and D4Y4 suicide attack variants. The P1Y1 Ginga ('Frances') twin-engined naval attack bomber/nightfighter entered production in 1943 at Nakajima (q.v.) factories. Yokosuka developed also the MXY-7 Ohka (Cherry Blossom) kamikaze piloted missile-bomb, derisively dubbed Baka ('fool' in Japanese) by the US Navy, and of which production by various manufacturers totalled about 800.

ZANDER & WEYL • UK

Established at Dunstable, Bedfordshire, was engaged in the design, manufacture and repair of sailplanes. Zander & Weyl built the Dart Flittermouse single-seat ultralight aeroplane in 1936. Built aircraft subsequently as Dart Aircraft Ltd (q.v.).

ZAVODY • Czechoslovkaia

The Skoda company was the largest industrial organisation in Czechoslovakia in the 1920s, manufacturing engines of indigenous design alongside licence-built Hispano-Suiza and Lorraine Dietrich aero engines, Dewoitine aircraft and Curtiss Reed propellers. Skodovy Zavody had a controlling interest in the Czech Avia company (q.v.) and in Ceskoslovenska Letecka Spolecnost, the Czech airline. Parent company has also made cars, firearms, etc.

Below: Zenair Zenith CH 2000
two-seat lightplanes

ZEEBRUGGE AERONAUTICAL CONSTRUCTION COMPANY • Belgium

This company designed and produced a two-seat light cabin monoplane and a two-seat fighter biplane in the mid-1920s.

ZENAIR LTD. • Canada

Formed 1974 and currently producing the Zenith CH 2000 certificated two-seat lightplane (first flown June 1993 and delivered in assembled form from 1994). Also markets the Zenith CH-100 single-seater, Acro CH-150 and CH-180 (aerobatic variants of CH-200), Zenith CH-200 two-seat lightplane and Zenith CH-250 long-range version, and Zenith CH-300 (Tri-Z) three/four-seat lightplane (as variant of CH 2000), all built from plans and/or kits.

ZENITH AIRCRAFT • USA

Formed in California in 1927 to specialise in the design and construction of high-performance commercial and military aircraft. A seven-seat passenger biplane designated Zenith Z6 was built.

ZENITH AIRCRAFT COMPANY • USA

Markets plans and kits for several versions of the CH-601 Zodiac two-seat low-wing cabin monoplane (first flown 1984), two-seat and twin-engined Zodiac Gemini CH.620 (first flown 1996), and Zenair STOL CH.701 two-seat utility cabin monoplane (first flown 1986, and certificated in Israel and Mexico).

ZENTRAL-AVIATIK UND AUTOMOBIL GMBH • Austria

This company produced the Aviatik B.1, one of the earliest purpose-designed combat aircraft, in 1914. The following year production on a large scale was initiated by Oesterreichische-Ungarische Flugzeugfabrik Aviatik (q.v.).

ZEPPELIN-WERKE LINDAU GMBH • Germany

This company was established under the patronage of Graf von Zeppelin to design and construct aircraft with Claudius Dornier as chief designer. The company's first product, the Rs 1 multi-engined flying-boat, was wrecked

before its first flight, but three differing examples were developed progressively, designated Rs II, Rs III and Rs IV. Other aircraft built by Zeppelin-Lindau included the C I, C II, D I and V I biplanes, and Cs I two-seat monoplane seaplane. Developed the Gs I commercial flying-boat after the Armistice, which was broken up on the instructions of the Allied Control Commission. In 1922 the company was renamed Dornier GmbH (q.v.).

ZEPPELIN-WERKE STAAKEN GMBH •
Germany

This company, located formerly at Gotha, built the largest aircraft to see service in the First World War, the Riesenflugzeug (giant aeroplane) 'R' series bombers. The Staaken design team evolved four-, five- and six-engined bombers, leading to the four-engined R.VI which was built by Automobil and Aviatik (q.v.), Ostdeutsche Albatros Werke and Luftfahrzeugbau Schütte-Lanz (q.v.) and carried out successful raids against Allied territory, dropping bombs as large as 2,200 lb (1,000 kg). A floatplane version of the R.VI, the Staaken L, was wrecked during trials in 1918.

Zlin 42 two-seat light trainers

An advanced four-engined all-metal monoplane airliner, the E.4/20, flew successfully in 1920 but was then destroyed by order of the Allied Control Commission under the terms of the Armistice.

ZLIN • Czechoslovakia

Zlinská Letecká Akciová Spolecnost formed 1934 as subsidiary of Bata Shoe Company. First aircraft produced was Zlin XII two-seat, low-wing cabin monoplane, followed by

Zlin 381, a licence-built Bücker Bü 181 Bestmann. The Zlin 22 appeared in 1947 as a two-seat trainer and was produced also in three-seat Zlin 22M version. Company name changed to Moravan (q.v.) in 1949, although products continued to be known as Zlins. See Moravan Inc.

ZMAJ • Czechoslovakia

Fabrica Aeroplana I Hydroplana Zmaj founded in 1927 by Jovan Petrovic to produce under licence the Hanriot H-41, Gourdou-Leseurre B-3 and Dewoitine D-27 fighters. Indigenous designs included a Wright-engined observation aircraft, an observation seaplane and the two-seat Fizir AF-2 Amphibian.

ZODIAC • France

First established in 1896, this company produced the Zodiac S2 two-seat biplane in 1912.

Below: Zenith Aircraft Zenair STOL CH.701

GLOSSARY

ABSOLUTE CEILING: The maximum altitude above sea level at which a heavier-than-air craft can be maintained in level flight.

ACLS: (i) Air cushion landing system, or (ii) automatic carrier landing system.

ADF: Automatic Direction Finding; utilising an automated radio direction finding (RDF) technique.

AEROBATICS: Voluntary manoeuvres, initiated by a pilot, other than those for conventional flight.

AERODROME: An area set aside for the operation of aircraft.

AERODYNAMICS: The branch of fluid mechanics dealing with air (gaseous) motion, and the reactions of a body moving within that air.

AEROFOIL (AIRFOIL): A body or structure shaped to obtain an aerodynamic reaction when travelling through the air.

AERONAUTICS: Concerned with flight within the Earth's atmosphere.

AEROPLANE (AIRPLANE): Meaning in modern usage a heavier-than-air powered craft.

AEROSTAT: A lighter-than-air craft.

AEW: Airborne early warning; aircraft equipped to give maximum advance warning of approaching hostile aircraft.

AFCS: Automatic flight control system.

AFTERBURNER: Thrust augmentation feature of a gas turbine engine.

AI: Airborne interception; radar device carried by military aircraft to aid location and interception of hostile aircraft.

AILERONS: Movable control surfaces, usually mounted in the trailing-edge of a wing adjacent to the wingtips, to control an aircraft's rolling movements.

AIRBRAKE: A drag-inducing surface which can be deployed in flight, perhaps for speed reducing or limiting, but see also spoilers.

AIRFIELD: More modern term for aerodrome, and applying more particularly to one used by military aircraft.

AIRFLOW: The movement of air about a body (aircraft) in motion.

AIRFOIL (AEROFOIL): A structure shaped to obtain an aerodynamic reaction in the air, thus affecting the performance of the aircraft.

AIRFRAME: An aircraft's structure, without power plant and systems.

AIRPLANE (AEROPLANE): Meaning in modern usage a heavier-than-air powered craft, as opposed to a balloon or glider.

AIRPORT: More modern term for aerodrome, and applying more particularly to one used for civil transport operations.

AIRSCREW: Now little-used word for propeller; believed to have originated to provide distinction from ship's propeller.

AIRSHIP: A powered lighter-than-air craft.

AIRSPEED: The speed of an aircraft through the air, relative to the air mass in which it is moving.

AIRSTRIP: A natural surface used for the operation of aircraft, often in an unimproved state.

ALTIMETER: An instrument, most usually an aneroid barometer, calibrated in metres and/or feet, to indicate an aircraft's height.

ALTITUDE: Height.

AMPHIBIAN: An aircraft able to operate from both land and water.

ANGLE OF ATTACK: Angle at which the air-stream meets an aerofoil surface.

ANGLE OF INCIDENCE: Angle at which an aerofoil surface is normally set in relation to the fore and aft axis of the airframe structure.

ANHEDRAL: Angle which the spanwise axis of an aerofoil makes to the fuselage when the wing or tailplane tip is lower than its root attachment point.

APU: Auxiliary power unit. Usually small engine carried on board an aircraft to provide an independent power source for such services as electrics, hydraulics, pneumatics, ventilation and air conditioning, both on the ground and in the air if needed.

ASI: Air speed indicator.

ASPECT RATIO: Ratio of the span to the chord of an aerofoil. Hence, a high aspect ratio wing has great span and narrow chord, and vice versa.

ASTRODOME: Transparent dome, usually on dorsal surface of fuselage, to permit celestial navigation by traditional means.

ASW: Anti-submarine warfare.

ATC: Air traffic control.

AUTOGYRO: An aircraft with an unpowered rotary wing, which autorotates as the machine is propelled through the air by a conventional power plant. `Autogiro' is the trade name for autogyros developed by Juan de la Cierva.

AUTOMATIC PILOT (AUTOPILOT): A gyroscopically-stabilised system maintaining an aircraft in level flight at predetermined heading and altitude.

AUTOROTATION: Automatic rotation of a rotary wing due to forward, or downward, movement of an autogyro.

AWACS: Airborne warning and control system, an advanced AEW aircraft, with additional facilities for deployment and control of defence, interception and counter-strike forces.

BALLISTIC MISSILE: A weapon which, in the terminal and unpowered stage of its flight, becomes a free-falling body subject to ballistic reactions.

BALLOON: An unpowered lighter-than-air craft, its direction of flight imposed by ambient airstreams.

BIPLANE: A fixed-wing aircraft with two sets of wings mounted, generally, one above the other.

BLEED AIR: Hot air, at high pressure, taken usually from the by-pass section of a gas turbine engine, for heating, de-icing and other useful work.

BLOWN FLAPS: Aerodynamic surface over which bleed air is discharged at high speed to prevent breakaway of the normal airflow.

BOUNDARY LAYER: Thin stratum of air nearest to an aircraft's external surface structure.

BOX KITE: Form of kite devised by Australian Lawrence Hargrave, used by many early constructors to provide rigid biplane structures.

BUFFET: Irregular, often violent, oscillations of an aircraft's structure, caused by turbulent airflow or conditions of compressibility.

CAA: Civil Aviation Administration (UK).

CAB: Civil Aeronautics Board (USA).

CABIN: Enclosed compartment for crew and/or passengers in an aircraft.

CAMBER: The curvature, convex or concave, of an aerofoil surface.

CANARD: Describes an aircraft which flies tail first, with its main lift surface at the aft end of its structure.

CANTILEVER: A beam, or other structure, supported at one end only, and without external bracing.

CATHEDRAL: Early word to describe anhedral, or negative dihedral.

CEILING: Normal maximum operating altitude of an aircraft.

CENTRE OF GRAVITY: (CG), the point on an aircraft's structure where the total combined weight forces act.

CENTRE-SECTION: The central panel, or section, of an aircraft's wing.

CHORD: The distance measured from the leading-to trailing-edge of an aerofoil.

COCKPIT: Compartment, originally open to the air, for accommodation of pilot and crew/passengers. Nowadays used informally by laymen to describe the forward part of the cabin, especially of an airliner, which is off-limits to passengers, and properly called flight deck.

COIN: Counter-insurgency aircraft.

COLLECTIVE PITCH CONTROL: Used to change simultaneously the pitch of all of a helicopter rotor's blades to permit ascent or descent.

CONSTANT-SPEED PROPELLER: One which governs an engine at its optimum speed, the blade pitch being increased or decreased automatically to achieve this result.

COWLING: The name of the fairing which, usually, encloses an engine.

CYCLIC PITCH CONTROL: Means of changing the pitch of a rotor's blades progressively, to provide a horizontal thrust component for flight in any horizontal direction.

DELTA WING: When viewed in plan has the shape of an isosceles triangle; the apex leads, the wing trailing-edge forming the base of the triangle.

DERATED: An engine which is restricted to a power output below its potential maximum.

DIHEDRAL: Angle which the spanwise axis of an aerofoil makes to the fuselage when the wing or tailplane tip is higher than its root attachment point (positive dihedral).

DIVE BRAKE: Drag-inducing surface deployed in a dive to maintain speed below structural limitations, or improve controllability (see airbrake).

DORSAL: Relating to the upper surface of an aircraft's fuselage.

DRAG: A force exerted on a moving body in a direction opposite to its direction of motion.

DRAG CHUTE: A heavy-duty parachute attached to an aircraft's structure which can be used to reduce its landing run.

DRONE: A pilotless aircraft, usually following a predetermined or programmed set of manoeuvres. See also RPV.

DROP TANK: An externally carried auxiliary tank, usually to contain fuel, which may be jettisoned if necessary.

ECM: Electronic counter-measures; airborne equipment to reduce the effectiveness of an enemy's radar or other devices which generate electromagnetic radiations.

ELEVATOR: Movable control surface, attached to the trailing-edge of an aircraft's tailplane (stabiliser) to control pitching movements.

ELEVONS: Movable control surfaces which act collectively as elevators, but differentially as ailerons.

ELT: Emergency locator transmitter; emits a homing signal from a crashed aircraft to simplify location for rescue services.

ENVELOPE: Container, usually flexible, or the lifting gas or hot air of an airship or balloon.

FAA: Federal Aviation Administration.

FAI: FÉdÉration AÉronautique Internationale.

FAR: Federal Aviation Regulations.

FIN: A fixed vertical aerofoil surface, usually a dorsal component of the tail unit, to provide stability in yaw.

FIRING: An addition to an aircraft's basic structure which is intended primarily to reduce drag.

FLAP: Most usually a wing trailing-edge movable surface which can be deployed partially to increase lift, or completely to increase drag.

FLAT-FOUR: Characteristic description of a horizontally-opposed four-cylinder engine; hence flat-twin, flat-six.

FLIGHT DECK: (i) Separate crew compartment of a cabin aircraft, or (ii) the operational deek of an aircraft carrier.

FLIGHT SIMULATOR: A ground-based training device to permit the practice of flight operations; often specific to a particular aircraft for detailed training.

FLOATPLANE: Aircraft which is supported on the water by floats; more usually termed a seaplane.

FLUTTER: Unstable oscillation of an aerofoil surface.

FLYING-BOAT: A heavier-than-air craft which is supported on the water by its water-tight fuselage.

FLYING WIRES (LIFT WIRES): External bracing wires, usually of streamline section, which carry the weight of the fuselage in flight.

FULLY-FEATHERING PROPELLER: One in which the blades can be rotated so that the leading-edge of each faces the oncoming airstream. This reduces drag if an engine has to be stopped in flight.

FUSELAGE: The body structure of an aircraft.

GLIDER: A heavier-than-air, fixed wing, unpowered aircraft for gliding or soaring flight.

HARDPOINT: A strengthened section of the under-wing or fuselage, intended for the carriage of external weapons or stores, usually on pylons.

HELICOPTER: A heavier-than-air craft with a powered rotary wing.

HELIUM: A non-inflammable lifting gas for lighter-than-air craft.

HIGH-WING MONOPLANE: An aircraft which has its single wing mounted high on the fuselage.

HULL: The water-tight fuselage or body of a flying-boat.

HYDRO-AEROPLANE: Early term for an aircraft which could operate from water.

HYDROGEN: The lightest known lifting gas, used to inflate balloons and airships, unfortunately highly inflammable.

IATA: International Air Transport Association.

ICAO: International Civil Aviation Organisation.

ICING: Condition arising when atmospheric moisture freezes on the external surfaces of an aircraft.

IFF: Identification, friend or foe; an electronic device to interrogate approaching aircraft.

IFR: Instrument Flight Rules; i.e. flight by reference to on-board instruments under conditions of poor visibility or darkness.

ILS: Instrument Landing System.

IN-LINE ENGINE: Engine in which the cylinders are one behind another, in straight lines.

INS: Inertial navigation system, in which highly sensitive accelerometers record, via a computer, the complex accelerations of an aircraft about its three axes, thus integrating its linear displacement from the beginning of a selected course and pinpointing the aircraft's position at all times.

ISA: Agreed International Standard Atmosphere (1013.2 millibars at 15°C) to permit accurate comparison of aircraft performance figures.

JASDF: Japan Air Self-Defence Force.

JATO: Jet-assisted take-off, utilising solid or liquid fuel rockets to augment the take-off power of an aircraft's engines. See also RATO.

JGSDF: Japan Ground Self-Defence Force.

JMSDF: Japan Maritime Self-Defence Force.

KINETIC HEATING: Heating of an aircraft's structure as a result of air friction.

KITE: Usually tethered heavier-than-air craft, sustained in the air by its aerofoil surfaces being inclined to the wind to generate lift.

LANDING WEIGHT: Normal maximum weight at which an aircraft is permitted to land.

LANDING WIRES: External bracing wires, usually of streamline section, which support the wings when the aircraft is on the ground.

LANDPLANE: A heavier-than-air craft which is equipped to operate from land surfaces only.

LBA: Luftfahrtbundesamt; the Federal German Civil Aviation Authority.

LEADING-EDGE: The edge of an aerofoil which first meets the airstream in normal flight.

LIFT: The force generated by an aerofoil section, acting at right angles to the airstream flowing past it.

LORAN: A long-range radio-based navigation aid.

LOW-WING MONOPLANE: An aircraft which has its single wing mounted low on the fuselage.

MAC: Military Airlift Command (USAF).

MACH NUMBER: Named after the Austrian physicist Ernst Mach, a means of recording the speed of a body as a ratio of the speed of sound in the same ambient conditions. The speed of sound in dry air at 0°C (32°F) is approximately 331 m (1087 ft)/sec; 1193 km/h (741 mph). Hence Mach 0.8 represents eight-tenths of the speed of sound.

MAD: Magnetic anomaly detector carried, for example, by maritime reconnaissance aircraft to locate a submarine beneath the surface of the sea.

MID-WING MONOPLANE: An aircraft which has its single wing mounted in a mid-position on the fuselage.

MONOCOQUE: Structure in which the outer skin carries the primary stresses, and is free of internal bracing.

MONOPLANE: A fixed-wing aircraft with a single set of wings, i.e. one wing on each side.

NACA: National Advisory Committee for Aeronautics. Now NASA.

NAF: Naval Aircraft Factory (US).

NASA: National Aeronautics and Space Administration.

NATO: North Atlantic Treaty Organisation.

ORNITHOPTER: Name for a flapping-wing aircraft. Only model ornithopters have flown to date.

PARACHUTE: Collapsible device which, when deployed, will retard the rate of descent of a body falling through the air. Used originally as a safety device, has been adopted for dropping troops, supplies, equipment, etc.

PARASOL MONOPLANE: A fixed-wing aircraft which has its single wing strut-mounted above the fuselage.

PAYLOAD: The useful load of an aircraft: cargo, passengers; in a military aircraft, its weapon load.

PITCH: The angle of incidence at which a propeller blade or rotor blade is set.

PORT: Left-hand side when facing forward.

PRESSURISATION: Artificially increased pressure in an aircraft to compensate for the reduced external pressure as the aircraft gains altitude.

PROPELLER: Rotating blades of aerofoil section, engine driven, each of which reacts as an aircraft's wing, generating low-pressure in front and higher behind, thus pulling the aircraft forward.

PROTOTYPE: The first airworthy example of a new aircraft design or variant.

PUSHER PROPELLER: Inaccurate but accepted description of propeller mounted behind an engine. It acts aerodynamically as described under propeller, and is thus a tractor in action.

PYLON: Structure attached to wing or airframe to carry load, e.g. engines or weapons.

RAAF: Royal Australian Air Force.

RADAR: Beamed and directed radio waves used for location and detection, as well as for navigational purposes.

RADIAL ENGINE: One in which the cylinders are mounted equidistant and circumferentially around a circular crankcase. Cylinders and crankcase are fixed, and the crankshaft rotates.

RAE: Royal Aircraft Establishment, formerly Royal Aircraft Factory.

RAF: (i) Royal Air Force, or (ii) Royal Aircraft Factory.

RAI: Registro Aeronàutico Italiano.

RAMJET ENGINE: An aerodynamic duct in which fuel is burned to produce a high-velocity propulsive jet. It needs to be accelerated to high speed before it can become operative.

RATO: Rocket-assisted take-off: virtually the same as JATO.

RCAF: Royal Canadian Air Force.

RDF: Radio direction finding; using the transmission from two or more stations to fix position of an aircraft by its bearing in relation to each.

RFC: Royal Flying Corps.

RNAS: Royal Naval Air Service.

RNZAF: Royal New Zealand Air Force.

ROCKET ENGINE: One burning liquid or solid fuel and carrying its own oxidiser, enabling combustion to continue outside of the earth's atmosphere.

ROLL: Movement of an aircraft about its longitudinal axis, representing a wing-over rolling action.

ROTARY ENGINE: Cylinders disposed as for radial engine, but in this case the crankshaft is fixed, and cylinders and crankcase rotate around it.

ROTOR: The rotating-wing assembly of an autogyro or helicopter, comprising the rotor hub and rotor blades.

RPV: Remotely piloted vehicles, directed usually by radio by a pilot in another aircraft or based on the ground.

RUDDER: Movable control surface, attached to trailing-edge of fin, to control aircraft movement in yaw.

SAAF: South African Air Force.

SAC: Strategic Air Command (USAF).

SAILPLANE: An unpowered heavier-than-air craft designed primarily for soaring flight.

SEAPLANE: A heavier-than-air craft which operates from water, and is supported on the surface of the water by floats.

SEMI-MONOCOQUE: An aircraft structure in which the outer skin is inadequate to carry the primary stresses, and is reinforced by frames, formers and longerons.

SERVICE CEILING: Normally height at which an aircraft can maintain a maximum rate of climb of 30 m (100 ft)/min.

SGAC: SecrÉtariat GÉnÉrale À l'Aviation Civile.

SKIN: The external covering of an aircraft's basic inner structure.

SLAT: Auxiliary aerofoil surface, mounted forward of a main aerofoil, to maintain a smooth airflow over the main aerofoil at high angles of attack.

SLOT: The gap between the slat and leading-edge of the main aerofoil, which splits the airflow and maintains a smooth flow over the main aerofoil upper surface.

SPAN: The distance from tip to tip of the wing or tailplane.

SPAR: A primary structural member of an aerofoil surface, from which ribs or frames are mounted to form the desired aerofoil contours.

SPINNER: A streamlined fairing over a propeller hub.

SPOILERS: Drag-inducing surfaces which can be deployed differentially for lateral control, or simultaneously for lift dumping to improve the effectiveness of landing brakes.

STALL: Condition which arises when the smooth airflow over a wing's upper surface breaks down and its lift is destroyed.

STARBOARD: Right-hand side when facing forward.

STOL: Short take-off and landing capability.

STREAMLINE: To shape a structure so that it will cause the minimum aerodynamic drag.

STRUT: Solid or tubular member, usually streamlined, used for bracing, as, for example, between the two wings of a biplane. Can be required to carry tension or compression loads.

SUBSONIC: Flight at a speed below that of sound.

SUPERCHARGER: A form of compressor, often turbine-driven, to force more fuel/air mixture into the cylinders of a piston-engine than can be induced by the pistons at ambient atmospheric pressure.

SUPERSONIC: Speed in excess of that of sound.

SV-VS: Soviet Military Aviation Forces (Soviets-kaya Voenno-Vozdushnye Sily).

SWEPT WING: Wing of which the angle between the wing leading-edge and the centre line of the rear fuselage is less than 90 degrees.

TABS: Small auxiliary control surfaces which can be adjusted to offset aerodynamic loads imposed on main control surfaces.

TAC: Tactical Air Command (USAF).

TAILPLANE (STABILISER): Primary horizontal aerofoil surface of tail unit. Can be fixed, or may have variable incidence, and its purpose is to provide longitudinal stability.

TAKE-OFF WEIGHT: Maximum allowable weight of an aircraft at the beginning of its take-off run.

THRUST: Force which propels an aircraft through the air; generated by conventional propeller or the jet efflux of a turbine engine.

TRACTOR PROPELLER: Propeller mounted forward of the engine. (See propeller.)

TRAILING-EDGE: The rear edge of an aerofoil.

TRIPLANE: Fixed-wing aircraft with three sets of wings, mounted one above another.

TURBOFAN: Gas turbine engine with large diameter forward fan. Air is ducted from the tips of these fan blades and by-passed around the engine, and added to the normal jet efflux to provide high propulsive efficiency.

TURBOJET: Gas turbine engine in its simplest form, producing a high velocity jet efflux.

TURBOPROP: Gas turbine engine in which maximum energy is taken from the turbine to drive a reduction gear and conventional propeller.

TURBOSHAFT: Gas turbine engine in which maximum energy is taken from the turbine to drive a high speed shaft. It can be used to drive a helicopter's rotor or any other form of machinery.

USAAC: United States Army Air Corps (predecessor of USAAF).

USAAF: United States Army Air Force (predecessor of USAF).

USAAS: United States Army Air Service (predecessor of USAAC).

USAF: United States Air Force.

USCG: United States Coast Guard.

USMC: United States Manne Corps.

USN: United States Navy.

VARIABLE-GEOMETRY WING: Wings which, fully extended, give the best low-speed performance for take-off and landing, and can be swept in flight to optimum positions for best cruising and high-speed flight performance.

VARIABLE-PITCH PROPELLER: Usually a propeller in which the blades can be set to two positions; a fine-pitch setting for take-off and landing, and a coarse-pitch setting for economic cruise performance.

VEE-ENGINE: One with two banks of in-line cylinders mounted with an angular separation on a common crankcase.

VENTRAL: Relating to the under-surface of an aircraft's fuselage.

VFR: Visual Flight Rules; i.e. flight under conditions of good external visibility, without dependence on aircraft instruments.

VSTOL: Vertical or short take-off and landing.

V/STOL: Vertical and/or short take-off and landing capability.

VTOL: Vertical take-off and landing capability.

WING-LOADING: The gross take-off weight of an aircraft divided by its wing area. A Boeing 747, for example, can have a maximum wing loading of 727.8 kg/m2 (149 lb/sq ft); a high-performance sailplane, such as the Scheibe Bergfalke, can be as low as 29.4 kg/m2 (6.02 lb/sq ft).

WING WARPING: Method of lateral control adopted by Wright brothers and many early builders/designers, in which a flexible wing is twisted (warped) to provide roll control as with ailerons.

YAW: Movement of an aircraft about its vertical axis, representing movement of its tail unit to port or starboard, to change the aircraft's heading.

INDEX

G

H

V